LIVING IN STYLE

LIVING IN STYLE

Fine Furniture in Victorian Quebec

GENERAL EDITOR

JOHN R. PORTER

THE MONTREAL MUSEUM
OF FINE ARTS

MUSÉE DE LA
CIVILISATION

Living in Style — Fine Furniture in Victorian Quebec was published on the occasion of the exhibition presented at the Montreal Museum of Fine Arts from March 4 to May 16, 1993 and at the Musée de la civilisation, Quebec City, from October 19, 1993 to April 24, 1994. The exhibition has been organized by the Montreal Museum of Fine Arts and the Musée de la civilisation in collaboration with Université Laval, with support from the Ministère des Affaires culturelles du Québec and Communications Canada's Museum Assistance Program. In Montreal, the exhibition has benefited from the promotional support of *La Presse*, Société Radio-Canada, CJMS, CKMF and CJAD.

This publication was co-ordinated by the Montreal Museum of Fine Arts.

Pierre Théberge, Director
John R. Porter, Chief Curator
Danielle Sauvage, Director of Communications
Paul Lavallée, Director of Administration

This catalogue is a production of the Publications Service.

Co-ordination: Denise L. Bissonnette
Translation: Jill Corner, Judith Terry, assisted by Roy Keys
Graphic design and electronic publishing: Dufour et Fille design, inc.
Photo-engraving and printing: Bowne de Montréal, inc.

All rights reserved.
The reproduction of any part of this book without the prior consent of the publisher is an infringement of the Copyright Act, Chapter C-42, R.S.C., 1985.

© The Montreal Museum of Fine Arts, 1993

Legal deposit - 1st trimester 1993
Bibliothèque nationale du Québec
National Library of Canada

ISBN: 2-89192-161-5

The Montreal Museum of Fine Arts
P.O. Box 3000, Station "H"
Montreal, Quebec H3G 2T9

PRINTED IN CANADA

Dedicated to my mother, and
to the memory of my father and of
ROBERT SHIPP PORTER
(Burwell, 1852 - Lauzon, 1919)
who was born in Cambridgeshire
in the reign of Queen Victoria

LIST OF LENDERS

Allan Memorial Institute, Montreal
Archdiocese of Quebec City
Archdiocese of Sherbrooke
Archives nationales du Québec, Centre de Québec et Chaudière-Appalaches
Archives nationales du Québec, Direction de Montréal, de Laval, de Lanaudière, des Laurentides et de la Montérégie
David S. Brown, antiquaire, Montreal
Canadian Museum of Civilization, Hull
Denyse Desroches, Granby
Léopold Désy, Saint-Antoine-de-Tilly
Environment Canada, Canadian Parks Service, Quebec region
Diocese of Chicoutimi
Raymond Fabien and Marthe Fabien-Lapalme, Anjou
Jourdain Fiset, Quebec City
Flaurence Joncas, Cap-Rouge
The Honourable Serge Joyal, Montreal
Jean-Claude Lachance, Granby
Alain Michel Laferrière, Saint-Clet
McCord Museum of Canadian History, Montreal
Ministere de l'Enseignement supérieur et des Sciences, Gouvernement du Québec
Monastère des Augustines de l'Hôtel-Dieu de Québec, Quebec City
The Montreal Museum of Fine Arts, Montreal
Musée de la civilisation, Quebec City
Musée des arts décoratifs/Château Dufresne, Montreal
Musée des Ursulines de Trois-Rivières, Trois-Rivières
Musée du Québec, Quebec City
Musée du Saguenay — Lac-Saint-Jean, Chicoutimi
Musée du Séminaire de Québec, Quebec City
Musée Laurier, Arthabaska
Musée Pierre Boucher du Séminaire de Trois-Rivières, Trois-Rivières
Petites Franciscaines de Marie, Baie-Saint-Paul
Mr. and Mrs. Joseph Sirois, Saint-André de Kamouraska
Soeurs de la Charité de Québec, Beauport
Soeurs de la congrégation Notre-Dame — Villa Maria, Montreal
Soeurs des Saints-Noms-de-Jésus-et-de-Marie, Montreal
Soeurs du Bon-Pasteur de Québec, Quebec City
Université Laval, Québec City

AND OTHER LENDERS WHO PREFER TO REMAIN ANONYMOUS.

THE AUTHORS

PATRICK ALBERT, conservator (furniture), Centre de conservation du Québec, Quebec City

JEAN-FRANÇOIS CARON, M.A., historian, doctoral candidate at the Université Laval

JOHANNE DAIGLE, Ph.D., historian, Professor at the Université Laval

CLAIRE DESMEULES, M.A., art historian, doctoral candidate at the Université Laval

DANIEL DROUIN, M.A., art historian, doctoral candidate at the Université Laval

MICHELINE HUARD, M.A., art historian, doctoral candidate at the Université Laval

YVES LACASSE, M.A., Curator of Canadian Art (Painting and Sculpture before 1960) at the Montreal Museum of Fine Arts

ALAIN MICHEL LAFERRIÈRE, conservator (furniture), Saint-Clet

GINETTE LAROCHE, Ph.D., art historian and ethnologist, Quebec City

RÉNALD LESSARD, M.A., historian, Archives nationales du Québec, Quebec City

GLORIA LESSER, M.A., art historian, Montreal

JOHN R. PORTER, Ph.D., art historian, Professor at the Université Laval, Chief Curator at the Montreal Museum of Fine Arts and director of the MOBIVIQ project

GYNETTE TREMBLAY, M.A., ethnolinguist, Quebec City

CLAUDE VALLIÈRES, art historian, Lévis

NATALIE VANIER, art historian, research assistant at the Montreal Museum of Fine Arts

NOTE TO THE READER

All dimensions are given in centimetres in the usual order, with height followed by width and depth (overall measurements).

The numbers in the margins refer to the illustrations; the numbers and titles in bold type refer to furniture in the exhibition.

The short titles appearing in the margin refer to the case studies and period documents found at the end of the essays.

Except where otherwise indicated, historical documents have been transcribed exactly. For the sake of authenticity, we have deliberately refrained from making corrections.

Throughout this volume, the £ symbol stands for the British pound sterling, which was divided into shillings and pence (penny in the singular). When money changed hands in nineteenth-century Quebec, French-speaking citizens sometimes used the words *chelins* and *deniers* instead of shillings and pence. In order to simplify things, we have used a shortened version for sums of money. Thus, the sum of 5 pounds, 4 shillings and 2 pence is given as à £ 5.4.2.

The illustration captions were written by Claire Desmeules and John R. Porter.

LIST OF ABBREVIATIONS

AJTR	Archives judiciaires de Trois-Rivières
AMMFA	Archives of the Montreal Museum of Fine Arts
ANQM	Archives nationales du Québec, Montreal
ANQQ	Archives nationales du Québec, Quebec City
ANQS	Archives nationales du Québec, Sherbrooke
ANQTR	Archives nationales du Québec, Trois-Rivières
CCFCS	Canadian Centre for Folk Culture Studies, Hull (Canadian Museum of Civilization)
DBC	*Dictionnaire biographique du Canada*
IOA	Inventaire des œuvres d'art du Québec, fonds Gérard-Morisset
MOBIVIQ	Projet de recherche sur le mobilier de l'époque victorienne au Québec (Université Laval, Québec)
MSRC	*Mémoires de la Société Royale du Canada*
NAC	National Archives of Canada, Ottawa
PUL	Presses de l'Université Laval
RHAF	Revue d'histoire de l'Amérique française
SRP	Service des ressources pédagogiques, Université Laval

CONTENTS

Preface 13
Acknowledgements 15
IN SEARCH OF OUR SHARED PAST 17
INTRODUCTION 19

I THE CONTEXT

QUEBEC SOCIETY IN THE VICTORIAN ERA 33
Ravenscrag, the Most Luxurious Home in Victorian Montreal 49
The Carved Mirror Frame of the Steamship Québec 53
The Bedroom Suite Created for the Prince of Wales in Montreal in 1860 55
The Reception Lounge of L'Université Laval, Quebec City 60

THE ARTS IN QUEBEC DURING THE VICTORIAN ERA 63
An Admirable Work Executed by a Woman 81
Comments on the Decoration of Churches by an Art Lover 82
A Parisian Sculptor in Montreal in 1849 83

II THE USERS

DOMESTIC WORLDS 87
The Spencer Wood Villa in 1851 132
The Baker-Gilmour House, Stanbridge, in 1882 134
The Tea Ritual 137
The Residence of Dr. Joseph Morrin, Quebec City, in 1839 139
The Passions of Businessman Hector Mackenzie 140
The Residence of Andrew McKay Smith, Sherbrooke, in 1871 141

COLOUR PLATES 143

THE HOMES, FURNISHINGS AND COLLECTIONS OF R. B. ANGUS 177

THE DRAWING ROOM 191
The Drawing Room of the L'Assomption Manor-House
    in the Late Nineteenth Century 223

THE DINING ROOM 225
On Table Manners 247
Excess in the Dining Room 248
The Sideboard of Jean-Thomas Taschereau and Respect for Family Tradition 249

THE BEDROOM 251

III THE FURNITURE MAKERS

THE FURNITURE MARKET IN QUEBEC 269
The John & William Hilton Manufactory in Montreal, in 1864 294
The Purchases Made by Madame Chapais in Quebec City, in 1866 295
François Gourdeau, Furniture Maker 299
Evidence of Owen McGarvey in February 1888 304
Recollections of Cabinetmaker Édouard Bertrand 305

BETWEEN WORKSHOP AND FACTORY 307

WILLIAM DRUM AND THE ADVENT OF INDUSTRIALIZATION 323

PIERRE DROUIN AND HONORÉ ROY, CABINETMAKERS 349

A WORLD OF EXCHANGE: PROVINCIAL AND INTERNATIONAL EXHIBITIONS 363
The Canadian Section at the Great Universal Exhibition, London, 1851 391
A Masterpiece of Marquetry by Cabinetmaker Pierre Roy in Dublin in 1865 392
The Owen McGarvey & Son Exhibit, at the
    Provincial Exhibition in Montreal, 1882 393
Cabinetwork at the Quebec Provincial Exhibition of 1877 395

IV THE FURNITURE

AN INDUSTRY OPEN TO THE WORLD 401

DIVERSITY, INNOVATION AND THE QUEST FOR COMFORT 413
Woods, Veneers and Finishes 432
Techniques Employed in the Making of Fine Furniture 435
Metal Furniture 438

THE PURSUIT OF ELEGANCE: DOMINANT STYLES AND THE EVOLUTION OF TASTE 441

DECORATIVE MOTIFS 465

THE VOCABULARY OF DOMESTIC FURNITURE 487

Select Bibliography 513
List of Art Works Presented in the Exhibition 521
Index of Names 522

Preface

The exhibition *Living in Style: Fine Furniture in Victorian Quebec* and the volume that accompanies it are the result of an important collaborative effort uniting the Montreal Museum of Fine Arts, the Musée de la civilisation in Quebec City and the Université Laval. In a formal accord signed in April 1990, the two museums agreed to develop a project focusing on the results obtained by a group of university researchers who had been working since 1986 under the supervision of John R. Porter, Professor at the Université Laval.

This joint endeavour was designed to respect the goals of our three institutions, to permit the valuable pooling of our resources and to contribute towards the diffusion of scholarly research on a subject situated at the point where art and material culture meet.

Given the disparate aims of an art museum and a museum of civilization, deciding which museological approach to adopt in mounting the exhibition *Living in Style* represented something of a challenge. However, after a process dedicated to arriving at original solutions, the three teams – directed by John R. Porter at the Université Laval, Yves Lacasse, Curator of Canadian Art (Painting and Sculpture before 1960) at the Montreal Museum of Fine Arts, and Line Ouellet, project head at the Musée de la civilisation – succeeded in reconciling a number of different but complementary traditions, techniques and views. In specific terms, the Université Laval has been responsible for research and writing, the Montreal Museum of Fine Arts for publication, conservation, photography and transport of the artefacts, and the Musée de la civilisation for the design and production of the exhibition.

One of the project's main goals was to throw new light on a largely neglected but extremely significant part of our heritage by situating it within its original historical, artistic and cultural context. It was felt that the household furniture of Quebec's *bourgeoisie* can not only be appreciated in and for itself but can contribute to our knowledge of life during the Victorian era.

Based on a dozen or so selection criteria, no less than 114 pieces of furniture were chosen for the exhibition. They are mostly Quebec made and intended for domestic use, exquisitely executed pieces that the Victorians referred to as "fine furniture" to distinguish them from more rustic and functional objects. In preparation for the exhibition, sixty-five per cent of the pieces underwent restoration, a task assumed principally by Alain Michel Laferrière and Estelle Richard at the Montreal Museum of Fine Arts, and Patrick Albert of the Centre de Conservation du Québec. The restoration of certain items was lengthy and complicated: the magnificent sideboard that once belonged to Hugh Montagu Allan of Montreal, for example, which had to be almost entirely rebuilt, and the large bookcase from Ravenscrag, a richly decorated piece measuring three and a half metres high by five and a half wide.

The exhibition also includes paintings, sculptures, drawings, engravings, stained glass, plans, tools, photographs and a wide variety of decorative art objects, all of which help recreate the surroundings in which Victorian furniture was normally found. As well as the Montreal Museum of Fine Arts and the Musée de la civilisation, from whose collections many of the items have been taken, some forty lenders generously agreed to contribute towards the success of our project. We are extremely grateful to them.

The exhibition circuit enables spectators to steep themselves in the domestic world of the Victorian *bourgeoisie*: from the splendour of the drawing room to the intimacy of the bedroom, via all the innovations the period had to offer. An abundance of visual support material combined with precise and succinct written documentation provide a deal of information regarding styles, furniture makers and users. An audio-visual presentation has also been prepared, which conjures up a way of life that combined strict adherence to etiquette with a growing interest in relaxation and comfort. The whole is presented in a simple and original contemporary setting that highlights the handsome workmanship, beautiful woods and rich carving characteristic of the finest furniture of the period.

The present volume, although it accompanies the exhibition and contains reproductions of all the furniture on view, has been developed independently. It is actually a general study of the subject, containing essays by a number of specialists from different fields all working under John Porter's skilful supervision. Several among them have gained their special knowledge of furniture as a result of their university studies and their participation in this project.

In its focus on the lifestyles and tastes of a period not long gone, this study examines a representative selection of the furniture produced by the hundreds of *meubliers*, cabinetmakers, carvers and decorators working in Quebec during Victoria's reign. With its wealth of images, many published here for the first time, the book provides a chance to explore and assess the significance of foreign influences, and conjures up all the elegance, comfort, originality, refinement, oddity and extravagance of this extraordinary era. In sum, it represents an important and original contribution to the furthering of knowledge in the field of the decorative arts and, as there has existed hitherto no general study of Victorian furniture in Quebec, an especially timely one.

To John Porter, who has acted as conceptor and overseer of the project since 1986, we offer our gratitude and our congratulations for having combined with such verve the roles of Guest Curator for the exhibition *Living in Style*, Professor at the Université Laval and, since 1990, Chief Curator at the Montreal Museum of Fine Arts. The quality of his leadership and the depth of his scholarly commitment have much to do with the success of the remarkable task he has shared with his fellow-members of the Université Laval MOBIVIQ team and his colleagues at the Montreal Museum of Fine Arts and the Musée de la civilisation in Quebec City.

Roland Arpin	Michel Gervais	Pierre Théberge, C.Q.,
director	*rector*	*director*
Musée de la civilisation	Université Laval	The Montreal Museum of Fine Arts

Acknowledgements

At the end of a long-term project such as this one, gratitude is inevitably due to many people – so many, in fact, that any attempt to list them can result in unfortunate omissions. My collaborators and I would therefore like to begin by thanking all those who have contributed in any way at all towards the mounting of the exhibition and the production of the volume that accompanies it. We are particularly indebted to all the friends, colleagues, specialists, lenders, curators, archivists and other professionals who over the years have encouraged us, received us warmly, shared their ideas with us, directed us towards interesting avenues of research and transmitted to us vital information.

In the early years of the project, we received research grants and backing from the Social Sciences and Humanities Research Council of Canada (1986-1988), from the Fonds pour la formation de chercheurs et l'aide à la recherche du Ministère de l'Éducation du Québec (1988-1990), and from the Budget spécial de recherche de l'Université Laval. In 1990, the Montreal Museum of Fine Arts and the Musée de la civilisation in Quebec City added their support to our project by contributing towards the development of an exhibition concept and the writing of a scientific study of fine furniture in Victorian Quebec.

On a more personal level, we would like to take this opportunity of saluting Georges-Pierre Léonidoff, Jean-Pierre Labiau, Éric Nicolai and Didier Prioul, four early collaborators who, after making significant contributions to the MOBIVIQ project, have moved on to other things.

Finally, without taking account of their various functions, we would like to express our special gratitude to the people whose names follow; without their cooperation, their generosity, their faith and their expertise, the results we have achieved would be considerably less than they are: Danièle Archambault, Henri Beaulac, Mario Béland, John Bland, Andréanne Bolduc, Claude Boudreau, Claude Brazeau, Réal Brisson, Raymond Brousseau, Jean Cannone, Paul Carpentier, Ruth Cathcart, Guy Champagne, Luc d'Iberville-Moreau, Philippe Dubé, Bernard Genest, Andrée Héroux, Serge Joyal, Yves Lacasse, Dorothée Lachance, Kenneth Landry, Line Ouellet, Ann McLaren, Paul-Louis Martin, Pierrette Maurais, Claude Poirier, Denis Robitaille, Guy-André Roy, Martine Tremblay, Luce Vermette and Diane Vincent.

John R. Porter

1
Notman Studio, Montreal, *Willie Matthews*, 1862
Photograph, McCord Museum of Canadian History, Montreal, Notman Photographic Archives (2557-I)

IN SEARCH OF OUR SHARED PAST

MORE THAN A CENTURY AWAY FROM US, LITTLE WILLIE Matthews of Montreal stands proudly before our eyes, thanks to the quintessentially Victorian magic of photography. Wearing a bow tie and holding his cap in his hand, clearly proud of his "Sunday best" clothes, he leans nonchalantly against the arm of an imposing Renaissance-revival armchair covered with black horsehair cloth in which his parents have probably just been photographed.

The Notman studio armchair, having been used as a prop for endless similar photographic sessions, passed through many hands before being acquired by the McCord Museum of Canadian History, and was recently restored to its pristine condition here at the Montreal Museum of Fine Arts. We have succeeded in tracking down much of the history of this evocative artefact, although some of the memories associated with it are lost for ever.

The story of this armchair echoes in a sense the history of all the furniture from the Victorian period in Quebec. Although with the passing of time much of it has disappeared, enough representative pieces have survived to enable us to retrace its development in general terms, while additional material is still being discovered. After all, even though little Willie's portrait is as lifelike as could be, it only captures a fleeting moment. Many more such moments would be needed to compose a true character sketch.

The same could be said of this first general account of fine Victorian furniture in Quebec, which is the result of an initial inventory, systematic research and analysis by a number of experts. Although our study relies on a wealth of new documentary and visual evidence in order to draw a fuller picture than the generally accepted one, it has demonstrable limitations, and points to the need for further research in a number of areas.

On completing this first stage of investigation, which has been an exciting task for us all, my colleagues and I are happy to think that other enthusiasts both professional and amateur will carry out further explorations into the lifestyle of Quebec in Victoria's reign. They will undoubtedly find, as we have done, a nostalgic delight in disinterring more of these shared memories lying dormant in our collective consciousness.

John R. Porter
Sillery, April 16, 1992

INTRODUCTION

Eclecticism, which is absurd in religion and philosophy, has always seemed to me essential in terms of literature. Insisting on the classical viewpoint means deliberately limiting one's intellectual horizon.

Octave Crémazie, 1867[1]

WHEN WE BEGAN, IN JUNE 1986, TO STUDY THE FINE furniture of Victorian Quebec (1837-1901), it was not because of its intrinsic aesthetic appeal, nor because we were determined at all costs to rehabilitate a part of our heritage that had been long neglected. Above and beyond a desire to cross the traditional boundaries of our discipline, this choice of topic sprang from the present cultural ambience. Like the Victorian era, the world of today is characterized by insatiable curiosity, constantly changing tastes, and a pronounced eclecticism in the field of interior decoration. For some years now our intellectual, political and cultural outlook in Quebec has also been increasingly sensitive to the mechanisms of interaction and to the international context. From this standpoint, Quebec furniture from the years 1840-1900 represents a remarkably eloquent expression of an immense, world-wide shift in thinking, a breaking down of the divisions between countries and cultures.[2]

However, the picture we are now able to paint of this area of our communal heritage is very different from the idea we had of it some six or seven years ago. We were then faced with a somewhat tenuous subject, represented by a small number of artefacts documented more by accepted ideas than by historical research. Unlike other aspects of our material and artistic culture, the furniture of Victorian Quebec has received remarkably little attention from historiographers.[3] Thus, the first thing we had to do was to start from scratch, reconstructing a reality that the people of Quebec had almost entirely erased from their collective memory. To read the entry on "Furniture" in the *Canadian Encyclopedia* published by Hurtig in 1985, one would think that "Victorian furniture" was a purely English Canadian phenomenon from provinces other than Quebec. It was as if the history of furniture in Quebec had mysteriously come to a stop in the 1830s and only started again in the twentieth century!

The explanation of this odd silence is not in itself a simple one. For practical purposes, it was the result of an ideological position widespread among the Quebec intelligentsia from the 1920s until the dawn of the 1970s. In their concern to preserve historical material linked to French traditions together with ensuring the survival of early forms of craftsmanship, they automatical-

2
John Henry Robinson (1796-1871)
Her Most Gracious Majesty, the Queen Victoria, 1845
Coloured engraving after a work by John Partridge (1790-1872), 67.1 x 54.3 cm
Musée du Québec, Quebec City, photo Nicole Savoie (A.42.75.E)

3
Georges T. Doo (1800-1886)
His Royal Highness the Prince Albert, K. G. & c., 1844
Coloured engraving after a work by John Partridge (1790-1872), 66.9 x 54.9 cm
Musée du Québec, Quebec City, photo Nicole Savoie (A.42.76.E)

ly rejected wholesale anything that smacked of British cultural imperialism or American-style industrialization. From Jean Chauvin through Gérard Morisset to Jean Palardy, the verdict on furniture associated with the name of Victoria, ruler of the British Empire, was severe and final.

In 1928 Chauvin stated his case in the following memorable phrase: "For us, the Victorian era conjures up stifling drawing rooms, massive doors hung with looped and tasselled curtains, rubber plants and palm trees, settees draped with rugs, cushions gilded like bishop's copes and a whole jumble of fussy, ornate knick-knacks."[4] Thirteen years later, Morisset devoted a page of his first general compendium to listing the names of several cabinetmakers who made "imitations" of an "artistic level" the author preferred not to describe.[5] Even more significantly, Morisset did not take the trouble to find, document or photograph furniture in the Victorian style for the enormous inventory of art works in the province of Quebec which he had just begun. On the other hand, he paid particular attention to traditional furniture, and many pieces were acquired by the provincial museum as a result of his recommendations. In the early 1960s Jean Palardy found this work a godsend when he was preparing his own monumental tome on the early furniture of French Canada.

Following Morisset, Palardy ascribed the start of the decline of Quebec traditions in about the 1830s to the emergence of the English Gothic revival:

> This marks the beginning of the decline of French Canadian architecture. The very distinctive and charming styles of the houses and churches of Quebec,

LIVING IN STYLE

4
Horatio Walker (1858-1938)
Interior of a House, 1886
Watercolour, 14.2 x 23 cm
Musée du Québec, Quebec City, photo Patrick Altman
(34.539.01)

which arouse such admiration today, were soon forgotten. The appalling churches put up since that time demonstrate this decline. Novelty took over, and our élite adopted almost anything new as long as it was not of local origin.

With the popularity of Gothic revival architecture, armoires with narrow Gothic panels, grotesque tables and fantastic armchairs were found even in country homes. The universal plague of Victorian and Louis-Philippe furniture and trimmings darkened Canadian interiors, and the most hideous styles of the nineteenth century were indiscriminately mixed. The whole of Canada was disfigured by this outbreak of bad taste.

In Quebec, traditional furniture received its death blow. The lure of ephemeral fashions and the consequent rejection of the past contributed to the loss of a French Canadian identity, and obscured the distinctive character of a whole people.[6]

This ideological stance, which went hand in hand with approving only of traditional furniture, helped to consolidate the enduring myth of Quebec as a rural society turned in on itself and resistant to change. This idea had long been reflected in picturesque and condescending popular pictures of the French Canadian *habitant* family in the farmhouse kitchen. Another result of this attitude was that an important section of our collective heritage was dispersed or fell into decay. Interest on the part of the public and of public institutions, which had been aroused on behalf of traditional furniture, evaporated into indifference and neglect.

From Montebello to the villa Cataraqui, innumerable Victorian residences lost most or all of their furniture during the twentieth century.[7] In 1921 it

5
The yellow drawing room of the Manoir Papineau, Montebello
Photograph
Archives nationales du Québec, Centre de Québec et Chaudière-Appalaches, collection initiale
(N-77-7-11-34)

6
Edgar Gariépy (1881-1956), Montreal
The yellow drawing room of the Manoir Papineau, Montebello
Photograph
McGill University, Montreal, Ramsay Traquair Archive
(101704)

was the granddaughter of the historian François-Xavier Garneau who raised the alarm when the contents of the seigneurial *manoir* of Louis-Joseph Papineau were in danger of being sold at auction. In an open letter addressed to premier Louis-Alexandre Taschereau, she insisted in vain on the importance of keeping house and contents together as a whole:

> I have stressed the historical value of Montebello, but what is also relevant is the intrinsic value of this estate, built in the purest French style, evoking the old manor houses with their plain but impressive lines, set amid splendid scenery, a genuine specimen of the seigneurial residence from the earliest days of the colony. The furnishings, perfectly intact and reverently preserved by his descendants, are also of great artistic interest. I beg of you, do not allow so beautiful a monument to the past to be dismantled; rather, make it the framework of a National Museum, a shrine illustrating for future generations our taste, our tenacity and our patriotism.[8]

From the 1930s on, the anthropologist and ethnographer Marius Barbeau was one of the few to take any interest in Victorian furniture: he interviewed an old cabinetmaker, collected some historical data, took a series of photographs and identified a group of suites of furniture he deemed worthy of interest; most of them he attributed to the workshops of William Drum and Philippe Vallière. In June 1935 he spoke to a Toronto collector about the furniture to be found in the archbishop's palace and the seminary in Quebec City, as well as the drawing-room suites belonging to Mrs. William Home on Laurier Avenue, Mr. Whitehead on Maple Avenue (avenue des Érables) and Mrs. Gordon Pfeiffer on the same avenue.[9] A month later, at Mrs. Pfeiffer's request, Barbeau recommended her thirteen-piece suite to the trustees of the National Gallery in Ottawa, pointing out that it had originally belonged to John Young, a friend of the painter Cornelius Krieghoff. In his letter he stressed the importance of this sort of nineteenth-century production, and lamented its all too frequent fate:

> It was an important industrial and artistic growth in itself. For many years now Montreal [. . .] dealers have been exporting this furniture by the car-load to Boston and New York, and palming it off as old French furniture.[10]

7
Console table with mirror from the original Desrochers Collection, Couillard Street, Quebec City
Photo ministère des Affaires culturelles du Québec, IOA

In some of his published books Barbeau included photographs of furniture and notes on some furniture makers. One of the eight Victorian pieces reproduced in his *J'ai vu Québec* (1957) was a magnificent mirror then attributed to Jean-Baptiste Côté, which had been drawn to his attention by Édouard Desrochers of Couillard Street in Quebec City.[11] Elsewhere, Barbeau evokes the memory of the furniture makers Vallière, Drum, "Puff" Roy, Narcisse Bertrand, Azarie Lavigne, Laurent Moisan, Joseph Lamarre and Octave Morel. He does not neglect to mention the accomplishments of his own father:

> A number of professional and folk carvers are still working in various parts of Quebec, although their art has lost its former usefulness and significance. My father, for instance, though a farmer, used to while away the winters in his workshop making fine furniture. That avocation was an invaluable recreation to him as a stimulus after summer labour on the farm. [...] To him this occupation was a pleasure from childhood to old age. Though he may be described as a folk carver, his taste for sculpture was derived from the old professional art of Quebec. He had known, as a young man, two professional carvers, the Dion brothers, while they were working on the decorations for his parish church.[12]

In 1970, a year after Barbeau's death, a bedroom suite made by his father Charles was acquired by the Museum of Man in Ottawa.

In retrospect, Marius Barbeau's efforts on behalf of Quebec Victorian furniture seem to have gone relatively unnoticed, and had no significant results. Thus, we do not know what has become of Dorothy Pfeiffer's furniture, nor of the fine bedroom suite of which O. C. Côté of Des Remparts Street, Quebec City, sent photographs to Ottawa.[13] The same is true of a drawing-room suite attributed to Louis Jobin, which the chief curator of the provincial museum described to the collector Paul Gouin in a letter of March 21, 1946.[14] Did it make its way to the United States or English Canada, after languishing in some shed, barn or basement? It was to just such a place that an interesting Naturalist-style sideboard had been relegated, when it was found and recorded

8
Charles Barbeau
Bed, about 1900
Painted basswood, 230.5 x 160.8 x 205 cm
Canadian Museum of Civilization, Hull (70-462)

in a photograph now in the Université Laval archives, in the bequest of the architect Sylvio Brassard.[15] A similar fate befell a walnut sideboard that appeared in two photographs published by *Le Petit Journal* on September 25, 1949. At that time this remarkable and finely carved piece was stored in the basement of the Notre-Dame de Montréal church. It had originally been commissioned, in about 1898, by Charles Brouillette, a merchant in Saint-Henri de Mascouche, from an unidentified sculptor. All that is left to us today of this vanished piece is a cryptic description that indicates how unusual it was:

> The sideboard is nine and a half feet high, seven feet eight inches wide and twenty-seven inches deep. The base is flanked by four doors carved with fishes hanging from a nail and birds with their wings outstretched. Between the doors and at each corner, large beavers seem to climb and gnaw the wood. The upper part of the base is carved with flower motifs, and the side panels with figures of

game. The handles of the drawers above the doors are carved in the shape of deer.

On the upper part of the sideboard are three mirrors in carved frames. A slab of marble imported from Italy adds a last luxurious touch.[16]

The general situation of Victorian furniture in Quebec, together with the particular cases referred to, naturally influenced the approach we took to the research, and meant that the task became part of a whole process of recovering what had been lost. We left no avenue unexplored as regards finding surveys and inventories, unearthing old pictures and designs, and building up a representative range of manuscript and printed sources. Some trails that at first seemed unorthodox or unpromising turned out to be very rewarding in the end.

9
W. B. Edwards, Quebec City
Bedroom suite, Des Remparts Street, Quebec City
Photograph
Canadian Museum of Civilization, Hull, Marius Barbeau Collection (90-607)

10
W. B. Edwards, Quebec City
Dressing chest from a bedroom suite, Des Remparts Street, Quebec City
Photograph
Canadian Museum of Civilization, Hull, Marius Barbeau Collection (90-606)

11
Sideboard
Photograph
Archives de l'Université Laval, fonds Sylvio Brassard (255-11-5.3)

12
Renaissance-revival sideboard from Saint-Henri de Mascouche
Illustration published in the *Petit Journal*, September 25, 1949
Photo SRP

These areas of investigation gave rise to several preliminary articles[17] and provided food for thought on the methodology of the various possible approaches to studying nineteenth-century *bourgeois* furniture. Reading foreign historians on the subject soon confirmed our sense of the polysemic nature of this furniture, and revealed how fragmented and specialized were the studies devoted to it. Some authors gave lengthy descriptions of the characteristics of the major styles, based on specially selected famous pieces,[18] while others dwelt on the formal and stylistic development of a broader range of significant pieces replaced in context.[19] The socio-historical approach produced studies in which furniture provided a way of analyzing decoration, lifestyles and social conditions, either on the international scale or in terms of specific countries.[20] In a work published in 1948 which is still relevant, Siegfried Giedion took a functionalist approach in studying the movement away from craftsmanship and towards mass production in the context of a concern for comfort.[21] Other writers of less ambitious monographs and articles have followed the careers of specific furniture makers[22] or examined the concrete aspects of their work: the tools and materials used, the working methods, and so on.[23] Completing the range of approaches are the compendiums on design,[24] the dictionaries of cabinetmakers[25] and works on furniture typology, the most notable of which is Nicole de Reyniès's book on domestic furniture published in 1987.[26] Faced with so many ways of approaching the subject, we decided on a multi-faceted method of evaluation, giving due consideration, in so far as was possible, to all the descriptive, analytical and symbolic aspects and thus to allow Quebec Victorian furniture to speak to us again.

As we pondered the question of methodology, we came up against the delicate question of the status of furniture in museums as well as in the art market.[27] Many art historians feel that furniture should be relegated to the basement of the Art History temple, far from the upper floors reserved for the noble arts of architecture, painting, and, though lower down, sculpture. The most entrenched think it almost sacrilegious to suggest that a piece of furniture made for a functional purpose could possibly be invested with the aura of an art work, even if it is unusually pleasing aesthetically. And yet a number of Victorian theoreticians held that art and decoration were one and the same, so that strictly speaking, by adding ornamentation to an everyday object, one could turn it into a work of art.[28] Such seems to have been the opinion held by the author of an article published in the Montreal newspaper *La Minerve* in 1866, which described a large decorated mirror frame carved by craftsmen of the famous furniture makers J. & W. Hilton of Montreal.[29] Referred to from the outset as a "superb work of art", this frame with a seafaring theme had been designed for one of the drawing rooms of the steamship *Québec*, and was elaborately carved with dolphins and seaweed, the arms of France and England, a heraldic beaver and a bust of Jacques Cartier, the celebrated navigator and explorer from Saint-Malo. In addition to describing this fine piece, designed by Arthur Mingeaud, a French-born artist, the author of the *La Minerve* article refers expressly to that extra richness which, in the Victorian era, could confer special status on some utilitarian objects. Thus the artist's talent and the craftsman's skill enabled the purchasers of their furniture to rise above their concern for ease, comfort and luxury, to "enjoy what is beautiful and pleasing", in short, to lay claim to good taste.

Fine furniture in Victorian Quebec as a subject lies somewhere between art and material culture: it may equally well be examined from an aesthetic viewpoint as from a socio-cultural one. To opt for just one of these approaches would be to compartmentalize in an arbitrary and unreal manner, and would limit the interpretation. In itself, fine furniture is a proper subject for a formal and stylistic analysis made in terms of similar productions at the same date. In evaluating what was derivative and what original, there is no denying the effect of outside influences at a time when there was so much trade and exchange both within the province and internationally. Above and beyond these factors, furniture cannot be disassociated from the historical, socio-economic and cultural context in which it is created and accepted. Not only does it provide information on the lifestyle, taste and social standing of its users, but it also reveals something of the craftsmanship, training and technical expertise of its makers. Separate from works of the Higher Art, often created for an élite, fine furniture in the Victorian era is a valuable indicator of the cultural dynamic of a society, in so far as it became part of the daily life of a wide range of individuals, from the producers to the owners, occasional users and even observers. From this standpoint, there is no denying the relevance of a study and an exhibition based on multidisciplinary research at the university level, which responds to the specific demands of both an art museum and a museum of civilization.

Just as the design of the exhibition is unique in its dual thrust, both aesthetic and educational, so also the companion publication, written by several authors, is unlike the usual catalogue in its layout, documentary content and images, and in its open-minded approach. We called on the expertise of art historians, historians in various special fields, ethnologists, sociolinguists, geographers and even specialists in nineteenth-century Quebec literature. Since real life is not compartmentalized, there could never be too many or too varied ways of trying to understand the lifestyle of a vanished age.

As our work progressed, we tried to free ourselves of some long-standing prejudices, to leave room for positive criticism that would transcend our present-day criteria of appreciation. We decided to employ certain terms that were current in the past but have fallen into disuse. One such is the word *meublier*, which could mean a manufacturer of furniture, a cabinet maker or a craftsman decorator – an upholsterer – specializing in furniture.[30] We also learned to appreciate the importance the Victorians accorded to words such as taste, elegance, luxury, wealth, progress and comfort. These were values regularly invoked by newspapers in the period 1840-1900, as can be seen in the following extract from an article published in connection with the provincial exhibition held at the Crystal Palace in Montreal in 1860:

> [The furniture section] is particularly attractive to those who like *comfort*. Indeed, is it not pleasant, when weary after a long day's work, to stretch out on a soft sofa smelling deliciously of wood and dream of distant, glamorous lands? Anyone who has ever felt like this should lose no time in going to see the magnificent *drawing-room suite* made by Mr. Pariseau of Montreal in beautifully carved walnut ornamented with remarkable taste and elegance.[31]

The text incorporates frequent quotations from and reproductions of contemporary documents – extracts from newspapers, house inventories, descriptions of companies and exhibitions, correspondence, and so on – together with case studies. These documents and studies should provide the reader with vital background information on the lifestyle of Victorian Quebec. They reveal a community living in a changing world, a society in which, though some values and cultural practices were generally upheld, this apparent consensus often disguised a multi-faceted, pluralistic social reality with ample room for individual ambitions and personalities to flourish.

John R. Porter

1   Extract from a letter to his friend the Abbé Henri-Raymond Casgrain dated January 29, 1867. The *Oeuvres complètes de Octave Crémazie* were published under the patronage of the Institut canadien de Québec (Montreal: Librairie Beauchemin, 1882), p. 54 (trans.).

2   Much of the present text is taken from a paper given in Rennes in 1988. John R. Porter, "L'objet matériel et ses contextes: le cas du meuble de l'époque victorienne au Québec", Proceedings of the conference "Les dynamismes culturels en France et au Québec", held in Rennes on June 2 and 3, 1988 (*Annales de Bretagne et des Pays de l'ouest*, vol. 95, no. 4 [1988], pp. 379-388).

3   See Georges-Pierre Léonidoff and John R. Porter, "La recherche universitaire et la mise en valeur des collections de mobilier victorien au Québec", *Muse*, spring 1986, p. 22.

4   Jean Chauvin, *Ateliers* (Montreal and New York: Louis Carrier and Les Éditions du Mercure, 1928), p. 139 (trans.).

5   Gérard Morisset, *Coup d'oeil sur les arts en Nouvelle-France* (Quebec City: 1941), pp. 43-44.

6   Jean Palardy, *The Early Furniture of French Canada*, translated by Eric McLean (Toronto: Macmillan of Canada, 1963), p. 393.

7   In this regard, see Paul Trépanier's editorial "Sauver les meubles" at the beginning of a special issue of *Continuité* (no. 51, autumn 1991) devoted to Victorian interiors.

8   *La Presse* of August 24, 1921, quoted by Paul-Louis Martin in *Rapport annuel de la Commission des biens culturels du Québec pour 1986-1987* (Quebec City: Les Publications du Québec, 1987), pp. 20-21 (trans.). As is apparent from the photograph by Gariépy reproduced here, much of the furniture was dispersed shortly afterwards.

9   CCFCS, Fonds Marius Barbeau, Dossier 54 (Drum et Vallière), letter from Marius Barbeau to L.-R. Wright dated June 4, 1935.

10   CCFCS, Fonds Marius Barbeau, Dossier 54 (Drum et Vallière), memorandum, May 1, 1935; see also the letter from Mrs. Gordon Pfeiffer to Barbeau dated April 25, 1935.

11   CCFCS, Fonds Marius Barbeau, Dossier 39 (Jean-Baptiste Côté), letter from Édouard Desrochers to Marius Barbeau dated January 24, 1946.

12 Marius Barbeau, "Laurentian Wood Carvers", *The Canadian Geographical Journal*, vol. 9, no. 4 (October 1935), p. 183.

13 CCFCS, Fonds Marius Barbeau, Dossier 54 (Drum et Vallière), three undated photographs taken by W. B. Edwards. The documents were sent to Barbeau after Côté moved from Buckingham to Quebec. The third photograph shows another bedroom suite.

14 In this document, held in the Archives du Musée du Québec, Rainville describes the suite as "one of the most beautiful sets of Victorian furniture" that he knows. He adds, "it consists of six chairs, two armchairs, a large sofa, a stool, a centre table and two console tables. It is in a perfect state of preservation" (trans.).

15 It is not known what became of this piece, which looked very similar to another sideboard kept in the priests' residence of the Collège de Lévis. See Georges-Pierre Léonidoff and Jean-Pierre Labiau, "Un mobilier sous influence", *Continuité*, no. 38 (winter 1988), p. 29.

16 "Suzor-Coté aurait-il sculpté ce buffet gardé à Notre-Dame?", *Le Petit Journal*, September 25, 1949.

17 See the last section of the bibliography of the present text.

18 E.g. Colette Lehmann, *Mobilier Louis-Philippe / Napoléon III* (Paris: Éditions Ch. Massin, n.d.).

19 E.g. Peter Thornton, *L'époque et son style / La décoration intérieure 1620-1920* (Paris: Flammarion, 1986); Simon Jervis, *Le style de la grande époque victorienne*, catalogue of a travelling exhibition organized by the Victoria and Albert Museum (Ottawa: National Gallery of Canada, 1974). The last-mentioned work covers not only furniture but all sorts of visual evidence from architecture, sculpture and other decorative arts.

20 E.g. Mark Girouard, *The Victorian Country House* (New Haven and London: Yale University Press, 1979); *Histoire de la vie privée* (edited by Philippe Ariès and Georges Duby), vol. 4 of *De la révolution à la Grande Guerre* edited by Michèle Perrot (Paris: Éditions du Seuil, 1987).

21 Siegfried Giedion, "Mécanisation et environnement humain", in *La mécanisation au pouvoir / Contribution à l'histoire anonyme* (Paris: Centre Georges Pompidou / CCI, 1980), pp. 233-421.

22 E.g. Ruth Cathcart, *Jacques & Hay, 19th Century Toronto Furniture Makers* (Erin, Ontario: The Boston Mills Press, 1986).

23 E.g. Lilly A. Koltun, *The Cabinetmaker's Art in Ontario c. 1850-1900* (Ottawa: National Museums of Canada, 1979, Collection Mercure, dossier no. 26).

24 E.g. Edward Joy, *Pictorial Dictionary of British 19th Century Furniture Design* (Woodbridge, Suffolk: The Antique Collector's Club, 1984 [c. 1977]); Joseph T. Butler, *Field Guide to American Antique Furniture* (New York and Oxford: Facts on File Publications, 1985); Christopher Payne, *19th-Century European Furniture* (Woodbridge: The Antique Collector's Club, 1985 [c. 1981]).

25 E.g. Denise Ledoux-Lebard, *Les ébénistes du XIXe siècle (1795-1889), leurs oeuvres et leurs marques* (Paris: Les Éditions de l'amateur, 1984).

26 Nicole de Reyniès, *Principes d'analyse scientifique / Le mobilier domestique / Vocabulaire typologique* (Paris: Imprimerie nationale, 1987), 2 vols.

27 In an article published in 1988, Daniel Meyer, Curator at the Château de Versailles, demonstrated that in the eighteenth century even the most ornate pieces of furniture carved by famous craftsmen were still considered merely utilitarian objects (*Connaissance des Arts*, no. 433, March 1988, pp. 86-97). Because of their rarity, some limited series of the eighteenth and nineteenth centuries came to be included in the category of art works, a category which, it should be remembered, is artificially based on the ideas of uniqueness — or rarity — and of authenticity, the latter criterion invalidating productions by more than one hand. This is the viewpoint defended by Michel Melot in a paper entitled "La notion d'originalité et son importance dans la définition des objets d'art", given at the Colloque international de Marseille on June 13 and 14, 1985. See Raymonde Moulin (ed.), *Sociologie de l'art* (Paris: La Documentation française, 1986), pp. 191-202.

28 See for example an article in the London *Builder* entitled "Is the Prevalent Taste for `Art Furniture' and Bric-à-brac Indicative of a Sound, Healthy Aesthetic Culture?", reprinted in *The Scientific Canadian*, November 1880, pp. 354-355. See also the documents reprinted in two books by Bernard Denvir published in 1984 and 1986 (London and New York: Longman) in the series "A Documentary of Taste in Britain": *The Early Nineteenth Century/Art, Design and Society, 1789-1852*; *The Late Victorian/Art, Design and Society, 1852-1910*.

29 Reprinted in the *Journal de Québec* of April 6, 1866, p. 2, this article is appended to the present text.

30 This term can be found in the *Französisches Etymologisches Wörterbuch* of 1969 in the entry on "mobilis" (63, 2a).

31 *L'Ordre*, September 10, 1860, p. 1 (trans.).

CHAPTER

I

THE CONTEXT

13
Viger Square, Montreal
Engraving published in *L'Opinion publique*, August 18, 1870
Photo SRP

QUEBEC SOCIETY IN THE VICTORIAN ERA

THE NINETEENTH CENTURY WAS THE AGE OF REVOLUTION. Throughout the western world uprisings (Germany, Italy, Spain, Ireland, Russia), revolts (France in 1830 and 1848) and civil war (the United States 1861-1865) threatened the status quo and undermined political systems, social order and foreign policies. The economy was particularly affected: the industrial revolution, technological inventions and mechanization changed the nature of work, working conditions and lifestyles.

Quebec society was not immune from these changes, and went through a tense period of difficulties and new hopes. Democracy was strengthened (the electoral tax was abolished and more people could vote), a province-wide marketing system was created, new regions (the Saguenay, the Laurentians) were developed, towns and villages expanded and municipal and educational institutions were established. The face of Quebec gradually changed as the province evolved from a primarily agricultural society to an industrial and urban one. Every town had its commercial centre, its public market, its factories, workers housing and middle-class neighbourhoods. Signposts along the back roads displayed the names of every saint in the Catholic calendar, and new parishes sprang up by the hundreds.

New means of transportation and communication increased trade and travel as never before. This was the railway era, the dawn of a new age, which would be better for some and worse for others. A few individuals would succeed in amassing huge wealth, but the majority faced an uncertain future. Quebec migrants by the thousands took the train to the more industrialized regions of New England, while others flooded in to Montreal and Quebec City, where the old urban structures could not cope with the influx. Other emigrants, fewer in number, went off to try their luck in the newly opened territories.

With this tremendous shift of population, lifestyles and living conditions altered radically, despite opposition from the ubiquitous Catholic clergy. Torn between tradition and progress, Quebec society was in a state of flux: crises, emigration and ideological conflicts characterized the century, and the results of prosperity were slow in coming. Tensions were exacerbated by the fact that two peoples lived side by side on the same territory. Conflicts between the two

14
Notman Studio, Montreal
Louis-Joseph Papineau (1786-1871), about 1860
Photograph
National Archives of Canada, Ottawa (C-21005)

15
Notman Studio, Montreal
George-Étienne Cartier (1814-1873), 1863
Photograph
McCord Museum of Canadian History, Montreal,
Notman Photographic Archives (7956-I)

took the form of racial confrontations between the English and the Canadiens, or disputes over language between English-speakers and French-speakers. The English had the backing of the all-powerful home country, Great Britain, which was the leading world power throughout the nineteenth century.

The astonishingly long reign of Queen Victoria, from 1837 to 1901, coincided with the apogee of the British Empire and left its mark on an entire era. When the young queen was crowned in 1837, a running battle was going on in her Canadian colonies.

FROM CANADA TO QUEBEC

Since 1791 the British colony had been divided into two provinces, Upper and Lower Canada. However, Canadians were finding the colonial yoke increasingly irksome, and French Canadians above all were demanding a more equitable form of representation and major political reforms. England's refusal to accede to these demands led in 1837 and 1838 to the Patriots' Rebellion led by Louis-Joseph Papineau. These uprisings were harshly quelled, and following the report of the special envoy, Lord Durham, in 1840 Great Britain proclaimed the Act of Union, which by uniting Upper and Lower Canada was seen primarily as a way of ensuring the gradual assimilation of French Canadians.

From this time onward reforms began to be implemented, granting the colony increased responsibility and political, administrative and economic autonomy as the mother country became ever less concerned with its Canadian subjects and abolished preferential tariffs. The leading political parties during this period were the reds, radical liberals who stood for a continuation of the Patriots' demands and for the principles of democracy, and the conservative blues, who were aligned with the clergy and consequently had more support.

The inability of coalition governments such as the Lafontaine-Baldwin administration to solve the colony's problems soon led prominent politicians, including John A. Macdonald and George Étienne Cartier, to start designing a new constitution, and in 1867 the Confederation was created. The reds and their leader, Antoine-Aimé Dorion, stayed aloof from this process, but the new Dominion, also called at the time La Puissance, came into being without any real opposition.

Various powers were delegated to the provinces in the social, cultural and even economic spheres. French Canadians, who had seen their minority rights guaranteed within the newly constituted country, were henceforth the majority in the province of Quebec.

16
The Widening of the Lachine Canal.
Work at the Saint-Gabriel Locks Being Supervised by
Messrs. Loss and McRae
Engraving published in *L'Opinion publique*,
December 6, 1877
Photo SRP

17
Notman Studio, Montreal
Vice-Regal Car, about 1878-1880
Photograph
McCord Museum of Canadian History, Montreal,
Notman Photographic Archives (994-View)

THE MOTIVE POWER OF THE CENTURY: THE RAILWAYS

To increase trade within a province as huge as Quebec, transport and communications had to be improved and developed. The telegraph, the mails, roads, rivers and railways made travel and communications faster and more efficient than ever before. By the late 1840s both Montreal and Quebec City had a telegraph service, and by the early 1850s Quebec had its own postal service and the postage stamp had been introduced.

To increase commercial use of the river system and to forward wheat and lumber to England, ships, now mostly built of steel and powered by steam, had first to find a way of crossing the rapids. In the late 1840s the canal system (Lachine, Rideau, Welland, Beauharnois) was completed, and between 1850 and 1851 a canal was dug between Montreal and Quebec City. In the second half of the nineteenth century rail transport superseded river traffic. Trains provided fast year-round service, and symbolized in a sense the spirit of the new age. Politicians and businessmen joined forces to improve the system, so that by the mid-nineteenth century all business policy was based on the railways. They were considered vital to industrialization, to economic growth, perhaps even as the basis of a continent-wide State. Several members of Parliament and ministers held shares in railway companies whose projects were financed by the state but carried out by private enterprise.

The Grand Trunk, the first great railway system which linked Sarnia, Ontario to Rivière-du-Loup, Quebec, opened in 1860. The second, the Intercolonial, running from Rivière-du-Loup to Halifax, Nova Scotia, was completed in 1876. The third (and last) of the great railroad lines, the Canadian Pacific, stretching from Montreal to Vancouver, was opened in 1885. The railway companies, with their networks of stations and plants, their thousands of employees and their financial structure (joint stock companies) ushered in the era of big business. Most economic development in the second half of the century was based on the construction of railway lines, which encouraged industrial growth and stimulated local industry and national markets, the lumber trade and colonization.

The railways also brought town and countryside together. The colonizing lines, as they were called at the time, made possible the development of distant regions such as the Saguenay, Lac-Saint-Jean, the Beauce and the Gaspé, which could only be reached by train. The railroad brought raw materials from the outlying areas into the big cities to be processed. It was by means of the railways that the textile industry was able to establish the sweating system, whereby clothing made in pieces in the factories was sent out to be made up by women workers in the nearby countryside. It was also the railway that made it possible for department stores such as Eatons (founded in 1880) to set up mail-order businesses so that rural inhabitants could order goods advertised in their catalogue.

Although the government invested heavily in railways throughout the second half of the nineteenth century, the roads were poorly maintained and frequently in a lamentable state. By the turn of the century Quebec had an excellent system of communications with the outside world, but communications within the province were still underdeveloped. The exception was Montreal. Situated at the centre of navigation between the Great Lakes and the Atlantic, its port handled a considerable volume of traffic. As a junction for railways running towards the east, the south and the west, the city gained even greater ascendancy over central Canada, while staying in close contact with the United States by means of lines by which many French Canadians emigrated to New England. This control over all the communications networks gave the metropolitan area increased power, making it disproportionately more influential than its rival, Quebec City, and the other urban centres of the province. Entire regions such as the Abitibi were not yet served by the railways and remained cut off.

THE INDUSTRIAL REVOLUTION AFFECTS THE PROVINCE

Steam power and iron had already revolutionized transport and communications, and their use in developing industries increased production as never before. The industrial revolution was thus made possible. Throughout the second half of the nineteenth century a new society gradually grew up, characterized by urban living, industry and the wage-earning class.

Agriculture, still the basis of Quebec's economy, was modernized little by little. A turning point came in 1875, when the province's farmers began to specialize in milk production. Advances in technology increased yields and led to the emergence of large, more market-oriented farms. Alongside this modern style of agriculture there grew up a kind of subsistence farming linked to the lumber industry. This was the period when William Price moved into the Saguenay and the lower St. Lawrence region to cut timber, which in the nineteenth century was mainly exported to England. Towards the end of the century, however, with the development of the pulp and paper industry a greater percentage of exports began to go to the United States.

But above all, the industrial revolution marked the changeover from an agricultural society to an urban, industrial one. Industrial development was primarily an urban phenomenon. Canadian industry was born on the banks

18
Samuel McLaughlin (1826-1914)
Montreal harbour, about 1866
Photograph
Musée du Québec, Quebec City (G-69.191-F)

19
Notman Studio, Montreal
Harbour from Custom House, Montreal,
about 1885-1889
Photograph
McCord Museum of Canadian History, Montreal,
Notman Photographic Archives (1941-View)

of the Lachine Canal around 1846. Once improvements to the canal were complete, the government made land and water-power resources available to industrialists. The initial period of development saw industries concentrated in the Montreal area. From the 1850s onward, industrialization was based on the flour trade, ironworks, lumber and the shoe industry, sectors that required cheap labour provided mainly by immigrants.

The world-wide slump of 1873-1879, caused by the collapse of the Austrian banking system, slowed down the process of industrial development. Bankruptcies multiplied, the timber industry went into decline, and there was growing unemployment. The financial sector in Canada was also affected. Many small banks disappeared or were taken over by large chartered banks

22
Notman Studio, Montreal
Thomas D'Arcy McGee (1825-1868)
Photograph
National Archives of Canada, Ottawa (C-51976)

D'Arcy McGee was born in Ireland and settled in Montreal in 1857. Appointed minister in 1863, he was considered one of the best public speakers of his time. He fell into disgrace, however, and died at the hand of an assassin on April 7, 1868.

23
Notre-Dame Street, Montreal, 1843
Engraving after a drawing by James Duncan (1806-1881), 25.9 x 38.5 cm
National Archives of Canada, Ottawa (C-1635)

traffic, administration, education and law and order became increasingly acute.

The municipal authorities were slow to intervene, preferring to leave the initiative to private enterprise. However, the municipalities gradually built up local infrastructures, and most large towns or cities could boast a number of public buildings: a town hall, law courts, post offices, fire stations, schools and hospitals. Travellers arriving at Viger station in Montreal or du Palais station in Quebec City could find board and lodging in big hotels. As a result of ever higher property values in the urban centres, neighbourhoods became more specialized. Business, administration and services tended to be concentrated in the city centre; workers lived close to the industrial areas, while *bourgeois* residences were built far from the factory chimneys and the overcrowded makeshift housing of the proletariat. Outside the cities municipalities developed in all regions of Quebec. From the mid-nineteenth century on, townships centred on parishes grew up, each with its own civil administration and social services. By the second half of the century there were hundreds of new parishes. Father Labelle, a 333-pound Titan of a man who became famous for instigating the development of the North (the Laurentians), founded some sixty of them.

By the end of the century the urban population of Quebec was double what it had been in the 1850s (see table). The population of Montreal grew from 90,323 in 1861 to 267,000 by 1901. Quebec City could no longer compete: during the same period, its population had only risen from 59,990 to 69,000.

* These statistics were taken from tables by J. Hamelin and Y. Roby, *Histoire économique du Québec, 1851-1896*, p. 292, and from P.-A. Linteau, R. Durocher and J.-C. Robert, *Histoire du Québec contemporain*, vol. I, p. 153.

The populaiton of Québec and its major urban centres from 1851 to 1891*					
	1851	1861	1871	1881	1891
Montreal	57 715	90 323	107 225	155 238	216 650
Québec City	42 052	59 990	59 699	62 446	63 090
Trois-Rivières	4 936	6 058	7 570	8 670	8 334
Sherbrooke	2 998	5 899	4 432	7 227	10 110
Québec as a whole	890 261	1 111 566	1 119 516	1 359 027	1 488 535

TO THE GLORY OF GOD: CHURCHES AND SCHOOLS

In nineteenth-century Quebec society eighty-five per cent of the population was Catholic. Among the other religious denominations, Protestants, mainly Anglicans, Presbyterians and Methodists, constituted the largest and best organized minority. What they had in common was a tendency to allow the laity greater freedom of initiative than did the Catholic Church. Generally speaking, Catholics and Protestants acted as separate groups quite cut off from one another. For the Catholic clergy, which had been proscribed after the English Conquest of 1760, the second half of the nineteenth century represented a new beginning.

After 1840 the religious authorities were permitted to create new dioceses and to train priests, and the clergy were granted economic privileges: church property was henceforth exempt from taxes. Following the failure of the Rebellions of 1837-1838, the British authorities seem to have decided in this way to ensure cooperation from the Catholic clergy and hence the loyalty of the French Canadian population. This favourable turn of events led to a remarkable resurgence of the religious orders. Over a fifty-year period (from 1851 to 1901), the number of men and women in religious orders rose from 893 to 25,332. Most of these were nuns, who constituted seventy-seven per cent of the clergy in 1901.

With this growth in its numbers and its means, the Catholic clergy took an increasingly important leadership role. The failure of the uprisings (which had been condemned by the religious authorities) and the lack of political and economic organization within Quebec society was to the advantage of the clergy. Mgr Bourget, appointed Archbishop of Montreal in 1840, dreamed of making his city a little Rome. His election gave more power to the clergy in all aspects of social, and indeed political, life. The creation of new dioceses (Trois-Rivières, Rimouski, Sherbrooke, Chicoutimi, Nicolet, Valleyfield) meant that the faithful were kept in closer contact with the clergy: the keeping of registers recording baptisms, marriages and deaths enabled priests to follow up on their parishioners from the cradle to the grave.

Religious fervour was not the only reason for the astonishing surge in ecclesiastical activity. There was no lack of work for the religious orders.

24
Bishops of the Episcopal Church in Canada Present at the Recent Synod Held in Montreal
Engraving after a photograph by Notman published in the *Canadian Illustrated News*, October 3, 1874
National Archives of Canada, Ottawa (C-61459)

25
Chaplain's office, Soeurs de la Charité de Québec
Photograph published in the souvenir album marking the 50th anniversary of the foundation of the Hôpital des Soeurs de la Charité de Québec (1849-1899)
Archives des Soeurs de la Charité de Québec, Beauport
Photo SRP

26
Louis-Philippe Hébert (1850-1917)
Father Joseph Michaud and Monsignor Ignace Bourget Studying the Plans for Montreal's New Cathedral in the Company of Several Notables, 1902
Bronze bas-relief, 87.4 x 183.3 x 15.5 cm
Musée du Québec, Quebec City, photo Patrick Altman
(A 77.207 S)
A bas-relief identical to this one adorns the monument to Monsignor Ignace Bourget that stands near the cathedral of Montreal.

Parish priests, still relatively few and far between in mid-century, turned their hands to all sorts of jobs in order to provide for the spiritual and material needs of their flocks. As they grew larger, the religious orders became more specialized. The nuns were mostly concerned with good works. There were so many unfortunates in need: the poor, orphans, the old, the sick, society's rejects who received no help from the civil authorities. Hospitals, poorhouses and orphanages were established, together with charitable organizations such as the Société St. Vincent de Paul. The zeal of the clergy in preaching, helping, nursing and consoling the faithful was as instrumental in uniting Quebec as were the railways in uniting Canada. The communications network of the Church throughout the province was highly effective. Through Catholic newspapers and Catholic schools, the ecclesiastical message was so widely disseminated that no Catholic could break the rules without being ostracized by society.

Of all the fields in which they worked, education was the primary concern of the Catholic clergy. As the public school system developed, their efficient

lobbying put a stop to any attempts at secularization, and especially to a state-controlled Ministry of Education (one was established in 1868 but closed down in 1875). The clergy also succeeded in infiltrating every level of the public school system. The first Catholic university, Université Laval, was founded in 1852 as a result of pressure from the clergy. In this regard, however, Protestants were better served. The two Protestant universities, McGill, founded in 1829 and Bishop's College, established in 1853, provided technical and scientific training, whereas Catholics were mainly exposed to the humanities and the classics, a background that produced fine public speakers, quick to take part in the major debates of the age.

IDEAS AND INDIVIDUALS

The political, economic and social upheavals of the nineteenth century gave free rein to the expression of diverse ideas about how societies develop. In Quebec, although there were various visions of society, the main ideological conflict was that between liberalism and ultramontanism. The former was a

27
Mother Marie-Anne-Marcelle Mallet and three of her protégés
Photograph
Archives nationales du Québec, Centre de Québec et Chaudière-Appalaches (P000-6/PN-M/3)
Mother Mallet (1805-1871), founder of the order of the Soeurs de la Charité de Québec, was deeply concerned by the fate of the poor and the orphaned.

28
Livernois Studio, Quebec City
The orchestra of the boarding school run by the Ursulines de Québec
Photograph
Archives nationales du Québec, Centre de Québec et Chaudière-Appalaches (P560/N78-10-15-406)

29
The University of McGill College, Montreal
Engraving published in the *Canadian Illustrated News*, August 26, 1882
National Archives of Canada, Ottawa (C-77307)

philosophy, initially inspired by the ideals of the French Revolutions of 1789, 1830 and 1848, which emphasized the value of liberty and the rights of individuals as opposed to groups. Ultramontanism, which grew up in reaction to liberal ideas, emphasized spiritual rather than materialist values, and called for the powers of the clergy in the secular world to be extended and strengthened.

The Institut canadien, a literary and philosophical society that debated the social issues of the day, was the main platform for the liberals, who gradually became more moderate in their outlook. Without being anti-clerical, they rejected the influence of the clergy in non-religious matters. However, the Church's hostility to liberalism lost the movement a great deal of its support among the French-speaking population. It was not until the turn of the century that the Liberal party of Wilfrid Laurier became popular with the electorate and came to office. Meanwhile, the liberals encouraged French Canadians to aim at progress through education, economic development and the advancement of science. Liberalism became the credo of a bourgeois society whose interests, values and beliefs gradually became paramount.

In reaction against liberalism, the ultramontanes took a more aggressive stance during the second half of the century, refusing to separate Church and state. Under Mgr Bourget's bishopric the ultramontane ideology was clearly defined. It was based on respect for authority, hierarchy and order, and preached obedience to the authority of parents, husbands, bosses and the Church, together with an obligation on the part of the ruling classes (noblesse oblige) to provide for the less privileged; values that were on the decline in the nineteenth century. Since it believed in papal infallibility and the inalienable right of the Church in matters of education, ultramontanism held that the clergy should be active in every field of civil society. In this context, French Canadian nationalist sentiments were inspired sometimes by liberalism and sometimes by conservatism. The problem of their survival as a people, accentuated by the failure of the Rebellions and the union of the two Canadas, led them to cultivate a certain romanticism and to a rediscovery of their past.

30
Wilfrid Laurier (1841-1919)
Photograph
National Archives of Canada, Ottawa (C-1977)

31
Celebrating Saint-Jean-Baptiste Day in Quebec City
Engraving published in *L'Opinion publique*, July 1, 1880
National Archives of Canada, Ottawa (C-75480)

32
Montreal - Their Excellencies at Villa Maria Convent
Engraving after a drawing by E. Jump published in the *Canadian Illustrated News*, February 8, 1873
National Archives of Canada, Ottawa (C-59005)

This engraving depicts a visit made by the governor general of Canada, Lord Dufferin, and his wife to Villa Maria, a girls' boarding school run by the Soeurs de la Congrégation de Notre-Dame.

Thus the traditional life of French Canada was depicted by journalists (Étienne Parent, *Le Canadien*, 1842), historians (François-Xavier Garneau, *Histoire du Canada*, 1845-1848), and novelists (Joseph Marmotte, *François de Bienville*; Philippe-Aubert de Gaspé, *Les anciens canadiens*; Napoléon Bourassa, *Jacques et Marie*; Antoine Gérin-Lajoie, *Jean Rivard le défricheur*). But for a people not much given to reading, it was their passion for political, patriotic and religious oratory that reflected the importance of nationalist sentiment in the nineteenth century. The religious aspect gave this nationalism an added dimension. The Catholic Church was linked to conservatism and represented tradition, the past, authority, dogma and restraint. The Protestant churches stood for values more often associated with liberalism: reason, liberty, progress, science, the future and social justice.

Egalitarian ideas made little headway in Quebec, which was at the time deeply conservative in social matters. This conservatism underlay the attitude of feminists at the turn of the century. Feminist thinking was based on the generally held belief that society was divided into two complementary but separate spheres of life: the public sphere (work, business, politics) associated with men, and the private sphere (the family, children's upbringing and education) associated with women.

The economic and social changes that took place during the nineteenth century shattered previously held beliefs about social norms. Everyday life was not immune from the new realities of an urban industrial society.

33
A. R. Roy, Quebec City and Lévis
Émile Bélanger and his brother Octave, about 1880
Photograph
Archives du Séminaire de Québec (Ph 89.375)
Photo W. B. Edwards Inc., Quebec City

THE ELECT OF THE HOME: WOMEN AND DAILY LIFE
In Quebec society during the Victorian era, it was women who were in charge of organizing the everyday life of the family. Like their mothers and grandmothers, Quebec women still had many children. In 1831 there were 271 births for every thousand women of childbearing age. After 1851 the birth rate began to drop slowly, and this trend continued up to the end of the century. Between 1851 and 1901, the number of births per year fell from 196 per thousand to 160 per thousand. This fall in the birth rate, which was to continue until the late twentieth century, began with the industrial revolution. Urban areas, Protestant families and the *bourgeoisie* were the first to be affected by it.

Another new phenomenon, women and children working for wages, had a more obvious effect on social mores. Many of the products previously made at home (clothing, bed linen, food, soap) were now made industrially. As mills opened in large numbers across the province, women and children streamed in to work in them. In Montreal in 1871 thirty-three per cent of industrial workers were women, and across the province as a whole by 1891 one of every five factory workers was a woman.

These employees must have had a better life than did women working as maids, for girls in large numbers left home to work in the factories. Towards the end of the century, *bourgeois* ladies were increasingly obliged to find their maids among the newly arrived immigrants, especially the Irish: sometimes they even had to pay their fare over. Better educated single women could become schoolteachers or office clerks. For the very poor, or those reluctant to put up with the working conditions of home or factory, there was always prostitution, a growing phenomenon. According to estimates made by the Montreal police, there were forty-one prosperous and well-established broth-

34
Jones at the Club
Caricature published in *Diogenes*, July 30, 1869
Photo SRP

els in 1871; by 1891 there were 102 of them. With the increase in poverty and homelessness, other women worked as volunteers to provide a range of services for the destitute.

There was little room for lay people in the area of social services, which being good works were monopolized by the Catholic religious orders. The nuns established all kinds of shelters, some even providing day-care services for children (in 1858 the Grey Nuns opened a nursery for infants whose mothers worked in factories). Ladies of the *bourgeoisie* offered similar services for Protestants. But for well-to-do women there were fewer and fewer possibilities of working. They were increasingly confined to the house at the very time when much of the work previously done at home was being taken over by industry, so that there was little for them to do. The political and religious authorities tried to persuade them that a woman's true place is in the home.

As economic, social and family problems proliferated, feminism was born out of the determination of women of the prosperous classes to become involved in helping the poor. By the turn of the century, women's issues were making headlines in the women's pages of the leading newspapers. Among the subjects debated were working women, access to higher education and the right to vote. The clergy and nationalist politicians believed, wrongly, that the emancipation of women would lead them to abandon family life. The solution they suggested to the problem of women was a re-evaluation of home life as the only true vocation for a woman. The home should be a refuge from the horrors and dangers of the industrial world. The privacy of the home was to be jealously guarded, in *bourgeois* residences built well away from working-class neighbourhoods. In order to exclude servants from the life of the family, staircases were built connecting their sleeping quarters to the kitchen.

The pleasures of home and the conveniences of domestic life were enthusiastically acclaimed, even though technological innovations to date consisted merely of running water and coal-burning stoves. Affluence and success were demonstrated in interior decorating and furniture. In their drawing-rooms ladies of good society offered their guests tea in the afternoon, leaving their husbands to amuse themselves in venues thought unsuitable for women, such as billiard rooms. The well-to-do and the new rich displayed their wealth in ornate interiors and elaborate décor, as well as in opulently stuffed and upholstered furniture that provided appropriate comfort for those who could afford it. The idea of Home Sweet Home, the intimate and comfortable domestic kingdom, was increasingly appealing to the middle classes.

★ ★ ★

The Victorian era in Quebec was marked by important changes as the society moved from a pre-industrial to a modern state. This was a sort of halfway stage, a time when the old and the new existed side by side. The weight of tra-

35

36

dition gave continuity to a mainly rural and farm-based society, an unequal community of two racial groups and two cultures, dependent on the larger nation surrounding it, a society that believed in the virtues of faith and family and in institutions hallowed by history. But the pressures of the modern age upset the balance of society: a people learning to live an urban, industrial, wage-earning existence saw new virtues in the concepts of liberty, individualism and private property, and believed that the establishment of democratic institutions was a sign of progress.

The nineteenth century marked the transition from the traditional to the modern age. In Quebec this transition was a slow and painful one that lasted for the whole duration of Victoria's reign, from 1837 to 1901. In every sector of society divisions appeared, tensions mounted and conflicts arose, characterized by stormy debate; fortunes were made and lost in the twinkling of an eye, and many were forced to pack up and take the train to an uncertain future. The end of the colonial system and the gradual adoption of parlia-

35
Ceremonial chair in the William and Mary style, about 1880.
Black walnut and tooled leather, 157.5 x 23 x 77 cm
Bishop's palace of Chicoutimi. Photo Christine Guest/MMFA
This high-backed formal armchair, with seat and back upholstered in tooled leather and armrests adorned with griffin's heads, served as the episcopal throne of Monsignor Dominique Racine in the first cathedral of Chicoutimi.

36
Renaissance-revival Speaker's chair, about 1879. White oak, 224 x 81.5 x 69 cm
Archdiocese of Quebec City, kept at the Musée du Séminaire de Québec. Photo Christine Guest/MMFA
This chair was used by the Honourable Joseph-Goderic Blanchet (1829-1890), who was Mayor of Lévis from 1855 to 1861, member of parliament in Ottawa from 1861 to 1875, President of the Legislative Assembly in Quebec City until 1871, and Speaker of the House of Commons from 1879 to 1882.

mentary institutions, the industrial revolution and urbanization, the railways and population migration, trade and communications networks, new institutions and public services: all these changes affected social interaction, lifestyles and living conditions.

It was this ever-changing context that produced the exuberance, the disparities, discrepancies and diversity so characteristic of the Victorian era. The eclecticism of the Victorian style was perhaps due to the fact that permanence in this world was no longer possible. Uncertainty led people to create defensive structures, to build for themselves homes as refuges, where they felt safe from setbacks and reversals of fortune. Home was still the best place to relax, to retreat from the hard, cold competitive ethos of the developing industrial world, and the concern for domestic comforts mirrors this need. The showy opulence and pomp of the houses of the well-off, the rich and the powerful of Victorian society symbolized their need for security and desire to affirm their new social standing by displaying to others the concrete evidence of their success.

Thus, the richly decorated ceremonial chairs of bishops and parliamentarians, the sumptuous décors of dining-cars, the luxurious furniture of public institutions as well as the lushly upholstered armchairs in the private drawing-rooms of prominent families, all bear witness to their time. The desire for comfort and luxury went hand in hand with the need to believe in future prosperity. By the turn of the century Quebec was entering a new period of prosperity as a result of foreign investment in the province's natural resources (American investment would soon outstrip that of the British). For the newly elected Liberals as well as for the capitalist owners of industrial and financial empires, the future looked rosy as liberalism triumphed over conservatism. The Catholic clergy and nationalist politicians took up a defensive position. Workers were asking for a share in the profits, and women were demanding their political rights. Quebec society had already changed, irrevocably.

Johanne Daigle

BIBLIOGRAPHY

Bernard, Jean-Paul, ed., *Les idéologies québécoises au XIXe siècle*, Montréal, Boréal Express, 1973.

Collectif Clio, *HHistoire des femmes au Québec depuis quatre siècles*, Montréal, Les Quinze, 1982.

Hamelin, Jean and Jean Provencher, *Brève histoire du Québec*, 3rd printing, Montréal, Éditions du Boréal, 1987.

Jean Hamelin and Yves Roby, *Histoire économique du Québec, 1851-1896*, Montréal, Fides, 1971.Linteau, Robert, René Durocher and Jean-Claude Robert, *Histoire du Québec contemporain*, vol. 1: *de la confédération à la crise*, Montréal, Éditions du Boréal, 1989.

Linteau, Robert, René Durocher and Jean-Claude Robert, *Histoire du Québec contemporain*, vol. 1: *de la Confédération à la crise*, Montréal, Éditions du Boréal, 1989.

Mathieu, Jacques and Jacques Lacoursière, *Mémoires québécoises*, Québec City, PUL, 1991.

Rudin, Ronald, *Histoire du Québec anglophone*, Québec City, Institut québécois de recherche sur la culture, 1986.

Ryerson, Stanley-Bréhaut, *Le Capitalisme et la Confédération*, Montréal, Parti Pris, 1972.

Têtu de Labsade, Françoise, *Le Québec, un pays, une culture*, Montréal, Éditions du Boréal, 1989.

Trofimenkoff, Susan Mann, *Visions nationales: une histoire du Québec*, Saint-Laurent, Éditions du Trécarré, 1986.

Vincenthier, Georges, *Histoire des idées au Québec*, Montréal, VLB, 1983.

Ravenscrag, the Most Luxurious Home in Victorian Montreal

When Scottish-born Hugh Allan (1810-1882) arrived in Montreal in 1826, he soon earned a reputation for business acumen. A wily and astute financier, he founded his fortune on shipping but also invested in industry, banking, railways, insurance and mining. In the 1860s and 1870s he became the richest man in Canada, with a fortune of between six and ten million dollars.[1]

Now at the height of his success, Allan naturally wanted to give it concrete expression in a form consonant with his social standing and financial fame. In 1861 he commissioned the architect Victor Roy to design a spacious Tuscan residence in the Renaissance-revival style, to be built on the southeast slope of Mount Royal.[2] From the high tower

37
Notman Studio, Montreal
Sir Hugh Allan
Photograph
Archives nationales du Québec, Centre de Québec et Chaudière-Appalaches (P600-6/PN-A-37)

38
Ravenscrag, the home of Sir Hugh Allan in Montreal
Engraving published in *L'Opinion publique*, December 12, 1872, Photo SRP

39
Notman Studio, Montreal
The large drawing room at Ravenscrag in 1911. Photograph.
McCord Museum of Canadian History, Montreal, Notman Photographic Archives (185,092 Misc-II)
The elaborate ornamentation and eclectic style of this room testify to the tastes of Hugh Montagu Allan and his wife, who redecorated Ravenscrag's interiors around 1890.

THE CONTEXT

of the house, which contained dozens of rooms, Allan had a commanding view of the whole city, including the port where he could see the ships of his own company, the Allan Line. To the initial plans the shipping magnate soon added a large conservatory and a huge ballroom, then an anteroom to the latter, and a billiard room.[3] By 1872, after these additions were completed, Ravenscrag[4] had become a gathering-place for all the notables of Montreal as well as for distinguished visitors to the city. For some forty years it was the setting for many memorable receptions, including suppers for a hundred followed by balls for over three hundred guests. The house and its grounds were spacious enough to accommodate every kind of social, cultural or political event, and its interior furnishings and decoration as sumptuous as could be desired.

Though little documentation has survived, there is no doubt that Sir

40
The ballroom at Ravenscrag
Illustration published in the magazine *Canadian Homes and Gardens*, August, 1926

41
John and William Hilton
Renaissance-revival bookcase from Ravenscrag, about 1864. Black walnut, 347.6 x 550 x 61.6 cm. Allan Memorial Institute, Montreal. Photo Christine Guest/MMFA
The general form of this piece recalls that of a bookcase inspired by the Italian Renaissance that was illustrated in the catalogue of the Great Exhibition held in London in 1851.

42

44

45

43

46

42
Rococo-revival centre table from Ravenscrag
Private collection, United States
Photo John Bigelow Taylor

This exquisitely-crafted table was purchased at the Hôtel des Encans de Montréal in August 1986.

43
Head of Jacques Cartier, detail of figure 41
Photo Christine Guest/MMFA

44
Caryatid, detail of figure 41
Photo Christine Guest/MMFA

45
Trophy representing Literature and History, detail of figure 41
Photo Christine Guest/MMFA

The family name of the famous poet Lord Byron (1788-1824) appears on the right-hand page of the book.

46
The dismantling of the Ravenscrag bookcase in August 1992, prior to its moving and restoration, by a team of technicians from the Montreal Museum of Fine Arts
Photo Bernard Brien/MMFA

THE CONTEXT

Hugh Allan turned to the very best firms and craftsmen in the city for the interior decoration of his home. It is quite possible that he enlisted the services of James Thomson, a well-known cabinetmaker and interior decorator of Scottish extraction who worked regularly for the wealthiest citizens of Montreal.[5] The equally famous Hilton company was certainly called on, in particular in 1867 for a "ravishing" marquetry-work bedroom suite.[6] Three years earlier a trade magazine had called the library built for Ravenscrag by John and William Hilton "the most magnificently fitted up of any in Canada".[7] It is quite likely that the design of this Renaissance-revival room and the carving of its bookcases were entrusted to Arthur Mingeaud, a French-born artist who was at that time chief designer and woodcarver with the firm of Hilton.[8]

In November 1940 Sir Hugh Montagu Allan (1860-1951), Sir Hugh Allan's eldest son, donated the house, outbuildings and grounds of Ravenscrag to the Royal Victoria Hospital, whose trustees turned the enclave into a psychiatric institution, the Allan Memorial Institute. To this end, in 1943 major renovations were begun which when completed left only three rooms of the old interior relatively intact: the hall, a bedroom in the tower, and the library. With a few exceptions that include an impressive sideboard ordered by Sir Hugh Montagu in about 1890, little is known of the fate of the original furniture and woodwork.[9]

Today, the stately library built by the Hiltons still stands witness to the taste, wealth and interests of Ravenscrag's first owner. Allan obviously had a hand in the choice of subjects for the carvings, from the twin caryatids on either side of the fireplace to the four circular trophies on the doors of the lower bookcases. The full-breasted caryatids could well be mermaids,[10] while the reliefs from left to right symbolize Commerce, the Fine Arts, Literature and History, and lastly the State. At the top of the bookcase the bust of the sailor, explorer and discoverer Jacques Cartier is an indication of the continuum of history in which Allan saw himself as a part. The three[11] terrestrial globes surmounting the woodwork emphasize the international scope of the financial empire created by the shipping magnate.

John R. Porter

---

1 See the biography of Sir Hugh Allan by Brian J. Young in collaboration with Gerald J. J. Tulchinsky in *DBC*, vol. 11 (1881-1890) (Quebec City: PUL, 1992), pp. 5-17.

2 Despite claims in some publications, the architectural design was not entrusted to John William Hopkins. Guy Pinard clearly explains the reasons for this slight, and evaluates the contributions of the various architects who worked on the building and extensions of Ravenscrag. Guy Pinard, *Montréal, son histoire, son architecture*, vol. 2 (Montreal: La Presse, 1988), pp. 173-179.

3 The ball room and conservatory were designed by Victor Roy and Alexander G. Fowler, while John William Hopkins and Daniel Wily were responsible for the billiard room and the anteroom to the ball room. Répertoire d'architecture traditionnelle sur le territoire de la communauté urbaine de Montréal, *Architecture domestique, T. 1: les Résidences* (Montreal: Service de la planification du territoire de la CUM, 1987), pp. 18-25.

4 This evocative name was that of the Marquis of Lorne's residence in Scotland, near Hugh Allan's birthplace. See François Rémillard and Brian Merrett, *Demeures bourgeoises de Montréal* (Montréal: Éditions du Méridien, 1986), p. 80.

5 We know from Marius Barbeau's interview with the cabinetmaker Édouard Bertrand in about 1930 that Thomson also worked for George Stephen and Peter Redpath. The "Allan" mentioned by Bertrand could be either the father, Hugh, or his son Hugh Montagu.

6 *La Minerve*, April 6, 1867, p. 2.

7 *Montreal Business Sketches with a description of the City of Montreal*, published by the Canada Railway Advertising Company (Montreal: M. Longmoore, 1864), p. 78.

8 He was in Hilton's employ by 1864 (*The Gazette*, March 30, 1864, p. 2). Before coming to Montreal, Mingeaud had worked in Paris and New York. By 1869 we find him in Quebec City, working initially for William Drum. He opened his own workshop in the Saint-Roch district in 1872.

9 We have reason to be grateful to Luc d'Iberville-Moreau, Director of the Musée des arts décoratifs de Montréal, for helping to preserve many important pieces at a time when few people were aware of their value.

10 The arms of one of the library armchairs are carved in the shape of dolphins.

11 The top of the middle section of the bookcase was previously surmounted by a large wooden globe, which had later to be moved when a false ceiling was installed. Eric Nicolai, *Rapport préliminaire sur les meubliers Hilton de Montréal*, unpublished text produced by the MOBIVIQ team in January 1989.

The Carved Mirror Frame of the Steamship Québec, Designed by Arthur Mingeaud for the Montreal Firm of Hilton in 1866[*]

Walking by the window of the Hilton shop on Great St. James Street, one cannot help noticing a mirror with a frame that is undoubtedly the handsomest of its kind in Canada. This superb work of art has been created for one of the lounges in the *Québec*, the fine steamer built last year in the port of Sorel.

The Richelieu Navigation Company, not content with providing all possible comfort for its passengers, was determined also to make these comfortable surroundings beautiful and charming too. The company turned to the firm of J. & W. Hilton for the fitting up of this splendid steamship, and asked them to create a new and elegant kind of decor for the lounges. This aim was achieved, thanks to the skilled craftsmen who worked from excellent designs created by the firm's head designer.

It is apparent at first glance that Mr. Arthur Mingeaud learned his trade in a wider world of choice and taste than can be found here in Montreal. This perfectly executed and even more skilfully designed frame is not of the heavily ornate kind in which imagination substitutes for artistry and skill. Although deliberately simple, it portrays admirably well the subjects it depicts, and is perfectly appropriate to its setting.

At the two lower corners can be seen two dolphins and seaweeds, symbols of sea-faring. On one side are displayed the arms of England with a trophy of flags and armour, and on the other the arms of France, also surmounted by armour and a sheaf of standards. These pendant carvings evoke the goodwill that exists between the two great nations, which is daily strengthened by the union of the two peoples on the soil of Canada.

Nor are the arms of Canada forgotten; the industrious beaver is

47
Louis-Prudent Vallée, Quebec City
Interior of the steamship *Québec*: the main lounge, about 1870
Photograph
National Archives of Canada, Ottawa (C-35637)

---

[*] Article published in *La Minerve* (Montreal), and reprinted in the *Journal de Québec* on April 6, 1866, p. 2 (trans.).

48
The Richelieu Company's Steamer Quebec Leaving the Wharf at Montreal for Quebec
Engraving published in the *Canadian Illustrated News*, July 30, 1870
National Archives of Canada, Ottawa (C-50342)

found building his dam at the base of the frame, setting an example of hard work, organization and concord.

This superb frame is surmounted by a bust of the celebrated navigator Jacques Cartier, who was the first to bring trade and industry to this beautiful land of Canada; the bust is surrounded by an exquisitely designed and carved garland of maple leaves.

The Richelieu Navigation Company is to be congratulated on this fine vessel, which will be launched once the ice breaks up. The firm of Hilton also deserves felicitations on having chosen not only to decorate the passenger lounges in a luxurious manner, but to do so with artistry and taste, displayed in the faultless execution of artist Mingeaud's skilful design.

The Bedroom Suite Created for the Prince of Wales in Montreal in 1860

On August 25, 1860, before more than forty thousand people, Albert Edward, the Prince of Wales, opened the Victoria Bridge in Montreal. This "masterwork of modern times",[1] called the eighth wonder of the world, constituted a year-round link between Montreal and the south shore of the St. Lawrence. As Gloria Lesser notes, the bridge also offered "the advantage of joining and unifying the British territories of North America and of providing them all with direct communication to the United States and to the major Atlantic ports"[2].

The completion of the bridge — which from the start was intended to be named after Queen Victoria — seemed an ideal occasion for inviting Her Majesty to Montreal. Unable to accede to this request in person, the Queen sent her son, the future King Edward VII (1841-1910), to represent her. In the summer of 1860, therefore, the Prince visited the Maritimes, Upper and Lower Canada, and even some cities in the United States.[3] However, Montreal, then the richest and most densely populated city in British North America, was the most important stopover of the trip. The Prince's visit aroused a great deal of interest, and among the elaborate preparations for it special attention was paid to the furniture provided for the Prince and his entourage. Much of it was commissioned from the Toronto firm of Jacques & Hay, the leading cabinetmakers of Upper Canada.[4]

While in Montreal, the Prince stayed in Rosemount, the residence of the Hon. John Rose (1820-1888), Commissioner of Public Works, whose responsibility it was to organize the royal visit. The interior decoration of Rosemount, which was situated to the north of McGregor Avenue between Simpson and Redpath streets, was specially renovated for the occasion.[5] According to the Montreal newspaper *The Pilot* of August 23, 1860, "the supervision of the decorations was entrusted to Messrs. Lawford & Nelson, Architects, of Place d'Armes; the painting and decoration was done by Messrs. McArthur and Spence; while the manufacture of the furniture was by Messrs. Jacques & Hay of Toronto." Three weeks earlier, the editorialist of *The Globe* had written at length about the furniture created for the Prince, after visiting the firm of Jacques & Hay:

49
The Prince of Wales Laying the Last Stone of the Victoria Bridge over the St. Lawrence River
Engraving after a drawing by G. H. Andrews published in the *Illustrated London News*, October 6, 1860
Bibliothèque municipale de Montréal
Photo Brian Merrett/MMFA

50
Jacques & Hay Co. (active 1835 to 1870)
Rococo-revival bed, 1860
Curly maple, bird's-eye maple and basswood,
178 x 156 x 218 cm
The Montreal Museum of Fine Arts, gift of Mrs. David M. Stewart (1989.Df.4 a-e) Photo Christine Guest/MMFA

THE CONTEXT

51
Jacques & Hay Co. (active 1835 to 1870)
Rococo-revival wardrobe, 1860
Curly maple, bird's-eye maple and basswood,
253 x 153 x 59 cm
The Montreal Museum of Fine Arts, gift of Mrs. David
M. Stewart (1989.Df.5) Photo Christine Guest/MMFA

52
Arms, detail of figure 50
Photo Christine Guest/MMFA

"We had an opportunity yesterday of inspecting the set intended for the bed-room which will be occupied by the Prince in the residence of the Hon. Mr. Rose, during his stay in Montreal. This is now almost complete, and will be sent off to its destination without delay. All the articles are of beautiful curled maple, which has been made to take on its highest degree of polish. The maple, the emblematic wood of Canada, is a material exceedingly well adapted for an elegant and cheerful style of bed-room furniture, and when its capabilities are made the most of by such superior workmanship as can be had at Messrs. Jacques & Hay's Factory, the articles turned out will give our distinguished visitors no mean idea of the beauty of our Canadian woods and the skill of our Canadian artisans. Coming to particulars, there is first, a French bedstead, bearing on the head and foot-boards a good deal of carving, but not too much to destroy the simplicity which a good taste would desiderate in furniture for a bed-room, even though a Prince's. At the top of the head-board are the shield of the Prince of Wales, and coronet, supported by a scroll of maple leaf, with scrolls beneath of the rose, shamrock and thistle intertwined, and the Prince's crest, all carved work. On the foot-board, in the centre, is the Prince's crest (the well known tuft of feathers), surrounded by a wreath of the rose, shamrock and thistle, combined with the maple leaf. On each of the side-panels of the foot-board is a pleasing design, symbolizing the idea of rest — a beautifully carved bird, resting with folded wings in a nest hung upon a branch. The posts, which are of bird's-eye maple, have also a good deal of carving, and contrast with the

53
Notman Studio, Montreal. Bedroom suite made by William Drum for the Prince of Wales on the occasion of his visit to Quebec City in 1860. Photograph McCord Museum of Canadian History, Montreal, Notman Photographic Archives (MP 2276)

54
Notman Studio, Montreal. Bed from the suite made by William Drum for the Prince of Wales on the occasion of his visit to Quebec City in 1860. Photograph McCord Museum of Canadian History, Montreal, Notman Photographic Archives (MP 1980)

other parts of the bed-stead, by being somewhat darker in colour. The wardrobe is an exceedingly fine-looking article – the beautiful polish of its large doors, in which not a single flaw can be seen, being especially observable. It is divided into several compartments, and is surmounted by the Prince's crest. There is next a dressing-table, with large cheval glass. On each of the pedestals is the Prince's crest, and a scroll of maple leaves. The glass is surmounted by the Prince's shield, the maple leaf, &c. The wash-stand was incomplete when we saw it, not having received the marble slab which will cover it. We trust it will be covered not with foreign, but with Canadian marble, so that the distinctive character of the entire set, as being of home production and home manufacture, may not be destroyed. There is also a pretty little writing-table, on the standards of which are carved the Prince's crest and shield, surmounted by a coronet. And the set is completed by a luxurious couch and easy chair, covered with rich brocatelle, in green and gold, and a few other chairs, stuffed, also covered with brocatelle. The whole, as we have stated, is of curled maple, and, we believe we are safe in saying, surpasses in beauty, simple elegance, and finished workmanship, anything of the kind ever before manufactured in Canada."[6]

Three other bedroom suites, "nearly of the same pattern, but of different materials", were made by the same firm for the Prince's stopovers in Ottawa, Toronto and Niagara Falls.[7]

Shortly after the departure of the Prince of Wales, the furniture made for his visit was put up for sale at auction, and the newspapers hastened to stress how unusual an event this was to be:

"Those desirous of obtaining a souvenir of H.R.H. the Prince of Wales, should embrace this opportunity, as the articles have obtained a historic interest; and it is an opportunity which will not be met with in a life-time."[8]

We know little about the history of the bedroom suite made for the Prince's stay in Montreal between its sale at auction in the fall of 1860[9] and its acquisition 110 years later by Mrs. May B. Stewart through Fraser Bros. Ltd. of Montreal.[10] In 1989, Mrs. David M. Stewart presented the Montreal Museum of Fine Arts with five pieces from this famous twelve-piece suite – a bed, a wardrobe, a dressing chest, a washstand and a chair[11] – which her late husband had inherited from his mother.

The bedroom suite designed by the firm of Jacques & Hay for the Prince of Wales's stay in Montreal is mainly in the rococo-revival style, with some decorative elements taken from the Renaissance revival. Handsome though the set is, it is nevertheless surprising that the work

55
William Drum (about 1808-1876)
Renaissance-revival cabinet, about 1860
Veneers of burl oak, burl walnut, bird's-eye maple, curly maple and black walnut
153 x 80 x 61.5 cm
Canadian Museum of Civilization, Hull (981.50.1)
One of Drum's business cards is still stuck on the underside of each of the cabinet's two drawers (see figure 301).

was not commissioned from a local company such as the fine cabinet-making firm of Hilton. In Quebec City, on the other hand, it was William Drum, the city's leading furniture maker, who was entrusted with making the bedroom suite for the Prince's visit to the capital. The bed chamber was installed in a room in the Parliament building, and a journalist writing in *The Globe* gives the following description of its furnishings:

"A French bedstead of black walnut, with sheets of finest linen, has been provided for the repose of our illustrious visitor. The posts are square, and, if it is allowable to use such language, in the Italian style. The foot-board is adorned with a well executed carved crest of His Royal Highness. There are no hangings yet, but there are going to be — they will be attached immediately the Prince arrives. Two tables, one with a large mirror, the other with a marble top, are beautiful specimens of cabinet work. The chairs are of the same material as the rest of the furniture — black walnut, with covers of crimson silk."[12]

Only two old photographs of William Drum's bedroom suite have come down to us. However, it is quite possible that the superb cabinet made by Drum and acquired by the Canadian Museum of Civilization in 1982 from a London collector is the one presented to the Prince of Wales by the Governor General before he left Montreal,[13] of which a brief description appeared in the *Quebec Mercury* on August 23, 1860:

"Yesterday afternoon His Excellency presented to His Royal Highness a splendid cabinet composed of and also containing finely finished specimens of the woods of Canada, collected by the Woods and Forests Department under direction of the Honble. Commissnr. Vankoughnet. The cabinet has been constructed by Mr. Drum at short notice, and is nevertheless a beautiful piece of workmanship fit to adorn a palace. The carving is richly and thoroughly finished and the contrast presented by the black walnut and white woods interspersed in the ornamentation of the exterior has a splendid effect. The blocks inside represent 66 specimens of our woods, one side planed, the other side polished."

Natalie Vanier and Yves Lacasse

1   As described by Alphonse Lonclas, *Notice historique sur la famille royale d'Angleterre: le pont Victoria et le Palais de l'exposition publiée en l'Honnneur (sic) de la Visite de S.A.R. le prince de Galles au Canada* (Montreal: Imprimerie Sénécal et frère, 1860), p. 4 (trans.).

2   Gloria Lesser, "En 1860, le Prince de Galles inaugure le pont Victoria", *Vie des arts*, vol. 26, no. 105 (winter 1981-1982), p. 38 (trans.).

3   For a detailed account of the tour, see Henry James Morgan, *The Tour of H.R.H. The Prince of Wales Through British North America and The United States. By A British Canadian* (Montreal: Printed for the compiler by John Lovell, 1860), 271 pp. On this subject, see Stanley Triggs et al., *Le pont Victoria Un lien vital/Victoria Bridge: The Vital Link*, exhib. cat. (Montreal: McCord Museum of Canadian History, 1992).

4   On Jacques & Hay see: Sheila M. Smith, "Jacques & Hay Cabinet Makers 1835-1885", master's thesis in art history presented to the University of Toronto, 1968, 60 pp.; John Mackinnon, *A Checklist of Toronto Cabinet and Chair Makers, 1800-1865* (Ottawa: National Museums of Canada [National Museum of Man], 1975, Mercure collection, File no. 11), pp. 69-72 and 77-97; and Ruth Cathcart, *Jacques & Hay. 19th Century Toronto Furniture Makers* (Erin, Ontario: The Boston Mills Press, 1986), 96 pp.

5   A detailed description of the renovation in *The Montreal Herald* is cited in the *Morning Chronicle* (Quebec City) of August 18, 1860 (p. 2) and in Morgan, *op. cit.*, pp. 103-106.

6   *The Globe* (Toronto), August 2, 1860, p. 2.

7   *The Globe* of August 2, 1860 stated that the Ottawa suite was of oak, the Niagara Falls one of cherry wood and the Toronto one of walnut. The bed of the last-mentioned suite is held in the Canadian Museum of Civilization in Hull (inv. no. 988.22) and is, except for the wood used, identical in every respect to the suite created for Rosemount, which now belongs to the Montreal Museum of Fine Arts.

8   *The Gazette* (Montreal), September 24, 1860, p. 3.

9   This sale was announced for October 31 in *The Gazette* (October 31, 1860, p. 3), although the catalogue of the sale in question, a copy of which is in the municipal archives of the city of Montreal, is dated September 27.

10 The furniture came from the estate of Marjorie Caverhill.

11 In 1970 Mrs. May B. Stewart gave two chairs from her seven-piece set to the McCord Museum of Canadian History. This institution also holds a pedestal table donated in 1930 by the Misses McLennan, which was probably part of the same suite. It is possible, however, that the chest of drawers with mirror was part of the furniture provided for a member of the Prince's entourage, and not part of the suite in the Prince's own bedroom.

12 *The Globe*, August 18, 1860, p. 2.

13 One of Drum's business cards was found under each of the two drawers of the cabinet.

56
Interior of the cabinet, detail of figure 55
Photo Christine Guest/MMFA

The Reception Lounge of L'Université Laval, Quebec City

L'Université Laval, founded by the Séminaire de Québec, was the first French-language university in North America. It was granted a royal charter in 1852 through the good offices of the Governor General, Lord Elgin, Queen Victoria's representative in Canada. In October the authorities of the Séminaire commissioned from the painter Théophile Hamel a "standing portrait to be placed in the main reception room of the future university in recognition of the Institution's first members." The large painting was completed the following spring and temporarily displayed in the Parliament building, but was destroyed when Parliament burned down in 1854. Fortunately, two small versions of it are still extant; one of these, dated 1852, was given to the university by Sir Francis Hincks in December 1876. The painting depicts the Earl of Elgin in ceremonial attire with his hand on the royal charter granted to the Séminaire de Québec in 1852. Behind the governor general can be seen the viceroy's chair of the upper chamber of Parliament. This ceremonial chair, executed in 1852 by the master carver Louis-Thomas Berlinguet and his son Louis-Flavien from designs by the cabinetmaker William Drum, was "a superb example of carving". It was covered in red fabric, with the royal coat of arms exquisitely embroidered in gold on the back by the Soeurs de la Charité de Québec.[1]

Had it not been destroyed, it seems probable that Hamel's great painting would have occupied a prominent position in the reception lounge of L'Université Laval's centre block, an impressive building designed by the architect Charles Baillairgé and completed in 1856. The interior decoration of the reception lounge on the first floor was not finished until October 1865. This was a huge room with a restrained décor in the neo-classic style; its general appearance is known to us from a photograph taken by Livernois in 1902. In the twentieth century the reception lounge underwent a number of changes to its plaster mouldings, light fixtures, floor (the marquetry work dates from 1911), curtains, and, of course, to what was displayed on the walls. Throughout the Victorian era the periodic addi-

57
Théophile Hamel (1817-1870)
Lord Elgin, 1854
Oil on canvas, 76.9 x 49 cm
Musée du Château Ramezay, Montreal (CR2396)
Photo Patrick Altman/Musée du Québec

Lord Elgin (1811-1863) was governor general of Canada from 1846 to 1854.

58
Livernois Studio, Quebec City
The reception lounge of L'Université Laval, about 1902
Photograph
Archives du Musée du Séminaire de Québec (T-33)

59
Rococo-revival settee from the reception lounge of the first Université Laval
144 x 250 x 90 cm
Séminaire de Québec
Photo Jean-Pierre Labiau / MOBIVIQ

tion and removal of pictures continually altered the appearance of the room, but it is rather difficult to date its various stages because of a lack of visual evidence. There is no doubt that the large portrait of Queen Victoria (a copy by Joseph Légaré executed in 1839 and acquired by the Séminaire in 1874) which is now so much a part of the room was only installed there in 1899 or 1900.[2]

Although no explicit reference to the subject has been found, it was almost certainly the cabinetmaker William Drum who was entrusted with making the furniture for the reception lounge of L'Université Laval in 1859. The firm's account books show that between 1854 and 1872 Drum received regular payments from the Séminaire de Québec.[3] The central fixture and a settee in the room, however, came from a donation by Dr. Charles-Eusèbe Lemieux, professor and later dean of the Faculty of Medicine.[4] It is noteworthy that the name of the cabinetmaker Philippe Vallière has traditionally been associated with these two finely made pieces. Aside from these items, the white marble table with marquetry inlay on which is displayed the papal charter granted to the university in 1876 by Pope Pius IX, and the rector's chair, the furniture of the reception lounge is not particularly institutional in appearance. It consists of a series of chairs and armchairs with two settees and a large centre table. To sum up, it is a numerically imposing ensemble, of fairly conventional workmanship and heterogenous in style, with Empire-revival, rococo-revival and Renaissance-revival elements.

The reception lounge of L'Université Laval was in the past used for official receptions of all kinds: political, religious, university or social. Here was held the annual reception on December 8, the Feast of the Immaculate Conception, to which were invited representatives of the British monarchy and the civil authorities, senior members of the Catholic clergy and prominent citizens. A spacious chamber with windows to the north and south, provided with ample furniture including two or three unusual pieces, the reception lounge in a sense mirrored the ideology of an institution of higher education conscious of the importance of its mission, which sought to demonstrate its attachment to certain values and its fidelity to tradition. These commitments were apparent to visitors from the various Italian and Quebec paintings on the walls. According to an official statement that appeared in the Université Laval yearbook in 1898, works of art in the reception lounge included an impressive painting of the *Immaculate Conception*, a copy of the portrait of Mgr de Laval, the first bishop of Quebec City and founder of the Séminaire, the likenesses of the first five rectors of the university[5] (including that of the Abbé Louis-Jacques Casault, its founder) and those of the first four "patron cardinals", as well as the standing portraits of Pope Pius IX and the Earl of Elgin, which were of very different sizes for the reasons already stated.

John R. Porter and Claude Vallières

---

1 The August 31, 1852 edition of the *Quebec Mercury* published a good description of the Legislative Assembly building, which was reproduced in French in the *Journal de Québec* on September 9 of the same year. As regards the part played by Drum and the Berlinguets, see a contract registered with the notary Joseph Petitclerc (ANQQ), under no. 6532 (March 6, 1852). For further information on the portrait of Lord Elgin, see the entry by John R. Porter in Mario Béland (ed.), *La Peinture au Québec 1820-1850*, exhib. cat. (Quebec City: Musée du Québec - Les publications du Québec, 1991), pp. 322-324.

2 Its presence in the reception lounge is first noted in the university yearbook for 1901. In the 1898 yearbook, the painting mentioned is still the large *Immaculate Conception*, painted in Italy in 1865-1866 by Vincenzo Pasqualoni (1819-1880). This hung opposite the large standing portrait of Pope Pius IX (1867) by the same artist.

3 There is, however, no mention of Drum's main rival, Philippe Vallière.

4 The year of the donation was not found in the documents consulted.

5 By Théophile Hamel, Pasqualoni and Eugène Hamel (three portraits).

THE ARTS IN QUEBEC DURING THE VICTORIAN ERA

DURING THE FIRST HALF OF THE NINETEENTH CENTURY, painting in Quebec developed considerably as a result of "new ways of looking at things" and "new perspectives".[1] This development, however, was still considered too slow by some contemporary critics, including the journalist Napoléon Aubin. In an article published in Quebec City in 1847, he expressed his regret at seeing talented artists still restricted to "utilitarian" genres such as religious paintings and portraits:

> [...] those who could give society a lead in the matter of taste make but poor use of their pride and display. Luxury is excusable when it encourages the arts and industry; it is by employing his wealth judiciously that the rich man can enable society as a whole to share in his pleasures, and of all people, artists are those whose happiness is the most inexpensively procured.
>
> [...] Let us suppose that a traveller who loves paintings visits one of our prominent citizens. He is shown into a drawing room, where he will find soft carpets, mahogany furniture, gold candelabra, a marble chimneypiece, thick curtains, and innumerable trifling knick-knacks that are both tasteless and ill-made. No paintings of any sort.
>
> [...] But if this traveller found your walls hung with pictures painted in Canada — local scenes, landscapes, historical paintings — showing even a modicum of originality, these works would undoubtedly provide the topic for an interesting conversation, would give the visitor a favourable notion of good society in Canada and of the status of the arts here, and might even induce him to take home some work of art as a souvenir. Everyone would discover new pleasures if public taste were influenced in this way, and everyone would benefit from the spirit of competition thus engendered, since men of tact and imagination would find thereby, at the very least, a means of distinguishing themselves from those whose only attribute is money.[2]

The same attitude is found some months earlier in reaction to an exhibition of 179 paintings organized by the Montreal Society of Artists, a group of seven English-speaking painters who wished to stimulate interest in the arts. In a long article published in *The Pilot and Journal of Commerce* on January 29, 1847, a critic laments the weakness of the art market, the poverty of artists, and the slowness of the British colony, in comparison with the United States, to provide the necessary infrastructures.³ When the French sculptor Charles Bullet visited Montreal two years later, a journalist from *La Minerve* expressed the same concern, and pleaded for a "small academy of drawing and sculpture" to be promptly established.

Despite the shortcomings pointed out by the press, the colony was not entirely devoid of talent in the field of the arts. There were, in fact, a significant number of knowledgeable art lovers and collectors in the province, men such as Benaiah Gibb in Montreal and Henry Atkinson in Quebec City.⁴ The latter, in addition to his passion for European art, antiquities and the decorative arts, encouraged local artists like the sculptors Leprohon and Berlinguet and the landscape painter Joseph Légaré. Over the years, Légaré himself built up a large collection of European canvases and prints, which he displayed to the public in a gallery described as "a delightful place of resort" by artists and art lovers.⁵ On the death of his widow in 1874, the collection was left to the Université Laval, where it formed the basis of a distinguished art gallery.

As a result of its developing economy and the increased movement of goods, people and ideas, Victorian Quebec was soon involved in an unequivocal process of decompartmentalization, opening up and diversification in the field of the arts. By 1881 the progress achieved since 1847 was obvious, according to John George Bourinot:

> [...] We must also look to the signs of general culture that are now exhibited on all sides, compared with a quarter of a century ago, when the development of material interests necessarily engrossed all the best faculties of the people. The development of higher education, together with the formation of Art Schools, Museums and Literary Societies, is illustrative of the greater mental activity of all classes. [...] It is no longer considered a sign of good taste to cover the walls with oils and chromos whose chief value is the tawdry, showy gilt which encases them and makes so loud a display on the walls of the *nouveaux riches*. In the style of public buildings and private dwellings, there is a remarkable improvement within twenty years, to indicate not only the increase of national and individual wealth, but the growth of a cultured taste. The interior decorations, too, show a desire to imitate the modern ideas that prevail abroad; and in this respect every year must witness a steady advance, according as our people travel more in the older countries in Europe and study the fashions of the artistic and intellectual world. There are even now in prosaic, practical Canada, some men and women who fully appreciate the aesthetic ideal that the poet Morris would achieve in the form, harmony, and decoration of domestic furniture.⁶

Two years later, in *The Dominion Annual Register and Review*, the publisher Henry J. Morgan expressed himself in much the same terms, noting with particular pleasure the new customs regulations that enabled works of art to circulate more freely, the success of three exhibitions held in the handsome gallery of the Art Association of Montreal, and the development of the design schools established by the Board of Arts and Manufacture of the Province of Quebec.⁷

However, in terms of art the Victorian era was a long transition period, dur-

60
Jules-Ernest Livernois (1851-1933), Quebec City. The picture gallery, Université Laval, Quebec City, about 1890
Photograph
Archives du Séminaire de Québec

ing which people vacillated between the prestige associated with the noble forms of the past and an inclination towards the expressions of modernity. While the rediscovery of the art of past centuries led to a flood of copies and pastiches, this fashion for evoking the past also went hand in hand with a penchant for novelty, for anything that came from abroad. The fluctuations in fashion were further affected by the great number and variety of practising artists, as diverse in their backgrounds as in their training and specialities. Close study showed us that there was no point in trying to find common characteristics within this heterogenous artistic community, which was in addition highly mobile. Furthermore, mediums, styles and genres were equally diverse, and frequently mingled in works that could only be called eclectic.

To tackle this multi-faceted reality, we shall endeavour here to establish a few guidelines in terms of the evolution of taste, and will evaluate the part played by both conservatism and innovation in the art of Quebec during the Victorian era. In so doing we shall try to avoid generalizations, noting changing contexts and the vital but variable socio-economic status of those who commissioned works of art. We also noticed a quite marked social and ethnic division between French speakers and English speakers as regards artistic interests, perceptions and sensitivities. For one group, the societal aspect of art was automatically more important than individual commitment, while for the other, the opposite tendency was true.

SEPARATE WORLDS
From 1880 onwards, the large fortunes made by a handful of the *grands bourgeois* of Montreal, mainly as a result of investing in the transcontinental Canadian Pacific Railway, enabled them to build up considerable personal collections of art works. Men such as Sir William Van Horne, Sir George A.

61
Louis-Philippe Hébert (1850-1917)
Sir George Alexander Drummond (1829-1910),
about 1886
White marble
The Montreal Museum of Fine Arts, gift of the family
of Sir George Alexander Drummond (1923.460)

62
Gabriel Max (1840-1915)
The Raising of Jairus's Daughter, 1878
Oil on canvas, 123.3 x 180.4 cm
The Montreal Museum of Fine Arts,
gift of Lord Atholstan (1920.117)

Drummond, Charles Hosmer, James Ross, Richard B. Angus and Lord Strathcona surrounded themselves with paintings by old masters and by contemporary European and North American artists.[8] Of them all, it was probably Sir George Drummond whose interests were the most varied, ranging from Constable and Turner to Rodin, the Barbizon School, the Hague School, Corot, Gustave Doré and Meissonier, and including a real enthusiasm for the Impressionists Raffaëlli, Monet and Degas. His eclectic tastes even embraced Benjamin Constant's orientalism, Whistler's aestheticism, and the edifying academicism of the German painter Gabriel Max (1840-1915), whose canvas *The Resurrection of Jairus's Daughter* he acquired. For this painting he commissioned from a Montreal ornamenter an elaborate oak frame incorporating an inscription in Hebraic characters which read "Damsel, I say unto thee, arise."

Among the English-speaking *bourgeois* élite of Montreal, an appreciation of art was fostered by the annual exhibitions of the Art Association, the predecessor of the Montreal Museum of Fine Arts. Founded in 1860, the association had eighty members, but only acquired its own exhibition gallery, in Phillips Square[9], in 1879. Members were especially partial to Canadian landscapes, although art from abroad was often preferred by the affluent. When *Crown of Flowers* by William Adolphe Bouguereau (1825-1905) was exhibited in 1887, it met with an enthusiastic reception from the press and public alike. Two years later, R. B. Angus presented this painting, along with five others, to the Art Association of Montreal. A number of collectors in Quebec City were also fascinated by European art. One of them, the wealthy merchant Richard R. Dobell, acquired *The Lady of the Lake*, a marble sculpture by the English artist John Adams-Acton (1830-1910) which had been reproduced and discussed in the London *Art Journal* in 1876. This piece, inspired by a poem by Sir Walter Scott, echoed the Victorian enthusiasm for the Middle Ages.

However, not all the well-to-do were equally passionate about art. The

64
William-Adolphe Bouguereau (1825-1905)
Crown of Flowers, 1884
Oil on canvas, 162.9 x 89.9 cm
The Montreal Museum of Fine Arts,
gift of R. B. Angus (1889.17)

63
Opening of the Art Gallery, Montreal, by His Excellency the Governor General and Her Royal Highness the Princess Louise
Engraving published in *L'Opinion publique*,
June 12, 1879
Photo SRP

Montreal businessman Hector Mackenzie was not particularly discriminating in his choice of canvases, watercolours, prints, chromos and photographs to adorn the walls of his house at 961 Sherbrooke Street. His eclecticism was more a desire for ostentation, which was gratified by a few important paintings, including works by Canadian landscape artists such as Adolphe Vogt and Cornelius Krieghoff (1815-1872).

Krieghoff had done much to develop a taste for genre painting and landscapes among his English-speaking Canadian clients.[10] As a founding member of the Montreal Society of Artists in 1846, he exhibited there no less than forty-eight works, which hung alongside works by Martin Somerville, Andrew Morris, William Sawyer and James Duncan. One of Krieghoff's canvases, *Officer's Trophy Room*, is an unusual painting demonstrating a marked

THE CONTEXT

65
John Adams-Acton (1830-1910)
The Lady of the Lake, 1864
Marble, 229 cm (with pedestal)
Musée du Québec, Quebec City, gift of William Dobell
(G-36.30-S)

66
Jules-Isaï Benoit de Livernois (1830-1865), Quebec City
Cornelius Krieghoff
Photograph
McCord Museum of Canadian History, Montreal

taste for accumulation, an overabundance of detail and exoticism. Despite the small size of the room, we sense in the officer, A. A. Staunton, a craving for adventure to which the artist, a great traveller himself, was naturally drawn. In 1853 Krieghoff settled in Quebec City, where for some ten years he was enormously successful. One of his commissions was to paint the vignettes for a large carved-wood reredos to be placed behind the Speaker's chair in the chamber of the Legislative Assembly in the new parliament building. This remarkable rococo-revival piece, which was destroyed in a fire in 1883, comprised nine landscapes depicting the lumber trade, a vital component of the economic activity of Quebec at that time.

Following in the footsteps of artists like Légaré, Krieghoff and Duncan,

67
Cornelius Krieghoff (1815-1872)
Officer's Trophy Room, 1846
Oil on canvas, 46 x 65 cm
Royal Ontario Museum, Toronto (954.188.2)

68
The Wood Trade by Cornelius Krieghoff,
about 1860
Photograph
Archives du Séminaire de Québec (Ph.87.669)
Photo W. B. Edwards Inc., Quebec City

many other painters sought to profit by the growing public appetite for genre scenes and landscapes. In 1865 William Raphael (1833-1914), a former pupil at the Berlin Academy, took advantage of the eclectic setting of the "Industrial and Artistic Section" of the Montreal provincial exhibition to present a view of Bonsecours Market which was praised, with some reservations, by the critic of *La Minerve*:

> A Mr. Raphael has on display a view of Bonsecours Market that his great namesake could not have painted without jeopardizing his reputation. This piece has many fine qualities; but why, in all the *Bonsecours Markets* (and they are legion) painted by Raphael, Duncan and others, are Canadians depicted in clothes and attitudes that are far from being those of the present day?[11]

69
William Raphael (1833-1914)
Immigrants at Montreal, 1866
Oil on canvas, 67.5 x 109.6 cm
National Gallery of Canada, Ottawa

70
Lucius O'Brien (1832-1899)
Sunrise on the Saguenay, 1880
Oil on canvas, 90 x 127 cm
National Gallery of Canada, Ottawa

The following year Raphael painted a similar work entitled *Immigrants at Montreal*. Above and beyond its relative verisimilitude, this picture is significant in that it demonstrates how open to the outside world Quebec society was at this time. In terms of the arts, this open-mindedness is seen in the acceptance of many painters newly arrived from abroad, such as the Germans Otto Jacobi and Adolphe Vogt. Their landscapes began to be painted from an "art for art's sake" perspective and, like those of other Canadian artists, were increasingly appreciated for their intrinsic pictorial qualities. They also reflected a widening of horizons in the sense that they depicted distant places and remote parts of the country that were now accessible thanks to new means of transport. At the provincial exhibition of 1865 the watercolourist Washington F. Friend showed views of Lac Saint-Charles and Cap Trinité as well as several pictures of *Niagara Falls*. Between his trips to Europe the brilliant colourist Allan A. Edson explored the forests, mountains and rivers of the Eastern

Townships, where he spent his childhood; in the early 1870s he agreed to execute drawings for *L'Opinion publique* and the *Canadian Illustrated News*. In 1882 public curiosity was gratified by the appearance of *Picturesque Canada*, a two-volume illustrated publication on which many artists had collaborated under the direction of Lucius O'Brien (1832-1899). The latter also produced a wide range of paintings remarkable for their picturesque and atmospheric effects (e.g. *Sunrise on the Saguenay*, 1880). Some years later O'Brien was one of the landscape artists who took the Canadian Pacific Railway to go and capture in paint the grandeur of the Rocky Mountains.[12] During the same period Horatio Walker became fascinated by the Île d'Orléans, a little world in itself that appealed to his poetic vision of rural virtues.

Just as public interest in landscapes was to a great extent stimulated by published pictures, so the work of the various landscape artists was influenced by all sorts of movements, from the English School to the Barbizon School, the academicism of the German School and the approach of the American Hudson River School. At the same time, the impact of photography on artists such as Jacobi, Edson and O'Brien cannot be discounted.[13] Indeed, landscape photographs were beginning to be regarded as suitable for collections. Thus the 1882 inventory of the Baker-Gilmour house in Stanbridge in the Eastern Townships includes "Photographic views by Notman" and "Thirty-six stereoscopic views on glass" alongside landscapes by Edson, Vogt and Jacobi. This valuable documentary evidence is the more interesting because it reveals the tastes and interests of two collectors who lived far from the city.[14]

There is no doubt that the rapid development of photographic technology threatened the market for traditional portrait painters. In this regard it is interesting that such luminaries of the dark-room as Livernois in Quebec City and Notman in Montreal made use of painters to add the finishing touches to their negatives. Notman, for example, hired artists such as William Raphael, John Arthur Fraser and Henry Sandham. Napoléon Bourassa noted, referring to the early 1860s, that "until then portraits had been the only livelihood for Canadian painters; but since photographers invaded the world of art, it no longer constituted even their bread and butter."[15]

Bourassa's reference to "the world of art" is particularly relevant in regard to William Notman (1826-1891), a man of imagination whose photographs went far beyond merely reproducing the individual features of his sitters. He was simultaneously a chronicler of the events of his time, an observer of everyday life, a recorder of the home life of the *bourgeoisie*, a methodical portraitist and a master of the composite photograph. One of the last-mentioned compositions, his remarkable oil on sensitized canvas entitled *The Skating Carnival*, contains no less than sixty figures in costume. In addition to the technical expertise it demonstrates, the eclecticism and medieval richness of colour recorded in this display of virtuosity capture to perfection the particular tastes of the prosperous English-speaking middle classes, who were as receptive to anything new as they were to the charms of the past.

A COMMUNITY-CONSCIOUS WORLD

Within the French-speaking community of Quebec there were certainly art lovers and collectors, but far fewer of them than among the English-speaking community. On the contrary, it is generally acknowledged that French

71
Jules-Ernest Livernois (1851-1933),
Quebec City
Interior of the Livernois Gallery, 1886
Photograph
Archives nationales du Québec, Centre de Québec et
Chaudière-Appalaches (NV-65034)

Canadian traditions and cultural habits produced mainly, if not exclusively, art works of a public nature, particularly religious and commemorative art.

The Catholic clergy emerged from the Rebellions of 1837-1838 stronger than ever. From then on their power and involvement in many spheres of activity increased noticeably, and their influence was consequently significant in the fields of art and architecture. As a way of demonstrating his commitment to the Holy See, Mgr Ignace Bourget, the ultramontane Bishop of Montreal, had an impressive cathedral built that was modelled on St. Peter's in Rome. As regards paintings, those influenced by European art were also very popular, especially as the copying of religious works by French and Italian old masters had been common practice in Quebec since the late eighteenth century. Despite his advanced age, Antoine Plamondon (1804-1895) continued to make copies, variations and imitations from engravings reproducing the works of Raphael, Mignard, Titian, Domenichino, Guido Reni and Rubens, thus helping to broaden the artistic horizons of his compatriots.[16] Like other artists, both native and foreign, he produced many versions of Raphael's *Saint Cecilia* in the art gallery of Bologna, a subject that was highly popular during the Victorian era.[17] However, Plamondon had to contend with considerable competition in the realm of religious art. He took umbrage at the phenomenal success achieved by his compatriot Antoine-Sébastien

72
William Notman (1826-1891),
Henry Sandham (1842-1910) and
Edward Sharpe (active 1850 to 1871)
The Skating Carnival, 1870
Composite photograph printed on canvas,
135.9 x 95.2 cm
McCord Museum of Canadian History, Montreal,
Notman Photographic Archives
This work immortalizes the costume party on ice held at the Victoria Rink in honour of Prince Arthur. The skating rink, which was illuminated by some five hundred gas jets, had been opened in December 1862.

Falardeau (1822-1889) who, after winning the first prize in a competition for copies, was made a knight of the Order of St. Louis by the Duke of Parma. The works Falardeau brought back from Italy in 1862 were highly prized by *bourgeois* collectors because they had been copied, not from poor-quality prints or other reproductions in oils, but directly from the original old masters.

The Quebec painter Eugène Hamel (1845-1932) spent two sessions studying art in Europe, including four years in Italy. The academic training he received there gave him great prestige in the eyes of the clergy, in addition to which he was very receptive to his clients' wishes. He specialized in pious subjects that appealed to the sensibilities of the time, usually borrowing his compositions from illustrious predecessors or from fashionable Roman painters. It goes without saying that the latter in their turn profited by the penchant of the Quebec clergy for Italian art. Even though he never set foot on the soil of North America, a painter like Vincenzo Pasqualoni obtained many important commissions from this continent.[18]

Impressed by the architecture, frescoes, sculptures and paintings they had seen in Europe, some churchmen and superiors of religious orders wished to recreate in their own churches comparable interior decorations. To this end they encouraged foreign artists to emigrate here, or called on the services of Quebec artists who had trained in Europe. The results include the art work by Daniel Müller in the Gésu church in Montreal (1865-1866), by the German William Lamprecht in the church at Saint-Romuald (1868),[19] by Napoléon Bourassa (1827-1916) in the Nazareth home (1870-1872) and the Notre-Dame-de-Lourdes chapel (1875-1882), by Charles Huot in the Saint-Sauveur church in Quebec City (1887), by Edmond Meloche in the chapel of the Congrégation des hommes de la haute ville de Québec (1887), and the domes by Luigi Cappello — Ozias Leduc's first teacher — at Yamachiche and Trois-Rivières.[20] It is not surprising that these interiors are marked by various influences, and incorporate all sorts of references to European art. Daniel Müller, trained in the Düsseldorf School, showed his eclecticism by borrowing from Ingres as well as Overbeck and Gagliardi. Bourassa, influenced by the

73
Antoine Plamondon (1804-1895)
Saint Cecilia, 1878
Oil on canvas, 184 x 113 cm
Musée du Québec, Quebec City,
Photo Patrick Altman (A 73.568 P)

74
Antoine-Sébastien Falardeau (1822-1889)
The Triumph of Charity, with Christianity after Federico Barocci, 1860
Oil on oval panel, 37.5 x 37 cm, with four miniatures representing *Christ* after Carlo Maratta (1861), *Beatrice Cenci* after a painting formerly attributed to Guido Reni (1861), *Music* after Giovanni Martinelli (1861) and *The Sibyl* after Guido Reni (1861)
Musée du Québec, Quebec City (34.707)

75
Notman Studio, Montreal
Interior of the Church of Notre-Dame de Lourdes in Montreal, about 1884
Photograph
McCord Museum of Canadian History, Montreal, Notman Photographic Archives (1544)

religious austerity of the Nazarener movement, made great use of mystic symbolism, and embellished the interior of Notre-Dame-de-Lourdes in the manner of a medieval master craftsman.

In a different key, Bourassa was also influenced by Ingres's *Apotheosis of Homer* in creating his *Apotheosis of Christopher Columbus*, an ambitious project incorporating sixty-two historical and allegorical figures mostly borrowed from earlier works. This composition was among the many subjects that Bourassa suggested in vain to the provincial government for the interior decoration of the new Legislative Assembly building in Quebec City in 1883. Following his example, many other painters, including Eugène Hamel (1845-1932), Charles Alexander Smith, Marc-Aurèle de Foy Suzor-Coté and Henri Beau, submitted designs of a commemorative nature. Finally, in 1910, Charles Huot was awarded the much-coveted commission. The penchant for commemorative art that developed among the French-speaking élite in mid-century became widespread in Quebec society by the 1880s, and gave rise to the installing of many bronze monuments in public places. Despite their academic style, these works constituted a relatively novel addition to the

76
Eugène Hamel (1845-1932)
Jacques Cartier on Mont-Royal, 1885-1886
Oil on canvas, 35.2 x 77 cm
Musée du Québec, Quebec City

Quebec scene. Louis-Philippe Hébert (1850-1917), who began his career executing religious sculptures in wood, later achieved great success with this "new" genre based on a "new" material. In competition with other Canadian and foreign artists, he created some forty monumental sculptures including various historical figures for the façade of the Legislative Assembly building in Quebec City. His famous monument to De Maisonneuve on Place d'Armes in Montreal, unveiled in 1895 before a large crowd, was praised by the French sculptors Jules Dalou and Frédéric Bartholdi (who was the creator of the Statue of Liberty).[21]

Unlike Hébert, Louis Jobin (1845-1928) continued to work mainly in the old tradition of wood-carving. Armed with additional training acquired in the studios of New York and wide experience in the field of non-religious art, he sometimes ventured beyond the established norms in order to satisfy the expectations of his clients, both the *bourgeois* and the clergy. The organizers of the great nationalist parade for St. John the Baptist Day in Quebec City called on him in 1880 to help with the ornamentation of five floats, including one symbolizing Agriculture built from designs by the architect Paul Cousin in collaboration with the master cartwright Pierre Gauvin. Made "in the shape of an inverted Roman chariot",[22] the result was, in aesthetic terms, what we would today call kitsch.[23] Basically *revival* in inspiration, the Agriculture float was something halfway between intellectual and popular culture. With its hybrid aspect and profusion of disparate components, it was really a kind of pastiche and thus emphatically kitsch. Its main embellishment, the statue of Ceres, was in fact a copy with variations made from a photograph of the marble *Fortuna* in the Vatican Museum, itself a Roman copy of a Greek original. To turn her into a goddess of agriculture, Jobin changed the contents of the cornucopia or horn of plenty and armed her with a billhook, thus creating a hybrid mythological figure. The colours of the float are sugary and kitsch, with candy-cane tones and bold contrasts of complementary colours.

THE *BOURGEOIS* QUEST FOR GOOD TASTE

Bizarre though it looks to us today, the Agriculture float is a useful introduction to the delicate matter of good taste, a question that obsessed the middle classes, both French- and English-speaking, throughout Victoria's reign. The float designed by the Cousin-Jobin team was approved in 1880 by a special committee chaired by the famous architect Charles Baillairgé and composed of ten members, including draughtsmen and well-known artists. This com-

77
Louis-Philippe Hébert (1850-1917)
Monument to De Maisonneuve, 1895
Place d'Armes, Montreal
Photo Christine Guest/MMFA

78
Paul Cousin, Louis Jobin (1845-1928) and
Pierre Gauvin
The float representing Agriculture, 1880
Polychrome wood, metal and leather,
450 x 233 x 497 cm
Musée du Québec/Musée de la civilisation,
Quebec City (75.285)

mittee was specifically mandated to make sure that nothing should "shock the eyes of connaisseurs and judges of art and good taste".[24] In the Victorian era, any echo of the art of past ages was for a long time considered to be a guarantee of good taste. For the newly rich *bourgeois*, the cleric who had visited Europe or dreamed of doing so, the interior decorator who subscribed to foreign periodicals, just as for the established architect, appropriating and mastering the forms of the past was proof of a cultivated taste. As a result, the temptation to accumulate and combine influences was considerable, especially since the artifacts thus produced were in general almost universally accepted. Indeed, it was not until the 1880s that the occasional voice was raised on behalf of "the rules of good taste", protesting against the excesses of fashion and demanding a return to simplicity.[25]

In the field of the decorative arts, as in those of painting and sculpture, the Victorians' reverence for the entire range of forms handed down from past ages is very apparent. In Holy Trinity Cathedral in Quebec City, the memorial windows commemorating the city's third Anglican bishop borrow from medieval art for the ornamentation of the frame and from the Renaissance for echoes of images from the great Raphael.[26] The architect Eugène-Étienne Taché (1836-1912), a keen "revivalist", also indulged in an orgy of multiple references in designing his *Plan for an altar for the chapel of the Congrégation de Notre-Dame de Saint-Roch in Quebec City* in 1884. With its innumerable painted and gilded motifs — shields, crowns, flowers, angels, inscriptions and so on — this motley composition relies more on the effects created by abundant decoration than on a respect for the rules of style. In the eyes of his contemporaries, however, this altar "in the medieval style" reveals "superior talent and a truly artistic taste". In actual fact, it is mainly composed of Renaissance-revival elements similar to those Taché used in his designs for the Legislative Assembly building in Quebec City.[27]

Nor was the home immune from the prevailing fashion: little by little it too was invaded by decorators and gilders. In 1850 the Montreal firm of Lloyd and Roy was famous for its "finely finished ornamental and decorative painting", and its salons were "painted in the most handsome style and in tasteful colours".[28] In the same period, the silversmiths Savage & Lyman ordered from Bohle & Hendery of Montreal — Peter Bohle (1786-1862) and Robert Hendery (about 1814-1897) — a remarkable tea and coffee service to be presented to John Leeming in gratitude for his work as secretary-general of the provincial exhibition in Montreal in 1850. The rococo-revival style of this set, with its nature motifs — oak leaves, acorns, acanthus-leaf clusters, a squirrel — was novel in its day. Though restrained, the plant motifs are everywhere: on the teapot they are combined with the arms of Canada, framed by the symbols of commerce, industry and agriculture. The Leeming service, designed by the painter James Duncan, was unusual at a time when most silver plate for presentation purposes was imported from abroad.[29]

It was considered good form to display in one's home pottery and decorative art objects of all kinds, especially if they were mementoes of a romantic trip through Europe or demonstrated a fascination with exotic lands. In the manor-house at Montebello Louis-Joseph Papineau showed off his humanist interests and training in the classics by displaying elegant pieces of pottery and good reproductions of antique busts and equestrian statues, not to men-

tion a Diana the Huntress and a miniature of the *Apollo Belvedere*! His imposing whatnot was part and parcel of that concern for appearances so dear to the *bourgeois* in the Victorian era. Some, indeed, showed far less restraint than Papineau in accumulating objects and mixing styles, so that their homes sometimes resembled junk rooms or the catch-all sections of provincial exhibitions.

The love of valuable objects displayed to visitors in one's drawing room was already a characteristic of some prominent citizens at the start of the Victorian era. In the portrait by Théophile Hamel (1817-1870) of Madame René-Édouard Caron and her daughter, the nymphs by a fountain in a glass case seen in the background are evidence of this. The painting depicts woman in her role as hostess and educator, in conformity with the views of the age and with middle-class etiquette.[30] Infrequently, a lady might exhibit outside of the home pretty landscape paintings or "pictures in flowers, in oils, watercolours and pencil [revealing] neat, careful, meticulous and patient work",[31] but her part in the work was glossed over. In fact ladies were confined to the world of home, where they were to make use of their talents in drawing, music, dress-making and embroidery. In 1880 *bourgeois* society reacted with surprise and admiration to the work of a certain Mrs. Clifford of Quebec City, who had created a large sculptured frame to hold photographs of Queen Victoria, the Princess Louise and the Marquis of Lorne. This enthusiastic reception by the political authorities and the public was tinged with moral considerations that outweighed the intrinsic merits of the frame itself, an eclectic curiosity that combined old moiré fabric and gold thread with poetry and perfume!

In the field of the arts then, Quebec society as a whole happily shared the Victorian penchant for reviving old forms. Their enthusiasm was the greater because this fashion, often considered a sterile one in other countries, enabled Quebec to make up for lost time in the area of the visual arts. The old

79
Studio of Charles Clutterbuck, Stafford
The George Jehoshaphat Mountain Memorial (The Ascension, The Baptism of Christ, the Transfiguration and symbols of the Evangelists), 1864
Stained-glass window, triptych
Holy Trinity Cathedral, Quebec City
Photo Jean-Guy Kérouac

80
Eugène-Étienne Taché (1836-1912)
Design for an altar for the chapel of the order of Notre-Dame de Saint-Roch de Québec, 1884
Ink and graphite on paper, 49 x 40.5 cm
Archives nationales du Québec, Centre de Québec et Chaudière-Appalaches, fonds E.E. Taché (NC-83.8.29.2)

81
Bohle & Hendery (for Savage & Lyman)
Teapot, 1851
Silver, 10 x 8.5 cm
National Gallery of Canada, Ottawa

82
*Arts Trophy of the Montreal Firm
of Thomas F. G. Foisy*, 1889
Engraving published in K.G.C. Huttemeyer,
Les intérêts commerciaux de Québec et Montréal et leurs
manufactures (Montreal, K.G.C. Huttemeyer, 1889),
p. 104
Bibliothèque du Séminaire de Québec,
fonds ancien (210)
Photo W. B. Edwards Inc., Quebec City

colony, now a dominion, could thus fully renew its links with its European roots, while widening its cultural horizons. In so doing, the middle classes certainly brought great enthusiasm to discovering the treasures of the past, but they were also not averse to new, contemporary forms of expression. In this manner, Quebec gradually caught up with Europe and the United States. Home interiors and fine furniture naturally evolved along the same lines.

John R. Porter

84
Théophile Hamel (1817-1870)
Mrs. René-Édouard Caron and Her Daughter, 1846
Oil on canvas, 124 x 99 cm
Musée du Québec, Quebec City

83
Edgar Gariépy (1881-1956), Montreal
Whatnot from the yellow drawing room
of the Manoir Papineau, Montebello
Photograph
McGill University, Montreal,
Ramsay Traquair Archive (101672)

1   This is the sub-title I myself suggested for the major travelling exhibition organized by the Musée du Québec in 1991-1992. See Mario Béland (ed.) *La peinture au Québec 1820-1850* (Quebec City: Musée du Québec - Les publications du Québec, 1991).

2   *Le Canadien*, October 15, 1847, p. 2.

3   See John R. Porter, "Les perspectives du marché de la peinture: entre les besoins matériels et le goût de l'art", in *La peinture au Québec 1820-1850, op. cit.*, pp. 11-35.

4   See Porter, *op. cit.*, pp. 13-15. It seems that knowledgeable collectors could occasionally pick up first-rate art works on the local market. When Edward Maitland's effects were being sold off before he left for England, the auctioneer John Leeming advertised for sale "A very valuable painting by David of *Mohammed Appearing to Saladin*, and "a marble bust of Paris, with base, by Canova.", *L'Aurore des Canadas*, May 7, 1844, p. 3 (trans.).

5   AMMFA, John W. H. Watts Papers, "Scrapbook", p. 344 (letter from the collector Edward Taylor Fletcher to William Kingsford, December 24, 1889).

6   *The Intellectual Development of the Canadian People: An Historical Review* (Toronto: Hunter, Rose & Company, 1881), pp. 118-119.

7   Toronto: Hunter, Rose & Company, 1884, pp. 234-235, 240-241. As regards schools of applied arts designed primarily for the working class, the situation in Montreal has been well researched by Céline Larivière-Derome ("Un professeur d'art au Canada au XIXe siècle: l'abbé Joseph Chabert", *RHAF*, vol. 28, no. 3 December 1974, pp. 347-366). In 1871 and 1872, Chabert obtained from the government of France two collections of statues, models and drawings he needed for his teaching.

8   See Janet M. Brooke, *Discerning Tastes: Montreal Collectors 1880-1920* (Montreal: Montreal Museum of Fine Arts, 1989).

9   See Jean Trudel, "Une élite et son musée", *Cap-aux-diamants*, no. 25 spring 1991, pp. 22-25.

10 In connection with the Montreal provincial exhibition of 1860, the critic Gustave Smith aptly remarked that "The small number of genre pictures on display indicated clearly that this branch of art is not yet much cultivated in Canada, However, we have no doubt that a taste for it will shortly manifest itself." *L'Ordre*, November 14, 1860, p. 1 (trans.).

11 *La Minerve*, September 28, 1865, p. 1. See also the *Journal de Québec* of the same date (p. 3), which describes in detail the images in the painting.

12 See Dennis Reed, *Lucius O'Brien: Visions of Victorian Canada*, exhib. cat. (Toronto: Art Gallery of Ontario, 1990).

13 See Ann Thomas, *Canadian Painting and Photography, 1860-1900*, exhib. cat. (Montreal: McCord Museum of Canadian History, 1979), in particular the chapter on the influence of photography on landscape painting (pp. 87-104).

14 ANQS, file of notary Michael Boyce, no. 2324, July 17, 1882. See later in the present publication Claire Desmeules's remarks on this house, with accompanying photographs.

15 Napoléon Bourassa (1880), quoted in Roger Le Moine, *Napoléon Bourassa, l'homme et l'artiste* (Ottawa: Éditions de l'Université d'Ottawa, 1974), p. 221 (trans.).

16 See John R. Porter, "Antoine Plamondon (1804-1895) et le tableau religieux: perception et valorisation de la copie", *Annales d'histoire de l'art canadien*, vol. 8, no. 1 (1984), pp. 1-24.

17 See Denis Grenier, "La descendance québécoise de la *Sainte Cécile* de Raphaël: le rôle de la copie dans la diffusion d'un thème iconographique européen", *Annales d'histoire de l'art canadien*, vol. 12, no. 2 (1989), pp. 115-138.

18 Gérard Morisset, *Coup d'oeil sur les arts en Nouvelle-France* (Quebec City: 1941), pp. 88-89.

19 The person who bespoke this set, the Abbé Pierre-Télesphore Sax, had visited Rome in 1850-1851. "It was not until 1858, twelve years after the church was consecrated, the Father Sax decided to have the interior of the church *completed in fresco*. This was a new technique and somewhat risky in our climate, with its extremes of cold in the winter and of heat in the summer. However, frescoes had been used some years previously in decorating the church of the *Gésu* in Montreal, and seemed to have been found satisfactory.

While travelling in the United States, M. Sax went to consult the Benedictines, who are knowledgeable about the arts, and they gave him the name of W. Lamprecht, a young artist from Munich who had won the first prize at its famous school of painting; they recommended him as one of the best painters then residing in the United States. M. Sax got in touch with him and gave him the contract to decorate the interior of the church in fresco." Benjamin Demers, *La paroisse de St-Romuald d'Etchemin, avant et depuis son érection* (Quebec City: J.-A. K. Laflamme, 1906), pp. 251-252, (trans.).

20 See Ginette Laroche, "L'iconographie jésuite et ses implications culturelles dans l'art et la religion des Québécois (1842-1968)", doctoral thesis submitted to l'Université Laval in May 1990.

21 See Denis Martin, *Portraits des héros de la Nouvelle-France: images d'un culte historique* (Montreal: Hurtubise HMH, 1988), pp. 108-109.

22 *L'Événement*, June 25, 1880, p. 1.

23 "Kitsch" is defined as an aesthetic attitude or style characterized by the ill-assorted use of old-fashioned or popular elements considered in bad taste by the cultural establishment and mass-produced. Kitsch in art emerged in the last quarter of the nineteenth century. As an art of the masses as opposed to that of the avant-garde, kitsch can be identified by its mediocrity and approachability. It is closely tied to the triumph of middle-class mores, is conventional and far from being "art for art's sake". To paraphrase Abraham Moles, it is a kind of art that seeks its identity in its heritage, the values of the past, which are unquestioningly accepted as beautiful by a recently established *bourgeois* culture that is quite satisfied by variations on copies. It is a revivalist kind of art based on imitation. See John R. Porter, "L'oeuvre du statuaire Louis Jobin (1845-1928): au confluent de la tradition et du kitsch", *Vie des arts*, vol. 30, no. 122, pp. 48-51, 103; A. Moles and Eberhard Wahl, "Kitsch et objet", in *Communications 13 — les objets* (Paris: Seuil, 1969), pp. 105-129.

24 H.-J.-J.-B. Chouinard, *Fête nationale des Canadiens-français à Québec en 1880* (Quebec City: Imprimerie A. Côté, 1881), pp. 136-137.

25 See, for example, an article published in *Le Courrier du Canada* on December 2, 1886 (p. 2) on the interior decoration of churches.

26 See Ginette Laroche, "Les memorial windows: une mémoire de verre", *Annales d'histoire de l'art canadien*, vol. 9, no. 2 (1986), pp. 96-140.

27 See Mario Béland and Ginette Laroche, "L'odyssée de deux anges volants du Musée du Québec", *Annales d'histoire de l'art canadien*, vol. 11, nos. 1 and 2 (1988), p. 58-85.

28 *La Minerve*, August 12, 1850, quoted in John R. Porter, *L'Art de la dorure au Québec du XVIIe siècle à nos jours* (Quebec City: Garneau, 1975), p. 96.

29 See Ross Fox, *Pièces honorifiques de la collection Henry Birks d'orfèvrerie canadienne* (Ottawa: National Gallery of Canada, 1985), pp. 22-26.

30 As early as 1833 a newspaper article listed "the many essential occupations that consign drawing, music and the other beautifying arts to the boudoirs of the fair sex". *Le Canadien*, July 26, 1833, p. 3.

31 See the *Journal de Québec*, September 28, 1865, p. 3; John R. Porter, "Les perspectives du marché de la peinture...", *op. cit.*, pp. 31-32.

An Admirable Work of Art Executed by a Woman*

The Ottawa newspapers recently brought to the public eye an admirable work of art executed by Mrs. James Clifford of Quebec City. This creation, a masterpiece of its kind, has been on display for some time in the lounge of the Russell Hotel and in Rideau Hall, and all those who have examined it have been amazed to see that a woman's hand could unaided complete so sizeable and so perfect a piece of handiwork as this by Mrs. Clifford. It is a magnificently sculpted frame containing photographs of Her Gracious Majesty Queen Victoria, of the Marquis of Lorne and of Her Royal Highness the Princess Louise. The frame is four feet long, two feet high and four inches deep. In the centre is a magnificent cushion of antique moiré fabric on which appears a "facsimile" of the Queen's signature; above it is the royal crown in gold thread with representations of the Queen of England's diamonds. Mrs. Clifford broke 400 needles while stitching the crown on to the cushion. Just the perfume that scents the frame cost $14.

Below the cushion to which the photograph of Queen Victoria is attached are the following verses by M. Pamphile Lemay, embroidered in gold.

This magnificent frame was valued at $500 by the Marquis of Lorne on his most recent visit to Quebec City. We feel sure that such is less than the true worth of the creation, for Mrs. Clifford spent several months preparing the designs, and many weeks in creating the frame, which she sculpted herself.

We believe we speak for all who have been to see the tableau in offering our warmest thanks to Mr. Southgate for admitting to the lounge of the Windsor Hotel all the visitors who have flocked to admire this work of art by a young Canadian woman.

Mrs. Clifford has received several letters of congratulation from the Governor General and ministers of the Dominion, which we hope will have proved adequate recompense for her energy and courage.

In Mrs. Clifford French Canadians, and especially French Canadian ladies, have an example to follow, and we have good reason to hope that no-one will be averse to studying and examining this magnificent frame, which will soon be displayed at the St. Lawrence Hall and later at the Hôtel-de-Ville.

TRIBUTE

There is, in the Atlantic, an island of proud shores;
All ships salute it, and bruit its fame abroad.
It is an oasis in a savage wilderness
And the sun sheds a ray there always.
Its valleys are fertile, its cities magnificent.
Ships without number berth in its ports;
The din of its factories fills the air;
Bronze cannon defend its glory and its ancient fortresses.
Among the great who govern the earth, there is
A woman blessed by God. For half a century, faith
And honour have been the watchwords of her austere reign.
As she passes, she brings happiness
And when on all sides the people's hatred
Shakes thrones and judges kings,
She reigns in peace. Her secular throne
Finds its supreme support in the love of law.

Pamphile Lemay (trans).

---

* An article published in *La Minerve* (Montreal), May 14, 1880, p. 1 (trans.).

Comments on the Decoration of Churches by an Art Lover*

Fashion is a pitiless tyrant. Who would have thought it? Even sanctuaries are not safe from its infiltrations. And there, as everywhere else, fashion is frequently seen to be irrational, capricious, sometimes shameless, snapping its fingers at the requirements of good taste and propriety, and breaking all established rules and ancient customs.

For some years now it has been the fashion to decorate our churches.

But what could be better? you say. I suppose you bring in an artist decorator to put the finishing touches to the architect-builder's work, to place statues and bas-reliefs here and there, to divide the ceiling up with transverse ribs into sections with coffers, cartouches with trophies significant and otherwise, or by depicting these objects in paint where means are insufficient to afford bas-reliefs. Isn't that following the rules of art? I see nothing reprehensible in that.

Oh indeed! if that were the case; but matters are not usually arranged thus. Indeed, the word decorate, which I used earlier, was perhaps the wrong term; it might be more correct to say daub.

The artist decorator should have knowledge of which our interior decorators, or rather our church-daubers, seem to have no glimmering. Such a man will have been employed by an artist, perhaps, for some jobs carried out under supervision; then one day, he says to himself: "Why shouldn't I do this kind of work on my own account? I'd earn a lot more! I know perfectly well how to use gold, red, yellow, blue and so on, so why shouldn't I take on these jobs myself?"... And that's how he becomes an artist decorator.

But art has rules, confirmed by experience over the centuries, which have to be learned in order to be understood. Even good taste has to be trained, and refined by the study of masterpieces. Intelligence and commonsense are not always sufficient in forming taste; a certain training has to be undergone in order to acquire it.

However, our tactician decides to be an artist and sets to work. He knows how to apply colour, and you should see how he uses, and abuses, them: reds, yellows, gold and orange everywhere; it's bright, so it must be beautiful! A glance at those of our churches in Montreal and Quebec City that have been decorated in the past few years confirms that this was the guiding principle behind their interiors. Brightness was wanted, and was achieved; but beauty, true beauty as art and refined taste understand it, is absent. People have forgotten or do not know that beauty in art is always simple, restrained, more liable to impress us through its uniformity and in the harmony of its component parts than through flashiness and sallies; guns are not part of an orchestra!

The most lamentable aspect of the trend is that more often than not, those who employ these self-styled artists are themselves insufficiently knowledgeable to be able to guide their employees, avert mistakes, or insist that the rules of good taste be followed. A parish priest, say, has seen a church decorated with a profusion of colours, gilding and sumptuous marble; he wants to have his own church dressed up in the same manner; it's the fashion! Now Pierre, the churchwarden or syndic, is friends with Baptiste the dauber, and one must help one's friends. And so, without proper plans checked and approved by art scholars, without detailed specifications on how the work is to be done to make it sturdy and durable, the contract is thrown together, and Baptiste will have all the facilities he needs to fatten his purse. As long as the results are bright and shiny, what does it matter if he gives us images of Aeolus instead of cherubim, if he depicts unrealizable marble sculptures, if he gives us a frieze projecting from a cornice, if he creates trophies in which the rules of perspective are so flouted that it is not always possible to guess what the image is supposed to represent. Go to Sainte-Anne de Beaupré, Beauport, Champlain, Notre-Dame in Montreal, Saint-Jacques, among others, and you will see what I mean.

Far be it from me to reproach these workers for their lack of training; these poor people do what they can, they know no better. Besides, Baptiste daubed such-and-such another church, and everyone thought it beautiful. The priest of such-and-such another parish was of the same opinion and wanted to have

---

* An article published in *Le Courrier du Canada* (Montreal), December 2, 1886, p. 2 (trans.).

his church dressed up in the same manner. So he came to an agreement with Baptiste, and the latter repeated the process, using gaudy colours in a slapdash way.

What is just as unfortunate is that by proceeding like this, we are regressing artistically instead of progressing; we are ruining public taste and giving foreigners a poor notion of our level of civilization.

And that is precisely what struck the group of Frenchmen who came to Montreal recently after travelling to New York for the unveiling of the Statue of Liberty illuminating the world. After visiting the Séminaire de Saint-Sulpice, Villa-Maria and so on, they moved on to the churches, first entering Notre-Dame. What a huge nave, they said, and what a soaring ceiling, but why so much gilding? why all this heavy-handed painting? They then went to Saint-Jacques — the same profusion of garish colours and obtrusive decoration. Alas!, they said, is the love of the arts the last product of a civilized society?...

A Parisian Sculptor in Montreal in 1849*

The début of M. Charles Bullet, a sculptor from the Paris Academy, with a bust of Monsignor Bourget which is an impeccably executed perfect likeness, had given us only a limited notion of his abilities, although it may be said without exaggeration that his first piece might be envied by our leading North American sculptors.

During his brief visit to New York, M. Bullet created, to demonstrate his skill, a marble bust and a statuette of the sculptor *M. Brown*. Both these creations were accepted for display at the exhibition of the National Academy of Fine Arts in New York, where they were much admired by connoisseurs. Since the artist came to Montreal, our American neighbours have done their utmost to coax him southward, and indeed he might have accepted the flattering offers made him, had he not been committed to stay here to execute a bust of Monsignor Bourget in fine Italian marble. It is now up to us to keep him here, to encourage him, so no-one can say that the only distinguished sculptor who ever came here was obliged to seek other countries with more patrons of the arts than we have in Canada. A lone sculptor is easily kept busy!

Now that M. Bullet has just produced new evidence of his talent in the shape of a *St. John the Baptist* three and a half feet high, the public is called upon to judge a true work of art. Those who choose to stroll along Notre-Dame Street should deign to pause at number 29, where they will find a moment of great pleasure in viewing this grand and noble sculpture! One is struck with admiration at first glance, wondering how clay can be moulded and shaped thus, with such expressiveness, indeed, such life... This beautiful composition demonstrates what art is, to those of us who know it only imperfectly. Religious faith is apparent in the highest degree in this statue. The Saint's stance is confident and bold, with no tragic gestures, as befits a preacher; the expression on the face soars above the material of which it is formed. The gesture of the head, with the arm pointing to the sky, is so fine, so noble, the artist must have had one of those rare moments of ideal inspiration to handle his clay like that. We need not dwell on the perfect proportions of the figure: the articulation of the hands and feet, the sublime movement of the ankle, the modelling of the flesh to hint at the skin over the muscles and the muscles over the bones. It all comes together in perfect harmony, and constitutes in our opinion a work of the first order.

Since the Revolution in France has sent us one of her children, why should we not welcome him, especially when, in collaboration with our Quebec painter M. Hamel, he can develop the fine arts in our land? Let it not be said of us by our descendants that we rejected progress. Our poverty in the realm of the arts is apparent from the most cursory

---

* Article published in *La Minerve* (Montreal) and re-issued in *Le Canadien* (Quebec City) on December 26, 1849, p. 1, (trans.).

glance at our public buildings, both outside and inside. Look at the niches in our churches, too long denuded of statuary. Is the nature of our soil so unrewarding that it cannot yield any material worthy of the sculptor's chisel? Let us go into one of our churches. Where are the marble altars, the pulpits, the statues of saints, &c.? What do we find but wood carvings in poor taste, so coarse in style that it is impossible to find a single example of the Greek, medieval, Louis XIV or Louis XV styles. Everywhere there are meagre, pathetic scrolling and foliage motifs like bent, folded, cut-out tin-plate: everywhere gilding, tawdriness, painted decorations, nothing monumental, nothing truly rich or artistic. Look at our drawing rooms. Aside from a few families who have brought back one or two fine paintings and sculptures from their trips to Europe, what do we see? Some poor-quality lithographs tinted in red and blue. A few bad, shapeless plaster pieces cast in moulds and polished by people who do not know what sculpture is. There you have, more or less, the sum total of the art we possess, with the exception of the Bank of Montreal (an architectural masterpiece) and four bas-reliefs on the Banque du Peuple which were executed in London, not forgetting the fountain in front of the parish church, which is scarcely worthy of the little garden of a *petit bourgeois*.

Let us, then, make a start. It would be so easy to establish a small academy of drawing and sculpture where young people interested in the arts could spend an hour or two of an evening drawing and modelling copies of good prints and some statues and busts brought from Europe (which would cost very little). Expenses would be minimal: two teachers, the models, a studio, lighting, and a few small prizes from the province to be awarded to the students. In ten years or less, we should then see men of genius set off to travel Europe and later return to create masterpieces in their native land. Our little school would grow to eventually become as illustrious as those in France, Spain, Germany and Flanders. Are our fellow countrymen lacking in artistic aptitude? No. The past is there to prove it. How many talented wood carvers like Dauphin, Berlinguet, Auclair and others needed only a few lessons in drawing and the anatomy of shapes and modelling in order to rise to the level of the most famous sculptors. Are not the fine arts meant to regenerate a country, to excite the imagination of its people through one of those powerful experiences that transform every life? They can awaken in the soul a host of mysterious feelings and ingenuous emotions, open man's heart to a myriad tendernesses; in short, the arts can penetrate every nook and cranny of our workaday life, like the wildflowers mingled among hard-won crops.

CHAPTER

II

THE USERS

85
Notman Studio, Montreal. *Mr. MacDuff's Family*, 1874. Composite photograph
McCord Museum of Canadian History, Montreal, Notman Photographic Archives (11,119 Misc II)
The architectural decor of this composite photograph is virtually identical to the façade of Ravenscrag, at that time the home of Sir Hugh Allan.

DOMESTIC WORLDS

Bourgeois Values and Lifestyles in the Second Half of the Nineteenth Century

THE HOUSE:

... The plan of the house reflects the way of life imposed by the climate and by society; its appearance gives certain hints concerning the reigning trends in art; overall, it incorporates a host of revelations regarding public taste and the practices and customs of the domestic household, and offers countless glimpses of the nature of social relations.

César Daly, *L'architecture privée au XIXe siècle sous Napoléon III* (Paris: Ducher & Cie, 1870), p. 11 (trans.)

IT IS IMPOSSIBLE TO STUDY VICTORIAN FURNITURE IN isolation. Like many authors before me, I have been obliged to recognize the need to include in my study certain corollaries: for whom was this furniture intended, what function was it designed to fulfil, who made it, and how? Numerous questions arise concerning the situations and lifestyles of the people who used it — concerning, in other words, the domestic worlds they inhabited. It has been said that the Victorian house was an enormous "machine for living". If we are to fully appreciate the furniture, it seems to me crucial to examine whether this assertion can also be applied to Quebec and, if so, to discover just how the "machine" worked. It would be rash, however, to attempt to define a model specific to Quebec without situating it within the broader context of domestic life in the Western world. For it seems clear that things developed here very much as they did elsewhere. Throughout the West the same basic patterns developed, the same trends emerged, the same attitudes were adopted. Such a global analysis has the advantage of revealing clearly the particular nature of domestic life in Quebec, which was characterized by the ever-present duality of the English- and French-speaking worlds. Between these two extremes were all sorts of variations. Some features mirrored the domestic life of Britain, others had more in common with attitudes prevalent in France or the United States. This duality peculiar to the Quebec model had a marked effect on life in the province, on the factors that permitted the attainment of a certain standard of living and on the precise conditions necessary for its achievement. This chapter is devoted, then, to an examination of those who acquired and used the furniture, of their status, their aspirations and their possessions.

Without risk of over-generalization, the Victorian era can be approached by examining one of its most characteristic features: the phenomenon of specialization. Society's offices, professions and duties were becoming more and more specialized, and this led directly to a widening of the gulf between the major social classes. The process of specialization was embodied in the city itself, in the contrast between rich and poor neighbourhoods, between luxurious and modest homes. To a large extent, the *bourgeois* house — the prototypical dwelling of the Victorian era — grew out of the same process of

86
Notman Studio, Montreal
Mr. Gurd's country house on the banks of
the Rivière des Prairies, 1886
Photograph
McCord Museum of Canadian History, Montreal,
Notman Photographic Archives (81,030 Misc-II)

specialization and compartmentalization that marked Victorian society generally: town house, country house, *bourgeois* mansion, worker's cottage, semi-detached house and row house. In fact, the trend towards specialization was so strong that it affected various more detailed aspects of habitation, including the division and hierarchization of space, and the specialization of rooms, practices and furniture and, to some degree, of decorative objects.

This specialization was not the result of chance. The evolution of attitudes, customs and sensibilities during the nineteenth century had given rise to new practices and new needs that modified both lifestyle and the house itself. The search for "symbols" to represent the new class that had emerged, the growing need for domestic privacy and comfort, and the transformation of relations between men and women, parents and children, masters and servants, were the principal factors influencing lifestyle during the second half of the nineteenth century.

> THE BOURGEOIS:
> The bourgeois [...] was a kind of seigneur or English lord who dwelt in a magnificent mansion and lived in the most incredible luxury [...] They all possessed impressive carriages that women and children would watch from their doorways as they passed by, with an air of respectful admiration. These carriages were the only four-wheeled vehicles in the parish. When the curé [...] and Dr. Bénoni Guay each acquired a buggy – known as a "wâguine" – it caused quite a stir. Some people even found it rather odd, so ingrained in the collective unconscious was the idea that four-wheeled carriages were the exclusive prerogative of the English.
> Louis Fréchette (1839-1908), *Mémoires intimes* (trans.)

This childhood memory recounted by Louis Fréchette conjures up a clear picture of the social structure of the Victorian era, in which the *bourgeoisie* played such a dominant role. It was a structure characteristic of nineteenth-century Western society. In the early Middle Ages, when this new social class

first began to emerge, it comprehended the merchants and dealers that inhabited the fortified cities. And, as Rybczynski points out,[1] the reason for the *bourgeoisie* being at the heart of the question of household comfort is clear: while society's nobles resided in castles, its scholars inhabited monasteries and its serfs made do with humble shacks, it was the *bourgeoisie* who lived in houses.

The *bourgeoisie* was defined by the usual criterion of the ownership and possession of capital.[2] The main sources of capital behind the rise of the *bourgeoisie* in Quebec during the economic expansion that occurred between 1850 and 1914 were "the import-export business, commercial credit, real estate speculation, sea and rail transport, major public works like the railways and industrial production".[3] The *bourgeoisie* was the group that owned and controlled this capital. And where there is capital, there are merchants. The merchant class was undoubtedly the most representative *bourgeois* group of the period; they possessed, moreover, their own institutions and meeting-places. In the social structure of the nineteenth century, then, the *bourgeoisie* had replaced the aristocracy as society's ruling class.

The *bourgeois* class, expanding rapidly during the nineteenth century, included individuals whose social level and particular circumstances were determined largely by their economic situation and the power they wielded. But — and this is the source of the unique nature of Victorian society in the province — as well as the usual strata, Quebec society was composed of a wide variety of ethnic groups, which in turn influenced variations in circumstance. "Class was in fact only one of the elements in a social structure which continued to include differences between urban and rural life, between major cities and small towns, and in which differentiating factors and social networks depended also on ethnic origin, religion, family and the surrounding community."[4]

The Quebec *bourgeoisie* was made up of three large groups[5]: the *grande*, the *moyenne* and the *petite bourgeoisie*. The members of the *grande bourgeoisie*, first of all, who were relatively few in number, were of predominantly Anglo-Scottish descent and were concentrated in Montreal. They headed the country's most important institutions and businesses, which included banks, insurance companies, trust companies, railways, continental and international shipping lines, major industries and real estate projects. Next came the much larger group formed by the *moyenne bourgeoisie*, whose ranks swelled considerably during the Victorian era. This sector included people of English

87
A horse-drawn sleigh in front of Beauvoir, Richard R. Dobell's villa in Sillery, about 1890
Photograph
National Archives of Canada, Ottawa (C-4780 A)

88
Merchants' Exchange Refreshment Rooms
Engraving published in the *Canadian Illustrated News*, November 21, 1874
National Archives of Canada, Ottawa (C-61536)

and Scottish origin, but also some French Canadians and Irish. They were spread throughout the province's larger cities, and they played a role in all branches of economic activity at the regional level. Working principally as wood merchants, wholesalers, and managers of regional banks and mortgage loan companies, they were also active in provincial and municipal politics. At the bottom of the scale was the *petite bourgeoisie*, largely French-speaking but with a significant proportion of immigrants; this group included village or local tradesmen, the more well-to-do craftsmen and professionals, and the clergy.

During the Victorian era, though, these subdivisions were not necessarily of prime importance; the key concept was that of the middle class. For the middle class formed a sort of indeterminate zone, outside the limits of the other groups, an ever-changing and constantly growing mass whose precise nature, since it altered as the century advanced, it is not easy to define. We can say, however, that it included all those people who had succeeded in rising above their original circumstances but without joining the ranks of the truly privileged, represented by the *grande* and *moyenne bourgeoisie*. Mark Girouard is one of the few authors to offer a really adequate definition of the middle class: "Behind the middle-classes lay all that the Industrial Revolution was producing in the way of mines, factories, railways, ships, warehouses, banks and cities to contain and support them. As a result the number of newly rich people who were able to invest in landed property, to buy or build a house, and to set up as landed gentry was greater than it had ever been.[6]" The truth of this last assertion was proven all through the Victorian era. And, from the mid-nineteenth century until the outbreak of the First World War, the single-family house adapted to the needs of the middle class was to undergo a development and to experience a popularity quite without precedent.

The Baker Gilmour House, p.

STATUS AND ASPIRATIONS

As the *bourgeoisie* developed into society's ruling class, their way of life gradually became the general standard. Since their upward social mobility was rooted in money, members of the middle class set great store by all of life's more material aspects, everything that enabled them to proclaim their recent social promotion, and this gave rise to the emergence of a number of class signs.[7] By "class signs" I mean those features that help us to identify a member of the *bourgeoisie* and that enabled them to identify one another; in fact, this categorization through external signs is characteristic of middle-class life.

One of the ways in which members of the middle classes could display their new social advancement was to conform to the code of behaviour prevalent in the best society. Being a member of the *best society*, having *good manners*, being *well educated* — all were important components of middle-class respectability. The group that served as a model for the *bourgeoisie* was the old aristocracy, a highly ritualized sub-society governed by an extremely strict code of etiquette. These rules were developed by the aristocracy to facilitate recognition between themselves and differentiation from the other social classes, and they were adopted by the *bourgeoisie* for exactly the same reasons. However, owing to their very complexity, the rituals and regulations were full of snares for the newly rich, and their efforts to conform were never ending. They often turned for assistance in these efforts to books on etiquette and manuals on social comportment that described in detail everything that was to be done or not done in all conceivable circumstances.

The house and everything associated with it — the neighbourhood in which it was located, its size, the number and type of rooms, their lay-out, the number of servants, the quality and variety of the furniture, the silverware, the carriages — undoubtedly represented *the* most important classing sign among the *bourgeoisie*. It symbolized, *a posteriori*, the social status of its occupants.

Living a life, as they did, centred so very largely on "appearances", on everything touching the material aspects of human existence, and owing to the rituals that became increasingly explicit during the period, one of the main concerns of members of the middle class was to maintain their standard of living. Most of the expenses involved in keeping up the required lifestyle were associated with ceremonial displays or the basic running of the household.[8] Here again, the *bourgeoisie* were assisted by the numerous books dealing with the house that appeared throughout the nineteenth century. Many of these publications indicated in their title the income group for which they were intended.

> Clearly, one reason for the proliferation of this kind of book was the increased desire for status. Those income groups which previously did not aspire to any trappings of wealth now wanted to be told with precision how to behave and how to plan their budget. Secondly, houses did become more complicated. There was more space, there were more different kinds of rooms [...] On the other hand, organization was taken to enormous lengths.[9]

The middle class had become a world unto itself, governed according to its own highly specific rules. And the middle class in Quebec kept pace with the rest of the world. Of course, in certain circles traditional values continued to hold sway. But *bourgeois* society in Quebec was nonetheless very similar to *bourgeois* society throughout the West: its organization, its values and its lifestyle were virtually identical to those of the middle classes in England, Germany, Vienna, France and the United States.

The diary written between 1874 and 1880 by Henriette Dessaulles, a young middle-class girl from Saint-Hyacinthe, provides clear proof of this. The work is even more revealing, however, of the feminine world of which the author was part, so complex and so different from the world inhabited by men. The diary offers no clearly enunciated description of the framework supporting the life of the period, but it nevertheless provides countless insights into the middle-class world at the end of the Victorian era. In fact, this young girl's diary sketches an incisive portrait of a society and a period.

The Dessaulles family were typical members of the *moyenne bourgeoisie*. Descended from the early seigneurs of Saint-Hyacinthe, Henriette's father, Georges-Casimir, was both mayor of that city and president of the local bank. Through various alliances, including important marriages into the Papineau family, the Dessaulles gradually "took on the dimensions of a clan". In response to current tastes and new requirements, the family exchanged the old eighteenth-century seigneurial manor for a "Victorian" home, situated in the very centre of Saint-Hyacinthe. It was here that Henriette lived with her younger brothers and sisters, her father – often absent – and her stepmother, of whom she was not very fond. The rather strained relationship that evidently existed between the young girl and her stepmother throws a good deal of light on *bourgeois* life of the period. Her stepmother obviously attempted to instill in Henriette an awareness of her own rank, a devotion to respectability and a sense of decorum, and all the other values that were an integral part of a middle-class mentality at the time. Until she was ready to "come out" into society, on the completion of her convent education, the young girl spent her time reading and daydreaming in her room, taking country walks and exchanging visits with cousins living in Montreal. As Louise Saint-Jacques Dechêne points out in her introduction to the diary,[10] the life of this privileged class, with its balls and drawing-room entertainments held among family and friends, was reminiscent of English country life.

THE BOURGEOIS HOUSE

In fact, English country life was in many ways the source of the *bourgeois* lifestyle of the second half of the nineteenth century. Prior to the Victorian era, only members of the aristocracy and the *grande bourgeoisie* possessed both a town and a country house. This privilege was embodied in the luxurious villas and vast estates that dotted the countryside around Quebec City. The Victorian era, with its enormously improved systems of transportation, made a second home a possibility for all members of the *bourgeoisie*. In this period of increasingly marked social hierarchization, being a *bourgeois* meant first and foremost living in a suburb on the outskirts of a city, in a neighbourhood where one was surrounded by one's peers. The working classes, by contrast, continued to live close to their place of labour. In the years between 1840 and 1900, the separation between work and dwelling place occurred first of all among the wealthy, gradually filtering down, layer by layer, and reaching the lower echelons of society by the turn of the century.

In Quebec City, the development of the Grande Allée began in 1832, coinciding with the first cholera epidemic. From this period on, the town's wealthier citizens began to leave the downtown area to take up residence in healthier surroundings that combined the advantages of the country with proximity to the city. These new neighbourhoods quickly developed their own particular style of architecture, appropriately labelled "suburban". In Montreal, the rich neighbourhoods were clustered in the west, the poorer ones in the east, with the additional distinguishing ingredient of ethnic origin: the inhabitants of the rich neighbourhoods were predominantly English-speaking, those of the poor neighbourhoods French-speaking.

In the latter part of the nineteenth century Montreal superseded Quebec City, rapidly becoming the province's main centre for business and trade. From 1850 on, Montreal's *bourgeoisie* began to move away from the city's industrial and commercial sector to settle in the suburbs. The new, exclusively middle-class neighbourhood that sprang up as a result covered an area of roughly one square mile that came to be known simply as the "Square Mile". Between them, the inhabitants of this neighbourhood controlled seventy per cent of Canada's wealth, and from 1850 to 1930 a number of sumptuous *bourgeois* residences were built in the area. Jewel among this array of splendour created for the "money barons" of the time was Ravenscrag, home to Sir Hugh Allan.

residence of Andrew [?]ay Smith, p. 141

The same division of the various social classes into different neighbourhoods occurred in Sherbrooke. Here, the northern suburb was inhabited by the city's English-speaking *bourgeoisie*, while their French-speaking counterparts formed an enclave in the heart of the downtown area.

THE IMPACT OF PATTERN BOOKS ON THE MIDDLE-CLASS HOUSE

> ... The Victorian age became increasingly the age of the middle classes. Middle-class ideals, middle-class politics and middle-class morals came to dominate a large part of society. Perhaps the most characteristic expression of middle-class ideals was the detached house in both country and suburb. It was the dream of every businessman or professional man.[11]

When it came to selecting the style and decor of their houses, a number of models — together with all sorts of practical information — were available to the middle classes. These models appeared in various specialized publications, including architects' and builders' journals, women's magazines and, above all, pattern books. Such sources presented a wide range of houses suited to varying incomes; a good proportion of the dwellings were actually intended for less wealthy families, for the publications themselves were directed at the middle ranks of the *bourgeoisie*. This new form of literature, which transformed both domestic architecture and lifestyle during the second half of the nineteenth century, grew out of a philosophy that had emerged in England towards the end of the eighteenth century: the Picturesque movement. An innovative feature of this movement was that it gave the house — the house as home — a central position within its doctrine.[12]

These publications can be divided into two generations. The initial group, which appeared in the first half of the nineteenth century,[13] was aimed unequivocally at an affluent public. The second, on the other hand, published during the latter half of the century, quickly adapted itself to middle-class requirements. Pattern books became quite extraordinarily popular, both in England and the United States,[14] where pioneer Andrew Jackson Downing successfully adapted European models to the North American context. The books published during the Victorian era differed from the earlier ones in their inclusion of advice concerning the furnishings best suited to each type of house. These publications played a crucial role in the dissemination throughout the population at large of the tastes and values associated with the Picturesque movement.[15]

The popularity of these publications can be explained largely by the fact that they were a response to changes in the social structure that occurred in the latter part of the nineteenth century. They actually served as ideal vehicles of middle-class ideology,[16] contributing in a decisive way to the development of a specifically suburban architecture and lifestyle adapted to the needs of lower- and middle-income families who, thanks to better systems of transport and a general rise in standards of living, were moving out of the cities to settle on the outskirts.

The pattern books of the period focused principally on two types of dwelling intended for country or suburban living — the cottage and the villa — although they did also include designs for semi-detached and row houses. By raising the social status of the cottage and lowering that of the villa, the

89

Residence of Mrs I. Butters, Stanstead Plain, Stanstead Co., P.Q.
Engraving published in the *Illustrated Atlas of the Eastern Townships and South Western Quebec* (Quebec City, H. Belden, 1881)
Photo SRP

This elegant house, built in 1867 in Stanstead Plain, in the Eastern Townships, was the summer home of Mr. Butters, an American from Boston. It is reminiscent of a design for a villa created by Calvert Vaux in 1864.

90
Design for an Irregular Brick Country House
Engraving published in Calvert Vaux, *Villas and Cottages: A Series of Designs Prepared for Execution in the United States* (New York, Dover Publications, 1970 [Harper & Brothers, 1864]), p. 177
Photo SRP

books helped minimize the differences between the homes of the wealthy and those of ordinary people.[17] It was thus during the Victorian era that the cottage, once a humble rural dwelling, became the archetypical middle-class home. The pattern books offered models accessible to all, each one a testimony to the growing desire for privacy and comfort.

In the decade following 1840, the new house models were gradually introduced into Quebec through the medium of pattern books and American magazines brought into Canada by rail. While the pattern books themselves were for the most part read by a limited group made up of architects, engineers and a few members of the *bourgeois* elite, a few large-circulation American magazines — mostly farming, women's and gardening magazines — were publishing house plans from 1840 on. Quebec followed suit ten years later.[18] Moreover, it seems that there was reference to the content of the pattern books in the lectures held by Cercles agricoles (farming associations) all over Quebec.[19]

While the impact of these pattern books on Quebec Victorian architecture is beyond doubt, direct references to them as a source are not common. The memoirs written by Madame Béïque provide a rare example: "In the autumn of 1885, my husband purchased an island at Vaudreuil [...] When it came time to make the plans for the house, Judge Antoine-Aimé Dorion, who later became Chief Justice on the Appeal Court and who spent his summers in Vaudreuil, lent us several American magazines on architecture, which we went to pick up at his house on Sherbrooke Street."[20]

In the 1870s, architects began selling their plans by mail, taking advantage of the tremendous promotional support offered by specialized magazines. One such magazine, *The Canadian Mechanics' Magazine and Patent Office Record*, was published by George E. Desbarats in Montreal, starting on March 1, 1873. The magazine had a wide public, which included engineers, architects, builders, cabinetmakers and mechanics, together with manufacturers in the textile, paper, naval and mining industries, and all those concerned with the domestic field in general. The magazine often published plans for houses, and while

LIVING IN STYLE

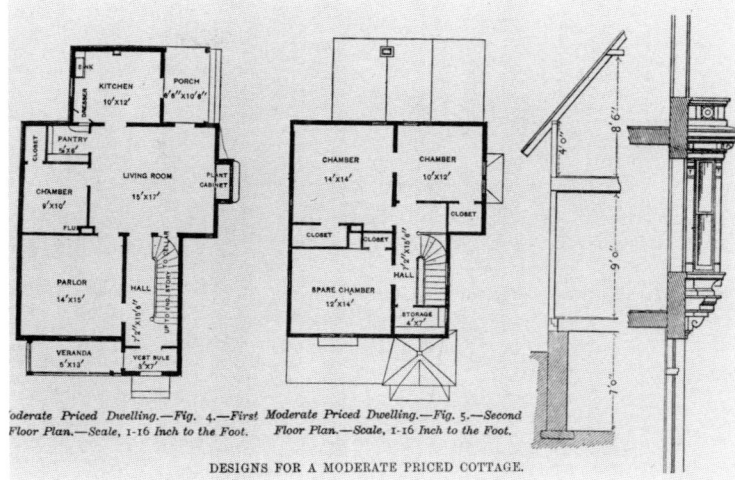

91
Design for Cottage
Detail: pattern for façade
Engraving published in *Scientific Canadian*,
March 1880, p. 88
Photo SRP

92
Designs for a Moderate Priced Cottage
Detail: patterns for ground floor
and sections
Engraving published in *Scientific Canadian*,
March 1880, p. 89
Photo SRP

some of the plans were quite elaborate, the majority were chosen because they were economical to build and offered a well-designed interior, ideally suited to the needs of an average middle-class family. In the vocabulary of the time, the word "cottage" was still used to describe a relatively small, modest house, while the term "villa" referred to a more luxurious, elaborate dwelling. Prices ranged from $900 to $14,000. As well as house plans, the magazine contained all sorts of advice on decoration, lighting and ventilation, plus information about new techniques, materials and fabrics currently on the market.

THE DETACHED HOUSE: COTTAGES AND VILLAS

The Picturesque aesthetic affected all aspects of British architecture, but, as Janet Wright points out, it had a particularly marked influence on "the small house erected in a rural setting or on the outskirts of a town". It actually gave rise to a new category of houses: villas and picturesque cottages. The theories of the Picturesque movement were applied to the cottage and the villa throughout the Victorian era, and made themselves felt in a predilection for nature and its integration into architecture (evident in conservatories, verandahs and gardens), the revival and adaptation of earlier architectural styles (especially the Gothic, Renaissance and Queen Anne), a taste for asymmetrical forms and the manipulation of light and shade. Picturesque principles were introduced into the province by British middle-class immigrants, and between 1850 and about 1880 they gave rise to a number of villas and cottages, especially in the Quebec City region.[21] Among these were several picturesque cottages built according to the principles of the Americans Andrew Jackson Downing and Alexander Jackson Davis, well-known pattern book authors. According to Stephan Muthesius, it was at this period that the symbol of the suburban house became truly established: the small villa and ornate cottage, traditionally associated with the deep countryside, were gradually adopted as suburban dwellings.[22]

The cottage, a creation of English Romanticism, was a small, modest house. It had its roots in the English peasant dwelling as transformed by the theorists of the Picturesque movement. It was popularized — adapted, that is, to more limited financial means than those of the aristocracy — by the pat-

THE USERS

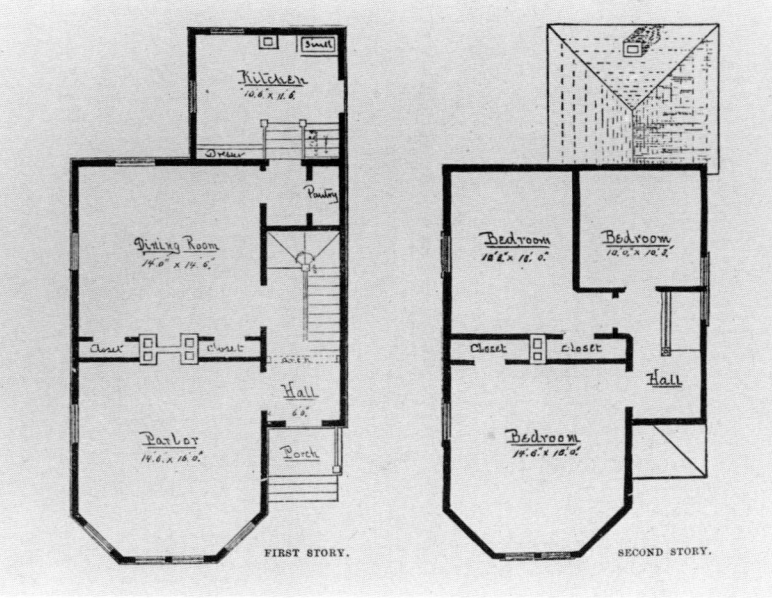

93
Design for a Cheap Cottage
Detail: pattern for façade
Engraving published in *Scientific Canadian*,
July 1880, p. 224
Photo SRP

94
Design for a Cheap Cottage
Detail: patterns for ground and first floors
Engraving published in *Scientific Canadian*,
July 1880, p. 225
Photo SRP

tern books. These publications invariably recommended that the furnishing and decoration of the cottage should remain extremely simple, for it was intended to encourage relaxation.

By the beginning of the Victorian era, several cottages had already been built on the outskirts of Quebec City, among them Kirk Ella and the Stuart Henry house. To begin with, the cottage's square, symmetrical plan was very simple. The ground floor consisted of a central entrance hall containing a staircase and giving onto four equal-sized rooms — a drawing room, dining room, library and kitchen — while the bedrooms were all on the second floor. However, under the influence of the pattern books, this basic plan soon became less regular and more complex. The need to position the house according to its best geographical orientation led to a greater flexibility in the plan's design. Irregular plans, often L- or T-shaped, began to appear and gradually to replace the rigid, central-corridor plan that had dominated residential architecture during the whole of the eighteenth century.

From the 1850s on, the distinction between the villa and the cottage became more marked, especially in the Quebec City region.[23] The term "cottage" came to designate a house that was more modest than a villa. Precisely because it was more modest, and thus better adapted to middle-class requirements, and also as a result of the many plans available in magazines, the cottage was an extremely popular residential form up until the start of the twentieth century.

The picturesque villa, also originally a country dwelling, differed slightly from the cottage. Faithful to its model — the Italian Renaissance villa — it was less rustic-looking than the cottage and was considerably larger and more elaborate. Being a far more costly residence than the cottage, the villa clearly did not appeal to the same public. The Butters house in Stanstead offers a typical example of a villa: its interior lay-out and appointment enabled its inhabitants to maintain a lifestyle of some elegance, although a rather more casual one than usual in a town house. There were more rooms than in a cottage — more reception rooms, but especially more bedrooms. This increased

size was the outcome of the fashion for visits to the country, very common during this extremely hospitable era. The villa, then, was designed to accommodate several guests at a time, and the lay-out of the rooms took into account the occupants' need for a certain privacy. The interior decor of this type of house was often in the rococo-revival style.

THE ROW HOUSE

The row house is another type of dwelling that originated in Britain and became widely popular during the nineteenth century. Created towards the end of the eighteenth century in response to the dense population of urban areas, where space was scarce, the row house was the ideal town house. From the 1870s on, row houses began to spring up in the suburbs of major cities, where land was divided in long, narrow lots. This type of house, inhabited frequently by members of the middle classes, came to be associated with this social group. In fact, in Great Britain and all her colonies, the row house became the quintessentially middle-class home. These houses, also called "terraced" houses in their country of origin, were set slightly back from the sidewalk, leaving a small strip of garden in the front. The façade of each house was generally identical with its fellows, and terraces of such dwellings would often line both sides of a street. In the late nineteenth and early twentieth centuries, a period of great eclecticism, the individual façades did occasionally vary, as in the terrace designed in 1903 by Stavely & Stavely for Quebec City's Du Parc Avenue, which included more prominent structures at either end. Elsewhere, row houses were sometimes built in small groups of two or three together.

95
Fred C. Wurtele (1842-1920), Quebec City
Row houses built on Quebec City's Grande-Allée by Joseph-Ferdinand Peachy in 1877-1879
Photograph
Archives nationales du Québec, Centre de Québec et Chaudière-Appalaches (P546/C-1)
These houses were demolished in the 1960s to make way for government buildings.

96
Harry (1848-1929) and Edward Black
Staveley (1877-1969)
Houses to Be Erected on Park Avenue, Quebec, for Mr. W. Sharpe, 1903
Archives nationales du Québec, Centre de Québec et Chaudière-Appalaches, fonds Staveley, plan 314-A
(NC 86-6-1)

The row house was a variation on the large English country house, but in a form adapted to limited space. Due to the narrowness of the lots, the row house could only extend in height and depth. The arrangement of the rooms followed a virtually unchanging plan. In fact, as Stephan Muthesius explains,[24] the basic plan employed all over Britain up to the beginning of the twentieth century was so simple it could be summed up in a few words: two stories of two rooms each. Variations included additional floors, a basement and/or a wing at the back. The Victorian row house was taller than its Georgian counterpart, owing to the number of bedrooms. However, while in England it might have had four or even five floors plus a basement, in Quebec it rarely rose over three. The interior lay-out, though, was virtually the same: the entrance hall with its staircase occupied only a narrow segment of the house. Set completely to one side, it opened onto the drawing and dining rooms, the two most important rooms in the house; visitors could thus immediately admire the best furniture, finest mouldings and most elegant chimneypieces the house had to offer. The entrance hall was rarely positioned centrally in row houses, although there were exceptions to this rule when the width of the lot permitted, as in certain houses on Laval Avenue in Montreal. The kitchen and other utility rooms were in the basement or at the back of the house, the main living rooms on the ground and first floors, and the bedrooms on the upper floors. The servants' rooms were in the attic.

During the 1880s, there was a new development that involved opening the house towards the back by locating one of the larger family rooms — usually the dining room — in the rear wing, with French windows giving onto the garden.[25] Where it was unfeasible to have the dining room opening onto the outdoors, architects began to combine dining and drawing rooms, separating the two with folding doors or an archway. This arrangement had the advantage of creating an illusion of greater space when the doors were open or, when they were closed, of increasing the feeling of cosiness. But the most positive effect of this lay-out was on the lighting. The drawing room usually possessed a bay or bow window giving onto the façade, and this served also to light the dining room, located further back and often windowless. In this case, if there was a rear wing it usually housed the kitchen and the maid's room.

97

98-99

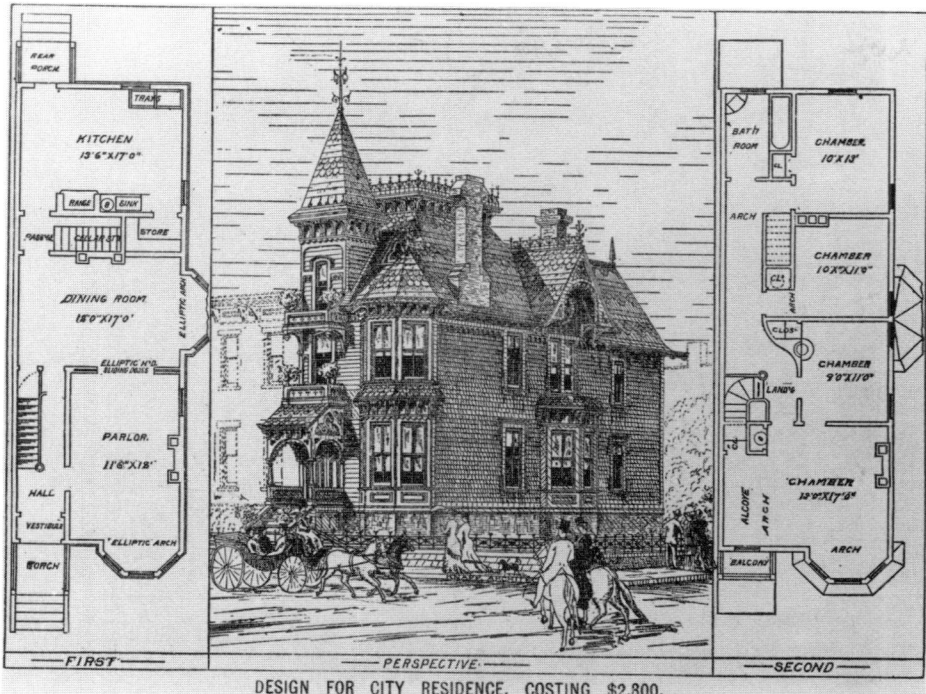

97

Design for City Residence, Costing $2,800
Engraving published in the *Canadian Mechanics' Magazine and Patent Office Record*, February 1878, p. 36
Photo SRP

"*Description of Cottage.* The first and second floor plans show the internal arrangement. On the first floor are parlor, dining-room, and kitchen. The parlor and dining-room each contain a fine semi-octagonal bay-window; that of the parlor affording a view through the street in either direction, and that of the dining-room giving the latter an exposure to the front street as well as in other directions. Under the main stairs is the dining-room china-closet, and the pantry dividing the dining-room from the kitchen contains the stairs to the cellar. A capacious kitchen store-room is provided, and wash-trays are fitted up in the kitchen, the dimensions of the latter affording ample room for laundry as well as for culinary purposes. The kitchen is fitted up with range, boiler and sink, and the several fire-places of the first floor are placed in the best positions for utility and effect. The sliding doors dividing the parlor and dining-room are finished with elliptical head, and trussed arches of the same form span the bay-windows. The second floor contains four sleeping-rooms and a bath-room, the former being each provided with closet and wash-basin. The bath-room is fitted up with bath-tub and water-closet, cased and trimmed up in hard wood. A close flight of stairs leads to the attic, which is very spacious, is well floored, and would afford fine bedrooms."

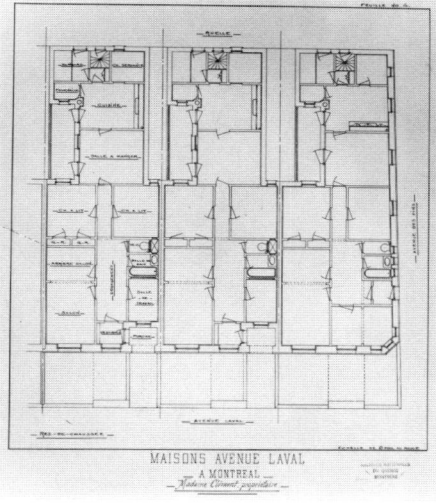

98

Houses, Laval Avenue in Montreal - Mrs. Clément, Owner
Detail: façade
Archives nationales du Québec, Direction de Montréal, de Laval, de Lanaudière, des Laurentides et de la Montérégie (plan 147-142)

99

Houses, Laval Avenue in Montreal - Mrs. Clément, Owner
Detail: plan of ground floor
Archives nationales du Québec, Direction de Montréal, de Laval, de Lanaudière, des Laurentides et de la Montérégie (plan 147-147)

The size of row houses varied according to the width of the lots available, but the smallest could be as narrow as sixteen feet. For their inhabitants, however, these miniature houses possessed everything they required: a drawing room, a dining room and bedrooms, and even a bathtub supplied with hot water by a series of pipes connected to the kitchen stove. A real house, in fact, entirely suitable for respectable people.[26] The height of the ceilings was usually around the permitted minimum: nine feet for the ground floor, eight feet six inches for the first floor and eight feet for the top floor.

THE SEMI-DETACHED HOUSE

The semi-detached house, another type of suburban residence, was popularized by John Claudius Loudon. The two halves of a semi-detached house usually reflected each other like a mirror image, each possessing exactly the same elements, but in reverse. Generally somewhat larger than a row house,

100

Harry Staveley (1848-1929)
Residences for Messrs. A. P. Doddridge and T. Houghton, Maple Avenue, Quebec, 1900
Detail: front elevation
Archives nationales du Québec, Centre de Québec et Chaudière-Appalaches, fonds Staveley, plan 284 (N78-8-134)

101

Harry Staveley (1848-1929)
Residences for Messrs. A. P. Doddridge and T. Houghton, Maple Avenue, Quebec, 1900
Detail: plan of ground floor
Archives nationales du Québec, Centre de Québec et Chaudière-Appalaches, fonds Staveley, plan 284 (N78-8-136)

102

Harry Staveley (1848-1929)
Residences for Messrs. A. P. Doddridge and T. Houghton, Maple Avenue, Quebec, 1900
Detail: plan of second storey
Archives nationales du Québec, Centre de Québec et Chaudière-Appalaches, fonds Staveley, plan 284 (N78-8-137)

100

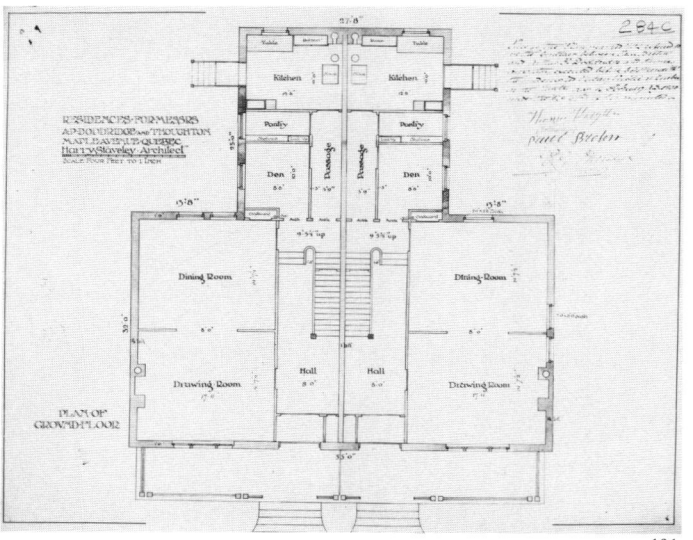

101

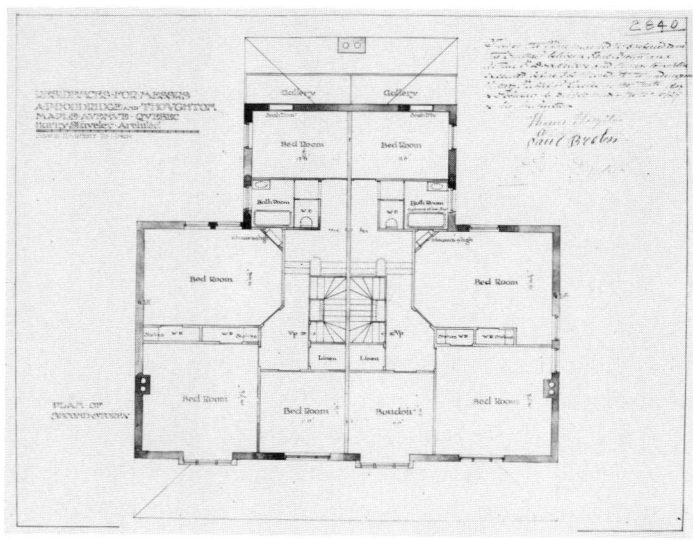

102

the semi-detached was in a number of ways a variant on the basic row house theme. It differed from it, however, in social significance. The social structure that characterized the Victorian era was to a large extent reflected in the various types of middle-class single-family homes: the detached house (villa or cottage) was at the top of the hierarchy, followed by the semi-detached, which was only joined to its neighbour on one side, with the row house bringing up the rear. Like the latter, the semi-detached house often possessed exterior architectural details that were an indication of the social status of its occupants; the bay window was just such an indicator, for it could either stretch from ground level right to the top of the building or, in a more economical version, remain limited to a single floor.

TECHNICAL INNOVATION AND DOMESTIC COMFORT

The middle-class Victorian house, whether detached, semi-detached or terraced, was almost invariably equipped with the latest technical developments in the fields of comfort and hygiene. Owing to the general rise in the standard of living that began in the 1870s as a direct result of industrialization, the middle classes were able to satisfy their growing taste for comfort and luxury. Although we may remain unimpressed today, the advances made in domestic comfort during the Victorian era were enormous, especially in heating, ventilation and bathroom installations. The house belonging to the wealthy merchant Cirice Têtu, built in 1852 on Sainte-Geneviève Avenue in Quebec City, possessed all the latest innovations. The architect, Charles Baillairgé, equipped the house with gas lighting, a central heating system designed with the help of the ironmonger Zéphirin Chartré, and hot and cold running water connected to the water closets and bathrooms.[27] The Têtu house, however, was unusually opulent for the period. The majority of houses in Quebec did not achieve such levels of comfort until the final three decades of the nineteenth century, as the 1896 *Montreal Star* advertisement and the reflections of Madame Dandurand in her diary of 1898 go to show:

> How easy everything is nowadays, and how happy these country girls ought to be in our houses – if only they were capable of grasping the notion of work. The gas stove that boils water in five minutes with no more effort than it takes to strike a match and turn a knob, no ashes, no mess; blazing hot water that pours out of the tap onto the dishes; stoves that never go out and that even a child could work. Yet with all this, they manage to do everything wrong. Servants are the curse of the century. I believe that with fewer conveniences but more faithful servants, our mothers achieved greater comfort.[28]

HEATING

Hot air and water furnaces existed from the beginning of the Victorian era. The coal furnace, located in the cellar, heated the various rooms via a system of pipes, radiators and air vents. Central heating was still costly to install and run, however, and remained beyond the reach of many households. In fact, even when such systems were installed, they were sometimes only used to heat part of the house. Kitchens were equipped with cast-iron stoves, which first made their appearance between 1840 and 1845. These coal-fuelled stoves were used for cooking, providing hot water and heating the room. Gas stoves began to appear during the 1880s, and the first electric stoves were exhibited in Chicago in 1893.

The main rooms of the house were always equipped with coal fireplaces, and in some cases these provided the main source of heat. This form of heating was inherited directly from the British, who traditionally accorded much importance to the fireplace, considering it the very heart of the house. Despite the improvement in domestic heating systems, even the more affluent did not give up the open fire. "Feeling [...] a general reluctance to adopt the stove as a system of heating, the Anglo-Saxons preferred to keep to the open fireplace, in which they burned wood or coal. This choice came naturally to them, for it was the traditional English way of heating."²⁹ While the stove played an increasingly large role in French-Canadian homes, the open fireplace continued to be a central feature of English-Canadian households.

The fireplace was thus a primary symbol of domestic comfort, and architects and builders paid a great deal of attention to its design and manufacture. The growing popularity of fireplaces was influenced by two major artistic trends: the Gothic revival, which re-focused attention on the huge fireplaces of medieval times, and the Arts and Crafts movement which, after about 1875, led to a renewed interest in the broad chimneypiece of the country cottage.³⁰ "This reverence for the 'hearth' was related to the notion of 'home', which was developing all through the 1800s and by the end of the century had become something of an obsession. In fact, the idea of 'hearth and home' emerged just as the hearth, in the real sense of the word, was on the point of disappearing..."³¹ By the turn of the century, the fireplace had become more of a symbol than an effective source of heat.

LIGHTING

> ... One day the news arrived that in Quebec City there was a new kind of lighting where you simply turned a knob and set a match to an iron pipe on which there was no tallow or whale oil, and not even any wick! [...] It was called gas.
>
> Louis Fréchette (1839-1908), *Mémoires intimes* (trans.)

Until 1845, candlelight was the most common form of lighting, despite the introduction of the oil lamp towards the end of the eighteenth century. The whale oil used to fuel these lamps was relatively expensive and they were hence employed only for specific activities, such as sewing or studying.³² With the development in 1859 of kerosene, a derivative of petroleum, these lamps came to be used more widely, for it proved to be a clean fuel that was less expensive than whale oil. Gas, employed initially only for street lighting and public buildings, was adapted for domestic use in the 1860s. Gas illumination was improved in 1887 by the introduction of Welsbach's incandescent gas mantle. As gas was dirty, had an unpleasant smell and provided a very harsh light, however, it was frequently used only in service rooms, like the kitchen, and in very dark areas like corridors and staircases.

Since gas was the first specifically *bourgeois* technology³³ and its principal users were members of the middle class, it tended to be seen by England's higher social ranks as rather vulgar, an innovation that reeked of the *nouveau riche*. They much preferred to stick to candlelight or the oil lamp. A British lady of some social standing wrote in her memoirs that at Belvoir Castle, until 1908, "There were at least three men assigned to looking after the lamps and candles, for we had no other form of lighting. We despised gas, although I don't remember why; because it was vulgar, I think..."³⁴ This form of snobbery was not echoed in North America, and many houses, ranging from the most luxurious to the most modest, were equipped with gas mantles. Nevertheless, the number of silver candelabras present in inventoried dining rooms³⁵ tends to indicate that the use of the candle endured among the affluent (at least in certain rooms) and that it actually served as a symbol of wealth, another emblem of their way of life.

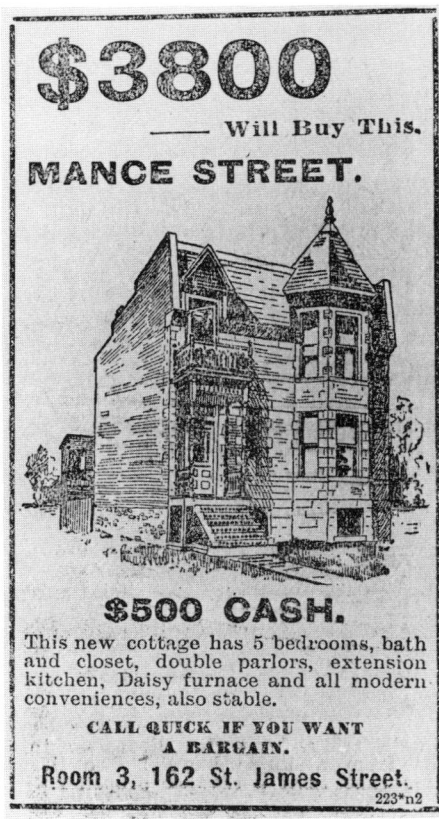

103
Advertisement for a town house, Jeanne-Mance Street, Montreal
Published in *The Montreal Star*, September 21, 1896
Photo SRP

Thomas Edison's discovery of electricity was presented to the public for the first time at the Philadelphia Exposition, in 1876. Philadelphia was actually the first city to be equipped with electricity, and it was followed during the 1880s by all the major cities of the United States. Electric lighting had its Canadian début in Montreal, in 1878. To begin with, however, only the most affluent could afford to have electricity installed in their homes. Domestic electric lighting did not become widespread until the decade following the turn of the century.

WATER SUPPLY AND BATHROOM INSTALLATIONS
Both contemporary studies and historical accounts indicate that North American homes were way ahead of their European counterparts in matters of comfort. From the 1850s on, both Montreal and Quebec City were equipped with a system of aqueducts and sewers. Moreover, North American central heating systems and bathroom installations seem to have been far better designed than those elsewhere. Here is the account of a French traveller who visited Montreal in 1908:

> In many ways the level of comfort is greater here than in Paris: even in the simplest of homes there are bathrooms, and special boxes to keep food cool during the hot weather. Ice is delivered every morning, just like milk or bread. The delivery man passes and throws one or more blocks onto every doorstep; and the servants come and pick them up with big iron tongs.[36]

This report takes on even greater significance when we recall that during the same period the great upper-class houses of England still employed water carriers. Using a wooden yoke borne across their shoulders, buckets suspended from either end, these men constantly carried water to the house in order to keep its many pitchers, basins, kettles and bathtubs filled, day and night.

The source of the remarkable middle-class concern with cleanliness during the nineteenth century was the *bourgeois* idea that cleanliness and respectability are indissoluble.[37] As the century unfolded, this idea — which derived directly from the principles of the Aesthetic movement — was gradually adopted by other sectors of society. By the end of the nineteenth century, the bathroom and water closet had become essential features of any house design. The bathroom, usually situated on the same floor as the bedrooms, contained a fixed bathtub supplied with hot and cold water by pipes that ran up from the basement. The water closet would occasionally be located on the ground floor, usually under the stairs.

The typical bathroom of today — one containing a bathtub, washbasin and toilet — first appeared in the United States around 1890. In England, and Europe generally, the toilet and washbasin were always entirely separate from the bath. Indeed, at the time it would have been considered quite unthinkable for the three items to be placed in the same room.

BOURGEOIS VALUES AND LIFESTYLES
Two fundamental and specifically *bourgeois* inclinations were the basis for domestic life during the second half of the nineteenth century: the great value set on the family and the need for privacy. These notions had a decisive

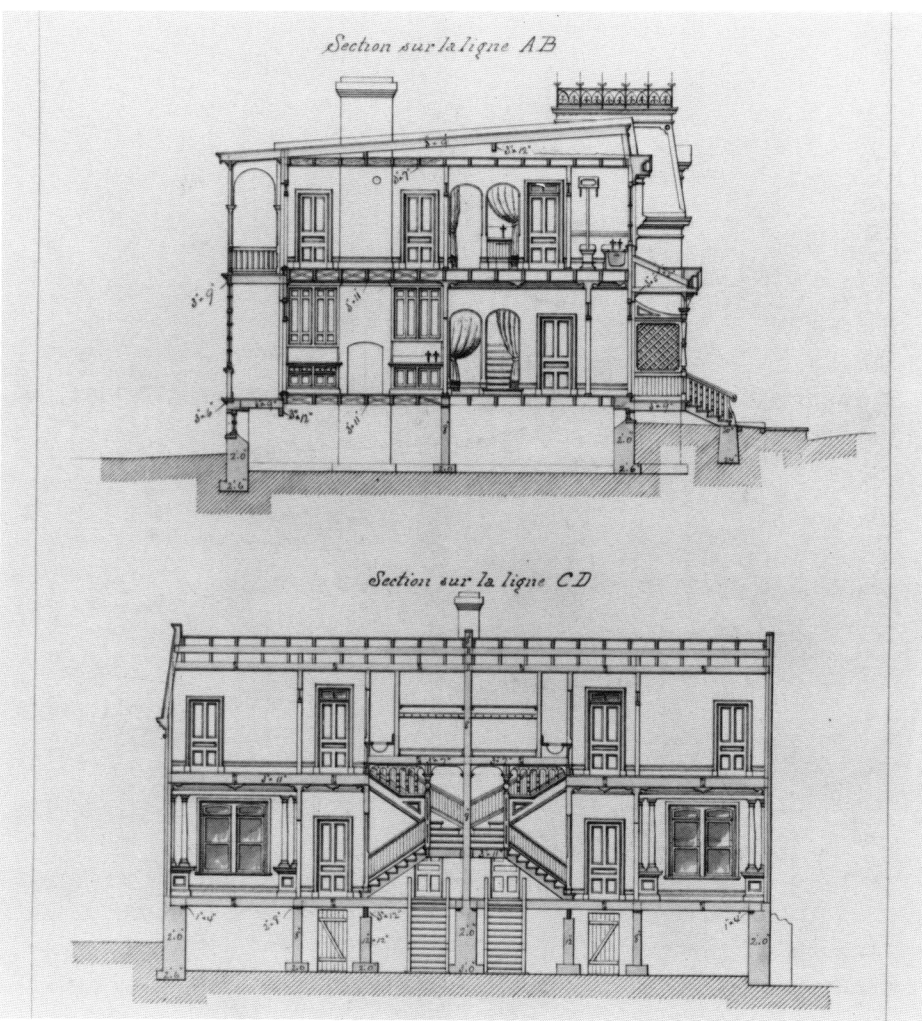

104
A. Préfontaine, architect
Thomas Préfontaine House, Longueuil, 1892
Detail: transverse and longitudinal sections
Archives nationales du Québec, Direction de Montréal, de Laval, de Lanaudière, des Laurentides et de la Montérégie (P 147-3)

effect on the middle-class house; they became, indeed, its very essence. In her essay "Manières d'habiter", Michèle Perrot says of the bourgeois house that it was simultaneously the physical centre of the family and the principal mainstay of social order. In other words, the house served not only as the family's dwelling and meeting place, but also as the public symbol of a couple's economic prosperity. Within this context, a luxurious interior was indispensable to happiness, and comfort a prerequisite of well-being.[38]

The upheavals caused by the industrial revolution had a direct effect on domestic accommodation. A refuge from the ever-growing pressures of work became a necessity. The workplace and the dwelling place therefore began to separate, giving rise to the first residential suburbs. The distance between city centres and these suburbs was welcomed, for the city was perceived increasingly as ugly, uncomfortable and even immoral.[39] This split between work and dwelling was the source of a new kind of domestic space, designed to protect the privacy of the family: the home.[40] In the second half of the nineteenth century, the house became the focus of an almost scientific interest, and the house and the family, seen as one, were the focus of much lofty sentiment.

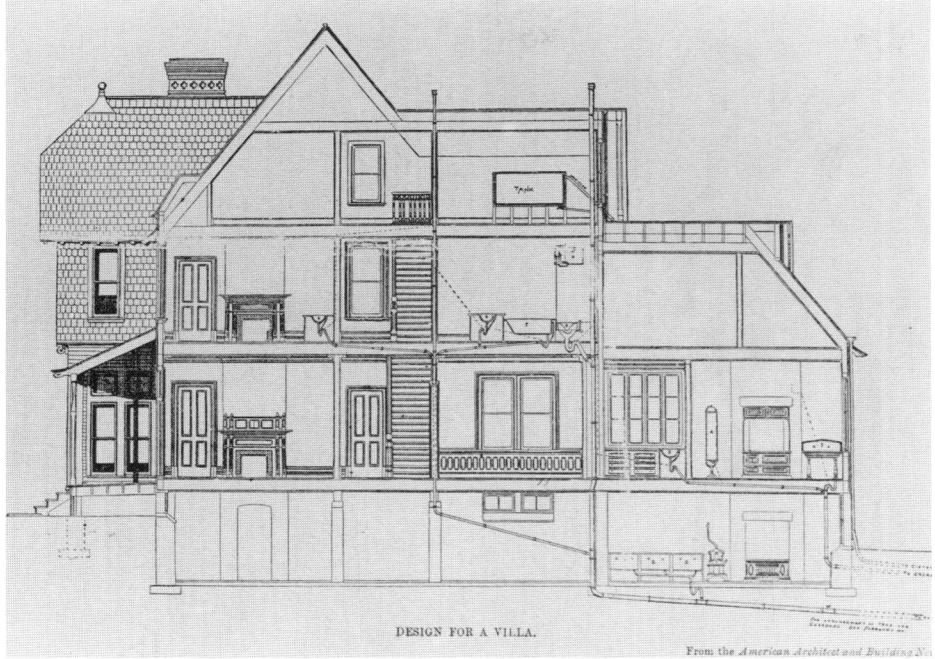

105
Design for a Villa from the "American Architect and Building News"
Engraving published in the *Canadian Mechanics' Magazine and Patent Office Record*, November 1878, p. 350
Photo SRP

THE CULT OF THE FAMILY

Within the middle-class world, then, the family became the object of a veritable cult. The family has been described as the main theatre in which nineteenth-century domestic life was acted out, supplying simultaneously "its leading characters and its principal roles, its customs and its rites, its intrigues and its conflicts".[41] In fact, the family was the bourgeois value that had the greatest impact on nineteenth-century lifestyles. Family life, with all that it implied (the veneration of home life, the importance of family ties, the formation of social networks of one sort and another), was, along with the notion of respectability, the cornerstone of the nineteenth-century middle-class world. The *bourgeois* house was a home, and for the first time in the history of domestic accommodation, spaces were set aside specifically for family activities.

The function and even the designation of the house's various rooms reveal much about the family's way of life. After the parents' and children's bedrooms, the dining room occupied a position of prime importance, for it was the scene of the family's daily gatherings. The drawing room, on the other hand, remained to some degree a showplace, site of a broader social activity than the one centred on the dining room.

The sense of family had a direct influence on the furnishing and decoration of each room. The goal was to create a warm, comfortable, even cosy environment. The arrangement of the furniture was thus less formal in the rooms used regularly by the family as a group. The interior decoration of these rooms was not merely for display. It included comfortable armchairs placed near the hearth, pot plants, caged birds and side tables bearing a host of useful objects: lamps, books, magazines, needlework…

"During the nineteenth century, the child was more than ever the centre of the family. The child was an object of investment on a number of levels:

106
A family gathered in the drawing room
Photograph
Archives nationales du Québec à Chicoutimi, fonds J.E.A. Dubuc (W-79-4-6)

The Victorian *bourgeois* house was first and foremost a home. In this group portrait, which includes members of several generations, the family is gathered around a portrait of a deceased ancestor.

emotional, of course, but also financial, educational and existential. As its heir, the child represented the family's future, its hopes and dreams, its way of coming to terms with time and with death."[42] Although the luxurious residences of the English-speaking bourgeoisie often boasted a nursery — and sometimes even two [43] — the children of Quebec's French-speaking middle-class were not relegated to separate quarters. They had their place in the dining room and even the drawing room, which often contained furniture designed especially for them. As a general rule they were allowed in the drawing room, or at least in the living room where the family gathered in the evening.

It is important to note that relations between parents and children had altered considerably under the influence of a new philosophy that set great store on maternal instinct and encouraged closer ties between mother and child. It was gradually being realized that children are not miniature adults to be constantly disciplined, but individual beings who must receive affection if they are to develop as they should. It is no surprise, then, that in accordance with this new view, the lives of middle-class French-Canadian women were centred around home and family. Madame Béïque's memoirs sketch a clear picture:

107
Living room of "The Cottage", Clarke Ave., Montreal, October 22, 1899
Photograph
National Archives of Canada, Ottawa (PA-123275)

My life as a married woman [she married in 1875] was like that of all the other French-Canadian mothers of my time. A life of repeated confinements, housework and child care... Having raised ten children, I had over twenty years of the daily routine of illness – my own or the children's – and of all sorts of worries, but also of family happiness.[44]

THE NEED FOR PRIVACY

The disposition of the interior space of the house was determined by the vital need for privacy. This need was new to the nineteenth century and increased as the century advanced. "A three-fold desire for family, marital and personal privacy gradually affected the whole of society, becoming extremely marked by the beginning of the twentieth century. It was embodied most noticeably in a widespread reluctance to submit to the effects of overcrowding and the involuntary social intercourse that results, and in a growing aversion for the panoptical effect of public places..."[45]

The quest for privacy, which allows the individual to choose between solitude and the company of others, was a major factor in the transformation of the house. It was the reason for the designation of rooms for specific functions (*bed* room, *dining* room), and of the limited access ensured by connecting corridors and staircases. It was also the source of the division of the house into distinct zones of activity: social life, private life and service.

As Monique Éleb-Vidal explains, the need for privacy was a more or less direct offshoot of the notion of modesty. Up until the nineteenth century, many activities took place in public, including washing and sleeping. People were never alone. Then gradually, during the nineteenth century, the freedom to isolate oneself from other members of the family, servants and possible visitors became a privilege of the wealthy. There are numerous references to this new freedom in the literature, personal diaries and etiquette manuals of the period, embodied in the latter in the complex visiting rituals they advocated.

THE USERS

108
Notman Studio, Montreal
Library of Mrs. Annie Morrice's house,
Montreal, 1899
Photograph
McCord Museum of Canadian History, Montreal,
Notman Photographic Archives (128,255-II)

THE VARIOUS ROOMS: CIRCULATION, LAY-OUT AND SPECIALIZATION

The double function of the *bourgeois* house as social symbol and home meant that it had to fulfil two roles: it had to advertise the status of its occupants while simultaneously preserving their privacy. Under the combined impact of the two requirements, the middle-class domestic interior became gradually more hierarchized, compartmentalized and specialized, while at the same time its design and furnishings were conceived with an ever more attentive eye to physical comfort. The arrangement and function of the rooms, staircases and hallways were often determined by strategies of encounter and avoidance.[46]

The defining of a family space thus involved not only separation from the servants, but also a physical division between the private rooms reserved for family life and the other more formal rooms intended for public display. Parallel to the development of this spatial division of the *bourgeois* house was the advent of mass-produced furniture, whose use and arrangement were virtually fixed in advance by a spatial codification that confirmed the function of each room and reinforced its classification as a public or a private space.[47]

The most important factor in the transformation of the nineteenth-century house were circulation patterns. In order to respect privacy, each room had to have a separate entrance; there was no longer any question of going through one room to reach another. This led to the abandonment of the successive plan and the symmetrical positioning of the rooms that it entailed. The corridor became a major element in movement from one part of the house to another. The circulation patterns in a *bourgeois* house were to be determined in part by questions of decorum, as the various books on etiquette made abundantly clear.

LIVING IN STYLE

109
Notman Studio, Montreal
Library of Mrs. Annie Morrice's house,
Montreal, 1899
Photograph
McCord Museum of Canadian History, Montreal,
Notman Photographic Archives (128,255-II et 128,256-II)

110
Notman Studio, Montreal
Interior of Rotherwood, the Hague house,
Montreal, 1890.
Photograph
McCord Museum of Canadian History, Montreal,
Notman Photographic Archives (92,622 Misc-II)

In a work published in 1870, which remains one of the basic sources in the study of domestic architecture under Napoléon III, César Daly outlined the rules governing the interior disposition of the rooms. He put great emphasis on circulation patterns and was very specific about the type of rooms suitable

THE USERS 109

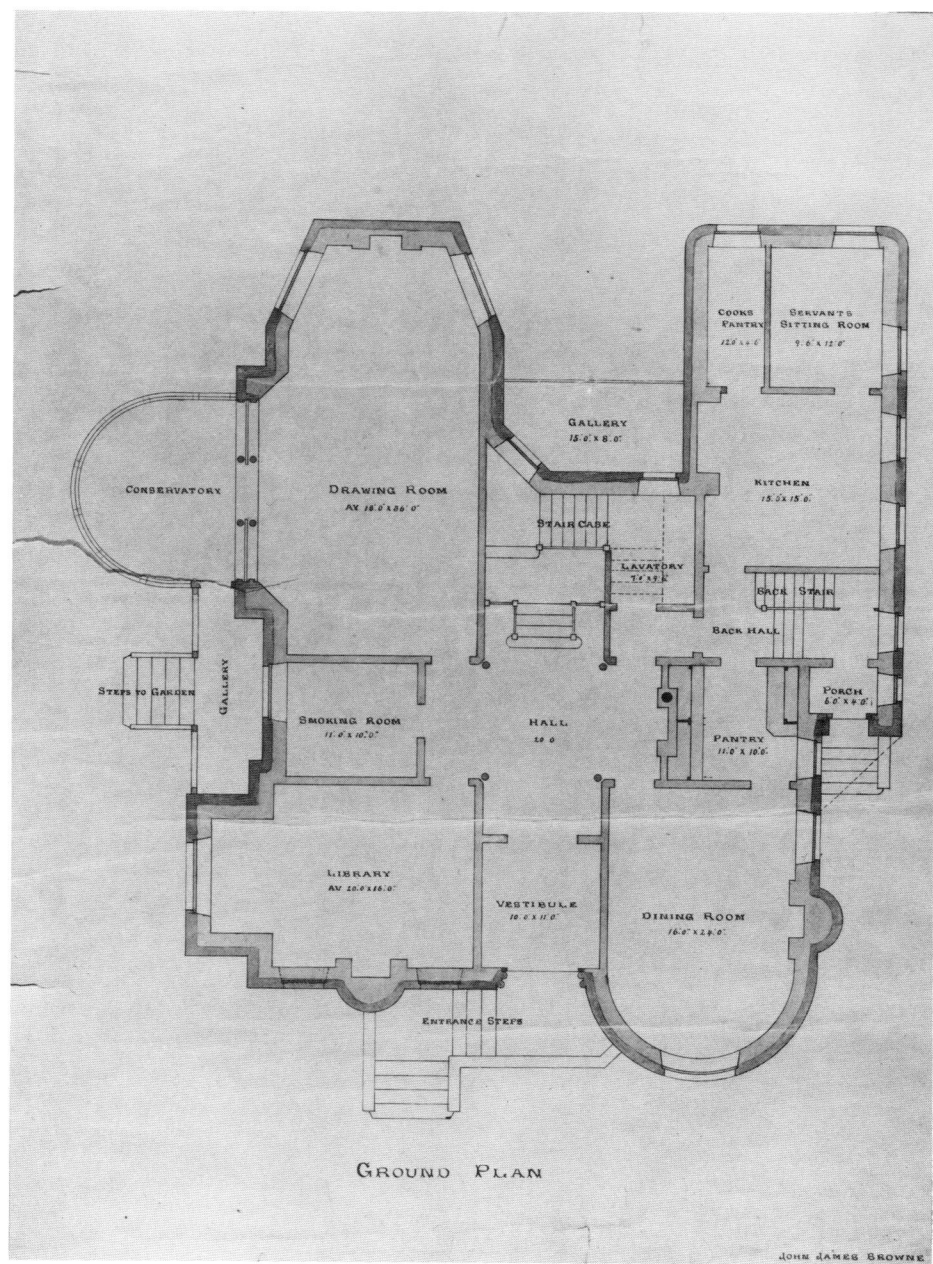

111
John James Browne (1837-1893)
Plan for a suburban villa, about 1892
Detail: plan of ground floor
Archives nationales du Québec, Direction de Montréal, de Laval, de Lanaudière, des Laurentides et de la Montérégie (plan 148-125)

This plan for a suburban villa illustrates clearly the division between the service rooms and the rooms inhabited by the family. Note the main staircase and the back stairs, employed by the servants.

for each floor and each area. In fact, all the writers of the time endorsed the same principle: the layout of the rooms should be extremely carefully planned. Most of the house plans of the period show the same division into broad areas: the reception rooms, such as the drawing and dining rooms, are mostly on the ground floor and in other easily accessible areas; the private rooms, such as the bedrooms, are generally on the first floor; the service rooms, such as the kitchen and servants' quarters, are in the basement or attic, or in a separate wing.

Clearly, then, Victorian standards of propriety required that the various activities of the house take place in well-defined areas. Except during formal encounters, the family was to remain separate from the guests. Servants and members of the family should never meet one another by chance. The former had their own quarters, located at some distance from the family's rooms. As Hermann Muthesius explains, the position of the staircases was a crucial factor in avoiding casual encounters between masters and servants. The house's main staircase was reserved for the exclusive use of the family and their guests. Everyone else circulating through the house, including servants and tradesmen, was obliged to use the back staircase. These back stairs, also called the service stairs, ran through the house from cellar to attic, and their main function was to provide access to the servants' rooms, usually situated on the topmost floor. Only the most modest homes were without a service staircase.

The closed plan house, with its compartmentalized and hierarchized space, both conditioned and was conditioned by the highly ritualized lifestyle of its users. From about 1870 on, however, there was a gradual opening up of house design. The open plan, which resulted among other things from a new way of grouping volumes, was promoted by both the Aesthetic and the Arts and Crafts movements. These movements were a reaction against the opulence and excessive ornamentation that had characterized the interiors created between 1850 and 1860, and both favoured a return to simplicity and purity of line in furniture design and interior decor.

The open plan centred around the hall/living room, a new type of room introduced by the architects Shaw, Webb and Nestfield in England, and Richardson in the United States. This room was of considerable size and completely dominated the design of the house; in fact, it carried echoes of the great halls of the baronial castles of the past. This large living room was generally equipped with a fireplace, a carved-wood staircase broken up into several flights, a beamed ceiling, wood-panelled walls and stained-glass windows. Comfortably furnished with upholstered armchairs and a thick carpet, the room created a powerful atmosphere of cosiness, informality and "hominess". In houses possessing such a room, it automatically became the centre of family life and it was here, rather than in the drawing room, that the company would gather before a meal.

Although examples of the open plan began to appear in England and the United States from the 1870s on, Quebec was somewhat slow in taking up the new idea, despite the fact that a number of such houses were discussed in specialized magazines. With a few rare exceptions, like the Montreal residence of George Stephen, built between 1880 and 1883, most of the houses in the province whose plans were centred around the hall/living room were built around the turn of the century. Moreover, they were almost all commissioned as residences for members of the English-speaking *bourgeoisie* of Quebec City or Montreal.[48]

THE SPECIALIZATION OF ROOMS
Until the late eighteenth century — and in some cases into the mid-nineteenth — the use of the various rooms in Quebec houses remained fluid and multi-functional. The traditional domestic interior of the period consisted of a kitchen, a large room, bedrooms and several smaller rooms; the number of bedrooms and small rooms varied according to the financial means of the owner and the size of the house. The houses of the more affluent were in

112
Remodelled Hallway
Engraving published in the *Scientific Canadian*, May 1879, p. 137
Photo SRP

"We offer the accompanying illustration as an example of remodelling. In the original house the stairway was narrow and enclosed. This has been removed, and a new staircase in hardwood introduced, with fire-place and settle at the foot of the same, and at the end of the settle the old hall clock. The upper portion of this fire-place has the brick-work exposed, the lower portion being encased for mirror, etc., and above the mirror a small sconce mirror. As will be noticed, the doorways into the principal rooms from this hall are without doors; a curtain of heavy material, hung to a rod with rings, forms a means of shutting off the view from the hall when desirable. The end of the main hallway is marked and divided by a newel column bracketed each way.

"We are indebted to Bicknell & Comstock, New York, for our illustration and description, from one of their latest publications, entitled 'Woolett's Old Homes Made New', containing twenty-two plates of exteriors and interiors."

113
Notman Studio, Montreal
Carved oak staircase and Gothic-style gallery in the Baumgarten house, McTavish Street, Montreal, 1904
Photograph
McCord Museum of Canadian History, Montreal, Notman Photographic Archives (C 151,888-4-II)

The house of Alfred Baumgarten (1842-1919), built in 1887, was purchased by McGill University in 1926. When the building was transformed into the McGill Faculty Club, in 1935, the Gothic gallery was demolished.

stone rather than wood, and they were larger, more comfortable and better furnished than those of lesser fortune.

During the first half of the nineteenth century, however, Quebec architecture came under the English influence: the number of rooms increased and their functions became more clearly defined, their names more specific. The houses of the *bourgeois* elite gradually began to include rooms with extremely precise functions, such as the drawing room, the dining room, the library, the boudoir, the billiard room and the conservatory.

Between 1840 and 1900, this specialization of the domestic interior increased and spread gradually throughout all levels of society. The house itself, in its size, its type and the number of rooms it contained, still remained an ideal symbol with which members of the *bourgeoisie* could advertise their status. The houses built by Montreal's upper classes towards the end of the nineteenth century served exactly this purpose. However, the average middle-class house in Victorian Quebec contained few rooms with highly specialized functions. It centred around the two basic spaces that had come into widespread use during this period: the drawing room and the dining room. There might occasionally be a boudoir or a library, although the latter was more often found in the homes of the English-speaking *bourgeoisie*. The drawing room, the dining room and the master bedroom are thus the most representative areas of the Victorian house. As such, they are the focus of a more detailed study in the present volume.

It is interesting to note that traditional labels such as *salle* (large room), *chambre* (room), *cabinet* (small room) and *chambre de compagnie* (visitors' room) persisted throughout the Victorian era among working-class French-speaking people, both in the country and the city.[49]

The specialization of rooms was accompanied by a specialization of furniture and even of users. Among the upper classes, men's and women's roles were becoming increasingly differentiated; men were associated very much with the outside, public world, while women, owing to their role as wives and mothers, were confined to a growing degree to the house.

114
Dinner Given to Lord Lisgar by the Citizens of Montreal
Engraving published in the *Canadian Illustrated News*, July 6, 1872
National Archives of Canada, Ottawa (C-58681)

115
Expectation
Engraving published in the *Canadian Illustrated News*, January 6, 1872
National Archives of Canada, Ottawa (C-58430)

Reflecting the contrast between the masculine and feminine worlds, the rooms in a Victorian house were clearly stamped with the imprint of one or the other. The drawing room was feminine. It was the place where the mistress of the house received her guests, and this function was mirrored in its decoration: it had to be welcoming, warm and comfortable, the colours subdued and the materials fine. The dining room, on the other hand, was considerably more masculine. This was no doubt due to the custom which decreed that the men remain at table after the meal, to smoke and talk, while the women retired to the drawing room. The billiard room, very popular at the period, was the room in which the master of the house would gather with his friends to smoke and play a game of billiards. In houses of sufficient size, other rooms were set aside for the exclusive use of either men or women. Madame might retire to her boudoir or morning room, while the gentleman of the house could withdraw to his library, sitting room or smoking room.

In Quebec, then, houses where the rooms were assigned highly specialized functions belonged mainly to the upper-class elite, which, although it included a few French Canadians, was predominantly English-speaking. The most opulent houses, built mainly in the last third of the nineteenth century, were of English inspiration and provide proof of Quebec's receptivity to foreign models. The rooms in these houses were always arranged around the entrance hall and passageway, and their functional range was remarkable: they might include a large and small drawing room, a smoking room or library, a billiard room, a conservatory, a breakfast room, a morning room, a nursery, a sewing room, dressing rooms, a picture gallery or a music room. Some rooms, such as the sitting room, were widely used but only among English-speaking people. Of course, all these houses possessed numerous bedrooms.

SERVANTS: A NECESSARY EVIL

> It was, of course, the servants who ran the complicated "machines" of the larger houses.
>
> Stephan Muthesius, *The English Terraced House*

THE USERS

116
C. A. Muerrle, Toronto
Library in the home of Colonel MacPherson, Quebec City
Photograph
National Archives of Canada, Ottawa (PA 51701)

117
Notman Studio, Montreal
Library of Rotherwood, the Hague house, Montreal, 1902
Photograph
McCord Museum of Canadian History, Montreal, Notman Photographic Archives (142,237-Misc-II)

118
Notman Studio, Montreal
Mr. Wood's sitting room, Montreal, 1863
Photograph
McCord Museum of Canadian History, Montreal, Notman Photographic Archives (9175-I)

119
J. Hill, Montreal
Smoking room or "cosy-corner" of the Harrison Stephens house, The Homestead, Montreal
Photograph
McCord Museum of Canadian History, Montreal, Notman Photographic Archives

In Victorian England, servants represented the foundation-stone that supported the whole structure and equilibrium of the house. Without them, the *bourgeoisie* could never have maintained their enormous houses so full of furniture and objects, for the upkeep was endless and the mistress of the house did not generally undertake any domestic tasks.

Nevertheless, not all Victorian households boasted a large staff. Even though wages at the time were low, the number of servants employed in a house was a very clear indicator of social status. A study of domestic servants in Canada's urban areas shows that in 1871 only ten to fifteen percent of households were able to afford one or more live-in servants.[50] When we consider, moreover, that of this relatively low percentage only two to four percent

120
Notman Studio, Montreal
Picture gallery of the James Ross house, Montreal, 1901
Photograph
McCord Museum of Canadian History, Montreal, Notman Photographic Archives (137,813-II)

121
J. Hill, Montreal
Music room of the Harrison Stephens house, The Homestead, Montreal
Photograph
McCord Museum of Canadian History, Montreal, Notman Photographic Archives

had more than one,[51] it becomes clear that Quebec houses during the Victorian era were hardly over-populated with servants: "… Of course, in the best neighbourhoods the proportion was somewhat higher, reaching nearly seven percent in Quebec City and Montreal; but even that was quite modest."[52] Those who did employ several servants – all residents of the major cities' most affluent neighbourhoods – were mostly in business, but included as well some professionals, civil servants and people of private means.[53]

THE USERS

122
Notman Studio, Montreal
Servants in the garden of Weredale,
the home of L. J. Seargeant, Montreal
(detail), 1885
Photograph
McCord Museum of Canadian History, Montreal,
Notman Photographic Archives (78,325-II)

Among the Victorian *bourgeoisie*, the possession of a conservatory and the employment of a large number of servants were both indications of wealth.

123
Notman Studio, Montreal
Serving tea, 1888
Photograph
McCord Museum of Canadian History, Montreal,
Notman Photographic Archives (88,120 Misc-II)

According to *bourgeois* conventions of the time, a woman had to employ the services of at least one all-purpose maid for the family to dissociate itself from the working class and join the ranks of the lower middle classes, or *petite bourgeoisie*.[54] A modest-income family would employ a maidservant who came daily. However, a typical middle-class family would generally employ a live-in maid, accommodated in a small room in the attic or basement. Such a servant worked extremely hard: every day from dawn to dusk she was kept busy preparing and serving meals, seeing to the upkeep and cleaning of the whole house, and obtaining all the necessary supplies. In some cases, she also took care of the children and worked in the garden. It was a harsh life indeed for these "maids of all work", who laboured fifteen to eighteen hours a day, constantly at the beck and call of their employers.

Another facet of the increased specialization so widespread during the Victorian period was the establishment of a strict hierarchy among domestic servants. As the work of each staff member became more clearly defined, so did the distance between the various ranks increase. Although this hierarchical system achieved its apotheosis in England, it also existed in France:

> Formal behaviour is as carefully controlled as the etiquette governing a court. It is taught by special instructors; everything is planned, everything is regulated, even the hierarchy of the domestic servants, who are divided into the upper staff and the lower staff; the two do not mingle, but eat at separate tables [...] Each type of service has a corresponding position and each position is held by two people, in case of negligence or illness. No servant will agree to undertake a task outside their allocated duties, however urgent the need. Of the many servants employed, the masters see only those whose tasks necessitate personal contact. Each of these is called by a special bell [...] But it must be admitted that it is only with English servants, serving English masters, that this system has achieved its most excruciating perfection.[55]

A large house, belonging to a wealthy member of the *bourgeoisie*, usually

LIVING IN STYLE

employed a butler and a housekeeper, each in charge of various members of the lower staff. These two, together with the mistress's lady's maid and the master's valet, were the four most senior staff members, and they took their meals in a different room from the rest of the servants.

The separation of the family from the domestic staff was another peculiarity of Victorian middle-class life. Servants, although omnipresent, had to be invisible. Until the eighteenth century domestic servants had been part of the family, sharing the same living space as their employers. Then a difference of social status gradually began to make itself felt: servants still inhabited the same space, since this was unavoidable, but they were required to keep themselves as separate as possible. For example, a servant no longer slept near his master's bed, but in a small room adjoining the employer's bedroom. During the Victorian era things became even more clear cut, and there was absolute segregation between servants and masters. Physical barriers were erected, which reinforced the moral ones already in place.[56]

Servants' bedrooms were situated in the attic or basement, or in a separate wing. Service areas were set apart from the residential rooms and were reached by different access routes: there were service staircases and main staircases, service or back doors and main doors, front passages and exits and back ones. Houses were equipped with a system of bells, with a different ring for each room. When the servants' duties took them into any of the residential rooms, they were obliged to use the service stairs and to be as discreet as possible. This system reached its zenith in large English houses with many servants, where there developed two quite distinct realms: the world of the masters and the "below stairs' world" portrayed in the popular television show *Upstairs Downstairs*.

While the strict separation between the residential and service areas of a house was a question of status, the number of distinct access routes for servants – staircases, corridors and doors – was an indicator of a house's degree of luxury.[57] In fact, a house without a service staircase was by definition a modest house. In small middle-class homes, the service area usually consisted solely of the kitchen and an adjoining maid's room.

The segregation of domestic servants during the Victorian era was partially the result of the increased distinction between the social classes that developed during the nineteenth century. Members of the bourgeoisie were proud of their status and anxious to assert their rank in any way possible. For them, servants were members of the common mass. As Monique Éleb-Vidal explains, the bourgeoisie were obliged to accept the presence of domestic servants, whom they considered their inferiors and whose personal habits were different from their own. And, since thresholds of susceptibility and standards of hygiene did not develop at the same rate within society's various classes, during that period "servants, who were of the people, symbolized dirt. They were seen as dirty both by birth and because of their role as handlers of refuse".[58]

Of course, employers were not always indifferent to the fate of their servants, but middle-class sensibilities were much offended by objectionable smells and dirt. The following quote from Henriette Dessaulles captures the ambivalence quite effectively:

> I cannot stand cooking smells; I wish that everything were always shiny and clean and that all the housework were done by fairies, for I'm sorry for the poor servants who spend their lives tidying up after us. I'm sorry for the cooks who spend their days in the boiling heat cooking our meals and I'm sorry for the washerwomen who scrub and scrub to produce lovely clean dresses for us *literally* "by the sweat of their brow"! (March 13, 1879)[59]

The kitchen was usually located apart from the main rooms and never adjoined the dining room, for it was out of the question that cooking smells be allowed to reach the rest of the house. In England, in fact, the kitchen was used exclusively for the preparation of meals, with all cleaning activities taking place elsewhere. English kitchens did not even possess a sink; this item was located in the back kitchen or scullery, a small room used for washing dishes and vegetables, and for preparing poultry, game and fish. The kitchens of large English houses actually included a series of small rooms with various specific functions: a scullery, a larder for each type of provision, a bakehouse, a servants' dining room and a pantry.

Except in the richest of *bourgeois* houses, which possessed extensive domestic quarters, servants were generally inadequately accommodated in Victorian times. There are many contemporary documents and accounts that confirm this sad state of affairs. Claudette Lacelle sums up the situation thus:

> They [the servants' rooms] were also poorly ventilated and lit, since the windows were small and some rooms only had a dormer or a skylight; the rooms were usually damp and ill-heated as well, most of them being icy cold in winter and [unbearably hot] in summer. Also, they were badly furnished and decorated, for they usually only contained an iron bedstead with a rotten mattress, old mismatched furniture and a small stained mirror. In addition, they were generally located in the most out-of-the-way corner of the house…[60]

In Quebec, domestic servants were employed mainly by English-speaking people living in urban areas. At the end of the nineteenth century, only a few members of Montreal's *bourgeois* elite (very wealthy merchants and businessmen) employed large numbers of servants, and their houses were designed to accommodate them. The most elaborate domestic quarters might have included a laundry, one or more pantries, a larder, a kitchen, a scullery or back kitchen, a servants' hall, a cook's room, a kitchen maid's room, one or more maid's rooms, a parlour maid's room, a servants' bathroom and a coachman's room.[61] The only service room apart from the kitchen in most French-Canadian homes during the Victorian era was the *dépense*, or larder, a very small room used to store provisions. Previously, this room was sometimes known as the *cabinet de cuisine*.

INTERIOR DECORATION AND LUXURY: VICTORIAN TASTE

While the service rooms were usually ill-lit, poorly heated and inadequately furnished, the residential rooms, in sharp contrast, were meticulously, comfortably and even luxuriously decorated. Between 1840 and 1900, the appointments of these rooms reflected the same increase in specialization that governed their function and position in the house. The interior decor of a room now accentuated its purpose. From this period on, the bedroom, drawing room and dining room were quite distinct, for the various spaces were defined by a use of different mouldings and furniture, reinforced by diverse types of upholstery fabrics, drapes and ornaments.[62] Of course, interiors varied according to the financial resources of the owners. But all of the latter, whatever their means, were highly susceptible to fashion trends and major aesthetic movements.

Victorian taste was, by definition, *bourgeois* taste. It was a manifestation of the gradual opening up of the world that characterized the period, and it reflected the development of knowledge, attitudes and aesthetic sensibility that was the result. The *bourgeoisie* loved to show off, which explains their penchant for things flashy, flamboyant and ostentatious. For them, taste was bound up with social advancement; but it was also determined by a pre-established code of conventions diffused widely in all sorts of specialized publications (including pattern books, home economics guides and books on etiquette and comportment). To have good taste was to be conventional, for taste was identified with what was proper and appropriate: a degree of luxury quite acceptable for the upper ranks was considered unsuitable for those lower down the scale. Finding the right level, the "happy medium", was a question of propriety and respectability. And the middle classes had to look no further for a model than Queen Victoria herself, for she represented the perfect embodiment of the middle-class "good taste" of the period.[63] At her own instigation a number of her interiors were reproduced, first pictorially and later photographically. They thus became models for the *bourgeoisie*, since the royal family was the ideal exemplification of middle-class values.[64]

"GOOD" AND "BAD" LUXURY

This preoccupation during the Victorian era with the idea of "good taste" had its source in the two quite distinct notions of luxury prevalent at the time: the good and the bad.[65] Bad luxury, first of all, was that which resulted from a desire to show off. It was condemned by *bourgeois* morality because it smacked of the parvenu. Good luxury, on the other hand, was related to comfort, convenience and well-being — in other words, to family values. It grew out of the idea of the house as a refuge, where one could be happy surrounded by one's nearest and dearest. This was the conception of luxury central to Victorian middle-class morality. In fact, having good taste was proof of distinction. *Bourgeois* morality was ostensibly opposed to exaggeration in matters of decoration and to the excessive accumulation of objects, for they were seen as detrimental to a desirable family atmosphere.

In light of all this, the resolutions of the young wife of Raoul Dandurand, made prior to her move to Montreal in 1885, take on even greater significance:

> I have my own ideas on luxury and the lifestyle of my future compatriots, the ladies of Montreal. Because of my reputation and the place Raoul has made for himself in Montreal, I will probably be occupying a quite prominent position in society. My present disposition, however, is not to follow the path taken by everyone else. I am no less concerned with my comfort than all these fine ladies, only I understand the notion differently. Firstly, giving religion the priority it merits, I would be very reluctant to fill my house with expensive ornaments and frivoli-

ties when there were people around me, even members of my own family, who lacked the means to give their children a good education. And instead of following or even anticipating the burdensome fashions that have one change one's furniture, one's house and even one's street as easily as one's hat, I would devote the sums required by such exigencies to the purchase of beautiful books, subscriptions to good magazines, instructive travel or the theatre [...] Of course, it is easy to be led astray – "the treacherous goad of example" as the good Virgil puts it, that pushes you into the vortex in spite of yourself.[66]

Books on etiquette and comportment played an important role in the education of the middle classes in matters of taste. These publications propagated the idea that good taste was a sign of good upbringing and respectability:

Endeavour, as far as your position and your entourage permit [...] to banish from your house any trace of that "luxury for effect" which is based on intrinsic value, on the cost of objects rather than their true beauty. Understand that good taste resides in a love of simplicity, harmony and elegance, and that nothing is more antithetical to it than flashiness on the one hand and the display of wealth on the other. Be therefore modest in your furnishings, as you should be in your own appearance [...] My only wish is to convince you that a taste for the rich is not the same as a taste for the beautiful and that only the latter can be permitted in your surroundings, for it alone denotes the superior intelligence that is the result of a perfect upbringing [...] Your furnishings should be simultaneously simple and becoming, of plain materials but graceful and elegant shapes; everything should be tasteful and should conjure up that sense of order, of harmony that the mind seeks in all things...[67]

TASTE, LUXURY AND ACCESSIBILITY

The concept of good taste went through a number of metamorphoses during the Victorian era, to which the succession of historical styles that emerged during the period were linked.[68] The different phases of taste, closely associated with the notion of accessibility, were the result of the fact that "luxury was continually being redefined to preserve the distinction between classes".[69] Industrialization, or rather the mechanization of the techniques used in the manufacture of furniture and other consumer goods, led to mass-production and accessibility to a much wider public. What had once been reserved exclusively for only the most wealthy was now within the grasp of less fortunate groups. As a result, "the emergence of a class of bourgeois consumers in the wake of the Industrial Revolution has been traditionally perceived as the source of a decline in taste, especially in the area of interior decoration".[70]

Mass-produced luxury items were purchased principally by the middle classes, who, with their new-found, industrially-based wealth, were eager to decorate their homes taking full advantage of all the innovations of their age.[71] In their advertising, furniture dealers often stressed the wide range of merchandise available, suited to all sorts of homes and pocket books.

In Quebec, there was much moralistic opposition to luxury at the time, for it was seen as the cause of the exodus of French Canadians that began in the 1840s. The following observation appears in a report prepared by the Parliamentary Committee of the Province of Canada in 1849: "Luxury is spreading in the most deplorable manner throughout the provinces, into which there have been poured, in a profusion unprecedented in this country, manufactured articles from abroad that are for the most part quite useless..."[72] By the 1860s, luxury had reached rural areas: "...luxury in clothing, food and carriages has moved from the towns to the villages, and from there to the rest of the countryside".[73] What made this development even harder to accept was the fact that the countryside had been seen as the last bastion of "virtue", in contrast to the city, already considered for some time a "hotbed of corruption".

The rococo-revival style dominated the period for many years. This is understandable, for the style was closely linked to the monarchy, that model of the *bourgeoisie*. As the century advanced, however, new styles and trends emerged. These were easily accessible to the general population, and the most affluent made efforts to distinguish themselves from the masses. Thus the Renaissance-revival style, associated with the wealth, power and prosperity of sixteenth-century Italy, replaced the rococo-revival in the interiors of the wealthiest members of the *bourgeoisie*.

The following example illustrates the phenomenon of accessibility and how it affected the taste of the period. In reaction to the exaggerated ornamentation and excessive accumulation of objects that had marked much of the Victorian era, some theoreticians rebelled and began to advocate a return to simplicity and restraint in furnishing and interior decoration. This gave rise to a massive reform movement that radically transformed furniture design, hitherto trapped by the aesthetic conventions of the past.[74] However, despite the catchwords of simplicity and restraint, only the most prosperous could afford to follow the extremely expensive new fashion, and it quickly became the luxury style of the late nineteenth century.

In its assimilation of this drive towards reform, which flourished between 1875 and 1900, Quebec was influenced primarily by Charles L. Eastlake, one of the leaders of the British movement. Eastlake was the author of an extraordinarily popular guide to interior decoration called *Hints on Household Taste*, which had considerable influence on the population at large. First published in England in 1868, the book was re-edited numerous times and by 1881 was in its sixth American edition. Eastlake favoured a return to simple lines and to well-designed, well-constructed furniture; he also sought to instill sound principles while rejecting the reductive conventions governing the taste of the time:

> ...People whose taste is guided by mere custom sit down to dine upon an oaken chair before an oaken table with a turkey carpet under their feet, and a red flock-paper staring them in the face. After dinner the ladies ascend into a green-and-gold-papered drawing-room to perform on a walnut-wood piano, having first seated themselves on walnut-wood music-stools, while their friends are reclining on a walnut-wood sofa, protected from the heat of the fire by a walnut-wood screen. A few years ago, all these last-mentioned articles of household furniture were made of rosewood.[75]

Eastlake actually saw taste conventions as ridiculous and strove to make people realize that even if their aesthetic choice was different from that of their neighbours, this did not necessarily mean that the principles of "good taste" were being flouted. The Eastlake style became extremely popular in the United States, where it was often combined with the Renaissance-revival style.

124
An advertisement for the firm of Frederic Lapointe of Montreal
Published in the *Montreal Star*, August 30, 1897
Photo SRP

125
Notman Studio, Montreal
Conservatory of the George Stephen house, Drummond Street, Montreal, 1884
Photograph
McCord Museum of Canadian History, Montreal, Notman Photographic Archives (73818-II)

THE LUXURY OF SPACE AND A TASTE FOR NATURE: THE CONSERVATORY

Another manifestation of luxury was the proliferation of distinct spaces within the house, of rooms with specific functions.[76] A large house with many rooms, and especially extensive domestic quarters, was a sign of prosperity. But for the very wealthy who sought continually to distinguish themselves from the masses the room that best symbolized affluence was the conservatory. As Charlotte Gere points out, a conservatory — or winter garden, as it was called at the time — required a large staff and costly upkeep, for it was used to cultivate rare plants all year round. In its very extravagance, the conservatory was perfectly suited to Victorian taste. It often contained exotically-inspired furniture or furniture made of wrought iron. Here, wicker or bamboo pieces could blend nicely with objects of oriental influence, while the architecture of the room itself was often Moorish or Alhambresque in style.[77]

In the late nineteenth and early twentieth centuries practically none of the residences that lined Quebec City's Grande Allée possessed a conservatory. Even though it was a wealthy neighbourhood, space was at a premium, and the house belonging to Charles Langelier was alone in boasting a winter garden. As was often the case, the Langelier conservatory was connected to the most important room in the house — the large drawing room. Several of the houses on the thoroughfare did possess solariums, however, which opened onto the dining room. "Situated at the back of the house, often the only possibility when making such an addition owing to the narrowness of the lots, the solarium did not possess the same function as the conservatory, but was the result of the same desire for contact with the outdoors during inclement weather."[78]

Conservatories first began to appear in the 1850s, but from 1880 on they were more commonly attached to the house and were larger and more comfortable owing to improvements in heating and ventilation systems. The architecture of the villas in the area surrounding Quebec City was also marked by the modernity of the Victorian era,[79] and several of them were adorned by these large steel and glass structures: Cataraqui had a conservatory in 1856 (enlarged in 1866), Bois de Coulonge in 1860, Kirk Ella in 1876 and Highlands in 1897. The luxury embodied in this special room is captured in the following comment, made in 1882: "…What, indeed, can be more gratifying, during the arctic, though healthy, temperature of our winter, than to step from a cosy drawing-room, with its cheerful grate-fire, into a green, floral bower, and inhale the aroma of the orange and the rose, whilst the eye is charmed by the blossoming camellia or virgin daphne, all blending their perfume and exquisite tints."[80]

This type of luxury gradually spread throughout society's lower echelons, but in a modified form. While the conservatory remained a privilege of the very rich, a reduced version of it could be seen in middle-class houses in the bay windows that frequently lit the main rooms and that were filled with a profusion of plants and flowers and often a caged bird.

126

THE HOUSE AS A SHOWPLACE: HIERARCHIES OF DECORATION

Some of the rooms in a bourgeois house, such as the entrance hall, the drawing room or parlour, the dining room, and to a lesser extent the master bedroom, possessed considerable symbolic importance. It was not enough that they be situated in a strategic position in the house, of an acceptable size and adequately lit: their appointment had to reflect certain fundamental principles. Most of the ornamentation was concentrated in the entrance hall, the main staircase, the drawing room and the dining room because these were the house's public areas, seen most frequently by visitors. Thus, the hierarchy that governed the lay-out of the rooms was echoed in their furnishing and decoration:

> …The Victorians expressed the gradations of status with meticulous care. Guests were admitted to the best room – the parlour; this would contain the most expensive and expansive furnishings in the house, probably arranged around a marble fireplace. As you moved away from this room towards the back and the top of the house you would notice not only the furnishings and appointments shrinking and cheapening but also fixtures such as the skirting boards, plaster cornices and fireplaces.[81]

The entrance hall played a key role in the *bourgeois* house. Usually preceded by a vestibule, the hall served as the pivot for internal circulation, giving onto all the main living rooms including the drawing room, dining room and library or office. As various pattern book authors pointed out, the entrance hall was the first – sometimes the only – room seen by visitors and as such had to be decorated and furnished with great care. It was here that outsiders received their initial impression of the house and its occupants.

127-128

The hall also served as the transitional space between the public and private rooms. For reasons of privacy, it was recommended that the staircase, which led to the bedrooms, should not be positioned actually in the entrance hall but adjacent to it. This arrangement was not all that common in Quebec, although it was seen occasionally – for example, in the Dobell house in Sillery, between about 1870 and 1890. Some houses possessed a hall divided

129

126
Home, Sweet Home
Engraving published in *The Canadian Home, Farm and Business Encyclopaedia*, 1884
National Archives of Canada, Ottawa (NL-17576)

127
Notman Studio, Montreal
Entrance hall, with Christmas decorations, of Thornhill, the Lyman house, McTavish Street, Montreal, 1888
Photograph
McCord Museum of Canadian History, Montreal, Notman Photographic Archives (MP 411-14)

128
Notman Studio, Montreal
Entrance hall of Rotherwood, the Hague house, Montreal, 1890
Photograph
McCord Museum of Canadian History, Montreal, Notman Photographic Archives (92,623 Misc-II)

into two sections – sometimes forming an L shape – separated either partially or completely by a door, and in these cases the staircase was located in the second section. The hall of the Stuart Henry house was of this type. This arrangement allowed the house's inhabitants to move freely between their bedrooms and the ground-floor living rooms without fear of encountering visitors or strangers in the entrance hall. This solution was nevertheless restricted to the most luxurious residences, and the majority of Quebec houses possessed an entrance hall that gave directly onto the main staircase.

The hall stand, sometimes called a coat-and-umbrella or hat-and-umbrel-

129
Entrance hall of Beauvoir, the Richard R. Dobell house, Sillery, about 1890
Photograph
National Archives of Canada, Ottawa (C-4780 B)

la stand, was a distinctive feature of small entrance halls. Introduced in the early nineteenth century, hall stands gradually became increasingly ornate, especially those made of cast iron. Some consisted simply of an iron pole on a base or a flat fixture attached to the wall. Others included a small shelf in wood or marble, a drawer for clothes brushes, a mirror and even a bench for sitting. All bore pegs for hats and many included a space for umbrellas. During the 1860s a new type of stand appeared. Made of bentwood and of very simple design, it was used extensively in public places such as hotels, restaurants and offices. As well as the stand, entrance halls also often contained a console table surmounted by a mirror, one or more wooden chairs for use by servants and visitors, a grandfather clock — a custom inherited from the eighteenth century — and a barometer.

The drawing room, often a blend of the good and the bad, was the place where Victorian household taste reached its fullest expression. Prior to the nineteenth century only the most affluent possessed a drawing room, for it was synonymous with luxury and wealth. It is therefore not surprising that the aristocratic drawing room, characterized by a chimneypiece and a large pier glass, was imitated by the *bourgeoisie*, who saw it as an ideal place in which to parade their prosperity. As the Victorian era advanced, however, the drawing room became common even in more modest circles.

"The desire of the middle classes to keep up appearances was often still concentrated in this space, which was decorated and furnished with ostentatious luxury but which was actually used only rarely, and whose ornaments and furniture were often kept covered."[82] This attitude was exemplified in the drawing rooms or parlours of turn-of-the-century working-class houses, which had not yet become family living rooms but were reserved exclusively for special occasions, such as funerals, visits from the *curé* or engagement parties.

This use of space struck some contemporary writers as extravagant, especially those who compared Canadian lifestyles with French:

THE USERS

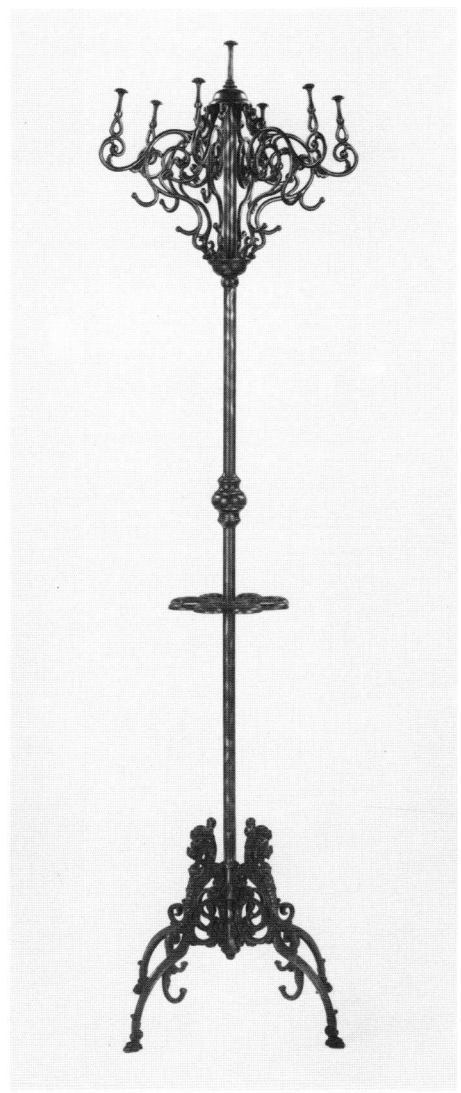

130
Hat and umbrella stand, about 1860-1890
Cast iron and brass, 193.5 x 41 x 41 cm
Vincent-d'Indy Music School, Soeurs des Saints-Noms-de-Jésus-et-de-Marie, Montreal
Photo Christine Guest/MMFA

131
Naturalistic hat stand, about 1880
107 x 90 x 34 cm
Private collection, Coaticook
Photo Christine Guest/MMFA

…The average Canadian woman is oriented far more towards public life than private. Comfort is sacrificed to appearance. Even in the most modest, least affluent homes, the family [...] will share a single bedroom in order to maintain a dining room and a parlour. Everything is sacrificed to these two rooms; there is a piano even if no-one in the house plays. This instrument is even more common than in France.[83]

The mouldings and other fixed decorative elements (ceiling roses and chimneypieces, for example) that adorned the rooms of a Victorian house had a primarily practical function. The broad mouldings running up the sides and along the tops of doorways covered the join between the plaster and the wood. The skirting boards that ran along the bottom of the walls were designed to protect the plaster from damage caused by furniture and feet. Similarly, the dado rail (a wall moulding some distance from the floor) protected the wall from damage by chairs, and the moulding surrounding paintings had the same protective purpose.

However, in Victorian homes these fixed decorative elements also played a role in the identification and hierarchization of rooms. For example, a ser-

LIVING IN STYLE

132
Eastlake-style hall stand, about 1880–1900
Black walnut, figured walnut veneer and brass,
219 x 125 x 38 cm
Saint-Nom-de-Marie Boarding School, Soeurs des
Saints-Noms-de-Jésus-et-de-Marie, Montreal
Photo Christine Guest/MMFA

vant's bedroom would obviously not possess the same ornamentation as that found in the drawing room or dining room. The fireplace, a central feature of every room, symbolized very clearly the decreasing hierarchy of Victorian decoration: "The marble fireplace would become a slate fireplace, then be

133
Rococo-revival mirror
Gilded wood, 295 x 125 cm
Musée de la civilisation, Quebec City (89-51)
Photo Christine Guest/MMFA
This mirror was originally accompanied by a console table.

reduced further to a cast iron one, until its final manifestation in the servant's room at the very top of the house – a mean little thing with a plain wood surround, designed to burn as little coal as possible."[84]

The extraordinary care and attention paid by members of the middle classes to the decoration of their homes had its source at least in part in the idea of the house as a refuge and shelter from the less congenial aspects of the outside world, especially work.[85] Each piece of furniture was designed for a particular purpose and intended for a particular room. Previously, furniture had been both multi-functional and moved regularly from one room to another. But as the rooms became more specialized, so did the furniture. Chairs for the hall, and suites for the drawing room, boudoir, dining room or bedroom now became commonplace; and the same specialization could be

128 LIVING IN STYLE

observed in the furniture intended for country houses, conservatories and verandahs.

One of the dominant features of interior decoration in the second half of the nineteenth century was the tendency to accumulate furniture and objects of all sorts. Despite the fact that it contravened middle-class morality, this approach, so evident in the typical *bourgeois* home, actually originated with Queen Victoria herself. For it appears that after the death of Prince Albert in 1861 the Queen gave full rein to her taste for masses of objects, creating a cluttered, overcrowded look that became the model for the interiors of the period.[86] Accumulation became virtually the "guiding principle in the interior composition of space".[87] Some rooms ended up looking more like antique shops than living areas, for it did not end with furniture: paintings, silverware and porcelain, bronzes, miniatures, photographs and souvenirs of all kinds, trophies, numerous vases, lamps and knick-knacks, piles of books, stained-glass in the windows, a profusion of pot plants and cut flowers, caged animals and objects made of wax or paper on display under glass domes all contributed towards the general effect of the room.[88]

However, in spite of the apparent confusion, nothing was left to chance in matters of decoration. The pictures were carefully divided into categories: oil paintings, watercolours, genre scenes, still lifes and portraits. Watercolours and tapestries were considered most suitable for the drawing room, while oils were recommended for the dining room as they were thought to induce conviviality and ease digestion. Reproductions and photographs of classical subjects were spread throughout the house.[89]

Claire Desmeules

1   Witold Rybczynski, *Le confort: cinq siècles d'habitation* (Montreal: Éditions du Roseau, 1989), pp. 36-37.

2   Paul-André Linteau, "Quelques réflexions autour de la bourgeoisie québécoise, 1850-1914", *RHAF*, vol. 30, no. 1, June 1976, p. 57.

3   Paul-André Linteau, René Durocher and Jean-Claude Robert, *Histoire du Québec contemporain: de la Confédération à la crise (1867-1929)* (Montreal: Éditions du Boréal, 1989), pp. 184-185 (trans.).

4   *Ibid.*, p. 183 (trans.).

5   I am using here the classification suggested by P.-A. Linteau in "Quelques réflexions autour de la bourgeoisie québécoise, 1850-1914", pp. 55-66.

6   Mark Girouard, *Life in the English Country House* (New York: Penguin Books, 1980), p. 268.

7   For more on this question see Monique Éleb-Vidal and Anne Debarre-Blanchard, *Architectures de la vie privée: maisons et mentalités, XVIIe - XIXe siècles* (Brussels: Archives d'architecture moderne 1989).

8   Stephen Mennell, *Français et Anglais à table, du Moyen Âge à nos jours* (Paris: Flammarion, 1987), pp. 298-299.

9   Stephan Muthesius, *The English Terraced House* (New Haven/London: Yale University Press, 1982), p. 40.

10   Fadette, *Journal d'Henriette Dessaulles 1874-1880* (Montreal: Hurtubise, 1971), with an introduction by Louise Saint-Jacques Dechêne, pp. 15-16.

11   Roger Dixon and Stephan Muthesius, *Victorian Architecture* (London/New York: Thames and Hudson, 1985), p. 47.

12   Danielle Pigeon, "L'influence des catalogues de plan dans l'architecture domestique des Cantons de l'Est: 1840-1880", master's thesis, Université du Québec à Montréal, 1982.

13   Between 1790 and 1835, over sixty pattern books were published in England alone.

14   Between 1800 and 1840, twenty different editions of pattern books were published in the United States. During the 1850s the number rose to ninety-three, and in the 1870s fifty-eight new publications appeared. As the number of publications rose, moreover, their cost went down: from an initial $2 to $3, the selling price dropped to 35 cents a copy or less. See Clifford E. Clark, Jr., "The Vision of the Dining Room: Plan Book Dreams and Middle-Class Realities", in *Dining in America 1850-1900* (Amherst: The University of Massachusetts Press, 1987), pp. 145-146.

15   Janet Wright, *L'architecture pittoresque au Canada* (Ottawa: Canada Parks, 1984), p. 23.

16   Danielle Pigeon, *op. cit.*, p. 57.

17   *Ibid.*, p. 16.

18   In Quebec alone, at least six farming magazines published house plans regularly: *Le Journal d'agriculture* (Montreal, 1851); *Le Journal d'agriculture illustré* (Montreal), which printed plans by the architect Alphonse Raza between 1884 and 1895; *Le Journal du cultivateur* (Montreal, 1855); *La Semaine agricole* (Montreal, 1869); *La Revue agricole* (Montreal, 1862-1863); and *Farm & Home* (Canadian edition, Montreal, 1899-1901). Danielle Pigeon, *op. cit.*, p. 121.

19   Danielle Pigeon, *op. cit.*, p. 122.

20   Madame F.-L. Béïque, *Quatre-vingts ans de souvenirs* (Montreal: Éditions Bernard Valiquette/Éditions A.C.F., 1939), p. 47 (trans.).

21   France Gagnon Pratte, *L'architecture et la nature à Québec au XIXe siècle: les villas* (Quebec City: Musée du Québec, 1980), p. 116.

22   Stephan Muthesius, *op. cit.*, p. 248.

23   France Gagnon Pratte, *op. cit.*, p. 109.

24   For more on this subject see Stephan Muthesius, *op. cit.*

25   *Ibid.*, p. 97.

26   Hermann Muthesius, *The English House* (New York: Rizzoli, 1987), p. 147.

27   Lise Drolet, "La maison Cirice-Têtu", *Continuité*, no. 37, fall 1987, pp. 44-46.

28   Madame Raoul Dandurand, née Joséphine Marchand (1861-1925), *Journal-Mémoires*, unpublished typescript, p. 106 (trans.).

29   Marcel Moussette, *Le chauffage domestique au Canada des origines à l'industrialisation* (Quebec City: PUL, 1983), p. 160 (trans.).

30   Robin Guild, *The Victorian House Book* (New York, Rizzoli, 1989), p. 146.

31   Anne Martin-Fugier, "Les rites de la vie privée bourgeoise", in *Histoire de la vie privée: de la Révolution à la Grande Guerre* (Paris: Seuil, 1987), p. 211 (trans.).

32   John Maass, *The Victorian Home in America* (New York: Hawthorn Books, 1972), p. 23.

33   Witold Rybczynski, *op. cit.*, p. 156.

34   Quoted in Charlotte Gere, *L'époque et son style: la décoration intérieure au XIXe siècle* (Paris: Flammarion, 1989), pp. 54-56 (trans.).

35   I am referring here to the inventories drawn up after a death, one of the most important sources available for a study of lifestyles in Quebec during the second half of the nineteenth century.

36   Jean Lionnet, *Chez les Français du Canada* (Paris: Plon, 1908), p. 108 (trans.).

37   Stephan Muthesius, *op. cit.*, p. 55.

38   Michèle Perrot, "Manières d'habiter", in *Histoire de la vie privée...*, pp. 307-309.

39   Stephan Muthesius, *op. cit.*, p. 42.

40   Ursula Paravicini, "Les deux versants de l'intimité domestique: rôle des femmes et incidences spatiales du XIXe au XXe siècle", in *La maison. Espaces et intimités*, Proceedings of the conference held at the Académie d'architecture de Paris, November 28 and 29, 1985 (Paris: École d'architecture Paris-Villemin, 1986), p. 288.

41   Michèle Perrot and Anne Martin-Fugier, "Les acteurs", in *Histoire de la vie privée...*, p. 88 (trans.).

42   Michèle Perrot, "Figures et rôles", in *Histoire de la vie privée...*, p. 146 (trans.).

43   The villa Cataraqui, for example, had both a day and a night nursery, in accordance with the approved British model.

44   Madame F.-L. Béïque, *op. cit.*, pp. 43-44 (trans.).

45   Michèle Perrot, "Manières d'habiter", in *Histoire de la vie privée...*, p. 320 (trans.).

46   *Ibid.*, p. 310.

47   Ursula Paravicini, *op. cit.*, p. 290.

48   There are a number of examples of this type of plan in Quebec City, mostly situated on the Grande Allée and built around the turn of the century: the Marsh house (1899), the Holt house (1899-1900), the Harcourt-Smith house (1908) and the Hamilton house (1908); in Montreal, the George Stephen house (1880-1883) was one of the earliest examples.

49   Evidence for this has been drawn principally from after-death inventories and the literature of the period.

50   Claudette Lacelle, *Les domestiques en milieu urbain canadien au XIXe siècle* (Ottawa: Canada Parks, 1987), p. 109.

51   *Ibid.*, p. 115. The author reports that, according to the census of 1871, there were fifty-one families in Quebec City and seventy-five in Montreal (all residents of the Saint-Antoine neighbourhood) who employed four servants or more.

52   *Ibid.*, p. 111 (trans.).

53   *Ibid.*, p. 113.

54   Ursula Paravicini, *op. cit.*, p. 293.

55   Mademoiselle E. Dufaux de la Jonchère, *Le savoir-vivre dans la vie ordinaire et dans les cérémonies civiles et religieuses* (Paris: Librairie Garnier Frères, 1883), pp. 40-41 (trans.).

56   Monique Éleb-Vidal and Anne Debarre-Blanchard, *op. cit.*, p. 253.

57   Monique Éleb-Vidal and Anne Debarre-Blanchard, *Architecture domestique et mentalités. Les traités et les pratiques au XIXe siècle*, research report, Secrétariat de la Recherche architecturale, ministère de l'Urbanisme, du Logement et des Transports, Paris, 1984-1985, p. 165.

58   Monique Éleb-Vidal and Anne Debarre-Blanchard, *Architectures de la vie privée...*, p. 254 (trans.).

59   Fadette, *op. cit.*, pp. 209-210 (trans.).

60 Claudette Lacelle, *op. cit.*, pp. 151-152 (trans.).

61 This example is taken from the after-death inventory made in 1901 of the Montreal merchant Hector Mackenzie, referred to elsewhere in this book.

62 François Loyer, *Paris XIXᵉ siècle: l'immeuble et la rue* (Paris: Hazan, 1987), p. 220.

63 Charlotte Gere, *op. cit.*, p. 222.

64 *Ibid.*

65 This passage on the two conceptions of luxury is a summary of the ideas developed by Monique Éleb-Vidal and Anne Debarre-Blanchard in *Architectures de la vie privée...*, pp. 261-262.

66 Madame Raoul Dandurand, *op. cit.*, p. 123 (trans.).

67 Comtesse Drohojowska, *De la politesse et du bon ton ou devoirs d'une femme chrétienne dans le monde* (Paris: Victor Sarlit, 1860), pp. 18-19 (trans.).

68 For the sequence of the various historical styles that emerged during the Victorian era, see the chapter devoted to them elsewhere in this book.

69 Monique Éleb-Vidal and Anne Debarre-Blanchard, *Architectures de la vie privée...*, p. 275 (trans.).

70 Charlotte Gere, *op. cit.*, p. 52 (trans.).

71 *Ibid.*, p. 222.

72 Report of the Parliamentary Committee of the Province of Canada published in 1849, quoted in Albert Faucher, "La notion de luxe chez les Canadiens français au dix-neuvième siècle", *Délibérations et Mémoires de la Société royale du Canada*, 1973, p. 176 (trans.).

73 *L'Écho du Cabinet de lecture paroissial*, June 15, 1866, quoted in Albert Faucher, *op. cit.*, p. 176 (trans.).

74 The design reform movement, also known as the Aesthetic movement, comprehended the Eastlake style, "art furniture", the Japanese influence, the Arts and Crafts Movement and Art Nouveau. Its main protagonists were Charles L. Eastlake, William Morris, William Burges, Norman Shaw and A. H. Mackmurdo.

75 Charles L. Eastlake, *Hints on Household Taste* (New York: Dover Publications Inc., 1986), pp. 72-73.

76 Monique Éleb-Vidal and Anne Debarre-Blanchard, *Architectures de la vie privée...*, p. 270.

77 Charlotte Gere, *op. cit.*, p. 102.

78 Danielle Blanchet, *Découvrir la Grande Allée* (Quebec City: Musée du Québec, 1984), p. 104 (trans.).

79 France Gagnon Pratte, *op. cit.*, p. 129.

80 James McPherson LeMoine, *Picturesque Quebec. A Sequel to Quebec Past and Present* (Montreal: Dawson Bros., 1882), pp. 380-381; quoted in France Gagnon Pratte, *op. cit.*, pp. 221-222.

81 John Marshall and Ian Willox, *The Victorian House* (London: Sidgwick & Jackson, 1989), p. 60.

82 Monique Éleb-Vidal and Anne Debarre-Blanchard, *Architectures de la vie privée...*, p. 270 (trans.).

83 Adrien Loir, *Canada et Canadiens* (Paris: E. Guilmoto, 1908), p. 81 (trans.).

84 John Marshall and Ian Willox, *op. cit.*, p. 60.

85 *Ibid.*, p. 58.

86 Charlotte Gere, *op. cit.*, pp. 24-25.

87 Michèle Perrot, "Manières d'habiter", in *Histoire de la vie privée...*, p. 335 (trans.).

88 R. W. Symonds and B. B. Whineray, *Victorian Furniture* (London: Studio Editions, 1987), p. 100.

89 John Marshall and Ian Willox, *op. cit.*, p. 69.

The Spencer Wood Villa in 1851[1]

Henry Atkinson was born in England in 1790. Britain's maritime trade activities were severely curtailed when Napoleon imposed the Continental System in 1806. As a result of the blockade, Great Britain found itself cut off from its traditional wood supplies; shipbuilders and wood merchants like the Atkinson brothers were among the first to leave the homeland to settle in Canada. At that time, the country possessed virtually limitless supplies of wood, and the Canadian lumber trade was protected by preferential tariffs. In 1812, at the age of twenty-two, Henry Atkinson arrived in Quebec City, where his brother Anthony was already owner of a shipyard. The following year, Henry purchased a concession in Cap Rouge with his brother William; the two went into partnership with George William Usborne and set up a new business that did trade with England. Henry built himself a luxurious residence at the cove of Sillery, on a plateau overlooking his lumberyards. A few years later, he handed the villa, Redcliff, over to his brother William and set off on an extended trip to Europe.

In 1835, on a visit to England, Henry Atkinson purchased the Spencer Wood estate in Sillery, unoccupied since 1826, whose heirs lived in London. He took advantage of his trip to acquire works of art, antiques and other rare pieces for his new villa. Atkinson also brought back with him plants and seeds for the grounds of the estate, which he planned to develop along the lines of the great domains he had visited on his travels through Europe. English gardens were the height of fashion at the time. On his return, Atkinson made changes to the villa itself and, with the help of his gardener, designed a vast park.

But it was not until 1846 that Spencer Wood became really famous. This was the year that Henry Atkinson brought over a gardener from Scotland called Peter Lowe. Together, the two embarked on a programme of scientific horticulture. Atkinson, who was something of an innovator, built an enormous greenhouse over three hundred feet long, which was heated by an ingenious system he developed himself. The produce grown in the Spencer Wood greenhouses — flowers, plants, fruit and vegetables — won awards at horticultural fairs in Montreal and even gained mention in the *Illustrated London News*.

However, after 1846 the hitherto flourishing lumber industry began gradually to decline, and Atkinson was forced to take certain financial steps to avoid disaster. In 1849, therefore, he sold most of his estate to the government, who intended to make it the Governor's official residence. The project was postponed for two years when the seat of government was transferred from Montreal to Toronto, but in 1852 the government was re-established in Quebec City. The previous year a major auction had been held at Spencer Wood. Thanks to one of the two auction catalogues,[2] we are able to gain quite a clear idea of the contents of the villa. There are six rooms inventoried in the catalogue: the hall, the dining room, the two drawing rooms, the library and the breakfast parlour. Between them, they contained numerous pieces of mahogany and rosewood furniture, several large mirrors with gilt frames, a number of Brussels carpets and a profusion of art works and antiques; the library, moreover, contained an impressive collection of books. The detailed contents of these rooms are given below exactly as they appeared in the catalogue, with the exception of the books, which are too numerous to be mentioned here.

ENTRANCE HALL

1. A small Mahogany Table
2. A Looking-Glass, old gilt frame, 4ft. 6 by 2ft 8
3. Six Mahogany Chairs
4. Two Mahogany Hat-Stands
5. One Hexagon Hall-Lamp, chain and hook
6. One Rare Buhl Clock (Louis XIV), beautifully inlaid Ormolu, on Tortoiseshell, on a rich Bracket Pedestal, with a Bronze Gilt Figure of Urania;
7. One Floor-Cloth
8. One Upright Hall Stove [...] for wood or coal
9. One Floor-Cloth, on stair-entrance
10. One do on stairs
11. One Stair-Carpet and Cover
12. 13 Brass Stair-Rods
13. Shakesperian Floor-Cloth, on landing
14. One Rustic Table, from Stratford upon Avon Crabtree
15. Two do Chairs, do
16. One American Stove, for wood or coal
17. One Stove Pan for ditto
18. Two Bronzed Statues and Pedestals, in niches, 5 feet high
19. Two Views of Carouge, rich frames, painted by Légaré
20. Two Views of Carouge, painted by Légaré

DINING-ROOM

21. One, London-made, Mahogany Sideboard [...] with side closets
22. One, London-made, set of Mahogany (Telescope) Dining Tables, for 20 persons
23. A Camera Obscura in Case
24. One Table Cover
25. One extra size fine Damask Table Cloth for 24 persons
26. One do do do
27. One Mahogany Cellaret, 20 bottles
28. Two Elegant Italian Marble Vases, with handles
29. One Plate Warmer
30. One Hearth-Rug
31. One Fender
32. One Set Polished Fire-Irons
33. Two, Round, Mahogany Pedestal Corner Closets, french polish
34. One Carved Black Walnut, Pier-Table, with carved gilt border of fruits, and Marble slab
35. One Pier Looking-Glass, French Plates
36. One Chimney Looking-Glass (French)
37. One ormolu, 14 days Clock, with Stand and Shade

38 Two very elegant Bronze Figures, on Marble and Ormolu Pedestals, supporting Branches of Lilies and Roses, for 3 candles each, […] bought at Fonthill Abbey
39 One Mahogany 4-shelf Waggon, on Castors
40 Ten Mahogany Chairs, moveable Hair-covered Seats
41 Two do Armchairs do, to match
42 One Mahogany, Red Leather-covered, Easy-Chair, falling-back, sliding seat
43 A set of Five Japan China Ornaments, consisting of 3 Vases and Covers, […], with 2 Beakers - a rare and fine set
44 Two Berlin Iron Statues of Napoleon and Frederick the Great
45 Two Richly Moulded Plated Candlesticks and Shades, for the open air or open windows
46 Two Set Red and White Damask Window-Curtains; Gilt Pins - Ropes and Tassels - with Gilt Cornices and Muslin
47 Two White Spring Sun-Blinds
48 One Gothic Pattern, 4-light, Bronze Lamp, with Shades, Chain and Hook
49 One New Floor-Cloth
50 One Dining-Table Carpet
51 One Mahogany Barometer and Thermometer
52 One Richly Carved Plated Lamp […] for Sideboard or Table - Very elegant

DRAWING-ROOMS

53 One Brussels Carpet, 20 by 19 ft.
54 One Fender
55 One Set Fire-irons
56 One Hearth-Rug
57 One Splendid Looking-Glass, on the Mantel, French Plate, 5ft. 9in. by 4ft., with new Carved and Gilt Frame
58 Two Bronze and Gilt Chimney Candelabra, for 5 lights each
59 One Very Elegant White Dresden Centre Vase, of Porcelain, mounted with Ormolu, Swan-neck Handles
60 Two White Marble Eggs, or Ormolu Tripods, Marble Pedestal, fitted for Candles - The above 3 articles of Taste, were brought from Fonthill Abbey
61 Four small Gilt Candlesticks, Antique Pattern
62 Two Rare And Curious Marquetrie Flower-Stands, inlaid with Flowers, Gilt and Ormolu Mounting - These articles of Louis XIV were obtained at Fonthill Abbey
63 Two Blue Silk Bell Pulls
64 One Round Rosewood Centre Table
65 One Rosewood Sofa Table
66 Two Blue and White Flower Vases and Covers
67 Two Berlin Iron Statuettes of Napoleon and Frederick, on Pedestals
The following articles, taken together, would adorn any Pier, or space between two Windows, in America:
68 Two Bronze and Gilt Candelabra for 6 Candles
69 One Magnificent Copy in Berlin Iron of the Warwick Vase, on Pedestal
70 Three largest size Japan China Vases and Covers, […] with 2 Beakers - Forming A Set of great beauty, rarely seen in Europe
71 One Looking-Glass French Plate, […] standing on -
72 A Mahogany richly carved Pier Table, from a Greek design, with Pedestal shelf, for China, and Marble Slab
73 Two Window Settees, with Chintz Covers
74 Two Sets Blue and White Damask Curtains; Gilt Cornices
75 Two White Spring Sun Blinds
76 Two Hair-Stuffed Ottomans, […] with Covers
77 One Mahogany Chess-Table on Castors, with two Drawers
78 One Set of Chessmen
79 Two Mahogany Card Tables
80 Bagatelle Board, complete
81 One Backgammon Board, complete
82 One Berlin Iron Inkstand, Napoleon's Tomb
83 One Curious Chinese Bronze Vase and Cover, on an Open Carved Wood Pedestal
84 One exquisitely formed Tripod Burner, in Berlin Iron
85 One Round Seagliola Table - painting, Infants playing with a Goat - on a Carved Pedestal of Black Walnut, surmounted by an exquisitely carved Wreath of Roses. By Leprohon
86 Two Mahogany Fauteuils, on Castors, covered with Morocco
87 Eight Mahogany Hair-covered Chairs, Moveable Seats
88 One Mahogany Couch, Hair-covered, Moveable Mattrass
89 One Mahogany Hair-covered Rocking-Chair
90 One Gilt Lamp, with Two Burners, Shades, Hook and Chain

SECOND DRAWING-ROOM

91 One richly Carved Centre Lamp, with 4 burners, Shades, Hook and Chain, The Neptune Pattern
92 One Magnificent Inlaid Roman Table, White Marble, containing 5 Circles intersected by Black Marble radii from a centre Onyx, dividing the whole into 140 receptacles for that number of the rarest specimens of Marble known, and encircled by a Green Marble Inlaid Band, with a descriptive Catalogue - Supported on a plain Mahogany Stand
93 One Brussels Carpet, 19ft by 20ft
94 One Rosewood and Ormolu Round Tripod-Stand, containing a Rich Japan Plateau, of 21 inches diameter from Fonthill Abbey
95 One Large Japan Bowl
96 One Model, to a Scale, of the Celebrated Bucentaur, made for Mr. Atkinson, in the Venetian Arsenal, by permission expressly obtained from that Government - Believed to be unique in America
97 Five Pieces, forming a light set of 3 Vases, and 2 Beakers […] of very beautiful Japan Ware, Fillagree Tops
98 One Looking-Glass, French Plate
99 One Black Walnut Carved Pier Table, Shell Front, with a Carved Border of Grapes, Gilt, and White Marble Slab
100 One Hair-stuffed Ottoman and Cover
101 One finely Carved Lamp-stand, from a Greek design, […] Bronzes. By Berlinguet
102 One Jobson's English Franklin Grate on Rollers to replace handsome Harp Pattern, Gilt Fire-Dogs, with two Brass Fenders
103 Two Statues on Pedestals
104 One English-made Six-fold Wind-Screen, Mounted with Canadian Maps, standing, when open, 8ft. 6in. high by 10ft. wide
105 One Six-fold London-made Wind-Screen, Mounted with Excellent Maps, on both sides
106 One Mahogany German-made Musical Clock, with Spare Cylinders, to play 42 Tunes in all - This Clock was sold, by Raffle, at Bath, for 80 Guineas
107 One Mahogany Piano Forte
108 One Æolian Harp

LIBRARY

109 One Air-tight Stove, Pan and Pipes
110 One Floor-Cloth
111 One London-Made Library Table, with four Drawers
112 One London-Made Chair, with Cane-seat, Back and Sides, and moveable Morocco Cushions, with Reading-Table, and Candlestick, made to rise or fall
113 The Library Fittings, nearly new, of Mahogany, forming two Sets, which may be had together or single; made to hold 2,000 Volumes together
114 One magnificent Bust, in Parian Marble, of Cicero
115 An Antique and Unique Set (of the 5th century) of the Twelve Caesars, purchased in Rome, being admirable Busts and resemblances; in Marble
116 One Etruscan Vase, excavated in the vicinity of Naples
117 One do do
One Spy-Glass and Stand, to unscrew

BREAKFAST PARLOUR

162 One Neat Bronze 2 Light Lamp, Shades, Hooks and Chains
163 One French Polished Pedestal Table for dining 6 persons
164 One Hair-Stuffed Settee […] Back & Cushions covered with Blue Moreen
165 One Carpet
166 One Floor-Cloth
167 One Stove Grate
168 One Set Fire-Irons
169 One Looking-Glass, French Plate
170 Two Classic-shaped Bronze Candlesticks
171 Four Small Bronze do
172 Two Bronze Pastile Burners
173 Six Mahogany Hair-covered Chairs
174 Two do do Arm, to match
175 Two Extra Large Indian China Vases & Covers
176 One Mahogany Pier Table, Closet, Marble Top
177 One Portrait of Byron, in a Gilt Frame, glazed
178 One *Le Naufrage*, after Vernet, do do
179 One *Death of Nelson* do do
180 West's celebrated *Death of Gen. Wolfe*, framed and glazed to match this sett, engraved by Wollett and is considered by Amateurs the finest effort of the Art, Proof copies have been repeatedly sold in Paris, at 1000 to 1100 frcs.
181 One Penn's *Treaty with the Indians*
182 One *Battle of Waterloo*
183 One *Madonna della Siggeola*, after Raphael
184 One Set Red Moreen Curtains, with Top, Pins, &c., Complete

Claire Desmeules

---

1 Most of the information concerning Henry Atkinson and the Spencer Wood villa comes from the article by Renée Gagnon-Guimond entitled "Henry Atkinson: Gentilhomme et baron du bois", *Cap-aux-Diamants*, vol. 4, no. 3, fall 1988, pp. 19-22. I would also like to thank Mrs. Guimond for her valuable assistance regarding the Spencer Wood catalogue.

The Baker-Gilmour House, Stanbridge, in 1882[1]

The Baker-Gilmour house, located in Stanbridge, in the Eastern Townships, was originally the home of the banker John Carpenter Baker and his wife, Ann Letta Augusta Stanton. On Baker's death in 1882, the house became the property of their daughter, Mary Jane, who was married to Arthur Henry Gilmour, also a banker and an associate of his father-in-law. The house and its contents thus represented a family inheritance that was passed on from generation to generation.

In 1976, Arthur de Cresse Gilmour, grandson of Mary and Arthur Henry Gilmour, bequeathed the house's original drawing-room suite to the Canadian Museum of Civilization. The photographs of the Baker-Gilmour house shown here were taken by him during the 1930s. At that time – as one of the photos shows – the drawing-room suite was in the picture gallery. When he bequeathed the suite, Mr. Gilmour informed B. Riley of the Canadian Museum of Civilization that the picture gallery had remained unchanged since about 1865. It contained works by, among others, Mower Martin, Wyatt Eaton, Allan Edson, Adolphe Vogt, A. H. Wyant, Duncanson and Perry.

The after-death inventory of J. C. Baker,[1] drawn up in 1882, corroborates Gilmour's remarks and provides extensive information about the living conditions of a middle-class family residing in the country. The house itself was a large two-storey building with carved wooden balconies encircling both floors. The ground floor consisted of the entrance hall, a dining room, a small drawing room, an office, a bedroom and a pantry – a utility room used to store china and miscellaneous household equipment. There was certainly also a kitchen, although it is not mentioned in the inventory. On the upper floor there was a passage leading to four bedrooms and a picture gallery. In addition, the house had a cellar, used to store perishables and to contain the refrigerator. The inventory also mentions outbuildings, including stables and a stone cowshed.

The family's affluence is indicated by the fact that all the rooms were extremely comfortably furnished, especially the drawing and dining rooms. Among the objects found in these luxurious rooms were carpets, curtains, a console table with a mirror, a Renaissance-revival drawing-room suite, a sideboard, an extending dining table, a pianoforte, an organ, bookcases and large quantities of books, together with quantities of fine porcelain, silverware and table linen. The inventory also throws light on another interesting feature quite characteristic of a *bourgeois* way of life: the house's owner was an enthusiastic art collector. The bulk of his collection was kept in the pic-

134
Lambkins Furniture Co. (attrib.)
Renaissance-revival settee from the original picture gallery of the Baker-Gilmour house in Stanbridge, about 1865
111.5 x 156 x 58 cm
Canadian Museum of Civilization, Hull (A-4896-a)
This settee is part of a drawing-room suite that also includes two armchairs and four easy chairs. The ensemble was probably made in the Eastern Townships by the Lambkins Furniture Co. of Riceburg.

---

1 ANQS, registry of notary Michael Boyce, no. 2324, inventory following the death of Ann Letta Augusta Stanton and John Carpenter Baker, banker, resident of Stanbridge, July 17, 1882.-

135
Arthur de Cresse Gilmour, Stanbridge
The living room of the Baker-Gilmour house during the 1930s
Photograph
Canadian Museum of Civilization, Hull (76-5031)

ture gallery, but the walls of all the main rooms were adorned with paintings.

The selection of art works is fully in tune with the tastes of the period: we see a penchant for the Picturesque, an interest in Antiquity — with its accompanying phenomenon of reproduction — early examples of photography and numerous chromolithographs. However, the Baker collection also represented the new painting that had developed in Canada following Confederation. Landscapes predominated, and there were many images of rivers, waterfalls, mountains, valleys, creeks, sunsets, and studies of storms and cloud-filled skies. But there were also a number of genre scenes, portraits and sculptures. Apart from the fact that the evaluations and details concerning the frames have been left out, and some abbreviations have been completed, what follows is an exact transcription of the gallery inventory. In 1882, the gallery's contents were valued at $ 5,225.

Owlshead by D.
On the St Ann, small
Rec of the tropics
Chagnon mountain & Orford lake
Composition with color
Falls of Yellow river
Niagara Falls by moonlight & two others
Photographic views, by Notman
Thirty six stereoscopic views on glass
Prangs chromos
Proserpine head by Eaton (oil painting)
Apollo Belevedere
Council of War, Roger
Canadians trio, Krieghoff (oil painting)
Chaudière Falls
Sunset at Sea
Spring Sunset, Edson
Scene on the Mississipi River, Edson, oil
Boys playing toss, oil
Sly peep
Cows in Stable (A. Vogt)
Landing St Helen's Island (H.S.) [Henry Sandham?]

Study (old man's head), Eaton, oil
Five portraits
Nude figure
Sunday R. Valley (oil)
Shower in the valley
Road Scene Elms
The moral lesson (J.O. Eaton)
Kittmany Creek (A. H. Wyant)
Blustering day (L. M. Wiles)
Twilight (L. M. Wiles)
Appletree in Blossom
Stem bridge & wine
Coming storm in harvest, A. Vogt
Cleaning horses
Fox (Martin's oil)
Falls of Latron (Jacobi, watercolour)
Morning early autumn on the Mississipi river & cattle (Edwin's oil)
Greek girl on porcelain
Between Toulon & Venice
View of Lake George (watercolour)
The Confidence, M. Wright (oil)

A rare volume, M. Wright (oil)
New York News boy, by Eaton
Two buds medallion, J.D. Perry
Marble Bust of Horace Greely
Marble figure "The Beggar Maid"
Two chromos of Boston
Marble figure, Merry Christmas (Perry)
Two small landscapes
One medium size landscape
Florentine
A lot of small pictures
Terra Cotta, Bush
A. True Demise[?] & fair (Eaton)
Old man's head study
A lot of loose pictures (Eaton)
Sea Saw snow[?] & Boots

136

137

138

136
Arthur de Cresse Gilmour, Stanbridge
The drawing room of the Baker-Gilmour house during the 1930s
Photograph
Canadian Museum of Civilization, Hull (76-5032)

137
Arthur de Cresse Gilmour, Stanbridge
Some of the works in the picture gallery of the Baker-Gilmour house during the 1930s
Photograph
Canadian Museum of Civilization, Hull (76-5030)
The portraits are of Mary Baker, daughter of Mr. and Mrs. John C. Baker, her husband Colonel Arthur Henry Gilmour (above), Ann Letta Augusta Stanton and John Carpenter Baker (below).

138
Arthur de Cresse Gilmour, Stanbridge
Another view of the picture gallery of the Baker-Gilmour house during the 1930s
Photograph
Canadian Museum of Civilization, Hull (76-5034)
The large painting by Adolphe Vogt entitled *Coming Storm in Harvest* can be see in the centre of the photograph.

The Tea Ritual

It is an affair of considerable importance among our neighbours across the Channel, and the girl or young woman who displays skill in this gracious art gains a reputation as an accomplished woman.

Comtesse Drohojowska, *De la politesse et du bon ton ou devoirs d'une femme chrétienne dans le monde* (Paris: Victor Sarlit, 1860), p. 45 (trans.).

As soon as there is mention of the ritual of tea-drinking, we think automatically of the English ceremony of "afternoon tea". By the mid-nineteenth century, the habit of taking tea — accompanied by cakes and other light refreshments — in the late afternoon, usually at a regular hour, had become an integral part of the British upper- and middle-class way of life.

Nevertheless, this afternoon event, which provided an opportunity for relaxed conversation in the drawing room or garden, remained a relatively simple affair: not much was required in the way of preparation, service was accomplished without the help of servants and the number of guests remained limited.

However, as certain period photographs show, the tea ritual sometimes took a more sophisticated form during the Victorian era; in fact, tea could become the focus of a fully-fledged reception.[1] This form of tea-taking, as described in certain French books on etiquette available in Quebec at the period, differed markedly from the British approach, especially regarding the time of day it took place.[2]

A distinction was made between private tea parties, consisting of between six and twenty people, and tea parties proper, attended by twenty to forty. Any event uniting a larger number of people was no longer a tea party, but a musical evening or dance — a ball or concert — depending on the type of entertainment offered to the guests. Invitations were sent six or seven days before the reception, and it was sometimes specified that the party would be a regular event taking place every week or fortnight. Such invitations were valid for the whole season, but unless one was an intimate of the family it was considered ill-mannered to attend every time.

139
Notman Studio, Montreal
Tea being served in the drawing room of the William McFarlane Notman house, Montreal (detail), 1890
Photograph
McCord Museum of Canadian History, Montreal, Notman Photographic Archives (92522-Misc II)

140
Notman Studio, Montreal
Tea being served in the garden at Trafalgar, home of the Williams family, Trafalgar Avenue, Montreal, 1888
Photograph
McCord Museum of Canadian History, Montreal, Notman Photographic Archives (MP 233/75)

TEA PARTIES
The guests, ranging in number from twenty to forty, were dressed as for musical evenings: women wore low-

Pl. 2

Pl. 3

Pl. 4

Pl. 2   Charles-Olivier Bédard, ROCOCO-REVIVAL SOFA (fig. 173), Musée de la civilisation, Quebec City

Pl. 3   Charles-Olivier Bédard, ROCOCO-REVIVAL LADY'S CHAIR (fig. 175), Musée de la civilisation, Quebec City

Pl. 4   Detail of plate 3

Pl. 5
ROCOCO-REVIVAL WHATNOT (fig. 179), Musée de la civilisation, Quebec City

Pl. 8

Pl. 9   Renaissance-revival sideboard (fig. 358), Musée du Séminaire de Québec

Pl. 8   Francis-Pierre Gauvin, Naturalistic sideboard (fig. 429), Musée de la civilisation, Quebec City

Pl. 10   Lower left-hand door of a Renaissance-revival sideboard (detail of fig. 200), Musée de la civilisation, Quebec City

Pl. 11   Naturalistic sideboard (fig. 206), Canadian Museum of Civilization, Hull

Pl. 11

Pl. 12

Pl. 13

Pl. 13
RENAISSANCE-REVIVAL BED (fig. 222), Jean-Claude Lachance and Denyse Desroches Collection, Granby

Pl. 12
RENAISSANCE-REVIVAL BED (fig. 221), Denyse Desroches Collection, Granby

Pl. 14

156　　　　　　　　　　　　　　　　　　　　　　　　　　　　　　　LIVING IN STYLE

Pl. 15

Pl. 16

Pl. 17

Pl. 18

Pl. 19

Pl. 14	RENAISSANCE-REVIVAL BED (fig. 211), Canadian Museum of Civilization, Hull
Pl. 15	LEFT-HAND SECTION OF A RENAISSANCE-REVIVAL "RÉCAMIER"-STYLE CHAISE-LONGUE (detail of fig. 216), Canadian Museum of Civilization, Hull
Pl. 16	FOOT OF A RENAISSANCE-REVIVAL "RÉCAMIER"-STYLE CHAISE-LONGUE (detail of fig. 216), Canadian Museum of Civilization, Hull
Pl. 17	PART OF THE BACK OF A RENAISSANCE-REVIVAL OCCASIONAL CHAIR (detail of fig. 215), Canadian Museum of Civilization, Hull
Pl. 18	PART OF THE UNDER-FRAME OF A RENAISSANCE-REVIVAL WRITING TABLE, (detail of fig. 217), Canadian Museum of Civilization, Hull
Pl. 19	RENAISSANCE-REVIVAL BEDSIDE TABLE (fig. 214), Canadian Museum of Civilization, Hull

LIVING IN STYLE

Pl. 20

Pl. 21

Pl. 22

Pl. 21
Detail of plate 20

Pl. 22
Detail of plate 23

Pl. 23
Charles Barbeau, BED (fig. 8),
Canadian Museum of Civilization, Hull

Pl. 20
Owen McGarvey, EASTLAKE-STYLE BED
(fig. 233), McCord Museum of Canadian
History, Montreal

Pl. 23

LIVING IN STYLE 159

Pl. 24

Pl. 24
Omer Marchand and the sculptors Bouthier and Proulx,
RENAISSANCE-REVIVAL HOTEL SIDEBOARD (fig. 250), Raymond Fabien and Marthe Fabien-Lapalme Collection, Anjou

Pl. 25
TERM, TELAMON AND GROTESQUE, detail of plate 24

Pl. 26
EASTLAKE-STYLE HALL STAND (fig. 132), Sœurs des Saints-Noms-de-Jésus-et-de-Marie, Montreal

Pl. 27

Pl. 28

Pl. 29

Pl. 30

Pl. 27 John and William Hilton, Trophy representing Commerce adorning the Renaissance-revival bookcase from Ravenscrag (detail of fig. 41), Allan Memorial Institute, Montreal

Pl. 28 John and William Hilton, Trophy representing Literature and History adorning the Renaissance-revival bookcase from Ravenscrag (detail of fig. 41), Allan Memorial Institute, Montreal

Pl. 29 John and William Hilton, Trophy representing the State adorning the Renaissance-revival bookcase from Ravenscrag (detail of fig. 41), Allan Memorial Institute, Montreal

Pl. 31
John and William Hilton, Trophy representing the Fine Arts adorning the Renaissance-revival bookcase from Ravenscrag (detail of fig. 41), Allan Memorial Institute, Montreal

Pl. 30

John and William Hilton, Cariatid adorning the Renaissance-revival bookcase from Ravenscrag
(detail of fig. 41), Allan Memorial Institute, Montreal

Pl. 32

164 LIVING IN STYLE

Pl. 32
William Drum, RENAISSANCE-REVIVAL CABINET (fig. 55), Canadian Museum of Civilization, Hull

Pl. 33
INTERIOR OF THE CABINET, detail of plate 32

Pl. 34
Detail of plate 32

LIVING IN STYLE

Pl. 35

Pl. 37
UPPER PART OF A ROCOCO-REVIVAL MIRROR (detail of fig. 133),
Musée de la civilisation, Quebec City

Pl. 35
ROCOCO-REVIVAL CONSOLE TABLE WITH MIRROR (fig. 360), Serge Joyal Collection, Montreal

Pl. 36
TERM, detail of plate 35

LIVING IN STYLE

Pl. 38

Pl. 39

Pl. 38
William Drum, BALLOON-BACK CHAIR (fig. 427),
Canadian Museum of Civilization, Hull

Pl. 39
HUNZINGER CHAIR (fig. 380), Augustinian monastery of the
Hôtel-Dieu de Québec

Pl. 40
OCCASIONAL CHAIR, AESTHETIC MOVEMENT (fig. 445),
McCord Museum of Canadian History, Montreal

Pl. 40

Pl. 41
Philippe Vallière, Rococo-revival rocking chair (fig. 283), Musée de la civilisation, Quebec City

Pl. 42
CEREMONIAL CHAIR IN THE WILLIAM AND MARY STYLE (fig. 35), Bishop's palace of Chicoutimi

Pl. 43
RENAISSANCE-REVIVAL LADY'S CHAIR (fig. 171), Musée de la civilisation, Quebec City

Pl. 44

Pl. 45

Pl. 46

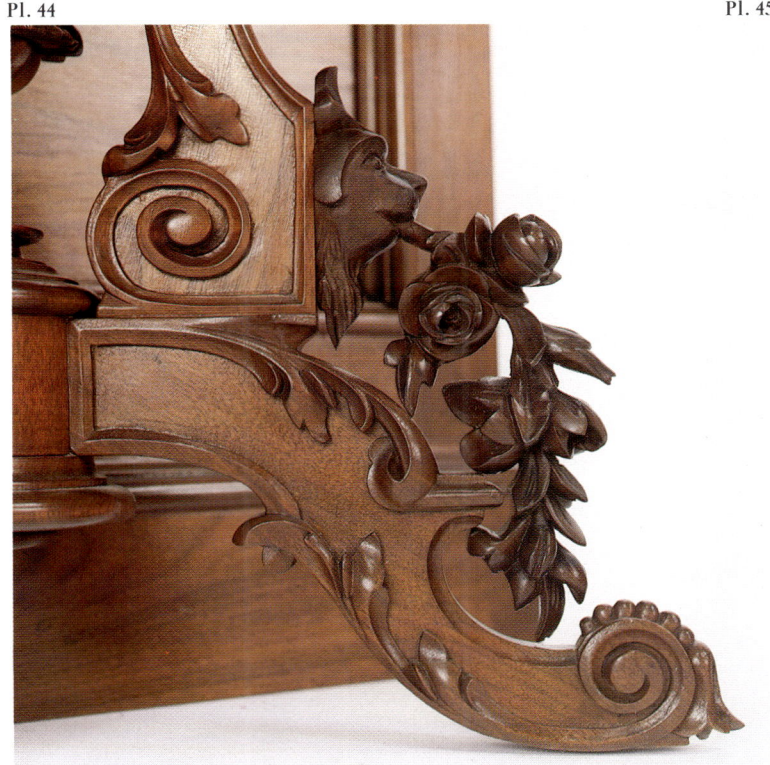

Pl 47

Pl. 44   Detail of plate 42

Pl. 45   François Gourdeau, Part of the under-frame of a Renaissance-revival games table (detail of fig. 295),
         The Montreal Museum of Fine Arts

Pl. 46   François Gourdeau, Foot of a Renaissance-revival lady's chair (detail of fig. 291),
         The Montreal Museum of Fine Arts

Pl. 47   François Gourdeau, Part of the under-frame of a Renaissance-revival console table with mirror (detail of fig. 293),
         The Montreal Museum of Fine Arts

LIVING IN STYLE   171

Pl. 48

Pl. 49

Pl. 48
Griffin's-head armrest of a rococo-revival bergere chair (detail of fig. 425), Musée Pierre-Boucher du Séminaire de Trois-Rivières

Pl. 49
Armrest of a ceremonial chair in the William and Mary style, detail of plate 42

Pl. 50
Francis-Pierre Gauvin, Chimera adorning a naturalistic sideboard, detail of plate 8

Pl. 50

172   LIVING IN STYLE

Pl. 51
FOOTBOARD OF A ROCOCO-REVIVAL BED (fig. 462),
Musée de la civilisation, Quebec City

Pl. 52
William Drum, BEAVER ADORNING THE BACK OF A CHAIR,
detail of plate 38

Pl. 53
BEAVER ADORING THE APRON OF A ROCOCO-REVIVAL SIDEBOARD
(detail of fig. 199), Musée du Saguenay-Lac-Saint-Jean, Chicoutimi

LIVING IN STYLE   173

Pl. 54

LIVING IN STYLE

Pl. 55

Pl. 56

Pl. 57

Pl. 58

Pl. 55
BACK OF AN ELBOW CHAIR IN THE CHIPPENDALE STYLE (detail of fig. 390),
Petites Franciscaines de Marie, Baie Saint-Paul

Pl. 56
Thomas Fox, LOWER RIGHT-HAND SECTION OF A RENAISSANCE-REVIVAL SIDEBOARD (detail of fig. 362), The Montreal Museum of Fine Arts

Pl. 57
BACK OF A SECOND EMPIRE FLY CHAIR (detail of fig. 394),
Musée de la civilisation, Quebec City

Pl. 58
ROCOCO-REVIVAL TILT-TOP GAMES TABLE (fig. 391),
McCord Museum of Canadian History, Montreal

Pl. 54
ROCOCO-REVIVAL DRESSING TABLE WITH MIRROR (fig. 325),
Canadian Museum of Civilization, Hull

LIVING IN STYLE   175

Pl. 59

Pl. 60

Pl. 59
INNER DOORS OF THE VESTIBULE OF THE ANGUS HOUSE, 240 DRUMMOND STREET, MONTREAL (fig. 143), (detail) Canadian Museum of Civilization, Hull

Pl. 60
LANDSCAPE (fig. 490), Musée de la civilisation, Quebec City

THE HOMES, FURNISHINGS AND COLLECTIONS OF R. B. ANGUS (1831-1922)

Quiet in demeanor, he is purposeful and unconsciously exerts an influence which makes for domination. That this domination is always used to good purpose and for the benefit of his country stands to his high credit."[1]

KNOWN INTERNATIONALLY AS A HIGHLY PROMINENT, respected financier and director of the Canadian Pacific Railway (CPR), R. B. Angus's support of institutions, art and museums after 1880 ran parallel to his build-up of a significant private collection of art and decorative art objects, which he ensconced in a series of spectacular late nineteenth – and early twentieth – century city and country homes, unfortunately now all demolished.

Richard Bladworth Angus was born on May 28, 1831 in Bathgate, Scotland near Edinburgh. The eighth child, and fifth son of twelve children, he was educated at Bathgate Academy in the stern ways of his Presbyterian fathers.[2] His father, Alexander Angus (1789-1856), was probably a draper, and his mother, Margaret Forrest (1798-1883), was also likely from Scotland. R. B. Angus's long financial career in Canada began when he came to Montreal at twenty-six years of age from Manchester, England, the mill town where he had worked in a bank and met his future wife, Mary Anne Daniels (1833-1913), the daughter of a wine merchant, whom he married on June 13, 1857. In the summer of that same year, the Anguses arrived in Montreal by steamer.

As was the custom in well-to-do British families, for those sons whose birth order dictated their destiny and their extraneous value in the family business, the later-born were often judiciously planted in strategic locations in the colonies as emissaries of their fathers, and to consolidate family associations abroad. Sent with letters of introduction, these young men were indentured to institutions to learn a trade or business from the ground up.

As part of the process of education of the well-off, it was customary, as an apprentice, to match one's mode of living to the circumstances of position and salary commensurate to one's peers – to establish social contacts with young men in similar circumstances, and to learn the mores of an institution and its clientele by identifying oneself with them. Thus through self-discipline, social learning, interaction and modelling, the humble but well-born clerk, in natural Darwinian fashion, could methodically ascend the business ladder with a solid background in commercial practices, in tandem with the social skills and attitudes necessary for eventual leadership and service in the business and social community at large.

In 1857, R. B. Angus joined the staff of the Bank of Montreal as bookkeeper-clerk at a salary of $600.00 a year, groomed to learn the banking business. The country's oldest banking establishment, chartered in 1817, the Bank of Montreal had recently built its head office in Place d'Armes (1845-1846). Angus rose steadily in the ranks, learning its institutional methods. The Bank of Montreal gave to Canada its first system of organized finance and its first domestic currency. Its Scottish directorate had adapted certain distinctive features of Scottish banking, one of which was the maintenance of numerous branches by a few banks of large capital, enabling the extension of banking services to communities in every part of the country.

After four years Angus was placed in charge of the Chicago agency (1861-1863), and subsequently became an agent for the Bank in New York (1863-1864), thus spending the better part of the American Civil War in the United States. At age thirty-eight, twelve years after initially joining the Bank, he had risen to the position of general manager and was known for his tact, foresight and business acumen.

In 1877 R. B. Angus and Scots-born George Stephen (1829-1921, later Lord Mount Stephen), president of the Bank of Montreal, travelled to Chicago on Bank business, along with Donald Alexander Smith (1820-1914), who later became Lord Strathcona and Mount Royal. On impulse, they continued on to St. Paul, Minnesota to meet Ontario-born railwayman James J. Hill, known as "The Empire Builder" for his creation of the St. Paul, Minneapolis and Manitoba Railway. They turned that railway into the profitable Great Northern. The depression of 1873 had hit America hard, and emigration on an unprecedented scale had created the need for mass transportation and settlement. Having witnessed the states of Illinois and Iowa grow from prairie to developed communities, they envisioned a similar potential for the Canadian West and Midwest, following the construction of a Canadian transcontinental railway.

In 1879 R. B. Angus resigned from the Bank of Montreal, and along with others, bought out Dutch interests in the St. Paul, Minneapolis and Manitoba Railway. He then moved to St. Paul for a two-year period, assuming the position of vice-president of the Railway. This successful business venture provided him with a considerable fortune.

Never a political opportunist — nominally Conservative, in fact — Angus nonetheless joined in 1880, along with George Stephen, Donald Alexander Smith and Duncan McIntyre, the syndicate whose task it was to build the CPR under the tenure of the first Canadian prime minister, conservative Sir John A. Macdonald. The contract was awarded to those financial and organizational experts who underwrote the CPR with their profits from the St. Paul, Minneapolis and Manitoba investment, which further enhanced their fortunes. Under Macdonald's national policy of Canadian tariff protection, the building of a transcontinental railway would promote large-scale immigration to the West. "The Railway would promote east-west trade, while the growing population of the West would provide the necessary markets for Canadian manufactured goods and a ready source of raw materials for the growing industries of central Canada".[3] James J. Hill recommended William Cornelius Van Horne (1843-1915) of Milwaukee as builder of the Railway; Van Horne was director-general during its construction period, Stephen the first president, and Angus, the vice-president.

As planned, the Railway created a physical link between the different regions of the country, forging the social and geographical connection between east and west. Angus's management of the Railway has become part of the history of the American and Canadian Northwest. His enlightened policy of settlement and industrial expansion, with strategically placed Bank of Montreal branches, expanded the capitalization of both the Bank and the CPR. After completion of the CPR in 1885, R. B. Angus continued to contribute to its development, acting as director until his death.

To build a fine house has always been one of the first impulses of the rich. Once their fortunes were consolidated, and political and patriarchal hegemony assured, in the 1880s these railroad magnates built pretentious mansions that heralded the plutocracy they espoused. George Stephen built his sumptuous home on Drummond Street in Montreal from 1880-1883 (now the Mount Stephen Club); R. B. Angus began "240 Drummond" in 1882; Van Horne, who had purchased John Hamilton's home on Sherbrooke and Stanley Streets in 1889, began modifying it in 1890 (it was demolished in 1973). Donald Smith's Scottish baronial home on Dorchester Boulevard near Fort Street was enlarged in 1885 and 1887-1888 by Hutchison & Steele, and demolished in 1941. Duncan McIntyre constructed his home in 1889 on the east side of Drummond Street, near Pine Avenue (demolished about 1930).[4]

In 1910, at age eighty-two, Angus returned to the Bank of Montreal as president; he had been the youngest general manager and was now the oldest president that the Bank had ever had. He retired from the presidency in 1913, but remained active in various companies, especially the CPR which named the Angus Shops after him in 1904. When Angus died in 1922 at the age of ninety-one, he was the last survivor of the original CPR syndicate.

THE HOMES AND RESIDENCES
By the middle of the nineteenth century, private fortunes were being built through profits made possible by the industrial revolution in rail and shipping. Wealth from land, natural resources, trade and finance resulted in the stratification of society. The parvenu, described by Americans Edith Wharton and Henry James, was distinguished from the nobility by "conspicuous consumption", a term coined by Thorstein Veblen to characterize his attitudes and behaviour. For those émigrés whose course had been more or less preordained, progress came about in an even more predictable manner.

Angus's systematic rise to fortune can be traced in his numerous changes of living quarters, according to status earned through position, salary, and a Victorian desire for mobility and material expansion: from rooms probably rented in a lodging-house in the downtown area close to the Bank of Montreal in the early emigration period, to the commissioning of city and country residences from established Canadian architects in the 1880s and at the turn of the century.

From 1860 to 1861, while a clerk at the Bank of Montreal, R. B. Angus lived with his wife and their first-born child, Edith (1858-1907), in low-income housing for the working-class in a mixed-income area on Aylmer Street. We can assume that they lived in the lower flat on the right-hand side of a brick or stone fourplex. As he rose to assistant accountant at the Bank of Montreal from 1861 to 1862, Angus and his wife moved to Richmond Place, St-Antoine

Street, with their new family member, Maud Mary (1860-1946), in what was considered an upper-class district situated north of Richmond Street, west of Guy Street and south of St-Antoine Street – before the CPR literally relegated this area (now Little Burgundy) to the wrong side of the tracks. After their return from Chicago and New York City, from 1864 to 1865, when Angus was assistant manager at the Bank of Montreal, the family lived at 12 City Councillors Street, with infants Kate Jane (1862-1870) and Bertha (1864-1949), in a small, modest single-family residence. The appointment of Angus as interim manager from 1865 to 1868 necessitated yet another move to 32 City Councillors Street (1 Clyde Terrace), a single-family dwelling in a row of five houses in a substantially middle-class area. Here, Donald Forbes (1866-1943) and Elspeth Hudson (1868-1938) were added to the growing family.[5]

The oldest Montreal versions of attached two-storey houses, the brick duplex containing one flat on each floor, often built in pairs, were based on a style which originated in Scotland. Victorian duplexes were erected in Montreal in the 1860s, and today about eighty percent of Montrealers still live in joined dwellings.[6]

According to David B. Hanna, the well-to-do of the Victorian era espoused an attitude which was the exact opposite to their modern counterparts: they rented their living premises until they were fabulously wealthy and had accumulated enough capital to buy a home without a mortgage, employing a property manager to run the necessary daily affairs.[7]

Unfortunately no photographs exist of Angus's substantial landscaped detached brick-on-stone house and stables on Ontario Avenue (now avenue du Musée), where the family resided in the 1870s when he was general manager of the Bank of Montreal. The collection of family photographs in albums may have been only of slight interest for the Anguses, as none seem to have survived. One daughter, Kate, had died prematurely in 1870, but the births of Margaret Forrest (1871-1956), William Forrest (1873-1951) and David James (1875-1948) completed the family unit, and all were comfortably sheltered in this spacious home. Plans for a conservatory, made in 1876 by architects John W. Hopkins and Daniel B. Wily, are indicative of Mrs. Angus's great interest in horticulture.

"240 DRUMMOND"

> "We are taking advantage of the sleighing to lay down stone for the foundations of our proposed new house and we have just begun to study the plans".[8]

R. B. Angus's three-storey home, located at 3450 Drummond Street, known as "240 Drummond" even when it was later renumbered several times as of the late twenties, was situated between Sherbrooke Street West and McGregor Avenue (now Docteur Penfield), and stretched from Drummond to Mountain Streets. The home and stables were constructed by architects John William Hopkins (1825-1905) and D. B. Wily in 1883-1884 and the house was "opened" in 1885. It was intact and still in the hands of the Angus family until 1945.[9]

By the early 1880s, wealthy Montrealers such as R. B. Angus moved away from the inner city to the area bounded by Dorchester Boulevard to the south, Mount Royal to the north, Bleury Street and Park Avenue to the east, and Guy Street and Côte des Neiges Road to the west. "The district came to

142
Charles L. Baker
The Angus house, also known as
"240 Drummond", Montreal, 1943
Photograph
Frederick F. Angus collection

be known as the Square Mile (since the 1930s) and the Golden Square Mile (since the 1950s) although it is unlikely either name was used during the neighbourhood's golden age".[10]

John William Hopkins was born and served his articles of clerkship in Liverpool. He emigrated to Canada in 1852 and settled in Montreal. In 1890, at age sixty-five, Hopkins assumed the presidency of the newly-formed Quebec Order of Architects, having reached his glory-days in the 1870s as a Canadian architect well-versed in the Victorian eclectic tradition, with stores, public buildings and clubs, commercial buildings such as banks and insurance companies, and private residences all to his credit. Before he accepted the Angus commission for "240 Drummond", Hopkins had already designed the Crystal Palace on St. Catherine Street in 1860, St. Paul's Church of Scotland on Dorchester Street (until it merged with St. Andrew's Church in 1920), and the first Art Association of Montreal building on Phillips Square with architect D. B. Wily in 1879, along with other prestigious undertakings. Furthermore, J. W. Hopkins had previously been under contract to the Bank of Montreal. In 1876 Hopkins had also built the conservatory for Angus's Ontario Avenue home, and further research may reveal the house plans to be possibly by his hand as well.

"240 Drummond", R. B. Angus's romantic, baronial home, loosely based on the Vanderbilt mansion in New York, featured polychromatic Scottish red brick, with Scottish beige cut sandstone trim for the main cornices, windows with Tudor lapels and carved Tudor rose drip-stones, window consoles and string courses. Local greystone was designated for the base course and stairs extending to the first storey. Slate was appointed for the roof and copper for the finials. In the spirit of architectural Revivalism, the architects aimed at duplication of a style and a "lifestyle". This home featured combinations and free interpretations of British architect Richard Norman Shaw (1831-1912) and Romanesque Revival architecture, incorporating fashionable Flemish gables and a romantic conical medieval tower. A conservatory faced west,

143
Inner doors of the vestibule of 240 Drummond Street, Montreal, about 1884
Oak, glass, copper and lead,
258.5 x 229.4 x 16 cm
Canadian Museum of Civilization, Hull, gift of Mary W. Angus (A-6316 a-d)
Photo Christine Guest / MMFA

and a sun room faced the river to the south. A coach-house was entered via the Drummond Street approach.

Richard Norman Shaw's functional yet distinctly modern type of domestic architecture, known as Queen Anne Revival, was often based on the Dutch and Queen Anne architectural styles of the sixteenth and seventeenth centuries. Houses in this style often feature "asymmetrical compositions of verandahs, corner towers, projecting wings with a great variety of window types, capped by steep and complicated roofs of dormers, intersecting gables, and conical roofs".[11] Leslie Maitland concluded that Canadian architects and their clients turned the Queen Anne Revival style compatibly Canadian by adapting it to the climate, materials, landscape and culture. It was a comfortable residence designed according to the plan, the exterior appearance subordinated to the interior arrangement, harmony combined with contrast between the various features of the house and its surroundings.

The entrance of "240 Drummond" faced south toward the river, the Drummond Street front being in reality the side elevation. The prominent front gable included a Richardsonian Romanesque (American architect Henry Hobson Richardson, 1838-1886) round-arched portal surround, whose piers incorporated pillars of polished red granite with Tudor rose capitals, and a tympanum with carved beige sandstone Tudor rose reliefs. The main door was carved in oak in the medieval linenfold pattern. The inner door leading to the hallway had a double-door and side panels of stained glass set within dark oak frames, and a wood carving in dark oak fit into a segmental frame over the glass, whose subject was ornately-carved dragons. A centrally placed plant figure allowed the side lights a degree of compositional self-sufficiency with a highly abstract geometrical pattern.[12]

There were bay windows, and a balcony over a bay window is mentioned in the architects' account books. Dormer windows were used for the third storey, sash windows for the second, and Art Nouveau glass was inserted into the transoms on the ground floor. A narrow, ornamental verandah with ironwork was situated over the front entrance. Architectural ornamentation included beige sandstone bas-reliefs of intertwined roses and thistles on the chimney breast and beige sandstone Tudor roses as friezes, the thistle symbolizing Angus's heritage, and the rose for his English wife.

Along with its elaborate entrance porch and adjacent cloak room, also with stained glass windows, the house contained a generous front hall with a drawing room to the left and a library to the right. On the first floor was a breakfast room, a billiard room and numerous bedrooms.

Architectural woodwork for the interior included wainscotting, a main staircase with carved baluster, handrail and newel post; cornices and architraves, doors and column plinths; mantles for various rooms including the library, for which built-in bookcases were especially designed by the architects. Panelling was used on the three storeys: dark oak for the first floor, light maple as wainscotting for the second floor, and still lighter panelling for the third. For the first storey, the Tudor rose was continued as a decorative motif for ceiling friezes in dark oak, while Tudor roses in painted wood as friezes again decorated the second storey ceilings. Mahogany was used as panelling and for bookcases in the library.

After R. B. Angus died in 1922, nine years after his wife, the home went to their oldest son, Donald Forbes. In 1943, photographs of the exterior, the hall and the library were taken as a souvenir by his widow, Mary Henshaw Angus (1868-1959), before the home was sold. "240 Drummond" was demolished in the summer of 1960.

While the philosophy of interior decoration during the late 1870s and 1880s was still based upon historical roots, styles were mixed more harmoniously even in cases where functionalism was combined with the irregular balance of the Picturesque. There was a greater concerted collaborative effort on the part of architect and craftsman to create a more cohesive decorative result. And while the woman's influence in the home was certain, in the case of Mary Anne Angus, it was hard to detect.

Accessories in the home were meant to educate as well as to adorn; even the fine arts of painting and sculpture were often treated as accessories possessing narrative and didactic functions. The interior of "240 Drummond" featured a mélange of artefacts which incorporated such diverse accoutrements as Turkish, Persian and Chinese carpets, Chinese Ming and Japanese Imari porcelains, Japanese prints and silk scroll paintings, Persian and Indian miniatures, Greek Tanagra figures, Turkish ceramics from Iznik, Italian and

144
Charles L. Baker
Hall and Stairway
(view of the wall to the right), 1943
Photograph
Frederick F. Angus Collection

Armless hall bench with Italianate panelled frame, on castors, upholstered in damask, with loose silk cushions. Oak stair wainscotting continuing to the second storey. The plant foliage in the foreground hides a carved newel-post with the head and body of a lion, designed by Edward Maxwell in 1898 when the stairway was altered and its risers were lowered. On the stairway wall are a series of five paintings by the Scottish painter, Noel Joseph Paton (1821-1901). *The Lowrie Dens of Yarrow*, while the painting on the uppermost part of the wall cannot be identified. The *Portrait of Mary Henshaw Angus* (1868-1959) of R. B. Angus's daughter-in-law, wife of Donald Forbes Angus, who inherited "240 Drummond" when R. B. Angus's wife, Mary Anne Angus died in 1913, is the work of the French-born portrait painter of the English School, Alphonse Jongers (1872-1945). The conversion of the home from gas to electricity probably commenced tentatively, which perhaps explains the curious choice of a globe surrounded by incandescent bulbs.

Hispano-moresque majolicas, Delftware, and most importantly, Angus's eclectic painting collection, along with English Jacobean and eighteenth-century furniture, French Louis XV and Louis XVI furniture, and even a chair of "pseudo-Egyptian" style. Some of these paintings, works on paper, and deorative art objects were given to the Montreal Museum of Fine Arts as gifts or bequests,[13] in some instances from family descendants.

In the entrance hall, over the second-floor landing at the top of the dark oak panelled staircase with an ornate oak Italianate bannister (Edward Maxwell lowered the steep stair risers in 1898), was a window of stained glass panels, based upon Alfred Tennyson's *The Lady of Shallott*, depicting the imprisoned heroine who watches and waits for a lover who may never arrive, a theme dear to the Pre-Raphaelites.[14]

On the back window wall of the hallway, a frame was created for a panelled screen of eight landscape scenes of Scotland painted on glass panels, dated 1693, divided in the centre by leaded glass panels, each with a different floral motif possibly of William Morris origin. Angus's nostalgia for his homeland presumably motivated this acquisition, which he made either directly, or through Cottier and Company.

On the stairway lit by sumptuous gas lamps, the *Portrait of Mary Henshaw Angus*, by the popular French-born portrait painter of the English School, Alphonse Jongers (1872-1945) — who had arrived in America in 1897 and worked in Montreal — displays an aesthetic impulse absorbed from English portrait painting.

The library featured a small semi-circular mahogany writing table and chair of Victorian vintage, crafted by an expert but unknown cabinetmaker. These pieces fit nicely into the recess on the first storey created by the tower, beneath a cornice of what seems to be brass metal openwork with classical foliate design, probably the work of the same metal craftsmen who had made the brass fireplace hood, fender and owl andirons. As in the entrance hall, tapestries covered the wall above the dado, and the ceiling was of plain gold leaf set within coffered panels. Alphonse Jongers's companion *Portrait of Donald Forbes Angus* hung over the mantle. When Donald Forbes took possession of the house in 1922, Jongers's works were placed in the library and on the staircase, respectively. To that painting's left was a landscape by Welsh artist Richard Wilson (1814-1882). On the opposite wall, centred over a mahogany bookcase designed by the architects, was the French Barbizon painter Jules Dupré's (1812-1889) landscape, *A Stormy Sea*. The mahogany built-in bookcases and library mantle were designed by Hopkins and Wily and, according to Frederick F. Angus, likely made by carvers in the Hochelaga Workshops of the CPR. As status symbols, railroad cars were unsurpassed and CPR carvers might have taken on outside contracts.

In the dining room, lincrusta was used for the ceiling in panels of gold Art Nouveau configurations on a dark-green ground, set within coffered panels with the Tudor rose at each corner, in another tone of gold on a lighter green ground and a Tudor rose frieze between the wall and ceiling. The dining room was furnished in the eighteenth-century English Georgian style and included a handsome George III mahogany sideboard, a Georgian dining room table and Chippendale-style mahogany chairs. Imported Spode porcelain was used as a dinner service, probably set on a table base of linens typical of the period. Venetian amber glass was etched with the initials R.B.A. and similarly monogrammed Regency silver was selected as flatware.

The drawing room at "240 Drummond" was decorated in the spirit of the Second Empire. Extant furnishings include neoclassical Louis XVI bergères, a Second Empire cabinet of black lacquer, marquetry and gilt, and a hinged curio table with a glass top – probably specifically designed for Angus's collection of Japanese swords and *tsuba* (sword-guards), whose blades were usually signed. Bronze figurative sculptures on pedestals included *The Gleaners*, by French sculptor Étienne-Henry Dumaige (1830-1888), and a bronze *Cleopatra and Attendants* by an unknown sculptor, mounted on a marble base. Angus also collected Italian Renaissance majolica and Islamic plates to adorn his walls; it was fashionable to hang these dishes around the borders of the ceiling. Eighteenth-century Dutch Delft vases, Chinese seventeenth-eighteenth century sang-de-bœuf vases and scent bottles, many now in the collection of the Montreal Museum of Fine Arts, originally in the city residence of R. B. Angus, were probably decoratively placed over mantles or chests.

PINE BLUFF, SUMMER RESIDENCE OF R. B. ANGUS
In its form and ideology, Pine Bluff, the Angus country residence on Bout-de-l'Isle (Senneville), facing Lake St. Louis (in the area now known as the West Island), built by father-and-son architects J. W. and E. C. Hopkins in 1886-1887, corresponded in spirit to American landscape architect Andrew Jackson Downing's (1815-1852) vision of the simple life in a rural setting for a country gentleman. The summer home thus reflected the urge for blissful domesticity and the growing vogue in hygiene, informed by the Wordsworthian beneficial effects of nature and clear air.

Pine Bluff was built in the Shingle Style, a country style popular around 1880, according to American art historian Vincent Scully, as the Americanization of the Queen Anne style, characterized by shingled surfaces.

145
Charles L. Baker
Library of 240 Drummond Street, Montreal, 1943
Photograph
Frederick F. Angus Collection

In the late nineteenth century the Shingle Style bordered Montreal's rivers and lakes, as well as the Atlantic seaboard.[15]

Pine Bluff burned to the ground in 1899 and, while photographs of the exterior do exist, it is impossible to reconstruct that home's contents. In 1901 R. B. Angus requested Edward Maxwell to clear the debris and to build a new home over the site.[16]

CHÂTEAU ANGUS

Château Angus, the second Pine Bluff completed in 1902, is an example of late-Victorian Edwardian mansions (Edward VII, 1901-1910) which bespoke the feudal castle, reflecting the changing countryside in an age of capitalist transformation. This "faux" château was built by Edward Maxwell in ashlar masonry with the main concerns, logically, being fireproofing and solidity. By this time, furthermore, a French château for a country cottage represented the ultimate in aesthetic leisure in the architecture of capitalism. This immense architectural project, which cost Angus $128,007.83, included specially designed furniture and fittings, carpets and curtains. Let it be recalled that there was no income tax until 1916, and even then it was considered but a temporary measure of the Robert Borden conservative government.

Sometime before 1910 R. B. Angus had his own steam launch, the *Namo*, and he was an early owner of the new locomobile of about 1910. The estate included stables, a potting house, greenhouses, a gardener's cottage, a peach house, an ice house, a hen house and an outhouse on the grounds. There were also boathouses, a windmill, a gate lodge, a garage, a laundry and some cottages. The grounds were entrusted to the renowned American landscape architect Frederick Law Olmstead, Jr. (1870-1957), who worked on the property from August 1899 to November 1900. In 1902, after the fire and the building of the new Maxwell house in Senneville, he did more work for Angus.[17] Unfortunately, no photographs exist of Olmstead's landscaping.

146
Notman Studio, Montreal
Pine Bluff, The R. B. Angus summer residence, Bout-de-l'isle (Senneville), 1887, by John William (1825-1905) and E. C. (active in Montreal 1870-1896) Hopkins.
McCord Museum of Canadian history, Montréal, Notman photographic archives (MP171/81)
A wide verandah continued around the entire house, including the entrance portico. Roses in urns flanked lakefront and side entrances, announcing Mrs. Angus's great interest in horticulture. This two-storeyed home countained on the first floor, a spacious hall that opened to the drawing room with a bay window affording a lakefront view, and to the dining room, the latter adjoining the pantry and servants' quarters located next to the kitchen, situated at the far end of the first floor. On the second storey, in the central hall area, generous walls were provided as picture gallery space for R. B. Angus's painting collection. There was a master bedroom with a balcony for the view of the lake, and adjacent dressing room. On this floor were six other bedrooms and servants'room, a commodious bathroom, and numerous fireplaces.

The interior design of Château Angus bore no relation to the architectural style used for the exterior, which was less refined. The architect was responsible for the classicizing mood evoked by the Palladian double stairway with its ample landing. Maxwell drew from such historical sources as the English Neoclassical tradition, from Anglo-American and Canadian sources, the William Morris craft tradition, and the sinewy lines and shapes of Art Nouveau. In so doing, he echoed the more systematic selectivity of the 1890s and turn of the century, championed by the Paris-trained architects who had come under the influence of the École des Beaux-Arts principles. Richard B. Angus died in that elaborate home in 1922, and Château Angus was demolished in the early 1950s.

The amassing of works of art by Montrealers such as R. B. Angus, and the sumptuous homes they built to accommodate these collections, bespeak the aspirations of the select group who cultivated these ideals at the turn of the century. Angus's homes were repositories for the art he collected, whose themes probably destined their logical sites: seascapes and landscapes for country home walls, and old masters and portraits for the city home. From the 1880s, he began to bestow princely gifts on numerous causes, confirming his triumph as both a patriot and a benefactor. His earliest gifts to the Art Association of Montreal date from 1879, the year the first Art Association of Montreal was built, on Phillips Square.

Gloria Lesser

147
Edward (1867-1923) and W. S. Maxwell (1874-1952)
Perspective view for the main house of the Richard B. Angus estate, Senneville, 1903
Watercolour and graphite on wave paper, 44,4 x 72.6 cm
McGill University, Montreal, Maxwell Archive
Photo Brigitte Ostiguy

The new cut-stone villa, in the château style, had a rigorously symmetrical façade and turrets flanking the main entrance.

147

1   *Montreal Pictorial and Biographical* (Montreal: S. J. Clarke Publishing Company, 1914), p. 8.

2   Acknowledgment must be made of the considerable assistance provided by Frederick F. Angus, great-grandson of R. B. Angus in the preparation of this essay. He contributed many of the photographs, as well as providing much of the interpretation of the material for the text. Much of the detail and accuracy of the text and captions may be attributed to his personal interest.

3   Craig Brown, "The Nationalism of the National Policy" in R. Douglas Francis and Donald B. Smith, *Readings in Canadian History: Post-Confederation* (Toronto: Holt, Rinehart and Winston, 1990), p. 35.

4   See Christina Cameron, "Domestic Interiors: Parks Canada's Designated Houses in Québec", *The Canadian Collector* 20 (1985), pp. 51-55. Martin Eidelberg, "The Canadian Connection: Parisian Art Nouveau Designer Edward Colonna Spent Much of His Life in North America", *The Canadian Collector* 19 (1984), pp. 22-24. Allan Pringle, "William Cornelius Van Horne: Art Director, Canadian Pacific Railway", *Journal of Canadian Art History* 8 (1984), pp. 50-78. François Rémillard and Brian Merrett, *Mansions of the Golden Square Mile: Montreal 1850-1930* (Montreal: Méridien, 1986). Service de la planification du territoire de la Communauté urbaine de Montréal, *Répertoire d'architecture traditionnelle sur le territoire de la Communauté urbaine de Montréal: architecture domestique 1. Les résidences* (Montreal, 1987).

5   Thanks to David B. Hanna, Professor of Urban Geography, Université du Québec à Montréal, for assistance in the interpretation of Goad, Pinsoneault and Hopkins atlases and City of Montreal assessment rolls.

6   The exhibition *Domicile: Montreal*, held in Montreal's Vieux Port from June 22 to September 2, 1990 concentrated on the history of Montreal's joined dwellings. See Henry Lehmann's review in *The Gazette* (Montreal), July 21, 1990.

7   Communication from David B. Hanna, to Gloria Lesser, September 10, 1990.

8   Letter from R. B. Angus to his son Donald Forbes Angus at school in Leamington, England, March 12, 1882. Montreal, private collection of Frederick F. Angus.

9   Bibliothèque de la Ville de Montréal, salle Gagnon. Account book for the Montreal office of John W. Hopkins and his partner D. B. Wily from 1873-1895. Lot 101. Dated 1882 and 1883, ledger nos. 121, 122, 125.

10   Joshua Wolfe, "Whole of Square Mile District Deserves Protection", *The Gazette* (Montreal), July 18, 1987.

11   Leslie Maitland, "Queen Anne Revival: A 19th Century Essentially British Style Became Comfortably Canadian", *The Canadian Collector* 21 (1986), p. 48.

12   The entire door frame and glass are in the collection of the Canadian Museum of Civilization, Hull, as a gift of Mary W. Angus, 1975.

13   According to Ruth Jackson, former curator of Decorative Arts, the Montreal Museum of Fine Arts, in conversation with the author, the Mrs. Charles F. Martin bequest in 1956 [Margaret Angus Martin] was the most important of the family bequests.

14   Further research may perhaps attribute these panels to William Morris.

15   France Gagnon Pratte, *Country Houses for Montrealers, 1892-1924: The Architecture of E. and W. S. Maxwell* (Montreal: Méridien, 1987).

16   For a photograph, refer to Désiré Girouard, *Lake St. Louis Old and New* (Montreal: Poirier, Bessette, 1893).

17   No drawings were deposited in the long Library of Congress file in Washington D.C. Refer to Library of Congress, Manuscript Division, Olmstead Associates Inc., B. 23, Job no. 214 and B. 35, Job no. 440.

CHANGES IN THE SOCIO-PROFESSIONAL STATUS AND THE PROPERTIES OF MONTREALER RICHARD B. ANGUS

	POSITIONS HELD	YEARLY SALARY AND ALLOWANCE	RESIDENCES	YEARLY RENT OF PROPERTIES
1857	Bank Clerk, the Bank of Montreal (BM)	$600		
1858	Assistant accountant (BM)	$850		
1860	Bank clerk (BM)	$1,000	43, Aylmer (fourplex)	$120 (rental value)
1861		$1,200 + $400	3, Richmond Place, St. Antoine	$180
1861-1863	Chicago, accountant for BM	$2,000		
1863-1864	New York City, second-class agent for BM	$2,400		
1864	Assistant manager (BM)		12 City Councillors Street (small single-family residence)	$300
1865	Interim manager (BM)	from $2,800 + $800 in 1865 to $5,000 + $1,000 in 1867	32 City Councillors (1 Clyde Terrace) (single-family dwelling in a row of 5 units)	$300
1868	General manager (BM)	$8,000	Great St. James Street (quarters in the BM)	$500
1872		from $9,000 + $1,000 in 1872 to $15,000 + $1,200 in 1873	27 Ontario Avenue (detached home)	$24,000 (property value)
1876-1879	Leaves the service of the BM in 1879	$25,000		$30,000 (including new conservatory)
1879-1881	In St. Paul, Minnesota, vice-president of a railway company			
1881	Canadian Pacific Railway Incorporated (CPR)		21 Côte-des-Neiges Road (detached home)	$800 (rental value)
1882	Second vice-president (CPR)			
1884-1922	Vice-president (CPR) in 1886; Director (CPR) (1888-1915) President (CPR) (1911-1915)		240, Drummond (detached home and stables) (J.W. Hopkins and D.B. Wily, architects)	$75,000
1886			Pine Bluff (summer residence) [built in Senneville by J.W. and E.C. Hopkins, architects; burns in 1901]	
1903			Château Angus (new summer residence on the site of Pine Bluff [Edward Maxwell, architect]	

THE DRAWING ROOM

WHEN THE WORD *SALON*, FROM THE ITALIAN *SALONE*, first appeared in France in the seventeenth century, it was used to describe a very different room from the one familiar to us today. This two-storey-high apartment of impressive size was divided in the early eighteenth century into two rooms called "the company salon" and "the family salon". As it lost its stately connotations during the second half of the eighteenth century, the salon spread to other classes of society and acquired a very specific function, gradually becoming a room kept exclusively for entertaining guests.

In his *Dictionnaire de la décoration*, published in Paris in 1890, which studies the origins of different rooms in the house together with fabrics, furniture and other aspects of interior decoration, Henri Havard clearly defined the role of the salon under the heading "apartment":

> Today, in terms of rented accommodation, the word "apartment" is more specifically used to designate a group of rooms for lodging but not for entertaining. An apartment, therefore, never includes a salon.[1]

Although the function of the salon remained fixed in France, such was not the case in England and the United States, where the division of the space into two sections radically influenced the development of the room. In England the salon or drawing room was more influenced by the "family salon", a more comfortably furnished room in which people could read and work, whereas in the United States, where the double influence was felt, the drawing room was used either as a richly decorated reception room or as a more relaxed and informal space.

In late-eighteenth-century Europe the drawing room and those who used it had evolved considerably, as had its function. In Quebec, however, drawing rooms were rarely found, and almost exclusively in the homes of the upper classes. Contrary to the practice elsewhere, this room was not kept just for visitors and formal gatherings; in fact, it remained a multifunctional space until the activities it was used for were moved to other rooms in the house. In short, before the Victorian era only the upper classes were able to afford a house big enough to keep one room solely for visitors. For ordinary people,

148
The Parlour Kitchen 50 Years Hence
Engraving after a drawing by E. Jump
published in the *Canadian Illustrated News*,
January 4, 1873
National Archives of Canada, Ottawa (C-58959)

the drawing room or parlour could still be the bedroom, the dining room or the study as well. This is clear from the sofas with pillows and bedspreads, the "dining tables", sideboards and desks so often found in this all-purpose room. In some country houses this was the case until the very end of the nineteenth century. Thus, in the house of Johnny Désilets, a farmer of the parish of Notre-Dame du Mont-Carmel, the "salon" housed a commode and a bedstead with its mattress next to a mirror, a table and small vases, all standing on a wool carpet with a red flower pattern and two checked runners, together with four paper blinds and two muslin half-curtains.[2]

The upper classes, committed to the rules and proprieties of Victorian etiquette, considered the practice of entertaining, eating and sleeping in the same room as unforgivably ill-bred, like entertaining one's guests in the kitchen. This was the attitude ironically portrayed by the cartoonist of the *Canadian Illustrated News* in a drawing sub-titled "The Parlour Kitchen 50 Years Hence".[3] Gradually going down the social scale, the parlour did not reach the homes of the lower classes — city workmen and small farmers — until the very end of Victoria's reign.

It should be kept in mind that in Victorian Quebec this room was variously called, in French and in English, the *chambre de compagnie*, the *salle d'entrée*, the *parloir*, the *salon*, the drawing room, the living room, the sitting room or the parlour! Thus the best-appointed and most luxurious room in the house took on the various European names for its functions. Eventually usage became restricted to one term — the drawing room or parlour — which corresponded to the more restricted use that was made of the room.

Many after-death inventories make it plain that in Quebec it was only very slowly that the room began to be reserved for a special use,[4] and that the words "drawing room" and "parlour" came into general usage.[5] Indeed, it was not until halfway through Victoria's reign that this room was kept solely for visitors and for big family gatherings. Although houses were now being designed to divide family from servants and to create specific spaces for specific functions, the drawing room or parlour was for decades a multifunctional room, even when it was decked with the latest innovations in the way of furnishings and decoration.

A SHOWCASE ROOM

In Europe and elsewhere, literary men and women such as Jules Simon and Louise D'Alq saw the need for devoting their talent to composing manuals on good manners and the proprieties in order to help people to behave correctly in society. These handbooks, which explained in detail the prevailing etiquette in "good society", did not deal only with matters such as how many guests to invite to a given occasion or the protocol to be observed for each occasion. They were also ethical guides that touched on subjects as diverse as tolerance, economics, religion, the upbringing of children, wifely duties and so on.[6]

Such books were even more necessary since, as a way of laying claim to superior social standing, everyone wanted to have a drawing room, even if it turned out expensive and was only sporadically used.

In a revealing publication entitled *La comédie du feu*, Louise D'Alq, the French authority in matters of etiquette,[7] insisted that it was foolish to have such a room unless one had the means to make proper use of it.

> An exaggerated politeness towards visitors, which tends towards unmannerliness, is frequently seen now that everyone has to have a drawing room, although they do not use it and skimp on the most vital things: thus we have the comedy of lighting the fire. It's winter, and you arrive numb with cold, especially if you

---

THE PARLOUR

Over all the furnishings the dust holds sway,
The Venetian mirrors have shed their charm;
There lingers still, like old Parmese perfume,
The bitter sweetness of a long-known sachet.

And never more across the silence flow
Piano tunes in a rhythmic lullaby;
Mozart and Mendelssohn, wed in sweet harmony,
Are but heard in dreams in sleepy evening's glow.

But the poet, wandering in gross ennui,
Opening windows to the night's clear force,
Alone, fists clenched, and with the wildest glance

Suddenly imagines, haunted by remorse,
A solemn great ball, evolved from fantasy,
Where he thought he saw his dead parents dance.

Émile Nelligan*

* "Le salon", from *Poésies complètes 1896-1899* (Montreal and Paris: Fides, Collection du nénuphar, 1952), p. 89. Translation from *The Complete Poems of Émile Nelligan*, collected and translated by Fred Cogswell (Montreal: Harvest House Ltd., 1983), p. 24.

have come in a carriage. You politely leave your coat or your furs in the entrance hall; and the maid leads you into a drawing room with no fire burning. The lady of the house comes shivering out of her bedroom, which is heated to a bare thirty-five degrees [Fahrenheit]. "What! Hasn't the fire been lit yet? But I gave orders for it to be done!" she exclaims, pretending to be surprised and making a show of going towards the bell pull. You demur: "Please, don't put yourself out for me; I'm in a hurry, and only have time to say hello." "Really? You're in a hurry? What a pity! It would have been so agreeable to have a chat with you! I must certainly order the fire to be lit." Another gesture towards the bell pull. [...] You leave, having caught a chill and feeling furious with your friend, while she goes back inside to warm herself up in comfort, somewhat annoyed by your visit, which caught her out in flagrante delicto, economizing. [...] If we can't offer a comfortable drawing room, then let us dispense with it, and entertain our visitors in the dining room or bedroom. But this is advice that no-one will follow. Lighting the fires every day in several rooms of an apartment is also expensive [...]".[8]

Louise D'Alq was not alone in deploring the unbridled appetite for showy décor and extravagance; many authors, including the famous Sarah Ellis,[9] who wrote for middle-class women, warned their readers against "the ease with which luxury is becoming available to everybody."[10]

A debate arose between interior decorators and purveyors of every kind of novelty on the one hand and the arbiters of good taste and restraint on the other. The resultant polemic raged furiously and sometimes bitterly until the early twentieth century. Every nuance in expressing beauty and elegance was invoked, instructing the new rich and reminding the hereditarily wealthy about errors in taste and propriety. It was, indeed, the old confrontation between wealth and good breeding. As Mrs. Ellis wrote:

> If our supreme desire is to cut a good figure in the eyes of the world by behaving according to generally held notions, the arrangement of our homes will be such as to display to our friends and acquaintances everything that can give them an inflated idea of our standards of luxury and elegance; if, however, our goal is to achieve for ourselves and those around us the maximum of true happiness, we shall have to follow a very different path. It is from the latter point of view that the following chapter is written; those who choose to adopt the other system have only to consult a silversmith or a furniture dealer.[11]

This debate, which began on the other side of the Atlantic, was closely followed in North America. Linked by both language and culture to France, England and its neighbours to the south, Quebec soon adopted the styles, fashions, etiquette and comportment necessary for a "proper" drawing room. This room was, it must be remembered, the most important one in the Victorian *bourgeois* home, and nothing was left undone that might enhance and embellish it. Visitors to the drawing room had to comport themselves with propriety, just as the furnishings and decoration had to conform exactly to the social status of its owners.

> After accepting as one of her primary duties the need to ascertain the precise position she holds in society, and to strive to live up to it, a woman should think seriously about the means she must employ to achieve this end.[12]

149
Notman Studio, Montreal
Mrs. Vaughan's drawing room,
Montreal, 1893
Photograph
McCord Museum of Canadian History, Montreal,
Notman Photographic Archives (100,243 Misc-II)

The increasing number of drawing rooms, the excesses of interior decoration, and the new ability of the middle classes to purchase decorative objects: all these trends constituted a challenge to the elegance and luxury that had traditionally characterized the drawing rooms of the upper classes. So etiquette books insisted on moderation, discretion and restraint, in an attempt to re-establish the distinction between the *bourgeoisie* and the *nouveaux riches*.

These books were written especially for the wife who, as lady of the house, held sway over the drawing room which she herself had designed from start to finish.

> A drawing room, in the usual acceptation of the term, is substantially a lady's room. It is there she presides and reigns supreme as mistress of the mansion and queen of her company. As a rule, she fills it with articles of bijouterie and knick-knacks — articles which ladies of taste are sure to admire. Rare cabinets, beautiful and exquisite receptacles for everything and for nothing; shells, mounted in gold and ormolu, etc.; easy chairs, couches, ottomans, and every appliance for elegant comfort and cosy chat. The style of its decorations should be in accordance with its general aspect when in use — light, cheerful and rich.[13]

As well as being responsible for furnishing and decorating the salon appropriately, a wife had the duty of organizing and directing the activities which took place there. She had therefore to bring together a group of people who would not only validate her husband's standing but also gain for her a certain reputation.

> The drawing room is the ladies' instrument, and it is there that they must reign supreme. A husband may be a good advisor, but from the wings; while the performance is going on, he is simply a bit player, at most a stage manager. The wife is the star turn. Some ladies hold such paltry receptions in their drawing rooms that one goes there as if to hard labour, and only because one must.

THE USERS

150
In the Drawing Room
Engraving published in *Country Patterns 1841-1883*, Donald J. Berg (ed.), (Pittstown, New Jersey: The Main Street Press, 1986), p. 113
Photo SRP

Other ladies resort to recitations or music. When the music is good, one cannot but approve; but a concert is not a social occasion. [...] You may ask: But what constitutes a drawing-room reception? It is not an English rout, where a hand shake and a cup of tea is the only entertainment offered; it is not a concert, something better experienced in the *cafés-chantants* of the Champs-Élysées; it is not one of La Fontaine's fables recited by a dashing blade or a simpering miss: I would rather ask to be part of a regional delegation and have the whole of La Fontaine, and the whole of Florian on top of that, recited to me by babies of eight to ten. You ask me what should take place in a drawing room? I'll tell you: conversation.[14]

In short, the drawing room was the primary showcase for social representation, reflecting family and financial success; it was a place to display one's taste and good breeding.

ETIQUETTE, OR THE QUESTION OF GOOD FORM

Most middle-class women had an At Home day, a day on which they made sure to be at home with the drawing room tidy in case visitors should turn up. The art of "holding a salon" consisted partly in knowing how to invite the right people at the right time. For more formal receptions, guests received an engraved invitation at least a week before the event.[15] This card stated the time at which the occasion would begin, and the nature of the suggested entertainment, so that guests could make sure to be properly attired. Only those who could not attend were expected to reply as soon as possible.

Without being quite as complex as table manners, drawing-room etiquette imposed numerous rules to do with the correct attire, behaviour, times at which to arrive or leave and the length of visits, as well as activities and conversation.

It should be noted at the start that, although appropriate drawing-room comportment was different for men and women, and for young and old,[16]

LIVING IN STYLE

151
New Year's Visiting in Canada
Engraving published in the *Canadian Illustrated News*, January 2, 1875
National Archives of Canada, Ottawa (C-62494)

some rules applied to everyone. One had, for example, to simulate extreme pleasure on being introduced to the other guests, and "always applaud what the lady of the house applauds".[17]

> On entering the drawing room and approaching people, a joyous demeanour is indicated, even with persons to whom one is indifferent, as soon as one establishes a social relationship with them. While the host and hostess go through the motions of advancing to meet their guests, shaking hands with them and settling them in the best seats, the guests should respond with enthusiasm. If social equality is to be disregarded during these proceedings, it is from the host that the hint is to be taken, since by visiting his home the guest has evinced a desire to see him, and therefore should show himself grateful.[18]

Arrivals and introductions were also governed by rigid etiquette. A guest ought never to enter the drawing room during a musical performance, and should not address anyone before greeting his host and hostess. In Quebec, introductions followed American etiquette; that is, the host spoke first to the person to whom another guest was being presented, rather than to the person being presented, as is the French way.[19]

Once seated where his host and hostess had indicated, the guest ought never to shuffle his feet, for fear of damaging the carpet, nor touch the objects laid out on tables, and above all, never cross his legs, stretch his arm along the back of a chair or sofa, nor slouch in his chair.[20]

It should be added that the chairs and settees in the drawing room were most carefully arranged, and that who sat where was governed by the importance, class, sex and age of the visitor. Thus it was out of the question for a gentleman to sit on a sofa beside a lady or girl. Men also had to give up their seats for newcomers. Indeed, they mostly remained standing and helped to serve the ladies.

FROM PRIVATE GET-TOGETHERS TO GRAND BALLS

It should first be noted that attire,[21] as well as the length of the visit[22] and the number of guests, varied with the occasion. For a private get-together with friends, known to French-speakers as *thé à l'américaine*, afternoon tea was served in the drawing room at five o'clock. Friends of the household served themselves tea, wine or liqueurs, and light refreshments were invariably offered.[23]

Informal dances for about six to thirty guests, for which a single invitation was issued for the whole season, took place every week or fortnight.[24] When a larger number of guests was invited, the occasion became more of a reception. Depending on the entertainment offered – dancing, theatre, or music – invitations were sent out so that people could, if necessary, decline an invitation considered inappropriate to their position or breeding.

As a general rule, books of etiquette recommended arriving early, that is, about nine o'clock, although in France it was thought improper to arrive before eleven. Also, in Quebec a buffet was rarely served at such functions. Although considered necessary in polite society in France, such a meal proved difficult to implant here, being dismissed as "an indulgence bad for the health".[25] When a buffet was served, the men stood beside the table and served the ladies seated around the room.

Etiquette books published in Quebec also disapproved, although without open condemnation, of big dances which "do not seem in keeping with the Christian spirit",[26] where ladies danced the waltz or the polka wearing very low-necked dresses and allowing themselves to be held somewhat too closely by their partners. The waltz was barely tolerated, and the polka condemned, by the Catholic clergy.

Playing cards was also considered a dubious activity, and described as "the shame of our drawing rooms, immorality contrary to good form and civilized behaviour".[27] However, despite these exhortations to prudence and moderation which constantly warned gamesters against the lure of gain, card parties were very popular in Quebec society, as is apparent from the ubiquitous card tables in every Victorian drawing room. Robertine Barry,[28] one of the first columnists for the weekly women's pages of the newspaper *La Patrie*, reported to her readers the extravagant behaviour of Montrealers:

> At almost every evening party a gaming table is set up in a corner of the drawing room or boudoir. I have even heard that some ladies always carry a pack of cards in their pockets, and that others are bored to death at parties where the game of Bluff is not played.[29]

As well as dancing, conversation and games,[30] music was a common amusement. Indeed, the piano played a vital part in the Victorian drawing room in Quebec, where it testified to the correct upbringing received by every girl of good family. Unless asked so to do, the lady of the house never performed herself. It was usually her daughter who initiated the evening's music, while the hostess confined herself to providing piano accompaniment for any guest who had been asked to sing.

At the end of the evening, people took their leave according to a specific ritual in which everyone put on an act. When a guest rose to take his leave:

> ...the host, on the other hand, remains seated, apparently reluctant to rise, and tries to detain his guest. He finally gets up, feigning regret, to escort him to the door. However much one may long to see guests leave, good manners require us not to allow them to depart without uttering the formula: "What's this? You aren't leaving already! Do stay a little longer!"[31]

THE COST OF PRESTIGE AND OF KEEPING UP APPEARANCES
As regards luxury and extravagance, Quebec was the equal of the old mother country, whose way of life was so envied. In 1847 an article by Napoléon Aubin published in the Quebec City newspaper *Le Canadien* reported on "the extraordinary richness of our drawing rooms" as follows:

> There are in Canada a host of well-off families who spend considerable sums of money on furnishings which are then hidden away uselessly in a richly decorated drawing room that is opened only once or twice a year.[32]

Aubin deplored the all-too-common lack of paintings by Canadian artists, and described the "soft carpets, mahogany furniture, gilt candelabra, marble chimneypiece, thick curtains and, for ornaments, innumerable trifling knick-knacks displaying neither taste nor talent."[33] It seems clear that furnishing and decorating a drawing room represented a considerable investment. The large number of after-death inventories studied show that as a rule, proportionately more was spent on this room than on all the other rooms in the house, and that this held true for both French- and English- speakers of all social classes.

It appears that some of the new rich would stop at nothing to be in fashion. Thus Marie Aglaé Bilodeau,[34] the wife of a prosperous Quebec City hardware dealer, happily chose very expensive furniture for her drawing room. This room was furnished with a Heintzman cottage piano valued at two hundred dollars, and a drawing-room suite in red plush, consisting of a sofa and six chairs, all arranged on a tapestry carpet. The contents of this room were evaluated at $236.05, representing almost half the value of all the furniture in the house. On the other hand, in furnishing her boudoir with almost the same number of items — a settee, six chairs, a table, three picture frames and a carpet — Marie Aglaé chose them from a much lower price range, and the total cost came to only $10.75.

So one's drawing room was generally thought to be vitally important, and those with the means to do so followed fashion by regularly changing its contents and decoration.

152
Renaissance-revival sofa, about 1875-1890
130 x 220 x 90 cm
Augustinian monastery of the Hôtel-Dieu de Québec,
gift of Miss Blanche Côté
Photo Christine Guest/MMFA

VARIATIONS IN PRICE AND QUALITY, AND THE PHENOMENON OF IMITATIONS

Aware that drawing rooms, once the prerogative of the wealthy, were now becoming common among the middle classes and the less well-off, furniture makers and interior decorators, followed later by the department stores, began to offer this new clientèle a whole range of less expensive, even cheap, products. Fabrics such as moiré, satin, silk, velvet, plush, rep, damask, petit-point tapestry and wool embroidered with glass beads were replaced by printed calico, denim and cretonne. The same went for the choice of woods, which also determined the quality and cost of the furniture. Where necessary, the use of staining and varnish could create the illusion of rare and precious woods out of skilfully treated birchwood!

In addition to the quality of the wood and the fabric, the carving of the wood also helped to determine the value of furniture. Drawing-room suites decorated with full-blown roses, like the one owned by the Chapais family, were quite common, while those made to order or decorated by a master woodcarver indicated the possession of wealth. As a result of mechanization and new techniques that reduced production time, much furniture imitating luxury products was manufactured for an ever-larger middle class that wanted at all costs to appear to have a certain standing in the community.

152-153

The decorative elements of the drawing room, such as the carpets, stained glass, wallpaper and mouldings, were also doctored and faked with varying

153
Renaissance-revival settee, about 1870
Black walnut, 127 x 182 x 87 cm
Musée du Saguenay–Lac-Saint-Jean, Chicoutimi
Photo Christine Guest/MMFA

degrees of skill and success. Carpets of fake fur, silk paper in imitation of stained glass,[35] imitation marble wallpaper, oilcloth and fabric[36] deceived the eye, along with artificial flowers, prefabricated mouldings, glass imitating crystal, and pelmets of electroplating or repoussé copper which bore a vague resemblance to the gilded wood of olden times.

By the end of the Victorian era, this massive influx of mass-produced, fake and deceptive objects had to some extent invalidated and degraded real craftsmanship and authentic materials; above all, it detracted from the prestige associated with the everyday possessions of the upper classes. This alteration in the exchange value of things led the rich to review and re-state their aesthetic criteria in order to bring back discrimination and competition in matters of taste. Simplicity, plainness and harmony between style and material were henceforth to be new factors in the consumption of luxury goods, reintroducing values once associated with financial constraints.

AN OBJECT TO BE REVERED

Of all the pieces of furniture which acquired symbolic value during the Victorian era, the piano was undoubtedly the one with the most vital cultural connotations. All the distinguishing marks, demands and constraints of class such as prestige, good manners and wealth were linked with this instrument, endowing it with a special status. After all, what could tell you more about a man's social standing and the happiness of his home life than a photograph or an oil painting of his wife seated at the piano or teaching her daughter how to play?

It should be noted, however, that knowing the tonic solfa and having a little talent were not the only prerequisites for acquiring a piano. The testimony of the Canadian novelist and essayist Joseph Doutre[37] is very revealing in this respect. In one of his novellas entitled *Le Frère et la soeur*, he expresses astonishment that the lady of a house to which he is invited should know music:

THE USERS

154
Rococo-revival table piano, about 1860
Palisander, 97 x 202 x 100 cm
Bertrand Lavoie Collection, Quebec City
Photo Christine Guest/MMFA

155
Notman Studio, Montreal
Drawing room of a residence in Trois-Rivières, late nineteenth century
Photograph
McCord Museum of Canadian History, Montreal, Notman Photographic Archives (MP 1571-24)

156
Ludger Larose (1868-1915)
Family Scene: The Piano Lesson, 1907
Oil on canvas, 86.8 x 68.9 cm
Musée du Québec, Quebec City, photo Claude Bureau (77.26)

Our host ushered us into a drawing room which for richness and elegant taste was in every way equal to the splendours of the city. What surprised us more than anything was the overall quality of all those things that normally surround a well-bred woman. There were paintings still unfinished and embroidery in gold and silver thread. Sheet music was scattered on all the tables, and the instruments were there to prove that the music was not placed there just to impress. We were embarrassed at not being able to hide our astonishment.[38]

The piano soon became a highly significant decorative object, which sometimes cost as much as, if not much more than, all the rest of the drawing-room furnishings.

Its non-essential nature — it was not for sitting on nor for storage or dis-

play – also explains its fascination. Its apparent uselessness, and its dual impressiveness as evidence of both wealth and culture, made it almost a cult object throughout the Victorian era. Merchants such as Joseph Gadd and foreign manufacturers such as the New York Piano Company opened showrooms in Montreal devoted solely to pianos, harmoniums and organs. A rental system meant that such an instrument could be acquired by anyone, both in the city and in rural areas.

157-158

THE CONQUEST OF SPACE

Although it is risky to generalize, especially about an era as long as Victoria's reign, the history of how the drawing room developed can be summed up as a constant struggle to appropriate more space. This struggle took place in three stages, which can be defined as follows: leaving the wall, emphasizing surfaces, and filling the void. These three stages could, of course, overlap depending on the means and taste of each family. Indeed, like all evolutions, the appropriation of space did not take place in a linear and uniform manner, nor simultaneously in every stratum of society. Even if he wanted to follow the fashion in interior decoration, a man on a small salary could not necessarily afford the full range of drawing-room furniture available, which was generally much more expensive than other furniture.

Leaving the Wall

In terms of the layout of the home, the collapse of the traditionally linear arrangement of drawing-room furniture may be regarded from several points of view as the first major change that distinguishes the Victorian drawing room from that of previous centuries. Before the eighteenth century, the way drawing rooms, company rooms or reception rooms were used justified the strict arrangement of chairs along the wall, so as to leave the centre of the room clear for the assembled crowds of courtiers. The furniture, consisting mainly of chairs, was similarly appropriate to such functions. Indeed, this arrangement of chairs against the wall was so invariable that cabinetmakers

157
Exterior View of the New York Piano Company Building, 226-228 St. James Street, Montreal
Engraving published in L'Opinion publique, July 1, 1880
Photo SRP

158
Interior View of the New York Piano Company's Warerooms, St. James Street, Montreal
Engraving published in the Canadian Illustrated News, July 3, 1880
National Archives of Canada, Ottawa (C-75486)
The New York Piano Company's showroom was inaugurated by Oliver King, pianist to Princess Louise, during a major concert held on June 22, 1880.

159
Notman Studio, Montreal
The family of Andrew Allan
of Montreal, 1874
Composite photograph made from a picture taken in 1871 (64,070-I)
McCord Museum of Canadian History, Montreal, Notman Photographic Archives (333,015-II)
Andrew Allan can be seen sitting in the centre of the drawing room of his house Iononteh, on Peel Street.

rarely took the trouble to properly finish the backs of chairs and sofas.

The creation of a term like "centre table" expressed a new mobility and a new location. The evolution of the drawing room in function, size and use gradually brought about the invention of furniture better suited to a new concept of home life based on comfort.

A composite photograph of the drawing room in the Andrew Allan house, taken by Notman in 1871, illustrates this new tendency in interior arrangement. Although there are still many chairs with their backs to the wall, a central fixture and small occasional tables break up the space in the middle of the room. This more flexible, less regimented arrangement was more appropriate to the various activities that now began to take place in the drawing room. Groups of chairs and sofas around a writing table, a piano or a centre table created cosy groupings that encouraged relaxation and conversation.

By the early 1880s the centre of the drawing room was fully occupied, but the excessive accumulation of furniture which now cluttered the space gave a somewhat stifling impression of chaos. Etiquette books offered advice for those struggling with this grave problem, suggesting stereotyped arrangements in keeping with common practice and the type of furniture usually found in drawing rooms. Thus the *Manuel d'économie domestique* proposes the following arrangement:

> The seating should be arranged in a semi-circle on both sides of the fireplace and in front of it, with armchairs at each corner and other armchairs alternately with straight-back chairs. There should be a small foot stool in front of each armchair. The tables are placed all around the walls of the room, but sometimes one table may be positioned in the middle of the semi-circle of armchairs. A small table should be placed by the wall at the corner of the chimneypiece within reach of the lady of the house, who customarily sits in one of the corner armchairs while entertaining visitors.[39]

LIVING IN STYLE

160
Notman Studio, Montreal
Drawing room of Mrs. Annie Morrice's house, Montreal, 1899
Photograph
McCord Museum of Canadian History, Montreal, Notman Photographic Archives (128,252-II)

In time, people learned to adapt the quantity and variety of their furniture to the size of their drawing room, and tried to make the furniture harmonize with its surroundings by distributing the pieces more evenly. As in the "blue drawing room" of the Montebello manor-house, some furniture was arranged along the walls while other pieces gave interest to the central space without creating an impression of heaviness.

Emphasizing Surfaces

In addition to exploring the possibilities of the centre of the drawing room, people turned their attention to the various surfaces: walls, floor, ceiling. Interior decorators especially became enthusiastic about colour schemes, the harmonizing of curtains with carpets, and of course about the arrangement of the furniture within the general decoration scheme of the room.

From the 1850s onward wallpaper was generally imported from the United States, England and France.[40] By the end of the Victorian era, the choice available grew as Canadian manufacturers joined the fray.[41] Their wallpaper was very popular with customers, as were satin, silk and cretonne fabrics for covering walls. However, a growing concern for hygiene in the home[42] and ease of upkeep gradually banished materials that were hard to clean.

161
J. G. Parks (active 1865 to 1895)
The blue drawing room of the Manoir Papineau, Montebello, about 1885
Photograph
National Archives of Canada, Ottawa (PA-115907)

Interior decorators preferred to recommend painting the walls, as aside from being less expensive, this was easier to make harmonize with the carpets and upholstery fabric, and was less likely to clash with the furniture of varying styles often placed side by side in the same room. As a reaction against the excessive gilding of furniture and mouldings which was so prevalent in *bourgeois* drawing rooms in the early years of Victoria's reign, the concern with colour harmony soon became the burning question of the day, especially for interior decorators.

In drawing rooms the white and gold previously used so lavishly began to disappear. Large gilt mouldings began to look in dubious taste, and decorators confidently suggested less "vulgar"[43] ornamentation to their clients. They proposed to replace gilding with colours that would create a welcoming and peaceful atmosphere, or, as Andrew Jackson Downing suggested, to use gilding together with white only in town houses. In country houses a more discreet use of gilding was advised, together with colours such as pink, pearl grey and light apple green.

As happened when the centre of the drawing room was appropriated, this new use of colour was often appallingly overdone, as William Hodgson notes in one of the leaflets published in 1879 by *The Scientific Canadian, Mechanics' Magazine and Patent Office Record of Canada*:

> I am not astonished at the fact that many persons have grey and white drawing rooms, when I think of the hideous effects sometimes shown me as decorations, where, perhaps a pale emerald green, a grey and a ghastly pink – the very pink that will not harmonize with the crude green in question – are the colours employed. The hideousness of some decorations, so called, is beyond expression, and white walls are infinitely preferable to such.[44]

Despite the general wish to create a less pompous kind of décor, the strong colours then available made these rooms, already so overloaded with furniture and knick-knacks, look even more hectic and cluttered. One can easily imagine the effect created by these "up to the minute" drawing rooms which might well have lemon-yellow walls with blue-black dados or blue-grey with brown-orange.

> Harmony between the various decorations can be achieved in many ways. A ceiling in which blue prevails, or even a plain blue ceiling, a suitable coloured cornice, citrine walls and a rich maroon dado will produce a harmony. A ceiling blue-green, general effect, walls of low-toned yellow-orange, and a dado of deep purple-red, will produce a harmony. In both these cases the doors might be of bronze green, and the architraves black.[45]

Nor did the curtains help to brighten the atmosphere of the room. The use of fabrics such as moiré, damask and tapestry required impressive yardage. The ornate curtains of the early Victorian era, with their tassels, pelmets[46] and fringes became even more elaborate about 1860, when muslin curtains,[47] sometimes flowered, or lace curtains were added to the windows.

Window curtains were sometimes replaced by shutters or by blinds of painted canvas fixed or mounted on wooden poles with a spring-loaded mechanism like those of today. However, these roller blinds were considered less elegant than Venetian blinds,[48] which were originally installed both inside and outside the house. The patterns on blinds were the same as those found on wallpapers or in wall paintings. Large landscape scenes were created to order by firms such as S. F. Stoneham of Montreal, who offered "Tasteful transparent oilcloths for windows, in magnificent new patterns, made to order in any size, in gold, silver and various colours for churches, chapels, private residences and stores."[49]

The thick curtains obviously kept the room in semi-darkness, and to counterbalance this inconvenience, people began to match window curtains to the seating, or the seats to the carpet, if they were of various styles and fabrics. Later, wooden curtain rods with knobs on the ends, on which curtain rings could slide, replaced the massively architectural pelmets.

At the same time that curtains were becoming less massive, decorators were recommending walls painted in lighter colours.

> In houses closely surrounded, the light obtainable is so small in quantity that it is oftentimes requisite that the walls should be as light in tone as possible, in order that they may reflect all the natural light and diffuse it around. This is specially needful in houses where the back windows are of necessity filled in with stained glass, that the outlook, which is often none of the pleasantest, may be hidden.[50]

Despite the pastel shades in vogue, the effect of heaviness persisted in many drawing rooms, because of the wool, tapestry or velour carpets,[51] often covered with two or three smaller carpets, which added yet more textures and colours to an already overcrowded décor.

Moulding, the last bastion of Victorian luxury and elegance, was not swept away by the wave of simplification that overtook the drawing room about the 1890s. Redolent of wealth, recalling the state apartments of kings, the thick cornices, the wainscotting, the dados and coronas, the corbels and fluting were never really banished, even though this kind of moulding, which continued to be varnished or painted in dark colours, sometimes gave a grim look that the new decorators were now trying to remove.

162
Edgar Gariépy (1881-1956), Montreal
Interior of a house in Saint-Joseph-de-Soulanges (Les Cèdres), 1929
Photograph
Bibliothèque municipale de Montréal (G.2339)

163
Interior of the Manoir Larivière,
Saint-Michel de Bellechasse
Photograph
Archives nationales du Québec, Centre de Québec et Chaudière-Appalaches, collection initiale (GH-770-342)

Filling the Void

Although the tendency to make use of shelves and all available surfaces for displaying beautiful objects existed well before the start of Victoria's reign, it grew more exaggerated as the era went on, becoming quite outrageous and unrestrained.

After-death inventories prior to the 1840s show that decorative objects each had their place, often quite unvarying, and on the whole were all remarkably similar. The basic decorative objects to be found in the home were a few fine pieces of silverware, mirrors, prints and pictures, "mantelpiece ornaments" and "cornice ornaments".

At the beginning of the Victorian era, despite a relatively homogenous decoration scheme for drawing rooms and furniture arranged in straight lines, there soon appeared a plethora of small decorative objects – insects under glass, ships in bottles, Chinese card boxes, animals of crystal and vases of agate and alabaster – that seemed to announce an urgent need to fill up the void.

As soon as they arrived in Canada, the latest novelties such as telescopes, stereoscopes, microscopes, opera glasses, music boxes, vases of flowers, bouquet holders and cages of stuffed birds joined the ranks of lithographs, oil paintings, and the ubiquitous mirrors that multiplied to infinity the many objects cluttering the drawing room.

The taste for accumulating possessions led to the fashion for laying one thing on top of another: small carpets or rugs over larger ones, little pieces of

164
Notman Studio, Montreal
Drawing room of the A. R. Creeman house, Montreal
Photograph
McCord Museum of Canadian History, Montreal, Notman Photographic Archives (MP 204/76-2)

needlework or embroidery over chair backs, lace, runners or oil cloth on tables, drapes decorated with pompoms, beads and knots over chimneypieces, door curtains and vases, work boxes and card boxes, paintings, prints and knick-knacks began to invade every nook and cranny, every shelf or item of furniture.

This passion for accumulating things, this apparently unconquerable aversion to leaving any space unoccupied, nevertheless gradually gave way to a desire for a more welcoming ambience. As Edmond Rousseau wrote in 1918:

> As a result of this appetite for unbridled luxury and pleasure that has invaded not only the Côte de Beaupré but the whole province of Quebec, the town house – in which there is even a silver-plated bell, as well as fine horse-hair furniture and, naturally, a piano – has replaced "those hospitable white-washed houses" which so delighted the eyes and heart...[52]

Despite the excessive cost of decorating one's drawing room, and of the receptions held in it, which ate up fortunes very quickly, happiness, one of the essentials of life, was not entirely absent. For a long time elegance, luxury, good taste and a high profile had been the bases of social life. The plight of the intellectual middle classes, landed with their drawing rooms and obliged to observe the rigid rules of propriety, or perhaps in financial straits, made poverty seem almost enviable. The last word should go to Robertine Barry, who at the end of the century advocated a return to more human values:

> Better the poorest of cottages than this gilded panelling, stamped with the seal of implacable fate! It is often the most humble of homes that give us an image of happiness. Such homes are not crushed under the heavy weight of their own grandeur, but please us simply by their welcoming quality and a comfortable appearance that charms and enchants us.[53]

THE USERS

FURNITURE AND COMFORT

Simultaneously with this discovery of space, people were learning to appreciate comfort. The new concept of comfort made a particular difference to chair design, ousting the chairs with high, straight, uncomfortable backs typical of the early nineteenth century.

Contemporary photographs such as those of the "yellow drawing room" in the Papineau manor-house and of Colonel McPherson's drawing room confirm the wide variety of chairs and sofas to be found on the market, most of them comfortably stuffed.

The inventory of the drawing room of William Henry Brehaut of Notre-Dame-de-Grâce parish in Montreal also tells us a great deal. On a carpet evaluated at twenty dollars stood a centre table, a tête-à-tête, two sofas, two easy chairs, two hall chairs, four chairs covered in rep, a small table, a piano bench, two card tables, four shelves, a whatnot and a papier-mâché table as well as some strips of carpet and fire irons. This police magistrate's house was thus comfortably furnished in the fashion of the time: no fewer than five tables vying for room with eleven chairs, of which there were at least five different kinds!

Chairs and sofas, the key elements of drawing-room furniture, became even more important with the introduction, about the end of the nineteenth century, of new styles created in Europe. The arrival of central fixtures, ottomans, bergère chairs, settees, tête-à-têtes, confidantes and squat armchairs soon changed the appearance of the drawing room, the arrangement of which was based on what was usually called the drawing-room suite. As a rule, above and beyond individual variations and marketing fads, such a suite most often consisted of a sofa, father's armchair, mother's armchair, a side chair and a centre table. Nevertheless, during the course of the Victorian era the basic components of the drawing-room suite varied greatly according to social class. Although the amount of furniture in a suite was not strictly spelled out, there is no doubt that, depending on the purchaser's means and needs, the number of items could be considerable, as in the case of the Gourdeau suite in the Montreal Museum of Fine Arts.[54]

Among other fine suites that have survived is that of the Whitehead family of Quebec City, consisting of a sofa, two armchairs and six occasional chairs, and that of Zéphirin Paquet, acquired from the cabinetmaker C. O. Bédard of Quebec City in 1884, which includes a sofa, two armchairs, four occasional chairs and a games table.

Another drawing-room suite, preserved in the archbishop's palace in Chicoutimi, contains a far more impressive number of pieces. *Le Progrès du Saguenay* of June 19, 1890, reported that:

> During his latest trip to Montreal, Father Roberge, the archbishop's secretary, who had been asked by the citizens to purchase the drawing-room suite they wished to present to Monsignor Bégin, made his choice and arranged to have the furniture made to order. There will be sixteen pieces, all very valuable and worthy of the archbishop's apartments.[55]

This suite, in the Aesthetic movement style, cost over $400; it was given to mark the twenty-fifth anniversary, the following July 27, of the ordination of

165
Edgar Gariépy (1881-1956), Montreal
The main drawing room of the Manoir Papineau, Montebello, 1915
Photograph
National Archives of Canada, Ottawa (PA 115932)

In the centre of this principal reception room, which was known as the yellow drawing room, can be seen a large seating fixture surmounted by a bust of Louis-Joseph Papineau carved by his son-in-law, Napoléon Bourassa.

166
C. A. Muerrle, Toronto
Drawing room in the home of Colonel MacPherson, Quebec City
Photograph
National Archives of Canada, Ottawa (PA-51696)

Mgr Louis-Nazaire Bégin (1840-1925). It was intended for the drawing room of the new bishop's palace, the construction of which began in 1889 and was completed in the spring of 1890.[56]

Despite the increasingly common tendency to fill drawing rooms with new types of chairs and sofas in various styles and different fabrics, the fashion for matched suites seems to have lasted up to the last decades of the nineteenth century, as this article of 1882 makes plain:

168
Advertisement for the firm of William King & Cie of Montreal
Published in *La Presse*, May 23, 1885
Photo SRP
The furniture pictured is in a style inspired by the Aesthetic movement.

167
Renaissance-revival lady's chair, about 1870
Black walnut, 97 x 54 x 56 cm
Musée du Saguenay–Lac-Saint-Jean, Chicoutimi
Photo Christine Guest/MMFA

Easy chairs that come under the classification of "Gossip", "Occasional" or "Tête-à-tête" were comparatively unknown a dozen years ago. Almost the only style of furnishing the drawing room then adopted was: the couch or settee on one side, and the chiffonnier facing the eagle-crowned mirror on the other, and a glossy oval loo table in the center; the ladies' and gents' chairs on either side of the fireplace, and six small upright chairs arranged demurely around the remaining wall space. Such a stiff disposition of the leading reception room was eventually broken up by some, and the fashion came into vogue of filling this apartment with any oddments that had pretence to beauty or comfort. When once the fixed law of having a "set suit" was transgressed by the leaders of fashion, admission into the drawing room was obtained for a crowd of chairs of all names, shapes and sizes. Whilst the old style of a "suit to match" suits the

169
Renaissance-revival settee, about 1870
Walnut, 144 x 187 x 80 cm
Musée de la civilisation, Quebec City, gift of the estate of Alfred B. Whitehead (60-36)
Photo Brian Merrett/MMFA

170
Renaissance-revival armchair, about 1870
Walnut, 130 x 70 x 75 cm
Musée de la civilisation, Quebec City, gift of the estate of Alfred B. Whitehead (60-37)
Photo Brian Merrett/MMFA

171
Renaissance-revival lady's chair, about 1870
Walnut, 125 x 63 x 67 cm
Musée de la civilisation, Quebec City, gift of the estate of Alfred B. Whitehead (60-38)
Photo Brian Merrett/MMFA

The Musée du Québec owns a portrait painted by Ludger Ruelland (1827-1896) in which a certain Mrs. Eusèbe Moreau – born Marie-Rose Délima Lacasse (1828-1909) – is shown seated on a chair very similar to this one.

requirements of many people better than the "harlequin" arrangement referred to, it must be confessed that the latter gives greater scope for the inventive genius of the chair and cabinet maker to sit down and think out a new shape, with the assurance that if it is novel, pretty, and comfortable, it will gain admission into the market and probably have "a run".[57]

172
Renaissance-revival chair
(from a set of six), about 1870
Walnut, 109.5 x 51.2 x 53.3 cm
Musée de la civilisation, Quebec City, gift of the estate of Alfred B. Whitehead (60-39)
Photo Brian Merrett/MMFA

It was not only in creating new styles of drawing-room chairs that cabinet-makers demonstrated their inventiveness. The whatnot in numerous varieties of shape was extremely popular up to the end of the century. Although not a new phenomenon, the screens found in many drawing rooms in the 1860s were becoming basically decorative items considered essential to drawing-room décor from this period on. A screen belonging to the order of the

173
Charles-Olivier Bédard
Rococo-revival sofa, 1884
Walnut, 132.5 x 176.8 x 82 cm
Musée de la civilisation, Quebec City (87-2401-1)
Photo Christine Guest/MMFA

174
Charles-Olivier Bédard
Rococo-revival armchair, 1884
Walnut, 109 x 67 x 70 cm
Musée de la civilisation, Quebec City (87-2401-3)
Photo Christine Guest/MMFA

175
Charles-Olivier Bédard
Rococo-revival lady's chair, 1884
Walnut, 120.5 x 68 x 72 cm
Musée de la civilisation, Quebec City (87-2401-2)
Photo Christine Guest/MMFA

173

174

175

176

176
Charles-Olivier Bédard
Rococo-revival chair
(from a set of four), 1884
Walnut, 102.5 x 51.2 x 70 cm
Musée de la civilisation, Quebec City (87-2401-4)
Photo Christine Guest/MMFA

Sœurs de la Charité de Québec is surmounted by a bust of the Princess Louise, wife of the Marquis of Lorne, Governor General of Canada. It was made by Xavier Lachance of the Île d'Orléans, whose wife Caroline spent three years on the needlework depicting "Ahasuerus, King of Persia, and Esther".[58]

Furniture makers also produced large numbers of drawing-room tables of every shape and size: tables for playing cards at, for serving dessert on, or simply as occasional furniture to hold knick-knacks, photographs and prized souvenirs. The decoration on the apron and under-frame could be a matter of volume, as in the table from the Musée du Saguenay-Lac-Saint-Jean, or

177
Charles-Olivier Bédard, Quebec City
Rococo-revival games table, 1884
Walnut, 75.5 x 95.2 x 94 cm
Musée de la civilisation, Quebec City (87-2401-5)
Photo Christine Guest/MMFA

178
Love seat, Aesthetic movement, 1890
Black walnut, 108.5 x 146 x 70 cm
Bishop's palace of Chicoutimi
Photo Christine Guest/MMFA

179
Rococo-revival whatnot
Walnut, 150 x 103 x 35 cm
Musée de la civilisation, Quebec City (88-2750)
Photo Christine Guest/MMFA

180
Renaissance-revival screen, about 1880
Black walnut and tapestry, 208 x 102 x 43 cm
Sœurs de la Charité de Québec, Beauport
Photo Christine Guest/MMFA

The petit-point tapestry depicting "Ahasuerus, King of Persia, and Esther" was executed by Caroline Lachance, a pupil at the Sainte-Famille de l'Île-d'Orléans convent, run by sisters of the order of Notre-Dame. She worked on the tapestry for three years, from 1864 to 1867. The screen itself, which is of a somewhat later date, was carved by Caroline's cousin, Xavier Lachance of l'Île-d'Orléans.

181
Rococo-revival centre table
Black walnut and black burl walnut veneer, 76 x 122 x 87 cm
Musée du Saguenay–Lac-Saint-Jean, Chicoutimi
Photo Christine Guest/MMFA

182
Rococo-revival side table
Mahogany, 77 x 90 x 54 cm
David S. Brown, antiquaire, Montreal
Photo Christine Guest/MMFA

This side table once belonged to Senator Francis Edward Gilman of Richmond, Quebec.

183
Rococo-revival games table
75.7 x 102.5 x 57 cm
Private collection, Montreal
Photo Christine Guest/MMFA

This table is one of a pair. An almost identical pair is owned by the Augustinian monastery of the Hôtel-Dieu de Québec. These pieces show marked formal and stylistic similarities to the console table with mirror illustrated below.

184
Rococo-revival console table with mirror
79 x 142 x 61 cm (table); 160 cm (mirror)
Private collection, Coaticook
Photo Christine Guest/MMFA

185
Easel, Aesthetic movement,
about 1880-1900
Black walnut and black figured walnut veneer,
217 x 92 x 15 cm
McCord Museum of Canadian History, Montreal
(M992.47.1)
Photo Christine Guest/MMFA

The two metal decorations, one depicting a horse's head and the other a dog's head, probably symbolize a special interest in engravings showing scenes of riding and hunting.

openwork, as in the one from the David Brown Collection which belonged to the family of the lawyer and senator Francis Edward Gilman of Danville.

There were, in fact, numerous varieties of style and format for drawing-room tables, and the same patterns could also be applied to tables with quite different functions. Thus a console table was often provided with a pivoting folding top that turned it into a games table. A console table with mirror, on the other hand, could also be a highly elaborate display piece.

Small pieces of occasional furniture were also extremely popular because they took up less room and could easily be moved. Mostly invented in the late eighteenth century, they sprang into surprising prominence during the second half of the nineteenth century. For example, the gypsy table to the right of the easel in Colonel McPherson's drawing room was so popular an item that the design for it was published in the June 1882 issue of *The Scientific Canadian*, with the remark that "Though a gipsy table is such an ordinary piece

186
Elizabethan-revival canterbury
Black walnut, 58.2 x 66 x 47.7 cm
Private collection, Quebec City
Photo Christine Guest/MMFA

A canterbury is a small open-work rack used to store sheet music. It would have stood near the piano, which reigned supreme over the drawing room.

187
Interior of a Montreal residence, about 1890
Photograph
National Archives of Canada, Ottawa (PA-118136)

188
M. E. Robb, Granby
Drawing room of the Gabriel Marchand house, Saint-Jean-sur-Richelieu, about 1900
Photograph
Martine Brault-Genest Collection, Quebec City

In the photo can be seen Gabriel Marchand – son of Quebec premier Félix-Gabriel Marchand – and his wife Rose-Anna Chaput, with their daughter Marguerite.

188
of furniture, and so much in request, yet its manufacture is confined to but few makers".[59]

185 Among other items of furniture, easels became popular since they made up for the lack of wall space. Thus in the Hague house, works of art were displayed on the two easels and so did not upset the general layout of the drawing room. For those who owned a piano, a music rack was indispensable.

186 This contrivance, known as a canterbury in mid-Victorian times, was originally a somewhat cumbersome item. It had an upper shelf, a drawer and a series of vertical racks.

While in time most kinds of furniture became simpler, as form became more appropriate to use, or were soon adapted to conform to the latest style, mirrors, although just as popular as music racks and little tables, changed less with the vagaries of fashion. The drawing-room mirror, an impressive item of

THE USERS

considerable size and surrounded by a heavy moulding, was usually placed above the chimneypiece, above a console table or between two windows. In addition to reflecting light and creating an impression of space, its main function was to impress. Although mirror frames were generally influenced by the prevailing trend, it was not until the late 1860s that furniture makers began to make mirrors an integral part of furniture structure and of interior domestic architecture.

Sometimes flanked by shelves and designed to form part of the wall above the chimneypiece, as in Gabriel Marchand's house in Saint-Jean-sur-Richelieu, the mirror continued to be an important element of drawing-room décor for all classes of society throughout the nineteenth century, whether above the chimneypiece of the Spencer Wood villa, the Governor's official residence in Quebec City, or the fireplace of the cooper Benjamin Brien dit Desrochers.

Micheline Huard

1   Henri Havard, *Dictionnaire de l'ameublement et de la décoration*, vol. III (Paris: Maison Quantin, 1890), p. 479.

2   AJTR, registry of notary Pierre Désilets, no. 4657, after-death inventory of Dame Marie Willand and of the late Johny Désilets, April 26, 1892.

3   *Canadian Illustrated News* (Montreal), January 4, 1873, p. 13.

4   In order to identify the reception room, among all the rooms in the home, and to analyze its development throughout the nineteenth century, we had first to define how the room was used, no matter what it was called. We thus established that the drawing room, following the definition generally accepted in Europe, was kept exclusively for social activities, and that in order for this to be its function, the room should not contain tools or other objects which would imply that it was used for any other purpose. Above and beyond its name, it was because of being different from the other rooms in the house that this space was used to express, through the elegance of its furnishings and decoration, a certain standing in the community or social network.

5   Towards the end of the century, many architects' plans and after-death inventories were still referring to the drawing room as the visitors' parlour, visitors' drawing room, parlour, living room, and so on.

6   Long before Canadian writers and journalists had adapted these guides to etiquette to local realities, it was these books, published in England and France, that laid down the law for people in Quebec. The first Canadian etiquette books and women's pages did not appear until the very end of the century.

7   Best known for her first book, *Le savoir-vivre dans toutes les circonstances de la vie*, of which over 100,000 copies were sold, Louise D'Alq, also known as Louise D'Alquié de Rieupeyroux, went on to publish more than thirty works on the same subject. They include *La science et la vie, conseils et réflexions à l'usage de tous* (1875), *Le maître et la maîtresse de maison* (1882), and *L'horticulture au salon et au jardin* (1885), all of which were re-published. See J. Balteau, *Dictionnaire biographique français* (Paris: Librairie Letouzey et Ané, 1936), vol. II, pp. 320-321.

8   Madame Louise D'Alq, *Le savoir-vivre dans toutes les circonstances de la vie* (Paris: Bureaux des causeries familières [new ed.], 1886), pp. 279, 281.

9   This Englishwoman, born in Holderness, Yorkshire in 1812 and married to the writer and minister William Ellis, wrote a number of novels and some poetry, but mainly moralistic stories to put women on their guard against vanity, parental negligence, alcohol abuse and so on. Disappointed in the tepid reception given to her first novel *The Negro Slave* (1830), in 1832 she contacted Thomas Pringle, who agreed to carry her books in his libraries. Her stories, the most famous of which was *The Woman of England* published in 1839, were very realistic narratives, and she became very influential. Some of her works were published under her maiden name of Sarah Stickney, and others variously under Sarah Ellis, Sarah Stickney Ellis or just Mrs. Ellis.

10   Mrs. Ellis, *Devoirs et conditions des femmes dans l'état du mariage*, translated from the English by Gustave Brunet (Paris: Éd. Amyot, 1847), p. 191.

11   *Ibid.*, p. 202.

12   *Ibid.*, p. 188.

13 "Furniture and Decoration", *The Scientific Canadian*, October 1879, p. 302.

14 Jules and Gustave Simon, *La femme du vingtième siècle* (Paris: Calmann Lévy, 1892), pp. 24-25.

15 In France it was customary for written invitations to be delivered by servants, even for informal parties.

16 Before the age of eighteen young girls were allowed to appear in the drawing room only briefly. Ladies were always served first, and older people could choose to remain sitting while the host or hostess served them tea or introduced other guests to them. Ladies sat beside the hostess, and were expected to give up their seats to later arrivals. They were not obliged to offer a hand on being introduced to a man, but could simply give a gracious nod of acknowledgement. As for children, they never entered the drawing room except when invited to, and were never to stay there without parental supervision when guests were present.

17 *La vraie politesse et le bon ton plus particulièrement à l'usage des élèves des collèges, pensionnats, etc., etc., et de tous ceux qui entrent en société* (Montreal: Imprimerie Eusèbe Sénécal, 1873), p. 85.

18 Louise D'Alq, *op. cit.*, pp. 307-308.

19 Madame Sauvalle, *1000 questions d'étiquette discutées, résolues et classées* (Montreal: Beauchemin, 1907), p. 217.

20 *La vraie politesse et le bon ton, op. cit.*, pp. 54-55.

21 For daytime visits, male guests could wear a frock coat and coloured trousers. After six o'clock in the evening, as in France, a tail coat was obligatory, although in more relaxed circles a black dinner jacket was accepted. Except in the case of a very brief visit, rubbers were removed in the drawing room. For formal evening occasions both men and women wore pale-coloured gloves.

22 According to the etiquette book *La vraie politesse et le bon ton*, there were basically three types of visit: courtesy visits, friendly visits and charitable visits. The courtesy visit should never last more than ten minutes, and took place between one and five o'clock in the afternoon. Friendly, charitable or business visits could last longer, but one had to be careful not to impose. Charitable visits were paid for the following reasons: illness, weddings, funerals, births, and so on, as well, obviously, as visiting the poor. A *visite de digestion*, a term questioned in this book, had to be paid within a week of being invited to dinner or to a big reception. After a dinner, it was considered rude not to spend at least an hour in conversation in the drawing room.

23 During more formal visits, it was the lady of the house who served the tea or coffee herself, with the help of a daughter or of the young people present when the guests were too numerous. Liqueurs were also offered, to which the visitor helped himself.

24 These get-togethers were also called in French *huitaine* or *quinzaine*.

25 *La vraie politesse et le bon ton*, p. 78.

26 *Ibid.*, p. 78.

27 Jules Clément, *Traité de la politesse et du savoir-vivre* (Paris: Éd. Bernardin-Béchet, 1878), p. 162.

28 A friend of Émile Nelligan, and awarded the *Palmes académiques* by France, this journalist, born in L'Isle-Verte in 1863, worked for the newspaper *La Patrie* after 1891. Before her *Chroniques du Lundi* column began in 1900, a collection of her poetry entitled *Fleurs champêtres* was published by Les Éditions Beauchemin in 1895. She also founded, in 1901, *Le Journal de Françoise*.

29 Françoise [Robertine Barry], *Les chroniques du lundi*, (n.p., 1900), p. 122.

30 In Robinson's *Encyclopaedia* of 1882 drawing-room games are described in detail. The games referred to are almost all guessing games, with names such as Consequences, Adjectives, Crambo (a versification game), Definitions, How Do You Like It?, What Is My Thought Like?, Forfeits and Proverbs.

31 Louise D'Alq, *op. cit.*, p. 311.

32 *Le Canadien*, October 15, 1847, p. 2.

33 A carpet was considered a great luxury. The historian and playwright Antoine Gérin-Lajoie has one of his best-known characters, Jean Rivard, say: "For example, the purchase of the wool carpet you see in our drawing room was the subject of prolonged discussions between me and my wife. We bought it shortly after I was elected to Parliament, at a time when a number of my colleagues were visiting me." Antoine Gérin-Lajoie, *Jean Rivard le défricheur. Récit de la vie réelle* (Montreal: Éditions Hurtubise HMH [J. B. Rolland et fils, 1874], 1977), p. 327.

34 ANQQ, file of notary Joseph Allaire, no. 9636, inventory of Dame Marie Aglaé Bilodeau and of the late Jean-Ferdinand Dagneau, hardware dealer of Quebec City, July 27, 1901.

35 In its June 1880 issue (p. 203), *The Scientific Canadian* announced to its readers a new invention that had just appeared on the market. This was silk paper printed in rich and brilliant colours, which could easily be applied on to ordinary glass to create the same effect as stained glass.

36 *The Scientific Canadian*, April 1880, p. 113.

37 In addition to publishing novels, Joseph Doutre (1825-1886) also wrote short stories as well as literary and historical essays. The authors of the *Dictionnaire pratique des auteurs québécois* call his output "work of good sense and clarity". See R. Hamel, J. Hare and P. Wyczynski, *Dictionnaire pratique des auteurs québécois* (Montreal: Fides, 1976), p. 210.

38 Joseph Doutre, "Le Frère et la soeur" [1846], published in *Contes et nouvelles du Canada français 1778-1859* (Ottawa: Éditions de l'Université d'Ottawa, 1971), vol. 1, pp. 168-192.

39 Stella, *Manuel d'économie domestique* (Paris: Librairie Générale, 1890), pp. 78-79.

40 For example, the firms of Fabre et Gravel and of Zéphirin Chapleau, two Montreal booksellers with advertisements in *L'Almanach canadien de la ruche littéraire*, published by C. H. Walker in 1854, sold not only books, maps, atlases and mathematical and surgical instruments, but also "rolls of wallpaper" and "wallpaper pictures, very attractive and inexpensive, of the Descent from the Cross and the Resurrection of Our Lord".

41 *Almanach du nouvelliste* (Quebec City: N. S. Hardy, 1882), n. p.

42 Some foreign manufacturers such as Wm. Woollam & Co. of London adapted their products to new market demands. This company announced in 1885 that their wallpaper was "guaranteed free from Arsenic." See Henry J. Morgan, *The Dominion Annual Register and Review* [1884] (Toronto: Hunter, Rose & Company, 1885), p. xxiv.

43 "Furniture and Decoration", *The Scientific Canadian*, October 1879, p. 302.

44 William Hodgson, "Room Decoration", *The Scientific Canadian*, September 1879, p. 266.

45 *Ibid.*

46 Pelmets, also known as valances, required several yards of fabric and the services of a decorator to be properly installed. Loudon was critical of them, pointing out not only the excessive cost of installing them but also the fact that they accumulated dust. He suggested replacing the pelmet by a short valance formed of pleats or scallops finished with fringing or tassels. Taken from John Claudius Loudon, *An Encyclopaedia of Cottage, Farm and Villa Architecture and Furniture* (London: 1833), pp. 1274-1275, quoted in G. C. Winkler and R. W. Moss, *Victorian Interior Decoration* (New York: Henry Holt and Company, 1986), p. 52.

47 These lace or muslin drapes not only served a decorative purpose, but also filtered sunlight and kept insects out of the house. See A. J. Downing, *The Architecture of Country Houses* (New York: Dover Publications [1850], 1969), pp. 374-375 and Loudon, *op. cit.*, pp. 338- 341.

48 Called "folding Venetian blinds" by Loudon and "shutter blinds" by Downing, these were originally made of wood and attached to the outside of the house; however, Downing strongly suggested installing them also inside the house, since blinds kept curtains and carpets from being faded by the sun.

49 An advertisement for S. F. Stoneham (353 Notre-Dame Street) published in *L'Almanach de la semaine agricole pour 1870* (Montreal: Duvernay Frères, 1870), p. 22.

50 "Hints in Decoration", *The Scientific Canadian*, August 1881, p. 250.

51 Carpet manufacturers, who at the start of the Victorian era offered very little choice, soon provided a wider range of products: carpets of felt, wool, wool and canvas, tapestry, velours and small fur rugs as well as the usual woven rag rugs and oil cloths for floors.

52 Edmond Rousseau, *Deux récits. A Carillon; Dans un Yacht* (Quebec City: Charrier & Dugal, 2nd ed., 1918), p. 7.

53 Barry, *op. cit.*, p. 255.

54 According to the inventory of the Montreal furniture maker Joseph Guillaume Lamontagne in 1893, some suites could comprise ten or more pieces, excluding tables. ANQM, registry of notary Joseph Chartrand, no. 3724, inventory of Joseph Guillaume Lamontagne and of the late Philomène Laforest, October 9, 1883.

55 *Le Progrès du Saguenay* (Chicoutimi), June 19, 1890, p. 3.

56 On this subject, see *Le Progrès du Saguenay* of April 11, 1889 and July 31, 1890.

57 "How to make a gossip chair", *The Scientific Canadian*, September 1882, p. 278.

58 The order of the Soeurs de la Charité de Québec were given this screen by Madame Athala Gourdeau in 1954. It had always belonged to the family of Caroline Lachance, who had been a student at the convent of the Sainte-Famille on the Ile d'Orléans, run by the sisters of the Congrégation Notre-Dame.

59 "A Gypsy Table by a practical workman", *The Scientific Canadian*, June 1882, p. 179 (ill. p. 181).

The Drawing Room of the L'Assomption Manor-House in the Late Nineteenth Century in the Words of the Writer Robert de Roquebrune (1889-1978)*

My childhood years in Canada were spent in a world that has vanished. Those years between 1890 and 1905 passed as if in a completely different universe – not only remote from us in time, but remote in the appearance of things, in the way people thought, and the way they acted. So entirely has the world of my childhood disappeared, so alien has it become, that I can scarcely even remember it.

[...]

In our old house, surrounded by its gardens, we lived on a sort of island far from the rest of the world. We heard little of what went on outside. [...] In the midst of all this, we lived a profoundly peaceful, amazingly happy life. That big house, with its low-ceilinged rooms, its mahogany and velvet furniture, its black marble mantelpieces, and its oil lamps, was for years a really carefree home. The very fact that I was born into it predisposed me to happiness.

[...]

The name "manor-house", which at the end of the nineteenth century was still used for the old seigneurial dwellings of French Canada, was far more imposing than the actual structures it designated.

The Saint-Ours manor-house, at L'Assomption, came down to us from a great-grand-aunt on my mother's side. My mother was brought up in it, and it was from there that she was married. We were all born there too.

It stood about two miles from the village, on the highway to Montreal. It was a big stone house, with a long roof pierced by dormer windows.

[...]

From the end of the seventeenth century down to our own time this manor-house had been lived in by a good many people and, through inheritance and relationships, had passed from the Le Gardeurs to the Saint-Ours and from them to my mother. In 1790 it had been partly rebuilt by our great-grand-uncle, Charles Auguste d'Eschaillon de Saint-Ours.

[...]

The drawing room in the manor-house was filled with mahogany furniture. There were great, well-stuffed armchairs, their wood carved with roses in full bloom, their upholstery of red buttoned velvet. There were also card-tables and whatnots. Two huge, high-backed sofas stood at one end, on either side of the door. In front of the black marble fireplace there was a round table with an epergne.

This was a strange and complicated object. It consisted of a silver base supporting a number of glass vessels. I never knew what it was supposed to be used for, nor did anybody else. I am inclined to think now that it served no useful purpose at all. It was an "ornament". This showy piece struck me as a very handsome object indeed. Thus, at a very tender age, I showed a taste for useless ostentation and for the poetry of decoration.

The whatnots – there were two of them – lent an odd note to the room because of their shape. They were made of black walnut and had a typical Victorian ugliness. They dated from the time of my parents' marriage in 1874. A "whatnot" was a sort of table supporting a mirror, which was surrounded by little shelves of different sizes, the ones on top smaller than the ones below. On this curious monument it was customary to display bric-à-brac – objects in porcelain or bronze, which represented a stag running, a cat in a slipper, or a lady of olden times (but of what times? for the fashions were a little vague), and other articles of similar taste. There was also a Meissen china bouquet whose flowers were so fresh and bright that they rivalled the real flowers from our garden which mother used to set out on the mantelpiece in summertime.

The pictures in the drawing room were hung from thick cords of red silk, and to make them easier to see they were made to stick out from the wall at a sharp angle. This was done by means of a wedge fastened at the back.

A child is always likely to be affected by the contents of the house where sensibility first comes to him, but nothing makes so deep an impression as pictures, engravings and portraits.

[...]

---

* Extracts from *Testament de mon enfance* by Robert de Roquebrune (Montreal: Fides, 1958, 1979), pp. 11-16. English translation by Felix Walther, *Testament of My Childhood. Robert de Roquebrune* (Toronto: University of Toronto Press, 1964), pp. 1-5.

THE DINING ROOM

THE DINING ROOM MADE ITS APPEARANCE IN THE eighteenth century, during the reign of Louis XV in France and that of the first, second and third Georges in England, at a time when a need began to be felt for privacy and comfort in the home. Hitherto no specific room had been set aside for such a purpose. Tables could be dismantled, and noblemen and princes ate either in the great halls of their castles when there were many guests, or in the solar, chamber or antechamber when eating in private. From the eighteenth century on, it was considered essential for both the nobility and the *bourgeoisie* to have at least a salon or drawing room and a dining room. However, at that time the French and English had very different notions of comfort. French houses, despite changing somewhat to accommodate new concerns for comfort and privacy, were still rather formal. In England the Georgian house, on the other hand, was the product of "a period that combined domesticity, elegance and comfort more successfully than ever before".[1] Living mainly in the country, the English aristocracy of the eighteenth century developed a way of life unique to their class, centred on the home. Cut off from cities and urban recreations, they visited and entertained each other a great deal. As Rybczynski explains, "Since all these activities took place in and around the house, the result was that the home acquired a position of social importance that it had never had, before or since [...] but [...] in a curiously private way".[2]

The middle classes, seeking to imitate the aristocracy, copied their houses and their way of life. Consequently, the two most important rooms in the Georgian house were the drawing room and the dining room; indeed, many people had two of each, that is, formal rooms for entertaining guests, and more intimate ones for the family. It was representatives of this English *bourgeoisie* who constituted the cream of Canadian society through the nineteenth century. It was the British who imported neo-classical architecture and with it the Georgian house. As English influence increased in Quebec it naturally brought into the homes of the local *bourgeoisie* the drawing room and the dining room, those twin summits in the hierarchy of rooms in an English house. In adopting these rooms, the Canadian *bourgeoisie* also clung to the English way of life and to the strict etiquette prevalent in the English home. In more modest homes, usually those of the lower middle classes, the drawing room and dining room were often the only two recreation rooms in the house.[3]

THE HEART OF THE MIDDLE-CLASS HOME

> We entered the dining room where on a damask tablecloth stood crystal glasses and candles burning in little pink glasses, and the warm air was full of the delicious scents of rare flowers. We bravely tackled a long menu of dishes, and for two whole hours were served everything that could tempt the fussiest palate, the most exigent taste, while in our glasses claret and champagne sparkled and uplifted our spirits.[4]

The dining room, along with the drawing room, was the most important place for the family to gather from the mid-eighteenth century onwards. In the nineteenth century these rooms became the primary venues where family members foregathered at a moment in history when "the house became the home".[5] For Monique Éleb-Vidal, this new concept was linked to a new idea of family life, and "explains many things: the quest for comfort, for domesticity, for creating a space for families to be together".[6] In the course of the nineteenth century there emerged a new attitude to meals and to the room in which they were consumed. Etiquette books devoted whole chapters to good table manners, the decoration of the dining room, the serving of meals, and menus. "The dining room became the place for family gatherings, often specifically so, and the table was its focus. By the nineteenth century this arrangement had made of mealtimes a family ritual."[7] The dining room, therefore, was an area with a strong family connotation, in which children were introduced to the basic rules of behaviour and learned their table manners. In addition to this, in terms of appearances the dining room "was a most important place. Here the family displayed itself to its guests, set out its silverware and exhibited an epergne made by a fashionable silversmith. But meals also constituted a special time for social interaction: it was at table that business was discussed, ambitions revealed and marriages arranged."[8]

THE POSITION OF THE DINING ROOM

Clearly, then, the position of the dining room within the *bourgeois* home was too important to be left to chance. It had to be close to the drawing room, since that was where guests gathered before going in to table, and after the meal was over. This was a middle-class custom so widespread and so unvarying that it could well be called a ritual:

> As the guests arrive, they are received in the drawing room by the host, who introduces people to each other where necessary. [...] Once everyone has gathered in the drawing room and all the preparations are complete, a servant comes to announce that "Madam is served". The lady of the house then invites her guests to follow her; she accepts the arm of the highest ranking man present, and moves into the dining room, both doors of which are open. [...] Once the meal is over, the hostess rises. All those present do the same, with each gentleman offering his arm to the lady placed next to him, and they all return to the drawing room for coffee and to spend the rest of the evening there.[9]

189
A family Christmas dinner, 1899
Photograph
Archives nationales du Québec, Centre de Québec et Chaudière-Appalaches, fonds Delphine Verge-Bigué (N476-26)

190
J. Hill, Montreal
Dining room of the Harrison Stephens house, The Homestead, Montreal
Photograph
McCord Museum of Canadian History, Montreal, Notman Photographic Archives

Ideally, the couples passed through the hall, if there was one, on their way to the dining room. From a practical point of view, to make things easier for the servants, the dining room needed to be close to the kitchen but not right next door to it, for it would be in poor taste for the noise and smells from the kitchen to reach the reception rooms. The pantry thus played a useful role between the two rooms, and allowed the servants to put the finishing touches to dishes before they were presented at table.

Most of the etiquette books printed at the time came from Europe. The few published in Canada were obviously based on books from France and England, since the habits of European polite society were also followed here, as is apparent from the Marquis de Lévis's account of his visit to Canada in 1895:

THE USERS

On Saturday June 22 at seven o'clock in the evening we dined at the Spencer Wood villa, the residence of the lieutenant-governor of the province of Quebec. This is a large villa in the Italian style, half an hour's ride from Quebec City, set in a pretty estate planted with fine trees overlooking the St. Lawrence. Madame Chapleau, an English-Canadian lady, is very charming, and together with her husband did the honours of the house, the meal and the evening. They were ably assisted by chamberlains in black coats with blue silk lapels, who meet you at the door and show you to your place. The guests, thirty in number, were the cream of Quebec City society. [...] Canadian music was played during dinner. Lord Aberdeen gave the toast to the Queen of England, and then everyone rose; the ladies moved into the drawing room; the men stayed at table a while in order to smoke, and then joined the ladies in the drawing room, where the rest of the evening was spent in conversation until eleven o'clock. Then Lord and Lady Aberdeen withdrew, which was the signal for our departure.[10]

THE DEVELOPMENT OF THE DINING ROOM IN QUEBEC[11]
Between 1840 and 1900 increasing numbers of Quebec homes began to include dining rooms, as the merchant *bourgeoisie* came up in the world. By the end of the nineteenth century dining rooms were to be found in working-class homes: small ones, it is true, but dining rooms nevertheless. This slow process of democratization was linked to the enormous growth of the middle classes, for whom the possession of a dining room represented one of the primary symbols of social success. In order to analyze this development, we have followed the chronological divisions used by most specialists on the period: the early Victorian period (1839-1859), the mid-Victorian period (1860-1879) and the late Victorian period (1880-1901).

THE EARLY VICTORIAN ERA: 1839-1859
At the start of the era, the only Quebec houses to possess dining rooms were those of the élite, and what is more, of the English-speaking élite.[12] There was nothing unusual about this: even in Europe and the United States, until the 1880s a dining room was still the prerogative of the well-to-do. In the 1840s and 1850s, therefore, dining rooms were relatively few and far between, found only in the larger than average city homes of the English-speaking *bourgeoisie*. Except for a few unusually prosperous craftsmen and for those employed in the timber trade, the possessors of dining rooms in the mid-nineteenth century were mainly doctors, notaries and landowners, or simply gentlemen. Few French speakers had one, save perhaps for the occasional rare representative of the old French nobility living in the country. The latter would have a *salon* or a room used for the same purpose, but it was still sometimes called by the older name of *chambre de compagnie*.

The dining-room furnishings varied according to social group and the owner's means, as was to be the case throughout the Victorian era, but on the whole it was a fairly luxurious, comfortable and well-furnished room. Mahogany furniture predominated, perhaps as a hangover from the neo-classical period. In addition to the sideboard, usually the most expensive item in

191

191
J. G. Parks (active 1865 to 1895)
Dining room of the Manoir Papineau,
Montebello, about 1885
Photograph
National Archives of Canada, Ottawa (PA 115908)
On his return from exile in 1845, Louis-Joseph Papineau (1786-1871) settled on his seigneury of Petite-Nation, where between 1846 and 1850 he built himself a manor house. The luxuriously-furnished dining room included two sideboards that bore a selection of fine silverware and china.

the room, the furniture consisted of a dining table, a horsehair sofa, a set of eight to twelve chairs and a couple of games tables. The floor was often covered by a Brussels carpet in well-to-do homes, or by a simple oilcloth. The room was heated by the inevitable fireplace and also by a stove. The presence of easy chairs, a clock, games tables and the games themselves (*bagatelle* or backgammon) suggests that the room was used not only for meals but also as a family room after meals. Depending on the owner's means, the dining room contained lesser or greater amounts of silverware, porcelain and crystal. The homes of the better-off were lit by candles, the rest by oil lamps. Well-to-do craftsmen had cherry wood rather than mahogany furniture, Windsor or rush-bottomed chairs, and a sofa covered with chintz rather than horsehair or moiré.

DINING ROOM OF THE HONOURABLE PIERRE DE ROCHEBLAVE AND ANNE-ELMIRE BOUTHILLIER, MONTREAL, 1840[13]

One mahogany sideboard
one set of mahogany dining tables in three pieces
one mahogany breakfast table
twelve cane-bottomed chairs, two with arms
one fabric carpet about twenty-six *verges* in area

two mahogany games tables
one alabaster chimneypiece ornament
one Franklin stove
one copper fire-guard
one child's rocking horse
one old sofa covered in horsehair

It is significant that this inventory does not mention a lamp, but includes several silver candelabra with snuffers and snuffer stands. It was, therefore, a very "English" dining room, even though its owners were French-speaking.

DINING ROOM OF THE NOTARY ERROL BOYD LINDSAY AND MARIE-LOUISE PERRAULT, QUEBEC CITY, 1841[14]

One mahogany sideboard	one statue and two prints
one mahogany dining table	one Brussels carpet and a small carpet
one sofa and twelve chairs	
two child's chairs	two curtains
one fire-guard, shovel and fork	

"GRANDE SALLE" USED AS A DINING ROOM BY THE MERCHANT EZEKIEL HART AND FRANCES LAZARUS, TROIS-RIVIÈRES, 1843[15]

One mahogany sideboard	one flowered oilcloth for floor
one horsehair sofa	one copper lamp with crystal shade
one large mahogany dining table	two other copper lamps with crystal shades
eight cane-bottomed chairs	
one plain stove with pipe	one table with a [?] and trimming with *limaçon*
one fire-guard, one pair of tongs, one shovel and a poker	
	five frames or portraits
two pots of flowers and three pyramids	one oilcloth for table
	fifty-six flower pots
one small table with flower pot	

THE MID-VICTORIAN ERA: 1860-1879

During the 1860s and 1870s there was a sharp rise in the number of dining rooms, especially after 1865, which seems to have been a watershed year although we cannot tell precisely why. This increase was directly linked to the growth in numbers and influence of the merchant and tradesman class.[16] Whereas in the two previous decades scarcely one fifth of the sample group had a dining room, now it was a third of them. They were still mainly English-speakers, but the number of French-speaking owners of dining rooms had grown considerably. At the start of this period it was mainly prominent citizens who had them, but during the 1860s and 1870s the majority of those with a dining room were English-speaking tradesmen and merchants. French speakers who owned them were mostly professionals, civil servants and the *bourgeoisie*.

It was the merchant's dining room, whether he was anglophone or francophone, which was by far the most luxurious. Its furniture was of mahogany or black walnut, and it was amply provided with tableware – porcelain, crystal and silverware in profusion. Some English-speaking merchants even had two dining rooms, one used only for the evening meal and the other, called a breakfast room,[17] for the morning and midday meals. The dining rooms of shopkeepers and artisans were much more modest. The furniture was of yellow or silver birch or pine, the table was hidden under a table cover, the floor-covering was oilcloth or linoleum rather than a carpet, and there was no silverware, porcelain or crystal.

Dining-room furniture was much the same as in the previous two decades, consisting of a table, a sideboard, one or two sofas and games tables. From the 1860s on many dining rooms were lit by gas[18] and contained a clock, usually an American one. The décor also changed, becoming more elaborate. This was a period in which much attention was paid to dressing up windows

192
Notman Studio, Montreal
Dining room of the Skaife house, Montreal, 1908
Photograph
McCord Museum of Canadian History, Montreal, Notman Photographic Archives (170,556-II)

with drapes, lace curtains and slatted blinds. Mantelpiece and cornice had their appropriate ornaments, and plants and flowers proliferated. The abundant greenery so often found in the dining room not only served an aesthetic purpose but also provided welcome humidity to counteract the dry air resulting from the heat of the stove.[19] Various kinds of shelving and whatnots had been designed to hold plants since the start of the century, and flower vases were everywhere. In addition to the plants and flowers that constituted an essential part of interior decoration in the second half of the nineteenth century, many households had cage birds whose warblings enlivened the most frequently used room in the house. The walls were hung with paintings, "pictures" in gilt frames, and maps.[20] Many dining rooms also contained a bookcase, books and sometimes a desk.

Dining Room of the Merchant Thomas Tail and Sarah McDonald, Melbourne, near Sherbrooke, 1865[21]

One dining table	a carpet
two sofas	nine pictures
nine hair-seated chairs	one hanging lamp
one small stand	a sideboard

... Together with a great deal of crockery, silver glasses and dishes, two damask tablecloths, over a hundred books and two candelabra.

In the breakfast room, together with some silver cutlery, were:

one clock	three window blinds or jalousies
one breakfast table	four pictures
one occasional table	one stove with pipes
nine chairs	one carpet
one child's chair	

THE USERS

DINING ROOM OF THE MERCHANT PHILÉAS MÉTHOT AND
LOUISE WELLING, QUEBEC CITY, 1861[22]

One mahogany dining table	one set of cornice ornaments
twelve black-walnut chairs stuffed with horsehair	consisting of five different figures and three globes
one black-walnut armchair stuffed with horsehair	one Turkey carpet about thirty-six *verges* in area
one mahogany sideboard	one oilcloth for floor
one mahogany bureau with three drawers and bookcase	another carpet of flowered cotton
one small screen	two pairs of wool damask curtains with copper cornices
one cast-iron grate with small shovel and tongs	... Together with a great deal of silverware, crystal and porcelain

DINING ROOM OF JOSEPH DIONNE, LEGISLATIVE COUNCILLOR,
TROIS-RIVIÈRES REGION, 1860[23]

One two-piece folding table with imitation marble oilcloth	three *bancs à bouquets*
seven chairs, six wooden and one of cane	one old, worn carpet and two pieces of rag rug
two square softwood tables with table-covers	one tea-board and a small wooden coffer painted green

DINING ROOM OF JOHN HARRISON, IRONMONGER,
TROIS-RIVIÈRES, 1876[24]

One horsehair sofa	two gas chandeliers
six cane chairs	two vases
one dining table with cover	two lamps
one sideboard	[some cutlery, including some silverware]
one large mirror with gilt frame	
the dining room carpet	four tablecloths and three napkins, with six other small napkins
a clock	

THE LATE-VICTORIAN ERA: 1880-1901

By the last two decades of the nineteenth century the dining room was no longer a unique characteristic of the English-speaking *bourgeois* way of life, since it could be found in as many French-speaking as English homes. It is also significant that by now there were dining rooms in rural areas, in the houses of artisans and farmers as well as tradesmen and doctors. In the 1880s and 1890s the rapid development of the dining room was directly due to the growth of the middle classes. A dining room was now part of the life style of many different social strata, from the leaders of society, the *grande bourgeoisie* and civil servants to clerks, small shopkeepers, craftsmen and farmers. Anyone with adequate means had in his house a room used only for meals.[25]

Despite the relative democratization of the dining room by the late nineteenth century, the gulf between the various social classes was even wider than before. The difference between the upper-class dining room and that of the humble artisan had less to do with the kind and number of pieces of furniture therein than with the quality of the materials, the fineness of the

Excess in t
Dining roo
p. 248

workmanship, the fabrics used, and above all, the pictures and decorative objects, which in the one case would be originals and in the other cheap imitations. We know, for example, that in this period watercolours and needlework pictures were thought best for the drawing room, while in the dining room oil paintings, especially still lifes with game, were considered the best possible taste:[26] "...paintings of fruit, still lifes, and anything reminiscent of food, belonged in the dining room." Landscapes, rural scenes and portraits also had their place there, as Robert De Roquebrune suggests:

> The walls of the dining room were peopled, too, with a number of motionless figures. This silent, solemn company filled me with a secret terror. The subjects themselves overawed me and I was quite bewildered by the costumes in which these people were dressed. I was very astonished to learn that these were my father's great-grandparents. The portraits had been painted at different periods and some of the artists were obviously more gifted than others.[27]

Mahogany, much less in evidence than in the early and mid-Victorian eras, was found only in upper-class dining rooms. An example of this is the gift made to Lady Laurier, wife of the Prime Minister of Canada, by a group of ladies from Quebec and Ontario in 1897, which was a complete dining-room suite in mahogany valued at two thousand dollars. The fashionable wood at this time was black walnut, a clear indication of prosperity, but oak, ash and pine furniture was also common, as can be seen in an advertisement by H. P. Labelle & Co. in 1897. In working-class homes traditional furniture was still found, but even there, references to elements of fakery such as "a softwood imitation black walnut sideboard" or "an imitation marble oilcloth for the table" testify to the mimicry by which the middle classes tried to imitate the upper classes.

Dining-room furniture remained the same: an extending table, a sideboard, often a sofa and armchairs. In humbler homes – those of artisans, farmers and office clerks – there might be a sewing machine and icebox. In terms of decoration, there were two distinct trends. That of the 1860s and 1870s was exaggerated: curtains, blinds and even door curtains proliferated, as did *jardinières* for flowers and plants, bird cages, "frames" and "pictures" on the walls, tablecloths and napkins. On the other hand, the trend towards simplification advocated by the Aesthetic movement made a perceptible difference in dining rooms, as can be seen in the dining room of the Foster house. Members of the liberal professions had more modest dining rooms on the whole, except when they held two concomitant posts, such as lawyer and councillor, lawyer and sheriff or lawyer and translator.

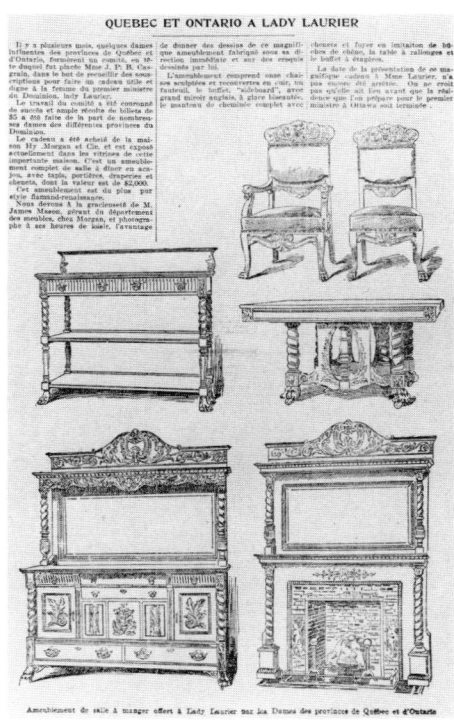

193
Dining-room Furniture Presented to Lady Laurier by the Ladies of the Provinces of Quebec and Ontario
Illustration published in *La Presse*,
August 28, 1897
Photo SRP

This furniture was intended for the Prime Minister's future residence in Ottawa. "The gift was purchased at the firm of Henry Morgan and Co. and is presently on display in the windows of this major retailer... The furniture is in the purest Flemish-Renaissance style. It is courtesy of Mr. James Mason, manager of Morgan's furniture department and an amateur photographer, that we are able to present sketches of this magnificent furniture, which was made under his direct supervision and according to his designs." (trans.)

DINING ROOM OF ELZÉAR GÉRIN-LAJOIE, LAWYER AND COUNCILLOR, TROIS-RIVIÈRES, 1887[28]

Brussels carpet extending also into the drawing room, 115 *verges* in area
one black walnut whatnot
seven black walnut dining-room chairs with leather seats
two black walnut armchairs with leather seats
one chair (hammock)
one black walnut dining-room table
two marble-topped tables in black walnut
one black walnut sideboard
one child's chair
two small black-painted *jardinières*

THE USERS 233

two large mirrors with black walnut frames
four pairs of curtains with rings and rod, three in the window embrasures and one in the doorway to the drawing room
two pictures (members of the Quebec National Assembly)
two pictures (Lord and Lady Dufferin)
one picture (American centenarian)
two gas chandeliers
one rug and a sheepskin dyed red
a bust of Charette
a Briet soda siphon
a complete porcelain service (for breakfast, dinner and dessert)
a silver tea service
an alabaster pot
a table cover in red wool
a screen
... And various pieces of crockery

DINING ROOM OF WILLIAM WATSON OGILVIE, MILLER AND FLOUR MERCHANT, AND HELEN JOHNSTON, MONTREAL, 1900[29]

One Turkish rug
twenty-two (22) dining room chairs
one dining room table
two dinner waggons
one oak cabinet
one folding screen
one small table and cover
one *jardinière* and plant
one pair candelabra
two cloisonné vases
two majolica vases
one photograph frame
one tray
two bronze (Hunting scenes)
three Doulton
[plated ware and glassware]
curtains, poles and shades

Oil Paintings in Dining Room

Cattle at Rest, by Gray
A Wayside Inn, by George Morland
Peasant Girl, by Hawkins
Farmyard, by Herring
Scene in Wales, by W. H. Paton
Solid Comfort, by Kotchenreiter
Flower Girl, by Munier
Camp Fire, by Otto Leyde
Grazing, by Otto de Thoren
The Hunter, by Anderson Hague
The Arab, by Scheyer
The Wind Mill, by Henry Kennedy
Hunting scene, *Gone away*, by Haywood Hardy
Hunting Scene, by Haywood Hardy
Buffaloes at Sunset, by Henry Bernard
In Lincolnshire, by E. King
Venetian Scene, by Santore
Venetian Scene, by Santore
The Bath, by Leberenz
Card Players, by Escosira
The Squire's Favorite, by Haywood Hardy
Scene near Bolton, by Nelson
Manx Fishing Village, by Peter Ghent
Washing Day, by Smith Hall
In Venice, by Way
The Gate, by Haywood Hardy
The Hayfield, Artist unknown

The breakfast room contained:

One carpet square
eight leather lined chairs
one sideboard
seventy pieces of plated ware
curtains, poles and blinds
one cabinet of plated ware
one black walnut dining table

Watercolours in Breakfast Room

Glen, by F. M. Belle Smith
Harbour Scene, Artist unknown
Bridge Scene, by Albert Hartland
Waiting, by C. Fitzgerald

194

Advertisement for the firm of H. P. Labelle of Montreal
Published in the *Montreal Star*, August 28, 1897
Photo SRP

195

Notman Studio, Montreal
Dining room of Mrs. Annie Morrice's house, Montreal, 1899
Photograph
McCord Museum of Canadian History, Montreal, Notman Photographic Archives (128,253-II)

The heavy draperies covering the door and the chimneypiece hangings contrast with the simplicity of the furniture and contribute towards the room's rather snug atmosphere.

Blarney Castle, by Albert Hartland
On the Conway, by Peter Ghent
Moonlight in Venice, by C. J. Way
In Wales, by Clinton Jones
Turnip Field near Conway, by Peter Ghent
Study in Rocks, by J. B. Tigh
On the Thames, by Albert Hartland
Five Copies of Hunting Scenes

DINING ROOM OF THE CARPENTER PROSPER BEAUMIER AND MARIE-DINA GUILBAULT, TROIS-RIVIÈRES, 1891[30]

Three chairs painted black
two rocking chairs painted brown with stuffed wings and backs
another rocking chair with rungs, painted yellow
four pictures in brown frames
one eight-day clock with cornice
one softwood table with cover
one softwood imitation black walnut sideboard with three doors and a double door
one softwood imitation mahogany *armoire*
two niches with statues of the Blessed Virgin and St. Joseph
the curtains of the two door frames of the room
[crockery, including a few items in crystal]
five coal oil lamps with globes
one pair of copper chandeliers
the dining room carpet with a rag rug runner
three small pots of artificial flowers

DINING ROOM OF THE BLACKSMITH EDWARD MCCARTHY AND MARY-ANNE MCGARR, MONTREAL, 1880[31]

Small pine table painted brown
eleven wood seat chairs
oval dining table brown with two leaves
oil cloth table cover
brown pine cupboard
three small coal oil lamps
six assorted pictures framed
four strips catalogne carpet
window curtains and fringe
... Together with crockery and various utensils

196
Notman Studio, Montreal
Dining room of Mrs. Foster's house, Montreal, 1897
Photograph
McCord Museum of Canadian History, Montreal, Notman Photographic Archives (119,061-II)

We can also compare the dining room of a summer residence with that in a city house thanks to the inventory of Thomas Davidson, manager of an insurance company, of 1901.[32]

DINING ROOM OF THE SUMMER RESIDENCE AT SUMMERLEA, QUEBEC

Lot of matting	mahogany dinner waggon
ash sideboard	bracket
oak dining table	hanging lamp
eight oak dining chairs	rustic flower stand
refrigerator	six framed pictures
round table and cover	lot of crystal

DINING ROOM OF THE CITY HOUSE ON PEEL STREET IN MONTREAL

Carpet (dyed)	two small vases
twelve oak dining room chairs	small liqueur basket
one sideboard	mirror
dinner waggon	tea-table
two pairs of rep curtains	mahogany dining room table
two curtain poles	table cover
brass chandelier	twelve pictures
four gas globes	five pictures (Leache's)

A SYMBOL OF SOCIAL SUCCESS FOR THE MIDDLE CLASSES

According to a study based on an analysis of pattern books and guides to interior decoration published between 1840 and 1900, a dining room became a real indication of social success for the middle classes in the years 1880 to 1901.[33]

If the middle classes rose in the social scale, it was thanks to money. However, since money alone could not enable anyone to rise socially, it was necessary to prove that one had taste, and the fact of possessing a well-furnished and well-decorated dining room constituted unquestionable proof of good taste.[34] By the end of the nineteenth century, to own a house with a separate dining room was therefore one of the main indices of social success for the middle classes:

> The dining room had become a central symbol for the attainment of middle-class status. Linen, silver and china which accompanied elaborate meals and stylized dining-room etiquette were now widely accepted as signs of having entered the ranks of the middle-class consumer society. [...] Although the front parlor still remained an important public space, the dining room had now come to represent the realization of artistic creativity, good breeding, and hospitality: only those whose jobs were secure and whose good taste was unquestioned could afford to enjoy an elaborate, multicourse meal, complemented by fine linens and silver. For them, a space earlier regarded a safe harbor for the family had been transformed into a showcase of middle-class accomplishment.[35]

Traditionally, the English dining room was a formal and dignified room. In addition to a welcoming fireplace, it often had wood wainscotting on the walls hung with oil paintings, preferably family portraits in heavy gilt frames. The heavy furniture, usually of highly polished mahogany, the high ceiling, the thick Turkey carpet and the frequent use of dark colours in the décor made the English dining room look warm and comfortable.[36] Perhaps because it gave the impression of a certain stability, it helped to confirm the new social status of people who had only just risen from the working classes.

FURNISHINGS
The furnishings of the Quebec dining room were not very different from the basic English model, which consisted of a dining table, usually extendable, with its accompanying chairs, a sideboard, a few occasional tables for dishes and two comfortable armchairs placed near the fireplace. Other items might include a screen to shield the company from draughts, and some other small occasional pieces. According to Muthesius,[37] it was unusual to find a settee or an easy chair in the late-nineteenth century dining room save in humbler homes, where the dining room was also used as a sitting room. This indeed was the case with most dining rooms in Quebec where, as in the United States, the dining-room furniture had much in common with that of the living room.[38] In addition to the sofa and armchairs, there were often a clock, a bookcase and books, games and games tables, a desk, a bird cage and many pot plants.

The custom of using the drawing room as a living room, and of considering it the most important room in the house was, according to Muthesius, more a phenomenon of the late nineteenth and early twentieth centuries. Until then it was customary to spend time in the dining room after the meal was over, and this was still the case at the end of the nineteenth century in many humbler homes in England, Canada and the United States. Unlike the upper classes, the middle class did not always have a drawing room. Even when a middle-class household had both a drawing room and a dining room, in winter the latter was often the only heated room in the house. It was where the family spent most of its time together in everyday activities: reading, working or talking. For this reason the authors of pattern books in the 1880s and 1890s recommended making the dining room an attractive and restful place with plants and flowers, whatnots to hold small decorative objects, and of course, a sideboard. They suggested using a somewhat richer, darker colour scheme than in the rest of the house, and building a china cabinet[39] into the wall of the room. Generally, however, the china cabinet was a discrete piece, known as a *vitrine*.

In Quebec it was, apparently, not just the middle classes who used their dining room as a living room. There is evidence that the old nobility of French stock also did so. The following was written by Robert de Roquebrune, in his childhood memoirs, about the dining room in the manor-house of the Saint-Ours family at L'Assomption in the late nineteenth century:

> The dining room was much more comfortable than the drawing room, so we spent a good deal of time in it. I can really remember it best as it was in autumn with the logs blazing in the fireplace, or in winter with the big stove growling away in one corner. Here in the evenings I had a chance to see my parents. My father would sit and read in his big arm-chair not far from the fire, and it could never get too hot for him. My mother would do her sewing or her darning near a little table, which held a lamp, her sewing basket, and a book or two. There would be long silences interrupted from time to time by animated snatches of talk, and all this while I played about on the carpet at their feet.[40]

THE TABLE AND CHAIRS

The dining-room table, usually rectangular or oval and extendable, is of English origin, often made of mahogany or black walnut. The dining-room chairs were often just of wood, cane-bottomed or Windsor-style, but balloon-back chairs (in mahogany or black walnut) were especially popular in the Victorian era because they were so comfortable: the rounded balloon-shaped back provided good support. Chairs like these were found in the drawing room as well as the dining room,[41] with silk, satin or damask covering in the former room and leather or horsehair in the latter. In the last third of the nineteenth century, however, the neo-colonial movement brought Chippendale and Queen Anne chairs back into fashion for the dining room, covered in morocco leather and sold in sets. A set usually contained two armchairs for the master and mistress of the house, placed at each end of the table. This English custom was also echoed in the drawing room and the library, with two comfortable leather armchairs beside the fire.[42]

THE SIDEBOARD

The sideboard was by far the most important piece of furniture in the Victorian dining room. It contained several drawers for the most valuable silver cutlery, and cupboards, in one of which alcoholic drinks were locked away. The primary function of the sideboard was, however, to display the handsomest items of silverware and porcelain the household possessed, which is why it unquestionably constituted the focal point of the room. At the start of the Victorian era it was plain and rather angular, but under the influence of the rococo revival it became more rounded and also more elabo-

197
Christmas dinner at 254 Olivier Avenue, Montreal, 1899
Photograph
McCord Museum of Canadian History, Montreal, Notman Photographic Archives (MP076-77)

rate in decoration. The upper section and the doors were often carved with still life scenes of hunting and fishing. With the Renaissance-revival fashion, which lasted from 1875 to 1900, sideboards became more massively architectural, but from the 1880s and 1890s the Aesthetic movement brought about a return to simplicity. The Eastlake style in particular led to less massive sideboards with less elaborate ornamentation using simple geometrical shapes; relief carving disappeared in favour of incised carving, appliqué motifs and the ornamental use of different kinds of wood. The sideboard from the Musée Laurier and the one from the Village québécois d'antan in Drummondville are particularly interesting examples. The former is of very polished workmanship in perfect keeping with Charles Eastlake's principles, while the latter is an excellent example of a local craftsman's interpretation of those same principles. During the last third of the nineteenth century it was not unusual to find in the dining room an alcove for a sideboard.

LIGHTING

Victorian etiquette books dwell at length on how to illuminate the dining-room table. As a general rule, they agree in stating that this is best done with candelabra rather than a lamp hanging from the ceiling:

> No matter how bright the light from gas globes or from a central gasolier, a formally set table must have candelabra with many lighted candles. The humblest of tables should not have less than two candles. Overhead lighting is crude and annoying: it makes the table look depressing and distorts people's faces, as does a camera, unless it is counterbalanced by ordinary lighting. When dinner takes place during daylight, everything should be in readiness to provide other sources of light quickly if the meal goes on a long time or the skies turn dark. But in every well-regulated household the blinds or curtains are drawn and dinner is eaten by candlelight. Only illuminated thus do the crystal and silverware, the decorative elements of the table, shine and sparkle in all their glory.[43]

THE USERS   239

198
Marius Barbeau, Ottawa
Balloon-back chairs from the priests' common room at the Sainte-Anne-de-la-Pocatière boarding school (about 1850-1880), 1951
Photograph
Canadian Museum of Civilization, Hull, Marius Barbeau Collection (J-9855)

199
Rococo-revival sideboard
Mahogany and mahogany veneer,
266 x 200 x 67 cm
Musée du Saguenay–Lac-Saint-Jean, Chicoutimi (A-76.146)
Photo Christine Guest/MMFA

The grapes, partridge, hares and fish that adorn this mahogany sideboard, together with the ermines that serves as its handles, constitute a rich decorative programme eminently suited to the function of the piece. The motifs have, however, been crafted in a rather naive style.

The Sideboard of Jean-Thomas Taschereau and Respect for Family Tradition

Throughout the long history of the Taschereau family, seigneurs in Sainte-Marie de Beauce, there is evidence of a continuous interest in porcelain and silverware. This tradition persisted from 1726, when the founder of the line came to Canada, down to the Victorian era. By making judicious marriages the Taschereaus became ever more wealthy. Inventories drawn up at regular intervals record their fine table services in green or flowered porcelain, their crystal decanters and dishes imported from France and England, their tableware in "*fayence de la Reine*", their silver-handled knives and forks, their tea and coffee services in flowered blue stoneware...

After the division of the property of Gabriel-Elzéar Taschereau in 1809, one of his sons, Jean-Thomas (1778-1832), married Marie Panet, daughter of the Speaker of the Legislative Assembly. Their son Jean-Thomas (1814-1893) in his turn married first the daughter of the legislative councillor Amable Dionne, and later the daughter of the Lieutenant Governor René-Édouard Caron. In 1843, as a young lawyer, Taschereau had his house in Saint-Louis Street demolished and replaced by a four-storey residence of stone. From that house, which stood near the present-day Château Frontenac, came a magnificent sideboard, which we can imagine today filled with the fine porcelain and silverware that must have impressed Jean-Thomas's distinguished visitors.

This sideboard was apparently bequeathed to his son Louis-Alexandre, the future premier of Quebec, and stood for many years on the second-floor landing of the family house on the Grande-Allée in Quebec City. On Louis-Alexandre's death it was inherited by his daughter Gabrielle, who placed it in the dining room of her new house, removing the two side supports in order to make room for a tea service. Charles, one of Gabrielle's brothers, was the next to inherit the sideboard, and it was through his son Michel that it was acquired by the Canadian Museum of Civilization in 1982. Since that time the piece has been restored to its original condition.

It seems that the Victorian Taschereaus excelled in the art of making a display, faithful to the family weakness for fine porcelain and silver cutlery.

Micheline Huard and
John R. Porter

206
Naturalistic sideboard, about 1860
Black walnut, mottled and burl walnut veneer,
250.5 x 196 x 65 cm
Canadian Museum of Civilization, Hull (982.33.1)
Photo Christine Guest/MMFA

This elegant sideboard is decorated with foliage, grape and rocaille motifs, all elements drawn from nature.

THE USERS

THE BEDROOM

IN FRENCH THE WORD *CHAMBRE* WAS ORIGINALLY USED FOR every room in the house without distinguishing between them. The term *chambre à coucher* seems to have sprung up in the mid-eighteenth century, the verb "sleeping" added to the word "room" reflecting the development in the use and organization of household space.[1] In Quebec, however, the medieval expression *chambre à lit*[2] lingered on to the second half of the nineteenth century. This usage was for a long time confined to the privileged classes, since the working classes could not necessarily afford a room used solely for sleeping. In the eighteenth century in both Europe and Quebec, many homes had only two rooms: one communal room for cooking, eating and working, and a second containing the bed of the master and mistress of the house, in which they also received visitors. The bedroom was the first room to be used for one specific purpose: sleeping. Thereafter, as *bourgeois* homes acquired other spaces with specific functions, such as drawing rooms and dining rooms, the number of bedrooms also multiplied.

THE INFLUENCE OF *BOURGEOIS* VALUES

In most Western societies, the increase in the number of bedrooms and their place in the Victorian home were phenomena closely linked to the *bourgeois* values of the time: the importance of family, and a growing need for privacy. As the *bourgeoisie* made of family and family values almost a religion, their homes needed specific places for displaying and protecting family life. Families were large in those days, and hospitality was considered a duty. The importance of staying on good terms with one's relatives, distant or close, led families of the prosperous classes to correspond with and visit each other regularly, so that their houses had to be able to accommodate guests.

The growing need for privacy was a determining factor in the greater number of individual bedrooms. Before the Victorian era, bedrooms were also often used as living rooms, but this habit disappeared with the new concern for privacy and the proliferation of individual bedrooms. The public health reforms of the nineteenth century also set at three the minimum number of bedrooms for a family — one for the parents, one for the daughters and a third for the sons[3] – thus guaranteeing the morality and decency vital to any respectable family.

Ideally, then, the Victorian home contained the main bedroom, which occupied the best position in the house, the children's rooms, which had to be close to the parents' room, the guest bedroom or bedrooms, and finally one or more bedrooms for the servants unless, as often happened, the latter simply slept in the kitchen or the attic. Bedroom furnishings and decoration varied according to who was using them. The master bedroom was naturally the best furnished and most comfortable, while the maid's bedroom, often relegated to the attic or the basement, was furnished with odds and ends of things unusable anywhere else in the house.

While the distribution of the bedrooms was affected by the arrangement of the ground-floor rooms, the fact that they were situated on the first and second floors of the house underscores a typically nineteenth-century respect for privacy. Each bedroom gave directly onto a landing or corridor. In keeping with the new concern for health and hygiene, and especially for the benefits of a well-aired house, bedrooms were supposed to be large, well-lit and with good ventilation.

THE MARITAL CHAMBER

Roger-Henri Guerrand says of the master bedroom: "The heavy veil cast over the slightest hint of sexuality in the early nineteenth century was made manifest in the creation of a sacred place, the marital chamber, a shrine to procreation, not to pleasure."[4] At the same time that the house itself was becoming a more private place, one space more than the rest began to express the privacy of the married couple away from their children: it was the master bedroom.[5]

> A man and a woman, once married, became [...] first a couple (an entity made manifest in the master bedroom) and then parents (a fact symbolized by the children's room or rooms and the family parlour). At the time, the marital bed was fit to be seen only if it remained encumbered by the sexual symbols that might have accrued to it, had the mentality of the time been susceptible to such notions of intimacy.[6]

From this standpoint, the furniture of the master bedroom has its own symbolism, as do those of the drawing room and dining room. The bed is by far the most important piece of furniture in the room.

THE DRESSING ROOM

In English houses it was customary for the master bedroom to give on to a small adjoining room called the dressing room, where the husband washed and dressed. It held all that was necessary for the purpose: commode, dressing chest, washstand and a fireplace, in front of which a portable bathtub could be placed. When the husband had his own dressing room, the wife used the bedroom for dressing. The dressing room sometimes became a sort of study, with a sofa, armchairs, a bookcase and work table, but this was rather rare. Dressing rooms began to appear in North American homes after the 1770s.[7] By the nineteenth century they were common in English and American homes, but here in Quebec were found only in English-speaking *bourgeois* houses until the late nineteenth or early twentieth century. Well-to-do French Canadians were more likely to have a *boudoir* next door to the master bedroom. A *boudoir*, however, was a different sort of room from a dressing room, and was differently furnished.

When her home had no *boudoir*, the lady of the house used her bedroom for the same purpose. The pieces of furniture she needed to dress — the dressing table and the wardrobe with its mirror — were placed near the window. Since in row houses the master bedroom was almost always above the drawing room, it often had a bay window. Both good lighting and good ventilation were considered vitally important.

From the 1880s on, this concern for health and comfort manifested itself in the bedroom in a preference for pale colours and cotton or silk curtains, and there was a fashion for built-in cupboards. Metal beds were rejected in favour of a return to wooden ones.[8] The dressing chest for the husband and/or the dressing table for the wife were always essential items. Bedroom furniture was mainly of oak, sometimes stained dark, and mahogany.

A SANCTUM FOR THE FAIR SEX

For a daughter of the *bourgeoisie* in the second half of the nineteenth century, her bedroom was a refuge. Reflecting the girl herself as an individual, it "was replete with symbols [and] became fused with the personality of its occupant, to whose autonomy it bore witness."[9] In her bedroom she kept innumerable personal possessions and mementoes, and there she spent hours writing letters and keeping her diary, reading, resting and entertaining her close female friends. All girls' bedrooms looked much the same: books, plants and flowers, perhaps a holy picture or statue in Catholic homes.

Like a charmed circle of the female world, the bedroom was the most concrete manifestation of a young girl's need for a refuge, a nook of her own where she could escape from the rest of the household. The furniture was usually very comfortable. In addition to the basic items — a bed, a commode and a washstand — there was often a writing table, comfortable armchairs and a chaise-longue.

> Here I am in my big bedroom, rediscovering all my bits and pieces with an almost insane joy I hardly dare describe, so silly do I find it. But between ourselves, my mirror helps me to get to know my own face again. I was beginning to forget it, and it is a strange sensation never to see oneself. My chaise-longue, my cushions, my dear little stove merrily burbling, my little altar, my books, the table where my papers have begun to pile up: all these are like so many little rediscovered delights, so sweet to me that I bless the horrid doctor for having insisted on my resting at home. (February 8, 1878)[10]

The bedroom constituted a sanctum for the ladies of the house since their menfolk never entertained in their own chambers. Of course, the lady of the house and her daughters only invited close female friends into this haven with its highly personalized décor full of mementoes, knick-knacks and cherished books, where one felt truly "at home". Other visitors were received in the drawing room, a place kept for more formal occasions. Drawing-room sociability was obligatory, whereas bedroom sociability was a matter of choice: "This evening [...] mother reproached me on my lack of *sociability*. Yes, I live in my lovely big bedroom, and I always find such a lot to do there that I don't spend a

207
Notman Studio, Montreal
Bedroom in the Masson house, Sherbrooke Street, Montreal, 1898
Photograph
McCord Museum of Canadian History, Montreal, Notman Photographic Archives (124,911 Misc-II)

great deal of time with the family. [...] It's very noisy downstairs, people chatter and argue about everything, about things that don't interest me."[11]

As a result of the codified etiquette and rituals governing private life, the washing and dressing required by propriety took place in the privacy of the bedroom. By the same token, certain garments and postures became taboo. The nightgown, for example, symbolized erotic intimacy, and could no longer be seen outside of the bedroom. Instead, the well-brought-up young woman wore a morning gown – generally a luxurious negligee – and only "let her hair down" in her bedroom.[12] "Never [...] was the female body so hidden as between 1830 and 1914."[13] The chemise or shift, pantaloons and corset were the attributes of modesty. This elaborate underwear made the process of dressing, a vital part of keeping up appearances, somewhat longer.

208

THE CHILDREN'S ROOMS

The nursery was very important in the English home. It was always separate from the rest of the house, and the children spent their time there away from the family until adolescence. Particular care was taken in planning the children's rooms to ensure that they were easily reached from the parents' private apartments: the boudoir and the master bedroom. The children slept in the nursery together with their nurse or nanny. In France the governess's bedroom was usually next door to that of her charge, and the door between was left open at night in case the child became unwell.[14] In Quebec nurseries were rare, except in a few English-speaking *bourgeois* homes. In the houses of the French-speaking *bourgeoisie* the children had their own rooms, or at least the boys and girls had separate bedrooms.

THE GUEST ROOMS

The presence of guest bedrooms in the Victorian *bourgeois* house was largely due to the English habit of going to stay in the country. This custom, like that

208
Notman Studio, Montreal
Miss Arnton's bedroom, Montreal, 1887
Photograph
McCord Museum of Canadian History, Montreal,
Notman Photographic Archives (83,187-II)
Ethel Arnton, daughter of a property developer, was a member of the Montreal Hunt Club and – as the décor of her room clearly shows – an enthusiastic fox hunter.

of visiting relatives and friends living in town, also became widespread here in Quebec. During such visits guests had as many obligations to their hosts as the latter had towards them, and etiquette books are very definite about the way to behave during these visits:

> Nowadays it is fashionable to spend the warmest weeks of the summer in the country. Usually you rent rooms or stay at an hotel; but you may occasionally be invited by relatives or friends to spend some time staying with the family. Here you must be even more careful than usual to behave with propriety. [...] We are

speaking here, of course, about Canada, where the upbringing, manners and etiquette found in good society are the same in the country as in town. [...] Do not show a gloomy face to your hosts, but show appreciation of everything: the house, the garden, the bedroom you have been allotted, the servants who look after you; fall in with the habits of the household as regards when you get up, eat and go to bed: try to give as little trouble as possible to those housing you, by adapting to all their customs.[15]

In this context, the bedroom had a special significance, since it was the only place where the visitor could be alone. The hostess had to prepare it with care, ensuring that everything was spotless and that the guest had a table with writing materials, some books, a washstand and a comfortable bed. The most comfortable guest rooms had one or two well-stuffed armchairs. It behoved guests not to be a burden to their hosts: ..."bring books with you so you can work or study, and thus you will be no trouble to your host and hostess on a rainy day or during the time you spend in your room."[16] Girls and young women were exhorted to observe the proprieties at all times, and were put on their guard against accidental meetings, since "a young woman, and especially a girl, cannot be too careful when in the country to avoid finding herself alone with the men who may be staying there at the same time as she."[17] To be prudent, she should avoid spending too much time on the stairs, in the corridors or in the drawing room at times when the rest of the company is not there. Before leaving her bedroom, she should take with her everything she might need all day, so as not to have to go back.

SPECIAL ROLES AND CUSTOMS
Although the bedroom was increasingly considered a private space as the century progressed, in mid-century it was still semi-public since life's most important events took place there. Only after the 1870s did the trend towards privacy become pronounced. Thereafter, even though the bedroom was still the setting for births, sickness and even death, the visitors brought by these events, which previously had included neighbours and friends, tended to be exclusively close family and medical practitioners.[18]

Births
Once a child was born, the bedroom became a sort of reception room where ladies – friends, neighbours and relations – came to pay a visit of either congratulation or condolence, as the case might be, to the newly delivered young mother.[19] Because of this custom, the role of the bedroom as a theatrical setting meant that its furnishings and decoration took on additional significance. *Bourgeois* ladies liked their bedrooms to look their best, which is why the wealthier among them paid a great deal of attention to their furniture and ornaments.[20]

Illness
Since anyone who fell ill was confined to the bedroom, sometimes for weeks or even months, the room had to contain, in addition to a bed, a night table, a table to eat at, a comfortable armchair, a good fireplace and room to write and even sew.[21] Chairs had naturally to be provided for possible visitors, as

209
Notman Studio, Montreal
Guest bedroom in the George Stephen house, Montreal, 1884
Photograph
McCord Museum of Canadian History, Montreal, Notman Photographic Archives (73,813-II)

when a sick person was unable to leave the bedroom, men were permitted to pay a visit to the sick room:

> In the plethora of etiquette books written for other countries, we are told that when a gentleman is invited to put his hat down, he should take care not to place it on the bed. This advice is irrelevant here, given that in Quebec no visitor is invited into a bed chamber except when someone is confined to bed through sickness. In that case, before entering the room, one makes sure to take off one's hat and hang it up in the passageway.[22]

The Doctor's Visit
The doctor was a familiar figure in nineteenth-century *bourgeois* life. More than just a social equal, he became a friend of the family and was paid heed to, especially given the growing importance of "women's diseases" in pathology.[23] Chlorosis or "green sickness", a form of anaemia that caused pallor in young girls, was undoubtedly the illness *bourgeois* families found most worrying. This strange sickness gave rise to the most imaginative diagnoses until, in the last third of the nineteenth century, people began to realize that it was due to a deficiency.[24]

210
Notman Studio, Montreal
Master bedroom of the George Stephen house, Montreal, 1884
Photograph
McCord Museum of Canadian History, Montreal, Notman Photographic Archives (73,812)
The room's wainscotting was in mahogany and bird's-eye maple.

Since chlorosis was associated with puberty, families found it doubly worrying, and the young girl was surrounded by an almost excessive solicitude until she was married. Restrictions were imposed, and the slightest feeling of faintness meant calling in the doctor. Henriette Dessaulles, a daughter of the *bourgeoisie*, was carefully watched by her family, and scrupulously recorded her fainting spells in her diary: "I feel weak. This morning as I was doing my hair I fainted. When I opened my eyes, I was in bed and papa was holding my hand and looking worried. I tried to smile at him, but he still looked very gloomy. The doctor came."[25] When he came to her bedside some months later, the physician told her again that she was not ill, but merely suffered from weakness. When Henriette said: "Did you know that I can't do my hair by myself any more?", he growled: "Too much hair, you must cut it. [...] I'm sending you to the seaside, and you'll come back plump and strong, won't you, my girl?"[26]

BEDROOM FURNITURE

When one thinks how much time was spent in the bedroom aside from the hours sleeping – time spent writing letters or a diary, reading and receiving friends, to say nothing of time spent sick in bed – the importance of having sufficient comfortable furniture is obvious. The bedroom had to be comfortable, but could not accommodate useless furniture. The basic items were a bed, a dressing table, a washstand, a bedside table and sometimes a wardrobe with a mirror. Additional pieces might include comfy armchairs set close to the stove or fireplace, a chaise-longue (often placed at the foot of the bed), a writing table and a prie-dieu. This last-mentioned piece of furniture, a symbol of ostentatious piety, had been very common in earlier centuries but had fallen into disuse. It came back into fashion in the mid-nineteenth century and remained popular until the end of the Victorian era.

The curtained four-poster bed of the early Victorian period soon became outmoded with the realization that bed curtains not only were dust traps and could house lice, but also constituted a fire hazard. In 1850 the American

211
Renaissance-revival bed, about 1870-1880
Curly and bird's-eye maple veneer, walnut, 287 x 180 x 221 cm
Canadian Museum of Civilization, Hull (A-566-a)
Photo Christine Guest/MMFA

212
Renaissance-revival wardrobe with mirror, about 1870-1880
Curly and bird's-eye maple veneer, walnut, 271 x 241 x 84 cm
Canadian Museum of Civilization, Hull (A-568)
Photo Christine Guest/MMFA

213
Renaissance-revival dressing table with mirror, about 1870-1880
Curly and bird's-eye maple veneer, walnut and marble, 229 x 145 x 68 cm
Canadian Museum of Civilization, Hull (A-567-a)
Photo Christine Guest/MMFA

214
Renaissance-revival bedside table, about 1870-1880
Curly and bird's-eye maple veneer, walnut and marble, 81 x 48.5 x 44 cm
Canadian Museum of Civilization, Hull (A-567-b)
Photo Christine Guest/MMFA

writer A. J. Downing noted that although the four-poster bed with curtains was still popular in England, it had been almost universally replaced in the United States by the "French bedstead", which was lower and had no curtains.[27] The bed from the Jourdain Fiset collection is a fine example of the latter from the 1840s and 1850s. Its shape still recalls the Empire style, but its rococo decoration places it in the early Victorian period. This concern for

THE USERS

215
Renaissance-revival occasional chair, about 1870-1880
Maple, 101.5 x 45 x 52 cm
Canadian Museum of Civilization, Hull (A-566 b)
Photo Christine Guest/MMFA

216
Renaissance-revival "Récamier" style chaise-longue, about 1870-1880
Curly and bird's-eye maple veneer,
98 x 193 x 77 cm
Canadian Museum of Civilization, Hull (A-566 c)
Photo Christine Guest/MMFA

217
Renaissance-revival writing table, about 1870-1880
Curly and bird's-eye maple veneer, leather,
75 x 122.5 x 68 cm
Canadian Museum of Civilization, Hull (A-570)
Photo Christine Guest/MMFA

health and hygiene brought about a vogue for metal beds made of iron or brass. These were very fashionable in the 1850s, 1860s and 1870s, while about 1875 there was a return to wooden bedsteads.

The general tendency, then, during the second half of the nineteenth century was to have a bed either devoid of curtains or with just short half-curtains or valances. The curtainless bed had stately head and footboards which soon became areas in which cabinetmakers, furniture manufacturers and wood carvers could display their skill. It should be remembered that the bed was the focus of the room which dictated the rest of the décor. Its position in the room was important. Whereas in France it was usually placed alongside the wall, with only one side open, in England and also in Quebec the bedhead was up against the wall with free space on either side. The bed also had to be situated so its occupants were not facing the window.[28]

As regards mirrors, the working classes had only tiny ones, and even these were considered luxury items. The *bourgeoisie*, on the other hand, could view

themselves in large cheval glasses or in the mirrors incorporated into wardrobe doors from the 1870s onwards. "A mirror invites contemplation, a look at oneself. It is in this private space that the individual prepares to meet the gaze of others; it is here that the presentation of the self is fashioned in terms of the social image of the body shown to the world."[29] There were also prohibitions associated with mirrors, such as the belief that leaving a mirror uncovered after a death brought bad luck.[30] Its erotic associations were powerful: since representations of the naked body were banned, a young girl ought never to look at herself nude.[31] Mirrors were nevertheless found everywhere in the Victorian home, from the drawing room to the bedroom. In this sense the wardrobe with mirror was a typically Victorian piece of furniture.

Early in this period it was common to place a small standing mirror or table swing mirror on the dressing table. It soon became attached to the dressing table and thence an integral part of it, so that the dressing table with mirror is also a Victorian phenomenon.

Until bedroom suites made their appearance in the mid-nineteenth century, the chamber pot was kept under the bed, or else formed part of a chair known as a close stool chair. The night table was so called because it was used to store the chamber pot during the night, near the bedhead.[32]

The washstand was an indispensable item of bedroom furniture until bathrooms began to be common in the late nineteenth and early twentieth century. It usually had a marble top to hold the basin, ewer, soapdish and tooth glass.

Although it was not actually part of the bedroom suite, the chaise-longue was only found in the bedroom, and indeed there was no reason for placing it in the drawing room.[33] It was in a sense a piece of furniture used for conforming to the proprieties, as the following extract indicates:

> A lady should avoid receiving a man in her bedroom if possible, and a young girl should not allow it for any reason. The doctor, an older close relative or a priest may be permitted to enter, but only if the girl or lady is too ill to get up. If the

218
Bed inspired by the Empire and rococo styles, about 1840-1850
114 x 128 x 212 cm
Jourdain Fiset Collection, Quebec City
Photo SRP

This "carriole" bed is typical of the mid-nineteenth century; the shape is derived from the Empire style, but the ornamentation is distinctly rococo in flavour. The beaver adorning the foot of the bed is a rare example of a specifically *québécois* decorative motif.

219
Advertisement for the firm of Russell Jones of Montreal
Published in R.S.W. Mackay, *The Montreal Directory for 1863-64* Montreal, John Lovell, 1863, p. 414
National Archives of Canada, Ottawa (C-120209)

220

Renaissance-revival bed, about 1875-1890
Black walnut and black burl walnut veneer,
218 x 168 x 217.5 cm
The Montreal Museum of Fine Arts, purchase, Hugh G. Jones Bequest (1988.Df.1)
Photo Christine Guest/MMFA

The relatively simple ornamentation of this bed is achieved mainly by an effective use of black burl walnut veneer. Burl wood, which comes from the point where a branch joins the trunk of a tree, is of great decorative value in the technique of veneering. This piece, with its restrained but imposing style and rounded corners, is proof that Victorian furniture could be extremely elegant.

221

Renaissance-revival bed, about 1870-1880
Black walnut and black figured walnut veneer,
259 x 158 x 231 cm
Denyse Desroches Collection, Granby
Photo Christine Guest/MMFA

Like the other pieces from the same suite (**226** and **227**), this bed shows a high quality of joinery.

222

Renaissance-revival bed, about 1870-1880
Black walnut, 230 x 170 x 212 cm
Jean-Claude Lachance and Denyse Desroches Collection, Granby
Photo Christine Guest/MMFA

As the veneer work on this bed illustrates, furniture makers were able to use machinery to obtain highly sophisticated decorative effects.

LIVING IN STYLE

223
Renaissance-revival bed, about 1875-1890
224 x 142 x 200 cm
Batiscan presbytery
Photo Jean-Pierre Labiau/MOBIVIQ

224
Renaissance-revival bed, about 1875-1890
230 x 133 x 201 cm
Musée du Séminaire de Québec, gift of Abbé G. Édouard Côté
Photo John R. Porter/MOBIVIQ

sickness is not serious enough to keep her in bed, she should lie on the chaise-longue and make the effort to sit up when visitors arrive. She should never receive visitors in her dressing gown or with her hair not done.[34]

A self-respecting woman received only a few visitors when she was ill. A newly delivered young mother received female visitors lying on her chaise-longue.[35] This piece of furniture was usually placed at the foot of the bed, and between it and the fireplace when possible.

Claire Desmeules

225
Rococo-revival dressing chest with mirror,
about 1840-1850
192 x 104 x 51 cm
Jourdain Fiset Collection, Quebec City
Photo SRP

226
Renaissance-revival dressing table with mirror, about 1870-1880
Black walnut, white marble and glass,
249 x 125 x 65 cm
Denyse Desroches Collection, Granby
Photo Christine Guest/MMFA

227
Renaissance-revival washstand,
about 1870-1880
Black walnut and white marble,
106 x 125 x 61 cm
Denyse Desroches Collection, Granby
Photo Christine Guest/MMFA

228
Notman Studio, Montreal
Mrs. Morrice's bedroom, Montreal, 1899
Photograph
McCord Museum of Canadian History, Montreal,
Notman Photographic Archives (128,254-II)

In her bedroom a lady might read, write letters, make entries in her diary or simply rest, and the appropriate furniture was necessary.

THE USERS 265

1 Pascal Dibié, *Ethnologie de la chambre à coucher* (Paris: Bernard Grasset, 1987), p. 143.

2 The expression *chambre à lit* was used in the Middle Ages to distinguish this room from the *chambre de parade* (state chamber) and the *chambre de parement* (robing chamber) in princely residences.

3 Stephan Muthesius, *The English Terraced House* (New Haven and London: Yale University Press, 1982), p. 48.

4 Roger-Henri Guerrand, "Espaces privés", in *De la révolution à la grande guerre*, (vol.4 of *Histoire de la vie privée*, Philippe Ariès and Georges Dulsy, eds.[Paris: Seuil, 1987], p. 334) (trans.).

5 Rivka Bercovici, "La privatisation de l'espace familial: la chambre à coucher conjugale au 19e siècle", in *La maison. Espaces et intimités*, Proceedings of the colloquium held at the Académie d'architecture de Paris, November 28-29, 1985 (Paris: École d'architecture Paris-Villemin, 1986), p. 353.

6 Monique Éleb-Vidal and Anne Debarre-Blanchard, *Architectures de la vie privée: maisons et mentalités, XVIIe - XIXe siècles* (Brussels: Archives d'architecture moderne, 1989), p. 188 (trans.).

7 Elisabeth Donaghy Garret, *At Home: The American Family 1750-1870* (New York: Harry N. Abrams Inc., 1980), p. 132.

8 Hermann Muthesius, *The English House* (New York: Rizzoli, 1979), pp. 224-231.

9 Alain Corbin, "Le secret de l'individu", in *De la révolution à la grande guerre, (vol .4)*,p. 440 (trans.).

10 Fadette, *Journal d'Henriette Dessaulles 1874-1880* (Montreal: Hurtubise, 1971), p. 149 (trans.).

11 *Ibid.*, p. 77 (trans.).

12 Alain Corbin, *op. cit.*, p. 446.

13 *Ibid.*, p. 447 (trans.).

14 Mlle E. Dufaux de la Jonchère, *Le savoir-vivre dans la vie ordinaire et dans les cérémonies civiles et religieuses* (Paris: Librairie Garnier Frères, 1883), p. 35.

15 *La vraie politesse et le bon ton* (Montreal: Eusèbe Senécal, 1873), pp. 96- 98 (trans.).

16 *Ibid.*, p. 99 (trans.).

17 Comtesse Drohojowska, *De la politesse et du bon ton ou devoirs d'une femme chrétienne dans le monde* (Paris: Victor Sarlit, 1860), p. 132 (trans.).

18 Elisabeth Donaghy Garret, *op. cit.*, p. 138.

19 *Ibid.*, p. 126.

20 These valances were often of silk, chintz, wool damask or bombazine.

21 Elisabeth Donaghy Garret, *op. cit.*, p. 126.

22 *La vraie politesse et le bon ton*, pp. 51-52 (trans.).

23 Alain Corbin, "Cris et chuchotements", in *op. cit.*, p. 595.

24 Alain Corbin, *op. cit.*, p. 571.

25 Fadette, *op. cit.*, p. 89 (trans.).

26 *Ibid.*, p. 108 (trans.).

27 A. J. Downing, *The Architecture of Country Houses* (1850), quoted in: Elisabeth Donaghy Garret, *op. cit.*, p. 119.

28 Hermann Muthesius, *op. cit.*, p. 92.

29 Alain Corbin, "Le secret de l'individu", p. 446 (trans.).

30 *Ibid.*, p. 423.

31 *Ibid.*

32 Elisabeth Donaghy Garret, *op. cit.*, p. 135.

33 Mlle E. Dufaux de la Jonchère, *op. cit.*, pp. 15-16.

34 Louise d'Alq, *Le savoir-vivre dans toutes les circonstances de la vie* (Paris: Bureaux des Causeries familières, 1886) vol. 2, p. 75 (trans.).

35 Baronne Staffe, *Usages du monde: règles du savoir-vivre dans la société moderne* (Paris: Victor Havard, 1893), p. 75.

CHAPTER

III

THE FURNITURE MAKERS

THE FURNITURE MARKET IN QUEBEC

The fine taste that has made such rapid progress in the past fifteen years has had a considerable effect on people's conception of art and music as well as the way they furnish and decorate their homes. The furniture trade has never offered more elegance and finesse than it does today, and in this regard we are more advanced than our forefathers.[1]

IN THE VICTORIAN ERA (1837-1901), CAUGHT UP IN THE TIDE of change that marked the evolution of Western societies during the nineteenth century, Quebec assimilated its share of change and innovation, always in its own way. The wave of industrialization, coming in a period characterized by a trend toward urbanization, rapid advances in transportation and technological progress in many areas, brought about profound changes in social and economic structures, affecting the way people lived in more than one respect. Different industries obviously experienced the effects of the transformation in production conditions differently and to varying degrees, depending on their scale. Of course, the furniture manufacturing industry was dwarfed by the food, leather and lumber industries.[2] Yet as a new reality began to take shape, this industry was not to go untouched, especially given the large number of craftsmen working in it and the variety of items produced.

According to the 1851 census, Canada East[3] had 311 furniture makers, while Canada West had 1,030.[4] The industrial census of Canada conducted twenty years later counted 1,108 employees working in furniture manufacturing firms in the province of Quebec, while the figure was 2,769 in Ontario, reflecting a significant increase in manpower in this trade. At this time, the Dominion of Canada—including the provinces of Nova Scotia and New Brunswick—counted a total of 4,366 employees working in this sector, with annual production valued at $3,580,978.[5]

In 1871, based on the number of firms and employees as well as production value, the Canadian furniture industry was dominated by Ontario, followed by the province of Quebec, which was nevertheless well ahead of Nova Scotia and New Brunswick (see table). The furniture industry in Canada was characterized by other disparities. Concentration of production in a few large cities was encouraged by the existence of a small number of large industrial-type firms that drew on abundant manpower. In Toronto, the largest furniture production centre in Canada, the well-known firm Jacques & Hay alone employed some 400 workers in 1866.[6] Alongside the large firms, both in the big cities and in outlying regions, were numerous smaller firms,

THE FURNITURE INDUSTRY IN CANADA IN 1871*						
	Number of firms and percentage		Number of employees and percentage		Production value and percentage	
ONTARIO	536	(63%)	2,769	(63.4%)	$2,306,070	(64.4%)
QUEBEC	218	(25.5%)	1,108	(25.4%)	$859,491	(24%)
NOVA-SCOTIA	52	(6%)	315	(7.2%)	$252,460	(7%)
NEW BRUNSWICK	48	(5.5%)	174	(4%)	$162,951	(4.6%)
CANADA	854	(100%)	4,366	(100%)	$3,580,978	(100%)

some of which were operated by a handful of craftsmen or even a single individual. Despite the undisputed domination of large industry in terms of production value, the majority of Canadian firms specializing in furniture production in 1891 were still workshops and stores employing fewer than five persons.[7]

In Quebec, as in Ontario, the furniture market revolved around a core of large industrial concerns. The situation in Quebec City in 1871 is typical. According to the census data, William Drum had 120 workers in his employ, and his main competitor, Philippe Vallière, had ninety-seven. Together, these two companies accounted for seventy-four per cent of the employees working in the twenty-one firms listed in Quebec City. Though diminutive compared to their American cousins, the industrial firms in Quebec City were giants beside the many craft-type factories and workshops scattered across the province. In the next chapter, Rénald Lessard gives us a sweeping account of the 497 firms in Quebec in 1871, revealing the existence of a veritable mosaic of functions and production levels. Within this composite reality were many specializations, including production of a mainly utilitarian traditional style of furniture.[8] Still, without any doubt, throughout the Victorian era the market for fine furniture expanded and diversified as new clienteles emerged and new needs began to make themselves felt. It was precisely because of his ability to meet these changing needs that furniture maker John Hilton became the head of the largest industrial concern in Quebec at the time of Confederation.

Elizabeth Collard has given a detailed account of John Hilton's career.[9] In 1845, he ended a more than twenty year association with James and Edmond Baird to open his own firm under the name J. & W. (his son's name was William) Hilton. The company expanded rapidly thanks to the use of modern, hydraulic-powered machinery. In 1854, his spacious showrooms located along Saint-Jacques Street were being supplied by a large plant located in Saint-Germain Street, near the Saint-Gabriel locks on the Lachine Canal.[10] In the factory, dozens of employees toiled at machines or finished furniture by hand. Much of the production was destined for an upper-class clientele that included such notables as Peter McGill, Hugh Allan and John Molson, though sales were not limited to English-speaking Montrealers.[11] A founding member of the Institut des artisans de Montréal in 1845,[12] John Hilton surrounded himself with talented, competent people.[13] After his death in 1866, the company fell apart and closed down in 1872.

* Based on the Census of Canada 1870-71, vol. III (Ottawa: I. B. Taylor, 1875), to p. 307. Data on number of employees were compiled by the author, and include persons aged over 16 years (men and women) and under 16 years (men and women). Percentages were also computed by the author.

Hilton's counterpart in Quebec City was William Drum. In a later chapter, our contributor Jean-François Caron traces the history of this energetic character, whose firm successfully navigated through the three major phases of the industrialization process. Drum's main competitor Philippe Vallière (1832-1919) stayed with a more modest facility that specialized in high-priced fine furniture.[14] He also had a steam engine, which in 1871 generated 35 horsepower to run the different machines used in the production of furniture. The firm had ninety-seven employees — including ten women — a respectable figure which testified to the success Philippe Vallière enjoyed with the firm after taking over from his father, Jean-Olivier. The senior Vallière's shop had only five employees in 1851. Two years later, Philippe joined the firm, and he wasted no time convincing his father to equip himself with a steam engine. Until 1866, however, the firm operated with no more than twelve workers, a situation that changed quickly when Philippe found himself alone at the helm of the Saint-Vallier Street business.

Philippe Vallière continued to prosper until the end of the Victorian era, benefiting from the decline of the Drum company after 1876. From that time on, he no longer had any serious local competition. In response to the economic difficulties and population stagnation in Quebec City, the value of the furniture produced there dropped from thirty-two per cent to around ten per cent of the province's total output between 1871 and 1891. Conversely, Montreal increasingly established itself as a metropolitan centre in Quebec and Canada as a whole. As the country's chief business centre, its industrial base expanded quickly, catalysed by a favourable geographic location, the rapid growth of its urban population and new means of transportation. In 1881, the number of furniture manufacturers in the city doubled, while Quebec City languished. Montreal had a number of large furniture producers, including Charles-E. Pariseau, Azarie Lavigne (1841-1890)[15] — a former apprentice of John Hilton — J.A.I. Craig, George Armstrong, Noël Pratte — or Pratt — Adolphe Bélanger, H. P. Labelle and many others. But none of them

229
Philippe Vallière's cabinet and chair factory, Quebec City
Engraving published in *The City of Quebec Jubilee Illustrated 1837-1887* (Montreal, 1887)
Quebec City Archives (A-103/E 2350, 10010)

230
Notman Studio, Montreal
John Hilton (about 1791-1866), 1863
Photograph
McCord Museum of Canadian History, Montreal, Notman Photographic Archives (4869-1)

THE FURNITURE MAKERS

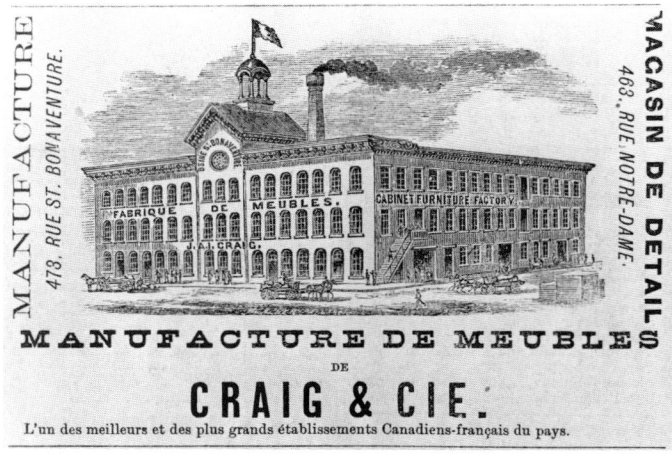

231
Advertisement for the firm of J.A.I. Craig of Montreal
Published in *L'Opinion publique*, December 12, 1878
Photo SRP

232
Examples of furniture sold by C. E. Pariseau, Canadian manufacturer, about 1870
Photograph
Canadian Museum of Civilization, Hull, Marius Barbeau Collection (58292)

equalled in size the plant of the Irishman Owen McGarvey's (about 1821-1897).[16]

In 1863, McGarvey moved to his final location on the corner of McGill and Notre-Dame Streets.[17] Already in business for some twenty years, he had outgrown his earlier premises at 1856 Notre-Dame Street, near Place d'Armes.[18] A commercial publication that came out in 1864 describes the ingenious layout of his new facility, which became a decisive factor in the firm's success.

> The premises he now occupies are capacious enough to all external appearance, but an inspection of the interior would impress the visitor with a somewhat different idea; for although they are three stories in height, and although every available foot of space is economized, they are scarcely found sufficient for the purposes of Mr. McGarvey's trade. The store is 97 feet by 60, and is owned by Mr. McGarvey. The premises are divided in two by a brick wall, but communication is provided for by means of folding doors.
>
> The first flat on the right hand side is used as a showroom. The furniture here on exhibition is of a beautiful description; and is remarkable alike for the taste of the workmanship and the excellence of the material employed. (...)
>
> From the first flat to the third, the store, on the right hand side, is used for the purpose of displaying the goods manufactured. The second flat contains a great variety of chamber sets of the best description. There are some fine specimens of marble-top tables, and also of sofas, made in the best possible manner, highly finished, luxurious and attractive. The price of the chamber sets varies from $18 to $200; the sideboards may be found to vary in much the same proportion. The third flat contains a very fine display of upholstery.
>
> The first flat, on the left hand side, is used as a store and packing room; immediately behind is the workshop, which runs up to the third storey of the building. The workmen employed consist of cabinet-makers, varnishers, upholsterers, carvers, etc. (...)
>
> The premises he now occupies not being extensive enough for his requirements, the proprietor intends, in Spring next, to open a new factory in Griffintown[19] (...) Mr. McGarvey began business on a limited scale, but by energy,

233

attention and a thorough system of management, has placed himself among the foremost cabinetmakers in the city.[20]

In fact, Mr. McGarvey soon became the biggest furniture manufacturer in Montreal, a status no one was able to contest after the bankruptcy of the Hilton firm. In 1876, he formed a partnership with his son John – who died in 1888 – taking on the name Owen McGarvey & Son; he continued to diversify his production and made extensive improvements to his business to remain the leader in the field. In 1891, six years before he passed away (and with him, his company), he completely renovated the storefront, proudly proclaiming that he could offer "the Largest, Finest and decidedly the Cheapest Stock of Parlor, Drawing Room, Library, Dining Room and Bedroom Furniture to be found in any Furniture Establishment in the Dominion of Canada or the United States"![21]

Following the lead of other manufacturers in the province, McGarvey was obviously not content with the Montreal market. Like furniture makers S. W.

233

Owen McGarvey (about 1821-1897)
Eastlake-style bed, about 1880-1890
Black walnut and black burl walnut,
228 x 153.5 x 188 cm
McCord Museum of Canadian History, Montreal, gift of Mrs. Audrey Smith (M987.66.3.1-2)
Photo Christine Guest/MMFA

This remarkable piece is part of an ensemble that also includes a washstand and a small dressing table in the same style. Owen McGarvey's stamp appears on the underside of the washstand's marble top.

234

Advertisement for the firm of Owen McGarvey of Montreal
Published in R.S.W. Mackay, *The Montreal Directory for 1865-66* (Montreal: John Lovell, 1865), p. 470
National Archives of Canada, Ottawa (C-120208)

THE FURNITURE MAKERS

235
M. and N. Hanhart
View of Quebec City, Canada, from the
Grand Trunk Railway Station (detail), 1862
Lithograph after a work by Cornelius Krieghoff
(1815-1872), 41.2 x 60.3 cm
McCord Museum of Canadian History, Montreal

Abbott and S. R. Parsons, he delivered goods "on carriages or steamboats". In 1856, he claimed that he was "equally prepared to fill orders for cane or wood chairs for export to Australia, California or to the markets of the South".[22] The same year, the firm J. & W. Hilton "exported" – no doubt outside Montreal – forty per cent of its production.[23] It manufactured a large quantity of mirrors, which were sold from the Gaspé to Sarnia. While accepting orders for the entire province, John Thornton acted as Montreal agent for John Woodward's huge factory in Sherbrooke. In the last decade of the century, cabinetmakers James Steel and W. R. Coysh carved out markets in the provinces of Quebec and Ontario, as well as throughout the Dominion. In Quebec City, Philippe Vallière was not to be outdone; in 1889, his markets extended "beyond Prince Edward Island in the East, and to all the Western provinces".[24] As early as 1871, he "accounted for a large share of the supply to the markets of Montreal, the Eastern Townships and New Brunswick". Like William Drum, he was able to bring his wares to the parishes on the lower St. Lawrence via the Grand Trunk, which, after 1860, connected Montreal to Rivière-du-Loup, with stops at Saint-Hyacinthe, Richmond and Lévis. To make further inroads into the Maritime Provinces, Drum[25] and Vallière would have to await the completion of the railroad in the early 1870s.

Alongside the larger industrial firms that dominated the scene, a host of small workshops and stores tried to eke out an existence, with varying success. As the chapter on Pierre Drouin and Honoré Roy later in this collection will illustrate, the life of the cabinetmaker is no sinecure. Better equipped and more skilled manufacturers of the calibre of Quebec craftsman François Gourdeau succeeded in winning a part of the well-to-do bourgeois clientele. It was chiefly for such customers, and "largely by request", that cabinetmakers like Gourdeau, Eugène Bistodeau and Pierre Roy produced "furniture of unsurpassed richness and finish".[26] Nevertheless, the competition they faced from large industrial firms and their machines was fierce, as the case of Pierre Roy, alias "Puff" Roy, testifies.

Ce que M. Puff, ébéniste, fait le plus souvent.

In an advertisement that appeared in March 1858, Roy claimed to "pride himself that the furniture items produced by his firm are able to compete with furniture from the best factories where steam and other inventions are used, in terms of both sturdiness, elegance and finish". In the columns of the satirical journal *La Scie*, he raised the stakes on January 29, 1864: "P. R. has always battled shops that make furniture using steam power, and he is certain that by his own energy he can rival them on all points, and dares hope that his efforts will be rewarded with a large clientele." In December of the same year, he invited the public to Quebec City to admire a fine piece of cabinetwork he had just completed, which was on display in the Glover and Fry store. However, his invitation ended with what amounted to a surrender before the conquests of the machine:

> If this kind of work is not appreciated, Pierre Roy proposes, if he finds a supplier or a good associate, to manufacture furniture in another, more modern, simple style, most of which will be made with steam-powered machines.[27]

If there was one production item where big industry definitely outclassed all its competition, it was the common wood or cane chair. These could be produced quickly and easily, in large quantities and at low prices by means of machinery. Moreover, the demand for this kind of unpretentious, utilitarian chair was constant, and came from all levels of society. Consequently, it was no surprise that first-class cabinetworking shops were interested in this sort of low-end, but highly lucrative production. Drum was able to produce almost 1,000 a week. McGarvey exported them abroad "in boxes containing a dozen each, in any desired quantity, on five days' notice, painted or plain". Most of the chairs were produced and assembled in the large plant run by the Irishman William Lynch at L'Épiphanie, not far from L'Assomption, though the finishing touches were applied in Montreal. According to *Montreal Business Sketches* of 1864, McGarvey was selling between 12,000 and 15,000 units a year. George Armstrong and the John & William Hilton firm were putting out "cane-bottomed chairs of every description, well-made, durable and cheap".[28] Formerly these were imported in large quantities from the United States; but now they can be made in Canada, in any number, of first-rate material and very cheap".[29] Quebec manufacturers were certainly not shielded from for-

236
Advertisement for the firm of François Gourdeau of Quebec City
Published in *L'Événement*, May 7, 1870
National Library of Canada, Ottawa (NC-11915)

237
Jean-Baptiste Côté (1832-1907)
What Mr. Puff, Cabinetmaker, Does Most Often
Woodcut published in *La Scie*, December 10, 1864
Photo SRP

This caricature depicts the cabinetmaker Pierre Roy "pulling the devil by the tail" [an allusion to the French expression "tirer le diable par la queue" – to have trouble making ends meet]. "Puff" Roy had already been the subject of caricatures in the two preceding issues of *La Scie*. In the November 25, 1864, edition there were no less than three used to illustrate the following satirical text, entitled Mr. Puff: "Mr. Drum represents a continual nightmare for citizen Puff, and the latter wishes to apprise the public of his nightly sufferings and of the annoying agitations that this nightmare causes him. To put a stop to his misery, Mr. Puff is leaving for the Celestial Empire. His aim is to find the recipe for a stain that will spark a revolution in furniture wood. He hopes to meet a real genius who will understand him and help him perfect all the schemes he has devised to make his fortune. Consequently, Mr. Puff – who is short of money – wishes to sell, prior to his departure, a piece of wood that is entirely unique in this country, a two-inch-square sample of lemon wood. Also, a huge collection of insects for the total destruction of the stuffing in sofas and other furniture, which he obtained this summer in his melancholy excursions to the lakeshore. Also on sale, by auction, to members of the Turf and Jockey Club, the magnificent stallion exhibited below – which has only been used till now to pull the fictitious hearse of this gentleman's workshop. Finally, this gentleman, wishing to leave behind a souvenir of himself, has consented to sell his battle helmet, nicknamed his 'arguing helmet', the very one that he used to wear on pay day. The gentleman, suspecting that his dear friend Morel will continue to copy his furniture designs, warns him that he has commissioned a certain gentleman to administer to him, in that area below the base of the spine, the kick illustrated below." (trans.)

THE FURNITURE MAKERS

238
Jules-Ernest Livernois (1851-1933),
Quebec City
The Côte d'Abraham in Quebec City (detail),
about 1885
Photograph
Patrick Altman Collection, Quebec City

239
The establishment of D. S. Rickaby, Saint-Jean Street, Quebec City, about 1880
Photograph
Patrick Altman Collection, Quebec City

eign competition. In 1862, furniture maker and merchant Thomas Craig sold 2,000 chairs from the Jacques & Hay factory in Toronto.[30] Nearly thirty years later, the Quebec City representative of Jacob & Josef Kohn of Vienna, D. S. Rickaby, sold "genuine Vienna chairs, which can be purchased at the same price as an imitation".[31]

In Quebec society of the Victorian era, competition, the conquests of the machine and compartmentalization of functions were to favour specialization of craftsmen and businesses. Conversely, new market needs and customer expectations fostered a degree of diversification. Furniture makers, both large and small, would thus open up sidelines. William Drum used his mills to supply the shipbuilding industry with timber. Philippe Vallière's firm was associated with an undertaker. This practice, which can be traced to England in the seventeenth, eighteenth and nineteenth centuries, was common among Quebec City and Montreal furniture makers who, in addition to selling wood or iron coffins, could also provide their customers with everything needed for the funeral cortege, from the hearse to gloves, veils and armbands.[32] Like John and William Hilton and Owen McGarvey, cabinetmakers sold mahogany planks, sculpted, gilt rosewood mouldings, windows and cornices in various patterns, or turned pieces of wood, not to mention the varnishes and paints used for finishing.

Furniture makers spared no effort to improve the beauty and physical comfort of the home. In the 1840s, Jean-Olivier Vallière began importing wallpaper from Europe.[33] Manufacturers like Vallière or Hilton did not skimp when it came to coverings on upholstered furniture. They offered their customers a wide selection of coverings, as well as drawing room curtains. In *La Minerve* of March 24, 1864, the Hiltons informed the public that they had "just received, on board the steamer Nova Scotian, their spring line of Brocatelle, Peking cloth, Rep, etc., Rep Curtains and embroidered Reps and Terry curtains, Lace Curtains from Nottingham, embroidered cloth for Tables or Pianos in the richest, most modern style." In the 1890s, cabinet-

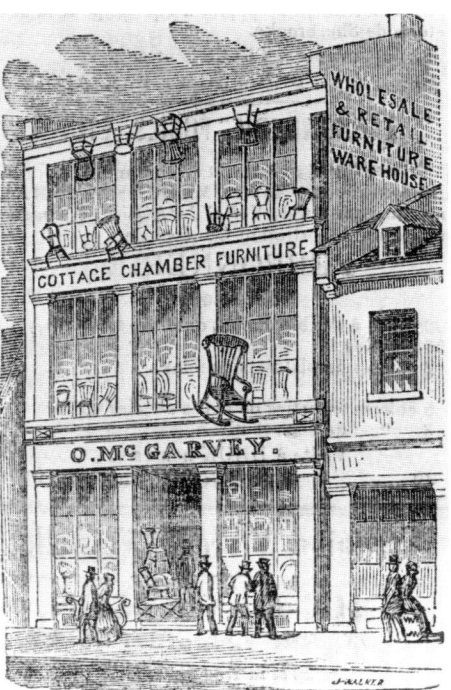

245 makers S. R. Parsons, W. Scott, James Steel and W. R. Coysh would continue to import tissue so that customers could choose their own coverings.³⁴ In fact, Coysh, Frederic Lapointe and partners Charland and Lahaise even offered a complete interior decoration service. From time to time, from the middle of the century, some cabinetmakers identified themselves expressly as "furniture makers and decorators" in their advertising, as was the case with William McMaster and R. William of Montreal in the 1850s. In 1870, manufacturer François Gourdeau of Quebec City announced that "he will also take care of decorating homes, and cutting, sewing and installing curtains, carpets and floor coverings, as well as installing cornices". On request, he would also make mattresses, feather beds, spring mattresses and quilted mattresses.

Toward the end of the century, the firm W. Scott & Sons built fine furniture and, in addition, imported oil paintings, watercolours, mantelpieces, screens and tiles. Lapointe added pianos to his list of offerings, while J.A.I. Craig opted for progress with "dynamo electro-magnetic machines" that were capable of generating electric light.³⁵ More conventionally, large firms and smaller shops alike offered their customers furniture repair services. In 1864, furniture-cabinetmaker Michel Roy of Quebec City claimed he was prepared to repair furniture in the home "wherever his services may be required", adding that "he polishes furniture in the French or English style,
244 and paints wood in all styles".³⁶ In Montreal, young Azarie Lavigne would do the same the following year, after leaving the Hiltons.

Aware of the advantages of diversification, other furniture makers were quick to venture outside the sometimes constricting bounds of the home furnishings market, especially when they could win prestige orders. This was the case with William Drum, who was commissioned to build furniture for

240
William Drum (about 1808-1876)
Hitchcock chair, about 1860-1870
Wood, stencil-painted, 85 x 47.5 x 41 cm
Mr. and Mrs. Joseph Sirois Collection, Saint-André de Kamouraska
Photo Christine Guest/MMFA

A Hitchcock chair is a light, easily-transported chair with a cane or rush seat, turned front legs and a railed back that often bears stencilled decorations. This type of chair, derived partially from Sheraton, was designed by the American Lambert Hitchcock (1795-1852), who established a chair factory in 1825 in Unionville (now called Rivington), Connecticut. This particular example was made by William Drum of Quebec City, as proved by the inscription "W. Drum Factory" that appears on the middle rail of the back.

241
Advertisement for the firm of Owen McGarvey of Montreal
Published in *Le Pays*, May 16, 1857
Photo SRP

242
Advertisement for the firm of George Armstrong of Montreal
Published in *The Gazette*, July 29, 1863
National Library of Canada, Ottawa (NL-17944)

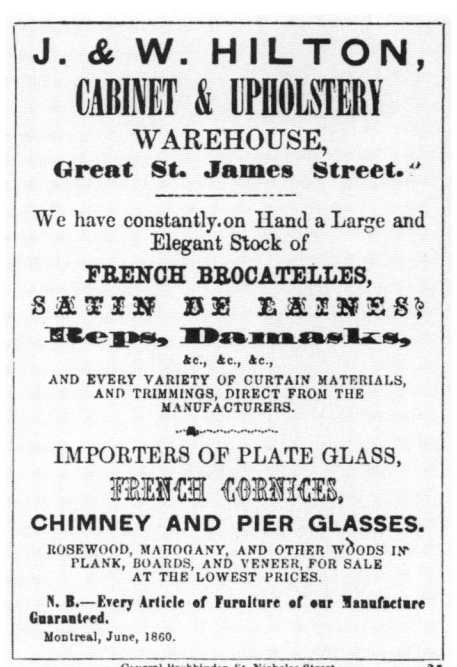

243
Advertisement for the firm of
J. & W. Hilton of Montreal
Published in the *Business Guide to the City of Montreal*
(Montreal: John Lovell, 1860)
Photo SRP

244
Advertisement for the firm of
Azarie Lavigne of Montreal
Published in *La Minerve*, March 28, 1865
National Library of Canada, Ottawa (L-11885)

245
Engraving illustrating an article on
W. R. Coysh of Montreal
Published in *Montreal Illustrated 1894...* (Montreal:
The Consolidated Illustrating Co., 1894), p. 259
Photo SRP

the Prince of Wales's apartments in Quebec City in 1860. A few years later, together with the firm Jacques & Hay of Toronto, he landed contracts to furnish Rideau Hall, the Governor General of Canada's residence in Ottawa. In 1879, Philippe Vallière, not to be outdone, was retained to furnish the viceroyal suite at the Citadel of Quebec City;[37] he also received government orders to furnish public buildings. There was also the lucrative hotel furnishings market.[38] In Montreal, the Hiltons catered to the needs of innkeepers Vardon and Hogan before doing the elegant decor of the drawing room and 130 bedrooms in the Ottawa Hotel.[39] In 1853, the new owner of the Keenan Hotel in Trois-Rivières awarded a contract to T. Rickaby.[40] Thirty years later, Philippe Vallière shared a large order to furnish the Château Frontenac in Quebec City with Hay of Toronto. Hotel furnishings were sometimes quite conventional, but could also be of the highest quality — witness a fine bed from the old Windsor Hotel, which opened in Montreal in 1878, and the imposing lobby piece designed by architect Omer Marchand in 1900. The scale model was done by a French sculptor named Bouthier, while the work was executed by a certain Mr. Proulx, who was also a sculptor.[41]

Furniture makers like Montrealers John Carlisle and David Tees specialized in producing office furniture, whereas for others this market was only a sideline. McGarvey, for example, was content to offer his customers magnificent writing desks and bookcases, while W. Scott & Sons catered to the specific needs of schools, colleges, hospitals and other public buildings. In 1862, Drum furnished the Banque Nationale building on Saint-Pierre Street in Quebec City.[42] The needs of the Catholic Church were quite varied, as can be seen from orders received by three cabinetmakers from Quebec City. In 1863, sculptor F.-X. Berlinguet designed and executed the episcopal chair for the Archbishop of Quebec City. Sixteen years later, the Grondines parish ordered a credenza from Hilaire Falardeau of Quebec City to exhibit paintings in the church in conjunction with the monthly cycle of religious festivals. In 1888, Philippe Vallière built the benches and confessionals for the Chapelle de la Congrégation. Thirty years earlier, he and his father Jean-Olivier had

246
The Prince's Parlor in the Government House, Quebec, Magnificently Fitted up by the Authorities of the City
Engraving published in *Leslie's Illustrated Weekly Newspaper* (New York), September 1, 1860
Quebec City Archives - Collection iconographique (A093/H1211, n°. 12739)

247
Renaissance-revival bed, about 1875-1890
257 x 164 x 212 cm
Presbytery of the Marie-Reine-du-Monde cathedral, Montreal
Photo ministère des Affaires culturelles, Montreal, Inventaire des biens culturels (75-1204)

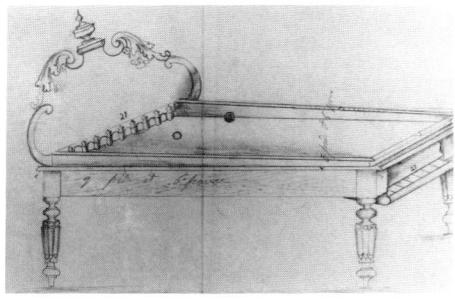

248
Dawson's Study
Detail of an engraving published in the *Canadian Illustrated News* August 26, 1882
National Archives of Canada, Ottawa (C-77309)
John William Dawson (1820-1899) was principal of McGill University for thirty-eight years, starting in 1855. He was the author of over 350 publications, mostly on paleontology, and was largely responsible for establishing McGill's reputation.

249
Pierre Drouin (1815-1860) or Honoré Roy (1821-1892). "Pigeon-hole" table, about 1860.
Crayon on paper, 32 x 40.5 cm
Environment Canada, Parks Service, Quebec region (EX 86.3.143). Photo SRP
This drawing may represent one of the "billiard tables" made in 1860 for the hotelier Jean L'Hoist. "Pigeon-hole" was an old English game that consisted of rolling balls across a table so as to get them into nine small openings situated at the opposite end. It was somewhat different from the game of *bagatelle*, in which the end of the table towards which the balls were directed was semi-circular and the balls were pushed with the aid of a billiard cue.

250
Omer Marchand (1872-1936) and the sculptors Bouthier and Proulx. **Renaissance-revival hotel sideboard**, 1900.
Oak, 285 x 360 x 60 cm
Raymond Fabien and Marthe Fabien-Lapalme Collection, Anjou. Photo Christine Guest/MMFA
Originally intended for the Château Laurier in Ottawa, this imposing hotel sideboard was never delivered. The commission was unexpectedly cancelled and the piece remained in storage in Montreal.

wrought the splendid woodwork in the cabin of a ship built in Quebec City, "from rosewood, bird's-eye maple and mahogany".[43]

Some furniture makers also produced for public places. In 1855, Alexis Michelot, "a distinguished French sculptor" who had only recently come to Canada, "executed a sideboard and various ornaments for the Alexandre restaurant" in Montreal.[44] The owner of the Éthier restaurant also engaged a French cabinetmaker, M. Escoubès, to create the decor for his establishment in 1874. Another Montreal furniture maker, Joseph-Ludger Clément of Notre-Dame Street, specialized in producing "Billiard, Pigeon Hole and Bagatelle Tables".[45] In Quebec City, craftsmen Pierre Drouin and Honoré Roy also produced billiard sets and other table games of their own design.[46] Renovations at a pharmacy on St. Lawrence Street in Montreal earned the owner, James Goulden, two illustrations and a favourable notice in the *Canadian Illustrated News* of September 16, 1871. Apparently, the pharmacist did not cut corners, and brought in the best workmen:

> The shelving, drawers, &c., were designed by Mr. Thompson, and executed by Messrs. Jacques & Hay, of Toronto; the counters were designed and made by Messrs. Hilton, of this city. They are of solid black walnut and ash, in oil, finely carved. The ceiling was frescoed by J. Underwood.

Similarly, photographer William Notman seems to have turned to an excellent cabinetmaker to decorate his studio in a manner in keeping with the expectations and prestige of his clientele. In a note he sent to the *Philadelphia Photographer* in December 1867, he remarked that photography studios

ought not only to be carpeted, but abound in suitable pieces of furniture and choice ornaments such as are usually seen in drawing or sitting rooms. If possible, let such be real, and so arranged that sitters may have somewhat of a home feeling.[47]

258-260   Naturally, cabinetmakers wishing to satisfy the specific needs of entomologists and ornithologists had to deal with problems of a different kind, and be prepared for some not-so-ordinary orders!

The market forced furniture makers to expand their facilities and diversify, taking every available measure in order to attract, satisfy and hold onto their clientele as well as to sell and replenish their inventory. Most took out advertisements in newspapers to offer their services, publicize their specializations, announce new items, boast about their products and advertise furniture auctions, lotteries and liquidation sales. In their advertising, some employed remarkable inventiveness. Owen McGarvey, with his flair for novelty, even found a way to establish connections between his production and a visit by the Prince of Wales in 1860, the formation of Sir John A. MacDonald's cabinet in 1878, provincial exhibitions and the end of the uprising in the northwest in 1885! Potential buyers strolling down Notre-Dame Street could not help but be attracted by the huge red rocking chair that graced his storefront for

261   decades. Around 1885, his competitors, W. C. Norman, M. X. Hicks and S. R. Parsons in Notre-Dame Street all used more neutral signs. During this time, in Quebec City, furniture maker C. O. Bédard had a footboard as a sign, a dis-

262-263   tinctive symbol he exhibited both in newspapers and on his letterhead.

During the 1850s, William Drum's firm maintained separate showrooms where customers could admire a complete sampling of his products. In his work of 1857, Willis Russell describes with obvious enthusiasm the six "Grand Show Rooms" in Saint-Paul Street, whose contents "could furnish an entire city, though it was piled high in a great confusion".[48] During the 1860s, Pierre Roy and other Quebec City furniture makers kept showrooms where they could display their wares. In Montreal, Hilton had a store separate from his shop as early as the 1850s. Until he went bankrupt in 1875, Charles E. Pariseau's store in Notre-Dame Street was supplied by a factory in Coaticook

251
The Maison Ethier, Notre-Dame Street
Engraving published in the
Canadian Illustrated News, April 18, 1874
National Archives of Canada, Ottawa (C-6192)

252
Hilaire Falardeau
Credence, 1885
232 x 112.5 x 64 cm
Church of Grondines
Photo Jean-Pierre Labiau/MOBIVIQ
This credence, intended "for the month of prayers", was made by a cabinetmaker from the Saint-Roch district of Quebec City. It was to be used to display the paintings of the Sacred Heart and of various saints including St. Anne during the month devoted to them in the liturgical calendar. In the book containing parish resolutions, curé Joseph-Stanislas Martel noted: "It would have been more beautiful if he [Falardeau] had followed my designs".

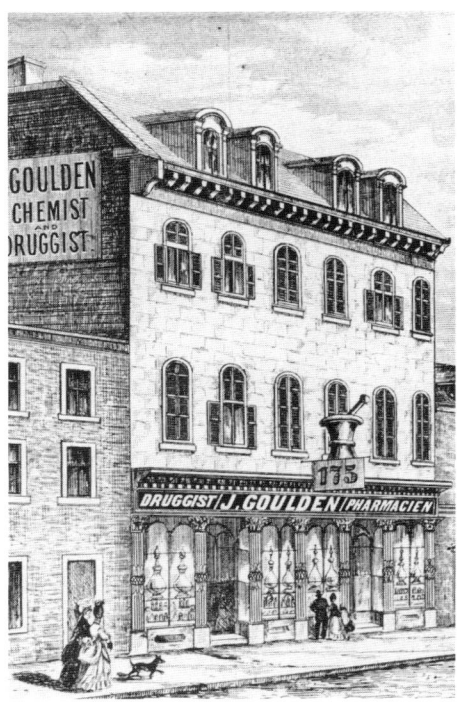

253
Jas. Goulden's Drug Store, St. Lawrence Main Street, Montreal
Engraving published in the *Canadian Illustrated News*, September 16, 1871
National Archives of Canada, Ottawa (C-56494)

254
Interior View of Goulden's Drug Store
Engraving published in the *Canadian Illustrated News*, September 16, 1871
National Archives of Canada, Ottawa (C-56493)

that was equipped with steam-powered machinery.[49] J.A.I. Craig's workshop was located on Saint-Bonaventure Street, while his retail store was on Notre-Dame Street, and H. P. Labelle had a similar arrangement. As larger stores opened, consumers were treated to an even broader selection. S. R. Parsons even grouped his furnishings according to their purpose:

> The first floor of the warehouse is devoted to dining-room and miscellaneous furniture, the second to drawing and chamber suites, the third to chamber furniture, while the fourth is utilized for workrooms, upholstering, etc.[50]

Perusing the some 250 pages of inventory in the Adolphe Bélanger stores located on Notre-Dame and de Brésoles streets, one is struck by the abundance and variety of home furnishings a single large furniture maker was able to produce.[51] This was later eclipsed by McGarvey's store, which, after it was renovated in 1891, regaled passers-by with an attractive free exposition of his products in two "Show Windows" that were called the largest in the world, and a fine series of "Bay Windows" on the upper level.

As might be expected, new consumption habits began to appear in the last two decades of the nineteenth century, mainly in Montreal proper. To appreciate the extent of the changes, one need only look through the long and eloquent description furniture-maker and decorator Frederic Lapointe offers of his firm and services in a pamphlet published in 1894:

> His warerooms occupy an imposing structure, with six floors and basement for storage and exhibit purposes, handsomely fitted and thoroughly organized in departments, giving the most realistic idea of the character and appearance of

LIVING IN STYLE

255
Notman Studio, Montreal
Mrs A. G. McDougall at the Photographer's, 1888
Photograph
McCord Museum of Canadian History, Montreal,
Notman Photographic Archives (MP-133/74-46)

256
Renaissance-revival armchair, about 1860
Black walnut and horsehair, 123 x 74.2 x 92.8 cm
McCord Museum of Canadian History, Montreal,
(UANO 123)

257
Notman Studio, Montreal
Mrs. Ross at the Photographer's, 1861
Photograph
McCord Museum of Canadian History, Montreal,
Notman Photographic Archives (2793-I)

258
Entomology cabinet
122 x 194.2 x 57 cm
Musée de la civilisation, Quebec City (34-9)

This cabinet was apparently first owned by Abbé Léon Provancher (1820-1892), a highly respected naturalist of the Victorian era. The piece later entered the collections of the now defunct Musée de l'Instruction publique, in Quebec City.

259
Ornithological display case, naturalistic movement, about 1890
Display of pheasants and grouse
Black walnut, 160 x 116 x 52 cm (case),
82 x 110 x 55 cm (table)
Université Laval, Sainte-Foy, succession
Martha Ada Boswell (LB1556)
Photo Christine Guest/MMFA

Both this and the following piece were possibly executed in Philippe Vallière's factory, which was next door to Quebec City's Boswell brewery. Both cases show the influence of naturalism, a movement associated with the rustic furniture so fashionable in the final decades of the nineteenth century. The desire to simultaneously imitate and domesticate nature was already evident in the ornamentation of a cabinet that the Parisian cabinetmaker Tahan had presented at London's Great Exhibition, in 1851.

260
Ornithological display case, naturalistic movement, about 1890
Display of small birds
Black walnut, 160 x 116 x 52 cm (case),
82 x 110 x 55 cm (table)
Université Laval, Sainte-Foy, succession
Martha Ada Boswell (LB1557)
Photo Christine Guest/MMFA

Both display cases present specimens of Quebec and North American birds, some of which are now extinct or endangered species. The birds are part of a collection started in 1880 and intended for a museum for public instruction. The collection, kept until 1962 at the Musée du Québec in Quebec City, was later displayed on the premises of the Commission des écoles catholiques de Québec (on Bourlamaque Street) before being transferred to the Université Laval in 1973.

the furniture in household surroundings. A large volume might be filled with descriptions of the beautiful goods handled by this house, the following being simply a few of the more prominent specialties: Here are to be found at all times a comprehensive and well-selected assortment of albums, book-cases, bric-a-brac, baby carriages, bed lounges, parlor suites, wooden and iron bedsteads, bedroom suites, chairs and rockers, cupboards, cradles, clocks, chests of drawers, carpets, dressing bureaus, doll carriages, divans, dining-room sets, easels, feather beds, hanging lamps, hat racks, lounges, mattresses, music stands, oil cloth, ottomans, pictures of all sizes, pianos, pillow-shams, door curtains, prie-dieu, parlor suites, rugs, shop stools, screens, student chairs, spring beds, sideboards, secretaries, sofas, kitchen, dining, centre, saloon and fancy tables, umbrella stands, wash stands, wardrobes, writing desks, etc. These goods are manufactured to Mr. Lapointe's immediate order in new, artistic designs in all the popular cabinet woods, while he makes a specialty of embodying the wishes and views of those about to decorate and furnish private residences, fitting up interiors in the most elaborate manner. [...] Mr. Lapointe, with characteristic enterprise, has recently issued a handsome illustrated catalogue and price list, the pictures in which abundantly prove that he is now handling lines of goods not only first-class in workmanship, but likewise in correct styles, tasteful, artistic and of most elaborate finish. He makes a specialty of high-class pianos, and controls the selling agency for the instruments turned out by such well-known firms as Weber, Decker & Son, J. P. Hale, New York Piano Co. and Vose & Sons, of Boston.[52]

During the same period, large department stores, such as the one Henry Morgan opened on Sainte-Catherine Street in 1891, came on the scene. The furniture department was located on the third floor. Those who preferred could also order furniture and other items by catalogue from the T. Eaton

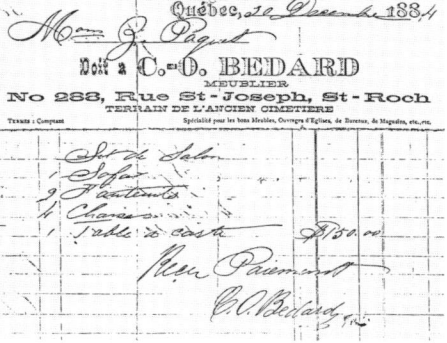

company in Toronto as early as the mid-1880s. During the Victorian era, this kind of shopping was prefigured by other variations: exchanges, reductions on large cash purchases, credit sales, wholesale prices, leasing with option to buy, and so on. Around 1890, Montreal's F. Lapointe offered a special discount to merchants from the city and countryside as well as "to any businessman". Meanwhile, Philippe Vallière in Quebec City was able to count on "several experienced travellers" to represent the interests of his wholesale and retail business from one end of Canada to the other.[53]

Then there is the matter of foreign competition. Since accurate figures are lacking, we must content ourselves with occasional allusions, which are infrequent enough for us to say that foreign furniture imports were fairly limited. From the outset we exclude merchants like G. Armstrong and James Steel who had their furniture made in Ontario shops.[54] Occasional appearances by Jacques & Hay of Toronto on the Quebec market belonged to the same interprovincial dynamic. However, local merchants were more sensitive about the presence of furniture from the United States. In 1864, John Thornton even issued a patriotism-tinged proclamation, asserting that his firm took care to use "our native woods" and that "this gentleman imports nothing whatever

261
Notman Studio, Montreal
Notre-Dame Street in Montreal, Looking East (detail), about 1885
Photograph
McCord Museum of Canadian History, Montreal, Notman Photographic Archives (1329)

262
Advertisement for the firm of Charles-Olivier Bédard of Quebec City
Published in the *Courrier du Canada*, January 22, 1881
Photo SRP

263
Bill of the furniture maker Charles-Olivier Bédard of Quebec City, 1884
Archives du Musée de la civilisation, Quebec City
Photo SRP

This bill, dated December 20, 1884, is for a drawing-room suite now in the collection of the Musée de la civilisation, in Quebec City (87-2401).

264
Advertisement for the firm of H. P. Labelle of Montreal
Published in the *Catalogue descriptif du Musée La Salle* (Montreal, 1892), p. 34
National Library of Canada, Ottawa (NL-17934)

from the States, being one of those who believe that our own resources and the skill of our native workmen are amply sufficient for all requirements".⁵⁵ Residents of the Eastern Townships, and in particular people living in villages located close to the US border (such as Stanstead), seem to have found it more economical to go south to buy furniture. In 1854, wholesalers and retailers Goss and Magoon of Sherbrooke imported their furniture from Portland and Boston.⁵⁶ A few years later, the Americans tried to invade the Canadian market themselves. In 1862, the New York firm Weil and Braunsdorf advertised in the columns of the Quebec City paper *Courrier du Canada* to promote its living room, library, dining room and bedroom furnishings, while manufacturers Daniels, Kendall & Company of Boston did the same in Montreal.⁵⁷

There is some indication that these isolated initiatives may have paid off. In April 1862, the Quebec City auctioneer A. J. Maxham was selling off "furniture of value from the famous MEEK shop in New York at the Bannockburn

house on chemin Ste-Foy, the residence of Mr. J. Nicol". The sale included a full rosewood living room suite, a mahogany dining room set and various bedroom pieces.[58] It should be remembered that in the 1850s, the renowned J. & J. Meeks firm rivalled with the no less famous New York shop run by John Henry Belter. To expand their clienteles, they would even copy each other's products. Thus the Belter dining room set acquired by a certain Fortier family of Quebec City in the Victorian era bore an uncanny resemblance to a typical Meeks design.[59]

The American presence continued into the 1870s, when J. M. Papineau of St. Lawrence Street imported new furniture "from the principal shops in New York, Buffalo and Boston".[60] In 1879, after six years of a depression that crippled the Canadian industry, the MacDonald government resolved to adopt a protectionist duty policy. At a special meeting of the Quebec City Chamber of Commerce called to discuss the new tariff, furniture maker Philippe Vallière said he was satisfied, though he seconded a motion to the effect that it was "regrettable that the government showed no preference toward industries in Great Britain over the United States, since the former has always kept its markets open to the mass of exports from these lands, freely, while the United States had for so long maintained a tariff that was hostile toward us".[61]

265
The Facade of the Establishment of Owen McGarvey & Son of Montreal
Engraving published in *Montreal Illustrated 1894...* (Montreal: The Consolidated Illustrating Co., 1894), p. 295
National Library of Canada, Ottawa (C-138078)

266
The Facade of the Establishment of Frederic Lapointe of Montreal
Engraving published in K.G.C. Huttemeyer, *Les intérêts commerciaux de Montréal et Québec et leurs manufactures* (Montreal: K.G.C. Huttemeyer, 1889), p. 128
Bibliothèque du Séminaire de Québec, fonds ancien (210)
Photo W.B. Edwards Inc., Quebec City

267
Henry Morgan's Store in Montreal
Illustration published in *Montreal Illustrated 1894...*
(Montreal: The Consolidated Illustrating Co., 1894), p. 300
National Library of Canada, Ottawa (C-138079)

268
Rocking chair, about 1895
Oak, 121.9 x 61.5 x 83.3 cm
Sœurs de la Charité de Québec, Beauport
Photo Christine Guest/MMFA

The armrests of this rocking chair are designed to accommodate newspapers and magazines. Often made of oak and adorned with machine-made ornamentation, chairs like this one sold in large numbers in major department stores in the late nineteenth century.

269
Hall stand in the Arts and Crafts style, about 1895
White ash, 209.5 x 76.5 x 38.7 cm
Sœurs de la Charité de Québec, Beauport
Photo Christine Guest/MMFA

During the 1890s this type of hall stand, combining mirror, pegs and a seat, was sold by large department stores like T. Eaton of Toronto. Although it is an inexpensive, mass-produced piece, the stand's simple lines, high-grain wood and functional look show a clear Arts and Crafts influence.

In 1864, the firm of Renaud, King and Patterson of Montreal would import "Austrian bentwood furniture", as did Quebec City's D. S. Rickaby, exclusive agent of Jacob & Josef Kohn of Vienna. In the meantime, the energetic Henry Shaw found an original solution that reconciled the public's infatuation with foreign furniture and his desire to promote local industry. The Reverend J. Douglas Borthwick explains the situation in his 1875 publication:

> [...] As salesman in the department of fine furniture, libraries or works of art he has few equals in this or any country.
>
> His store, Craig street near Victoria Square, is now the largest and best supplied emporium for the sale and display of fine furniture in the Dominion. Since the re-erection of his building, after the disastrous fire in 1872, Mr. Shaw has devoted the four principal flats of his immense store to the display and sale of furniture of a superior class, and several of the principal private residences of Montreal have been furnished from this favorite establishment. Mr. Shaw's plan has been to import from the best makers in New York and Boston, specimens of the finest work in Bedroom Suites, Drawing-room Suites, Bookcases, Wardrobes, Desks, &c., and sending the samples thus imported to some of our large city manufacturers, or to the factory with which he is connected at Bowmanville, he gives out by contract the work to be made from these articles stipulating that the material used must be perfectly sound and seasoned, and the workmanship as good as the sample. [...] In this way the most elegant and fashionable furniture is produced in a very excellent and superior manner, no way inferior to the imported articles, but at a great saving in cost; besides this plan which Mr. Shaw

has adopted, gives constant employment to between one hundred and two hundred skilful mechanics, most of whom are French Canadians returned from the United States, who brought their families back to swell the manufacturing population of our city. [...] Mr. Shaw's plan of reproducing the best New York or Boston styles, as well finished, at about half the cost, will have a tendency to check this habit of transferring our money and labour to increase the wealth and prosperity of foreign cities.

While traditional furniture continued to be used in less well-off quarters, the Victorian era witnessed a gradual generalization of functional furnishings for the main rooms of the house, and the emergence of a variety of more or less accessory pieces of furniture that contributed to comfort and appearance. The new consumption practices and the rapid changes in taste in some parts of society meant that home decorations were periodically renewed. In 1885, on the eve of her marriage to Raoul Dandurand, Joséphine Marchand speaks explicitly of those "onerous fashions that force you to change the furnishing of the house and street, like a hat"![62] Some cabinetmakers catered to the rich, and the very high prices of their superior-quality furniture were beyond the reach of modest incomes. James Thomson worked for the "leading representative citizens" of Montreal, including the Allans, Redpaths and Stephens. At the end of the century, W. Scott & Sons ministered to the caprices of James Ross and the Van Hornes, while W. R. Coysh boasted of the "patronage of the elite of the Dominion". One of them, or a cabinetmaker of their calibre, may have fashioned the remarkable dining room sideboard ordered by Hugh Montagu Allan around 1890.[63] On occasion, Owen McGarvey's advertising explicitly mentions a "Medium Class of Parlor, Dining Room, Library and Bedroom Suites, varying in price from $25 to $75".[64] While Renaud, King & Patterson built and sold "fine and medium furniture", H. P. Labelle was prepared to satisfy all budgets: his living room sets cost anywhere from $20 to $350, dining room sets from $18 to $300, and

270
Bed, Aesthetic movement, about 1880-1900
201 x 155 x 215 cm
Private collection, Stanstead
Photo Jean-Pierre Labiau/MOBIVIQ
According to oral tradition, this bed was part of a bedroom suite purchased in Boston.

271
John Henry Belter (1804-1863) (attrib.)
Rococo-revival drawing-room chair, about 1850
Black walnut, 101 x 50 x 64 cm
Private collection, Quebec City
Photo Christine Guest/MMFA
According to oral tradition, this drawing-room chair of laminated wood was part of a seven-piece suite ordered in 1850 from the New York firm of John Henry Belter by the Fortier family of Quebec City. It is, however, virtually identical to other pieces made at the same period by the J. & J. Meeks company (Eileen and Richard Dubrow, *American Furniture of the Nineteenth Century: 1840-1880*, [Exton: Schiffer, 1983], p. 99). An armchair very similar to this one is seen in a photograph of the entrance hall of Rideau Hall, the residence of Lord Aberdeen, Governor General of Canada, published in *The Canadian Magazine*, December 1898.

THE FURNITURE MAKERS

272
Advertisement for the firm of Daniels, Kendall & Co, of Boston
Published in *The Gazette*, August 13, 1862
National Library of Canada, Ottawa (NC-17940)

273
The Great Piano and Furniture Auction Rooms of Henry J. Shaw, Craig Street
Engraving published in the *Canadian Illustrated News*, May 1, 1875
National Archives of Canada, Ottawa (C-62669)

274
Advertisement for the firm of Frederic Lapointe of Montreal
Published in the *Catalogue descriptif du Musée La Salle* (Montreal, 1892), p. 1
National Library of Canada, Ottawa (NL-17931)

bedroom sets from $8 to $300! Always looking for new markets, Frederic Lapointe catered to the working classes, which now also found tasteful furniture accessible. In 1895, he made "the least expensive offer ever made": $198 for thirty-four pieces.[65] The next year, Perrault was asking only $50 for twenty-eight pieces, "a full set of furnishings for the home", including "a bedroom set, a dining room set, a living room set and a kitchen set".[66] In his testimony before the "Royal Commission of Enquiry into Relations Between Capital and Labour in Canada" in 1888, McGarvey noted quite incidentally that "furniture has become twenty-five to thirty percent cheaper" thanks to the effects of industrialization. Yet the fact remains that until the end of the Victorian era, domestic furniture accessible to everyone had a distinctly less sophisticated character than in the past, its utilitarian dimension often outweighing consumers' pretensions to elegance.

This survey of the Quebec furniture industry reveals a growing diversity during the reign of Victoria. The manufacturer's profile and professional status varied depending on the size of the firm where he worked, the nature of his products, related activities, the size of his clientele, the number of personnel and his equipment or machinery. What a contrast there was between the artisanal trade of a Pierre Drouin or an Honoré Roy and the way an employee would work in an industrial concern like the Drum plant! The former were not exactly strangers to the production line, but their routine was quite different from the turners, polishers, varnishers, upholsterers and machine operators who perpetually performed the same operations. Still, mechanization left room for a certain amount of manual labour, such that the best ornamental sculptors were able to maintain a profitable professional status.

Furniture makers also enjoyed a certain degree of mobility, made possible by apprenticeships, associations, growth of demand and the expansion of the industry and an increasing concentration of firms in large cities. Throughout the Victorian period, the furniture factories in Quebec City were located mainly in the north part of the Saint-Pierre district, not far from the docks of the Saint-Charles River. In Montreal, the firms tended to congregate on

275
Renaissance-revival sideboard, about 1890. White oak, 323 x 264 x 67 cm
Ministère de l'Enseignement supérieur et des Sciences, Gouvernement du Québec. Photo Christine Guest/MMFA

This sideboard bears an inscription establishing that it was commissioned by Hugh Montagu Allan (1860-1951), the eldest son of Sir Hugh Allan (1810-1882). The extremely fine workmanship of the carved embellishments indicates that some furniture makers called on leading artists to provide the carving for their pieces. This sideboard was formerly in the Jean-Marie Gauvreau Collection. Before it's restoration by the Montreal Museum of Fine Arts in 1992, it had been dismantled and stored in the Musée des arts décoratifs de Montréal. The inward-curving scrolls that originally completed the top have not been found.

276
Hipolito Zapponi (died 1894).
Philippe Vallière, 1876
Oil on canvas, 75 x 61 cm
Musée du Québec, Quebec City (46-171)
This painting was executed in Rome.

either side of McGill Street, and on Craig, Saint-Joseph and Notre-Dame Streets. For a cabinetmaker like Édouard Bertrand, the world of furniture had no boundaries. At the end of his apprenticeship with Noël Pratte, he worked for James Thomson, and then struck out for the United States. In Montreal, he made the acquaintance of sculptor and illustrator Charles Fichot, one of the many French craftsmen who, like Michelot, Mingeaud,[67] Escoubès and Bouthier, had come to America to seek their fortunes. In Quebec City, meanwhile, Philippe Vallière was doubly aware of the value of European tradition and resources for tasteful furniture. In fact, according to his obituary, he "made several trips to Europe. He studied cabinet making with the old-world masters, and brought into his firm a few French and Belgian workers who were regarded as genuine artists in their own countries".[68]

John R. Porter

A Description of the John & William Hilton Manufactory in Montreal, in 1864*

A visit to the manufactory of Messrs. Hilton, situated on Alexander Street, serves better than anything else to convey an accurate idea of the extent of their business, and the facilities they possess for carrying it out in all its branches, how so much can be done and so cheaply, with the aid of machinery. The buildings are large and well adapted for the purpose; and the number of men engaged is about eighty. On the first floor the steam engine is located; it is of twelve horse-power, and by means of belts running upwards through the ceiling, drives the necessary machinery on the upper flats. The visitor is bewildered on entering by the number of belts intersecting each other at every step, by the din of wheels, the screech of saws, and the whirr of rapidly revolving bits. At one bench is to be seen a lathe, into which a square of wood is this moment inserted, and in a few seconds comes out a handsomely turned post, round and symmetrical. Here a grooving machine takes a piece of stout board between its teeth, and in a few seconds has grooved on both sides, the upper and under, what it would take hand labour an hour to perform. The circular saw tears in a straight line through a plank what the human arm would require hours to separate. The upright saw, not broader than the smallest blade of a pen-knife, works up and down incessantly. There is no geometric curve or angle that it will fail to cut with lightning rapidity, let the wood be ever so tenacious; it is a wonderful piece of mechanism, and its effective power astonishing in the extreme. Next comes the planing machine. A piece of walnut plank over two and a half feet broad, and four feet long is fastened securely to a movable iron bed. Then it is drawn under the plane; this is composed of two sharp steel teeth, chisels, in fact, revolving horizontally with great impetuosity, and placed a considerable distance asunder. The board is moved backward and forward under the plane; if it is hard wood, a spark now and then will fly out, indicating the irresistible force and the strong resistance; but the machine overcomes every obstacle, and in a minute or two the board emerges, smooth and of equal surface in every part. Thus there is accomplished in a fraction of time what the human arm could not so efficiently perform in hours. Then there is the moulding machine, which moulds curves of every kind with astonishing rapidity; and leaves its indentations on the hardest wood, as if it were friable as chalk. The following is an enumeration of some of the machines incessantly at work in this factory: planing machine, surface machine, vertical sawing machine, moulding sticker, shaping and moulding do, circular saws, grooving saws, turning lathes, morticing lathes, tennening [sic] lathes. The machinery in this workshop is all of a modern character, and is capable of turning out finished material in the most rapid manner conceivable. There is a drying room connected with the establishment, to which the exhaust steam from the engine-house is conveyed by an underground pipe. Here the wood, before going to the workshop, is thoroughly seasoned, and by a process nowhere else in requisition in this Province. Separated from the machinery department by a yard, is the finishing and polishing department. Here the furniture receives the finishing touches preparatory to being placed in the market. In this building also is the carvers' shop, where a number of skilful workmen are busily engaged on those beautiful designs of birds, fruits, flowers, etc., which we see ornamenting first-rate specimens of the cabinet maker's art. Some of these patterns are of great beauty, and require for proper and effective development, great skill and long experience. There is now one branch of cabinet making, carried out by this firm, which is nowhere else practiced in this Province —enamelling. They are engaged in the manufacture of chairs, the backs of which are inlaid with ivory and mother of pearl, and which when finished combine the useful and ornamental in a manner rarely to be met with; as specimens of mechanical perfection in this business, they cannot be excelled. Enough now has, perhaps, been said to show that the Messrs. Hilton possess qualities for carrying out their trade scarcely to be surpassed in Canada.

---

* Taken from *Montreal Business Sketches with a Description of the City of Montreal* published by the Canada Railway Advertising Company (Montreal: M. Longmoore, 1864), pp. 79-81.

The Purchases Made by Madame Chapais in Quebec City, in 1866, for her House in Saint-Denis

During the 1840s, the businessman Jean-Charles Chapais (1811-1885) contributed in a major way to the development of the parish of Saint-Denis-de-la-Bouteillerie into a prosperous, well-organized village. In 1846 he married Georgina, daughter of Amable Dionne, a legal counsellor and wealthy merchant from Kamouraska. On the advice of his father-in-law, Chapais decided to embark on a political career, and he served as member for Kamouraska from 1851 until Confederation. After 1867, he held a number of posts, including deputy in Quebec City, senator and minister in Ottawa. Although relatively unobtrusive on the national scene, Chapais played an important role in the development of Saint-Denis and the surrounding region.[1]

In 1833,[2] Jean-Charles Chapais built a house in Saint-Denis, and the house underwent major repairs and alterations in 1866.[3] These renovations were behind Madame Chapais' shopping trip to Quebec City in July of 1866. The plan was also that at the end of her stay she would travel home with her daughters, Amélie and Georgina, who were pupils at the Ursuline convent. In the meantime, she visited a number of the Old Capital's commercial establishments in the company of her husband's *chargé d'affaires* Ferdinand Hamel, whom she refers to affectionately as her "gentleman escort". Despite the summer heat, Madame Chapais seems to have undertaken her task with considerable energy. At the importers Henry Goodwin & Co., she purchased porcelain dishware, wine glasses, crystal dishes and vases.[4] She also visited the ironmongers Bélanger & Gariépy, where she bought several different types of container and six "portmanteau hooks".[5] The main goal of her trip, however, was the purchase of furniture for various rooms in the house. To assist her, Ferdinand Hamel had previously prepared a list comparing the prices of Quebec City's two main furniture makers, William Drum and Philippe Vallière.[6]

On July 7, "Georgette" wrote to inform her "dear husband" that her final choices were not necessarily in accordance with his suggestions:

278
Madame Jean-Charles Chapais, née Georgina Dionne (1830-1888)
Photograph
Musée de la civilisation, Quebec City (68-931)

279
Neuville Bazin, Quebec City
The Chapais house,
Saint-Denis de Kamouraska, 1950
Photograph
Archives nationales du Québec, Centre de Québec et Chaudière-Appalaches, fonds de l'Office du film (E67/NN82362-50)

280
A corner of the drawing room in the Chapais house, Saint-Denis de Kamouraska, about 1950
Photograph
Musée de la civilisation, Quebec City (68-1328)

281
Philippe Vallière (1832-1919)
Rococo-revival sofa, 1866
Black walnut and horsehair,
102.3 x 196.7 x 91.1 cm
Musée de la civilisation, Quebec City (68-1189)
Photo Christine Guest/MMFA

282
Philippe Vallière (1832-1919)
Rococo-revival armchair, 1866
Black walnut and horsehair,
112.7 x 62.5 x 58.7 cm
Musée de la civilisation, Quebec City (68-1190)
Photo Christine Guest/MMFA

My purchases are proceeding well, but I'm dying of the heat and I am so shocked by the prices of things that it's all I can do to buy anything at all. I bought a luncheon service at Goodwin's, not the one you selected, for they could not give me more than twelve plates. With it I bought an all white set with a gold band that is very complete and a little less expensive than the other. I didn't take the dinner service; it is magnificent, but too enormously expensive. At Vallière's I took one of the black walnut bedroom suites that you chose. It will be for the downstairs bedroom. I took the small oak suite for the back room upstairs, the guest room. I assure you it will be perfectly adequate. I couldn't make up my mind to buy anything for my bedroom, it's too expensive and it's too much to buy at once. Perhaps things will be cheaper in the fall. Anyway, if ever I have to spend another summer like this one it won't kill me. I did not buy anything for the little girls' rooms either. I would prefer the oak table from Vallière's in walnut, but they couldn't make one for me, at least they couldn't have had it ready in a fortnight and since we have a wagon for all the other things it seems a shame not to transport everything at once. If you'd like me to take it

283
Philippe Vallière (1832-1919)
Rococo-revival rocking chair, 1866
Black walnut and horsehair,
104.4 x 64.4 x 88 cm
Musée de la civilisation, Quebec City (68-1191)
Photo Christine Guest/MMFA
In Quebec, the term "chaise berçante" (rocking chair) was used indiscriminately for chairs both with and without arms.

284
Philippe Vallière (1832-1919)
Rococo-revival chair
(from a set of six), 1866
Black walnut and horsehair, 96 x 51.5 x 50.5 cm
Musée de la civilisation, Quebec City (68-1192)
Photo Christine Guest/MMFA

285
Philippe Vallière (1832-1919)
Rococo-revival games table, 1866
Black walnut, 77 x 91 x 42.8 cm
Musée de la civilisation, Quebec City (80-4.1)
Photo Christine Guest/MMFA

telegraph Ferdinand. If not, I'll assume you'd prefer me to wait for one in black walnut at the same price. I took the chairs you wanted for the drawing room. It's impossible to buy anything at Drum's, it's exorbitant. Your wallpaper was very fine but did not suit the room at all, it was too dark. McDonald changed it for me and I took another

THE FURNITURE MAKERS

286
Philippe Vallière (1832-1919)
Rococo-revival games table, 1866
Black walnut, 77 x 91 x 42.8 cm
Musée de la civilisation, Quebec City (80-4.2)
Photo Christine Guest/MMFA
This table is identical to the preceding one, but its extending leaf has been opened to show the mechanism.

287
Philippe Vallière (1832-1919)
Corner whatnot, 1866
Black walnut, 163 x 75 x 42 cm
Musée de la civilisation, Quebec City (68-1304)
Photo Christine Guest/MMFA

that is also very nice and less expensive – 7/6. I will write to you again before I leave and send you a list of everything I have bought with the price of each article.7

Three days later Madame Chapais attended the end-of-the-year ceremonies at the Ursuline convent. The following day she returned to Saint-Denis with her daughters, with the hope of "finding [her] garden well on".8 For his part, the business manager Hamel organized the shipment by "wagon" – actually a railway carriage – of the "furniture and other merchandise" the following Saturday.9

The house in Saint-Denis, called "Mont Plaisir", was for many years the residence of the historian and politician Thomas Chapais, Jean-Charles' son. In 1950, Thomas Chapais' nieces, Élodie and Julienne Barnard, bequeathed his papers and art collection to the Quebec Government.10 In 1967, a first cursory inventory was drawn up of the furniture and objects in the house at the time of their purchase by the Ministère des Affaires culturelles. One year later the house was also acquired. It was classified as a historical monument in 1989 and since that time has been open to the public during the summer months. The drawing-room suite chosen by Madame Chapais, which now belongs to the Musée de la Civilisation, is one of the few that can be firmly attributed to the firm of the Quebec City furniture maker Philippe Vallière.11

John R. Porter

1   See Chapais' biography by Andrée Désilets in *DBC*, vol. 11 (1881-1890) (Quebec City: PUL, 1982), pp. 193-194.

2   ANQQ, registry of notary Michel-Honoré St. Jorre, April 17, 1833. Document referred to by Pierrette Maurais in "Recherche historique concernant la construction de la maison Chapais de Saint-Denis de Kamouraska et l'acquisition de son ameublement", unpublished report submitted in October 1990 for the MOBIVIQ project. Most of my notes and references are based on this report.

3   Julienne Barnard, *Mémoires Chapais* (Montreal: Fides, 1961), vol. 1, pp. 126-128 and 254-259.

4   Ministère des Affaires culturelles à Rimouski, Fonds maison Chapais de Saint-Denis, bill dated July 9, 1866. This bill was no doubt settled by F. Hamel after Madame Chapais' visit.

5   *Ibid.*, bill dated July 10, 1866.

6   Archives du Musée de la civilisation, Quebec City, Fonds Barnard.

7   Archives de l'Université Laval, fonds Chapais (trans.). In a letter dated July 10, Madame Chapais apologises to her husband for not sending the promised list.

8   *Ibid.* (trans.).

9   Archives du Musée de la civilisation, Quebec City, fonds Barnard, letter from Ferdinand Hamel to Jean-Charles Chapais, July 16, 1866 (trans.).

10   Several photographs were taken of the interior of the house on this occasion. ANQQ, fonds de l'Office du film, prints EC 67/NN-82350-50 to E67/NN82362-50 and E67/NN-82436-50 to E67/NN-82445-50. The drawing-room wallpaper, carpet and curtains are not the originals owing to the fire started by Christmas tree candles that occurred in 1925. The old wallpaper, which depicted a battle scene with the soldiers' uniforms standing out against a grey background, had to be replaced. The horsehair upholstery of the furniture was also damaged but was restored to its original condition.

11   Despite the rather vague references in Madame Chapais' letter – she talks of the "chairs" for the drawing room – a close examination of the prices mentioned in Ferdinand Hamel's letter (July 16, 1866) and the comparative list he had prepared earlier confirms this.

François Gourdeau, Furniture Maker

The careers of most of the furniture and cabinetmakers working in Quebec during the Victorian era remain shrouded in mystery. There are very few cases where specific works can be definitely attributed to particular creators, and documentary information about them is rare and fragmentary. All researchers have to work with is what they can glean from advertisements, directory listings, brief descriptions taken from censuses and occasional newspaper references. In spite of his importance and reputation, the manufacturer François Gourdeau (1840-1920) of Quebec City is no exception to the rule. We know very little about the details of his life, and the documentary evidence related to the few pieces known to be by him is cryptic and still open to a number of interpretations.

Son of the furniture maker Édouard Gourdeau and of Émérance Levasseur,[1] François-Xavier[2] Gourdeau was born on September 9, 1840,[3] probably in the parish of Saint-Jean-l'Évangéliste-de-Dorchester, today Saint-Jean-d'Iberville.[4] We learn from the census of 1861 that twenty years later François was living in the Saint-Roch district of Quebec City and working as a "furniture maker". After having apparently learned the rudiments of the trade from his father, he may have spent a few years in the studio of the sculptor Jean-Baptiste Côté (1832-1907) of Saint-Roch and possibly even visited the United States.[5] We know for sure, however, that he set up his own business in 1864, shortly after his marriage on November 25, 1863 to Philomène Chamberland of the parish of Saint-Roch.[6] For the following fifty years the name of the *ébéniste* or "cabinetmaker" François Gourdeau appears regularly in the city directories.[7] Following a brief retirement, he died in Saint-Roch on June 19, 1920, and was buried two days later in the Saint-Charles cemetery.[8]

François Gourdeau seems to have been a cabinetmaker of considerable energy, well able to compete with other frontrunners of the profession. At the age of thirty he was already head of a well-organized, well-equipped, versatile manufacturing business, and was fully conversant with foreign fashions. In the advertisement he ran in *L'Événement* from April 9, 1870, there is mention of the "improvements he has brought to his workshops, both as regards choice of materials and new craftsmen". The newspaper's editor, commenting on the advertisement, was extremely complimentary:

The establishment of Mr. F. Gourdeau, furniture maker-upholsterer, enjoys a remarkable reputation; and in truth we feel that to run an advertisement for him is really quite superfluous. The taste with which Mr. Gourdeau executes his commissions is well known. We have seen a number of drawing rooms furnished by him and we have noticed one in particular that stands out from all the rest; this drawing room, furnished in the French style, is one of the very finest of its type. There is no better to be in seen in either New York or Paris.[9]

Gourdeau, obviously flattered by these remarks, hastened to add to his advertisement a passage drawing "public attention to the fact that he has furnished a large number of Quebec City's leading drawing rooms and that any one of these is enough to class his establishment among the very best".[10]

On January 3 of the following year, as part of a series entitled "L'industrie à Québec", *L'Événement* published an article on cabinetmaking. The article naturally gave a good deal of space to the large businesses of William Drum and Philippe Vallière, but it also mentioned the smaller firms of "Messrs. Roy, Gourdeau and Bistodeaux, who manufacture – mostly on commission – furniture of a richness and finish rarely surpassed".[11] None of the seventeen other furniture-making establishments listed in the Quebec census of 1871 received similar mention.[12] We also learn from the industrial census that François Gourdeau's furniture factory was open twelve months a year, that it had a fixed capital of $1,000 and an identical floating capital, that it employed fifteen men and one woman, that it possessed both machinery for "sawing and turning" and a man-operated "mechanical complexity", that it had on the premises 6,000 feet of mahogany, black walnut, butter-nut, ash, oak and pine worth $2,500, and that it produced annually 800 pieces of furniture of different types worth a total of $7,500. In fact, Gourdeau's firm was Quebec City's leading establish-

ment in the "manufactory" class of furniture maker, and at the provincial exhibition of 1871 it was the only outfit of this type to compete alongside the industrial firms of William Drum and Philippe Vallière.

Even though the magnificent and extensive displays mounted by Drum and Vallière took up nearly all the space in the exhibition's "furniture department", Gourdeau succeeded in attracting attention with a fine drawing-room suite. Nazaire Levasseur (1848-1927), a journalist with L'Événement, spoke of it in the following terms:

This Elizabethan-style drawing-room suite is really pretty; the carving is virtually perfect. It was made a couple of years ago for a citizen of Quebec City, and Mr. Gourdeau, not having had time to prepare anything for the Exhibition, is presenting the set with the owner's permission. It has, moreover, won him an honourable mention.[13]

The newspaper Le Canadien had already made mention of the suite's "magnificent carving" and of Gourdeau's "talent and outstanding taste", while The Quebec Gazette, The Morning Chronicle and The Quebec Daily Mercury had all alluded to "sets of drawing room furniture of black walnut and most artistic design".[14] As far as we know, the provincial exhibition of 1871 was the only one in which Gourdeau won a prize — an honourable mention — and, in fact, the only one in which he participated at all. Drum and Vallière were the only furniture makers to take part in the Quebec City exhibition of 1877, and the editor of L'Événement noted Gourdeau's absence, recalling the "magnificent drawing-room furniture" he had presented in 1871.[15]

In June 1873, Gourdeau's business was seriously compromised by a fire that reduced "the whole workshop and its contents to ashes". Reporting on this terrible event, which almost ruined the cabinetmaker-entrepreneur, a journalist for La Minerve stated that when the fire broke out "Mr. Gourdeau had been on the point of delivering three walnut drawing-

288
François Gourdeau (1840-1920) and Rose-de-Lima called Mary Moreau (about 1858-1938)
Renaissance-revival screen, 1869-1870
Black walnut, tapestry and glass,
208 x 112 x 53 cm
Augustinian monastery of the Hôtel-Dieu de Québec
Photo Christine Guest/MMFA

289
François Gourdeau (1840-1920)
Renaissance-revival settee, about 1870
Black walnut, 144 x 195 x 68 cm
The Montreal Museum of Fine Arts, gift of the Succession J.A. DeSève (1986.Df.1)
Photo Christine Guest/MMFA

The general look of this piece, together with the shape of the legs, apron and back, all draw their inspiration from the Renaissance. Certain other elements, however, owe more to the Rococo-revival style.

room suites, to which he had only to put the finishing touches".[16] The article goes on to report how Quebec's citizens clubbed together to raise money to help Gourdeau re-establish his business. Ten years later Gourdeau was still employing at least fifteen workers,[17] and he responded to the needs of the community on several occasions with versatility[18] and generosity.[19]

Today, the only known works by Gourdeau are a drawing-room

290

291

292

290
François Gourdeau (1840-1920)
Renaissance-revival armchair, about 1870
Black walnut, 190 x 75 x 61 cm
The Montreal Museum of Fine Arts, gift of the Succession J.A. DeSève (1986.Df.2)
Photo Christine Guest/MMFA

291
François Gourdeau (1840-1920)
Renaissance-revival lady's chair, about 1870
Black walnut, 190 x 75 x 53 cm
The Montreal Museum of Fine Arts, gift of the Succession J.A. DeSève (1986.Df.3)
Photo Christine Guest/MMFA

292
François Gourdeau (1840-1920)
Renaissance-revival chair
(from a set of six), about 1870
Black walnut, 120 x 45 x 53 cm
The Montreal Museum of Fine Arts, gift of the Succession J.A. DeSève (1986.Df.7)
Photo Christine Guest/MMFA

screen, a twelve-piece drawing-room suite and a small dressing-table mirror. Even here, despite extensive research, the attribution and dating of the pieces are still open to revision, for although formal and stylistic comparisons are quite conclusive, the concrete evidence is sketchy and, as the reader will realize, secondary sources are contradictory.

It would not be possible to attribute any Quebec furniture of the Victorian era to Gourdeau's workshop were it not for a gift made to the sisters of the Hôtel-Dieu in Quebec City by the late Mrs. Arsène Roy, née Mary Moreau. Mrs. Roy bequeathed to her daughter Anne-Marie, who was Sister Saint-Nazaire at the Hôtel-Dieu, a very fine wooden screen decorated with a piece of needlepoint she had herself executed in 1870 when she was a pupil at the Jésus-Marie Convent in Sillery. From a note written by Mrs. Roy's son, Monsignor Lionel Roy, that is stuck on the back of the screen, we learn that:

The frame and the stand were both carved by Mr. François Xavier Gourdeau, of Saint-RochÎ in Quebec City. The complete set won first prize when it was presented at the Provincial Exhibition of 1873.

The information concerning Gourdeau handed down in the family and noted by Monsignor Roy is explicit enough to be plausible, but the note is inaccurate regarding both the year of the exhibition and the type of prize awarded to the cabinetmaker. In the light of the content of the note and the information already referred to, it seems reasonable to suggest that the screen belonging to the Hôtel-Dieu was part of the ensemble of drawing-room furniture submitted by François Gourdeau to the provincial exhibition in September 1871 for which he won an honourable mention. Even the execution of the needlepoint by Mary Moreau in 1870 seems to fit, for the suite exhibited in 1871 had been made two years earlier for "a citizen of Quebec City".

The carving and decoration of the Gourdeau screen display certain distinctive features, including the high relief head on the cresting and the richly carved plant and animal motifs on the base. From a stylistic and formal point of view, these elements bear a striking resemblance to those appearing on an imposing drawing-

THE FURNITURE MAKERS

293
François Gourdeau (1840-1920)
Renaissance-revival console table with mirror, about 1870
Black walnut, 212 x 81 x 15 cm (mirror),
77 x 84 x 42 cm (table)
The Montreal Museum of Fine Arts, gift of the Succession J.A. DeSève (1986.Df.7)
Photos Christine Guest/MMFA

294
François Gourdeau (1840-1920)
Renaissance-revival games table, about 1870
Black walnut, 78 (diam.) x 91 x 45 cm
The Montreal Museum of Fine Arts, gift of the Succession J.A. DeSève (1987.Df.3)

295
François Gourdeau (1840-1920)
Renaissance-revival games table, about 1870
Black walnut, 78 (diam.) x 91 x 45 cm
The Montreal Museum of Fine Arts, gift of the Succession J.A. DeSève (1987.Df.2)

room suite purchased by the Montreal Museum of Fine Arts in 1986-1987 from a Quebec City antique dealer. The suite is composed of twelve pieces, including a settee, a gentleman's armchair, a lady's armchair, six other chairs, a console table with mirror and two games tables. If we compare the screen to the carved heads that adorn the various seats in the suite or to the under-frames of its three tables, it becomes immediately evident that all the pieces were produced by the same workshop. In fact, it seems legitimate to wonder if the suite was not the very one for which Gourdeau won an honourable mention in 1871. An oral tradition going back many years that associates the suite with a prize would seem to support this hypothesis. Moreover, the suite once belonged to the notary and journalist Théophile Levasseur (1853-1936), whose older brother Nazaire was, we recall, very interested in Gourdeau's work during the 1870s.[20] Nazaire Levasseur may even have been the Gourdeau suite's first owner.

Until we possess further documentary information about François Gourdeau, the field remains wide open to speculation. One thing is certain, however: if the Hôtel-Dieu screen was indeed shown at the provincial exhibition of 1871, the suite of drawing-room furniture of which it was part must have been extremely similar in workmanship and style to the ensemble now belonging to the Montreal Museum of Fine Arts.[21] It is for this reason that we feel justified in dating the suite to about 1870 and in situating at around the same period the carving decorating the frame of a small mirror acquired recently by the same institution.[22]

John R. Porter and Yves Lacasse

295

1 They were married at Saint-Jean-d'Iberville, in the Richelieu valley, on November 21, 1842. Édouard's parents came from Saint-Pierre on Île d'Orléans and Émérance's from Saint-François, also on Île d'Orléans.

2 In the record appearing in the marriage register of the parish of Saint-Roch in Quebec City, dated November 25, 1863, Gourdeau is given the first name of François-Xavier. However, he was commonly referred to by the single first name of François.

3 François Gourdeau was born illegitimate. At the time of his parents' marriage, the curé of Saint-Jean noted in the register that he had "legitimized François, born on September 9, 1840" (trans.). His brother Édouard was baptized on December 26, 1842, five weeks after the wedding; at the time of the 1871 census in Quebec City, Édouard was twenty-eight and his older brother François was thirty.

4 See note 1. The receipt that the "furniture maker" Édouard Gourdeau signed before the notary Fabien Ouellet of Quebec City (ANQQ, no. 2419) on September 19, 1844, states that he lived in the parish of Boucherville.

5 In the transcription of Marius Barbeau's interview with the seventy-eight-year-old sculptor Joseph Carbonneau of Quebec City there is the following intriguing passage, which might be a reference to François Gourdeau: "Father J. B. Côté had some apprentices: one named Gourdeau who went to the U.S. (he was a good sculptor). . ." (CCFCS, Fonds Marius Barbeau, Dossier 39 [J. B. Côté], chez Carbonneau [trans.]). Carbonneau had himself been apprenticed to the furniture maker Ferdinand Arel. Édouard Gourdeau, François' father, worked regularly for William Drum and Philippe Vallière from the 1850s on (see the section on William Drum in Chapter 3). And as we learn from the 1871 census, Édouard Gourdeau the younger (François' brother) also worked as a furniture maker. From 1867, the names of the three furniture-making Gourdeaus appear in the Quebec City directory.

6 In *Cherrier's Quebec City and Levis Directory for 1882-1883* (p. 256), Gourdeau himself states that he started his own business in 1864.

7 His name appears for the last time in the directory for 1915-1916.

8 We are grateful to Rénald Lessard of the Archives nationales du Québec in Quebec City for having supplied the basic biographical information on François Gourdeau.

9 *L'Événement*, April 9, 1870, p. 2 (trans.). Gourdeau's advertisement ran until July 29, 1873 (Luce Vermette, *Répertoire des ébénistes des villes de Montréal et de Québec, 1850-1870* [Ottawa: Canada Parks, 1984], microfiche).

10 See *L'Événement*, May 7, 1870 (trans.).

11 A large part of this article was reprinted in the *Annuaire du commerce et de l'industrie de Québec pour 1873* by L. H. Huot (Québec City: L. H. Huot, 1873), pp. 20-23 (trans.).

12 For more on these other firms, see John R. Porter (ed.), *Les meubliers Pierre Drouin et Honoré Roy et l'industrie du meuble à Québec à l'époque victorienne* (Quebec City: Université Laval, 1989), Cahiers du CÉLAT, no. 10, p. 17.

13 *L'Événement*, September 18, 1871 (trans.). This information is confirmed by an article published in *Le Canadien* on September 13, 1871. Between 1867 and 1878, Nazaire Levasseur was successively reporter, assistant editor and editor-in-chief for *L'Événement* (see *L'Événement*, November 9, 1927).

14 See the editions of September 13, 1871.

15 *L'Événement*, September 25, 1877.

16 *La Minerve*, June 27, 1873.

17 The June 11, 1881 edition of *Le Nouvelliste* mentions the help offered by Gourdeau and fifteen of his employees to victims in the Saint-Jean-Baptiste district of Quebec City.

18 Gourdeau contributed towards the making of the "Char à Peintres" (painters' float) that was part of the Saint-Jean-Baptiste Day parade held in Quebec City on June 24, 1880. In the work by H.-J.-J.-B. Chouinard entitled *Fête nationale des Canadiens-français célébrée à Québec en 1880* (Quebec City: A. Côté et cie, 1881), pp. 487-488, Paul Cousin offers the following description: "The float was constructed by Mr. Gourdeau, furniture-cabinetmaker, of Église Street in Saint-Roch, according to the plans and specifications of Mr. P. Cousin, architect. The painting of the backgrounds, marbles and fresco decorations are by Messrs. Gauthier et Frères, painter-decorators of Saint-Joseph Street in Saint-Roch. The sloping base is encircled by a piece of canvas arranged like drapery, upon which appear the words *Painter-decorators*. Above this rises a regular monument of the Ionic order, complete with bases, pilasters, capitals, imposts, architraves, entablatures and pediments, entirely in wood, with the decorations and carvings of the order and the grounds painted in imitation of marble" (trans.).

19 In 1883, he executed the "beautiful cabinetwork" of the holder for the banner of the Union Saint-Joseph for the parish of Saint-Roch, of which he was a member (*Journal de Québec*, February 26, 1883).

20 For more about Théophile Levasseur, see his obituary in the April 16, 1936 editions of *Le Soleil* and *L'Événement*. The suite belonged successively to Théophile Levasseur, his niece Blanche Brochu, and the nephew of the latter whose wife, Mrs. Lucille Brochu, sold it to the Quebec City antique dealer Louis Zaor. According to Mrs. Brochu, oral tradition has it that the suite was purchased by Théophile Levasseur in Toronto, during an exhibition at which it won a first prize. Apart from the detail concerning the prize, this information is hard to reconcile with what we know of Gourdeau and of Levasseur.

21 The fact that in 1871 the Gourdeau suite was said to be in the "Elizabethan style" does not undermine our hypothesis owing to the extremely imprecise nature of such labels at the time. See chapter 4 of the present volume, "The Pursuit of Elegance: Dominant Styles and the Evolution of Taste", for a discussion of the various "revival" styles.

22 See below the insert in chapter 4 entitled "Techniques Employed in the Making of Fine Furniture in Victorian Quebec".

Evidence of Montreal Furniture Dealer and Maker Owen McGarvey Before a Royal Commission of Enquiry in February 1888*

Q.-How long have you been in business?
A.-About forty years.
Q.-We want to get to the bottom of a question and to make it short I will ask you direct: Can you tell us if the furniture used by the medium class of mechanics is dearer today than it was ten or fifteen years ago or if it is cheaper?
A.-That is the class of goods purchased, generally speaking, by mechanics, and the labouring classes.
Q.-The medium class, from medium to lower class?
A.-They are from twenty-five to fifty per cent lower now than they were fifteen years ago. The lower the grade the cheaper they are in proportion to quality.
Q.-And do you think those goods are just as well made now as they were before the advent of the National Policy?
A.-Probably they may not be so durably put together for the price. They are made to sell cheap, but they have got to about proportion, namely from twenty-five to fifty per cent cheaper.
Q.-Do you think these articles, these goods made by machinery, are just as good as those made by hand?
A.-Well, if the machinery is perfect they are just as good, of course, some portions of every article are made by hand.

* Extract from the *Report of the Royal Commission on the Relations of Capital and Labour in Canada: Evidence - Quebec* Part I, (Ottawa: Queen's Printer, 1889), pp. 726-727.

Q.-Do you manufacture?
A.-We manufacture furniture and deal in it.
Q.-Are wages as high now as they were twelve years ago?
A.-Very probably they are twenty per cent more than they were twelve years ago. We have from twenty to twenty-five men whom we pay from ten to thirteen dollars a week now. We paid them from eight to nine dollars then.
Q.-Do you use machinery in the manufacture of furniture?
A.-No.
Q.-Skilled work is largely if not wholly hand work?
A.-Yes; such as carving and the making of goods to order.
Q.-Do you use much machinery in the manufacture of this cheap or medium class furniture?
A.-We do not use machinery personally, but we contract with those that use it in the manufacture of this class of goods. Mr. Lynch, of L'Épiphanie, makes our chairs and common class of goods, and has done so for the last thirty years.
Q.-You say that certain classes of furniture are now twenty-five to fifty per cent cheaper than they were fifteen years ago?
A.-Yes.
Q.-Is it a better class of furniture?
A.-I have answered that question. Probably they may not be as durably put together, but they are a good serviceable article. For instance, articles which could be sold at that time for sixty-five dollars will sell now for twenty-five dollars wholesale and thirty-five dollars retail – namely, cheap parlour and bed room suites.
Q.-You find a market all over the Dominion for your goods?
A.-Yes; we sell a good class of furniture, and we ship to all parts almost. We ship to British Columbia, Manitoba, and all over the Dominion. We do not consign goods to agents, but parties purchase from us, and have them shipped to their address.
Q.-You ship wholesale out there, that is, parties buy it here and have it removed?
A.-Yes.
Q.-Do you find that there is an increasing demand – a greater demand – for high class furniture among the working classes than formerly?
A.-Yes.
Q.-Has the advance of the use of machinery in manufactories a tendency to cheapen articles of furniture?
A.-I consider it has cheapened articles very much, and also caused an increase in the number of hands employed; in fact, all classes of furniture are produced very much cheaper now than they were ten or fifteen years ago.
Q.-Is more machinery used now than was used ten or fifteen years ago?
A.-I do not know that more machinery is used, but there are always improvements being made in all classes of machinery every year.
Q.-Have the hours of labour

decreased in that branch of trade during the past fifteen years?
A.-No; it is the same as it has been during my time, namely, ten hours a day.
Q.-Is the furniture made of Canadian woods?
A.-Yes; except the veneers, which are imported from France and other places. That is French veneers, and veneers taken from other foreign woods.

Recollections of Cabinetmaker Édouard Bertrand as Recounted in an Interview Conducted by Marius Barbeau in About 1930*

Édouard Bertrand, who is eighty-six years old, was born in Montreal, but his ancestors came from Isle-Verte. His grandfather was a mason born in Quebec City. His father was a shoemaker.

I did my apprenticeship with the cabinetmaker Noël Pratte. In those days his workshop was on St. Lawrence Street, in Montreal; later he moved to Craig Street. I believe Pratte was born in Trois-Rivières; he was possibly related to John Pratte, of the Compagnie du Richelieu. He was French- rather than English-speaking. His was a medium-sized firm. He was just starting out when I was with him. He was a carver. He had worked for many years in New York. In 1859, the year before I joined him, his firm was located on St. Lawrence Street. I'm not quite sure, but I think he stayed in business until 1895. He built the Canadian Club house on La Gauchetière Street. I completed a four-year apprenticeship course. The fourth year I was earning $2.50 a week.

After that I worked at Thomson's on Saint-Jacques Street. Thomson was a cabinetmaker; he had many clients in Montreal. Thomson worked for the Allans, the Stephens, the Redpaths and other wealthy Montrealers. His work was the finest in the country. He was a Scot. He first had a firm in Toronto and later came to Montreal. There were no other carvers who stayed at Thomson's for thirteen or fourteen years. He had about fifty employees. The carvers were important in those days. For the sofas and chairs he employed ten cabinetmakers and ten or twelve carvers. At Pratte's they employed twenty-five or thirty people of whom ten to twelve were carvers. The carvers were from different backgrounds: some French Canadian, some French — even some Scots. Quite a mix. Much of the furniture was in the Louis XV and Louis XVI styles; it was mostly Renaissance.

Many of the workmen came from Drum or Vallière's firms, and from Quebec City generally. They were good craftsmen. Vallière's firm was excellent, and I knew several workmen who had done their apprenticeship there. We made the same furniture as in Quebec City. At Thomson's our furniture was mostly in the French style. Sometimes we did things in the Gothic style; these were more like English furniture.

In the United States, I worked for one of the best companies of the

---

* Edited and translated version of a typed transcript kept in dossier 64 ("Sculpteurs anciens") of the Marius Barbeau Collection at the CCFCS, Canadian Museum of Civilization, Hull.

THE FURNITURE MAKERS 305

time. I stayed there for a while, and then worked for some other firms. After that I joined Mason & Hamlin, and I stayed there thirty-seven years, carving organs and pianos. To start with, Mason & Hamlin only made organs. There are some of my carvings all over the world, because Mason & Hamlin made organs for many different countries.

During the interview, Barbeau noted the following pieces of furniture in Bertrand's home:

—An armoire cabinet in the Napoleon III Renaissance style, which was very common in Paris during the 1850s. The piece was designed by a Frenchman, Charles Fichot, who was a carver and designer. He was around my age, a little younger. He'd come from Paris and he'd been in Montreal for three or four years. He had no influence on the style here. I made the armoire based on his design. It's made of oak. I started it in 1882 and finished it some time later. At first I wanted to sell it, but finally I kept it for myself. At the bottom there are winged caryatids with round breasts that support the upper part; there are also pilasters. The piece is made of very fine oak and weighs between 250 and 300 pounds.

—An oak table in the style of the same period. Very fine.

—A small carved mahogany panel measuring twenty inches wide and ten inches high. The rough design was done in Paris and it was finished by Mr. Bertrand twelve years ago. It is a copy of a panel on a piece of furniture in the Louvre. I have seen it reproduced. Beautiful and well finished. There is a lyre in the centre, two female figures, two heads of cherubim, flowers, running decorations and fruit in the Renaissance style.

—In a finely-carved frame a portrait of his father, who died at eight-five, and his mother, who died at eighty-nine.

—Another even larger.

—A beautiful easel in the Japanese style made for a house in Boston.

—A hand mirror carved with maple leaves.

—A fine walnut hand mirror, very beautiful, with inlay on the back.

BETWEEN WORKSHOP AND FACTORY

Furniture making in the province of Quebec in 1871

DURING THE SECOND HALF OF THE NINETEENTH CENTURY, Britain's North American colonies were facing major changes. The formation in 1867 of a Canadian Confederation, uniting the provinces of Quebec, Ontario, New Brunswick and Nova Scotia, was the major political event of the period; economic upheavals also occurred, however, that were equally significant. Agriculture and forestry were still the foundation stones of the country's economy, but activities linked to the transformation of raw materials were developing and diversifying. The structure of labour was also changing. Generally speaking, it was a period of transition from craft to industrial production.

The process of industrialization normally moves through three stages: craft, manufacture and mechanized industry.[1] During the pre-industrial period production of goods was divided between many small, independent producers, who generally owned the means of production. Either alone or in partnership, assisted by a few employees, mostly apprentices, craftsmen accomplished the various stages necessary to the making of the product. At the manufacturing phase, the company was owned by one or more individuals who provided the capital and the means of production but who did not participate directly in the production process. The craftsman sold his labour, and his tasks became increasingly specialized. He was now either on salary or paid piece rates. The use of water and especially steam as sources of power grew steadily. Owing to the increased efficiency of the manufacturing process, goods could be mass-produced at lower prices. Finally, the introduction of machines marked the arrival of full-blown industrialization. Machines led to reduced costs, standardized production, and the employment of less qualified and often lower paid workers. The concentration of both the labour force and the manufacturing companies in cities hastened the urbanization of Canadian society. In Quebec, the proportion of urban dwellers went from 15% of the total population in 1851 to 36% in 1901.[2]

This development from craft, to manufacture, to industry occurred somewhat differently in the various economic sectors. In some cases stages were skipped, in others the three phases co-existed. Although in 1871 the furniture sector represented a production value of barely $1 million, out of Quebec's total manufacturing production of $77 million, it nevertheless clearly reflected the changes taking place.[3]

USING THE 1871 CENSUS: SOURCE AND METHODOLOGY

The federal census of 1871 remains the most useful document in studying the various businesses associated with the furniture industry during the Victorian era and attempting to determine their nature and that of their owners. This is because the statistics for individual manufacturing firms are less complete in the censuses of 1851 and 1861, while those from the censuses after 1871 have not been preserved or are not available. Moreover, the 1871 census contains information on the whole province and, unlike the later ones, the detailed schedules covering all the various towns and regions have been kept.

The census of 1871 was the first since Confederation, and it was designed to be as accurate as possible. The enumerators were sworn in, and anyone refusing "wilfully or without lawful excuse" to fill out to the best of their knowledge the schedules relating to them was liable to a fine of between ten and forty dollars. In addition, a *Manual Containing "The Census Act" and Instructions to Officers Employed in the Taking of the First Census of Canada (1871)* was provided for the census officers.[4] Finally, the census schedules were "communicated to the public in a condensed form, some time before the taking of the census, in order to allow everyone to acquaint himself with the questions which he is compelled by law to answer and be suitably prepared ahead of time."[5]

In order to avoid any confusion resulting from the mixing of various different types of information, nine separate schedules were prepared:

Schedule 1: Nominal Return of the Living
Schedule 2: Return of Deaths
Schedule 3: Public Institutions, Real Estate, Vehicles and Implements
Schedule 4: Cultivated Lands, Field Products, Plants and Fruits
Schedule 5: Live Stock, Animal Products, Home-Made Fabrics and Furs
Schedule 6: Industrial Establishments
Schedule 7: Products of the Forest
Schedule 8: Shipping and Fisheries
Schedule 9: Mineral Products

Schedules 1 and 6 have been used as the basis for this study of the furniture industry. Schedule 1 provides information regarding the names of the company owners, their age, trade or profession, sex, religion, family, and the presence of apprentices living under their roof. Schedule 6 contains information concerning the different types of business and their owners; the fixed and floating capital; the number of months worked per year; the number of employees, broken down by sex, age group and wage; the type of power source used and its par value; the type, quantity and value of raw materials used; and, finally, the type, quantity and value of the finished products. The census records the situation as it was on April 2, 1871, and the information concerning the production of the past year was to include data up to that day.[6]

The use of this rich source of information posed certain methodological problems. The first hurdle was to determine accurately which firms were actually linked to the furniture industry.

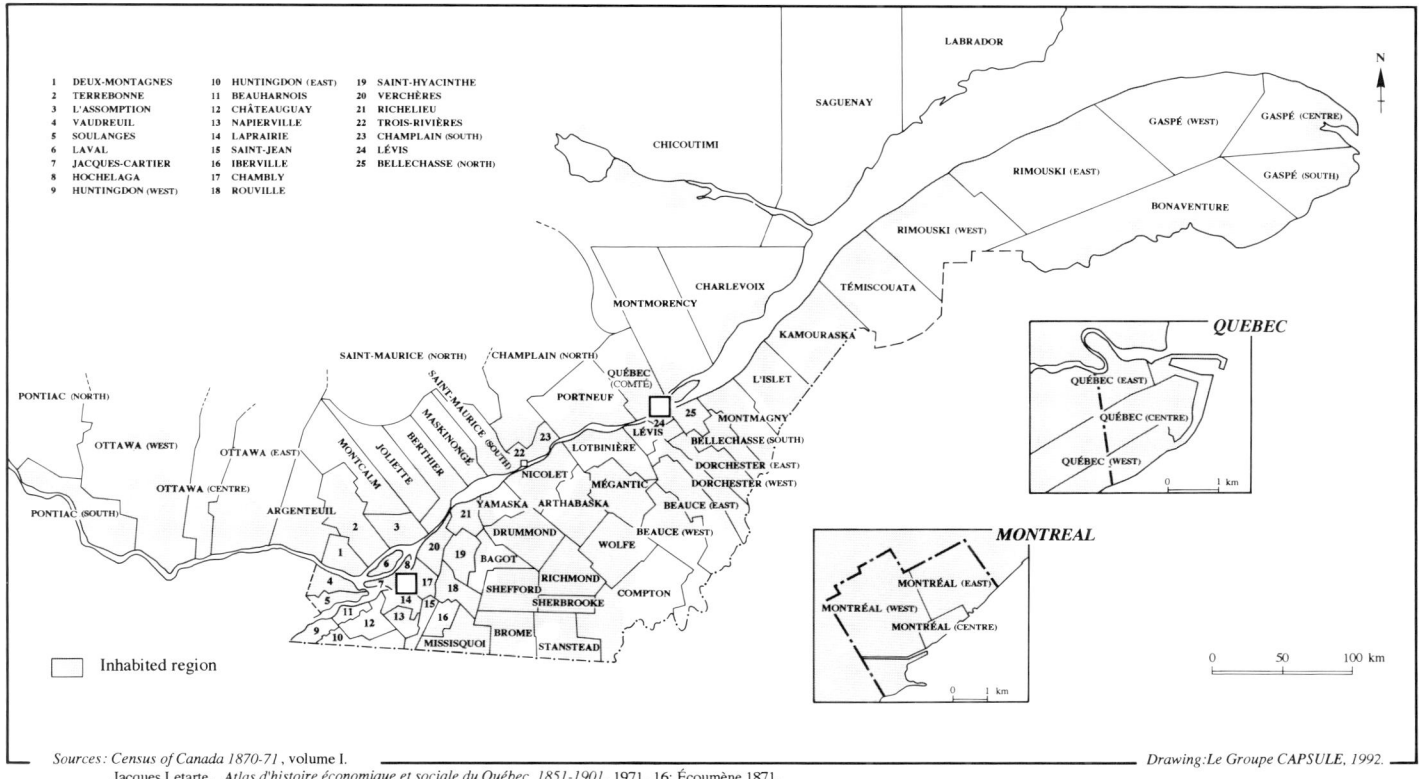

Census districts in Quebec, 1871
Drawing: Le groupe CAPSULE, 1992
Sources: *Census of Canada, 1870-71*
Jacques Letarte, *Atlas d'histoire économique et sociale du Québec 1851-1901*, 1971, 16: Écoumène 1871.

The definition of what constituted an industrial establishment was quite clear in the minds of the census officers: "An industrial establishment is a place where one or several persons are employed in manufacturing, altering, making up or changing from one shape into another, materials for sale, use or consumption, quite irrespectively of the amount of capital employed or of the products turned out."[7] Since in theory no minimum production value was required for inclusion in the census, a number of extremely small establishments were recorded. For example, the shop belonging to chair maker Stanislas Bergeron, forty-eight, at Saint-François, in the region of Yamaska, was included in the census despite the fact that it had only been open two months and the total value of the five dozen chairs produced so far was barely $15. And in Stoke, in the district of Richmond, joiner Joseph Lemire had a shop in which he had made a variety of wooden furniture consisting of six pieces worth a total of $15. In fact, several small establishments that appeared initially in the tables were later crossed out, either by an enumerator, a commissioner or a compiler, which seems to indicate that minimum criteria for the inclusion of an establishment were actually imposed by some or all of the census officers. Confirmation of this theory has not proved possible, however, with the material currently available. In any case, any firms that may have been left out were certainly extremely small, their production value representing only a small supplementary income for a single person.

The main problem concerns rather the capacity of the census officers to identify all the establishments linked in some way or another to the furniture industry. For people working in the furniture trade were often linked to the woodworking trade in general. Thus, of the 497 Quebec establishments linked to the furniture industry mentioned in the 1871 census, half do not define themselves as furniture makers (Table A). In fact, it is significant that the most frequently employed term, used by one quarter of those listed, is *boutique de menuisier*, or "joiner's workshop". This rather general term indicates the important, even predominant role played by small-scale craft work in the furniture trade and the versatility of many of its workers. The fact that we have included in our corpus not only those establishments that actually defined themselves as furniture makers, but also those that indicated that they did, in fact, produce furniture, means that our statistics are different from those compiled by the census officers and subsequently published.[8]

We faced a second major obstacle: the facts related to production are not always explicitly stated. A good number of enumerators employed the term *ouvrages de son métier* — "products of his trade" — without giving any further information about the nature of the products. Moreover, for some establishments that manufactured a range of goods, the census officers mentioned only the most important. It is therefore certain that a number of businesses have escaped our notice, especially joiners' shops.

Finally, in spite of the good intentions of the government and the census officers, several establishments were not recorded and a number of others did not provide all the required information or submitted, either wittingly or unwittingly, false declarations.[9] It is hard to believe, for example, that Félix Bigaouette, of Quebec City, had labour and raw materials costs amounting to only $1,250 when the value of his production was $24,000. Such a degree of profitability is quite unrealistic and completely incompatible with the figures submitted by his competitors.

Despite its limitations, however, the 1871 census possesses enormous potential. The parameters related to 497 businesses linked to the furniture industry, which have been card-indexed and then computerized, enable us to sketch a portrait of the Quebec furniture industry towards the middle of the Victorian era.

A GENERAL PICTURE OF THE QUEBEC FURNITURE INDUSTRY IN 1871

The 1871 census provides a picture of the manufacturing industries during a positive economic period, represented by the upswing (1870-1873) of a cycle that ended with the depression marking the years from 1873 to 1879.[10] The production value for the furniture sector was around $1 million, out of a total value of $77 million for Quebec manufacturing industries as a whole; this production value was distributed between 497 firms located throughout the province of Quebec. However, enormous differences can be observed from one region to another regarding the number of firms, the amount of capital involved, the wages paid and the production value. While the cities of Montreal and Quebec were home to respectively only 8% and 4% of the businesses linked to the furniture industry, between them they produced 61% of the furniture made in the province — 34% and 27% respectively.[11] The full significance of this concentration is revealed when we consider that together the inhabitants of the two cities constituted only 14% of the province's total population.[12] There is another indication, moreover, of the predominance of these two urban centres: between them, the firms in Montreal and Quebec City accounted for 43% of the labour force and 61% of the production value of the Quebec furniture industry. This predominance was due to the presence in the two cities of a number of large firms.

Tables C and D give the list of firms whose annual furniture production represented a value of $10,000 or more. These firms accounted for two thirds of the total production value of the Quebec furniture industry at the time. It will be observed that seventeen of the twenty-three firms in this category, and virtually all the largest, were situated in either Quebec City, Montreal or Sherbrooke. Between them, William Drum and Philippe Vallière of Quebec City, and J. & W. Hilton of Montreal produced one third of the furniture manufactured in the province and accounted for nearly half of the total fixed capital invested in the Quebec furniture industry.

The furniture industry was therefore far from a homogeneous block. If we break it down, five types of firm emerge: large furniture factories employing fifty or more workers, firms with between seven and forty-nine workers, those with between four and six, those with two or three, and finally establishments with only a single employee(table E). This classification according to the number of employees seemed to us the easiest to arrive at and the most effective to use.[13] The categories focused on by the enumerators appear, by contrast, to depend on rather ill-defined criteria. For example, the distinction between *manufacture*, or "factory", and *boutique*, or "shop", varies depending on the region, the owner and the enumerator. Apart from the details concerning sources of power, there is no information at all given regarding each firm's equipment or the division of labour in the various stages of furniture production. Production value and fixed and floating capital struck us as useful indicators, although susceptible to error or deliberate omission.

A TYPOLOGICAL ANALYSIS OF FIRMS LINKED TO THE FURNITURE INDUSTRY IN 1871

Large Furniture Factories

Of the 497 Quebec firms linked to the furniture industry, four stand out clearly from the others. Together, William Drum and Philippe Vallière of Quebec City, and J. & W. Hilton and D. & J. Tees of Montreal produced more than all the 425 firms employing three workers or less. This gives an idea of the size of the companies. The investments required to keep these four factories in operation amounted to $305,500 in fixed capital and $101,800 in floating capital, respectively one half and one third of the fixed and floating capital for the whole of the Quebec furniture industry. As an indication of the huge sums required in setting up firms such as these, it is interesting to note that their fixed capital represented on average the equivalent of close to one year's production — at least double that required by the other categories of firm.

With one quarter of the furniture sector's labour force, these four firms manufactured one third of the goods produced by this industry in Quebec. The use of water or steam as a power source was an essential part of their operations. The firm of William Drum was a clear frontrunner, with an estimated annual production of $16,000 and 120 employees. However, the more modest company of D. & J. Tees, employing fifty-two people, nevertheless manufactured annually 10,000 chairs worth $7,500 and 6,000 beds valued at $30,000. These four firms were in operation twelve months a year and 8% of their employees were women over sixteen years old.

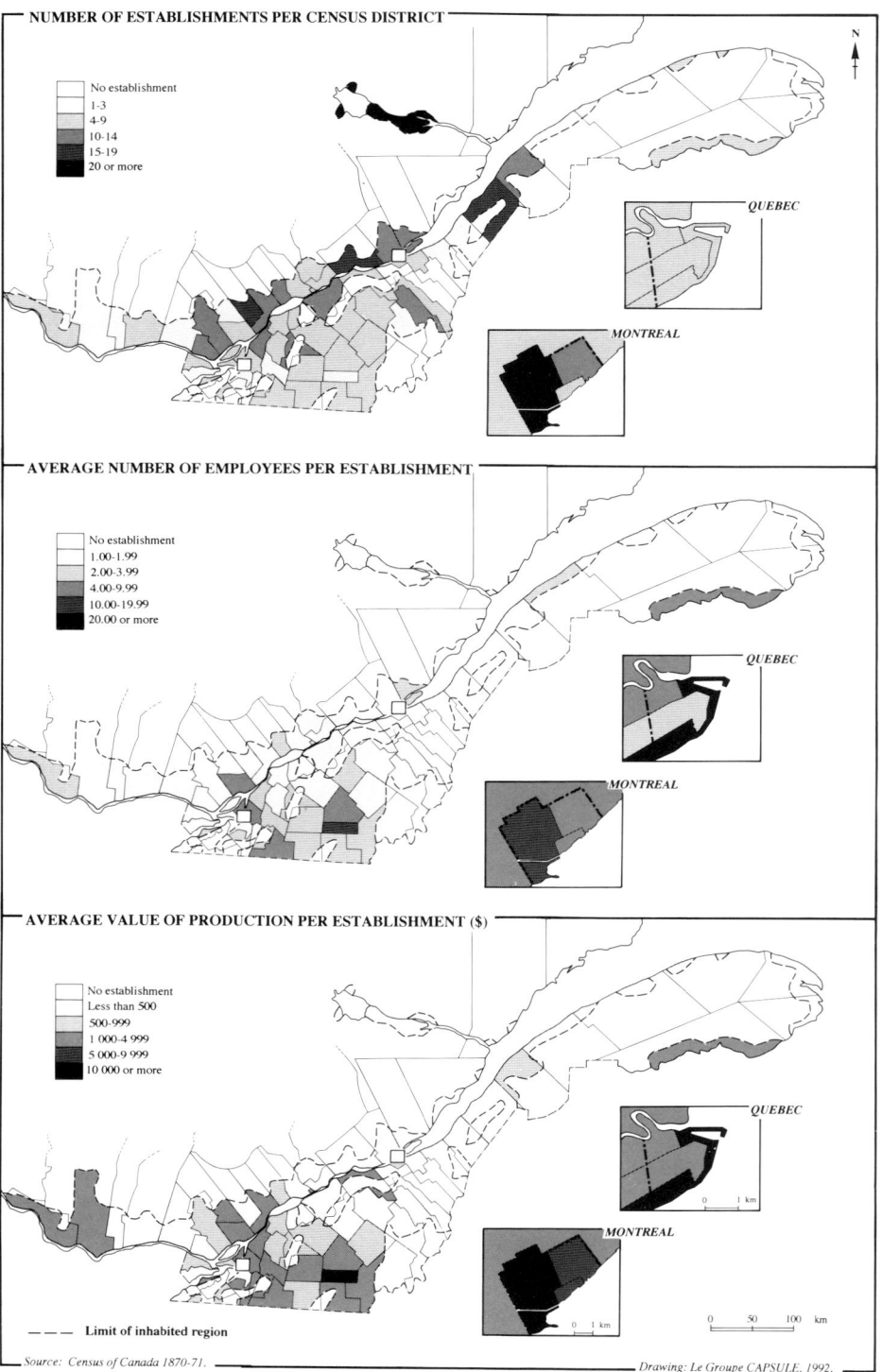

Quebec Furniture Industry, 1871
Drawing: Le groupe CAPSULE, 1992
Sources: *Census of Canada, 1870-71*

Firms Employing from Seven to Forty-Nine Workers

Firms employing between seven and forty-nine workers were found all over the province of Quebec, but the majority – and the largest – were concentrated in the cities of Montreal, Quebec and Sherbrooke, and in the census district of Hochelaga, near Montreal. The largest firm located outside these urban areas was without question that belonging to William Lynch, in L'Épiphanie, not far from Montreal. His company, which made extensive use of water power and employed thirty-six workers, manufactured annually $12,000 worth of chairs and other furniture. William Lynch, who identified

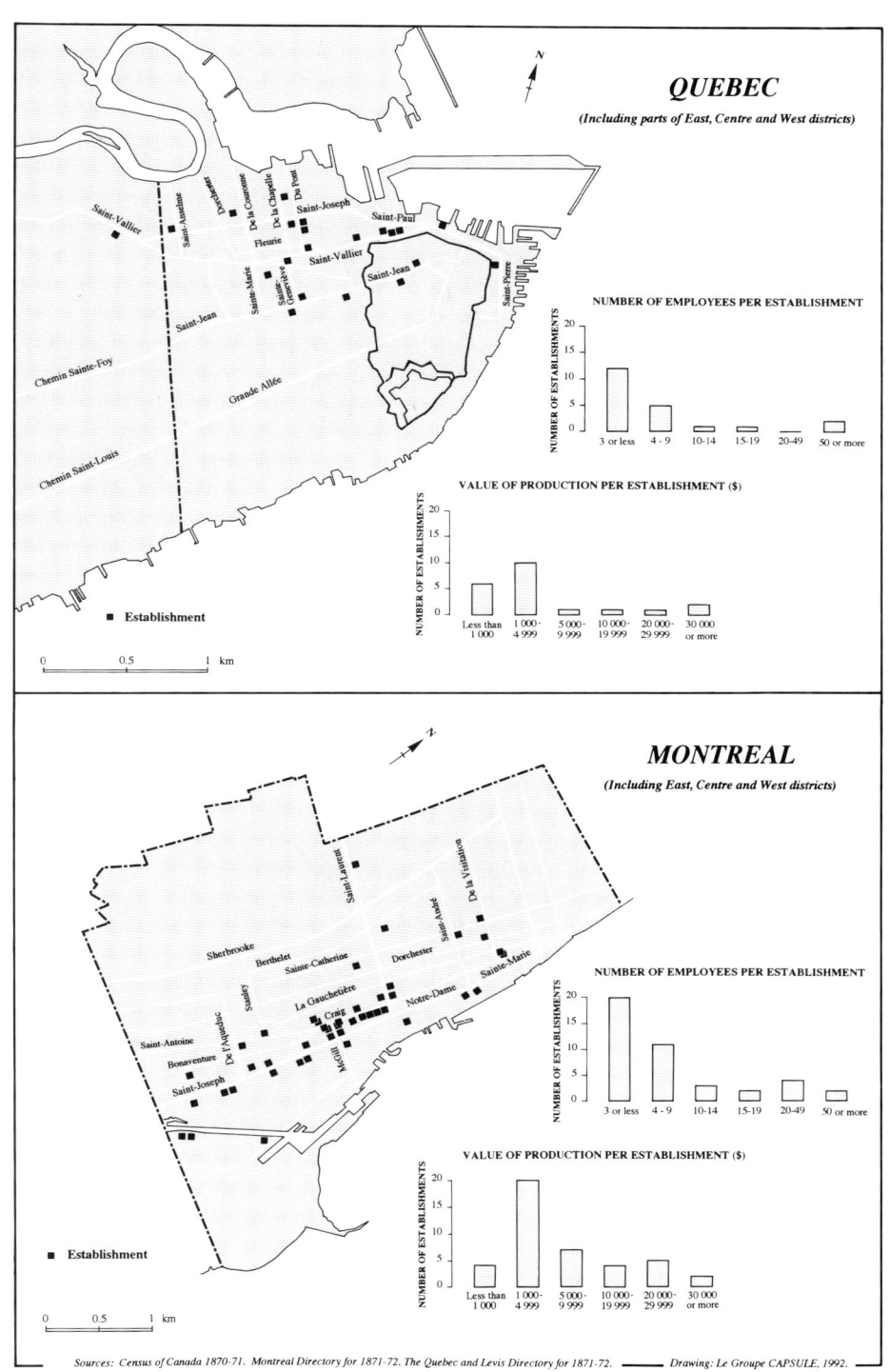

The Furniture Industry in Urban Areas, 1871
Drawing: Le groupe CAPSULE, 1992
Sources: *Census of Canada, 1870-71, volume 1, Montreal Directory for 1871-1872. The Quebec and Levis Directory for 1871-1872*

himself as a manufacturer, was a *Québécois* of Irish descent aged thirty-nine; he employed eight women in his company, which was extremely unusual for a firm in a rural area. Edouard Lynch, aged forty-one – probably his brother – is recorded as living under his roof. The firm attributed to Edouard was small, counting only two employees and producing furniture worth only $1,000.

The thirty companies falling into this category produced for about the same total value as the four large factories. The category includes a wider

THE FURNITURE MAKERS 313

variety of firms, but most of them are identified with the furniture industry. We thus find in this group eight furniture factories and four furniture works, together with four outfits identified as joiner's or carpenter's shops. The diversity of the situation is reflected in the declared profession of the various firms' owners. The category includes eight furniture makers, three manufacturers, two joiners, two dealers, a joiner-carpenter, a carpenter, a carpenter-farmer, a contractor, a merchant, a painter, a farmer and seven individuals whose profession is not given. Although the majority of the firms seem to have produced only furniture, at least nine manufactured other articles as well, including window frames, carriages, coffins, doors and other products made of wood. The relatively large size of the firms is indicated by the fact that twelve of them employed either water (6), steam (4), water and steam (1) or a horse (1) as sources of power. All of the firms except one were operational during all twelve months of the year. Women comprised slightly more than 10% of the labour force. In fact, two thirds of the women employed in the furniture industry were to be found in the seven to forty-nine employee category. In addition, nearly all the workers of under sixteen appear in this group. The firms in this category therefore lay somewhere between the large factories and the small-scale craftsmen's shops, possessing some of the characteristics of each.

Firms Employing from Four to Six Workers

The thirty-eight firms employing between four and six workers represent the upper end of the small-scale craftsmen's shops. Although almost half the firms in this category were located in the cities of Quebec and Montreal, they were to be found all over the province, especially in the western regions. Again, most of the firms specialized in cabinetmaking, but a number did manufacture other objects. Of the firms recorded in this category, only five are defined as factories, two thirds of them being referred to as shops. Only four firms made use of water and one of steam as a power source.

All the firms except one were operational twelve months of the year. There were virtually no women employees in this category of establishment.

Firms Employing Two or Three Workers

Firms employing three workers account for 86% of the companies linked to the furniture industry, those employing two or three, 29%. The craft element is very evident at this level: we observe the virtual absence of women, very little use of power sources other than manpower (only 15 cases out of 143), a good deal of activity related to furniture repair and a wide range of other activities. There are more firms identified as joiners' shops than as furniture makers. Among the twenty or so professions recorded by the owners of these firms the most common are joiner (46), furniture maker (41) — we have included in this group one *ébéniste*, one chair maker, and thirteen cabinetmakers — farmer (7), cartwright (6) and carpenter (5).

The heterogeneity of the firms with two or three employees can be illustrated by a few examples. Furniture maker Bruno Boucher was owner of a furniture factory in Notre-Dame-du-Portage, in the Témiscouata region. The firm employed three workers and used water as a power source. Annually, the firm produced two hundred beds, twenty-five tables, fourteen sofas and desks and five threshers, worth a total of $1,000. In Montreal, furniture maker Jean-Baptiste Duhamel produced in his shop, without any non-human power source, about a hundred pieces of furniture of various kinds worth a total of $900, together with the same number of coffins worth about the same amount. Another Montrealer, cabinetmaker John Ash, produced $500 worth of household furniture, but made repairs worth $1,000. Clearly, repair work accounted for a large proportion of this firm's business. In Deschambault, joiner Joseph Proulx made twelve pieces of furniture, three carriages, some window frames and some shutters, for a total value of $150. Finally, in Sainte-Famille, on Île d'Orléans, joiner Jean Pichet and his employee Onésime Lamothe (who lived under his employer's roof) built houses, made carriages and furniture and executed repairs of all kinds. Quite a varied picture!

Firms with One Employee
The 282 firms counting only a single employee represent 57% of the businesses linked to the furniture industry. However, their importance within the sector can best be judged from the value of their production, which was somewhere around 10% of the total production value of the Quebec furniture industry. The owners in this category defined themselves mainly as joiners (108), furniture makers (53), farmers (25), cartwrights (12), carpenters (11) or workers (11). Production was frequently seasonal, a fact not entirely explained by the presence of farmers in the group . The type and value of production varied widely from one firm to another. In Saint-Charles-Borromée, near Joliette, mechanic Christophe Capistran produced $1,000 worth of furniture in his "furniture factory". In Jeune Lorette, furniture maker Louis L'Heureux produced seventy-five dozen chairs worth $325 in his "furniture maker's shop". Finally, in New Richmond, in the Gaspé, cartwright Jean Lebuffe made wheels and tables and did a wide variety of repair jobs for a total value of $400. Many of these small craftsmen, who produced a broad range of products, also executed repairs. The frequent use of the terms *ouvrier* (worker) and *boutique d'ouvrier* (workshop) to describe individuals or their establishments is a clear indication of the lack of specialization of many of the people in this category, who adapted themselves to the needs of their clients and were, quite literally, "jacks-of-all-trades".

What conclusions may we draw from this broad sketch of the Quebec furniture industry? First of all, while the data from the 1871 census indicate the clear predominance of a handful of largely urban manufacturers, they also provide evidence of the continued existence of many small-scale craft firms, with wide-ranging and vaguely-defined activities, throughout the province of Quebec. Secondly, the picture that emerges is not one that shows a clear transition from craft to manufacture. It seems rather that the two forms of production co-existed, separated by an indeterminate area represented by the sixty-eight firms employing between four and forty-nine workers. It must be admitted, however, that the use of data from a single census necessarily provides us with a rather static view of the furniture industry. It is a view that can nevertheless be useful in adding another dimension to the more in-depth studies of the firms of William Drum and of Drouin and Roy, also included in this volume.

Rénald Lessard

TABLE A

\multicolumn{2}{c}{TYPES OF ESTABLISHMENT LINKED TO THE QUEBEC FURNITURE INDUSTRY IN 1871}		
Type of Establishment	Number	Type of Establishment	Number
1. Establishments defined exclusively as furniture makers			
Atelier d'ébénisterie et meublier	1	Cabinet shop	22
Atelier de meubles	2	Cabinet shop and repairs	1
Atelier de meubles communs	1	Chair maker	2
Atelier de meublier	7	Chair shop	1
Bedstead and chair factory	1	*Chaisier*	1
Boutique d'ébéniste	1	*Établissement de meublier*	1
Boutique d'ébénisterie	1	*Fabrique de meubles*	4
Boutique de chaises	1	Furniture	1
Boutique de chaises de cuisine	1	Furniture and chair factory	1
Boutique de couchettes et autres	1	Furniture and dealer manufacturer	1
Boutique de meubles	17	Furniture manufacture	1
Boutique de meublier	63	Furniture manufacturer	1
Cabinet and chair factory	1	*Manufacture de chaises*	3
Cabinet and chair shop	1	*Manufacture de couchettes de fer*	1
Cabinet establishment	1	*Manufacture de meubles*	18
Cabinet factory	5	*Manufacture de meubles et châssis*	1
Cabinet furniture shop	1	*Manufacture de meublier*	1
Cabinet maker	16	Manufacture of all kinds of furniture	1
Cabinet maker and repairer	1	*Manufacturier de meubles*	1
Cabinet maker's shop	1	*Meublerie*	4
Cabinet makers factory	1	*Meublier*	11
Cabinet making	1	Spring bed manufacturers	1
Cabinet making shop	1	Upholsterer	1
Cabinet manufactory	1	Upholsterer shop	1
		TOTAL: 209	

Type of Establishment	Number

2. Establishments defined as employed in cabinetmaking and other trades

Atelier d'ébénisterie tapissier 1
Boutique de charron et meuble 1
Boutique de charron et meublier 1
Boutique de menuisier et de meublier 3
Boutique de menuisier, charpentier et meublier 1
Boutique de meubles et voitures 2
Boutique de meublier et menuisier 2
Boutique de tonnelier et de chaises de cuisine 1
Boutique de voitures et de meubles 1
Cabinet shop paint shop 1
Charron et ébéniste 1
Fabrique de meubles et rouets 1
Factory of agricultural implements and furniture 1
Furniture and carpenter shop 1
Furniture and house builders 1
Furniture and wood shop 1
Manufacture de châssis, portes, jalousies, Meubles, etc. 1
Manufacture de voitures et meubles 1
Manufacturier de meubles et voitures 1
Mécanisme - Boutique de meubles 1
Meublier et menuisier 4
Office desk and coffin factory 1
Sash doors, etc, furniture shop 1
Undertaker and cabinet shop 1
Voiturier et meublier 1

TOTAL: 32

3. Establishments defined without reference to furniture making

Atelier de charpentier 1
Atelier de menuiserie 1
Atelier de menuisier 3
Boutique d'ouvrier 9
Boutique de charpentier 6
Boutique de charpentier et menuisier 1
Boutique de charron 11
Boutique de charronnerie 1
Boutique de forgeron et de menuisier 1
Boutique de menuiserie 36
Boutique de menuiserie et de voitures 1
Boutique de menuiserie et de voiturier 1
Boutique de menuiserie et de ferblanterie 1
Boutique de menuisier 116
Boutique de menuisier et de charpentier 3
Boutique de menuisier et de peintre 1
Boutique de menuisier et tourneur 2
Boutique de peintre 2
Boutique de sculpteur 1
Boutique de tourneur 1
Boutique de voitures et de forge 1
Boutique de voitures et de menuiserie 1
Boutique de voitures et peinture 1
Boutique de voiturier 1
Boutique ou se fabrique des rouets 1
Carpenter 2
Carpenter shop 4
Carpenter upholsterer 1
Charron 1
Establishment for sawing and planing wood and making matches 1
Finishing shop 1
House Carpenter 1
Joiner's work 2
Joiners shop 1
Manufacture de joujous 1
Manufacture de toutes sortes d'ouvrages en bois 1
Manufacture de voitures 4
Manufacture of doors and sashes 1
Manufacture pour tourner le bois 1
Marble cutters 1
Marble dealer 1
Mécanicien 1
Menuiserie 9
Menuisier 8
Moulin à tourner 2
Planing and carpenter shop 1
Turning machine 1
Voiturier 1
Voiturier et forgeron 1
Ware room 1
Work-shop 2

TOTAL: 255

4. No reference to the type of establishment

No reference 1

TOTAL: 1

GRAND TOTAL: 497

TABLE B

The furniture industry in the province of Quebec in 1871					
Regions (Census districts)	Number of firms	Fixed capital ($)	Floating capital ($)	Workers	Wages ($)	Production value ($)
Montreal (West)	25	164 766	82 065	301	92 019	282 095
Québec City (West)	6	285 000	84 800	242	49 880	265 100
Sherbrooke	2	13 000	3 000	34	9 354	53 000
Montreal (East)	10	5 590	3 050	74	14 126	51 650
Montreal (Centre)	7	23 060	16 525	29	10 334	38 175
Beauharnois	9	3 625	4 900	29	5 082	26 250
Hochelaga	7	7 200	4 850	60	8 950	22 960
Richmond	9	10 735	4 330	47	8 760	18 065
Stanstead	7	10 400	11 095	16	6 420	17 955
L'Assomption	9	6 365	965	51	8 800	17 830
Shefford	9	8 400	3 100	28	6 975	16 864
Quebec City (East)	9	3 834	3 300	36	5 055	16 340
Verchères	12	3 890	2 030	37	4 880	14 210
Missisquoi	5	5 435	7 115	25	4 585	13 360
Bonaventure	7	4 770	9 805	30	2 100	12 350
Berthier	10	2 610	1 670	13	1 835	11 980
Trois-Rivières	5	2 130	2 300	10	2 650	11 900
Compton	5	1 900	675	14	3 650	11 200
Quebec City (Centre)	6	2 050	4 950	15	2 950	10 500
Lotbinière	5	4 680	126	9	1 550	9 530
Chicoutimi	26	3 825	4 298	41	3 365	9 429
Bagot	10	4 320	1 930	21	4 280	8 185
Portneuf	17	2 955	255	33	4 432	8 095
Chambly	5	3 300	2 667	20	2 635	8 042
Témiscouata	13	1 785	297	15	2 205	7 070
Maskinongé	12	2 175	1 230	24	3 203	6 902
Terrebonne	11	3 400	1 292	18	1 893	6 840
Iberville	4	2 250	1 050	8	1 766	6 720
Joliette	17	1 464	925	23	2 656	6 466
Napierville	2	1 500	2 040	6	1 248	5 700
Pontiac South	4	740	1 000	10	1 860	5 500
Châteauguay	7	3 612	565	12	1 490	5 300
Kamouraska	16	1 965	410	23	2 624	5 064
Deux-Montagnes	11	2 360	680	14	1 662	4 830
Montmorency	10	1 384	739	20	2 037	4 674
Jacques-Cartier	8	2 165	800	10	658	4 450

Regions (Census districts)	Number of firms	Fixed capital ($)	Floating capital ($)	Workers	Wages ($)	Production value ($)
Drummond	8	1 100	675	10	2 074	4 330
Wolfe	6	2 010	415	8	1 640	3 950
Laval	8	2 002	1 472	13	2 370	3 920
Nicolet	10	870	207	11	1 704	3 845
Ottawa (West)	3	420	470	4	1 260	3 800
Brome	5	1 600	1 710	10	1 765	3 500
Saint-Hyacinthe	5	690	185	9	1 907	3 465
Montcalm	3	1 805	444	5	578	3 372
Rouville	2	1 540	2 005	7	1 414	3 090
Lévis	4	1 150	862	4	1 050	3 020
Quebec (County)	10	897	300	10	986	2 896
Beauce (East)	14	905	108,50	23	1 731	2 578
Vaudreuil	5	750	455	7	714	2 525
Richelieu	4	1 520	2 892	7	926	2 500
Yamaska	7	793	397	8	750	2 445
Ottawa (East)	8	980	430	10	1 170	2 400
Saint-Jean	2	350	220	3	450	2 300
Arthabaska	5	1 490	275	10	1 158	2 192
Saint-Maurice (South)	4	605	352	7	591	1 852
Mégantic	4	550	125	5	890	1 670
Champlain (South)	4	580	95	5	686	1 360
Laprairie	3	550	200	4	600	1 280
Huntingdon (East)	2	850	150	3	700	1 100
Bellechasse (North)	5	730	68	7	566	1 040
Dorchester (West)	5	1 315	393	5	385	1 000
Huntingdon (West)	3	228	37	3	475	785
Gaspe (West)	4	243	124	4	340	776
Rimouski (West)	2	1 075	500	4	330	760
Champlain (North)	4	570	168	5	428	733
Montmagny	3	320	260	3	30	644
L'Islet	3	165	98	3	200	550
Soulanges	1	350		1	100	400
Argenteuil	1	262	86	1	200	300
Beauce (West)	1	2		1	72	100
Ottawa (Centre)	1			1		58
Rimouski (East)	1	100	10	1	30	40
TOTAL	497	638 007	287 017,50	1 620	318 239	1 095 157

TABLE C

	Place	Type of establishment	Owner
	PRINCIPAL FURNITURE MAKERS IN THE PROVINCE OF QUEBEC IN 1871 *		
1	Quebec City	Cabinet & Chair Factory	DRUM, William
2	Montreal	Cabinet Factory	HILTON, J. & W.
3	Quebec City	Manufacture of all kinds of furniture	VALLIÈRE, Philippe
4	Montreal	Bedstead & Chair Factory	TEES, D. & J.
5	Sherbrooke	Sash Doors & Furniture Shop	LONG, William
6	Montreal	Office Desk & Coffin Factory	TEES, David
7	Montreal	Cabinet Factory	GAGE, G. T. & CO.
8	Quebec City	*Fabrique de meubles*	BIGAOUETTE, Félix
9	Montreal	*Atelier d'ébénisterie tapissier*	LAVIGNE, Azarie
10	Montreal	Cabinet Manufactory	CRAIG, Joseph
11	Montreal	Cabinet Maker	ARMSTRONG, George
12	Montreal	Furniture & dealer manufacturer	PARSONS, S. R.
13	Sherbrooke	Ware Room	TWOSE, Samuel
14	Sainte-Cécile	*Manufacturier de meubles et voitures*	DION, Eusèbe
15	Montreal	Spring Bed Manufacturers	WHITESIDE & CO.
16	Montreal	*Atelier d'ébénisterie et meublier*	PRATTE, Noël
17	L'Épiphanie	*Manufacture de meubles*	LYNCH, William
18	Quebec City	Cabinet maker	AREL, Ferdinand & CO.
19	Coaticook	Cabinet Shop	EWING, John
20	Montreal	*Manufactures de meubles*	PAPINEAU, Jean-Marie
21	Danville	Establishment for sawing and planing wood and making matches	BEIGNE, Joseph F.
22	Cox	*Atelier de menuiserie*	ROBIN, Charles & CIE
23	Coaticook	Cabinet Shop	MOORE, William

* This list includes all firms with a production value of $10,000 or more.
The terms found in the column headed "Type of establishment" are those used by the census officers.

TABLEAU D

	Owner	Fixed Capital ($)	Floating Capital ($)	Workers	Wages ($)	Power source	Production ($)
	Principal furniture makers in the province of Quebec in 1871 • Main characteristics						
1	DRUM	150 000	50 000	120	32 000	Steam	160 000
2	HILTON	40 000	20 000	74	25 000	Water	75 000
3	VALLIÈRE	100 000	20 800	97	11 440	Steam	64 000
4	TEES	15 500	11 000	52	20 000	Water	37 500
5	LONG	10 000	3 000	25	7 000	Water	37 000
6	TEES	10 000	4 000	12	5 150		25 000
7	GAGE	5 000	7 500	40	9 500	Steam	25 000
8	BIGAOUETTE	20 000	6 000	4	600		24 000
9	LAVIGNE	1 200	600	30	4 800		24 000
10	CRAIG	3 500	1 000	16	5 200	Steam	22 000
11	ARMSTRONG	37 000	8 000	18	7 500		20 000
12	PARSONS	700	400	5	2 000		18 000
13	TWOSE	3 000		9	2 354	Steam	16 000
14	DION	2 000	2 200	12	2 550	Water	16 000
15	WHITESIDE & CO.	6 700	10 000	6	2 000		12 500
16	PRATTE	2 000	800	20	3 200		12 200
17	LYNCH	5 000	600	36	200	Water	12 000
18	AREL & CO.	4 000	1 000	13	4 000		12 000
19	EWING	4 000	6 720	8	3 720	Water	10 000
20	PAPINEAU	32 040	12 000	10	3 120		10 000
21	BEIGNE	6 000	400	32	5 500	Water	10 000
22	ROBIN & CIE	4 000	9 000	24	1 200		10 000
23	MOORE	4 000	6 720	8	3 720	Water	10 000
	TOTAL	433 600	181 740	671	168 754		662 200

TABLE E

Type of establishment	Fixed capital ($)	Floating capital ($)	Months worked per year	Workers	Wages ($)	Production value ($)
BREAKDOWN OF FIRMS ACCORDING TO NUMBER OF WORKERS						
Firms with 50 workers or more (4):						
Total	305 500	101 800		343	88 440	336 500
Average	76 375	25 450	12	85	22 110	84 125
Firms with 7 to 49 workers (30):						
Total	154 290	76 832		488	101 203	332 700
Average	5 143	2 649	11,7	16	3 373	11 090
Firms with 4 to 6 workers (38):						
Total	71 365	53 675		179	36 156	140 650
Average	1 878	1 412	11,9	4,7	951	3 701
Firms with 2 or 3 workers (143):						
Total	58 024	33 871		337	51 271	173 306
Average	408	249	11,0	2,3	367	1 220
Firms with a single worker (282):						
Total	48 828	20 839		273	41 169	112 001
Average	177	795	9,6	1	158	403
TOTAL (497)	638 007	287 017		1 620	318 239	1 095 157

1 Paul-André Linteau, René Durocher and Jean-Claude Robert, *Histoire du Québec contemporain*, vol. I: *De la Confédération à la crise (1867-1929)* (Montreal: Boréal Express, 1979), pp. 138-148.

2 *Ibid.*, p. 151.

3 *Ibid.*, p. 143. Data for the furniture industry were taken directly from Schedule 6 – Industrial Establishments – of the 1871 census. NAC, RG 31, Statistics Canada, Federal Censuses, 1871 (available on microfilm at the ANQQ).

4 *Manual Containing "The Census Act" and the Instructions to Officers Employed in the Taking of the First Census of Canada (1871)* (Ottawa: Brown Chamberlin, 1871).

5 *Ibid.*, p. 11.

6 *Ibid.*, pp. 11-14.

7 *Ibid.*, p. 30.

8 While relying on the published summaries results in an over-simplified view of the situation, our corpus possesses the opposite disadvantage of including businesses that did not produce furniture exclusively. In these cases, since the capital employed, the number of workers, the wages paid and the production value can rarely be broken down according to the type of production, we have been obliged to use the firms' total figures. In an effort to reduce the impact of the phenomenon, we have calculated the minimum production value related to the manufacture or repair of furniture by adding up all the figures clearly linked to this field of activity. The total amounts to $861,798, a figure remarkably close to the one published in the census summaries – $859,491. This result represents a minimum. The situation was so different from one establishment to another that it is difficult to estimate the real total production value of the furniture industry. It was probably somewhere around $1 million. *Recensement du Canada 1870-71*, vol. III (Ottawa: I. B. Taylor, 1975), p. 307 and *passim*. See also John R. Porter, "L'industrie du meuble à Québec à l'époque victorienne", in John R. Porter (ed.), *Les meubliers Pierre Drouin et Honoré Roy et l'industrie du meuble à Québec à l'époque victorienne* (Quebec City: CÉLAT [Université Laval], 1989), p. 4.

9 Here are a couple of examples of these lacunae. In spite of two extremely thorough checks, it has proven impossible to find any trace in the industrial schedule of the Quebec City furniture maker Eugène Bistodeau. Nevertheless, in 1861 his business counted three employees, and in 1871 his firm was one of five mentioned in an article on cabinetmaking in Quebec City (*L'Événement*, January 3, 1871). See John R. Porter [ed.], *loc. cit..*, p.5. Nor is there any reference to the well-known Montreal furniture maker Owen McGarvey.

10 Linteau, Durocher and Robert, *op. cit.*, pp. 89-91.

11 The city of Montreal included the districts of Montreal (West), Montreal (Centre) and Montreal (East); the city of Quebec included Quebec (East), Quebec (Centre) and Quebec (West).

12 In 1871, the city of Montreal counted 107,225 inhabitants and the city of Quebec 59,699. The population of the province of Quebec was 1,191,516. It should also be noted that, with the exception of Montreal and Quebec City, there was at the time no city in the province with more than 8,000 inhabitants. The population of Trois-Rivières was 7,570 and that of Lévis 6,691.

13 "The number of people employed may be made up exclusively with members of the family of the proprietor [as is the case for most craftsmen, such as joiners, blacksmiths, shoemakers, tailors, etc., etc., (especially in the country)]; in other places the proprietor and family may not form part of the people employed." *Manual Containing. . .*, p. 31.

WILLIAM DRUM AND THE ADVENT OF INDUSTRIALIZATION

THE EIGHTEENTH AND NINETEENTH CENTURIES WERE marked by a new trend that shook western economies to their very foundations: the industrial revolution. All sectors were affected, including the furniture industry. Toward the end of the eighteenth century, the English invented machines to prepare wood, such as circular saws and planes, and it was not long before planing mills, where wood was prepared mechanically, began to appear.[1] The furniture industry benefited greatly from these innovations. Owing to its colonial status, Canada lagged somewhat behind other countries, and consequently the furniture sector did not really begin to feel the effects until the 1850s. In Quebec, one of the key players in the industrialization of the furniture sector was William Drum. After a career as a small-scale craftsman in the early 1830s, he was to become one of the biggest furniture manufacturers in Quebec. His firm would survive only a few years after his death in 1876.

William Drum is not an isolated case. In fact his career is illustrative of how the furniture sector became industrialized, and thus a study of the changes his operations underwent can be quite instructive, especially since no studies have ever been done of his case (or, for that matter, of other major Quebec furniture manufacturers). In analysing the strategies Drum adopted, we focus on the transformations that took him from shop to factory, and that made this craftsman a high-profile businessman in Quebec City. After a review of his career, we will analyze his facilities, his equipment and machinery, and then the manpower and working conditions in his plant, before we finally examine his production and marketing techniques.

At the outset, one small clarification is in order. At every stage in the development of his business, William Drum produced a wide range of furniture. Most of his goods, consisting mainly of chairs, were mass produced. The remainder included furniture of all kinds, all of high quality, and even prestige items. Consequently, in different documents from the period – manuscripts or printed matter – Drum portrays himself variously as a furniture maker, chair maker, furniture and chair maker or a furniture and/or chair manufacturer, regardless of the goods he was producing.

WILLIAM DRUM'S CAREER

William Drum was born in Northern Ireland sometime around 1808.[2] He was the son of Hugh Drum, a chair maker, and Elizabeth Wilson. He is believed to have come to Quebec City with his parents, who were from Moninghan, Ireland, but lived in Quebec City in 1826. Very little is known about his parents, and there is a simple reason for this. In September 1843, a drunken Hugh Drum murdered a cobbler in Saint-Charles Street, where he lived. He was sentenced to three years' hard labour in the Kingston penitentiary. When he was released from prison, he was a thorn in the side of son William, who was doing a brisk trade. The younger Drum thus shunted his father to the sidelines of Quebec City society and his immediate acquaintances by sending him to work in his Château-Richer mill. The first mention we have of Drum is his marriage to Esther Thompson in Quebec City on September 23, 1829. He would have been twenty one then, and was said to be a carpenter. It was probably about this time that he began to work as a chair maker. Unfortunately, nothing is known about his apprenticeship, but as a rule this would have been completed by the time he reached legal age,[3] which is when he married. Only six of the ten children born to the Drum-Thompson couple reached adulthood.

1829-1837: Craftsman

In 1831, William Drum moved to the Saint-Roch district, where he rented a house on Des Fossés Street and apparently opened his first shop. He hired his first apprentice on April 20, 1831. His business was still in the craft phase, which meant that he was an independent small producer who owned his means of production, hiring a few apprentices to help him. In November 1832, he formed a partnership with Jean-Olivier Vallière, another Quebec City furniture maker. They offered their customers a wide assortment of mahogany, rosewood and wicker furniture, painted or varnished, and all sorts of turned pieces "with all the good taste these can be given". Their shop was located at Drum's house on Des Fossés Street. The partnership was not to last long; it was dissolved by mutual consent on April 1, 1834. William Drum probably had plans to expand, since it was about then that he started hiring apprentices systematically: four in 1834, three in 1835 and four in 1836. In the May 2, 1834 issue of the newspaper *Le Canadien*, he claimed to be in possession of about eighty dozen chairs of all kinds, as well as various other pieces of furniture.

1837-1857: Manufacturer

In 1837, William Drum appears to have embarked on the second phase of the mechanization of his business, which was soon to become a manufactory. This phase can be divided into two stages: 1837-1845 and 1845-1857. On May 1, 1837, he moved to Saint-Paul Street, into more spacious premises. This new location was ideal. He set up shop across from the new Saint-Paul market, a site that was soon to become very popular. He sublet his old shop on Des Fossés Street to a grain dealer. In the lease, Drum stipulated that the lessee, James Coyle, would display chairs outside his store. Moreover, Coyle could not sublet to another furniture maker. William Drum thus secured exclusive rights to two points of sale. Also during this period, he began hiring more apprentices. Between 1837 and 1857 he had between ten and twenty-two working with him at any given time.

Nevertheless, 1837 was a recession year, and William Drum did not escape its effects. In fact, the transition appears to have been difficult. This is suggested by a contract he signed with an apprentice on January 5, 1838, in which he reserved the right to terminate the agreement if the economic situation did not improve. Luckily for both sides, the agreement was not broken. Once business began to turn around, Drum was ready to expand again. In November 1843, he signed an emphyteutic lease for the use of the lands and sawmill at Petit-Pré in Château-Richer, and installed equipment so he could turn parts and produce chairs. He hired his first apprentice, Jean-Baptiste Tremblay from l'Ange-Gardien, to work at the mill in December 1843. In October 1844, he had a building erected at the same site, where he installed machinery to manufacture nails in sufficient quantities to be sold. To this end, in January 1845, he entered into an agreement with John Shaw, a Quebec City hardware store owner, who was to provide the iron to produce nails and to sell for him. Even though he sold five nail machines in 1849, he continued producing nails at least until 1851. Drum ran his Château-Richer mill until 1868.

Like most people living in the lower town, William Drum was not spared by the great fire of May 28, 1845. Yet he was able to turn his fortunes around and expand a second time. First he purchased the lot he had been renting from James Hunt. He also acquired three other adjacent lots with their gutted buildings. These four lots accounted for most of the block formed by Saint-Paul, Saint-Charles and Lacroix Streets and Des Bains Lane. He took out a fifteen-year mortgage to pay for the properties. After the fire, the government had issued bonds at a preferred interest rate of 4% for Quebec City residents who had endured losses. William Drum took out a loan for £400, which he used to rebuild on top of the ruins. Business appears to have picked up quickly, for in 1854 he bought another lot in the same block, this time paying cash.

Lastly, throughout the period 1837-1857, Drum spread his name by taking part in several expositions, some of them major events, and winning a number of prizes. He was represented at provincial exhibitions in Montreal in 1850 and in Quebec City in 1853 and 1854, and later took part in the more prestigious world's fairs in London in 1851 and Paris in 1855.

1857-1876: Industrialist

With all these successes to his credit, Drum was ready to make the transition to mechanized industrial production, which he achieved in 1857. It was in *The Canada Directory for 1857-58* that he first advertised his steam factory.[4] He obtained a steam engine and about thirty of the latest woodworking machines.[5] In 1859, he purchased another property in Saint-Charles Street, in the same block as his other properties. He now owned more than half the block. The next year, his social status became greatly enhanced. Indeed, until then, he and his family had lived in the building where his shops were located, which was the norm for craftsmen. However, in January 1860, he bought a villa, Belvedere Lodge, on Saint-Louis Road on the outskirts of Quebec

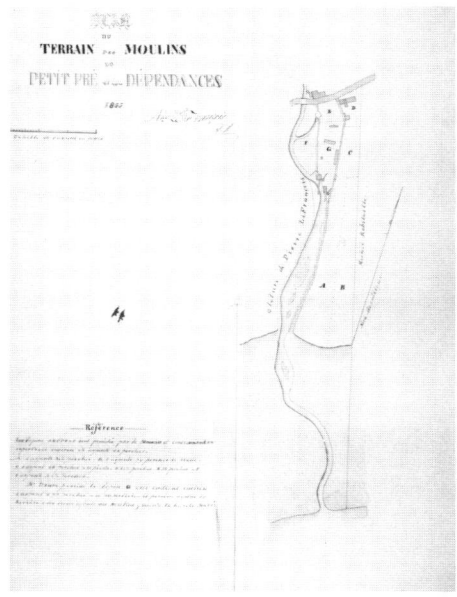

296
Plan of the Lands Belonging to the Moulins du Petit Pré and the Outlying Areas, 1855
Archives nationales du Québec, Centre de Québec et Chaudière-Appalaches, fonds Nicolas Lefrançois (NC83-6-1)

297
William Drum's New Factory on the Saint-Charles River, about 1870
Photograph
Ministère des Affaires culturelles, Québec, Direction générale du patrimoine (14771 555-3)
The main pavilion of the first Université Laval, built in 1855-1856 by the architect Charles Baillairgé, can be seen in the background.

City. Socially, this meant he had moved up from being a craftsman to a businessman. Moreover, he freed up vital space for his manufacturing facilities. In addition to his steam engine and many machine tools, his building now housed a warehouse, work areas for painting and upholstering and six showrooms.

The expansion was so rapid that in 1861, Drum provided work to 109 persons, including eighteen apprentices. In June 1865, he talked of retiring from business in favour of his son (probably Samuel-Wilson). The idea was abandoned, however, although Samuel-Wilson did become more active in his father's business. In 1866, the number of apprentices in the family business exceeded fifty for the first time, which suggests that business was brisk. Yet on the eve of Confederation and the opening up of new markets, he could not content himself with this success. He anticipated future demand and prepared to meet it. As a result, at the end of 1866 he bought from the John Molson estate a waterfront property and a large lot on the other side of Saint-Paul Street, along the Saint-Charles River. In May 1867, he issued a call for tenders to build a mill and furniture plant. He had a 100-horsepower steam "engine" and three boilers installed.[6] This new plant allowed him to separate the production and marketing functions. Indeed, apart from the paint shop, only the office, warehouse and showrooms remained in the old premises.

William Drum strode into the 1870s stronger than ever. In 1871, he hired 120 persons, including sixty-seven apprentices, and his furniture production was valued at $160,000. In addition to a wide selection of furniture, he produced between seven and eight hundred chairs a week, and could have produced as many as a thousand. Beyond the local market, he sold much of his production in Montreal, the Eastern Townships and the Maritime Provinces.[7] Then, about 1871, he opened a furniture warehouse in the Côte

298
A Fire at the Drum Factory, in Quebec City
Engraving published in L'Opinion publique,
September 11, 1873
Photo SRP

du Passage in Lévis, which he occupied until 1877. It is easy to understand how useful the Grand Trunk Railway's service to Lévis was for him, as well as the new markets opened up by Canadian Confederation. He was now uncontestably one of the biggest employers in the Quebec City area, the largest furniture producer in Quebec, and in Canada, second only to Jacques & Hay Co. of Toronto.

However, the 1870s were marked by events that would have a considerable effect on William Drum's company. A lengthy economic crisis began in 1873, striking both Europe and America. Moreover, on top of the crisis, disaster struck. On the morning of August 19, 1873, before his workers arrived, a fire broke out in the drying room, which was located above the boilers. The fire brigade reached the scene quickly, yet they were unable to control the blaze in its early phase. People had complained of a lack of water in the aqueduct for some days, but that morning the shortage had tragic consequences. Pumping water from the Saint-Charles River was attempted, but since hands were scarce at that time of the morning, it was a waste of effort. As the morning wore on, the fire spread almost completely out of control. There were several explosions, most notably in the building in which flammables such as paint and varnish were stored. It was not until eleven o'clock that a pump with adequate pressure was brought, but it was too late.

William Drum's losses were estimated at approximately $160,000, while the insurance policies he held with different companies totalled about $26,000. Whereas he had been able to profit from the 1845 fire, this time he suffered terribly. The consequences were disastrous, not only for Drum, but also for a hundred workers who had lost their incomes.

Shortly after the fire, William Drum formed a partnership with other Quebec City businessmen to found the Stadacona Bank, which was chartered on May 23, 1873. Because his insurance did not cover his fire losses, and his own savings were inadequate, he decided to rely on outside capital and change the legal status of his company. In October 1874, he announced his

299
The Ruins, After the Fire
Engraving published in L'Opinion publique,
September 11, 1873
Photo SRP

intention to convert his company into a limited company, and expand the business considerably. He decided to join forces with his partners in the Stadacona Bank and other businessmen to create the Drum Cabinet Manufacturing Company. The company received its charter on February 4, 1875. The solution Drum had chosen to overcome his problems was the best suited to the economic situation at the time, and fitted in with the trend toward industrialization. Thanks to the *loi sur l'incorporation des compagnies à fonds social*, it was possible to raise a large capital without too much risk, as shareholders' liability in the event of bankruptcy was limited to their investment. During this period, this new legal form was increasingly popular for companies. Drum made sure he retained control over the company by keeping 55% of the 3,000 shares (worth $100 each) that were issued for him and his family. Lastly, to make good use of all the machinery at its disposal, the new company had a charter issued to

> conduct general manufacturing, woodworking of all kinds and especially to manufacture all kinds of furnishings, tapestries, utility items, ornaments, etc., to purchase, sell and trade wood of all descriptions, construction wood, beams, planks, etc., etc., manufactured or not; to saw, cut, rabbet plane, flute, whitewash, sculpt, mortise, turn, work in relief, and all works of all description done at the mill and including carpentry and framing of houses; and also to make or manufacture parts of mirror glass of all descriptions, with full power to purchase, sell, trade all the items mentioned above and to engage in commerce or trade in such, and all other items included in or relating to any of the above mentioned branches of business, or any auxiliary branch of business relating to it which is not specially mentioned here.

However, Drum did not wait for the charter to expand his manufacturing activities and begin putting his machinery to good use. As early as 1870, he started preparing wood, as several receipts from the Séminaire de Québec indicate. In addition, in 1873 he sawed a large amount of wood for Quebec City shipyards.

The announcement of the creation of the Drum Cabinet Manufacturing Company was well received in business circles. For example, the 1875 report of the Bradstreet Company in New York, which specialized in credit ratings, noted that the new company had started up under good auspices, since the members of its board of directors were powerful financiers who also sat on the board of directors of the Stadacona Bank. The company's reprieve was short-lived, however, because in addition to having to cope with a sluggish economy, it lost its energetic director and founder. On May 12, 1876, Drum succumbed to what was then called "pulmonary congestion".[8] The directors then turned the management of the firm over to Thomas Craig.

1876-1891: Years of decline
Business was slow during these difficult years. The credit rating of the Drum Cabinet Manufacturing Company slid from "excellent" in March 1873 to "very high" in January 1875 and then to "good" in July 1879. Consequently, in June 1878 a general meeting of shareholders was called "to consider the urgency of closing the business of the Company". A decision was taken to liquidate the business, and on September 3, 1878, a sale "of the entire, varied assortment of the firm's furniture"[9] at drastically reduced prices was announced. On the same day, it was announced that "the 400-foot long dock on the St. Charles River, suitable for the lumber trade, which has been occupied for many years by the Drum Cabinet Manufacturing Company, and adjacent to the factory", was for rent.[10] In the meantime, Drum family members became mere shareholders, since Isaac Drum had taken his own life in July 1877 and Samuel-Wilson Drum had retired on October 1, 1878. Liquidation then got under way. In October 1888, the furniture factory, its machinery, the docks and land, as well as all rights and privileges over the latter were finally sold for $62,600 to H.-J. Beemer. Beemer was acting on behalf of the Quebec and Lake St-John Railway Company, which used the new acquisition to build a station and shops. On April 30, 1891, the Drum Cabinet Manufacturing Company was officially and legally dissolved.

Summing Up
William Drum was a special kind of businessman. Self-taught in business and the son of a craftsman, he was not accustomed to mingling in high society, and generally avoided worldly contacts. While he seems to have stayed away from gatherings of businessmen, he was by no means isolated from them. He was able to surround himself with influential people in the world of business as well as the political arena. His immediate circle included his son-in-law, Thomas-Hunter Grant, who held many positions including a seat on the Québec City harbour commission, and served as secretary of the Quebec City Chamber of Commerce for many years. His associates in the Drum Cabinet Manufacturing Company were also able to open many doors for him. Several of them sat on the Dominion Chamber of Commerce, the Quebec City Chamber of Commerce and the harbour commission, while others were shareholders or members of the board of directors of various

banks, corporations and companies, especially in the transport industry. Most of those who were active in politics were members of the Conservative Party, which was the party of choice for businessmen at the time, and William Drum was most certainly a supporter. Lastly, several were also associates of Drum's in the Stadacona Bank.

If we look back at the many financial transactions William Drum was involved in over the years, we note a rather conservative style of business. In all the transactions he made, he always exercised foresight and a great deal of caution. He always protected himself by asking for guarantees. For example, when he hired apprentices, he required a performance bond from their guarantors in the event the contract was not honoured. When he sold or leased furniture, he always took them as security. When he made purchases, he always protected himself. For example, when he purchased wood from a local farmer, the seller would have to guarantee the delivery date by mortgaging his properties, or those of a third party, for the value of the transaction. Lastly, at the end of the 1840s, he began lending money, which provided another source of income. Naturally, he always demanded guarantees. William Drum never hesitated to take legal action when anyone with whom he had dealings failed to live up to his obligations.

He was also extremely cautious in his investments. His portfolio was not very diversified, and he invested in sure values. The report by the executor of his will shows that his shares in the Drum Cabinet Manufacturing Company represented 55% of his investments. Another 39% was invested in five banks, including the Stadacona Bank, which he had founded. The remaining 6% was invested in five companies, three of which were in the transport sector. The same report shows that he had made loans worth approximately $11,275, and that he owned twelve properties. His debts were few, amounting to about 4% of the value of his estate, which was estimated at close to $280,000. At the time of his death, each of his four children received close to $67,000 after all debts were paid.

While hardly a typical case, William Drum is a good example of a small-scale craftsman who took advantage of industrialization to rise to the level of a large industrial producer and businessman. After this general review of Drum's activities, we can now take a closer look at how his move to industrialization affected his facilities and machinery.

FACILITIES, EQUIPMENT AND MACHINERY

William Drum's company is a fine example of industrialization in the furniture sector. As he progressed from craftsman to industrialist, he had to adapt his facilities to the increasingly diversified, complex machinery he was acquiring. His machines forced him to supply his factory with a source of energy, necessitating a diversification and division of labour. At every stage in his development, he was obliged to either move to new facilities or to build new ones that were better suited to his needs. An analysis of his various facilities and the machinery with which he worked tells us a great deal about the progressive mechanization of his company.

Facilities

Des Fossés Street, Saint-Roch district, Quebec City
From 1829 to 1837, the facilities William Drum rented on Des Fossés Street were perfectly suited to the needs of a craftsman. He worked on a small scale for a local clientele, using only manual tools and with very little capital. He thus lived with his family and a few of his men in a one-storey house with an attic, behind which stood a two-storey workshop, which also served as a warehouse and shop.

Saint-Paul and Saint-Charles Streets, Saint-Pierre district, Quebec City; Château-Richer
The first of two facilities William Drum occupied on Saint-Paul Street, from 1837 to the great fire of 1845, was similar to the one in Des Fossés Street, but more spacious in order to meet the needs of his new factory. Little is known about the building, except that, as Drum's business expanded, the new facility soon became too small, with the result that he moved the operation to Château-Richer. We have no description of the two mills that were located there, except for a surveyor's map of the lot where they stood. However, we do know that he used it to turn parts for chairs, and that he produced nails there (from 1845 to 1849). It must have been a fairly simple works, closely linked with the operation in Quebec City.

In a sense then, the 1845 fire that gutted the Saint-Paul Street workshop was almost a godsend for Drum. He took the opportunity it afforded to start building new facilities that same year, erecting a building on the rubble of the old premises. In 1853, based on plans by architect G. R. Browne, he built a second three-storey building on Saint-Charles Street, behind the other building. Another floor was added in 1856. This is probably when he introduced a steam engine to run his many machine tools. The two buildings formed a complex that prompted one contemporary observer to remark: "Possibly there is not another factory of the same description in all Canada which employs so many hands, covers a greater extent of ground, or turns out in the course of a year so much work as Mr. Drum's".[11]

The building in Saint-Paul Street was of stone, while the Saint-Charles Street structure was stone and brick. The latter was crowned by a brick chimney approximately ninety-five feet high. The two buildings were connected by a bridge, most likely at the second storey level. The building in Saint-Paul Street was used almost exclusively for sales, since it was located across from the marketplace. It contained six showrooms of about forty feet by thirty-six feet, which featured a wide variety of furniture for all tastes and budgets. The furniture was finished there: this we know from the presence of an upholstering room, as well as a painting and varnishing shop. It is understandable that these operations would have been located near the showrooms, since they constitute the final stages in furniture production.

The manufacturing operation was situated mainly in the second building, on Saint-Charles Street. The motive power produced by the steam engine was transmitted to this building. It comprised four storeys and a basement. The furniture shops were located in the basement and on the first two floors.

There were many machine tools here and on the other storeys. On the ground floor, insulated by a heavy iron door, was the kiln, which was heated by exhaust from the steam engine located nearby. The kiln gave on to the courtyard, where the wood was stored and where the engine room was located, between the two buildings, directly under the bridge. On the third floor was the chair shop with all the necessary machinery. The fourth floor was occupied by a warehouse, where unfinished pieces were probably stacked before painting and upholstering.

This was an industrial complex with a very rational organization of labour. First of all, the marketing and manufacturing functions were distinct, each located in a separate building. Moreover, all the machinery was located in a single building, with the finishing stages grouped in the commercial building, since they did not require any motive force. With this setup, the costs of installing the drive system were kept down, since the motive force was transmitted in one direction only. The division of labour was indeed obvious, with machine tools used to prepare the wood located on the lower floors, while those used in assembling and finishing furniture were located on the upper floor, the top floor being reserved for finished or near-finished furniture. William Drum's manufacturing facility was especially impressive, in that it also included the mills at Château-Richer, which ran steadily. The facility in Saint-Paul and Saint-Charles Streets remained in operation until 1867, when Drum had his Saint-Charles River plant built.

The Saint-Charles River plant, Saint-Pierre district, Quebec City
This new brick complex was similar to the previous one, but at 15,000 square feet,[12] it was larger and more modern. The outer walls were well provided with large windows. In addition, it was lit with candles, rather than oil. The new location enjoyed one major asset: it had direct access to the river. In addition to its dock, which was 399 feet long, it had a slide down to the river on its east side on which wood could easily be brought into or out of the adjoining sawroom. William Drum's plant, it will be recalled, sawed a great deal of wood for shipyards and other customers. Lastly, there was a large lot where wood was stored, and a few outbuildings, such as a shed for drying the wood, an office and several other sheds.[13]

The new mill on the Saint-Charles River was laid out like the old facility in Saint-Charles Street. The lower floors were used mainly for sawing wood, and the more detailed work was done on the upper floors. The basement was occupied by the steam engine room, whose ceiling was reinforced by a brick vault. There was also a forge to produce hardware for cabinet making or machinery. Wood was sawn here, and the sawdust was collected. On the ground floor, just above the steam engine, was the wood kiln. This room was two storeys high. On the same floor, wood was sawn, turned and planed, before being assembled on the second floor in the furniture shop. In addition to accommodating a warehouse, much of the top storey was used for varnishing, painting, gluing and stripping. Varnishing was done above the steam engine, an arrangement that proved disastrous in the 1873 fire.

We know how space was used in the Drum Cabinet Manufacturing Company (D.C.M.C.) from an insurance plan dating from 1875,[14] after the

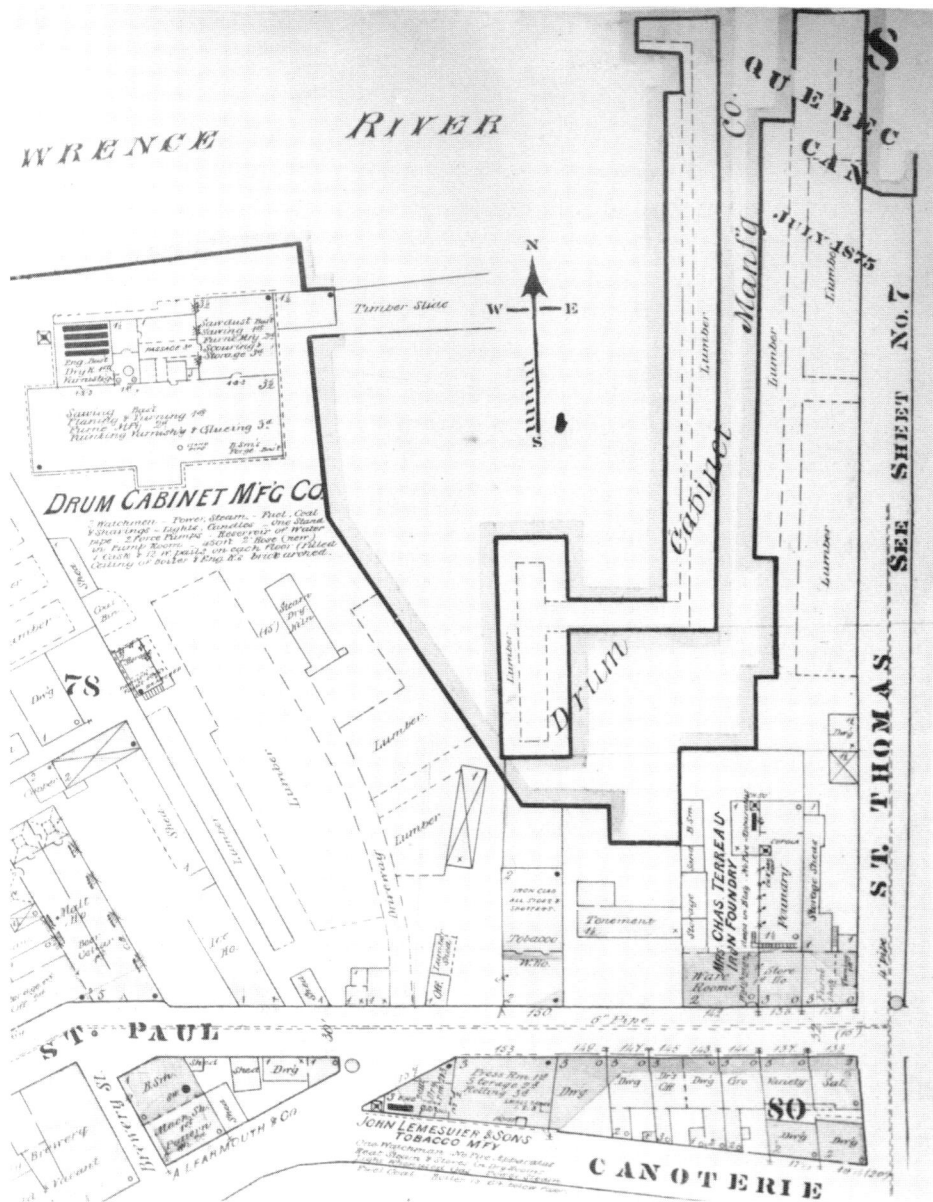

300
Plan showing the site of the Drum Cabinet Manufacturing Company, Saint-Paul Street
Plan published in the *Atlas Sanborn - Insurance Plans of the City of Quebec* (Quebec City, 1875), p. 8
Archives nationales du Québec, Centre de Québec et Chaudière-Appalaches (N1173-18)
The plan shows that the factory possessed a long jetty, a large inlet of water and a lumber yard.

1873 conflagration. Drum drew a lesson from this unfortunate event by adding fire-fighting equipment to later facilities, consisting of a supply column, two pumps and a water tank, and 450 feet of pipe, as well as four barrels and twelve fire buckets per floor. The firm most certainly did not have this kind of equipment in 1873, since the only pump mentioned in the reports of the event is one borrowed from the Quebec Rubber Company.

Lastly, we should note that Drum's industrial complex also included the old building in Saint-Paul Street, where the showrooms, upholstering and paint rooms remained, along with the office. When the D.C.M.C. liquidated its holdings in 1891, the Quebec and Lake St-John Railway Company, the new owner of the facilities, built a station on the site and used the old factory for servicing trains and as a grain elevator.

Mechanization

Steam engines

William Drum became a manufacturer in 1837, when he began to acquire machinery. From that time on, workers no longer handled the tools themselves, as machines took over most operations, performing them faster and more precisely. The machine tools could even perform more than one movement at a time, which workers obviously could not do. As Willis Russell remarked: "It seems indeed that man no longer labours by the sweat of his brow, as steam does all the sweating for him".[15] However, it was not out of compassion for his workers that Drum introduced machinery; rather, he sought to increase the quantity and improve the quality of his output. Although experienced cabinetmakers would always be necessary, if only for assembly, the workers now became machine operators, since they were confined to a single step in the production of a piece of furniture, that which was performed by their machine.

To drive the machinery, Drum needed a source of energy, and he chose hydraulic power over steam. In 1843, he moved to Château-Richer, where he was able to use hydraulic power equivalent to fifty horsepower at very low cost (£10 per year for fifteen years). The choice is easily explained. He apparently did not have enough capital to acquire a steam engine. Moreover, the Quebec City location was not well suited to the use of hydraulic power. Despite a strong current, the St. Lawrence River had a large tide, which left a wide sand bar along the bank. Building dikes or diversion canals would have entailed a considerable investment. The weak current in the Saint-Charles estuary, where Drum had his buildings, would have complicated things even further. For the time being, the question did not even arise, since Drum did not yet have access to the St. Lawrence or the Saint-Charles. Hence the appeal of the site at Château-Richer.

By the end of the 1850s, the situation had changed. Drum's capital was larger, and he had acquired more machinery. A substantial investment would be needed if he wanted to draw more profit from his operations. He had no choice but to move to steam. In addition to supplying regular power in all seasons, it would reduce heating costs in winter and provide an excellent source of heat to dry wood. About 1857, Drum therefore decided to mechanize his factory in Saint-Paul Street by installing a steam engine whose vertical cylinder was twelve inches in diameter, and had a thirty-two inch piston running up and down inside it. The flywheel was ten feet in diameter and fourteen inches wide, and drove a belt that relayed power to the shaft in the basement of the furniture shop in Saint-Charles Street. The engine room occupied a separate building in the yard between the two buildings that made up the manufacturing complex. William Drum acquired the engine in Quebec City, from the George Bisset foundry in Saint-Vallier Street. While the engine was certainly built by Bisset, it is unlikely that he designed it.

We do not know how many horsepower this new engine generated. Presumably, it was not a very powerful steam engine, since it had only one cylinder, and only drove about thirty machine tools, unlike the new steam engine installed in the mill on the Saint-Charles River, which was more powerful. In the 1871 census, Drum claimed that he owned a 100-horsepower steam engine. It was installed in the spring of 1869 by John McDougall of the Caledonian Works in Montreal at a cost of $700. In reality, it was not a new machine. McDougall merely modified a machine that had been installed earlier. He removed two cylinders and the regulator and replaced them with new ones. The new cylinders were sixteen inches in diameter, and accommodated a forty-two-inch piston. It was said to possess "all the improvements introduced in steam engines in recent years". The three boilers came from Robert Neil's works in the Saint-Roch district of Quebec City. In short, this steam engine had all the power necessary to drive close to one hundred machines.

Machine tools

Machine tools are tools or devices similar to those previously used by craftsmen, but which are manipulated or driven by a mechanism rather than the human hand. The craftsman is replaced by a worker who only supplies the tool with raw material to be processed, in this case, wood. When he introduced motive power into his facilities, William Drum wanted to equip himself with several machine tools. The two go together naturally. As early as 1857 he had thirty such tools. By 1873 he had a hundred, though these were probably a larger, more modern selection of the same tools he had in 1857. Willis Russell lists these tools in his description of William Drum's factory in 1857.

According to Michael-J. Ettema, machine tools used to manufacture furniture should be divided into three categories, depending on their function. First of all, there are machine tools used to prepare wood for assembly into furniture. Then come tools used to shape the wood and, finally, those used for decoration.[16] If we divide the machine tools in William Drum's factory in 1857 into categories, we get the breakdown given in Table 1.

First, we note that most of the machines owned by Drum fall in the first category. He owned a handful of tools in the second category, and just a few in the last. The first type had very little effect on furniture design, while the third category exerted considerable influence. It should be recalled that the use of machine tools made it possible to increase output while at the same time reducing costs. In a treatise on woodworking machines published in 1872, John Richards, an English engineer, noted that the more powerful the machine, and hence the harder the work it could do, the greater the savings it made possible.

On the other hand, if it was designed to carry out complex operations which required considerable adjustment, the savings were less. Consequently, production costs would be less if the first type of machine tools were used.

As we know, William Drum produced a wide selection of furniture. However, he leaned more toward mass production. As a result, he owned chiefly machine tools that were used to prepare wood for assembly into furniture, while there were only two machine tools for decoration. Since he produced fewer luxury items, he invested less in the latter machines, and found it more economical to hire craftsmen. In the first two categories, he owned almost all available types of machine tools, while in the third he had

TABLE 1

Preparation of wood for assembly into furniture	shaping	decoration
more than 4 circular saws	3 hand lathes	1 circular planing & moulding machine
2 Daniel's planers	2 self-acting lathes	1 moulding machine
1 surfacer	2 self-acting gauge lathes	
1 power tennonning machine	1 scroll saw	
1 mortising machine	1 scroll saw with gate	
1 tennonning & dowel machine		
x grooving machines		
x grinding stones		
x centre bitt machines		
x mortise machines with bitt & full swing		

only moulding machines. He appears to have had no spinning-moulding machines, carving machines or embossing machines.

Overall, we do not know where William Drum obtained his equipment. For his steam engines, he always did business with local producers in Quebec City or Montreal. In the case of his woodworking machines, he probably went to the United States, where there were several producers, such as J. A. Fay & Co. of Keene, New Hampshire, which moved to Cincinnati, Ohio sometime later, about 1862. Among his machine tools, Drum had two Daniel's planers. In an advertisement for J. A. Fay & Co. published after 1851,[17] we learn that Fay produced precisely this machine, and this model appears to have been one of the most advanced.

In short, William Drum seems to have used the most modern equipment in each of his production facilities. In addition, his facilities were always laid out in a way that made the most economical use of space. However, facilities and machinery are only one aspect of production in an industrial context. Manpower is also a very important factor.

MANPOWER AND WORKING CONDITIONS

In the industrialization process, the many changes that occur in a shop have a tremendous impact on the manpower engaged in the production process. Not only are the workers' tools transformed, and their work and role considerably altered by the division of labour, but they are faced with a new factory discipline with which they have to learn to live. It is a big leap from life in the shop to life in a factory, and it often proves difficult for workers. According to Sidney Pollard, an inability to adapt to these changes results in desertion by workers, or at least a problem of acute absenteeism that is characteristic of industrialization.[18] What was the situation at Drum's plant?

Manpower

Between 1830 and 1876, Drum hired as many personnel as he needed or as economic conditions dictated. In the 1830s, he employed only a handful of people, while in the 1871 census he claimed to have 112 workers in his employ. His manpower consisted of a few women, day labourers, apprentices, tradesmen and administrative personnel.

Women
Women played only a small role in the production process at Drum's plant. In 1861, he had only one female employee out of a total of 109 workers, while in 1871 he employed twelve out of a total of 120 workers. However, it is not known what role they played in the production process. At a time when women were confined to a small number of trades traditionally assigned to them, it would have been odd to find them handling machine tools. It is more likely that they were employed to braid wicker chair bottoms or sew hangings, draperies and upholstering cloth.

Day labourers
It is even more difficult to assess the importance of day labourers on the payroll. The census did not separate workers into categories, and since they were hired on a daily basis, as needed, they cannot be isolated from the other employees. Still, we have discovered seven employment contracts for day labourers between 1856 and 1859, the time when Drum was moving up to mechanized production, which is not surprising. In fact, this kind of manpower is better suited to mass production in an industrial context than in a small workshop.

Apprentices
Of the various kinds of manpower Drum employed, he clearly favoured apprentices. In fact, apprentices played a very important role during the many years he was in business. In forty-six years he hired 244 apprentices, who represented 17% of his employees in 1861 and as much as 56% in 1871 (see Table 2). During the period from 1830 to 1856 when Drum worked as a craftsman, he had 74, or 2.7 per year on average, while in the industrial period from 1857 to 1876 (the last year he hired apprentices), he had 170, or 8.5 a year on average. Since apprentices were taken on for several years, in the many years he operated his factory William Drum consumed a total of 1,295 apprentice-years for his production, which is considerable. Apprenticeships were very important, since they enabled him to renew his manpower. The master, in this case Drum, undertook to teach the apprentice the art and secrets of the trade. However, in an industrial context, when he had up to sixty-eight apprentices a year in his service in 1871, neither Drum nor his tradesmen were likely to fulfil the requirements of apprenticeship. He was probably able

TABLE 2

Number of apprentices employed by William Drum, 1830 - 1881					
Year	hirings per year	apprentices in service	year	hirings per year	apprentices in service
1830	0	0	1856	5	17
1831	1	1	1857	10	21
1832	0	1	1858	1	19
1833	0	1	1859	3	17
1834	4	5	1860	0	14
1835	3	8	1861	7	18
1836	4	11	1862	9	24
1837	4	14	1863	5	26
1838	1	13	1864	13	34
1839	0	12	1865	10	42
1840	1	10	1866	12	50
1841	5	14	1867	8	49
1842	3	14	1868	19	62
1843	5	16	1869	8	65
1844	3	18	1870	19	68
1845	3	19	1871	10	67
1846	4	22	1872	11	64
1847	1	19	1873	11	63
1848	6	20	1874	3	54
1859	4	19	1875	7	50
1850	4	21	1876	4	41
1851	8	22	1877	0	31
1852	1	20	1878	0	22
1853	4	20	1879	0	14
1854	0	19	1880	0	6
1855	0	15	1881	0	3

to do so until 1862, when he had on average fourteen apprentices a year working for him. From then on, the best bet is that he hired apprentices mainly in order to obtain docile, cheap labour power. The average age of the apprentices Drum hired was sixteen. An apprenticeship lasted 51 months on average. As a rule, age determined the length of the apprenticeship. The length was set so that the apprenticeship would be completed within a few months of the date the apprentice reached legal age (21 years). The younger the apprentice, therefore, the longer his training period. It is interesting to note that Drum hired mostly French-speaking workers: 64% of his 244 apprentices spoke French, as against 36% English-speaking. These figures are hardly surprising, since they closely reflect the proportions of the French- and English-speaking population of Quebec City during this time.[19] However, even though there were more French-speaking workers, Drum ran his business in English. This is shown by the fact that 46% of French-speaking workers concluded apprenticeship contracts in English, while only 3% of the English-speaking apprentices had contracts in French. Moreover, a chronological survey of the 244 apprenticeship contracts signed by Drum sheds more light on how his business functioned as regards manpower. For example, the autumn seems to have been the slowest period for his business. During the whole time in which he hired apprentices, from 1831 to 1876, the number of apprentices hired from September through December represented only 19% of the total, whereas January through April accounted for 43% of the total, April being the biggest month of the year.

The trades selected by young men entering into apprenticeships with William Drum tell us a great deal about the company's evolution toward industrialization. As we suggested earlier, the installation of the first steam engine in 1857 was the point at which Drum's company acquired the status of a mechanized industry. From that point on, industrialization inevitably brought with it a division of labour.

For the purposes of our commentary, we should state from the outset that painters included varnishers, and that manufacturers embraced all workers who claimed to be apprentice furniture or chair makers, and that machinists included those who were to learn how to work with any given machine. We have divided these three groups into two categories: apprentices hired up to 1856, and those hired as of 1857. The results are shown in Table 3, and an examination confirms that 1857 was the turning point in Drum's transition to the industrial model. We see that before 1857, Drum hired mainly apprentices in furniture making and manufacturing, according to the very general nomenclature of the trade. Apprentices in furniture making alone represented 66% of all those hired prior to 1857. If we add manufacturing apprentices, the figure rises to 84%. Moreover, between 1843 and 1858, fifteen of the latter worked or spent some of their apprenticeships at Château-Richer. Since we know that at this site, he only turned pieces to produce chairs – with very little equipment – this operation was definitely a factory.

As of 1857, job titles are more specific, indicating a specialization of functions. Drum then began hiring fewer apprentice furniture makers or manufacturers and more apprentice chair makers, upholsterers, turners, painters and, for the first time, apprentice sculptors and machinists. These specialized trades were to account for 61% of the apprentices hired in 1857 and after.

The case of apprentice painters and/or varnishers is especially interesting. Drum hired twenty-eight of them: one in 1849 and all the others after 1861. Prior to this date, he does not seem to have had any workers or apprentices specializing in this function. Moreover, between 1846 and 1853, before he hired apprentice painters, there is a clause in the contracts of twelve apprentice furniture makers stipulating that during their training period they had to spend a certain amount of time in the paint shop. The length of this period was generally from eighteen to twenty-four months. Yet during the same time there are contracts in which it is stated that the apprentice furniture maker will not have to do any painting. This function would have been regarded as compulsory in the chair manufacturing process, but evidently the men did not spend much time at it because it was both unpleasant and easy to learn. This is

TABLE 3

	Breakdown of apprentices by category of trade up to 1856 and after 1857 William Drum's operations from 1831 to 1876		
trade	number	number to 1856	number after 1857
furniture maker	113	49	64
chair maker	17	5	12
carver	25	0	25
turner	11	1	10
painter	28	1	27
upholsterer	22	4	18
manufacturer	16	13	3
machinist	10	0	10
unknown	2	1	1
total	244	74	170

proved by the case of an apprentice chair manufacturer who, due to his lack of talent for learning, in 1851 was assigned to spend the last four years of his apprenticeship painting and polishing.

By relying more on apprentices as a source of manpower, William Drum made a considerable contribution to the furniture industry. In forty-six years he alone trained 244 furniture craftsmen, that is, more than five a year, which is significant. Some of these individuals — Honoré Roy, François Bédard and Joseph Parent, to name a few — were even entered into the 1871 census as owners of their own factories. Others, such as Pierre Maranda and Joseph Monier, were to spend many years with Drum.

Specialized workmen

The different kinds of manpower described above could not have been effective without a core of specialists in various trades. We have found eleven contracts for tradesmen, including chair makers, furniture makers, carvers, painters and mill operators, for seven different individuals spanning the period from 1840 to 1874. Some of these were hired as foremen. Craftsmen were hired for periods varying from ten months to five years. According to their contracts, two of them were to teach their trade to apprentices. For example, Jacques Renaud undertook to "teach the trade of chair maker to apprentices... [and].. to work as well". The contract signed by carver George Hasley was more explicit. On the one hand, he had to "teach Mr. Drum's apprentices and day labourers who did not know the trade of sculptor or furniture maker". And on the other, he undertook to "make all patterns and models from drawings and not to do so for persons other than Mr. Drum except by the latter's written consent". Drum's cautious style is easily recognized here.

Édouard Gourdeau, meanwhile, was required to do more supervision. His contract of 1853 bound him for eighteen months to "furniture making and supervision of machinery and men" in both Quebec City and Château-Richer. In 1865, he returned for another three years in the same places, but this time to "run and manage the mill". Finally, in 1872, he signed a five-year contract for "general management of the establishment". Gourdeau seems to have been one tradesman who was in great demand, because he worked for Philippe Vallière between two contracts with Drum. When he entered into service with Drum in February 1872, he undertook to begin working on April 25 or, if he had not finished his work at Vallière, as soon as he could. Some skilled craftsmen seem to have enjoyed a certain amount of mobility between competing firms.

Lastly, we know from a variety of sources, including the press and certain notarized documents, of other tradesmen who also worked for Drum from time to time. Among them were carvers Louis-Thomas and Louis-Flavien Berlinguet, with whom William Drum did business in 1852 when he built the Speaker's Chair for the Parliament.[20] In 1871, we know that carver Arthur Mingeaud worked in Drum's shops.[21] Finally, one tradesman for whom Drum had a great deal of respect was his foreman Thomas Hunter. In his will, Drum left him an annual pension that was enough for him to take out a life insurance policy valued at $1,000, as well as $1,500 so that his two sons should learn a trade. These bequests testify to the esteem Drum felt toward Hunter in return for devotion and loyalty during many years of service.

Administrative personnel
To round out his team, Drum had an administrative staff: accountants, clerks and managers. Among these were, naturally, his sons Isaac and, above all, Samuel-Wilson.

In short, from 1830 to his death in 1876, Drum hired hundreds of employees. We can identify many of them: 244 apprentices, five day labourers, sixteen tradesmen, six administrative employees and seven individuals whose functions cannot be identified precisely. Added to these 278 employees were a dozen women. This list is most certainly incomplete, but it is nevertheless impressive, especially with regard to the number of apprentices.

Working Conditions
In general, the transition from shop to factory alters working conditions, making work more difficult. Without exculpating Drum, working conditions in his factory do not seem to have been worse than anywhere else. In fact, in some respects they may have been better. No documents have been found indicating that he employed children under the age of twelve or that he had persons working at home for him. Nor is there any indication that he physically mistreated any of his employees. Lastly, throughout the period under study, working conditions seem to have changed very little.

A number of constants emerge from a study of the 244 apprenticeship contracts and twenty employment contracts he signed. First of all, the work week in Drum's company was six days. There was no work on statutory holidays (Good Friday, Christmas and New Year's), and these days were not paid (except in the case of Charles Chrétien, whose contract specified that he would receive a salary). The workday was twelve hours long, which did not include one hour for lunch and an hour for dinner in some cases. The day thus often extended over fourteen hours. There was a summer schedule, from May 1 to November 1, and a winter schedule for the other six months of the year. In the summer, workers started their day at five, and in the winter at seven. We have only found one contract, from 1872, in which a ten-hour working day is stipulated. Lastly, throughout their training periods, apprentices could miss up to two weeks of work, without pay. Additional days would have to be made up at the end of their contracts.

As for wages, day labourers and craftsmen were paid on a weekly basis. The frequency varied with apprentices. Some were paid every six months, some quarterly; but generally they received their wages monthly. Masters usually supplied their apprentices with rooms and/or meals and/or clothes and/or shoes. Drum did not subscribe to this practice. He provided one or more of these services to twenty-nine apprentices only, all of whom signed contracts before 1858, that is, before the industrial period. Moreover, fifty-six apprentices received no wages. Only eight of them received one or more of the services described above. In other words, forty-eight young workers underwent their apprenticeships without receiving remuneration of any kind.

If all the salaries are brought down to the same scale, that is, in dollars a week, some comparisons can be made. The average weekly salary of a day labourer between 1856 and 1859 was $3.67. In the case of the tradesmen, as with the day labourers, we have only a few examples. Furthermore, these are quite spread out in time. Nevertheless, their wages are clearly much higher than the day labourers'. For example, a carver received $12 a week in 1865, a mill operator $9 a week in 1853, $9 in 1865 and $12 in 1872, while a foreman-chair maker earned $8.50 a week in 1874. Other tradesmen received $3 and $4 a week, so that the average weekly wage of all craftsmen combined, between 1840 and 1874, was $6.49, close to double what a day labourer earned.

The case of apprentices is easier to analyze given the relatively larger numbers. We have taken the average of their weekly salaries according to the eight groups of trades identified earlier, and we have divided them into pre-industrial and industrial periods. We immediately note that the average salary was higher in the industrial period than previously for almost all groups of trades. In spite of this, we note that as of 1857, when salaries were highest, they were less than half of what day labourers earned. If we add to that the forty-eight apprentices who received no compensation, it becomes obvious that apprenticeships were very profitable for William Drum. Lastly – and this is surprising – we note that the average weekly salary of English-speaking apprentices was lower than French-speaking apprentices, that of regardless of the period considered. We have found no explanation for this fact.

With regard to the security of workers in Drum's plant, there do not seem to have many accidents. In fact, unless such things were commonplace and nobody bothered to talk about them – which would be unusual – we have found only one mention of an accident during the entire period under study. The victim was the young apprentice Crispin Simard, whose right index finger and thumb were cut by a saw.[22]

Discipline

As we mentioned earlier, factory discipline presented the greatest difficulty for workers. As a result, Drum had to keep an eye on discipline in his plant, especially as regards punctuality. However, he did not have to administer sanctions in breaches of discipline or offenses by his employees. An act dating from 1817 stipulated that relations between masters and their employees in Quebec City, Montreal and Trois-Rivières were under the jurisdiction of justices of the peace, who were to make rules that the police would then enforce. In 1831, when the City of Quebec was incorporated, administration of this rule was transferred to the City Council, which was to have the same powers as justices of the peace. Finally, in 1866, the Quebec City Council enacted a "regulation concerning masters, assistants, apprentices, domestics, servants, day labourers, etc.".

This new regulation was very good for Drum and all other masters. It described all the misdemeanours employees should not commit: improper conduct, disobedience, laziness or desertion, absence without leave, negligence in performing one's duties or obeying the master's orders, squandering of the master's goods or endangering of his interests. These offenses were punishable by a fine that was not to exceed forty dollars, or the salary of several months of hard work for an employee at Drum's plant. The masters' only duty was to pay their employees for the work they did, without ever mistreating them or subjecting them to cruel treatment, failing which they risked incurring a penalty that was not to exceed twenty dollars or imprisonment for not more than thirty days – hardly commensurable with the penalties that applied to workers.

Whit this kind of regulation, in the event one of his employees committed a misdemeanour, Drum had only to complain to the police, who would make sure the accused appeared before the Recorder's Court. This may have happened on many occasions although we have noted only eight cases innewspapers from the period. This is not a large number, yet one fact catchesour attention: all the desertions took place between 1870 and 1874, when Drum's company was at its zenith and the workers were concentrated in theSaint-Charlles River plant. Four apprentices and four day labourers were involved. Three of the apprentices deserted at the age of nineteen, when they had completed more than half of their training period. The other apprentice was only thirteen years old when he ran off after just six months of work.

The relatively small number of cases of desertion leads us to believe that this was a rare phenomenon. To remove any temptation, in seventy of the 244 apprenticeship contracts he signed, William Drum included a clause to guarantee the punctuality of his apprentices. If an apprentice abandoned or deserted him, the latter's guarantor undertook to pay Drum a sum of money that was sometimes quite considerable. The average value of these bonds was $39, and they ranged from $3.25 to as high as $100. Nevertheless, as of 1850 they were $50. This is something that characterized the entire period under study. With this measure, the authority of the guarantor ensured the loyalty of the apprentices. He probably included this clause when he had sufficient doubt as to the good conduct of a future apprentice.

Lastly, despite the municipal regulation and the clause guaranteeing apprenticeship contracts, in some cases Drum and an apprentice would nullify their mutual undertaking by agreement. This happened eleven times, and in nine cases there was no guarantee clause.

From 1830 to 1891, the ground rules changed considerably in the furniture industry, especially in William Drum's firm. In his workshop, in his mechanized plant, by special order or mass produced, over the years Drum and his workers, apprentices, day labourers and craftsmen produced a long line of furniture. Our next task is to find out what was produced and how it was sold.

PRODUCTION AND MARKETING

What was actually produced in a furniture factory equipped with a powerful engine and a hundred machine tools, employing a hundred workers? To analyze Drum's production we will select a sample which, although insignificant in relation to his total production, nevertheless gives us a fairly good idea. Based on forty-nine documents of different kinds (bills, legal proceedings, furniture rental leases, public accounts) we have compiled 543 items for which we have descriptions and prices. There is often more than one copy of a given item in a single document, and so we have been able to establish a list of 2,928 pieces of furniture dating from May 1852 to May 1880.

Production

The tremendous variety of products immediately stands out . In fact, apart from chairs, we find a wide range of seat furniture, tables, commodes and desks, wardrobes, beds and washstands. According to the materials and their finish, these various types of furniture could be classed as luxury items. An examination of the different materials used will reveal some very fine woods indeed.

Alongside the production of furniture, there was what we might call accessories. Beginning in 1858, Drum produced a wide variety of mirrors and began making clocks (most certainly the bodies, but not the mechanism). Because Drum was manufacturing beds, he had to provide all the accoutrements. As a result, he produced a large quantity of mattresses, pillows, bolsters and quilts.

In America, the nineteenth century was heralded by the arrival of patented furniture. While Drum himself owned no patents, he was not to escape the trend. In fact, our list includes one barber's chair in 1858, as well as two "step-stool chairs" in 1870. In 1869, as a result of an agreement with M.G.D. Mayer, he produced a patented hammock-chair. It is described as a combination of comfort, economy and durability, in addition to being convertible. It could be transformed into a hammock, an armchair or a cradle as one pleased. And it only cost $2.60 – the ideal patented piece of furniture.[23]

For his wood, Drum used, in order of importance, black walnut, pine, grey walnut, ash, oak, mahogany, birch and tulipwood. Moreover, even though our list includes only six pieces of birch furniture (all of them chairs), several notarized deeds indicate that Drum used this wood abundantly, since he purchased large quantities of it. In addition, he demanded that the wood should be taken from the trunk, that it should be straight, free of knots, marketable and that it be delivered in specific lengths. With all these conditions, it is clear that the wood was not going to be burned. We therefore conclude that all the wood chairs where the material is unknown were from his mass production, and that they were made of birch, probably painted.

Apart from wood, some of the other raw materials used by Drum included cane and wicker, which were used to make various kinds of chairs. Although more rarely, he also used marble, from which he made table or washstand tops. Drum also employed cloth as a covering for upholstered pieces such as sofas, couches, settees, armchairs and chairs. He used canvas, cotton, cretonne, damask, rep, satin, terry and horsehair cloth. In addition, since he produced upholstered pieces such as mattresses, his list of materials includes feathers, rags, straw, horsehair and springs. Typical of nineteenth century furniture, several of the items he produced were on wheels.

With regard to markets, all indications are that William Drum was especially sensitive to the growing demand for fine furniture among the middle classes. Obviously this did not prevent him from mass producing chairs or making luxury furniture. It is intriguing to note that the wife of businessman and politician Jean-Charles Chapais found the prices of the chairs she saw at Drum's store "exorbitant" — so much so that she preferred to buy from his competitor, Philippe Vallière! Parallel to this, Drum also catered to an institutional clientele. For example, in 1852, he produced the Speaker's chair for the Parliament,[24] and between 1854 and 1872 he completed a number of contracts for the Séminaire de Québec. In a more prestigious line of activity, he produced furniture that was to be used by the Prince of Wales during his visit to Quebec City in 1860.[25] Two years later, he obtained a contract to furnish the Banque nationale in Saint-Pierre Street,[26] and in 1875, he executed a pulpit for the Église des Pères Oblats in Saint-Sauveur.[27] Lastly, in 1869 and 1879, his firm produced various pieces of furniture for different government ministries.[28]

Marketing

To market his vast inventory, William Drum had to keep warehouses and showrooms, but most important, he also had to publicize his products. He did this via three different methods: direct advertising, sales at auctions and participation in exhibitions and competitions.

Of these three approaches, he tended more toward direct advertising. Throughout his career, Drum regularly purchased advertising in newspapers and local directories, and sometimes in media with a much larger circulation. For example, in 1851 and 1857 he published advertisements in *The Canada Directory*, and again in 1871 in the *Dominion Directory*. Unlike some of his competitors, he never used illustrations in his advertisements.

The advertising style he used varied very little in more than forty years. The texts were short and described his services. The content of the advertisements changed very little over the years. In the 1830s, he began by thanking the public for their confidence and encouragement. However, after 1837, he dropped the polite phraseology. He would talk about his very broad assortment of furniture, as well as the quality of the materials and workmanship. Of course, he underscored his low prices and credit arrangements. He noted that, despite his large inventory, he still produced on order, guaranteeing fast delivery. Lastly, he spoke about the efficient layout and size of his factory.

Beginning in 1855, he added a few new notions to his advertising. He began emphasizing the variety of styles and the quality of the manpower he employed. In 1855, he even claimed that his employees worked under

301
William Drum's business card, found glued under a drawer of a cabinet presented to the Prince of Wales in 1860
Canadian Museum of Civilization, Hul (981.50.1)
Photo Christine Guest/MMFA
See fig. 55.

his personal supervision. By 1857, he was talking about his steam factory. In an innovative move in 1865 he held a huge month-long sale, offering a 10% cash rebate or a discount on three-month notes on all items in his stock.

After 1871, he specialized more than ever in mass production at his new factory. Thus, in 1871, an advertisement described his factory as "the most complete and expansive in the Province, since he is in possession of more than fifty of the most recent inventions in Labour Saving Machines, which are all being put to use: the establishment can supply all furnishings and objects possible in his line at reduced prices that defy all competition."[29] As for the competition, he probably had none in terms of prices, but as regards workmanship, there were certainly competitors specializing in luxury furnishings. Despite all Drum's boasting about his many machines, the public did not necessarily believe that these machines could equal the quality of manual work by craftsmen. As a result, in 1875, he announced that he had an assortment of furnishings "of all kinds, capable of rivalling with the best establishments in the city in terms of fine workmanship."[30] In addition, between 1837 and 1865, Drum announced that he was offering funeral services, as many other cabinetmakers did. We have found nothing that leads us to believe that Drum employed the services of travelling salesmen, even though he exported his products to the Maritime provinces, the Eastern Townships and Montreal. Did wholesale and retail dealers from these regions come and deal directly with Drum in Quebec City? We do not know. However, in May of 1860, Charles Robertson, a furniture dealer from Montreal, announced that he had in his possession furnishings made by different firms, including products by William Drum of Quebec City.[31]

William Drum had a real knack for marketing, and he never passed up an opportunity to advertise: when he entered into partnership with J.-O. Vallière or when they dissolved their company; when he moved; when he enlarged his premises; when he sold a new patented piece; when he planned special

302

events. For example, in December 1871, he invited people wishing to give Christmas or New Year's gifts to come and visit his cabinetmaking shops, where they would be assured of finding the most elegant furnishings at very reasonable prices.[32] Sometimes his advertising took on a novel twist. For example, in the 1851 Census of Canada (which he filled in like all good citizens), he used the "Remarks" section of the questionnaire to publicize his wares, writing: "Household office and cabinet work executed in all its branches and varieties (the best of materials and workmanship) with neatness and dispatch."[33]

Another technique used by Drum to promote his goods was auction sales, which he held several times – such as in May 1859, May 1861 and just before his death in May 1876.[34] Was this a spring tradition? Since there are no documents on the subject, we cannot draw any conclusions. One thing is certain: the events were well publicized, and this gave him an opportunity to exhibit his products outside his store. For a few days, he had two points of sale and exposure in the auctioneer's catalogue. The Drum Cabinet Manufacturing Company also held its own auction in 1879.[35]

Lastly – again in the interest of obtaining exposure – William Drum took part in a number of exhibitions and competitions held in conjunction with them. Once again, he benefited from the publicity surrounding these events.

In sum, Drum could not have reached the summit of his trade had he not been first and foremost a good craftsman, a master of his art in whom people could trust. Carver Louis Jobin may have described him as a hard man,[36] but he was no harder than the others. He simply watched out for his own interests. In the midst of the golden age of capitalism, he was a man of his times. If he had lived longer, would he have survived the economic crisis? It is difficult to say, but no matter what he did, he probably would have made the right decision.

Jean-François Caron

302
Advertisement by William Drum of Quebec City
Published in *Lovell's Canadian Dominion Directory for 1871*, Montreal, John Lovell, 1871, p. 30
Photo SRP

303
Advertisement by William Drum of Quebec City
Published in *Journal de Québec*, May 7, 1859
National Library of Canada, Ottawa (L-11717)

THE FURNITURE MAKERS

* This text was written in conjunction with the preparation of a doctoral thesis in history at l'Université Laval. It is the abridged version of a technical article with some 170 notes and references and ten tables, a copy of which has been deposited in the archives of Parks Canada in Quebec City. We have drawn upon documents kept in the ANQQ from the registers of the following notaries: Jacques Auger, Louis Bégin, William Bignell, Noël-B. Bowen, Archibald Campbell, Edward George Cannon, John Childs, J.-G. Clapham, Edward Glackmeyer, Josiah Hunt, Nicolas Lefrançois, Antoine-Ambroise Parent, Joseph Pelchat, Joseph Petitclerc, Louis Prévost, Cyrille Tessier, Michel Tessier and Augustin Vocelle.

1 Pat Kirkham, "Furniture Making and the Industrial Revolution, c.1750-1870", *Design and Industry. The Effects of Industrialization and Technical Change on Design* (The Design Council, 1980 [History of Design collection]), p. 28.

2 *Census of Canada*, 1851, Quebec City, folio 396.

3 Jean-François Caron, "Les apprentis à Québec de 1830 à 1849", Master's thesis, Université Laval, 1986.

4 John Lovell, *The Canada Directory for 1857-1858*, p. 559.

5 Willis Russell, *Quebec, As It Was, and As It Is* (Quebec City: P. Lamoureux, 1857), pp. 149-159.

6 L.-H. Huot, *Annuaire du commerce et de l'industrie de Québec pour 1873* (Quebec City: L.-H. Huot, 1873), p. 31.

7 *L'Événement*, January 3, 1871 and L.-H. Huot, *op. cit.*, pp. 20-22.

8 *Journal de Québec*, May 13, 1876; ANQQ, Anglican Cathedral, Quebec City, May 15, 1876.

9 *L'Événement*, September 3, 1878 (trans.).

10 *Ibid.* (trans.).

11 Russell, *op. cit.*, p. 153.

12 Huot, *op. cit.*, p. 20.

13 ANQQ, Atlas Sanborn, 1875, Quebec City, p. 8

14 *Ibid.*, pp. 8, 12.

15 Russell, *op. cit.*, p. 155.

16 Michael-J. Ettema, "Technological Innovation and Design Economics in Furniture Manufacture", *Winterthur Portfolio*, Vol. 16, Nos. 2-3 (Summer-Fall 1981), p. 207.

17 Reproduced in Brooke Hindle and Steven Lubar, *Engine of Change. The American Industrial Revolution, 1790-1860* (Washington, D.C. and London: Smithsonian Institution Press, 1986), p. 264.

18 Sidney Pollard, "Factory Discipline in the Industrial Revolution", *The Economic History Review*, Vol. XVI, No. 2 (1963), 2nd Series, pp. 254-271.

19 Antonio Drolet, *La ville de Québec. Histoire municipale. De l'incorporation à la Confédération (1833-1867)* (Quebec City: La Société historique de Québec, 1967 [Cahiers d'histoire, no. 19]), p. 103.

20 ANQQ, register of notary Joseph Petitclerc, no. 6532, March 6, 1852; contract between Louis-Thomas Berlinguet, Louis-Flavien Berlinguet and William Drum.

21 *L'Événement*, February 3, 1871.

22 *L'Événement*, March 25, 1872.

23 *L'Événement*, September 13 and 24, 1869.

24 ANQQ, register of notary Joseph Petitclerc, no. 6515, February 28, 1852; contract between William Drum and John Young for Queen Victoria.

25 *Journal de Québec*, September 6, 1860.

26 *Journal de Québec*, December 27, 1862.

27 *Journal de Québec*, May 11, 1865.

28 *Documents de la Session* (No. 1), for the years 1869, 1871, 1873-1879.

29 *L'Écho de Lévis*, August 2, 1871.

30 *Journal de Québec*, October 12, 1875.

31 *The Montreal Gazette*, May 19, 1860.

32 *L'Événement*, December 22, 1871.

33 *Census of Canada*, 1851, Quebec City, p. 396.

34 *Journal de Québec*, May 7, 1859, May 2, 1861 and May 13, 1876.

35 *L'Événement*, October 23, 1879.

36 John R. Porter and Jean Bélisle, *La sculpture ancienne au Québec. Trois siècles d'art religieux et profane* (Montreal: Les Éditions de l'Homme, 1986), p. 170.

PIERRE DROUIN AND HONORÉ ROY, CABINETMAKERS

ONORÉ ROY DIT BELLEAU (1821-1892) WAS ONE OF WILLIAM Drum's many apprentices, but was far from achieving as brilliant a career as his teacher. Indeed, had it not been for the acquisition by Parks Canada of part of his workshop stock, he might have remained forgotten by posterity. But in 1974 two of Roy dit Belleau's great-granddaughters gave the federal agency a collection of 144 documents[1] and a six-piece suite of furniture[2] made, according to family tradition, by Roy himself.

Although incomplete, the Roy dit Belleau bequest is particularly valuable since there is nothing else like it in any of our public or private collections. Because of its rarity, it was published complete in 1989, together with a detailed study of Honoré Roy and his first associate Pierre Drouin (1815-1860).[3] The following text is a condensation of that study, focusing on the conditions under which a cabinetmaker worked in the Victorian era with regard to life style, equipment, work patterns, production, clientele and competition.[4]

And yet Drouin and Roy were in no way different from the majority of nineteenth-century craftsmen who, in spite of the rapid development of big industries, went on as best they could turning out products to suit the current taste. In charge of an under-equipped and above all scarcely mechanized concern, vulnerable to the fluctuations of a generally difficult period and to clients who demanded massive credit, the two furniture makers were obliged, in order to survive, to rely on often ephemeral partnerships, on engaging apprentices and on frequent loans. Drouin, an energetic and entrepreneurial man, managed in the end to get out of the venture without loss, but Roy's small firm was only moderately successful, and in 1866 he went bankrupt.

PIERRE DROUIN: THE EARLY YEARS (1815-1844)
Pierre Drouin was born of Pierre Drouin and Marie-Louise Freys (Fraise)[5] on January 15, 1815 in Charlesbourg. At the time his father was working temporarily as a carpenter there, but he later returned to Quebec City and spent the rest of his life in the Saint-Roch district. He continued to practice his

304
Attributed to Honoré Roy (1821-1892)
Rococo-revival chair (from a set of four)
84 x 43 x 46 cm
Environment Canada, Parks Service, Quebec region
(X 74.90.2)

305
Attributed to Honoré Roy (1821-1892)
Rococo-revival settee
103 x 182 x 84 cm
Environment Canada, Parks Service, Quebec region
(X 74.90.6)

306
Attributed to Honoré Roy (1821-1892)
Rococo-revival centre table
76 x 97 x 123 cm
Environment Canada, Parks Service, Quebec region
(X 74.90.1)

The top, apron, legs and under-frame of this rococo-revival centre table form an elaborate interplay of curves and counter-curves. The piece is ornamented with various plant motifs _ including acanthus leaves, flowerets and roses _ that are characteristic of the Rococo-revival style.

trade, despite calling himself on occasion a "merchant". His last calling was that of "tobacconist", and he died on December 20, 1846 at the age of seventy-two.

We do not know what kind of education Pierre Drouin received, but given the fluency of his signature it must have been adequate. On December 6, 1833, at the age of eighteen, he was engaged as an apprentice furniture maker by Thomas Hobbs, a prominent Quebec City furniture manufacturer.[6] The nineteen-month contract provided for a salary of seven and a half shillings a week until the following May 1, and ten shillings thereafter. In accordance with custom, Drouin contracted to serve his master well, to keep his secrets, to obey any lawful order he was given, not to waste or lend his master's possessions, not to frequent taverns and gambling establishments, and not to be absent without permission.

This contract was in fact unusual from several points of view. It was of short duration, instead of the usual five or six years. It was also uncommon to begin an apprenticeship at the age of eighteen. And lastly, the salary was high, more than double the normal rate. Shortly after his contract expired, Pierre Drouin spent some time away from Quebec City, and in 1839 described himself as a "furniture maker presently resident in the city of Montreal".

From 1839 to 1843 Drouin established the bases for a successful career, which started with a contribution from his parents that brought him back to Quebec City for good. "Wishing to provide him with suitable premises", they made over to him on November 9, 1839, a thirty-two-foot-wide lot in the parish of Saint-Roch-de-Québec, bordered by Des Fossés Street and lying behind Saint-Joseph Street. The gift included the wooden house and shed on the property. Furthermore, at his parents' death Drouin was to receive the sum of £100 pounds in cash, all the household furniture and the kitchen utensils. In exchange, Drouin was to take care of his parents. However, if the legators and the legatee could not live amicably together, the legatee engaged to pay some compensation, including a life annuity.

At about the same time Drouin's business was expanding. In 1842 or perhaps earlier he went into partnership with the furniture maker François Drouin. Their workshop on Des Fossés Street, which "endeavoured to combine sturdiness with elegance", did both joinery work and cabinetmaking, producing bedsteads, cradles, sofas, love seats, chairs, sideboards and tables of all kinds. They regularly placed newspaper advertisements to increase their sales, and eventually hired at least two apprentice furniture makers, Olivier Elot dit Julien and Joseph Marcoux. The former began his four-year apprenticeship on March 1, 1842, the latter on the following May 1.

Enriched by his parent's gift and well established in his trade, Drouin could now think of marrying. On November 21, 1843 in Saint-Michel-de-Bellechasse he married Marie Paquet. This lady, the daughter of Amable Paquet, pilot, and Luce Brochu, had been married on January 8, 1839 to Simon Forgues, also a pilot. In 1843 she had sole care of a young child. Pierre Drouin's marriage naturally brought about a readjustment of the agreement signed four years earlier with his parents.

THE FIRM OF PIERRE DROUIN (1844-1853)
The year 1844 marked a turning point in Drouin's career. The company known as Pierre and François Drouin was dissolved on June 11, and François Drouin, who seems to have been in poor health, made over his share to his partner. Before the dissolution, all the household furniture in the workshop was sold at auction at their shop on Des Fossés Street.

Between 1844 and 1853 Pierre Drouin continued to work single-handed on the same premises, specializing in cabinetwork. On June 12, 1844 he informed the public that he had available "a very extensive assortment of Furniture of all kinds" which he was selling "at very low prices". All "orders entrusted to his establishment [are fulfilled] punctually". In 1847 he announced that his customers could obtain "at very advantageous prices all sorts of beds, furniture in refined taste made of impeccably seasoned materials." He also

Advertisement for the firm of Pierre Drouin of Quebec City
Published in the Journal de Québec, May 16, 1850
Photo SRP

advertised that he had among other stock "a considerable quantity of cane chairs gaily painted, others entirely of wood, rocking chairs, etc." On occasion he did not hesitate to make items other than furniture: in 1847 the merchant Hippolyte Dubord ordered from him "a wheel for a rudder four feet in diameter [...] with copper inlay depicting the rose, the thistle and the shamrock; [...] a fly-wheel with copper tips and stars and another star in the centre."

To maximize his profits, Drouin continued to work with great energy and, unlike most of his business competitors, placed regular advertisements in the newspapers. He also organized a lottery and rented out furniture.

In 1850 he set up a lottery in the form of a raffle for twenty pieces of furniture among 312 subscribers at five shillings a ticket. However, he had to postpone the original date of the raffle, April 30, because of a fire. He then added more prizes but, doubtless because the raffle aroused little interest, it did not take place on the following August 24 either. Nevertheless, the list of prizes demonstrates the variety of products made by Drouin: bookcases with twelve drawers, mahogany sofas, settees, wing chairs, mahogany desks with mirrors, mahogany sideboards, mahogany round tables, mahogany card tables, folding tables, dining tables, mahogany and walnut commodes, carved bedsteads, pier glasses and dressing mirrors, yellow birch chairs, gilded basket-work chairs and rocking chairs.

At the time leasing out furniture was not unusual, and Pierre Drouin did so at least twice during this period. In 1849 two Quebec City craftsmen leased from him, one "an imitation-pine dressing table", coloured, a butternut table, six wooden chairs and a "cradle chair", and the other a butternut dressing chest with seven drawers and six brown-painted wooden chairs.

Between 1842 and 1850 Drouin's clientele, although it included lawyers, merchants and doctors, consisted mostly of French-speaking artisans in Quebec City. Other customers included the Institut catholique, the Hôpital Général de Québec and the Chambre de lecture de Saint-Roch, as well as some from outside Quebec City.

The years 1844 to 1853 were not all lucky ones for Drouin. His premises fell prey to fires at least twice. On May 28, 1845, like many of his fellow citizens, he saw his property go up in flames in a fire that spread through the Saint-Roch neighbourhood. He managed to recoup in 1848 with the help of two successive government loans of £100. In April or May 1850 there was a second fire. The damage it caused is hard to assess, but it was extensive enough to oblige Drouin to cancel his raffle.

In 1863 three buildings stood on his property on Des Fossés Street. One, facing the street, was a two-storey red brick house with attics and an iron and tin roof, thirty-two feet wide by thirty feet deep; behind it was a one-storey wooden house twenty-six feet by eighteen to twenty feet with a shingled roof; and lastly there was a two-storey red brick building about forty-eight feet by fifteen with a tin roof, which was used as a furniture making shop. It was probably this last building that was erected in 1850.

The fire of 1850 may have been the cause of Drouin's urgent need of money. In any case, from September 1850 to the end of the year he was offering his stock of household furniture for cash at reduced prices.

In the years that followed, his business prospered once more: he acquired more property and engaged two apprentices. In 1847 the nuns of the Hôpital

Général de Québec had made over to him two lots on Saint-Joseph Street in the Saint-Roch-de-Québec parish. As a result of transactions made on November 21, 1851 and January 7, 1852, he became the owner, for seventy pounds, of two adjoining half-lots on Saint-Joseph Street. In 1851, in addition to his family, Pierre Drouin had beneath his roof a sixty-six-year-old chair maker, P. Turgeon, and an eighteen-year-old furniture maker, Alfred Deblois. That same year Drouin hired François-Xavier Morel as an apprentice furniture maker. The apprenticeship began on February 1, 1851 and was for four years, during which Drouin was to teach the young man his "trade or profession of a furniture maker & turner." On February 15, 1852 another apprentice furniture maker, the sixteen-year-old Augustin Caron, joined the firm. Now well established, on June 1, 1853 Pierre Drouin went into partnership with Honoré Roy, a furniture maker six years younger than he.

HONORÉ ROY DIT BELLEAU: THE EARLY YEARS (1821-1853)

Honoré Roy was born on March 1, 1821 in Quebec City. His parents were Étienne Roy, a baker, and Louise Géraux. Like Drouin, he seems to have had a fair education: at least, his handwriting is fluent.

On December 4, 1838, at the age of seventeen, young Roy was apprenticed to the furniture maker William Drum[7] on a four-and-a-half-year contract. His working hours were to be from seven in the morning until eight in the evening in winter, and from five in the morning until seven in the evening in summer. Roy agreed to serve his master well, to obey any legal order given him, not to be absent without permission, not to lend his tools to anyone, not to cause damage to his master's property nor allow anyone else to do so without warning his master, not to play cards, dice or any other games of chance that could cause damage to his master, not to frequent taverns or disreputable places, but to conduct himself as a good and loyal apprentice should.

For his part, William Drum engaged to treat Honoré Roy appropriately and to teach him "the Trade and Business of a Cabinet Maker in as much as he is capable or susceptible of learning". Drum paid him £7.10.0. in cash for the first year, £9 for the second, £11 for the third, £14 for the fourth year and £8 for the last six months. However, if Roy were absent from work for two weeks or so through illness or other reasons, he had to make the time up, after which Drum would pay him.

On January 21, 1845, less than two years before the end of his apprenticeship, Honoré Roy got married in Quebec City to Marguerite Clavette, daughter of the late Jean-Baptiste Clavette, who had been a carpenter, and sister to the furniture maker Charles Clavette. It was not a long marriage: Marguerite died on March 18, 1848 aged scarcely thirty-two, after giving birth in 1845 to Marie-Marguerite-Adéline and to Marie-Joséphine, also called Marcelline, a year later.

In 1851 Roy was living on Saint-Joachim Street in the Saint-Jean-Baptiste district of Quebec City and describing himself as a furniture maker. He inhabited a two-storey stone house together with his mother-in-law Marguerite Gagné, his sister-in-law Catherine Clavette, his daughters Marcelline and Adéline, his sister Joséphine Roy, and an eighteen-year-old furniture maker called Louis Roy whose connection with Honoré Roy is unknown.

On October 25, 1853 Honoré Roy was married again in Quebec City to Sophie Robitaille, widow of Joseph Routier by whom she had had a son, Joseph, in 1831. Although their marriage contract specified that they held their property jointly, Sophie Robitaille kept her bed and its furnishings, her clothes and underwear, a sofa stuffed with straw and covered in chintz, and a folding table in butternut.

The partnership with Pierre Drouin, which began five months before this marriage, seemed to augur well for it. The seven years the partnership lasted were important to the careers of both men.

THE DROUIN-ROY PARTNERSHIP (1853-1860)

On September 30, 1854, Pierre Drouin and Honoré Roy, both master furniture makers or cabinetmakers, went into partnership to operate, under the name of Drouin & Roy, a "furniture business" for "the making, sale and retail of furniture". This contract ratified an ad hoc arrangement in place since the previous June 1. Pierre Drouin was at the time the dominant partner, since the shop and workshop operated out of his Des Fossés Street property, and he provided the capital in stock for the business, evaluated at £1,258.11.11. It included 618 chairs, 409 bedsteads, thirty-seven tables, thirty-five sofas, thirty-three wing chairs, thirty-one mirror frames, twenty-seven washstands, thirteen commodes, eleven mattresses and ten settees, as well as six carved ornaments and two flywheels.

Besides furniture, Drouin's assets included a large quantity of materials and components for making furniture. The lumber, mainly walnut, was evaluated at some £306, and was stored in three places: on the Saint-Joseph Street lot near the Hôpital de la Marine, on the Sainte-Marguerite Street lot, and in the yard on Saint-Joseph Street.

Drouin also provided "all the gear from the three Furniture Shops [...] with everything needed for painting and turning"; this was evaluated at £150. And lastly, he brought to the business a horse, four carts, two four-wheeled carts, two sleighs and four sleds for delivery. To this investment equivalent to £1,258.11.11 he added £90 in cash when signing the agreement. Honoré Roy, on the other hand, seems not to have brought anything to the partnership, at least not in goods or money.

This partnership, which was to last ten years, was established on an equal basis. The profits and losses, after expenses, debts, the rent on Drouin's house (£60 a year), and the annual six-per-cent interest on the investment were deducted, were to be shared equally between the two men when the partnership was dissolved. In June every year an inventory was drawn up to evaluate how the business stood. Once this was done, each partner took from the profits, if they were big enough, the sum of a £100, and the rest was ploughed back into the company.

Although the exact number of people employed by the firm of Drouin & Roy cannot be ascertained, the following gives some idea of the composition of the staff in March of 1856.

> SITUATION IN MARCH 1856
> **Owners:**
> Pierre Drouin, aged 45, master cabinetmaker
> Honoré Roy dit Belleau, aged 41, master cabinetmaker
> **Craftsmen:**
> Jean Noreau, aged 45, painter hired in 1853
> Joseph Routier*, aged 25, furniture maker, son-in-law of Roy dit Belleau
> Louis Roy*, aged 23, furniture maker, boarding with Roy dit Belleau
> **Apprentices:**
> Alfred Deblois, aged 22, hired in 1851
> Augustin Caron, aged 20, hired in 1852 for 5 years
> François Jolin**, aged 19, hired in 1853 for 5 years
> Yves Giroux, aged 20, hired in 1854 for 2 years
> Thomas Leclerc dit Francoeur, hired in 1855 for 5 yearss
> J.-B. Giguère**, aged 17, hired in 1855 for 5 years
> * Presence unconfirmed but probable.
> ** Worked as a painter at the start of his apprenticeship.
> N.B.: For the years 1856 to 1860, the year Drouin died, no hiring contract has been found.

In 1856 Eustache Matte, a Quebec City merchant, and his wife Émérance Thivierge falsely accused Pierre Drouin of having bought from them 25,000 cigars and refusing to pay for them. The court threw out these allegations since, on the evidence of many witnesses, Pierre Drouin had never dealt in cigars. In fact, the plaintiffs had mistaken the son for the father, who had been a "tobacconist" and had died ten years earlier in 1846. It became apparent that this was either a misunderstanding or a fabrication.

However, the testimony of Pierre Drouin's witnesses sheds light on some aspects of how the Drouin & Roy business operated in 1856. Thus we learn that

> the workshop is in a building adjoining the defendant's house [...] There are greenhouses and a door that lead from the house to the shop. To enter or leave, [people] go through the workshop and sometimes through the defendant's apartments.

It is clear from some evidence that there was no lack of work. Jean Noreau, a painter working for Drouin & Roy, had only been "a couple of weeks at a stretch without working, the rest of the time [he] worked from morning to night in the defendant's workshop". Honoré Roy, who at the time lived "facing [Drouin's] house", said the same:

> I have been associated with the defendant as a furniture maker for some three years. We carry on our business in the defendant's house on Des Fossés Street in the Saint-Roch district of Quebec City. The workshop and the defendant's home are in the same building. Since I have been in partnership with the defendant scarcely a day has gone by, except for Sundays and holidays, that I have not worked in the defendant's workshop. I go to my job there every day.

In the years they were together, Drouin and Roy went on making and selling a wide range of furniture "created in the latest style according to the most elegant fashions of London and Paris". They claimed to hire only the best

308
Advertisement for the firm of Drouin & Roy of Quebec City
Published in the Journal de Québec, March 16, 1858
Photo Jean-Pierre Labiau/MOBIVIQ

workmen, to oversee all the work themselves, and to sell their furniture "at very low prices". They occasionally undertook more unusual orders. In 1853 Honoré Roy made an altarpiece for the Séminaire de Québec, while an inventory of 1861 lists ship's wheels and components.

The firm of Drouin & Roy, using both craftsmanship and industrial techniques, is a fair example of a small-scale factory.[8] The capital, tools and workplace belonged to the partners, while the workmen and apprentices worked for a salary. Most, if not all, tools were provided by the firm; in 1861 the value of these was over £50. The number of tools suggests that the men had to share them.

In addition to the separation between capital and labour, the company of Drouin & Roy also demonstrates the beginnings of division of labour, of specialization. The many furniture components listed in the inventories – mouldings, chair legs and backs, spokes for ship's flywheels, sections of washstands, bed posts, cross-beams and posts for cradles – indicate that the furniture was to some extent mass-produced as individual components with the help of a turning lathe and templates, and then assembled. That there was some division of labour is shown by the fact that the firm had at least one painter, while the two apprentice furniture makers had to do some painting at the start of their apprenticeships. However, given the small number of employees, the degree of specialization was far less and not so strict as in a big factory.

Finally, as opposed to industry, a firm like Drouin & Roy made little or no use of machinery. In 1861, for example, they had only one turning lathe and one shaper for making mouldings, evaluated respectively at fifty shillings and fifty-five shilllings, and these were the only pieces of equipment costing so much. According to the inventories, no source of power was used.

Drouin & Roy not only made furniture, they also sold it retail. They had a shop next to the workshop, and various sorts of transport for delivering their goods. Their clientele was similar to that of Drouin in the 1840s. In 1863, out of the ninety-one customers who owed the firm money and whose occupations are known, there were eight hotel-keepers, six carpenters, six furniture makers, five merchants, four joiners, three stevedores, three lawyers, three carters, three shoe-makers, three smiths and three fullers.[9] The rest were mainly of the artisan class. The hotel-keepers were favoured customers, being the most numerous and owing the firm the most money. Drouin & Roy provided them with bedsteads, billiard tables and ornaments among other things. Ninety per cent of customers were French-speaking and lived in Quebec City. In the 1863 account books only one institution appears, the Institut catholique.

The company did well until the premature death of Pierre Drouin on May 29, 1860 put an abrupt end to the partnership. According to the coroner's report, it was heart disease that killed him at the age of scarcely forty-five. He left a widow and five children aged from sixteen months to sixteen years.

When the firm of Drouin & Roy was officially dissolved in early May 1861, its affairs were in good order. The importance of credit is very apparent. Active debts amounted to £640, representing half of the assets which were calculated at £1,294. The latter amount included the effects of Drouin's shop in 1863 (£301), the goods sold in two auctions held in 1861 (£312), and the tools, lumber and furniture sold to Honoré Roy in 1861 (£342). Liabilities amounted to £624. The difference between assets and liabilities showed a surplus of £670, which is low in terms of the investment made by Drouin in 1853.

The balance-sheet of Drouin's possessions drawn up in 1863 shows assets of about £1,833 and liabilities of £742. His widow Marie Paquet owned a lot on Sainte-Marguerite Street purchased in 1860 and another with a shed on Des Fossés Street purchased in 1856. Honoré Roy, on the other hand, seems to have been quite poor, owning no property. His whole life long, all he ever owned was one piece of land, and even this he only had for less than two years. His poverty is apparent from the fact that in 1854, apart from his share of Drouin & Roy, he possessed only £27 worth of furniture and £4 worth of tools.

HONORÉ ROY TAKES OVER FROM DROUIN
Nevertheless, Honoré Roy showed no hesitation in taking over from Drouin. In February of 1861 he acquired for £342 the "tools, furniture & lumber for furniture" from his partner's estate, and also rented from Drouin's widow the ground floor of her brick house with all its attics on Des Fossés Street, the workshop behind it, the wooden building on Sainte-Marguerite Street and a lot in the same place, with all the apprentices there. Also in 1861 he hired Elzéar Barbeau as an apprentice furniture maker, François-Xavier Robitaille in 1863 and Charles Hamel at about the same time. He eventually moved with his family into the widow Drouin's house.

Roy's financial situation seemed precarious. In addition to the cost of tools and materials, he had several debts to face. He borrowed money frequently, and signed or endorsed a dozen or so promissory notes. The crisis came in 1863: he signed a bond for £50 in front of a notary, several of his promissory notes were unpaid, and six protests were brought against him.

TWO SHORT-LIVED PARTNERSHIPS (1864-1865)
HONORÉ ROY & CIE AND ROY & CLAVETTE
On May 20, 1864, Honoré Roy went into partnership with his stepson Joseph Routier to form Honoré Roy & Cie with the aim of "carrying on the trade & business of Furniture Making & Cabinetmaking". Routier, a thirty-three year-old bachelor, was the son of Sophie Robitaille's first marriage. At this time he was living in his stepfather's house and already had some experience working with Drouin & Roy.

The new company, which was to last two years, was founded on a basis of equality. The earnings, profits, expenses and losses were to be shared equally between the partners, although Roy was the senior of the two. His was the sole name in the corporate title, he alone could sign for the company and provided the business, materials and tools. Roy's investment, however, was not as large as that made by Drouin in 1854. While the latter had provided his own premises, a business valued at £1,258 and £90 in cash, Roy only had rented premises and capital equivalent to £424. This included: the furniture in the shop (£95.17.0); the furniture, finished and unfinished, and components in the workshop (£91.1.8); lumber consisting of black walnut, butternut, oak, yellow birch, cherrywood, camphor and mahogany, and black walnut and rosewood veneer (£180); and tools worth £59.3.0. The latter included planes,

309
Advertisement for the auction sale of furniture made by the late Pierre Drouin of Quebec City & Roy of Quebec City
Published in the Journal de Québec, May 18, 1861
Photo Jean-Pierre Labiau/MOBIVIQ

jointers, clamps, workbenches and saws as well as the workshop templates (£3), three boxes of wood templates and cardboard designs (£15), four books of furniture designs (£12) and a box full of sheets with furniture designs (£2.10.0). The templates, models and designs accounted for more than half the total value of the tools.

The firm of Honoré Roy & Cie did not last long: it was dissolved on January 23, 1865. Roy seems to have been in financial difficulties. He owed £35 to his partner and various sums to William Venner and other creditors. In fact, although the association was not officially dissolved until January 1865, Roy seems to have already found himself another partner in late 1864.

On November 14, 1864 Honoré Roy and Charles Clavette, his first wife's brother, took on Joseph Nolet as an apprentice furniture maker. The partnership with Clavette, a furniture maker, was made official on February 4, 1865. We do not know how long the new company, incorporated as Roy & Clavette,[10] lasted (probably only a short time), nor what it was like. An indication of Joseph Routier's standing at this time is that in January 1865 he was described only as a shop assistant.

ROY'S BANKRUPTCY (1865-1866)

Honoré Roy's affairs reached crisis point in 1865-1866. On December 16, 1865 he was obliged to hand over materials to the bailiff Édouard Lacroix for the sum of £12.[11] On January 10, 1866, in order to protect her property and her rights, his wife Sophie Robitaille applied for and obtained a division of property. The testimony presented in this case was crushing for Roy. Joseph Routier stated that his step-father was "in a poor way of business" and that all his goods had been repossessed and sold. He added that Roy was "insolvent & incapable of finding other business, or of carrying on any trade". He further testified that "[Roy] has been in difficulties for over a year, and has become insolvent through taking insufficient trouble over his business as a result of insufficient foresight, hard work & skill". His step-son finished by saying that Roy was in a position where he could no longer carry on any business since his creditors had lost all faith in him. The bailiff Édouard Lacroix, who had arrested Roy for monies owed to the municipal corporation, and the carter Évariste Manceau, corroborated Routier's evidence.

In accordance with the verdict handed down on January 10, the assets and liabilities of the property jointly held by Roy and his wife were totted up. Since the communal estate was "more burdensome than profitable", Sophie Robitaille renounced it on January 31, and the court sanctioned this decision on February 19. In accordance with the verdict of January 10, 1866 and the proceedings then instigated, she claimed £24.17.5 from her husband, and when he refused to pay she obtained, in March and in May of 1866, a distraint on his property. It was not until July that, after refusing to do so in May, Sophie Robitaille agreed to have the sheriff sell the seized goods. The sale brought in only £4.6.0, which was scarcely enough to cover the costs.

HONORÉ ROY AND SOPHIE ROBITAILLE "FEMALE FURNITURE MAKER" (1866-1877)

Although they went on living together, from then on Honoré Roy and Sophie Robitaille kept their economic affairs separate, at least officially. A

study of the transactions, however, raises a number of questions. In 1866 Honoré Roy once again rented the wooden house on Des Fossés Street where he had lived with his family from 1856 to 1864. In 1868 he rented two workshops on Sainte-Marguerite Street. He also hired some apprentice furniture makers: Thomas Cardinal in 1869, Alphonse Laroche in 1872 and Joseph Richard in 1873. For her part, Sophie Robitaille managed the property she had inherited from her parents, took on Adolphe Souci as an apprentice furniture maker in 1866, rented out in her own name in 1870 the Des Fossés Street house leased by her husband in 1866, and finally, in 1872, described herself as a *meublière*. Given the lack of information available, it is hard to tell whether there was any link between Roy's business and that of his wife. It is, of course, possible that Sophie Robitaille was simply letting her husband use her name. The role played by Joseph Routier is also uncertain. In 1866 he was living with his mother and step-father, and indeed at that time the goods seized from Honoré Roy were left there in his care. On November 16, 1875 he went into partnership with the merchant Thomas Donohue to set up a business as furniture makers in Quebec City. The company was incorporated as Joseph Routier & Compagnie. In 1877 Joseph Routier, Sophie Robitaille and Honoré Roy were all living together on Des Fossés Street in the rented house, and at the same date a document attests to there being a workshop and shop in the building. Also in 1877 Marie-Esther Grenier, who owned the Des Fossés Street house, demanded $104.25 from Sophie Robitaille for several months of

310
Honoré Roy and his associate Joseph Routier
Photograph (ferrotype), 10 x 6.2 cm
Environment Canada, Parks Service, Quebec region
(EX 86.3.83)
Routier is shown holding a scaled-down model of a rocking chair in his right hand; Honoré Roy is holding a carved beaver that has recently been discovered in the home of one of his descendants.

311
Business card of Drouin & Roy altered by Honoré Roy of Quebec City
Lithograph on waxed cardboard, 7.9 x 11.1 cm
Environment Canada, Parks Service, Quebec region
(EX 86.3.95)
Photo SRP
Honoré Roy has written his first name in ink over the name of his former associate.

312
Pierre Drouin (1815-1860) or Honoré Roy (1821-1892)
Eagle (template)
Crayon on perforated paper, 20 x 38.3 cm
Environment Canada, Parks Service, Quebec region
(EX 86.3.106)
Photo SRP

THE FURNITURE MAKERS

unpaid rent. In October a verdict was given in her favour, and her tenant's goods were seized.

The federal census taken six months earlier allows us to draw a fairly accurate picture of the Des Fossés Street concern, but it is difficult to be sure whether it includes Sophie Robitaille's and Joseph Routier's business. Out of the twenty-one furniture-making establishments in Quebec City in 1871, that belonging to Honoré Roy was classified as being in the lower category in regard to the fixed capital ($334, 13th), the working capital ($200, 14th), and the number of employees (3, 10th), as well as the annual value of the raw materials used ($140, 17th) and the annual value of production ($800, 16th). The workshop produced about two hundred items a year including chairs, commodes, sofas and tables.

THE LATER YEARS OF HONORÉ ROY (1878-1892)

What Honoré Roy did after 1877 is still in doubt, but he seems to have practiced his trade until the end of his life. In 1879 he rented an apartment on the upper floor of a two-storey brick house on Saint-Dominique Street in the Saint-Roch district, at the corner of Saint-Dominique and Des Fossés Streets, and lived there until the early 1890s. On December 28, 1892, the day of his death, he had been living for a short time at 192 Saint-Jean Street and working in his workshop at 191 Saint-Vallier Street. Sophie Robitaille died in her turn a few months later, on March 1, 1893. Joseph Routier, her only child, died a bachelor on September 28, 1900.

The lives of the furniture makers Honoré Roy and Pierre Drouin brought them neither glory nor renown. Indeed, had it not been for the accidental preservation of some of their history, both men would doubtless have remained anonymous, as did most of their brother craftsmen. Nevertheless, a limited number of cabinetmakers, endowed with outstanding business acumen, imagination or professional skills, did succeed in rising above their peers and earning short-lived or lasting fame through their participation in events which, in Victoria's day, always attracted the crowds: the provincial and international exhibitions.

Rénald Lessard

1   These documents are: 64 lithographed plates from the *Garde-Meuble* by Désiré Guilmard, 36 drawings, 22 prints, 10 labels, 4 photographs, 4 templates, 3 pages of an invoice and 1 calligraphy exercise.

2   Four chairs, one drawing-room settee and one drawing-room table.

3   John R. Porter, Rénald Lessard and Jean-Pierre Labiau with the collaboration of Georges-Pierre Léonidoff, Micheline Huard and Claire Desmeules, *Les meubliers Pierre Drouin et Honoré Roy et l'industrie du meuble à Québec à l'époque victorienne* (Quebec City: Université Laval, Cahiers du CÉLAT, 1989) no. 10, 197 pages.

4   For further details, see the original study by Rénald Lessard (pp. 43-87), which is accompanied by an impressive scientific analysis with 170 notes and references. With Mr. Lessard's consent, I condensed the main points of his study for the purpose of this publication (J. R. Porter).

5   Jocelyn Milot states, incorrectly, that he was born in Quebec City on September 22, 1810, (Quebec City: PUL, 1985), *DBC*, vol. VIII, p. 262.

6   Contract of Pierre Drouin and Thomas Hobbs, December 6, 1833 (ANQQ, registry of notary Louis Panet, no. 5727).

7   Contract of Honoré Roy and William Drum, December 17, 1838 (ANQQ, registry of notary John Childs, no. 868).

8   Paul Mantoux, *La révolution industrielle au XVIIIe siècle. Essai sur les commencements de la grande industrie moderne en Angleterre* (Paris: Éditions Génin, 1959), pp. 13-16.

9   There were also two apprentices, two tax collectors, two writers, two notaries, two silversmiths, two turners, two saddlers, two sail makers, two boat builders, two shop assistants, a tinsmith, a grocer, a bailiff, a printer, a teacher, a *manchonnier*, a timber merchant, a plumber, a painter, a pilot, a policeman, an upholsterer, a sculptor, an insurance salesman, a baker, a customs official, a roofer and a carter.

10 On July 13, 1864 Roy had sold to Clavette a batch of furniture evaluated at £11.9.0 consisting of a sofa, a large square table, a washstand, two rocking chairs, a clock, a wardrobe, two commodes and two wooden chests.

11 These materials consisted mainly of planks and beams of oak, butternut, ash, black walnut, cherrywood, yellow birch, cedar, red maple, mahogany and camphor wood.

313
Bird's-eye View of the Site of the Montreal Provincial Exhibition (detail)
Engraving after a drawing by Eugene Haberer published in *L'Opinion publique*, September 29, 1881. Photo SRP

A WORLD OF EXCHANGE: PROVINCIAL AND INTERNATIONAL EXHIBITIONS

PRIOR TO 1850, ARTISTIC, AGRICULTURAL AND INDUSTRIAL exhibitions were already being organized locally in the principal cities of Lower Canada. The holding of the first great universal exhibition, in London in 1851, led to the development of a well-defined formula that was copied, on a smaller scale, by leading industrialized cities in many countries across the world, including Canada. The impact of the London exhibition was rooted in the simplicity of its concept: the goal was to assemble, in one place and for a specific length of time, the products of industry, agriculture and the arts, giving particular emphasis to natural resources.

The exhortations of Prince Albert, aimed at encouraging people all over the world to participate in London's Great Exhibition, sparked an enthusiasm in Quebec that led to the organization of the first provincial agricultural and industrial exhibition, held in Montreal in 1850. Moreover, during the same period many similar events took place in other Canadian cities.[1] During the second half of the nineteenth century, thirty such exhibitions were held in the province of Quebec with the goal of encouraging and stimulating Quebec production.

The fashion for provincial exhibitions endured until the close of the century, and the events attracted a huge number of participants. Organized at irregular intervals, the exhibitions were generally held during the first few weeks of September. For a period of three or four days, the exhibition sites were invaded by tens of thousands of visitors.

Following the model of the international exhibitions, the exhibits were examined by judges, and those considered to be the best in their class were awarded prizes and medals. There was a wide range of competition categories, including the agricultural, which consisted largely of animals, farming implements and agricultural produce. This latter section was extremely popular with the public throughout the period that concerns us. The horticultural exhibition also attracted many visitors and became something of a focal point of the autumn event. The fine arts section brought together works by the majority of Quebec's most popular artists, together with the creations of a few talented foreigners. The range of products displayed in the industrial

314
The Building for the "Industry" Section of the Montreal Provincial Exhibition of 1873
Engraving published in the Canadian Illustrated News, September 27, 1873
National Archives of Canada, Ottawa (C-59364)

315
Cover of the Guide to the Montreal Provincial Exhibition of 1884
Engraving published in 1884, Grande Exposition de la Puissance ouverte à l'Univers à Montréal du 5 au 13 septembre (Montreal: John Lovell, 1884)
Library of the Séminaire de Québec, fonds ancien (212)
Photo W. B. Edwards Inc., Quebec City

category was enormously varied. The programme of the 1871 provincial exhibition held in Quebec City divided the industrial category into thirteen more or less homogenous classes:

314

> Class 1: marquetry, cabinetwork and other woodwork, surgical instruments, musical instruments, etc. Class 2: coachwork, etc. Class 3: machines, manufactured metals, tools, equipment, etc. Class 4: building materials, pottery, tiles, slates, buttons, glassware, etc. Class 5: drawings, painting, sculpture, statuary, engraving, lithography, photography, fine arts materials, etc. Class 6: paper, printing, binding, paper-making, etc. Class 7: leathers, leather-making, rubber, etc. Class 8: oils, varnishes, chemical products and their preparations, etc. Class 9:

geology and natural history. Class 10: soaps, groceries, provisions, tobaccos, biscuits, etc. Class 11: manufactured articles in wool, linen and cotton, fishing equipment, furs, etc. Class 12: ladies' section. Class 13: manufactured domestic articles.[2]

The provincial exhibitions created a good deal of publicity for those who participated. They also had positive economic implications for the organizing city, due to the large number of visitors. During the second half of the nineteenth century, Montreal became the economic centre of the province and increasingly gained monopoly over the provincial exhibitions, frequently winning out over the cities of Quebec, Sherbrooke and Trois-Rivières.

FURNITURE MAKERS IN THE PROVINCIAL EXHIBITIONS
Inspired by the desire to have their creations admired by the general public and awarded the recognition of official prizes, close to eighty furniture makers took part in the thirty provincial exhibitions held in the latter half of the nineteenth century. This may seem like a small number when we consider the hundreds, even thousands of individuals that according to provincial industrial and nominal censuses were working in the furniture industry during the Victorian era. However, it included some of Quebec's best known and most prolific cabinetmakers.

Many different types of furniture maker participated in the exhibitions, reflecting the wide range of people working in the province's industry: the group included general craftsmen, upholsterers, carvers, factory owners, dealers, importers and workers in related trades. It is interesting to note the presence of an apprentice and of a handful of ladies[3] in the "furniture" class, together with a number of craftsmen not normally associated with the furniture-making trade.[4] Other participants created unique pieces worthy of public display simply through a love of the craft. For example, as a young man Joseph-Honoré Gignac created a writing desk made of 13,500 pieces of wood from seventy-three different varieties of tree.[5]

We shall not, for the purposes of this essay, consider as furniture makers participating in the provincial exhibitions either manufacturers of metal furniture,[6] school and office furniture,[7] and miniature and toy furniture, or others whose creations were of only secondary importance and might confuse the general picture.

With the exception of a few furniture makers working in the country, or based in Ontario or the United States, the craftsmen who participated in the provincial exhibitions came from either Montreal or Quebec City. According to their family names, the vast majority of them were English-speaking. With the exception of a few prosperous manufacturers and dealers based in Montreal and Quebec City, they generally presented works at only a single exhibition.

THE PRINCIPAL PARTICIPATING FURNITURE MAKERS
FROM MONTREAL
The most frequent participants in the provincial exhibitions were without question the firms of John and William Hilton (father and son) and Owen McGarvey (later Owen McGarvey & Son). These companies also shared the

316
Joseph-Honoré Gignac
Moorish-style writing desk, about 1880
Marquetry, 200 x 137.5 x 65 cm
Private collection, Saint-Rédempteur
Photo Michel Gilbert

317
Advertisement for the firm of Owen McGarvey & Son of Montreal
Published in the Montreal Star, September 19, 1891
Photo SRP
This advertisement mentions the fact that the McGarvey firm had participated in a number of exhibitions, both in Canada and abroad.

318
Advertisement for the firm of H. A. Wilder & Co. of Montreal
Published in the Montreal Star, September 12, 1896
Photo SRP

319
Advertisement for the firm of H. P. Labelle of Montreal
Published in the Montreal Star, September 15, 1896
Photo SRP

lead for the number of pieces of furniture exhibited during the second half of the nineteenth century. Between 1850 and 1870, the Hiltons presented a total of close to sixty individual pieces or suites of furniture in ten provincial exhibitions held in Montreal. And when McGarvey retired in 1896, after some fifty prosperous years in business, he had also presented about sixty pieces or suites in five Montreal exhibitions (1855, 1857, 1858, 1882 and 1884). In addition, these two leading furniture-making families met with some success in a number of international and universal exhibitions.

Another furniture maker, Adolphe Bélanger, made notable achievements in the exhibitions of 1880, 1882 and 1884. Although Bélanger's production was not on the same scale as that of the Hiltons and the McGarveys, he nonetheless qualifies as a major participant, for he presented about fifty pieces and suites in these three exhibitions. Other important exhibitors, classified in descending order according to the number of items presented, are James Thomson (1863, 1865 and 1880), H. A. Wilder & Co. (1893, 1895 and 1896), William Scott (1882), W. F. Dogherty (1881 and 1884) and Renaud, King & Patterson (1893). Manufacturers who presented a relatively small but nevertheless significant number of pieces include Azarie Lavigne (1873 and 1881), H. J. Shaw & Co. (1881 and 1884), Henry Morgan (1882), Noël Pratte (1868 and 1881), Frederick Carlisle (1853, 1857 and 1858), Joseph Forget called Despatis (1857, 1858 and 1860) and James Morrice (1850, 1857 and 1860).

The remaining fifty or so exhibitors were not inferior in either the originality of their presentations or the quality of their furniture. The common factor uniting these manufacturers, dealers and craftsmen was that they either exhibited rarely or presented very few items. For example, two important furniture stores located on Notre-Dame Street, the ones belonging to J.A.I. Craig (who also had a factory on Saint-Bonaventure Street) and H. P. Labelle (who also owned a furniture factory), are virtually absent from the Montreal exhibitions. Craig only exhibited four pieces in the 1880 exhibition, while Labelle presented a few at the exhibition in 1893. Another furniture maker, André Molinelli, who participated hardly at all (a single piece is listed for the exhibition of 1865) succeeded in making his mark through the originality of his style. A point worth noting is that not a single piece of house furniture was presented by a Montreal furniture maker at the provincial exhibitions held in Quebec City. Finally, another major manufacturer and dealer located on Notre-Dame Street, C. E. Pariseau, never presented any of his creations at the provincial exhibitions.

THE PRINCIPAL PARTICIPATING FURNITURE MAKERS
FROM QUEBEC CITY

The clear leaders in the "furniture" class of the provincial exhibitions held in Quebec City were the manufacturers William Drum and Philippe Vallière. Drum takes first place for both the number of participations (furniture by him was in competition at the local exhibitions of 1850 and 1853, and at the provincial exhibitions of 1854, 1871 and 1877) and the number of pieces or suites exhibited (close to thirty altogether). He also participated in the Montreal exhibitions of 1850 and 1870 – although he only presented a total of three pieces – and was active on the international scene. Philippe Vallière, exhilarated by all the attendant publicity,[8] took an active part in the exhibitions of 1871, 1877 and 1887. He exhibited a total of at least twenty individual pieces and suites of furniture.

Of the remainder there is little to be said, for very few Quebec City furniture makers participated in the exhibitions, and the exhibitions themselves were few and far between. François Gourdeau did present a few pieces, including a two-year-old drawing-room suite at the exhibition of 1871.[9] Evidence indicates that this was the suite now owned by the Montreal Museum of Fine Arts. Rather surprisingly, Pierre Roy, a well-established furniture maker from the Saint-Roch district, only took part in a single exhibition, the one held in Montreal in 1865. He exhibited a centre table,[10] but the piece received no awards.

Participants from elsewhere in the province included someone called Héribel, from Saint-Hyacinthe, who took part in the 1865 exhibition in Montreal, and the Huntingdon firm of Beyd & Co., who showed in the 1893 exhibition, also in Montreal. Undoubtedly his success at the 1855 exhibition held in Sherbrooke, encouraged Samuel Twose of the Eastern Townships to enter the 1863 one in Montreal. The participation of the Ontario-based Oshawa Cabinet Factory was particularly notable in the Montreal exhibitions of 1860 and 1881. Finally, the Statt company of New York presented works in the Montreal exhibition of 1873.

THE MAIN CATEGORIES OF FURNITURE IN THE
PROVINCIAL EXHIBITIONS

In the "furniture" class emphasis was placed on special or "display" pieces. Furniture of this type was usually found in the reception rooms of a *bourgeois* house. Precious woods, rich fabrics and finely-executed carving endowed this furniture with all the attributes of elegance and good taste. Generally accessible only to the wealthiest members of Quebec society, furniture of this class invariably reflected the tastes of the time, echoing the fashions and styles popular in Europe and the United States.

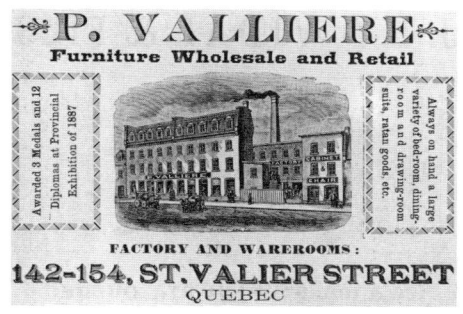

320
Advertisement for the firm of Philippe Vallière of Quebec City
Published in L'Indicateur de Québec et Lévis 1891-1892 (Quebec City: Boulanger and Marcotte, 1891)
Photo National Library of Canada, Ottawa (NC-17932)

321
Furniture Department of the British Section
Engraving published in the Illustrated London News, June 8, 1867
Bibliothèque municipale de Montréal
Photo Brian Merrett/MMFA
This engraving was published during the universal exhibition held in Paris in 1867.

Drawing-room suites, ideal symbols of their owners' social success, offered furniture makers the chance to display all their art and skill. In recognition of the important role played by these "symbols", the prizes awarded in this category were particularly enticing. Drawing-room furniture thus monopolized the attention of both judges and critics, and of the furniture makers themselves.

However, opulence and wealth had also to be displayed in the dining-room furniture – especially the sideboard – and the pieces adorning the principal bedrooms, and exhibition participants were evidently keen to display particularly high-quality items in these categories also.

As the growing needs of the *nouveaux riches* led to an increase in the number of rooms and, as a consequence, a greater variety of furniture, new categories of furniture were introduced. For example, the entrance hall, boudoir, office and library soon boasted their own particular range of appointments. From this period on, any form of innovation – in design, execution, comfort or style – meant certain success, both with the general public and the judges.

DRAWING-ROOM FURNITURE

A number of stylistic choices were available when it came to adorning the main room of the house, ranging from the rare to the ordinary, the distinctly odd to the highly functional. Members of the middle classes generally chose a drawing-room suite that included a sofa, armchairs, several straighter chairs and a selection of tables. They might also opt for a settee, an ottoman or love seat, or an S-shaped couch variously known as a "tête-à-tête", a "companion chair" or a "conversation chair". Other pieces commonly found in this important room included cabinets, desks, screens, mirrors, whatnots and miscellaneous tables chosen for their elegant design and fine workmanship.

There was also a good deal of diversity in the precious woods from which these furnishings were made. Black walnut, the preeminent Quebec variety, was much favoured by furniture makers, but rosewood, ebony and mahogany were also extremely popular. In upholstery fabrics, the fashion was for coarse silk brocade in crimson, red or green; brocaded cord; horsehair; red or green damask; green pekin; crimson or green silk rep; crimson, gold or red satin; and pale blue, natural, olive, gold, red or green silk. As to the designs, a whole host of new patterns were available in the second half of the nineteenth century, plus many others inspired by the styles of earlier periods.

At the provincial exhibition held in Quebec City in 1877, the "furniture" class offered for the admiration of visitors two suites by Philippe Vallière, both awarded first prize. One, a "true work of art", was covered with red damask and ornamented with several garlands of roses intertwined with mixed foliage. The decoration and fabric of the chairs and settee were identical, and even "the most practised eye was unable to perceive the smallest difference".[11] It is clear from the description that this ensemble was in the rococo-revival style so popular at the time. The other drawing-room suite was covered in green damask and adorned with gilded rails.

DINING-ROOM FURNITURE

For the sumptuous suites required for the dining room, furniture makers generally employed rosewood, oak, marquetry or black walnut. We can glean information on some of the pieces displayed in the 1882 exhibition from contemporary newspaper articles. For example, we know that a certain William Scott won first prize for his dark oak dining-room set, whose table was adorned with bronze shelves and painted tiles. And in the same category there was an adjustable table that could be extended to a length of eighteen feet. This piece was a recent production of the McGarvey store, as were the black walnut chairs covered in leather that accompanied it.

The main function of the sideboard was to hold china and silverware. It was generally made of precious woods such as mahogany, oak, bird's-eye maple or different types of walnut, and the sideboard's various surfaces were often richly carved or decorated with some handworked material fashionable at the time. A number of furniture makers used glass as an additional material, and gilding was occasionally employed to highlight the decorative carving. More often than not, these pieces displayed a highly specialized iconography considered suitable to their function, which included hunting and fishing scenes, flowers, bunches of fruit and cornucopia.

In honour of the Prince of Wales's visit to the Montreal exhibition of 1860, the Oshawa Cabinet Factory of Western Canada submitted an extremely elaborate sideboard. The central panel and cupboard doors were adorned with mirrors, garlands and scrollwork. The crown and sides of the central panel were decorated with a profusion of bunches of grapes, cornucopia and flowers, and the main shelf was supported by additional scrollwork.

BEDROOM FURNITURE

Visitors to the exhibitions were faced with an impressive array of choices when it came to those items of furniture associated with sleep and daily ablutions. Normally, bedroom displays included beds, commodes, chiffonniers and a variety of washstands. But that was not all. Year after year, the bedroom furniture on view included suites that might also comprehend a wardrobe, with or without a mirror, desks, tables, chairs, and various types of couch designed for reclining that served as an alternative to the bed. Again, the fur-

322

The Crystal Palace at Montreal, Inaugurated on Saturday, August 25, 1860, by His Royal Highness the Prince of Wales
Engraving published in the New York Illustrated News, September 8, 1860
Photo SRP

niture in this category was made of a wide range of woods. Black walnut continued to be popular, but mahogany, rosewood, oak, bird's-eye maple, ash, butter-nut, pine and basswood were also used, together with a few more exotic varieties. Some items were gilded, enamelled, painted, carved or artistically decorated with painted scenes. Marble shelves and mirrors were also often integrated into furniture used for storage.

At the Montreal exhibition of 1858, Jean-Marie Papineau presented a suite of pine bedroom furnishings painted in black and gold and decorated with scenes executed by an artist called Cotter. It is not impossible that this "Cotter" was actually E. T. Cotton, who was responsible for the decoration of a suite of bedroom furniture now in the collection of the Canadian Museum of Civilization.[12] Whatever the case, here is what a journalist writing in *La Minerve* said of the 1858 ensemble:

323-325

> In the realm of fine furniture, it is not possible to import from abroad anything that surpasses the finish and the admirable and elegant designs that adorn these pieces. It is acknowledged that with this collection Mr. J. M. Papineau joins the ranks of the very best furniture makers in Montreal, and perhaps in the whole of Canada. The amount of work that has gone into the pieces on view, the sums they must have cost and the paintwork and designs that decorate them are all clear testimony to Mr. Papineau's skill and enterprise.[13]

323
Rococo-revival bed, about 1860
Detail of the head
Black-lacquered basswood, polychrome paint,
148 x 161 x 211 cm
Canadian Museum of Civilization, Hull (982.16.1)
The painted decoration on this bed was designed to commemorate the Prince of Wales's visit to Montreal in 1860 for the opening of the Victoria Bridge. The view of the bridge is signed by E. T. Cotton.

Of all the items of bedroom furniture, the bed was awarded particular attention, and during the nineteenth century specific needs led to the development of a host of different types. These ranged from simple iron bedsteads to four posters suitable for a royal chamber, like the one presented by Drum at the exhibition of 1877 – beautifully carved and with magnificent curtains falling majestically from its summit – for the trifling sum of $120.[14] In 1882, McGarvey, always abreast of the latest innovations, exhibited a bed-lounge, a practical multi-purpose article for use in an office, library or "bachelor" apartment, or in large families. At the same exhibition, also at McGarvey's extensive display, the public were able to admire a folding bedstead covered in dark morocco leather. Two years later, the same manufacturer exhibited a sofa bed covered in crimson velvet.

In contrast to the extremely elaborate bedroom suites available, consisting of numerous pieces, the firm of Baker and Julien designed a compact "box" arrangement that combined all the different elements. At the exhibition of 1881, they won first prize for a folding cabinet that included a bed (also folding), a washstand, a wardrobe, a bureau with a mirror and a bookshelf. This rather odd contraption was applauded in the following terms: "The best description we can give of it is that in a large room, by means of this combination, three or four persons may have entirely separate apartments containing all the comforts included above."[15]

ENTRANCE HALL, LIBRARY AND OFFICE FURNITURE

In the early provincial exhibitions some displays included a few coat stands, often combined with umbrella and hat stands,[16] together with library tables and desks, various types of bookcase, and a wide range of office furniture. Furniture makers were evidently concerned to develop new forms in this category, and to add new uses to the basic functions of the usual pieces. Generally speaking, furniture in this class was made of walnut, oak, mahogany or cast iron.

324
Rococo-revival washstand, about 1860
Black-laquered basswood, polychrome paint,
104 x 106 x 46 cm
Canadian Museum of Civilization, Hull (982.16.3)
Photo Christine Guest/MMFA

TABLES

Year after year, dozens of tables of widely diverse shapes and functions were displayed for the appreciation of the crowd. There was always considerable interest shown in consoles, which were often accompanied by a mirror, and in pedestal tables, both of which were considered a chic addition to any Quebec interior. Magnificent dining tables and centre tables – also called drawing-room tables – were subjected to close scrutiny, for they had become absolute "musts" for any self-respecting *bourgeois* household. There were also a few rare library tables, and a host of others for private or small group activities, such as card tables, tea tables,[17] chess tables and billiard tables, all highly tempting to those wishing to be at the pinnacle of fashion. Ladies were faced with a bewildering choice of writing tables, work tables and dressing tables designed especially for them, which were available every year in the most up-to-date styles.

Even discounting tables made of marquetry, a wide variety of woods was employed in the manufacture of these many tables. Furniture makers commonly used mahogany, rosewood, ebony, bird's-eye maple, various types of walnut (especially black walnut), elm and pine. Moreover, other materials were often combined with the precious woods. Some table tops were made of marble or limestone, and glass and certain precious metals were also sometimes used. Other tables were painted so as to imitate mahogany or oak, or even marble, while some were adorned with painted historical scenes. Many were carved with motifs of zoological, botanical or anthropomorphic

325
Rococo-revival dressing table with mirror, about 1860
Black-lacquered basswood, polychrome paint,
115 x 110.5 x 53.5 cm
Canadian Museum of Civilization, Hull (982.16.2)
Photo Christine Guest/MMFA

inspiration. And as well as the usually geometrical shapes, there were a few tables of distinctly unusual form.[18]

But of all the many tables available, it was the marquetry table, veritable mosaic of precious woods, that reigned supreme. Some of the pieces in this medium produced by furniture makers and craftsmen for the provincial exhibitions were examples of true virtuosity. And it was painstaking and arduous work, as Louis Lecomte, a young artisan from the Saint-Sauveur district

326
Advertisement for the firm of Owen McGarvey & Son of Montreal
Published in La Patrie, September 18, 1896
National Library of Canada, Ottawa (NL-17948)

of Quebec City, confided to a journalist from *L'Événement* during the provincial exhibition of 1877:

> He devoted himself every evening for thirteen months to the execution of this table, which must have required the patience of an angel and considerable skill. The table is three feet in diameter and is composed of 2,649 pieces; the craftsman employed thirty-eight different types of wood in its making. His plan was to make a flower design inside a frame. He has achieved his aim: he was able to obtain hard wood in all sorts of shades, and has succeeded in portraying a magnificent bouquet of flowers, whose colours harmonize admirably. The pedestal is also in marquetry. The table's polish could not be better, and the smoothness of the surface is remarkable. The piece has been admired by all who have seen it. The young craftsman is asking $200, and adds that he would not be prepared to undertake another for the same price. I quite believe him.[19]

The most spectacular marquetry table was included in Owen McGarvey's display at the exhibition of 1882. As well as being composed of 9,000 pieces of black walnut and a variety of other woods, the table's octagonal top was decorated with carved shells and sixteen radiating diamond shapes encircling eight scenes depicting a variety of subjects.[20]

CHAIRS

The production of chairs with many different functions flourished during the period of the provincial exhibitions. And as the functions became more numerous, so did the shapes become more varied. Alongside standard items in many different styles were a number of patent chairs, developed in response to users' increasingly specific needs. As in the other categories of furniture, the chairs presented in the exhibitions aimed at luxury, comfort and uniqueness of design, rather than the simple domestic usefulness required by most Quebec households. Chairs as such did not constitute a category at the provincial exhibitions. Instead, there were a number of more specific categories – such as "best armchair", or "best dining-room chairs" – which varied considerably from year to year. Owen McGarvey presented the most impressive number of chairs in the Montreal exhibitions, and was responsible for introducing a wide variety of styles and types.

OTHER FURNITURE

Among the other types of furniture displayed by the many exhibitors in the "furniture" class, there was a marked preference for various kinds of cabinet, businessmen's desks, ladies' writing desks and whatnots. Additional items included in the class were easels, lecterns, screens, frames of all sorts, flower stands or jardinières and ladies' workboxes. Finally, the category was completed by a number of articles we shall not be discussing in detail, among them harmoniums, organs, pianos, piano stools, music stands and canterburys, clocks, mantelpieces and a variety of mirrors.

STYLISTIC ECLECTICISM

In the Quebec of this period, there was the same continuing propensity for revivalist styles that existed in Europe and the United States. This is confirmed by the content of the provincial exhibitions, which were a reflection of what was most popular and most frequently purchased by the province's wealthiest citizens. Some contemporary documents make mention of the styles of particular pieces on display, occasionally providing sufficient detail to enable us to distinguish one style from another.

In 1850, at the Bonsecours Market, Reed & Meakins presented some fourteenth-century-style chairs, also referred to as "antique". The same chairs were on view at London's Great Exhibition, in 1851, and were reproduced in a special issue of the *Art Journal* published that same year.[21] At the local exhibition held in Quebec City in 1853, the furniture maker François Lafleur, whose firm was located on the Côte d'Abraham, exhibited a bedstead in the Louis XV style. Twelve years later, at the Montreal exhibition, the Renaissance seems to have been the major source of inspiration, with a sideboard in this style by André Molinelli attracting particular attention. James Thomson also exhibited a sideboard and a centre table that included Renaissance-inspired elements in their design, together with a whatnot labelled as being in the "classical" style. In 1870, William Drum made an attempt to break into the Montreal market, exhibiting drawing-room furniture said to be in the purest of "Parisian" styles.

At the 1871 exhibition held in Quebec City the competition between Drum, Gourdeau and Vallière in the "drawing-room furnishings" category was fierce. The three vied for first place, the two former each presenting a complete drawing-room suite in the Elizabethan-revival style, the latter opting for a Louis XV-style ensemble. At the exhibition of 1873, the Montreal furniture maker Azarie Lavigne submitted a Greek-revival wardrobe and a Louis XV-style drawing-room suite. In 1877, Drum and Vallière were once again rivals in the race for medals, and both again submitted drawing-room furniture in the Elizabethan-revival style. Vallière, however, was more ambitious, exhibiting in addition two other drawing-room suites, one in the "American" style and another in the "French".

The many styles on view at the 1880 Montreal exhibition testify to the eclecticism of the period. Owen McGarvey's display included a complete bedroom set in the Queen Anne-revival style, an Eastlake-style sideboard and a Gothic-revival clock, together with a host of other items. A little further on, R. Constantine was exhibiting two cabinets, one Queen Anne revival and one inspired by the Empire style. Among the objects displayed by James Thomson were a Queen Anne-revival bedroom suite and a chair labelled as "Japanese" style. Finally, the picture was completed by J.A.I. Craig's submission of a set of boudoir furniture in the Louis XVI style.

The Louis XVI style was also the choice of Azarie Lavigne for the dining-room suite he exhibited in 1881, and Owen McGarvey was faithful to the Queen Anne style in the table and music cabinet he presented in 1882, and to the Eastlake style in the sideboard he submitted that same year.

THE MAIN CONTENDERS IN MONTREAL
Between 1850 and 1870, the largest number of important prizes given at the Montreal provincial exhibitions was won by the Hiltons. This father-son partnership, which began in 1845 and lasted until the John's death in 1866, received numerous money prizes, as well as a good number of diplomas, first and second prizes, and other types of award. Moreover, as sole owner of the

327
Armchair made by Reed & Meakins of Montreal and Presented by the Ladies of That City to Queen Victoria
Engraving published in Industry of All Nations: The Art-Journal Illustrated Catalogue (London: George Virtue, 1851), p. 199
Library of the Montreal Museum of Fine Arts
Photo Christine Guest/MMFA
In the illustrated catalogue the chair is wrongly attributed to the Hiltons.

THE FURNITURE MAKERS

328

Provincial Industrial Exhibition of Canada, Held at Montreal. The North Hall

Engraving after a drawing by Martin Somerville published in the Illustrated London News, November 23, 1850

Bibliothèque municipale de Montréal
Photo Brian Merrett/MMFA

In the foreground can be seen the drawing-room furniture by John and William Hilton that was chosen for the Great Exhibition held in London in 1851.

329

Provincial Industrial Exhibition of Canada, Held at Montreal. The South Hall

Engraving after a drawing by Martin Somerville published in the Illustrated London News, November 23, 1850

Bibliothèque municipale de Montréal
Photo Brian Merrett/MMFA

Agricultural produce occupied an important place in the provincial exhibitions. Fruit, vegetables, tools and machinery were exhibited alongside ornately-framed paintings and elegant furniture.

family firm William Hilton was extremely successful at the 1868 and 1870 exhibitions. He died in 1876.

During the Hiltons' "reign", the major prize-winner at the Quebec City exhibitions, William Drum, made an attempt to break onto the Montreal scene by competing at the exhibitions of 1850 and 1870. Owen McGarvey, for his part, began to show works at the exhibitions of 1855, 1857 and 1858, not

331

330

without a certain success. The Hiltons' predominance reached its highest point in 1863 and 1865, years in which the firm won about fifteen major awards.

The most complete and varied display put on by the Hiltons was presented at the Montreal exhibition of 1865, when visitors could admire some thirty pieces and groups of furniture produced in their workshops. Of this record number of articles six were awarded first prizes by the judges, and the firm also won two seconds and a special prize.[22] James Thomson likewise did well at this exhibition, winning three first prizes.[23] And at the same event, a rather unusual sideboard — "a low buffet of black walnut, Renaissance style, with carving depicting a variety of hunting and fishing themes"[24] — which seems to have inspired a number of Montreal cabinetmakers, confirmed the talent of furniture maker André Molinelli, who had recently arrived in the city and set up shop on St. Lawrence Street. This single participation by Molinelli in the provincial exhibitions attracted considerable attention; a journalist of the *Montreal Weekly Witness* wrote of the prize-winning piece:

> A. Molinelli, cabinet-maker, of St. Lawrence street, contributes only one article, but that article is worth a legion of such monstrosities as we have before now seen paraded at Provincial Exhibitions. It is a sideboard, and without disparagement to other contributors, we are disposed to give it the palm over every other one on view. The design has been carefully made and consistently carried out, whilst the fingers of the workman have executed with a rare adroitness and effect the conception of the designer's brain. It is difficult to indicate special points of excellence, since the whole is so meritorious and even in its effect upon

330
Advertisement for the firm of Azarie Lavigne of Montreal
Published in La Minerve, March 9, 1874
National Library of Canada, Ottawa (NL-17943)

331
The Montreal Exhibition. Interior of the Main Building
Engraving published in the Canadian Illustrated News, September 30, 1882
National Archives of Canada, Ottawa (C-77374)
As in a number of other major Canadian and American cities, a building was erected in Montreal inspired by the Crystal Palace designed by Paxton for London's Great Exhibition of 1851. In 1880 the Montreal version, built in 1860 after plans by John William Hopkins, was transported from Sainte-Catherine Street to near Jeanne-Mance Park. It was destroyed by fire in 1896.

THE FURNITURE MAKERS

332
Poster for the provincial exhibition held in Montreal in 1884
214 x 108 cm
Bibliothèque nationale du Québec, Montreal

333
Advertisement for the firm of H. A. Wilder & Co. of Montreal
Published in the Montreal Star, August 21, 1897
Photo SRP

334
The Quebec Provincial Exhibition
Engraving after a drawing by William Ogle Carlisle published in the Canadian Illustrated News, October 7, 1871
National Archives of Canada, Ottawa (C-56518)

the eye, and for that very reason it may not at first strike the observer so forcibly, a condition which attaches itself to most of the acknowledged master-pieces of art.[25]

William Hilton took the lion's share of the awards yet again during the 1868 and 1870 exhibitions. With these final contributions, he brought to a close a twenty-year period of success on the Montreal provincial exhibition scene, years punctuated by submissions to the London and Paris competitions that added to the already considerable prestige of the famous firm. During the decade following 1870, the province of Quebec went through a serious economic depression. The slump affected the furniture industry like any other, and a number of manufacturers were obliged to close down. Only a single provincial exhibition was held in Montreal during this period, in 1873. The Hiltons were no longer active, and Owen McGarvey did not participate. This left the field clear for Azarie Lavigne, an ex-employee of the Hiltons, to display all the latest products from his St. Lawrence Street store, to win two first prizes, and to publicize his success in a major advertising campaign.[26]

By the early 1880s, the economy had begun to pick up and Montreal, given an additional boost by the railway that now linked it to Quebec City and Ottawa, organized four major provincial exhibitions, held one after the other in 1880, 1881, 1882 and 1884. As far as the "furniture" class was concerned, 1880 was the year of Adolphe Bélanger, while 1881 was dominated by the Dogherty firm.[27] However, it was the furniture displays of 1882 and 1884 that went down in history as the most important of all the provincial exhibitions held in Quebec between 1850 and 1900, both in terms of the number of pieces presented and the press coverage they received. These two major exhibitions also fully established the prestige and influence of the firms of Owen McGarvey & Son and Adolphe Bélanger.[28]

Visitors who passed through the doors of the "Crystal Palace", which housed the exhibition of 1882, were able to admire close to a hundred pieces and groups of furniture, of which almost half were part of Owen McGarvey &

336

Son's celebrated display. Some ten furniture makers – notable among whom were Adolphe Bélanger and William Scott – competed in about fifty different categories. This explains why so many first prizes were awarded: nine went to Bélanger, eight to McGarvey and three to Scott. Where one received the gold medal in a given category, another was awarded the silver. It was at the 1884 exhibition that McGarvey and Bélanger competed for the last time, the former winning four first prizes and five diplomas, the latter ten first prizes and a silver medal.

The Montreal exhibitions of the last decade of the nineteenth century, held virtually every year, were transformed into enormous fairs. The various classes and categories in the industrial section soon outstripped the number of pages available in the newspapers, and the journalists assigned to cover the events considerably reduced the number of specialized articles devoted to them. In fact, it seems that the general public and the media had to some extent lost interest in Quebec furniture. This indifference was no doubt the result of the growing mediocrity of the designs, the retirement of certain major furniture makers and the increased availability of consumer products.

THE MAIN CONTENDERS IN QUEBEC CITY

In Quebec City the displays of William Drum and Philippe Vallière dominated the provincial exhibitions, clearly reflecting these firms' industrial and commercial success. However, the provincial exhibition of 1871 was the scene of a particularly fierce confrontation that put the critical faculties and aesthetic judgement of journalists and public alike to a severe test and sparked lively arguments rooted in differing criteria of "good taste". The displays of Drum and Vallière were ardently defended in the newspapers of the time by their English- and French-speaking compatriots, episode following episode almost like a serialized novel. Attempts were even made to influence the judges' decision by invoking public favour. The considerable wealth of one of the makers, Drum, allowed him to present furniture designed especially for the exhibition, while the other, Vallière, succeeded in executing a suite of furniture of superior quality simply through hard work, in spite of more limited resources.[29]

Good sense seems to have triumphed over this example of "racial jealousy", for Drum and Vallière shared the first and second prizes equally between them. As to the triumph of "good taste", so difficult a concept to define, it resided surely in the capacity of the judges and some journalists to

335

335
Canadian Trophy for the Paris Exhibition
Engraving published in the Illustrated London News, April 13, 1878
Bibliothèque municipale de Montréal
Photo Brian Merrett/MMFA

336
Grand Panorama of the Great Exhibition. North-West Portion of the Nave
Engraving after a daguerreotype by Claudet published in the Illustrated London News, January 3, 1852
Bibliothèque municipale de Montréal
Photo Brian Merrett/MMFA
This view shows the British furniture section.

THE FURNITURE MAKERS

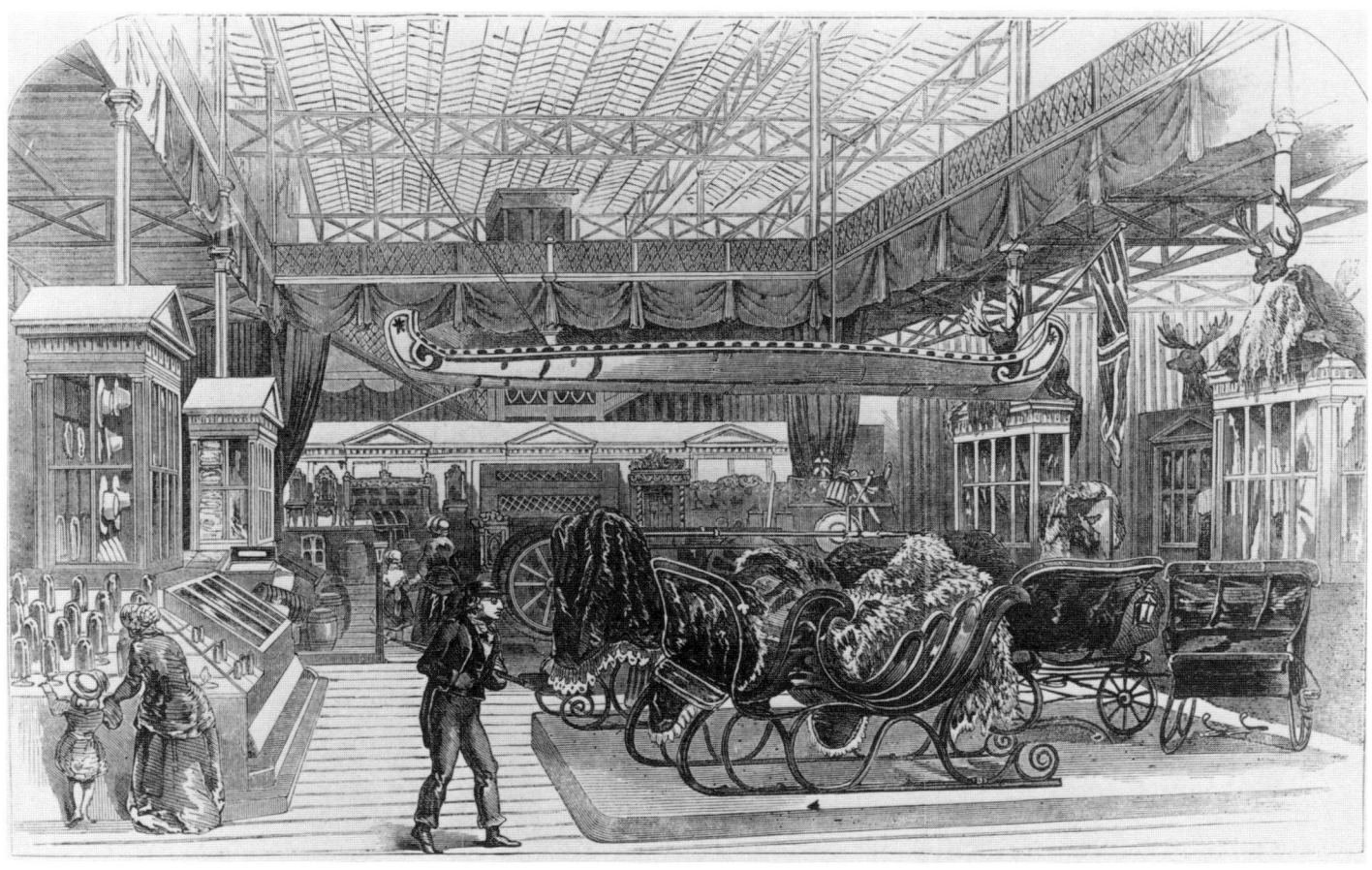

337
The Canadian Court
Engraving published in the Illustrated London News, May 31, 1851
Library of Bishop's University, Lennoxville
Photo SRP
Here, the display of Canadian furniture can be seen in the background.

acknowledge the quality of Quebec City's furniture industry rather than in the glorification of one style over another.[30] Drum and Vallière were once again rivals at the exhibition of 1877, but there was no repetition of the controversy of 1871.[31]

THE PARTICIPATION OF QUEBEC FURNITURE MAKERS IN INTERNATIONAL EXHIBITIONS

Participation in the major international and universal exhibitions held during the second half of the nineteenth century was a source of some pride to Canada's government, officials, organizers and exhibitors. The country eagerly accepted invitations from abroad, as well as reserving display space in the majority of the exhibitions held. From 1867 until the turn of the century, the Canadian presence at these events grew steadily. The design and lay-out of the stands displaying Canadian products also improved progressively, influenced by the fashions of the day and the resources and effort invested. A number of Quebec furniture makers, for the most part English-speaking, took part in these major international expositions. It seems, however, that their works were largely overshadowed by other Canadian products – in particular raw materials, which were of prime interest to other nations – not to mention the furniture produced by major European and American manufacturers.

The representatives of the Quebec furniture industry present at London's Crystal Palace in 1851 were largely members of Montreal's English-speaking community, as indeed were most of the organizers of the Canadian

338

Furniture by J. & W. Hilton presented at the universal exhibition held in London in 1851
Engraving published in Industry of All Nations: The Art-Journal Illustrated Catalogue (London: George Virtue, 1851), p. 119
Library of the Montreal Museum of Fine Arts
Photo Christine Guest/MMFA

The catalogue states: "The pieces are made of black walnut, boldly carved, and the chairs are covered with gold and crimson damask."

339

The Trophy Erected in the Middle of the Canadian Section, in the "annexe du bord de l'eau", Composed of the Contributions of the Exhibitors of Forestry Productions
Engraving published in Joseph-Charles Taché, Canada at the Universal Exhibition of 1855 (Toronto: Lovell, 1856), frontispiece
National Archives of Canada, Ottawa (C-137772)

delegation. Furniture makers such as Allen, Cameron, Hammond, Hilton, Morrice, Ramsay & McArthur, Readhead and Reed & Meakins, almost all of whom had been in business since the mid-1840s, submitted between them about thirty pieces of furniture, mostly intended for the drawing room. The items included various types of chair and armchair, sofas, a companion chair, a selection of tables and consoles, a chiffonnier and a bedstead. These pieces seem to have more effectively aroused the curiosity of the British public than the admiration of the judges. And the same was true for the only exhibit from Quebec City — six chairs submitted by William Drum.

At the universal exhibition held in Paris in 1855, the number of participating Quebec furniture makers dropped sharply. Nonetheless, the event included works by Drum, the Hiltons and McGarvey — a rare conjuncture —

340

Jean-Baptiste Returning from the 1876 Exhibition with His Prizes

Engraving after a drawing by Henri Julien (1851-1908) published in L'Opinion publique, October 19, 1876

Photo SRP

In the province of Quebec, the character of Jean-Baptiste symbolized all French Canadians, much as the people of England were symbolized by John Bull.

341

The Game and Fur Trophy in the Canadian Court

Engraving published in the Illustrated London News, August 14, 1886

Library of Bishop's University, Lennoxville

Photo SRP

The hunting trophy presented at the Colonial and Indian Exhibition held in London in 1886 conveyed something of the exoticism associated with Canada's wide open spaces.

the latter exhibiting for the first time at such an event. The two former manufacturers were each awarded a second-class medal for pieces that research indicates were the same as those exhibited in London a few years earlier. As for McGarvey, he received an honourable mention for a series of rocking chairs. As well as the items already mentioned, the exhibition included a glass table by the Montreal glassmaker J. C. Spence and a chair by a certain Captain Rhodes of Quebec City.

The furniture maker Pierre Roy of Quebec City is the only representative of the province known to have submitted a work to the international exhibition held in Dublin in 1865. This event, on a somewhat smaller scale than those of London and Paris, nevertheless provided Canadians with an opportunity to display the country's raw materials to an Irish public. Pierre Roy and the Toronto firm of Jacques & Hay each presented a marquetry table whose top was composed of a veritable mosaic of Canadian woods.

Dublin, p. 392

At the Paris universal exhibition of 1867, the honour of representing the Quebec furniture industry fell once again to three English-speaking manufacturers from Montreal: Owen McGarvey, James Thomson and Barrington & Perry. The former received an honourable mention for his overall presentation, about which contemporary sources give no details. The two others submitted respectively a table and a coat rack.

The selection of works presented by William Drum at the universal exhibition held in Philadelphia in 1876 was by far the most interesting submission of Quebec furniture. The display consisted of a set of boudoir furniture, two bedroom suites and a sideboard. How did Drum fare when it came to the awarding of the medals? We do not yet have the answer, although we do know that R. Hay & Co. of Toronto won a silver medal for a sideboard, and J.A.I. Craig of Montreal received a bronze for his display cabinets.

340

THE PARTICIPATION OF THE McGARVEYS IN INTERNATIONAL AND UNIVERSAL EXHIBITIONS

After 1870, it seems that fewer and fewer representatives of the Quebec industry were keen to try their luck on the international scene. Was it that the conditions for admission had become too complicated? Was the selection process more severe? Was there a falling off of interest in exhibiting abroad? Was the foreign competition too strong? Were quotas imposed? We have, as yet, answers to none of these questions. One thing is clear, though: only a single firm was prepared to ignore all such considerations and to continue to participate actively in major international expositions: the Montreal manufacturer McGarvey.[32] The firm submitted furniture to the Paris universal exhibition of 1878, to the one held in Antwerp in 1885, and to the colonial and Indian exhibition that took place in London in 1886. Their contributions earned the firm a series of first prizes, and silver and bronze medals, together with quite a selection of diplomas and certificates.

It seems clear that we cannot attribute the low participation of Quebec furniture makers in international and universal exhibitions to a lack of information, for the formula was a well-known one, used frequently in the various provincial and national exhibitions. Moreover, the Canadian government took advantage of its official press network to encourage potential exhibitors to take part, as well as making a number of appeals in various newspapers. The latter also published both articles from abroad and pieces signed by Canadian representatives. And a few Quebec furniture makers did succeed in making a small showing on the international scene. But there was little reason to imagine that such contributions might lead to an opening up of new foreign markets. All Quebec exhibitors could hope for was the opportunity to use press reviews of their international displays as support for their local advertising.

LOCAL PRESS COVERAGE OF QUEBEC FURNITURE PRESENTED AT PROVINCIAL EXHIBITIONS

The provincial exhibitions were extremely popular and generated a good number of reviews in the newspapers of the period. These reviews throw valuable light on contemporary attitudes towards Victorian furniture in Quebec. Critics seem to have had two main preoccupations: the formal and aesthetic aspects of the furniture on the one hand, and its functionality and originality on the other.

The fine furniture of the period was intended to embody such values as "beauty", "elegance", "luxury" and "wealth", and the pieces presented at exhibitions were designed to inspire the admiration of those who saw them. These often extremely expensive articles were expected to convey an impression of distinction, sumptuousness and magnificence. Participating manufacturers generally presented their most elaborate pieces: those that had cost the most to make and had taken the longest; those that had required the skills of the best carvers and the highest paid painter-decorators; those for which the finest woods and the most luxurious fabrics had been used to execute the most refined designs. Moreover, in creating these works Quebec furniture makers frequently drew inspiration from the various revival styles so popular at the time in France, Great Britain and the United States and so much admired by their clients.

The innovative aspects of the pieces were evaluated in terms of such notions as "convenience", "comfort", "durability", "progress", "strength", "utility", "diversity" and "variety". Closely associated with the needs of the *nouveaux riches* and with recent advances in technology, these concepts became integral to the furniture produced here. An exhibition piece would thus gain the favour of the critics if it satisfied a need, if it was synonymous with comfort, if it was robust and hard-wearing. Moreover, it would often belong to a set of varying pieces all marked by the same functionality.

Reviewers also sometimes made mention of the furniture makers themselves. The furniture industry employed hundreds of workers in Montreal and Quebec City, and the exhibitions provided journalists with an opportunity to encourage their efforts and stimulate the production of the various workshops, factories and industrial outfits, as was done for other sectors of the economy. However, when the time came to select the winners in the various categories a partisan spirit often took hold, and views were frequently influenced by whether the reviewer wrote for a Montreal or a Quebec City newspaper, or whether the paper was published in French or English.

LOCAL PRESS COVERAGE OF THE PRODUCTIONS OF MONTREAL FURNITURE MAKERS

The reviews sparked by the Montreal exhibitions throw a good deal of light on the principal criteria by which furniture was judged during the Victorian era. For instance, one journalist noted that Noël Pratte's display at the Montreal exhibition of 1868 offered "comfort and solidity at reasonable prices", while William Hilton's presented "all the elegance of the most refined luxury".[33] During the Montreal exhibition of 1880, a journalist writing for *The Gazette* underlined the "richness of effect, taste in design, variety [and] utility" of the works presented by Owen McGarvey.[34] This list of qualities does not, however, seem to have moved the journalist from *La Minerve*, who dwelt on quite different aspects of the McGarveys' display for that year:

> The collection of Mr. Owen McGarvey looks a bit like a bazaar. It is not that the pieces are inferior, but they are there in such profusion that it spoils the overall effect. From among this disparate group we noticed a chair made of horn, furniture made of gold-inlaid ebony, other pieces in walnut inlaid with enamel, etc. All this is very rich, but is more fantasy than luxury.[35]

Apart from the many diverging opinions, the most extensive review is the one dealing with McGarvey's large display at the Montreal exhibition that took place two years later, in 1882. Another article published in *The Gazette* covers all the principal criteria considered important in appreciating Quebec furniture toward the end of the Victorian era. This article, which appeared initially in English, was largely translated and published as an official statement in *La Minerve*.[36]

LOCAL PRESS COVERAGE OF THE PRODUCTIONS OF QUEBEC CITY FURNITURE MAKERS

In articles on fine furniture published in the Quebec City newspapers of the period, we find the same preoccupations as those expressed by Montreal journalists. Articles published in *L'Événement* in 1871 and 1877 make reference to a number of the notions mentioned earlier. However, what is most striking on reading some of the Quebec City articles is their chauvinistic tone, especially during the provincial exhibition of 1871. In fact, this tone had been set as early as 1860, when a journalist from the *Journal de Québec*, who had visited the Crystal Palace, wrote:

> The furniture I saw there was nothing special; the carving is poor and crude. What difference is there between all this and some of the most recent pieces produced by the workshops of Mr. Drum?[37]

This partisan spirit reached a climax when four Quebec City papers published similar articles during the exhibition of 1871. No Montreal furniture makers had accepted the Quebec City authorities' invitation to take part. The Old Capital was facing something of an industrial slump, however, and was counting on its furniture industry to help pull it out of the depression. On September 13, the following words appeared on page 2 of *Le Canadien*:

> We must say at the outset that our Quebec City furniture makers have proven themselves first-rate and we can only regret that Montreal's manufacturers saw fit to abstain from coming to compete with them, in the fear perhaps of being eclipsed (trans.).

The following day, page 2 of the *Journal de Québec* continued in the same vein:

> At the forefront of our Quebec City manufacturers, both for quality and enterprise, are Messrs. Vallière and Drum, who own two of the largest cabinetmaking establishments in Canada and can easily defend the honour of our city against all comers (trans.).

On the first page of the September 18 edition of *L'Événement*, we may read:

> I would like very much to have seen Montreal's furniture makers alongside those of Quebec City; this would certainly have offered greater variety, but in truth I do not believe that quality of workmanship, excellence of design and good taste can be taken much further in this field than they have been by the craftsmen, one might even say the furniture artists of Quebec City (trans.).

Finally, on September 21, *L'Opinion publique* published on page 462 this extravagantly positive review:

> Have you seen the furniture produced by Vallière, Gourdeau and Drum? What choice of woods, what polish, what tooling! what taste in the shapes and proportions! I have never seen anything like it before. Of course, Quebec City has the best cabinetmakers in the Province (trans.).

During the same exhibition, another debate absorbed the attention of readers. This was the dispute between *The Morning Chronicle*, an English paper published in Quebec City, and *L'Opinion publique*, a French paper published in Montreal. On September 13 and 14, the English paper published two articles in support of William Drum. According to the decision of the jury, the prestigious first prize for drawing-room furniture was awarded to Philippe Vallière, the young Quebec City manufacturer; however, according to *The Morning Chronicle* the prize should have gone to Drum, for he had executed an extremely expensive drawing-room suite especially for the exhibition. The *Chronicle*'s position inspired the wrath of *L'Opinion publique*, in particular of journalist André-Napoléon Montpetit:

> An English newspaper of this city seems to wish to criticize the verdict of the jury, who awarded a greater number of prizes to Mr. Vallière than to Mr. Drum. This is wrong; it shows a want of tact towards the judges, all of whom are eminently competent men and several of whom are masters of their craft. To each his own, we say. The jury employed to judge the relative merits of the furniture would perhaps not be able to appreciate the literary qualities of the *Chronicle*'s articles; similarly, we question the extent of the publication's knowledge of cabinetmaking.
>
> If the article were signed by men as expert in the field as those on the committee, then we would be more disposed to pay attention. As it is, the paper's criticism is simply an expression of disappointment, or possibly racial jealousy.
>
> While not denying Mr. Drum's obvious merits, we are swift to defend our young compatriot, who, through energy and sacrifice, and with relatively limited financial resources, nevertheless competes successfully against solid fortunes, major capital and unlimited credit.
>
> It is in relation to the awarding of the drawing-room furniture prize – the most important of all – to Mr. Vallière that the *Chronicle* voices its complaints against the jury. I took the time to examine the two selections extremely carefully, and I acknowledge that they are both perfect, although each in its own way. As there is only one prize, the issue was decided largely by taste, and taste decreed in favour of Mr. Vallière. The gentlemen at the *Chronicle* may well have heard the comments to which they refer; but for our part, we were witness on a number of occasions to expressions of exclusive admiration for Mr. Vallière's furniture. But we thought it wise to disregard them. After all, if notice were taken of all the opinions emitted, true merit would never be established. Throughout the Exhibition, I heard repeated comments to the effect that the bedroom suite in black walnut and bird's eye maple by Mr. Vallière deserved first prize; and yet the award went to Mr. Drum. However, the French papers did not protest and were very careful not to insult members of the jury by questioning either their honesty or their competence.[38]

This article is a reasonably accurate reflection of the competitive climate that reigned during the provincial exhibitions held in Quebec during the second half of the nineteenth century. Moreover, it gives us a glimpse of the problems faced regularly by judges required to make decisions based on a notion as subjective and as arbitrary as "good taste"!

LOCAL PRESS COVERAGE OF QUEBEC FURNITURE PRESENTED AT INTERNATIONAL AND UNIVERSAL EXHIBITIONS

The articles appearing in Quebec newspapers on the various Canadian submissions to international and universal exhibitions generally devoted little space to the furniture industry. The emphasis was usually on the progress made in Canada's various economic and industrial sectors, especially those related to raw materials, such as the mining and lumber industries. This is hardly surprising in view of Canada's trade relationship with the industrialized countries. On the subject of Quebec furniture shown abroad, most

342

Grand Panorama of the Great Exhibition. South-West Portion of the Nave (detail)

Engraving after a daguerreotype by Claudet published in the Illustrated London News, January 3, 1852

Bibliothèque municipale de Montréal
Photo Brian Merrett/MMFA

This image offers a view of the Canadian section at London's Great Exhibition of 1851. A wide variety of products are mentioned in the engraving's caption: silks, furniture, carpets, sledges, blankets, casks of wheat, flour, etc., a bark canoe, Perry's fire engine, tanned porpoise hides, a case of native gold from the south-eastern side of the Green Mountains, iron, lead, silver ores, and a complete collection of Canadian minerals.

journalists exhibited a resignedly realistic attitude towards the enormous gulf that separated it from the highly prestigious products of Europe and the United States. Still, encouragement was not lacking for those rare Quebec furniture makers who tried their luck on the international scene.

What seems to have caught the attention of the Quebec press during the London exhibition of 1851 was not the many pieces submitted by the province's manufacturers, but an anecdote featuring Prince Albert and the Queen herself. It seems that while the royal couple were visiting the exhibition's Canadian section, they were shown some armchairs by Reed & Meakins that bore a sign on which someone had been unwise enough to write, "For England's Queen, from the Ladies of Canada". This was an inexcusable example of lese majesty, for Victoria was in fact Queen of the United Kingdom. Despite the monarch's polite smile, Canada's officials were seriously embarrassed, and rather desperately attempted to justify the presence of chairs that "could hardly appear to advantage at Windsor Castle"[39] by speaking of the need to promote Canadian wood.[40] Opinions expressed in *Le Canadien*, rather more direct, left no doubt as to the meagre chances of Quebec furniture at the London exhibition:

> Among our furniture, there are a few excellent items; but today the fashion is for the early Renaissance style and heavy carving, and artists introduce high-relief figures wherever they can. Our furniture also possesses the fault of seeming flimsily constructed and skimpily designed. Austria will quite clearly win the honours in this section, although England and France will not be far behind.[41]

At the Paris exhibition of 1855, the Canadian representative Joseph-Charles Taché adopted a similarly realistic attitude towards the submissions of Quebec furniture. A true cosmopolitan, he waxed extremely enthusiastic about the splendid creations of French craftsmen on view before the exhibition's thousands of visitors. *La Minerve* reproduced Taché's article in its edition of December 22, 1855:

> The industries related to furnishings and decoration constitute the 24th class, in which Canada has thirteen exhibitors;[42] but apart from the interest sparked by the beauty of the "ribboned" maple used for a chair, some upholstery of embroi-

dered moose hide, which was admired, and the curiosity shown in our rocking chairs, which do not exist in Europe, it was impossible to obtain even the briefest mention; in fact, after having referred to only four pieces of foreign furniture out of the whole exhibition, of which one was designed by a Parisian artist, one serious critic, extremely well-disposed towards foreign entries, wrote that "the other countries have nothing in this section [the furniture section] that is worth mentioning". In this class of the Exhibition, success is limited to France and especially to Paris, and the only criticism offered to the class of exhibiting cabinetmakers is that they did not show ordinary furniture, for everyday use. The richness and beauty of this vast array of French furniture is indescribable.[43]

Quebec critics generally took much the same stance throughout the latter half of the nineteenth century. The success that received the greatest attention from critics was McGarvey's winning of two important medals at the exhibition held in Antwerp in 1885. Sir Charles Tupper, secretary of the executive committee for the exhibition of Canadian products, described McGarvey's works as "artistically made", "reasonably priced", " simple, neat and solid". He was a pragmatist, however, and concluded his assessment with the following moderate remarks:

> A wide selection of Canadian furniture, adapted to European tastes and entrusted to reliable agents, would undoubtedly result in considerable trade in no time at all. European buyers generally prefer to see what they are going to purchase, and photographs and engravings etc. of furniture would only cause problems and put an end to the market at the outset.[44]

FOREIGN PRESS COVERAGE OF QUEBEC FURNITURE PRESENTED AT INTERNATIONAL AND UNIVERSAL EXHIBITIONS

During the second half of the nineteenth century, France – closely followed by the United Kingdom – dominated the fine furniture industry. And while the provincial exhibitions were showcases for luxury items accessible only to Quebec's wealthiest citizens, the international and universal exhibitions reflected all the magnificence of the great courts of Europe. In fact, the major powers were more interested in getting their hands on Canada's natural resources than in encouraging its "curious products", and European and American critics showed little interest in Quebec-made furniture.

In London, in 1851, there was some acknowledgement of the pieces on view in the Canadian section, although the chief object of interest seems to have been the indulgent "smile" of Queen Victoria. The reviews published in the *Illustrated London News* refer to this event at least twice,[45] going on to note the rather unusual appearance of the furniture produced by the "Canadian colonists". The prestigious English art magazine the *Art Journal* published prints of a few pieces from the Canadian section of the 1851 exhibition in its special issue devoted to the show – a signal and unique honour; readers were even offered a glimpse of the famous chairs presented to the Queen by "the ladies of Montreal".[46]

Apart from these few anecdotal mentions, however, the harvest is poor. There seem to have been no further foreign references to Canadian furniture submissions until 1885. Sir Charles Tupper collected a few reviews that appeared that year in various European newspapers concerning the Canadian section of the Antwerp exhibition. The qualities sought at this event seem to have been "elegance", "sumptuosity", "richness", "solidity", "comfort", "progress", "innovation" and "good taste". Despite some very positive remarks, however, the astonishment expressed by Europeans regarding Canadian workmanship seems to have been universal. Here are some observations that appeared in *L'Indépendance belge*:

> There is certainly plenty of contrast, but what strikes us first and foremost is the degree of progress, one might almost say of perfection, that this country has achieved. What is astonishing to the visitor is to see, from a place where we thought such things quite non-existent, furniture of an elegance and comfort beyond reproach, entirely appropriate for a drawing room in Brussels or Antwerp. It should be added that these pieces are not so like our own that they cannot be distinguished.[47]

The general tone of the European critics did not alter until the end of the nineteenth century: there was much enthusiasm for Canadian woods but little interest in the furniture itself. An article published during the Paris universal exhibition of 1900 by the Parisian critic Henry de Varigny summarizes quite accurately the foreign attitude to fine furniture produced in Quebec during the Victorian era:

> By the furniture assembled in the Canadian pavilion, it may be judged that this country produces fine wood. The pieces are solid, a little heavy for those with a taste for the "modern style"; but of good quality, and very reasonably priced. I have even been told that the marked prices are a little high, and that the same pieces can be had in Paris for less. So much the better, from the consumer's point of view. For the rest, one cannot be too surprised: the forests of Canada are perhaps the largest in the world; and the trees can be cut and transported without difficulty, thanks to the many rivers to be used as power, and the large roads; finally, labour is not too expensive. Given all this, Canadian furniture can compete successfully with that made by Europeans in Europe, at least for ordinary, everyday items; art furniture is something else, however.[48]

Daniel Drouin

1   Early in October 1850, the city of Quebec hastily organized a local agricultural and industrial exhibition with the goal of presenting awards to the samples that would represent it at the provincial agricultural and industrial exhibition in Montreal a few days later.

2   Programme published in the *Journal de l'Instruction publique*, August 1871, p. 103 (trans.).

3   An apprentice of C. W. Meakins, an associate of the Reed & Meakins firm, was awarded a prize of two English pounds for a cradle presented at the 1850 Montreal exhibition. At the same exhibition a lady called Warren, daughter of a Montreal organist, received one pound five shillings for a pine centre table. At the exhibition held in Quebec City, in 1853, the Misses Cochrane and Taylor, of that town, were awarded respectively a prize (unidentified) and a diploma for frames and benches, and a chair embroidered with wool.

Lastly, at the 1877 exhibition in Quebec City, a lady called Farley showed a table decorated with Chinese designs executed in watercolour.

4   For example, at the local exhibition held in March 1855 in Montreal, the well-known Montreal painter-glassmaker J. C. Spence presented a drawing-room table made of inlaid glass. The piece did not win him any awards, however.

5   An article in the August-September 1931 issue of the magazine *La vie forestière* indicates that Gignac was awarded a gold medal for the writing desk at the provincial exhibition held in Montreal in 1880. Our efforts to obtain confirmation of this in contemporary newspapers have proven fruitless, however. Joseph-Honoré Gignac was a leading Quebec City wood merchant towards the end of the nineteenth century. In addition to his business activities, he published a book in 1912 entitled *Les arbres indigènes du Canada*.

6   Among those in this category were William Rodden, who presented cast iron furniture at the Montreal exhibitions of 1853, 1857 and 1858, and the firm of Meilleur & Cie, which displayed work at the 1863 Montreal exhibition.

7   The most important manufacturers in this category were members of the Tees family, from Montreal; their various firms were spread over several generations and formed a number of different associations. They took part in about ten provincial exhibitions, as well as several elsewhere in Canada and abroad.

8   Vallière took advantage of the success he achieved at the provincial exhibitions to increase his advertising.

9   According to an article on page 2 of the September 13, 1871 issue of *Le Canadien*, François Gourdeau borrowed the suite from the wealthy Quebec City merchant for whom he had made it two years before. And according to *The Herald* of September 17, 1873 (p. 2), Azarie Lavigne did the same in Montreal with a Louis XV drawing-room suite.

10   An article that appeared in *Le Courrier du Canada* on October 2, 1865 (p. 5) states that "there is not a single exhibitor from Quebec City in the cabinetwork products" (trans.). However, in the *Catalogue of the Provincial Exhibition at Montreal, September, 1865* (Montreal: John Lovell, 1865, 64 pages), Roy is clearly listed on page 47 (cat. no. 31).

11   *Le Courrier du Canada*, September 19, 1877, p. 2 (trans.).

12   However, as the bedhead is decorated with an image of Victoria Bridge, we know this suite cannot date from earlier than 1860.

13   *La Minerve*, October 2, 1858, p. 2 (trans.).

14   *L'Événement*, September 25, 1877, p. 2.

15   *The Montreal Star*, September 19, 1881, p. 4.

16   Owen McGarvey won first prize at the 1880 exhibition for a black walnut coat and umbrella stand, which included a "British" mirror six feet high and three feet wide, flanked on either side by panels of French walnut.

17   A variety of tea table was presented by the Doghertys at the 1881 exhibition in Montreal: exhibited as a "five o'clock tea table", it won a first prize.

18   Owen McGarvey presented a hexagonal table at the 1880 exhibition and an octagonal one two years later. The Perry firm of Quebec City caused a sensation at the exhibition held in their hometown in 1894, at which they presented a table in the shape of a book.

19   *L'Événement*, September 24, 1877, p. 2 (trans.).

20   The September 20, 1882 edition of *The Gazette* reported (p. 5) that the eight panels represented an Indian chief, George Washington, birds and flowers.

21   One of the six chairs presented by Reed & Meakins to the "Queen of England" is reproduced on page 199 of this catalogue. Unfortunately for its creators, the *Art Journal* attributed the chair to Hilton. Moreover, as well as giving the wrong maker, the editors of the catalogue made a mistake in the Hilton firm's name, giving it as "W. & B. Hilton" instead of "J. & W. Hilton".

22   The first prizes were won by a suite of drawing-room furniture, a suite of enamelled bedroom furniture, a rosewood whatnot, a centre table, a sofa and an easy chair. The second prizes went to two bedroom suites, one painted and the other mahogany. Finally, the special prize was awarded to a set of boudoir furniture and a gilded mirror.

23   Thomson can be considered a serious rival of the Hiltons in the Montreal provincial exhibitions, for the furniture he submitted to the scrutiny of public and judges alike was extremely finely-executed work very similar to that presented by the Hilton firm. In 1865, Thomson won first prizes for a black walnut bedroom suite, a walnut dining-room table and a set of chairs.

24   *La Minerve*, October 3, 1865, p. 1 (trans.).

25   *Montreal Weekly Witness*, September 30, 1865, p. 2. Molinelli won a first prize for this sideboard. James Thomson presented two, one of which was awarded a second prize.

26   That Lavigne was among the advocates of Molinelli's work is made clear by his advertisement on page 3 of the April 26, 1869 edition of *La Minerve*, in which he stated that "the furniture will be in the Molinelli style, so admired and so fashionable in Montreal" (trans.).

27   In 1880, Bélanger captured the most prizes, closely followed by J.A.I. Craig, James Thomson and R. Constantine. The following year, the judges looked favourably on H. J. Shaw & Co. as well as the Dogherty Brothers.

28   Despite the fact that Adolphe Bélanger presented fewer pieces than Owen McGarvey, and participated less often, if we examine the primary sources carefully we realize that Bélanger was awarded more first prizes than his English-speaking rival.

29   In 1871, Philippe Vallière was awarded the first prize in the category of drawing-room furniture of "not less than four articles". The same year, Drum won the first prize for "reasonably-priced" drawing-room furniture.

30   A number of interesting articles elucidate the opinions being expressed in the context of this "dispute". Among them, in chronological order, are those appearing in *The Morning Chronicle*, September 13, 1871, p. 2; the *Journal de Québec*, September 14, 1871, p. 2; *The Morning Chronicle*, September 15, 1871, p. 2; *L'Événement*, September 18, 1871, p. 1; and finally *L'Opinion publique*, September 21, 1871, p. 462.

31   As in 1871, Vallière won first prize for the best luxury drawing-room furniture, Drum for the best reasonably-priced drawing-room furniture.

32   Philippe Vallière did, however, submit a small selection of chairs to the international exhibition held in Kingston, Jamaica, in 1891.

33   *L'Événement*, September 19, 1868, p. 2 (trans.).

34   These words appear in an article published in the September 20, 1880 edition of *The Gazette* (p. 2). The full extract reads as follows: "It must, however, be said that Messrs McGarvey & Son's collection forms the largest on exhibition; that in point of value, richness of effect, taste in design, variety, utility and effective grouping, it is exceedingly creditable, and must add considerably to the fame of even this the oldest furniture house in the city, and especially so when it is considered that all the articles shown are simply taken from the ordinary stock, not one of them being made for the exhibition specially."

35   *La Minerve*, September 21, 1880, p. 2 (trans.).

36   See *La Minerve*, September 29, 1882, p. 3.

37   *Journal de Québec*, August 30, 1860, p. 2 (trans.).

38   *L'Opinion publique*, September 21, 1871, p. 462 (trans.).

39   *Le Canadien*, October 23, 1850, p. 2 (trans.).

40   The same argument was employed subsequently in an article on page 2 of the May 2, 1865 edition of *La Minerve*. Speaking of a table presented in Dublin by Pierre Roy, the journalist wrote: "The execution of this remarkable jewel is a tribute to the talent of Mr. Roy, and we feel sure that as well as testifying to the astonishing progress made by Canada's cabinetmaking industry it will serve to highlight once again the value of our native woods" (trans.).

41   *Le Canadien*, October 3, 1851, p. 2 (trans.).

42   Among these, seven were from the province of Quebec.

43   *La Minerve*, December 22, 1855, p. 1 (trans.).

44   *Documents de la session. Vol. II. Deuxième session du sixième parlement du Canada. Session 1888*, p. 25 (trans.).

45   The *Illustrated London News* refers to the famous smile in its May 3 (p. 372) and May 31 (p. 494) editions of 1851.

46   *The Industry of all Nations 1851. The Art Journal Illustrated Catalogue* (London: George Virtue, 1851), pp. 119, 199. On page 119 there is a centre table, a chair, an upholstered armchair and a sofa, all by the Hiltons. On page 199, there is an image of one of the chairs presented to the Queen. Attributed here to the Hiltons, they were actually made by Reed & Meakins.

47   *L'Indépendance belge*, September 13, 1885 (trans.).

48   Henry de Varigny, "Le Canada et son exposition", *L'exposition de Paris (1900)* (Paris: Montgredien et Cie, 1900), vol. III, p. 207.

The Canadian Section at the Great Universal Exhibition, London, 1851*

A hundred years ago, supposing a great international and industrial exhibition to have been possible at that time, Canada would have furnished a very different assortment from that with which she now presents us. Then we should have had a rude and miscellaneous lot of native manufactures and native finery, something after the fashion of that now collected in the Tunis Bay – a wigwam, some wooden or horn spoons, rough earthen pots, a few embroidered moccasins, a few tomahawks, and a dozen or so of scalps and other military trophies; but nothing indicative of the natural resources of this vast and almost virgin tract of territory, nothing that spoke of the honest industry or intelligent enterprise of its inhabitants. Very different from this, however, is now the case. Civilisation has begun its useful work in the far west; European industry has planted the spade there, and some of the fruits are now before us – speaking much and creditably for the past, but speaking still more cheeringly of what is yet to come.

The Canada division is situated to the south side of the Western Nave, next beyond the East Indian division. Its products are not so showy, but are yet more valuable as evidences of social wealth and social advancement. They are the spoils of peace, not of war, the industrial beginnings of a junior branch of the great civilising family of the universe, not the gaudy remains of an effete barbarism, which has been demolished, but not yet replaced by anything better. The Canadians send us abundant samples of natural wealth drawn from the bowels of the earth – specimens of iron, copper, and silver ore, besides a case of native gold obtained from the gravel on the south-east side of the prolongation of the Green Mountains; specimens of magnesite rock, of stones of fine quality for the purpose of lithography, of agates, soapstones, gypsum, slates, and serpentines. Of timber there is a large assortment (the major part forming a large pile in the midst of the main avenue) – oak, curled ash, bass-wood, black walnut, pine, curled maple, bird's-eye maple, hemlock, elm, spruce, &c., all fine specimens, and of which the black walnut struck us as especially beautiful, both for its colour, its rich and varied grain, and the high degree of polish of which it is susceptible. The maples also are extremely rich, and, as well as the black walnut, are well adapted for furniture and other decorative works. Of agricultural products we have numerous samples, the Canadian exhibitors evidently attaching a due importance to this branch of their national wealth: barrels filled with corn, Indian meal, barley, oats, peas, beans, flax, potatoes preserved for sea voyage; with Siberian oil-seed, hemp, hops, and sugar from the maple tree, all show the varied richness of a land which, put to good account, might effectually relieve the distress of the older communities of the world.

Lastly, in unmanufactured, or but partially manufactured products, there are specimens of moose hide and leather, moose deer's head and horns, calf-skin, porpoise-skin, &c.

In addition to these resources of natural wealth, the Canadian colonists are favourably represented as regards their skill of handicraft – particularly as relates to furniture and articles of domestic and general use. Of furniture there are several most creditable specimens – substantial in make, whilst aiming at some trick of style in decoration, which, although of course not claiming to compete with the more finished and artistic articles of luxe produced in London, Vienna, and Paris, show an aptness of handling, which a little study of improved models, abundant opportunities for which the present Exhibition affords, will doubtless, in future, direct more happily. Amongst the articles of furniture deserving of especial mention, from the loyal associations connected with them, are half-a-dozen chairs, the seats and back worked in worsted and silk by the ladies of Montreal, "for England's Queen". There are also a handsome pianoforte and some other musical instruments, showing that Saxon industry in Canada does not intend to restrict itself for the future to mere articles of utility.

In the midst of the room are some very stylish sleighs, with harness and sleigh-robes complete; and a fire engine of unusually large proportions, and remarkably elegant design and workmanship, capable of throwing two streams of water 156 feet high, or a single stream 210 feet high. There is attached to it a box containing necessary tools, and with a seat for the accommodation of the firemen, but this adds greatly to the length, and, although a useful contrivance for the comparatively open thoroughfares of Montreal, would hardly do for crowded London streets.

Amongst other matters which the visitor will remark in this collection, are some interesting models, including one of a wooden bridge, having an arch of 250 feet span; a Canadian trading canoe, made of course of bark — a remarkably fine specimen of this class of boat; shipbuilding crooks and futtocks; specimens of cordage; various tools and articles of cutlery; samples of carpeting, blankets, and grey cloth; fine cloths and satinettes; patent leather trunks, bound with brass ribs, and remarkably substantial; cooking and parlour stoves; a church bell, made from the copper of Lake Huron; some excellent printing types; a new description of copying-press; snow-shoes and moccasins; and even some articles of jewellery and some specimens of artificial teeth.

---

* Taken from the Exhibition Supplement to the *Illustrated London News* of Saturday, May 31, 1851, pp. 494-495.

A Masterpiece of Marquetry by Cabinetmaker Pierre Roy of Quebec City at the International Exhibition held in Dublin, Ireland, in 1865*

We have reason to believe that Canada will be advantageously represented at the International Exhibition to be held shortly in Dublin, Ireland, if not in the quantity at least in the quality of the objects shipped recently to that destination. Among these, we must mention a centre table, produced by the workshops of Mr. Pierre Roy, a furniture-cabinetmaker from Saint-Roch. This table is a masterpiece of marquetry. The top is composed of fitted segments of all the varieties of wood that grow here. In the middle there is a round piece in bird's-eye maple with, in the centre, a beaver in the same black walnut as the surrounding ring. Fourteen parallelograms in white oak, copper beech, plain black walnut, curly red maple, silver birch, curly walnut, butternut, yellow birch, hard ash, black bird's-eye walnut, grey elm and red birch radiate from the central section out to the circumference; a strip made of fir, grey spruce, red spruce, hemlock, red cedar, cedar, white pine, red pine, alder, white oak, poplar, apple-wood, hawthorn and wild plum-wood encircles the fourteen parallelograms. A broad border of several different varieties of black walnut runs around the outside edge of the table top. The pedestal, in the so-called Elizabethan style, is in artistically-carved black walnut. The execution of this remarkable jewel is a tribute to the talent of Mr. Roy, and we feel sure that as well as testifying to the astonishing progress made by Canada's cabinetmaking industry it will serve to highlight once again the value of our native woods.

---

* Article published in *La Minerve* (Montreal), May 2, 1865, p. 2 (trans.).

The Owen McGarvey & Son Exhibit, Presented at the Provincial Exhibition of September 1882, Held in Montreal's Crystal Palace*

On entering the main building almost the first exhibit which attracts attention is that made by Messrs. Owen McGarvey & Son, who occupy the entire end of the gallery facing the principal entrance. Both from its comprehensive character and tasteful arrangement, it claims and has received much admiration, as well as the warmest encomiums of praise from all beholders. Messrs. McGarvey & Son are steady exhibitors, and each year shows a decided advance in point of variety and general excellence. This year the firm has spared neither trouble nor expense, the result being a collection of articles extremely diversified in character and all artistic to the last degree. In arrangement and general effect a *coup d'oeil* of great richness and beauty is apparent at a glance.

It would occupy far too much of our available space to notice this grand exhibit as it deserves, but it would be unpardonable not to endeavour to give some description of it, however inadequate words may be to represent it properly. But at the outset it should be stated that the whole exhibit is taken from stock, and fairly represents the class of goods which can ordinarily be seen in the warerooms of the firm every day in the year. Commencing our description, we first notice the dining-room set in black walnut, which bears the stamp of solidity and usefulness. It is upholstered in leather, and the chairs are of quite a new design, combining substantiality with novelty. The table is, of course, extension in character, but worked by a spiral screw, and can be extended 18 feet without trouble, and yet be as firm as a rock. The accompanying sideboard is of Eastlake pattern, massive, handsome and eminently useful. The panels are of French walnut; it has plate-glass backs, two glass-front cabinets for silverware, and other conveniences. Next we notice the bedroom set, which is the theme of universal admiration. The bedstead is of black walnut, with French walnut finishings. The panels are very chastely carved, with designs representing ivy, oak, rose and vine, and otherwise richly decorated. The bureau is made to match, the drawers of which are all finished with bird's-eye maple, and both it and the bedstead are embellished with polished French walnut pillars, with floral capitals, and the washstand is a combination of toilet cabinet, somno and usual other accessories. The chairs are in keeping, the whole forming a *suite* of unparalleled beauty.

But the beauty of the foregoing is quite eclipsed by the drawing-room furniture, which is entirely of ebony and gold, with engraved panelling sumptuously upholstered in raw silk of a new pattern with olive silk plush trimmings. The framework of this set is especially commendable for its elegant appearance and the whole *suite* is of exceeding richness. A divan is got up in similar manner and each arm of the frame is adorned with a grotesque head holding heavy brass pendants – a decided and pleasing novelty. Next to the divan stands a *vis-à-vis* in ebony and gilt richly finished with old gold and crimson satin, and a fancy reclining chair of new design covered in crimson satin and old gold plush, a most handsome and inviting seat. An ebony Queen Anne style table stands close by with coloured marqueterie top especially noticeable for its original design, magnificent clean finish and perfect colour blending. Three gilt chairs, two in gold and one in silver are remarkably elegant, the former trimmed with crimson and blue satin, and the latter in royal blue satin with peacock-blue silk plush. Then we see an ebony gilt easel and portfolio having an appropriately engraved panel; two marble-topped gold gilt tables with handsome stands; two jardinieres with marqueterie panels, quite new; a beautiful ebonised cabinet with bevelled plate glass front; a music cabinet with heavy raised engraved panel and embossed plush panel under upper shelf, which completes the set. The whole of this *suite* is rich beyond description and fit for the use of royalty itself.

Passing on the miscellaneous articles we see a parlour cylinder desk, with cabinet and mirror front – very useful for a lady; two more Queen Anne style music cabinets, with marqueterie panels; a very pretty Davenport; the side drawers of which are finished in mahogany; a horse-shoe hanging hat-stand, with plated pins and diamond-shaped mirror — a novel idea; two remarkably chaste gilt mirror brackets, with pretty scrolls; a handsome mantel mirror, with richly gilt frame, which, with many other *objets d'art*, form a fitting background for this elaborate exhibit. Here again an *embarras des riches* meets us in the shape of five different wall brackets of original and beautiful design, a Swiss college clock, unique in ornament and interest. For materfamilias troubled with cross babies a clock cradle, which on being wound up swings for two hours, ought to be specially interesting. (Happy thought — Won't this solve the baby crying question?)

Now we turn to the rattan work, of which seven specimens are shown. Six of these are chairs, all of different styles and finished in various coloured bronzes, such as silver, gold, green, &c; the remaining specimen is a swing cot of entirely new design in bronze gilt. This finishing, which, by the way, has only just been introduced, adds greatly to the effect of these articles.

Getting back again to the ornamental exhibits, our attention is drawn to a worktable, the envy of all lady visitors. It is beautifully fitted with every convenience, has a mirror under its cover, the top of which is handsomely embellished with monogram and design in marqueterie. Gentlemen of literary habits, or those wishing for an especially comfortable chair should feel grateful to Messrs. McGarvey for introducing their reading chair, which is easily adjustable to any angle. It is made of solid black walnut, and appropriately upholstered in raw silk and plush reversible cushions. Given this chair, an interesting book or a pleasant companion, elysium is within reach. For devotional or ornamental purposes a very pretty prie-dieu in black walnut and gilt, trimmed in olive and crimson plush, with cabinet for books and an ornamental cross entwined in its rich framework, would be just the thing.

In the way of bed lounges, a combination-bed is exhibited. This is a really practical design, and discounts all others. As it stands it is a handsome office or library lounge, got up in black walnut and leather. But by a simple movement this innocent-looking article blooms into a real bed — not a make-shift, but a bed upon which anyone may sleep the sleep of the just in perfect comfort. For families cramped for room and bachelors occupying chambers this lounge is a treasure.

A chair formed of polished Texas cattle horns ingeniously arranged and richly upholstered is shown, which would make a beautiful addition to any room, and also a richly-carved pedestal table of black walnut with inlaid octagonal top. The outer border of this table top is formed of carved shells, and remaining design is formed of coloured marqueterie containing not less than nine thousand pieces of wood. Its centre is occupied by a sixteen pointed star of diamond shape and six different coloured woods, and grouped round this are eight panels representing as many various subjects, such as an Indian chief, George Washington, birds and floral designs. The whole design is extremely pleasing and the figures are remarkably clear and well brought out — indeed it is a splendid piece of art workmanship.

At the head of each stairway leading to the gallery and contiguous to the principal exhibit, Messrs. McGarvey show a quantity of chairs which represent the wholesale department of their large business. This might fittingly be called the "evolution" part of the exhibit, for it includes this necessary article of furniture in all stages of existence, from the commonest to the most costly and highly finished.

In closing this notice we cannot but congratulate Messrs. McGarvey & Son on the comprehensive character of their exhibit, its tasteful arrangement, the high quality, richness and style apparent in the goods; the usefulness as well as elegance everywhere discernible and the general excellence of the whole. And it may fairly be added that as this exhibit is a sample of what the firm keep ordinarily in stock, purchasers of high class furniture cannot fail to meet with what they require in the warerooms of these exhibitors.

The judges, evidently recognizing the value of the exhibit, have awarded it not less than fifteen prizes, eight firsts and seven seconds.

---

*   Article printed in *The Gazette*, September 20, 1882, p. 5.

Cabinetwork at the Quebec Provincial Exhibition of 1877*

Let us now look at the cabinetwork, and the effect it is likely to have had on visitors, especially those from abroad. If it has won compliments, as I am sure it has, then this is only just. Quebec is proud home to a number of firms that have contributed towards the province's fine reputation in the field of cabinetmaking. I can mention the companies of Drum and Vallière, and, on a lesser scale, of Gourdeau; only the latter did not exhibit works this year; at the 1871 Exhibition in Quebec City, Mr. Gourdeau put on a very fine display; this year, only the two former presented works; alone, they occupied the full width of the left wing, to a depth of some feet.

So many people, rich and poor alike, must have been set dreaming by this luxurious furniture! I feel sure some poor unfortunates who sleep on little more than a pallet have felt envious of those able to afford the superb double beds in the finest black walnut, with their rich canopies decorated with caryatids, finials and rosettes. And that others, who have only a few humble wooden chairs to their name, have sighed longingly before these armchairs and sofas upholstered with silk brocade, in tones of red, white, green and crimson! The Drum firm exhibited a set of drawing-room furniture in black walnut and red silk brocade, and another Elizabethan-style drawing-room set, in crimson silk brocade with a gold edging. A marvellously stylish bedstead, with finely executed carvings and a magnificent canopy whose sumptuous curtains sweep majestically down from the top, was positioned at an angle to the display, blocking off the corner of the pavilion. It was going for the trifling sum of $120. It is beautiful, it is superb; but when you sleep well, a passerby was heard to say, the humblest camp bed is just as good and you hardly notice the difference. Possibly so! but it seems likely that the comment came from someone not in a position to purchase the piece.

Among Drum's drawing-room furniture there was a tea table, with beautiful marquetry work and a gilt pedestal; in the centre of the piece is a star whose points of mahogany, white wood, walnut and bird's-eye maple radiate out from the centre, each stretching a distance of ten degrees towards the circumference.

In the middle of the display was a large looking-glass, made of French plate. There were also several other pieces of furniture in the English style, chairs, settees, and a sideboard worth mentioning; the chairs were covered in real Moroccan leather.

The artist Mr. Eugène Hamel had the good notion of hanging a few of his best canvases in this display; they were portraits; that of the Reverend Mr. Thomas Hamel, a bust; of the Honourable Mr. Ross, president of the Legislative Council, a three-quarter work; two busts of women, and a biblical study of *The Visitation*; also in the same room were hung two landscapes and the *Virgin and Child* by Mr. Rob. Morgan, a number of models of mechanical designs by Mr. Bender, a wooden model of the boat most recently launched by Messrs. McKay and Warner on the St. Charles River, and three watercolour paintings belonging to Lieutenant Colonel Strange.

At the edge of the dividing wall separating the displays of Drum and Vallière could be seen a charmingly fresh and poetic painting called *La Posta d'Amore*, the love letter. It shows two pretty women — which goes without saying, for the artist is hardly likely to have made them ugly — two pretty women, then, one of whom is mysteriously placing a note inside a tree trunk — a note either you or I would certainly be happy to receive — while the other stands guard; it is quite charming. I will not say it is worth framing, for it is already framed, and richly so. This painting is an original by Louis Cappelli.

It was impossible to pass on without taking a look at two pianos made in Canada by Mr. F. Oisel, who has been established for some years in Quebec City and who has gained full rights to that city by marrying a French Canadian lady. Mr. Oisel is one of our most skilled makers of musical instruments. He has practiced his craft in two of the world's most famous manufactories, which are invariably placed *hors concours* at all the universal exhibitions owing to the superiority of their products: the Parisian firms of Pleyel and Erard. These firms use only the highest quality materials in the fabrication of their instruments and employ only the finest craftsmen. Having worked for these companies, then, endows Mr. Oisel with first-rate qualifications. He clearly wished to take

AN INDUSTRY OPEN TO THE WORLD

> He has in his establishment a craftsman very recently arrived from Paris who has brought him much knowledge and who is ready to execute furniture of all types, such as Boulle furniture, very fashionable in Paris, rosewood furniture in the Renaissance and Louis XIV, XV and XVI styles, furniture in mahogany and black walnut, in marquetry, mosaic and Gothic revival – everything that is most up-to-date, in fact. There are also furniture designs that allow visitors to make their own choices.[1]

THIS EXTRACT FROM AN 1864 ADVERTISEMENT RUN BY furniture maker Pierre Roy accurately reflects the situation of the furniture industry in Victorian Quebec: it was an industry based largely on historical styles, responsive to changing fashions and to "novelty", dominated by the tastes and whims of an increasingly wide public, employing both indigenous and exotic materials; in sum, an industry open to the world that was marked for many years by the particular influence of France. Through its unprecedented typological diversity, this historically-oriented furniture industry nevertheless left room for innovation, not only in its production methods, but also in its "American" preoccupation with physical comfort, its receptivity to the various reform movements and its occasional use of decisively "Canadian" decorative motifs.

The adjective "Victorian" corresponds to no particular style, but evokes rather a situation of constantly shifting and changing eclecticism. And if it was a situation that confused even the Victorians themselves, they were nonetheless aware of the advances being made in furniture design during their era. Reviewing the various pieces submitted by cabinetmaker Philippe Vallière to the provincial exhibition held in Quebec City in 1877, a journalist spoke in the following rather vague terms of the "considerable progress" that they revealed:

> Looking at these luxurious objects, we realize straight away the gulf that separates them from the formal pieces employed by our fathers; in those days, the taste was simpler, less refined; the armchairs were heavier, the beds more massive; once the furniture was in place, it was not often moved; but over the past few years taste has developed . . . In the furniture of twenty or thirty years ago, there was nothing that could compare to the harmonious symmetry, the beauty, the elegance and the sumptuousness of the pieces being produced today.[2]

The journalist makes mention elsewhere of pieces in the "Elizabethan", "English", "French" and "American" styles, and exclaims, "So many people, rich and poor alike, must have been set dreaming by this luxurious furniture!" Fifteen years later, another reviewer noted the presence of furniture in the "Eastlake" and "Queen Anne" styles at Owen McGarvey's display at the

343
Double cabinet, late eighteenth century
Pine, 249 x 154.7 cm
The Montreal Museum of Fine Arts, gift of Miss Mabel Molson (1938.Df.13)

provincial exhibition in Montreal.³ This enthusiastic admirer employed a series of highly colourful expressions to convey the diversity, quality and distinction of the furniture, claiming that it offered an "*embarras des riches*" [*sic*], that "elysium" was "within reach" and that the articles were "rich beyond description and fit for the use of royalty itself". These remarks are interesting for what they reveal about the ambitions and ideals of a society in which, for all classes, the much-desired "good life" was somehow embodied in furniture similar to that employed by the monarchs and nobles of the past. All this was not lost on Quebec furniture makers, and their advertisements are full of references to furniture described as "tasteful", "high class", "fancy", "rich", "elegant" and "finely finished". Moreover, many of the advertisements make specific reference to the Louis XIV, Louis XV, Louis XVI and Queen Anne styles. At the same time, there is an obvious leaning towards innovation and

344
Regency serving table, about 1800-1830
Mahogany, pine and figured maple,
91 x 125 x 63.5 cm
The Montreal Museum of Fine Arts, gift of Miss Eleanor Hardisty-Smith (972.Df.2)
This serving table was purchased in Montreal in about 1868 by Donald Alexander Smith, who later became Lord Strathcona. It was originally one of a pair; the second table is now in a private collection.

any styles likely to improve the aesthetic or physical well-being of the user. As houses acquired additional, and more specialized, rooms, this trend led to a considerable increase in the types of furniture available, which were often functional but sometimes strictly decorative.

Quebec society, progressively more open to the outside world, was an active participant in the mechanisms of exchange that characterized Western societies generally. Owing to its status as a colony and later as a province in a British dominion, Quebec was naturally much influenced by international fashions governing the styles and decor of domestic life. In its unique way, it assimilated both the traditions of the old countries of Europe and the modern innovations of its American neighbours. In the realm of furniture, the growing receptivity to diverse outside influences caused a break in the slow rhythm that had characterized the development of our industry – one rooted in the French and English traditions – during the eighteenth century and the early decades of the nineteenth.[4] With the exception of a few enduring pockets of traditionalism, source of a somewhat heterogeneous production, the Victorian era was marked by a sharp break, even an explosion, in the evolution of taste. In the steady progression of art in earlier times, the appearance of a new style was the signal to abandon the one that had gone before. The Victorians, however, were reluctant to give anything up, and their passion for historical "revival" led to the coexistence of many different styles, all of which could be displayed as proof of their "good taste".

In a context of fierce competition, Quebec furniture makers who wished to retain and expand their market had no choice but to evolve, to keep up-to-date and to move with the times in order to satisfy a discerning public well versed in foreign fashions. In their advertising, novelty was something of a leitmotif we read of furniture that is "new", "in the new taste", in "the latest taste", of "new types", "in fashion", "in the most modern taste", "fashionable". . . For even if a piece of furniture is inspired by a historical style it can still seem "new" or "modern" to the person who feels they are discovering

THE FURNITURE

345

Advertisement for the firm of Jean-Olivier Vallière of Quebec City

Published in the *Journal de Québec*, June 24, 1853

Bibliothèque nationale du Québec, Montreal

346

Advertisement for the firm of Jean-Marie Papineau of Montreal

Published in *La Minerve*, July 12, 1856

National Library of Canada, Ottawa (NL-11856)

and recognizing its elegance! A maker like Jean-Olivier Vallière, then, paid attention to the changing tastes of his clientele. Not content with importing luxurious upholstery materials from abroad, he also obtained "patterns" that enabled him to sell a wide range of "furniture in every style", corresponding to the "varying tastes" of his "distinguished" clients.[5]

345

The universal exhibitions obviously had an enormous impact on the evolution of taste in Western societies. Leading countries used them as an opportunity to display their most remarkable and most recent products. These were subsequently reviewed in newspapers and reproduced in widely-circulating magazines. It is therefore understandable that echoes of the exhibitions held in London in 1851 and in Paris in 1855 should be felt in both the advertising and the creations of Montreal and Quebec City furniture makers. In 1856, J. M. Papineau was offering for sale "only furniture manufactured by himself according to the tastes of the Exhibitions of Paris and London, and which, as such, could adorn the foremost drawing rooms".[6] For their part, N. Veniere-Nicol and J. B. St-Laurent of Quebec City, ex-employees and successors of cabinetmaker François Lafleur, offered "an assortment of household furniture in the latest taste of London and Paris".[7] Engravings of furniture exhibited in London in 1851 were even employed by some Quebec makers in their advertising. For example, the *Art Journal* reproduction of a ceremonial or "state" chair by M. Jancowski of York, England, was associated on different occasions with the names of Pariseau,[8] Roy and McGarvey. It also served as a source of inspiration to Louis-Thomas and Louis-Flavien Berlinguet, charged by William Drum in 1852 to execute the viceroy's throne for the Upper Chamber of the Quebec parliament. On the back of this red-covered chair were "the royal armorial bearings magnificently embroidered by the Soeurs de la Charité de Québec"; the chair can be seen in the background of Théophile Hamel's 1852 portrait of Lord Elgin.[9]

346

347

348-349

The Quebec City furniture makers Pierre Drouin and Honoré Roy both subscribed to the *Art Journal*, published in London, and to the *Garde-Meuble ancien et moderne*, a Paris-based publication that was started in 1839 by the designer Désiré Guilmard and that continued after his death in 1885.[10] This decorating magazine contained information about different cabinetmakers' creations, especially those presented at the universal exhibitions.[11] Taking full advantage of their access to the magazine, Drouin and Roy were able to claim in their advertising that their furniture was "executed in the latest taste and in the most elegant style of London and Paris".[12] During the 1870s, furniture makers François Gourdeau and Azarie Lavigne promoted their products in a

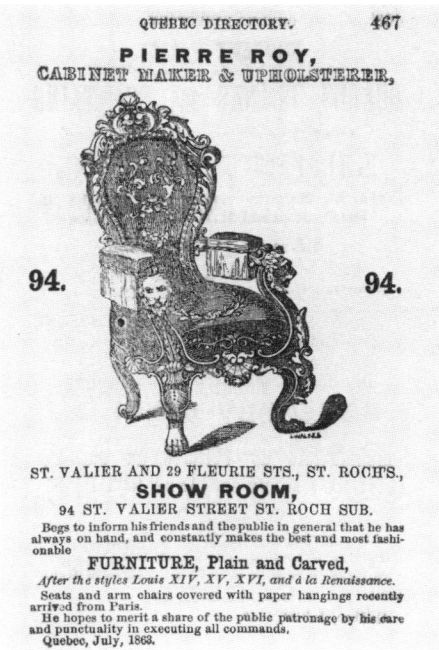

similar fashion by referring to Guilmard's "plans of furniture and furnished rooms" and to the "numerous, new and magnificent patterns and designs for furniture" received from Paris.[13]

There is no question, then, that plates from the *Garde-Meuble* served as models for Quebec furniture makers. By adjusting and adapting them, they were able to come up with numerous variations, ranging from the extremely sober to the elaborately carved, depending on the wishes, means and tastes of the individual client. For example, the makers Drouin and Roy drew their inspiration for a settee whose design has come down to us from plate number 456 of the *Garde-Meuble*. If we compare the drawing and the engraving, we can see that some sections have been copied directly from the model, while the central part of the back, the rear apron and the under-frame of the seat have all been modified. In another case, plate number 441 of the same publication has been used in the design of a dining-room sideboard. Here, the upper section of the back has been entirely eliminated, while the ornamentation of the main body of the piece has undergone a number of alterations; for example,

350-351

352-353

347
Armchair bearing the royal coat of arms presented by Jancowski at London's Great Exhibition in 1851
Engraving published in *Industry of All Nations: The Art-Journal Illustrated Catalogue* (London: George Virtue, 1851), p. 54
Library of the Montreal Museum of Fine Arts
Photo Christine Guest/MMFA

348
Advertisement for the firm of Pierre Roy of Quebec City
Published in G. H. Cherrier, *The Quebec Directory for 1863-64* (Quebec City: John Lovell, 1863), p. 467
National Archives of Canada, Ottawa (C-120205)

349
Advertisement for the firm of Owen McGarvey of Montreal
Published in R.S.W. Mackay, *The Montreal Directory for 1867-68* (Montreal: John Lovell, 1868), p. 511
National Archives of Canada, Ottawa (C-120202)

THE FURNITURE 405

350

Renaissance-style drawing-room settee, about 1851
Chromolithograph published in the *Garde-meuble ancien et moderne: collection de sièges* (Paris: D. Guilmard, 79th issue, plate no. 456)
Environment Canada, Parks Service, Quebec region (EX 86.3.18)
Photo SRP

351

Pierre Drouin (1815-1860) or Honoré Roy (1821-1892)
Drawing-room settee
Crayon on paper, 39.5 x 50.5 cm
Environment Canada, Parks Service, Quebec region (EX 86.3.107)
Photo SRP

352

Dining-room sideboard (Renaissance), about 1851
Chromolithograph published in the *Garde-meuble ancien et moderne: collection de meubles* (Paris: D. Guilmard, 76th issue, plate no. 441)
Environment Canada, Parks Service, Quebec region (EX 86.3.26)
Photo SRP

353

Pierre Drouin (1815-1860) or Honoré Roy (1821-1892)
Sideboard
Crayon on paper, 25.5 x 34 cm
Environment Canada, Parks Service, Quebec region (EX 86.3.128)
Photo SRP

the fish adorning the right-hand door of the prototype appear on the adapted version's central door, which in the original consisted of a glass panel.

It seems that this way of proceeding was common among Victorian furniture makers, at least in Canada and the United States. Like Drouin and Roy, various members of the Lejambre family, of Philadelphia, based their works on plates from Désiré Guilmard's *Garde-Meuble* or on illustrations published in London's *Art Journal*.[14] Another Philadelphia cabinetmaker, Daniel Pabst, created a splendid sideboard (now in the Philadelphia Museum of Art) modelled after plate number 29 of the *Cabinet Makers' Album of Furniture*, published in 1868 by the American Henry Carey Baird. It seems, moreover, that in illustrating his catalogue of patterns, the publisher Baird "appropriated" plates originally published by none other than Désiré Guilmard![15] This provides yet another clue to the decisive French influence on nineteenth-century cabinetmaking. Still extremely evident in the exhibitions of 1855 and 1867, this ascendancy gradually diminished after 1870, owing to the changing political climate, foreign competition, industrialization and the evolution of taste, particularly in

354-357

England and the United States. In Quebec, the impact of French models was as profound as it was long-lasting. For proof, one need only leaf through the plates published in the *Garde-Meuble ancien et moderne* during the 1850s: in the ornamentation and general form of the furniture, as well as the fabrics and the iconographical details, we see constant echoes of the chairs, armchairs, settees and sideboards that adorned Quebec drawing and dining rooms during the Victorian era. An instance is the rococo-revival console table with mirror belonging to Serge Joyal: although not identical, it is obviously closely related to the Louis XV piece from the French workshop of Bourdon the elder, exhibited in London in 1851, of which Guilmard published a lithograph in about 1852.

359-360

Nevertheless, it would clearly be an over-simplification to attribute everything to the French influence. As early as 1853, Jean-Olivier Vallière stated explicitly in one of his advertisements that he used "patterns of French, German, English and American furniture".[16] An avowal as simultaneously suggestive and cryptic as this at least has the advantage of reminding us that the systematic study of the sources of Quebec Victorian furniture is a task yet to be accomplished. Quite apart from the contents of the many furnishing periodicals, largely scattered here and there on separate sheets, there undoubtedly exists a wide variety of specialized works and treatises containing written and visual information that could throw light on this important question. In its January 1878 edition, Guilmard's *Garde-Meuble* itself identifies a number of promising avenues of research by naming and briefly describing the following collections: *Le portefeuille pratique du fabricant de sièges*, *Le carnet de l'ébéniste parisien*, *Sculptures de fantaisie*, *Marqueterie et Boule*, *Album du tourneur parisien*, *Le portefeuille pratique de l'ébéniste parisien*, *Album du sculpteur parisien*, *Album gothique*, *Album du fabricant de billards*, *La décoration au XIXe siècle / Décor intérieur des habitations* and *L'histoire de l'ornement* by D. Guilmard, together with the various manuals by Roret.

With rare exceptions and excluding the pieces published as engravings, it appears that the majority of Quebec furniture makers did not have direct

354

Drawing-room armchair and chair in the Renaissance style, about 1853

Chromolithograph published in the *Garde-meuble ancien et moderne: collection de sièges* (Paris: D. Guilmard, 90th issue, plate no. 523)
Bibliothèque Forney, Paris

355

Settee with tripartite back, about 1855

Chromolithograph published in the *Garde-meuble ancien et moderne: collection de sièges* (Paris: D. Guilmard, 99th issue, plate no. 576)
Bibliothèque Forney, Paris

356

Settee (new model), about 1856

Chromolithograph published in the *Garde-meuble ancien et moderne: collection de sièges* (Paris: D. Guilmard, 107th issue, plate no. 624)
Bibliothèque Forney, Paris

357
Dining-room sideboard-dresser (new model), about 1855
Chromolithograph published in the *Garde-meuble ancien et moderne: collection de meubles* (Paris: D. Guilmard, 100th issue, plate no. 587)
Bibliothèque Forney, Paris
An inscription states that the plan of this piece was supplied by its manufacturer, Balny jeune.

358
Renaissance-revival sideboard,
about 1880
Walnut and burl walnut, 310.5 x 204 x 61 cm
Musée du Séminaire de Québec,
gift of Abbé G. Édouard Côté
Photo Christine Guest/MMFA

contact with foremost examples of contemporary foreign cabinetwork, particularly those presented at the universal exhibitions. Until 1905, when its owner, Major Godfrey Rhodes, left England and installed the piece in his villa called Cataraqui in Sillery, Quebec, the famous sideboard executed by Thomas Fox for the London international exhibition of 1862 was only known here through the official catalogue published by the *Art Journal*. Thirty-five years earlier, at the villa called Kirk Ella, situated opposite Cataraqui, Edward Burstall had put up for auction "all his household furniture, great in quantity and high in price, consisting of furniture for the drawing and dining room, made for the most part in England, by Gillow of London".[17] In the mid-nineteenth century this famous old firm was renowned for its rococo-revival work and was well represented at the various universal exhibitions. It was also

at an auction that the painter Marc-Aurèle de Foy Suzor-Coté acquired the very fine French sideboard now in the collection of the Musée du Séminaire de Québec. Created by "a cabinetmaker of repute", this piece of furniture was purchased in Paris during the 1880s by the businessman and politician Pierre Garneau; it still bears the mark of the furniture maker C. O. Bédard, who apparently undertook some repair work on the piece around that time.[18]

Information relating to other auctions held during the 1860s confirms the presence in Quebec of furniture made by prestigious New York manufacturers like Ebbinghousen and J. & J. Meeks.[19] During the next decade, a period when Montrealer Henry Shaw was importing fine pieces from New York and Boston's leading manufacturers and having less expensive copies made locally, the influence of American furniture on the Quebec industry was both clear and direct. At the same time, Quebec makers naturally also had access to pattern books, catalogues and other publications containing images of the creations of their American counterparts. In June 1876, the editors of the *Canadian Mechanics' Magazine* published in their journal some ten pages of furniture designs taken from the *Boston Cabinet Maker*; before identifying the various models, they outlined their goals as follows:

358

363

359

Console table and mirror frame in the Louis XV style (gilded wood), about 1852

Chromolithograph published in the *Garde-meuble ancien et moderne: collection de meubles* (Paris: D. Guilmard, 82nd issue, plate no. 479)

Bibliothèque Forney, Paris

An inscription states that this piece was presented at the London exhibition – probably the one held in 1851 – and that it was made by Bourdon the elder.

360
Rococo-revival console table with mirror

Stained pine, varnish and gold leaf, 266.7 x 160 x 58.4 cm

Serge Joyal Collection, Montreal

Photo Christine Guest/MMFA

As is the case for much furniture, the origin of this ensemble is unknown. These outstanding, richly carved pieces are, however, perfect examples of the Rococo-revival style.

THE FURNITURE

361
Sideboard by Thomas Fox presented at the universal exhibition held in London in 1862
Engraving published in the *Art-Journal Illustrated Catalogue of the International Exhibition* (London: James S. Virtue, 1862), p. 255
Library of the Montreal Museum of Fine Arts
Photo Christine Guest/MMFA

362
Thomas Fox (active about 1839-after 1862)
Renaissance-revival sideboard, 1862
Figured walnut and boxwood,
262 x 213.4 x 64.1 cm
The Montreal Museum of Fine Arts, purchase, funds bequeathed by Dr. and Mrs. Max Stern (1990.Df.6)
Photo Christine Guest/MMFA
This sideboard belonged until 1972 to Major Godfrey Rhodes' daughter Catherine, who was married to the painter Percival Tudor-Hart (1873-1954).

It is our intention in future numbers to give one page of illustration to this branch of mechanical labor, which we have no doubt will be appreciated by cabinet-makers in country places, who have not the same advantages as those residing in large towns.[20]

Other articles published in Canadian newspapers and periodicals during the 1880s prove that Quebec furniture makers were aware of and receptive to the revivalist trends that marked the last two decades of the nineteenth century. It was a period during which the furniture industry and domestic interior decoration reflected an exoticism and an eclecticism that were virtually boundless. As well as exploiting to the full all new inventions and materials, manufacturers borrowed from every conceivable decorative and stylistic repertoire, from Turkey to Japan, from the Middle Ages to modern times. As early as 1850, a remarkably prophetic political cartoon showed an exotic image of the cabinetmaker François Lafleur, alias "the flower of furniture makers", seated in an armchair of indefinable style. Lafleur, who

364
Le carillon. The Representatives and the Represented, 1850
Featured in the caricature: François Lafleur furniture maker
Lithograph, 27 x 22.6 cm
McCord Museum of Canadian History, Montreal (M5961)

363
Furniture Designs
Engraving published in the *Canadian Mechanics' Magazine and Patent Office Record*, June 1876, p. 172
Photo SRP

proclaimed himself ready to provide "classical drawing rooms or drawing rooms in whatever period one might care to specify", foreshadowed in his own way the broadening and opening up of the Quebec industry that was to characterize it throughout the Victorian era.[21]

John R. Porter

1 *La Scie*, January 29, 1864 (trans.).

2 *L'Événement*, September 25, 1877, p. 2 (trans.).

3 *The Gazette*, September 20, 1882, p. 5.

4 See Jean Palardy, *Les meubles anciens du Canada français* (Paris: Arts et métiers graphiques, 1963); Donald Blake Webster, *English Furniture of the Georgian Period* (Toronto: McGraw-Hill Ryerson, 1979).

5 *Journal de Québec*, June 24, 1853 (trans.).

6 *La Minerve*, July 12, 1856, p. 4 (trans.).

7 *Journal de Québec*, June 25, 1859, p. 3 (trans.).

8 *La Minerve*, May 2, 1852, p. 3.

9 See my entry on this painting in the catalogue *La peinture au Québec 1820-1850*, Mario Béland (ed.) (Quebec City: Musée du Québec – Les Publications du Québec, 1991), pp. 322-324.

10 Denise Ledoux-Bernard, *Les ébénistes du XIXe siècle 1785-1889, leurs oeuvres et leurs marques* (Paris: Les Éditions de l'amateur, 1984), p. 173.

11 The *Garde-Meuble* was published every two months (six issues a year), and each issue consisted of nine plates divided into three categories (seats, furniture and fabrics). It is difficult to identify the various plates from the category numbers, especially as the individual plates are not dated. Only the title page of each issue bore the date of publication, the issue number and the list of plates contained therein. Owing to the practical usefulness of the plates, it is extremely rare to find groups of plates still accompanied by their original title page. In fact, only five or six title pages have been traced to date in the partial series examined in Quebec City, Paris and New York. Based on the clues they provide, and taking into account the journal's publication schedule, we have come up with the general dating hypothesis employed in the technical data accompanying the plates reproduced below.

12 *Journal de Québec*, March 16, 1858. The Roy dit Belleau collection, acquired in 1974 by Canada Parks (now the Canadian Parks Service), contains sixty-four lithographed plates from the *Garde-Meuble*, the earliest dating from 1844 (35th issue) and the most recent from 1852 (81st issue). See the "Catalogue raisonné du fonds Roy dit Belleau", drawn up by Jean-Pierre Labiau in John R. Porter (ed.), *Les meubliers Pierre Drouin et Honoré Roy et l'industrie du meuble à Québec à l'époque victorienne* (Quebec City: Université Laval, Cahiers du CÉLAT, 1989), no. 10, pp. 91-93.

13 *L'Événement*, May 7, 1870; *La Minerve*, March 9, 1874, p. 1 (trans.).

14 See Peter L. L. Strickland, "Furniture by the Lejambre Family of Philadelphia", *The Magazine Antiques*, March 1978, pp. 600-613.

15 *Victorian Gothic & Renaissance Revival Furniture: Two Victorian Pattern Books Published by Henry Carey Baird*, intro. by David Hanks (Philadelphia: Athenaeum Library of Nineteenth Century America, 1977). This work reprints in their entirety the *Cabinet Makers' Album of Furniture* and the *Gothic Album for Cabinet Makers*, both published originally in 1868. A photograph of the Pabst sideboard under discussion is reproduced just before the introduction in which David Hanks reveals the probable origin of the illustrations published by Baird in 1868.

16 *Journal de Québec*, June 24, 1853 (trans.).

17 *Journal de Québec*, September 19, 1870, p. 3 (trans.).

18 Archives of the Musée du Séminaire de Québec, Fonds Suzor-Coté.

19 *Journal de Québec*, April 14, 1862, p. 3; *La Minerve*, April 23, 1864, p. 3.

20 *Canadian Mechanics' Magazine*, June 1876, p. 187.

21 *Journal de Québec*, June 16, 1849, p. 3.

DIVERSITY, INNOVATION AND THE QUEST FOR COMFORT

... hands the like of which will never more be seen, hands that mould mahogany, that play tunes upon yellow birch, that seduce exotic woods — magician's hands.
Sébastien Japrisot[1]

VICTORIAN FURNITURE GREW OUT OF TWO FORMS OF production: small-scale craft and industrial manufacture. This aspect aside, however, the furniture, owing to its diversity and eclecticism, is extremely hard to classify. In this it resembles those who commissioned, purchased and used it. Lifestyles and domestic customs were changing at remarkable rates during this period, and no social group, living in either the country or the city, remained immune. The increasing ubiquity of the house's three main rooms generated needs that resulted in the appearance on the market of a wide range of furniture of differing functions and styles. This is reflected in the advertisement run by the furniture maker Ferdinand Arel in 1870. It could also be detected in 1853, in Jean-Olivier Vallière's rather muddled list of products, which included "Sophas, Settees, Bedsteads, Armchairs, Chairs, Couches, Ottomans, Commodes, Sideboards, Bureaus, Bookcases, Bureau Dressing Tables, Chiffonniers, Drawing-room Tables, Card Tables, Pier Tables, Mirrors, Washstands".[2] Among the wealthy, the diversification and specialization of rooms made the list of possible "fine, utilitarian and fancy furniture" almost infinitely long. The dual quest for beauty and comfort was laced with all kinds of whims and eccentricities. Taken far beyond the requirements of physical well-being, the material environment was dominated by the desire to "show off" and was frequently the scene of over-furnishing and a quite extraordinary accumulation of objects.

Contemporary newspapers and especially the 350 after-death inventories studied from across Quebec (which reflect a broad spectrum of socio-economic and language groups) make mention of hundreds, even thousands of items related to the various activities of everyday life, including furniture for storage, conservation, display, protection, decoration, rest and support, not to mention the interminable catalogue of seat furniture. The typological inventory drawn up by my colleague Gynette Tremblay is more than eloquent on this subject. But behind the stark numerical listings of the notaries, one sometimes gains a vivid glimpse of domestic worlds where daily life was punctuated by habits and cultural customs closely bound up with the use of one specific piece of furniture or another. To capture something of this more inti-

ATELIER DE MEUBLES.

J'AI l'honneur d'informer le public et mes pratiques que j'offre en vente un assortiment exceptionnellement choisi de Meubles de toutes sortes, de tous patrons. Ces meubles ne laissent rien à désirer de plus complet sous le rapport de l'élégance et du fini et quant aux prix, je n'ai qu'un mot à dire, c'est que jusqu'à aujourd'hui la pratique m'a toujours fait observer qu'ils étaient excessivement bas en comparaison des autres.

L'ASSORTIMENT CONSISTE EN :

MEUBLES DE SALON.—Sofas, Chaises Canapés, Tables de Centre, Tables à Cartes, Berceuses, etc., Tabourins en Acajou, en Noyer Noir, Gris, Simples, ou avec Sculptures, avec Couvertures en Velours, Crin et Damas.

MEUBLES DE SALLE A DINER :—Sofas, Canapés, Chaises en Canne, Tables à Dîner, à Coulisses, Buffets de toutes grandeurs et de toutes formes, avec ou sans sculptures.

MEUBLES DE CHAMBRE A COUCHER :— Couchettes de tous modèles, en Noyer de toutes variétés, en Acajou, Commodes, Garde-Robes, Canapés, Berceuses, Prie-Dieu, Chaises-Canapé, Tables à Toilette, Lavemains.

— AUSSI —

Une grande quantité d'autres Meubles de Goût, d'utilité et de fantaisie.

☞ Prix très modestes.

F. AREL, Meublier,
Rue St. Paul.

Québec, 7 déc. 1870.

365
Advertisement for the firm of Ferdinand Arel of Quebec City
Published in *L'Événement*, December 7, 1870
National Library of Canada, Ottawa (NL-11917)

The Old Arm Chair*
I love it, I love it, and who shall dare,
To chide me from that Old Arm Chair;
I've treasured it long as a holy prize,
I've bedewed it with tears, and embalmed it with sighs,
Tis bound by a thousand bands to my heart,
Not a tie will break, not a link will start;
Would ye learn the spell? a mother sat there,
And a sacred thing is that Old Arm Chair,
I sat and watched her many a day,
When her eyes grew dim, and her locks were grey,
And I almost worshipped her when she smiled,
And turned from her Bible to bless her child;
Years rolled on, but the last one sped,
My idol was shattered, my earth star fled;
I learn'd how much the heart can bear,
When I saw her die in that Old Arm Chair,
Tis past! tis past! but I gaze on it now,
With quiv'ring breath, and throbbing brow;
Twas there she nursed me, twas there she died,
And memory flows with lava tide,
Say it is folly, and deem me weak,
While the scalding drops start down my cheeks,
But I love it, I love it, and cannot tear,
My soul from a mother's Old Arm Chair.

mate vision, one must leaf through a novel of the period, submerge oneself in the memoirs of one of its representatives or savour the charms of a poem like "The Old Arm Chair".

On another level altogether, the extraordinary diversity of Victorian furniture is corroborated by the woods, veneers and varnishes, the techniques and the hardware employed in its making. Examination of the artefacts soon reveals evidence of methods often dominated by technical innovation and influenced by industrial production procedures; methods torn between the makers' occasional flights of virtuosity and their all-too-frequent goal of dazzling the clientele. The furniture-making industry obviously had to face difficulties and major changes rooted in the demands of the market and the vagaries of fashion. The situation was exacerbated by the fact that the basic preoccupations of the maker were no longer restricted to questions of style, adherence to the rules of the trade and traditional woodworking: he had both to come to terms with an increasing number of new materials and to take account of the new desire of his clients for comfort and efficiency.

Woods,
Veneers
Finishes
p. 432

Techni
p. 435

---

* Anonymous poem published in the *Business Guide to the City of Montreal with a Collection of Popular Songs* (Montreal: John Lovell, 1860), p. 24.

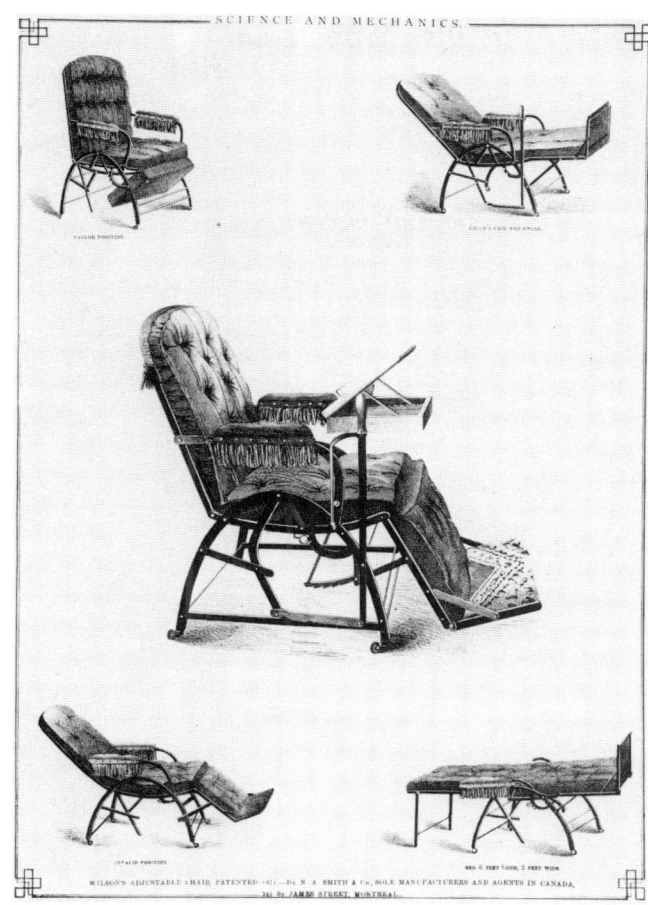

THE "AMERICAN" PURSUIT OF COMFORT AND EFFICIENCY

In the article on "furniture" in the 1899 *Dictionnaire du commerce*, French contributor Émile Clerc notes aptly that "among the innumerable new pieces of furniture launched onto the market each year, few are worthy of attention", most efforts being the result of "heterogeneous formulae obtained by combining earlier styles". Clerc does add, however, that "some foreign countries, especially America, concern themselves with the production of multi-purpose pieces".[3] In fact, the United States had been the source of much innovation during the preceding decades, especially in the realm of function and comfort. But their products were often more remarkable for their usefulness and ingenuity than for their elegance, which perhaps explains the relative indifference of Europeans towards patent furniture. Due to its geographical proximity to the United States, Victorian Quebec participated, although to a small degree, in the research initiated by the Americans.[4] The major manufacturer McGarvey, for example, parallel to his efforts to satisfy the requirements of a clientele that valued above all passive comfort and historically-oriented display, devoted some attention to adjustable and convertible furniture and the more active pursuit of comfort.[5]

Siegfried Giedion is the author of a most enlightening study of nineteenth-century constituent or patent furniture that was radically inventive and creative. At the outset, he distinguishes it from all the "transitory" variations based on historical forms that grew out of *bourgeois* taste and fashions.[6] In fact, the main priority of patent furniture was the pursuit of comfort rather

366
Fireside chair, about 1890-1900
Wood and upholstery, 90 x 61 x 60 cm
Jourdain Fiset Collection, Quebec City
Photo Christine Guest/MMFA

367
Wilson's Adjustable Chair, Patented 1871
Engraving published in the *Canadian Illustrated News*, December 28, 1872
National Archives of Canada, Ottawa (C-58944)

368
Francis George Coleridge
(active 1856 to 1871)
The Borderers Ante Room Any Evening between 8.30 and 11 p.m.
Watercolour, gouache, black ink and graphite on blue paper, 22.7 x 33.9 cm
National Archives of Canada, Ottawa (C-102485)

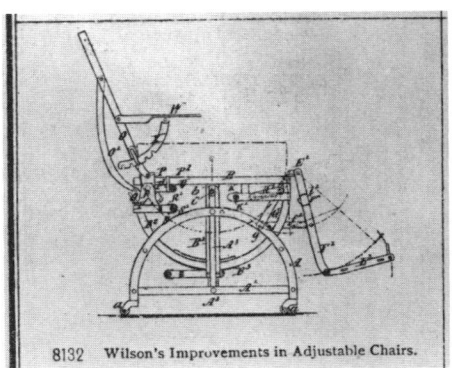

369
Improvements in Adjustable Chairs
Illustration published in the *Canadian Mechanics' Magazine and Patent Office Record*, December 1877, p. 196, patent no. 8132
Photo SRP

On April 14, 1881, the pharmacist M. G. Edson of Montreal referred to these improvements in an illustrated advertisement he published in *Le Moniteur du commerce*; he recommended the Wilson chair in the following terms: "Convenient for the Drawing Room, the Library, as a Lounge Bed for invalids, a Child's Cradle, a Bed or Sofa, combining elegance, lightness, sturdiness, simplicity and comfort. Wilson's Adjustable Chair has been known to the public for a number of years and has received Prizes, Medals and Diplomas at various Exhibitions, both in Canada and the United States, including a Medal and a Diploma at the Centennial Exhibition, a First Prize and a Diploma at the Provincial Exhibition in London, Ontario, in September 1877, a Medal in Paris in 1873, one in Toronto in 1880, and one in Montreal the same year." (trans.)

370
Advertisement for the firm of W. W. Moore of Montreal
Published in the *Canadian Illustrated News*, January 27, 1883
National Library of Canada, Ottawa (C-138203)

371
Adjustable armchair, patented in 1890, 1892 and 1897
103 x 110 cm (extended); 33 x 34 cm (foot-rest)
Léopold Désy Collection, Saint-Antoine de Tilly
Photo Christine Guest/MMFA

than of beauty. The new desire to adapt seating to the various positions of the human body, stimulated by the creative energy and curiosity of mid-nineteenth-century America, resulted in a panoply of inventions of all kinds.

It was, however, in England, starting in the 1820s, that the coiled spring came to be widely used in the fabrication of seats whose main object was comfort. As I. Grant notes, "a typical comfortable seat from around the middle of the century either had a visible wooden frame in precious wood adorned with rococo-revival ornamentation, or a frame of common wood entirely concealed beneath layers of padding and upholstery fabric".[7] This latter type is illustrated by a small Victorian fireside chair from a private collection in Quebec City. The slope of the back of this armless easy chair corresponds to the half-sitting, half-lying attitude that constituted the typical nineteenth-century position of relaxation. Going beyond the quest for passive comfort, patent furniture designers aimed to produce adjustable furniture that, through the manipulation of moveable components and distinct planes, could be adapted to the various positions of the human body.

It is still possible to find in Quebec barbers' and dentists' chairs similar to the conventional models used widely in the United States prior to the 1860s: in these pieces, only the head-rest, back and foot-rest are adjustable and sepa-

rate.[8] Making increasing use of mechanization, American inventors soon distinguished the two types of chair, giving them a far greater degree of flexibility and adjustability. As a result of the growing preoccupation with domestic comfort, these innovations had a direct effect on the fabrication of household seating. The best illustration of this is the famous Wilson chair, which was patented in the United States in 1871 and put on the market in Quebec the following year. A large illustration of the chair appeared in the December 28, 1872 issue of the *Canadian Illustrated News*, accompanied by the information that Dr. A. N. Smith, of St. James Street, was the only licensed Canadian manufacturer. It also showed five of the seventy different positions capable of being adopted at the time by the rather bizarre metal-framed object, which could be transformed at will into an invalid's chair, a drawing-room armchair, or a bed for adults or children! The article's popularity in both the United States and Canada was no doubt bolstered by the various improvements made to it during the 1870s.[9] The December 1877 edition of *The Canadian Patent Office Record* lists the alterations on which George Wilson took out an additional sixteen-year patent.[10] In 1883, the Montreal manufacturer W. W. Moore lauded the chair's comfort, versatility, ease of storage and transport, and even the beauty and richness of its upholstery! In their presentation of "Wilson's improved physicians' and surgeons' chair" at the provincial exhibition held in Montreal in 1881, the firm of M. G. Edson & Co. stressed rather the object's more technical qualities:

> It is especially adapted to gynecological practice and is adjustable to almost any position. It has upwards of 100 different changes, which are all effected by one handle at separate shafts with screw-motions.[11]

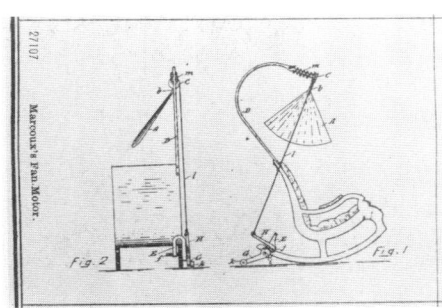

372

Smoker's chair with adjustable back,
about 1890-1900
Wood and imitation leather, 110 x 68 x 107 cm
Sœurs du Bon-Pasteur de Québec
Photo Brian Merrett/MMFA

373

The same chair in the reclining position
Photo Brian Merrett/MMFA

374

Fan Motor for Rocking Chairs
Illustration published in the *Canadian Magazine of Science and the Industrial Arts*, August 1887, p. 434, patent no. 27107
Photo SRP

The patent taken out by Moïse Marcoux on July 2, 1887, was valid for a period of five years.

THE FURNITURE

375
Suspended crib
Engraving published in the *Album de la Minerve*,
February 1, 1872
Photo SRP

It is possible to trace the existence of a number of other patented seats designed with the same goal of comfort but in more conventional styles and with a greater regard for elegance. The adjustable rocking chair from the Léopold Désy collection, which still bears patent stamps dated August 19, 1890, May 10, 1892, and September 21 and November 30, 1897, can be placed in a number of different positions depending on the whim of the user. The adjustable-backed smoker's chair in the collection of the Soeurs du Bon Pasteur in Quebec City is another example that was a perfect response to a requirement typical of the Victorian *bourgeoisie*. The rococo-revival piece, which is luxuriously upholstered in buttoned leather and has a reclining back, also possesses a special arm designed to hold all a smoker's accessories. Although this anonymous *fumeuse* is of a quite late date, it is worth noting that the firm of J. & W. Hilton had already attracted attention with a similar piece at the provincial exhibition held in Montreal in 1865.[12] By the 1880s, a number of furniture makers had become interested in the form.[13]

New developments aimed at increasing the comfort of invalids also undoubtedly had a direct influence on the shape of certain pieces of household furniture. Owen McGarvey, for example, before introducing innovations into his easy chairs intended for middle-class homes, had concerned himself with the well-being of the sick. In 1860 his store was carrying "convenient invalid chairs, of different types, and in which the occupant, by moving a tube with their left hand, can obtain cool or hot air; on their right is a desk for writing and reading, which can be pushed away at will."[14] To make the summer heat easier to bear, Moïse Marcoux of Saint-Eugène-de-Grantham invented a "fan device for rocking chairs", but it does not appear to have been put on the market.[15] One particularly unusual item in this category is the articulated chaise-longue that furniture maker James Thomson had photographed by Notman in 1891; one end of this richly upholstered oddity was designed to swing round to form an armchair.[16] The adjustable reading chair that the firm of Owen McGarvey & Son put on the market at the time of the provincial exhibition of 1882 was perhaps more in accordance with the true spirit of patent furniture. Even though it was "made of solid black walnut, and appropriately upholstered in raw silk and plush reversible cushions", it was also "easily adjustable to any angle".[17] It seems quite possible, in fact, that it was the less complicated forerunner of the modern pivoting, reclining office chair.[18]

The furniture created during the Victorian era was as varied as the activities and customs that gave rise to it. It is hard to know what to think of the "suspended crib" whose merits were promoted in 1872 in the *Album de la Minerve*, a "family magazine" devoted to fashion, home economy, literature, the fine arts, embroidery and music.[19] The article reads:

> The use of suspended cribs, so convenient and so popular in Europe, is practically unknown in Canada. They can be found in iron; but at prices ranging from $15 to $25. We are reproducing today the design of a crib that should become popular because it can be had at a reasonable price. The execution of this particular plan might possibly prove expensive, for the model is in carved black walnut. But it is an easy matter to suggest something simpler to the maker. The upright at the head of the crib is supported on two feet, while the other has only

376
Notman Studio, Montreal
Adjustable chaise-longue made by
Thomson (first position), 1891
Photograph
McCord Museum of Canadian History, Montreal,
Notman Photographic Archives (94,472-BII)

377
Notman Studio, Montreal
Adjustable chaise-longue made by
Thomson (second position), 1891
Photograph
McCord Museum of Canadian History, Montreal,
Notman Photographic Archives (94,473-BII)

378
Notman Studio, Montreal
Adjustable chaise-longue made by
Thomson (third position), 1891
Photograph
McCord Museum of Canadian History, Montreal,
Notman Photographic Archives (94,471-BII)

379
Notman Studio, Montreal
Interior of Rotherwood, the Hague house, Montreal, 1890
Photograph
McCord Museum of Canadian History, Montreal, Notman Photographic Archives (92,622 Misc-II)

one. The bar projecting from the top is not essential, but of use only if one wants to add a curtain or muslin. It would be quite easy to have a structure composed of nothing but the two uprights.[20]

Still in the realm of children's furniture, Owen McGarvey offered a number of curious inventions. In 1882, obviously having devoted some thought to mothers, he exhibited a "clock cradle, which on being wound up swings for two hours".[21] Two years earlier he had launched "a decided novelty in the shape of a children's combination chair, which in a remarkably small space and by as remarkable a piece of ingenuity forms at pleasure a hobby horse, child's high or low chair, and a team of horses".[22]

Its oddness apart, this latter piece shows a concern for convenience, moveability and space-saving, all common themes in writings of the period. The American of German descent, George Hunzinger, responded to these same preoccupations by designing ingenious folding chairs in various styles that were sufficiently elegant to cause them to be much in demand; they adorned a variety of locations, including the homes of wealthy private citizens like the Papineaus of Montebello and the Hagues of Montreal, and the Quebec City gallery belonging to the photographer Jules-Ernest Livernois.[23] On a more popular level, Hunzinger took advantage of the long-standing penchant of the

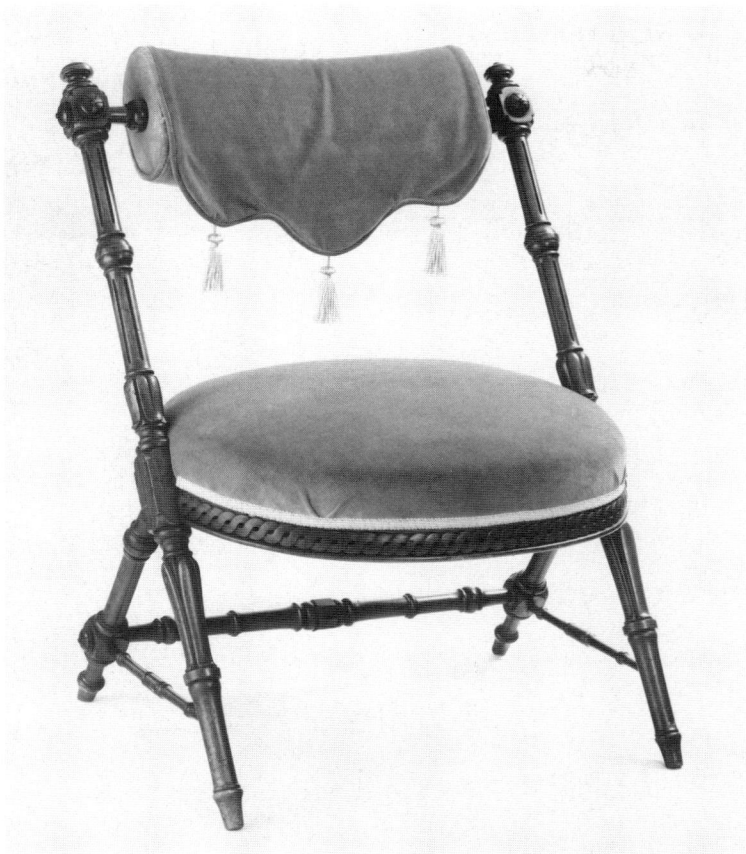

381　American middle classes for reclining and rocking chairs by patenting a "platform or spring rocking chair" in 1882. He was obviously not the first to explore this avenue, for such chairs had been in production since the late 1860s, but his invention offered the particular advantage of being less cumbersome, less noisy and altogether more comfortable than the traditional rocker.[24]

In a similar vein, the Montreal firm of Tees & Cie exhibited in 1880 an ingenious swivel bookcase, suitable for drawing-room or office and capable of holding between a hundred and a hundred and twenty large folio volumes, including those made for sheet music. Made of mahogany or walnut, in one or other of "twelve different patterns", this "vertical box, with shelves and compartments, turning on a vertical axis" was notable for its "undeniable usefulness".[25] Two years later, still obviously preoccupied with questions of convenience and space-saving, McGarvey attracted attention with an extending table equipped with a "spiral screw", which guaranteed its solidity even when it was stretched to the maximum length of eighteen feet.[26] The sole aim of the much less sophisticated folding bed put on the market by George Armstrong was to be practical, comfortable, strong, inexpensive and easy to store. And with much the same goals in mind, the Quebec City maker
382　William Drum had been producing since 1869 (by arrangement with a certain G. D. Mayer) a "patent hammock chair". This article, which sold for $2.60, was said to offer the dual advantage of being comfortable and convertible into a hammock, an armchair or a crib.[27]

As Giedion so rightly points out, while "the wealthy had no need of a chaise-longue that could be converted into a crib, or a bed that could become

380
Hunzinger chair, about 1870
126 x 63 x 56 cm
Augustinian monastery of the Hôtel-Dieu de Québec
Photo Christine Guest/MMFA

This type of chair, first marketed by George Jacob Hunzinger (1835-1898) and available in a variety of forms, is notable for the simplicity, economy and comfort of its design.

381
Platform rocker, about 1885-1900
Birch and coiled spring mechanism,
104 x 68 x 58 cm
Musée des Ursulines de Trois-Rivières (L 1992.2.M)
Photo Christine Guest/MMFA

The rocking movement of the chair patented by Hunzinger in 1882 was achieved by two coil springs mounted on a fixed base. The rocker illustrated here is one of the inexpensive, mass-produced versions sold widely by department stores like T. Eaton of Toronto.

THE FURNITURE

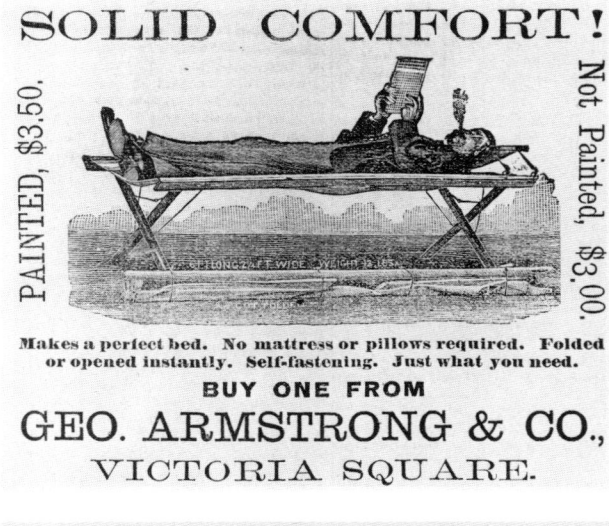

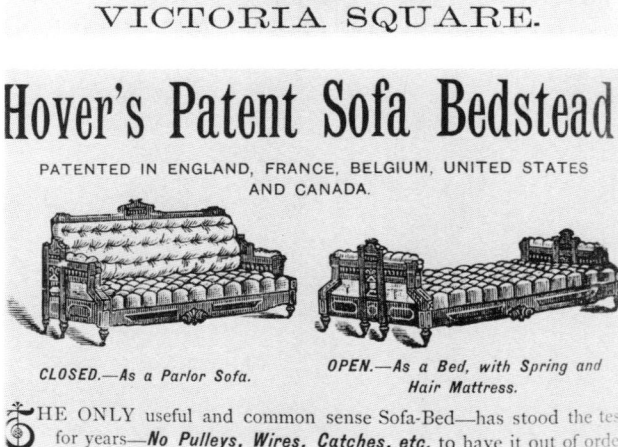

382
Advertisement for the firm of George Armstrong & Co. of Montreal
Published in *The Gazette*, September 3, 1880
Photo SRP

383
Advertisement for the Universal Commode Cabinet firm (detail)
Published in *The St. Lawrence Hall Montreal City Guide* (Montreal: The Canada Bank Note Company, 1885), p. 104
Bibliothèque municipale de Montréal

384
Advertisement for the firm of N. G. Valiquette of Montreal
Published in *La Presse*, September 12, 1896
National Library of Canada, Ottawa (NL-17952)

a closet", the same could not be said of those classes of society where many domestic needs had to be met in a restricted space. As the members of these groups, too, were concerned with comfort, they turned naturally to the convertible furniture that had been developing at the same time as adjustable furniture. Thanks to the multi-purpose, metamorphic nature of such pieces, it was possible to take best advantage of the often limited living space of city apartments and combine several functions in a single article of furniture, at a smaller overall cost.[28]

Among all the various types of furniture, it was the bed that was the focus of the most skill and originality. McGarvey, always open to innovations of all kinds, made a number of successful contributions. At the exhibition of 1882, he presented a "combination-bed" that a journalist from *The Gazette* described with wholehearted enthusiasm:

> This is a really practical design, and discounts all others. As it stands it is a handsome office or library lounge, got up in black walnut and leather. But by a simple movement this innocent-looking article blooms into a real bed — not a makeshift, but a bed upon which anyone may sleep the sleep of the just in perfect comfort. For families cramped for room and bachelors occupying chambers this lounge is a treasure.[29]

Two years later, he exhibited a version of "Plimpton's sofa bed, rightly upholstered in crimson velvet", "a piece of furniture suggestive of unalloyed comfort".[30] In 1886, a trade publication noted that "Messrs. Owen McGarvey

& Son also are the sole manufacturers, exclusive for the Province of Quebec, of the Ottoman Lounge Bed and Sofa-Bed and Ideal Parlor Sofa, which have a large sale and are popular with the trade and those using them".[31]

Another item available at the period was Hover's famous sofa bedstead, which was patented in France, England, the United States and Canada. Produced by The Universal Commode Cabinet Co., located on Saint-Sacrement Street in Montreal, this piece was said to be both "a perfect bed" and "an elegant sofa".[32] Some ten years later N. G. Valiquette of Sainte-Catherine Street began marketing another patented sofa bed for the drawing-room, which was promoted as "the champion" of the genre. Nevertheless, in the field of convertible furniture it achieved nothing like the virtuosity of an article that had been exhibited by the firm of Baker and Julien fifteen years before: "a folding cabinet combining a holding bed, washstand, wardrobe, mirror desk and book-rack", which won its inventors a first prize.[33]

However, the unquestioned leader in the field of "metamorphic" furniture was the Montreal firm of W. F. Dogherty, makers of the "Metropolitan Folding Bedstead", patented on February 28, 1881. Easy to move, open and close, occupying the minimum of space, hygienic and strong, it was said to be the cheapest and best-looking folding bed ever invented! It was available in a wide range of models, all of which could be radically transformed:

> By the use of specially made patent castors, the easy movement of the largest bed is secured. When in use as a bedstead it meets the requirements of the most fastidious; when closed, it represents handsome furniture so perfectly that not the slightest suspicion of its real purpose is suggested... The transformation of the bedroom into a sitting or dining-room, parlor or library is thus made complete. It can be as readily and cheaply transported from room to room or elsewhere as an ordinary bureau, and when folded is made to represent a bureau, sideboard, desk or parlor organ, bookcase or other furniture, and is made in all the above styles.[34]

There is no doubt that research undertaken in the area of adjustable and convertible furniture during the Victorian era contributed to domestic comfort and the quality of life, even if it also produced a number of inventions that were useless, bizarre or even frankly grotesque.[35] We hardly know what to make of the "sofa and bric-à-brac combined" for which Owen McGarvey held the exclusive patent for Canada and the United States,[36] or of the chair-coatstand on which Guillaume S. De Bonald of Berthier-en-Haut took out a five-year patent on January 9, 1877.[37] In contrast to the futility of such odd objects, though, we must acknowledge the originality and extraordinary usefulness of an article like the sewing machine,[38] which soon became an essential element of most middle-class Victorian households. From the 1850s on, considerable energy was devoted to producing variations[39] and innovations on the basic theme, by a number of different companies. One of these, Raymond's Sewing Machine Factory – run by Charles Raymond, an American who settled in Guelph, Ontario, in 1862 – manufactured several models and succeeded in cornering quite a segment of the market.[40] An advertisement published in 1874 by Hector Pageau, the company's only licensed agent in Quebec, stressed both the machine's safety and its ergonomic properties: the "Raymond" was not only "easy to drive", but was

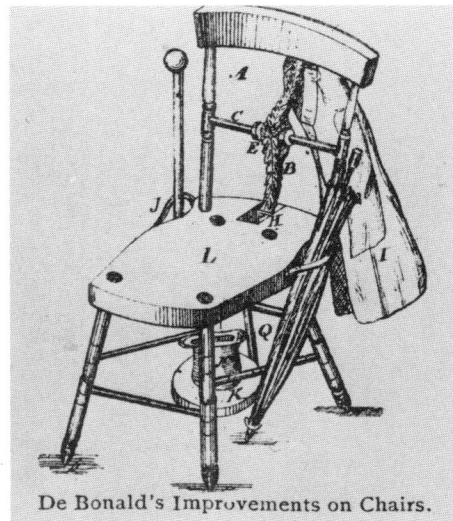

385
Improvements on Chairs
Illustration published in the *Canadian Mechanics' Magazine and Patent Office Record*, February 1877, p. 30, patent no. 6934
Photo SRP

The patent taken out by Guillaume S. De Bonald on January 9, 1897, was valid for a period of five years.

386
New Raymond sewing machine, about 1900
Walnut and figured veneer, 101.3 x 90.5 x 42.5 cm
Musée de la civilisation, Quebec City (88-2749)
Photo Christine Guest/MMFA

387
The same machine in the open position, without the cover
Photo Christine Guest/MMFA

388
Notman Studio, Montreal
Sofa by the manufacturer
R. N. Tombyll, 1892
Photograph
McCord Museum of Canadian History, Montreal, Notman Photographic Archives (99,066 Misc-II)

389
Notman Studio, Montreal
Love seat by the manufacturer
R. N. Tombyll, 1892
Photograph
McCord Museum of Canadian History, Montreal, Notman Photographic Archives (99,067 Misc-II)

actually said to "soothe the user rather than tiring her".⁴¹ In fact, Pageau would also have been justified in mentioning the sober elegance of this functional piece, in which wood, cast iron and the various elements of hardware necessary to its functioning are pleasingly fused.

Although during Victoria's reign innovations were particularly evident in the field of patent furniture, they were not restricted to this unique category. They came, in fact, in many forms, and influenced short-lived furniture just as much as "compositional". The increased diffusion of stylish furniture was thus significantly boosted by the new facility offered by machinery in a number of areas, including the making of mouldings, turning, the stamping out of decorative motifs and stencil work. As new materials emerged, the applications of those already known were being fully developed and systematized. One need only think of the castor, which, although in use since the late seventeenth century, is generally associated with the Victorian era: originally made of metal, it was during the period that concerns us that versions made of porcelain and earthenware were developed.⁴²

Springs, another item that already existed, also became far more widely used in the padding of mattresses, easy chairs and other upholstered seats.⁴³ Well supported by this new form of suspension, the fabrics employed to cover the furniture reached new heights of refinement, splendour and economy. Brocade, pekin, rep (of silk, wool or cotton), terry cloth, chintz, embroidery, brocaded cord, horsehair, damask (of silk or wool), silk plush or brocaded silk, satin, cretonne, velvet, leather, red morocco leather and denim⁴⁴ were all on offer, the eventual choice depending on the resources and tastes of the client. Padded seat furniture in unusual and original shapes, buttoned and covered with expensive fabric, obviously remained the prerogative of the most affluent members of the *bourgeoisie*, who were eager to parade their wealth and their good taste. It was undoubtedly among this privileged group that R. N. Tombyll found buyers for the remarkable upholstered pieces he had photographed by the Notman studio in 1892.⁴⁵

390
Elbow chair in the Chippendale style, about 1890

Wood, mother-of-pearl inlay, 103 x 63 x 66 cm
Petites Franciscaines de Marie, Baie-Saint-Paul
Photo Christine Guest/MMFA

During the second half of the nineteenth century, a dining-room suite almost always included two chairs with arms intended for the master and mistress of the house and placed at each end of the table. This particular chair is part of a five-piece dining-room set.

391
Rococo-revival tilt-top games table

Papier-mâché and mother-of-pearl,
68.5 x 65 x 54.6 cm
McCord Museum of Canadian History, Montreal, gift of F. Cleveland Morgan (M18974)
Photo Christine Guest/MMFA

392
Rococo-revival tilt-top games table

Papier-mâché and mother-of-pearl,
72.2 x 67.3 (diam.) cm
McCord Museum of Canadian History, Montreal, gift of F. Cleveland Morgan (M18972)

THE FURNITURE 425

393
Chair
Papier-mâché and mother-of-pearl;
cane seat, 86.7 x 51.5 x 57 cm
McCord Museum of Canadian History, Montreal,
gift of F. Cleveland Morgan (M18984.1)

394
Second Empire fly chair, about 1860-1870
Ebonized wood, mother-of-pearl inlay and gilding, 83 x 46 x 39 cm
Musée de la civilisation, Quebec City (81-5)
Photo Christine Guest/MMFA

The term "fly chair" was used for a lightweight novelty chair that did not match the rest of the furnishings. This example, made of ebonized wood and decorated with mother-of-pearl inlay, was probably imported from France.

Papier mâché, an essentially Victorian curiosity, proved to be one of the period's most interesting and popular discoveries in the realm of decorative furniture. Sheets of this material, made according to a pressurizing process developed in England, were often "japanned", or finished in black lacquer in imitation of the Japanese technique. Before being covered in numerous layers of hardened varnish, the papier mâché was ornamented with mother-of-pearl inlay, printed gold-leaf decorations and painted floral, grape, foliage and landscape motifs.[46] During the first half of the nineteenth century, papier mâché was employed almost exclusively for small decorative articles; however, as the result of technological innovations, whose extraordinary possibilities in the field of furniture were demonstrated at the Great Exhibition held in London in 1851,[47] use of the material increased and diversified dramatically. A number of English furniture makers, especially in the Birmingham area, began to systematically study the potential of papier mâché, and in this were swiftly followed by certain French firms and a few American ones located mostly in Connecticut.[48]

It is certain that some papier mâché furniture was imported into Quebec, but there is as yet no evidence to show that there was any produced in the province. The most that can be asserted is that in 1864 the firm of John & William Hilton introduced a decorative technique that also made use of mother-of-pearl:

There is now one branch of cabinet making, carried out by this firm, which is nowhere else practiced in this Province – enamelling. They are engaged in the manufacture of chairs, the back of which are inlaid with ivory and mother of pearl, and which when finished combine the useful and ornamental in a manner rarely to be met with; as specimens of mechanical perfection in this business they cannot be excelled.[49]

At the provincial exhibition held the following year, the Hiltons presented "three pearl inlaid chairs".[50] It seems likely that the decoration of these articles was similar to that seen on the backs of the chairs in the Chippendale-style dining-room set now in the collection of the Petites Franciscaines de Marie in Baie Saint-Paul. In any case, the genuine examples of papier mâché furniture that have been identified in Quebec's various public and private collections are all relatively typical examples of the genre as far as shape and decoration are concerned. Of the three small rococo-revival tables belonging to the McCord Museum of Canadian History, the one with the top bearing floral decorations has been executed with considerably less skill than the two others, which both possess a checker-board top. The two richly-decorated moulded chairs kept at the same museum are apparently of English manufacture,[51] while the pair of elegant fly chairs belonging to the Musée de la civilisation are in the Second Empire style and may be of either French or English origin.

Metal furniture lent itself to a both wider and more functional range of uses than articles in fragile papier mâché, and although much furniture of this type was imported into Quebec, a considerable quantity was also manufactured here in the province. It is therefore worth examining in some detail the various innovations imposed on this age-old material by the Victorian furniture industry.

Quebec was generally very receptive to foreign furniture that made use of new materials. At the universal exhibition held in Paris in 1870, the Americans were particularly proud of their perforated plywood chairs.[52] In

395

Examples of Bent Wood Furniture
Engraving published in the *Canadian Mechanics' Magazine and Patent Office Record*, December 1876, p. 372
Photo SRP

This illustration appeared in a section entitled "The Illustrated Family Friend", which the editors of the *Canadian Mechanics' Magazine* had added to their magazine in August 1876, stating that it would be "lighter in character, but not less instructive or useful, as it will be the means, we hope, of creating a taste for literature and science, and for many of those pleasant and useful arts, suitable for both sexes, which are so much practiced in the mother country and in Europe, and which have tended, in so much a degree, to improve and benefit nations.

396

Rocking chair, about 1900
Oak splints, wood, 104 x 68 x 58 cm
Musée de la civilisation, Quebec City (89-3087)
Photo Christine Guest/MMFA

The use of oak splints in the construction of this rocking chair derives from a time-honoured method previously limited to basket-weaving. This novel use of a basketry technique is typical of the innovative spirit of furniture-making in Victorian Quebec.

397
Wickerwork Platform Rocker Illustrating a Description of the Firm of Philippe Vallière (1832-1919)
Illustration published in K.G.C. Huttemeyer, *Les intérêts commerciaux de Montréal et Québec et leurs manufactures* (Montreal: K.G.C. Huttemeyer, 1889), p. 200
Library of the Séminaire de Québec, fonds ancien (210)
Photo W. B. Edwards Inc., Quebec City

The text accompanying the illustration opens as follows: "Modern furniture is marvellous in its art and elegance, and the improvements brought about over the past twenty-five years have been most marked." (trans.)

398
Advertisement for the firm of William King & Cie of Montreal
Published in *Le Monde illustré*, December 3, 1887
Photo SRP

399
Armchair, late nineteenth century
Wicker, 121.5 x 75 x 71 cm
Flaurence Joncas Collection, Cap-Rouge
Photo Brian Merrett/MMFA
This armchair is part of a set that once belonged to Dr. Martineau of Grosse-Île.

July of the same year, the furniture maker D. S. Rickaby announced that he was the only authorized agent for the "seat in Perforated Marquetry (Veneer) by Gardner".[53] Quebec citizens also showed a liking for the lightness, elegance and inexpensiveness of the bentwood furniture developed by the German-born Michael Thonet, who settled in Vienna in 1842. Thonet's participation in London's Great Exhibition in 1851 contributed in a major way to the international recognition of his work. By 1866, he had agents in Budapest, Paris, London, Berlin, Hamburg, Rotterdam and Brno. Following the expiration of his imperial patent in 1869, dozens of his designs – including the famous "Thonet" chair – were copied by a number of rival firms, notably Jacob and Josef Kohn, of Vienna.[54] In 1890, D. S. Rickaby was their official agent in Quebec.[55] Fourteen years earlier, the presence of furniture by Thonet and Kohn at the Philadelphia Exposition did much to increase the popularity of

400
Edmond Vandry, Quebec City
Tom Russell, Robert Shipp Porter, John William Porter and John Russell at the photographer's,
about 1898
Photograph
Private collection, Sillery

401
Notman Studio, Montreal
The conservatory in the George Stephen house, Montreal, 1884
Photograph
McCord Museum of Canadian History, Montreal, Notman Photographic Archives (73,817-II)

402
Notman Studio, Montreal
John Thomas Molson (1837-1910), about 1862
Photograph
National Archives of Canada, Ottawa (PA-125775)

bentwood furniture in the United States.[56] No doubt inspired by this presentation, *The Canadian Patent Office Record and Mechanics' Magazine* reproduced a few examples in its December 1876 issue. An advertisement dating from 1889 stated that McGarvey himself had in stock "a complete selection of much-admired bent furniture from Vienna (Austria)".[57]

In his publicity for the 1887 Christmas season, the Montreal *meublier* William King advertised various types of "fancy furniture", including "bentwood chairs from Vienna (Austria)" and "newstyle chairs in Chinese cane". This is an especially interesting bit of information, for it throws light on yet another facet of Victorian taste and fashion: the category of often exotically-inspired furniture made of various kinds of organic material. Items made of animal horn — including articles in American buffalo horn, designed to evoke the Wild West — were typical examples of this kind of furniture.[58] And here again McGarvey was prepared to go to any length to satisfy his clients' whims: in September 1880, visitors to his store could examine a "library chair, formed of eight buffalo horn tips, highly polished, the back being formed naturally by the curve of the horn, upholstered in red morocco leather".[59]

Flights of Victorian fancy reached even greater heights in a large variety of house and garden furniture made of rattan, wicker, cane and even ash splints.[60] As well as being light, sturdy and relatively cheap, such materials could be easily twisted and turned into any shape conceived by the fertile imagination of the designer. While cane — generally reed or rattan bark — was used for chair seats, long, flexible strips of rattan, reeds and other plants were used to model seat furniture and tables of all kinds. The selection of furniture available ranged from rocking chairs[61] with Hunzinger-inspired mechanisms to delicate drawing-room pieces; from elegant seats for the photographer's studio to whole suites designed to grace the conservatory or garden. In 1882, Owen McGarvey, ever-sensitive to fashion trends, exhibited six different models of basketwork chair rather unusually finished in tones of silver-bronze, gold and green.[62]

Wicker furniture, especially during the last few decades of the nineteenth century, was to some extent a reflection of the taste for "nature"; similarly, rustic furniture, especially as understood by the followers of A. J. Downing, echoed an interest in "the environment".[63] Ironically, these assemblages of branches selected for their individual shape can actually be seen as attempts to domesticate nature.[64] Some designers obviously yearned for dominance over more than simply the decoration and furnishing of the house! And nature did offer a certain aesthetic comfort, even if it fell a little short on the physical.

John R. Porter

1 *Un long dimanche de fiançailles* (Paris: Denoël, 1991), p. 118 (trans.).

2 *Journal de Québec*, June 24, 1853 (trans.).

3 Émile Clerc, "Meubles", in *Dictionnaire du commerce, de l'industrie et de la banque*, Yves Guyot and A. Raffalovich (eds.) (Paris: Guillaumin, 1899), pp. 786-787 (trans.).

4 The ten Quebec patents we have been able to trace dating from between 1873 and 1891 concern for the most part the fabrication of seats and convertible furniture (nos. 2685, 2782, 2800, 6934, 7044, 8132, 26791, 27107, 29273 and 36959). See *The Canadian Patent Office Record and Mechanics' Magazine* (1873-1880) and *The Scientific Canadian Mechanics' Magazine and Patent Office Record of Canada* (1880-1891). This sample is undoubtedly far from complete, as other sources cited below attempt to show.

5 His participation in the Montreal provincial exhibition of 1882 offers convincing proof of this interest. *The Gazette*, September 20, 1882, p. 5.

6 Siegfried Giedion, *La mécanisation au pouvoir: contribution à l'histoire anonyme* (Paris: Centre Georges Pompidou, 1980). See chapter 5, entitled "Le mobilier constitutif du dix-neuvième siècle", pp. 332ff.

7 I. Grant, "Le XIXe siècle", in *Histoire du mobilier* (Paris: Éditions Atlas, 1984), p. 195 (trans.).

8 Giedion, *op. cit.*, pp. 350-355. A barber's chair found in the attic of the Séminaire Saint-Sulpice in Montreal was photographed by the Inventaire des biens culturels du Québec à Montréal Service in 1978. There is also a dentist's chair in the collection of the Musée de la civilisation in Quebec City. It is known, moreover, that William Drum made a barber's chair in 1858, and the Roy dit Belleau collection kept at the Canadian Parks Service includes a typolithographed illustration of a dentist's chair with a reclining back and a separate foot-rest. See John R. Porter (ed.) et al., *Les meubliers Pierre Drouin et Honoré Roy et l'industrie du meuble à Québec à l'époque victorienne* (Quebec City: Université Laval, 1989), Cahiers du CÉLAT, no. 10, pp. 119 and 161 (ill. 85).

9 Giedion, *op. cit.*, pp. 357-359.

10 Patent no. 8132, pp. 192 and 196 (ill.).

11 *Montreal Daily Star*, September 19, 1881. The Wilson adjustable chair had already been exhibited by A. N. Smith in 1873. See *The Montreal Herald*, September 19, 1873.

12 *The Montreal Herald* of September 27, 1865 carried the words, "One smoking chair, and admirers of the weed will find every convenience about this chair".

13 At the exhibition of 1881, M. G. Edson & Co. were awarded a first prize for a "Smoking lounging chair". *Montreal Daily Star*, September 20, 1881.

14 *L'Ordre*, August 1, 1860 (trans.).

15 *The Canadian Patent Office Record*, August 1887, pp. 404 and 434 (ill.), patent no. 27107.

16 The photographs bear the inscription "copy of Lounge for Mr Thompson, feb. 6, 1891". James Thomson, whose name was often written with a "p" in contemporary texts, appears on the list of cabinetmakers included in *Lovell's Montreal Directory* for 1890-1891 and 1891-1892.

17 *The Gazette*, September 20, 1882, p. 5.

18 See Giedion, *op. cit.*, pp. 345-346.

19 See the front cover of the present work.

20 *Album de la Minerve*, July 1, 1872, pp. 157-158 (trans.). The text continues with a detailed description of the crib, accompanied by another drawing.

21 *The Gazette*, September 20, 1882, p. 5.

22 *The Gazette*, September 20, 1880, p. 2.

23 See Richard W. Flint, "George Hunzinger", *Nineteenth Century Furniture: Innovation, Revival and Reform*, intro. by Mary Jean Madigan (Watson: Guptill [Art and Antiques Book], 1982), pp. 124-131.

24 *Ibid.*, p. 129. The length of the arc-shaped "bends" on a traditional rocker could be an annoyance where space was restricted.

25 *L'Événement*, September 28, 1880 (trans.). A swivel bookcase surmounted by a bust of Queen Victoria can be seen in a photograph of the Hague house taken in 1902.

26 *The Gazette*, September 20, 1882, p. 5.

27 See *L'Événement*, September 13 and 24, 1869. Jean-François Caron has succeeded in tracking down the original patent in the archives of the patent office in Hull.

28 Giedion, *op. cit.*, pp. 360-370 (trans.).

29 *The Gazette*, September 20, 1882, p. 5.

30 *Montreal Daily Star*, September 12, 1884, p. 5.

31 *Industries of Canada, City of Montreal, Historical and Descriptive Review, Leading Firms and Moneyed Institutions* (Montreal: Gazette, 1886), p. 117.

32 See *Le Canard*, April 12, 1884, p. 4 (trans.). The same company also marketed "universal cabinets" made of black walnut, ash, cherry-wood or mahogany, which could be placed in any washstand, bedside table or commode. This invention, patented on January 15, 1884, was said to combine "elegance, healthfulness and comfort". *Le Canard*, May 10, 1884, p. 4 (trans.).

33 *Montreal Daily Star*, September 19 and 20, 1881.

34 *Industries of Canada...*, p. 157.

35 For more on this, see Giedion, *op. cit.*, pp. 336 and 362.

36 *Industries of Canada...*, p. 117.

37 *The Canadian Patent Office Record*, February 1877, pp. 20 and 30 (ill.), patent no. 6934.

38 On the somewhat obscure origins of the sewing machine, see "The Early History of the Sewing Machine", *The Canadian Patent Office Record and Mechanics' Magazine*, November 1873, pp. 236-237; and "The Sewing Machine", *ibid.*, March 1878, p. 72.

39 In 1873, the furniture maker-inventor Onésime Saint-Amand and Joseph Woodley of Quebec City applied for a patent on a sewing machine. *The Canadian Patent Office Record*, October 1873, pp. 158 and 169 (ill.), patent no. 2641.

40 See Martha Eckmann Brent, "A Stitch in Time: The Sewing Machine Industry of Ontario, 1860-1897", *Bulletin d'histoire de la culture matérielle/Material History Bulletin* (Ottawa: National Museum of Man, Spring 1980), pp. 1-32 (on Raymond, see pp. 11-15).

41 *Journal de Québec*, September 3, 1874, p. 3 (trans.).

42 John Gloag, "Castors or Casters", in *A Complete Dictionary of Furniture* (New York: The Overlook Press, 1991), p. 193.

43 "Spring Upholstery", *ibid.*, p. 636.

44 *Quebec Daily Mercury*, September 11, 1895, p. 2.

45 R. N. Tombyll's name appears in *Lovell's Montreal Directory* for the first time in 1891-1892, featured on the list of cabinetmakers; at that time, his establishment was located at 566 Craig Street.

46 A good description of the process can be found in *Exhibition of the Works of Industry of All Nations, 1851. Reports by the Juries* (London: William Cowles & Sons, 1852), p. 549.

47 *Ibid.* and Shirley Spoulding De Voe, *English Papier Mâché of the Georgian and Victorian Periods* (Middletown: Wesleyan University Press, 1971).

48 Joseph Butler, *American Antiques 1800-1900: A Collector's History and Guide* (New York: The Odyssey Press, 1965), pp. 78-79.

49 *Montreal Business Sketches...* (Montreal: M. Longmore and Co., 1864), p. 81.

50 *Montreal Herald*, September 27, 1865.

51 See De Voe, *op. cit.*, p. 179.

52 Giedion, *op. cit.*, p. 334.

53 *L'Événement*, July 9, 1878, p. 4.

54 See Christopher Wilk, "Thonet and Bentwood", in Madigan, *op. cit.*, pp. 118-123.

55 *L'Électeur*, November 10, 1890, p. 3.

56 Wilk, *op. cit.*, p. 122.

57 *La Minerve*, December 6, 1889, p. 1 (trans.).

58 Butler, *op. cit.*, p. 88.

59 *The Gazette*, September 20, 1880, p. 2.

60 See Katherine Menz, "Wicker", in Madigan, *op. cit.*, pp. 132-139.

61 In 1880, McGarvey had in stock "lady's and gentleman's rattan rocking chairs with new platform rockers, looking very inviting for a nap". *The Gazette*, September 20, 1880, p. 2.

62 *The Gazette*, September 20, 1882, p. 5.

63 Butler, *op. cit.*, pp. 86-87.

64 See *The Canadian Patent Office Record and Mechanics' Magazine*, September 1875, p. 267; October 1875, p. 317; October 1878, p. 320.

Woods, Veneers and Finishes

According to a somewhat simplistic but widespread view, the furniture produced in Quebec during the Victorian era was necessarily heavy and elaborately decorated, made of dark woods with a highly polished finish. However, an empirical examination of the artifacts' woods, veneers and finishes reveals a rather more complex situation.

To begin with, it is important to emphasize the wide variety of both local and exotic woods employed by the furniture makers working between 1840 and 1900. Examination of contemporary documentary sources and the furniture itself reveals the presence of the following varieties: black walnut, butter-nut, maple, oak, elm, ash, yellow birch, basswood, pine and cherry wood on the one hand, and mahogany, rosewood, ebony, camphor wood, palisander, tulip wood, zebra wood and cocobolo on the other. Of the two categories, local and exotic, walnut and mahogany were the most frequently used.

The situation regarding the furniture itself is also a dual one, for some pieces produced were examples of joinery (*menuiserie*), others of cabinetwork (*ébénisterie*). The joinery pieces are generally of solid wood, while the cabinetwork makes frequent use of precious woods, often in the form of veneers.[1] This said, certain pieces produced during the period that concerns us combine the two approaches in some quite outstanding examples of workmanship (see especially the sideboard by F. P. Gauvin belonging to the Musée de la civilisation).

During the first half of the nineteenth century, the penchant for woods with a pronounced grain led to the development of veneering techniques able to provide striking effects at a reasonable cost. Several local tree varieties were used to make veneers of quite interesting pattern. Through careful cutting, figured or crotch walnut,[2] sections of curly or bird's-eye maple,[3] the pith rays of oak and the intricate motif of burl elm[4] could all be put to use in the production of very fine veneers. That the levels of skill achieved in the field were considerable is indicated by the participation in the provincial exhibition held in Montreal in 1850 of "a young Canadian furniture maker from Quebec City", who had invented a machine to make sheets of

403
Renaissance-revival sideboard (detail), about 1870
Walnut and walnut veneer, 291 x 176 x 54 cm
Musée régional de Vaudreuil-Soulanges
Photo Christine Guest/MMFA

bird's-eye maple.⁵ This inventor, as an article in the Quebec City newspaper *Le Canadien* made clear, was none other than Onésime Saint-Amand. The article went on to say that Saint-Amand had produced an

...indigenous product of the greatest importance for industry and commerce and ... [which] should definitely be featured in the London exhibition. This product, a result of his ingenuity, which makes use of one of Canada's natural products, the tree that is its national emblem, was a large roll of bird's-eye maple veneer, accompanied by a highly-polished sample of the same veneer actually put to use. Mr. Saint-Amand has invented a machine that permits the removal of hundreds of feet in a single piece, and has set up a steam-run workshop to do just that. Maple veneer can be employed highly effectively in decorative furniture as a substitute for veneers of mahogany and other exotic woods; and instead of having to import them, at considerable cost, Canada, thanks to Mr. Saint-Amand, can now obtain veneers that are less expensive, of finer quality and found locally; they can even be exported.⁶

It is not known whether or not these internationalist hopes were realized, but there is no doubt that Saint-Amand took full advantage of his machine as far as the Quebec market was concerned.

As well as the local varieties, costly exotic woods sometimes known in French as *bois des isles* (island woods), such as mahogany and rosewood, were extremely popular. An 1861 inventory of the workshop of Honoré Roy dit Belleau lists forty-seven sheets of mahogany plywood and a batch of rosewood plywood, together with 185 plywood sheets of black walnut.⁷

As time went on, there was a growing preference for woods with a less pronounced grain, better suited to highlighting the work of decorators and carvers, whose role was increasing in importance.⁸ This development led naturally to a profusion of elaborately ornamented furniture, of which the Whitehead suite belonging to the Musée de la civilisation is an example. For this type of work, black walnut was definitely the most popular wood. Apart from the fact that it was easily available, its subtle grain and deep, warm colour were perfectly in tune with current tastes.⁹ In addition, it is a wood that carves easily and takes a very good polish. Other varieties were also employed, of course, but there was a widespread partiality for the darker woods; this preference was so general that varieties such as maple, oak, butter-nut and yellow birch were sometimes stained in imitation of other woods.¹⁰ The wavy grain of the yellow birch lent itself particularly well to the imitation of mahogany.

During the Victorian era, there were a number of methods for adding a "finish" to furniture. The finish is the plain or decorative coating employed to protect the wood fibres from liquid and dirt. This protective layer can be transparent, semi-transparent or opaque, coloured or uncoloured; all the possible combinations thus offer an extremely wide range of finishes. In 1880, *The Furniture and Cabinet Finisher*, published by Jesse Haney & Co., could be purchased for fifty cents from F. N. Boxer on Saint-Denis Street in Montreal.¹¹ Broadly speaking, finishes could be divided into the three categories of oils, waxes or varnishes. Although transparent and semi-transparent finishes were very common, furniture was also sometimes painted in a solid colour, entirely or partially gilded, or decorated with stencilled motifs.

PLACAGE !
Placage en noyer noir,
" en acajou,
Moulures en noyer noir et acajou
Cannes pour fond de chaise.
Le tout bien assorti et à vendre en gros et en détail par
ONÉSIME ST. AMANT,
Meublier,
rue Richelieu, faubourg Saint-Jean.
12 nov 1861   1331

404
Advertisement for the firm of Onésime Saint-Amant of Quebec City
Published in the *Journal de Québec*, January 2, 1862
National Library of Canada, Ottawa (L-11726)

Oil finishes bring out the colour of the wood but do not create a shine. The most commonly used, linseed oil, tends to yellow with time; the more frequently it is applied, the more it tends to alter the colour of the wood. Natural tung oil has less of a tendency to yellow and repels water better, but it was not widely employed. Wax finishes result in a rather soft, non-resistant finish that deteriorates rapidly. Whether it is coloured or not, the thin coat of wax applied to the wood's surface must be polished in order to achieve a shine. To retain a good appearance on wax-finished furniture, it is necessary to re-polish them regularly, which was obviously not practical in the case of extremely elaborately carved pieces.

As the result of the various advantages they offered, varnishes were generally preferred to either oil or wax finishes.¹² Spirit and oil varnishes are the two main categories of varnish, and there are a number of sub-categories arising from different combinations of the two. Spirit varnishes are derived from dry resins — often shellac — dissolved in alcohol so as to obtain a liquid that can be applied in a thin coat. As the varnish is applied the solvent evaporates and the resins regain their original characteristics. This type of varnish is relatively easy to prepare and apply, and results in a high lustre. Unless it has been bleached, shellac is of an orange colour that tones in well with various types of wood. It is not very resistant to water and alcohol, however, and is not employed for certain types of furniture. Oil varnishes, which generally contain linseed or tung oil, are more elastic and more resistant to abrasion. Resins and solvents are sometimes added to oil varnishes to accelerate the drying process and increase their resistance to dust. However, they result in a softer surface than spirit varnishes, and cannot be brought to such a high polish. The greater the proportion of oil in a varnish, the more durable but the less shiny it will be.[13] It is hardly surprising, then, to find that a large percentage of Quebec Victorian furniture was given a spirit varnish finish. The guarantee of a beautiful shine and easy maintenance through simple polishing was sufficient to outweigh any inconvenience caused by the finish's lack of durability.[14]

The degree of colour of a varnish depends on the relative fineness of the resins employed in its composition. Generally, however, the varnish used was sufficiently transparent to reveal the beauty of the wood's grain and colour. Owing to the aging of the resins and accumulation of dirt on the surface, the varnish on pieces of furniture that have come down to us with their original finish does not always retain its initial transparency. However, contrary to what is generally believed, it is possible to thoroughly clean the surface of a piece of furniture and to restore its original character without actually removing the varnish (a whatnot belonging to the Musée de la civilisation underwent such a cleaning). It is more difficult, though, to treat the resins so as to correct small cracks in the surface and restore a uniform finish; this task can only be successfully accomplished by a professional restorer.

The preceding observations offer merely a brief overview of the finishing techniques employed in Quebec during the Victorian era. *Meubliers* and cabinetmakers were traditionally disinclined to share their expertise, preferring to keep for themselves certain "trade secrets" and the advantages they entailed. Our only recourse in attempting to reconstruct their techniques is to refer to recipes published in various treatises and periodicals, hence the importance of preserving the furniture's original finish wherever possible. To strip a piece of furniture of its finish is actually to remove an element of its character and history that no modern varnish could possibly replace.

Patrick Albert and John R. Porter

---

1   The French words *ébéniste* (cabinetmaker) and *ébénisterie* (cabinetwork) were first employed towards the end of the seventeenth century to distinguish *menuisiers en ébène* (ebony joiners) — who specialized in working with precious woods — from other furniture makers. Before long, *ébénistes* began to develop special techniques designed to economize valuable woods, including the technique of veneering — the laying down of very thin layers of precious wood over a body of a more ordinary variety. In their advertising, some Quebec furniture makers of the Victorian period identified themselves as *meublier* (furniture maker), some as *ébéniste*, some as both. See, for example, the advertisement run by François Lafleur and Jean-Baptiste Saint-Laurent in *Journal de Québec*, March 30, 1844.

2   The irregular fibres of figured or crotch wood come from the place on a tree where a branch joins the main trunk.

3   Curly and bird's-eye maple are derived from trees that have had an irregular growth pattern.

4   Burl wood comes from a dome-shaped growth on the trunk of a tree; it shows a pattern composed of rings and spots against a dark, curly ground.

5   *La Minerve* quoted in *Journal de Québec*, October 22, 1850, p. 2. In January 1874, Edwin R. Whitney of Bolton applied for a patent for a new machine for cutting wood for veneers (*The Canadian Patent Office Record and Mechanics' Magazine*, February 1874, pp. 230-231, patent no. 3036).

6   *Le Canadien*, October 14, 1850, p. 2 (trans.). In the census of 1851 (p. 1 782), it is stated that in his workshop located in the Saint-Jean district, Saint-Amand used "1 steam to drive a machine" (trans.).

7   ANQQ, register of notary Jean-Baptiste Pruneau, no. 5121, February 16, 1861. See John R. Porter (ed.) *et al.*, *Les meubliers Pierre Drouin et Honoré Roy et l'industrie du meuble à Québec à l'époque victorienne* (Quebec City: CÉLAT [Université Laval], 1989), pp. 185-189. Excerpts from the *American Cabinet-Maker* dealing with marquetry and veneering are featured in the April (pp. 110-111) and July 1880 (pp. 227-228) issues of *The Scientific Canadian*.

8   See the article "Fashion in Woods", *The Scientific Canadian*, December 1882, pp. 375-376.

9   An article in the *Album de la Minerve*, May 15, 1873, pp. 318-319, asserts that "furniture in dark wood is the height of fashion" (trans.).

10   We have discovered a number of practical recipes for staining, darkening or imitating different woods. See the *Album de la Minerve*, January 1872 (p. 728) and May 27, 1873 (p. 532); *The Canadian Patent Office Record and Mechanics' Magazine*, February 1874 (p. 349); *Canadian Mechanics' Magazine and Patent Office Record*, May 1877 (p. 151), December 1877 (p. 366) and August 1878 (p. 240); *The Scientific Canadian*, April 1879 (pp. 105-106).

11   See *The Scientific Canadian*, October 1880, p. 313.

12   An article by Z. T. Anstett, entitled "Varnish, and the Materials used in its manufacture", originally published in the *Druggists' Advertiser*, was reproduced in *The Canadian Mechanics' Magazine and Patent Office Record* in June 1878, p. 191.

13   For more on this subject, see A. Romain, *Nouveau manuel complet du fabricant de vernis de toute espèce* (Paris: L.D.V.D. Inter Livres, 1987) (re-edition of a manual by Roret); F. N. Vanderwalker, *Wood Finishing, Plain and Decorative* (New York: Drake Publishing Inc., 1976), pp. 153-176.

14   Practical advice on polishes appears in the *Canadian Mechanics' Magazine and Patent Office Record*, December 1877, p. 367; *The Scientific Canadian*, January (p. 18), March (p. 88), April (pp. 105-106), and September (p. 275) 1879, March (p. 82) and November (p. 335) 1881.

Techniques Employed in the Making of Fine Furniture[*]

It is generally relatively easy for an experienced eye to recognize the style, origin and period of old furniture. This is far less true, however, for pieces from the Victorian era, a period during which the "revival" of earlier styles and even their all-out imitation were rife. To discover the truth in such cases, experts are sometimes obliged to closely examine the furniture's various material components.

One of the most distinctive features of Victorian furniture is the way in which it was constructed. For centuries, woodworkers had employed techniques that enabled them to assemble furniture without the assistance of any metal elements whatever; traditional construction, based on the mortice-and-tenon joint, was used exclusively. During Victoria's reign, though, cabinetmakers witnessed the transition from the small-scale craft workshop equipped with "classical" tools to industrial-style production in which machinery played an increasingly large role.

As the result of various technological developments, devices and techniques necessary to furniture production were accessible to nineteenth-century *meubliers* more easily and at a lower cost. Saw-mills equipped with circular or ribbon saws permitted the rapid manufacture of perfect planks, far more regular than those produced traditionally by pit-sawyers. Screws, rather than being fashioned with a file, were now manufactured automatically using a metal-working lathe. Nails, previously crafted individually by a blacksmith, were now also produced mechanically with the aid of shears.[1] In sum, furniture makers could now rely on a variety of materials that made the assembly of their creations a good deal easier. This was particularly significant in light of the fact that for economic reasons they were under pressure to produce more and more quickly. All these elements, then, led to important modifications in the fundamental conception of furniture.

Allowing for the inevitable exceptions, it is possible to identify a certain number of characteristics peculiar to fine furniture in Victorian Quebec that enable us to distinguish

405
François Gourdeau (1840-1920)
Dressing table mirror, about 1875
The Montreal Museum of Fine Arts, gift of Henri Beaulac (1990.Df.5)
Photo Brian Merrett/MMFA

406
François Gourdeau (1840-1920)
Components of a dressing table mirror, about 1875
The Montreal Museum of Fine Arts, gift of Henri Beaulac (1990.Df.5)
Photo Brian Merrett/MMFA

In a gradual move away from traditional methods, glue and metal elements were now used in the assembling of furniture to speed up production. However, many pieces still included hand-carved decoration.

407
François Gourdeau (1840-1920)
Renaissance-revival chair
(from a set of six), about 1870
Detail: the interior of the seat
Black walnut, 120 x 45 x 53 cm
The Montreal Museum of Fine Arts, gift of the Succession J.A. DeSève (1986.Df.7)

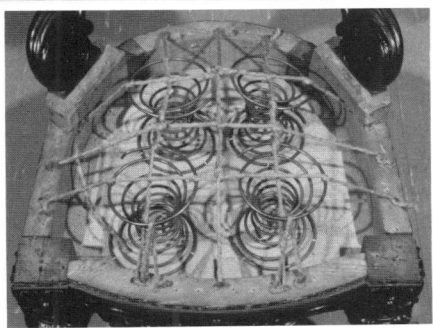

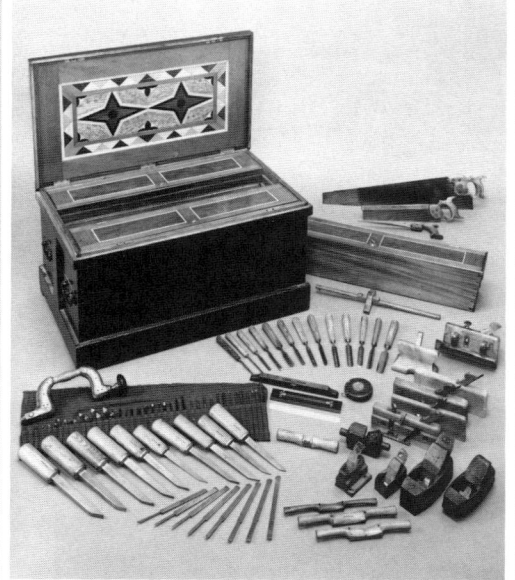

it from so-called "traditional" furniture. These general properties have been derived from the empirical examination of a number of pieces included in the present exhibition.

In the past, the framework of a piece of furniture — a cupboard for instance — formed a solid whole. During the Victorian era, although frames were still constructed using mortice-and-tenon joints, the tongue-and-groove technique was increasingly popular, the elements being quicker to produce with a machine. The panels of the piece were inserted into the grooves, but were sometimes also secured with screws at the back. The use of the dowel, a round piece of wood between a quarter and half an inch in diameter that was inserted into holes pierced at various points within a joint, became more widespread. In order to simplify construction, all the elements of a single article — a commode, cupboard or washstand, for example — were made separately and then assembled with the help of screws or nails. Moulding, once an integral part of the furniture, was applied and held on with nails or, in the case of large pieces, screwed on from the back. Very often articles were assembled using butt-joints, whereby two flat surfaces of wood were glued with animal glue and held in place with clamps until they dried. Nails were used where necessary to solidify the joints. Bottoms (of cupboards, drawers, etc.), once rough-hewn and thick, became much thinner, which offered the advantage of lightening the article as a whole. On the other hand, a frequent disregard for proportion and inadequate joining techniques meant that many pieces were far from stable. Things were particularly bad in the realm of seat furniture — chairs, armchairs and sofas. General structural flimsiness, exaggerated curves, poorly inserted dowels and butt-joint construction — often masked by a pleasing exterior — were the source of much shoddy work. These problems were often exacerbated, moreover, by the additional strain caused by an excessive use of springs in the upholstery.

Once part and parcel of the furniture, ornamentation was now screwed or glued onto the flat surfaces. This was the case for many carved elements, which were often made separately and affixed later. Without these applied decorations, numerous sideboards, bookcases and bedsteads from the period would appear extremely plain. Veneers, which became fashionable during the early decades of the nineteenth century, could now be produced by special machines, considerably reducing their cost. Veneering techniques, it will be recalled, involve the gluing of thin layers of precious or unusually-grained (burled or figured) woods

408
Eastlake-style bed, about 1880-1900
Detail of the head
176 x 152 x 200 cm
Musée du Séminaire de Québec
Photo Jean-Pierre Labiau/MOBIVIQ
The use of machinery led to the increasing stylization of decorative motifs.

409
Tool box belonging to an English cabinetmaker, about 1850
55 x 90 x 55 cm
Glenbow Museum, Calgary
The inside of this box is decorated with marquetry work. It is divided into nine drawers and four compartments, and holds 160 tools of various kinds. It belonged successively to the English cabinetmakers J. Williams and J. W. Floyd. The tool box was brought to Canada from England in about 1910 by the latter's grandson.

on a base of a more common variety. Similarly, pre-machined sections could be added to different articles to create unusual and striking shapes: these might be decorated with carving executed with the aid of a pantograph, ornamental elements taken from architecture or geometric motifs executed with a stamping die.[2] Moreover, there was a good range of well-manufactured, high-quality hardware that could be used to adorn furniture, which included "tear drop" handles, porcelain knobs, decorative cast iron fittings and castors.[3]

The equipment used by different cabinetmakers varied widely, as a comparison of the articles used by the *meublier* Honoré Roy dit Belleau and the manufacturer William Drum proves.[4] Even the craftsman benefited from progress, due in part to the appearance on the market of convertible planes that could be fitted with different blades. Rather than cluttering up his bench with all manner of planes, the modern *meublier* could purchase a "Stanley", which came equipped with about sixty different blades, the whole stored in a container no bigger than a shoe box! By using various combinations of blade, a craftsman could produce many different types of moulding.

Needless to say, the advent of new tools and machines did not entirely undermine the essential role of handwork. Apart from the rough-planing and the various preparatory operations, the furniture maker still undertook the assembling and hand-finishing of the pieces he produced. In fact, the Industrial Revolution allowed the cabinetmaker's art to reach new heights. No longer obliged to waste time and energy sawing, cutting and planing, some makers took advantage of the situation to devote themselves wholly to the design and decoration of their creations. For others, though, the increased fragmentation and anonymity of the various tasks, the demands of the market and the sometimes alienating new technologies had an opposite and negative effect, especially as regards the handing down of traditional craft techniques.

Alain Michel Laferrière and
John R. Porter

410
Stanley-type multi-purpose tool
15.5 x 30.5 x 19 cm
Alain Michel Laferrière Collection, Saint-Clet
Photo Christine Guest/MMFA

For more information about this multi-purpose tool, see the book by Alvin Sellens entitled *The Stanley Plane: A History and Descriptive Inventory* (The Early American Industries Associations, 1975)

Text based on notes and observations recorded by the cabinetmaker Alain Michel Laferrière.

1 The so-called "wire-nail" did not appear, however, until the end of the nineteenth century.

2 Victorian furniture makers had available to them – through catalogues and other sources – a host of machine-made decorative elements in different sizes and woods. There was also a wide range of mouldings on the market designed to adorn the house's various rooms. As early as April 1856, Owen McGarvey was offering for sale "a large assortment of Sheets of Mahogany, Grained Wood and Mouldings, carved in different patterns". *Le Pays*, April 1, 1856, p. 3 (trans.).

3 Baldwin and Clark were notable among the manufacturers of these items.

4 On June 23, 1862, readers of the *Journal de Québec* were informed in an advertisement that the ironmonger S. J. Shaw of Saint-Jean Street "still has in stock a wide assortment of tools for furniture makers and joiners, from the famous factory of W. Greaves and Sons" (trans.).

Metal Furniture

The use of iron became widespread during the nineteenth century. As the result of advances in technology, particularly the development of stronger alloys, it found an ever-growing range of applications, from the construction of trains, ships and large buildings, to the manufacture of gratings and railings, handrails, light fixtures, bathtubs, furnaces, stoves, utensils, pots and pans, pipes and hardware of all descriptions. Domestic interiors also came under its influence, and many Victorian homes in Quebec contained iron furniture of one sort or another, of either local or foreign manufacture.

Among the iron furnishings recorded is a wide variety of hall furniture — hall racks and stands or hat, coat and umbrella stands — designed to fulfil one or several of the various obvious functions. Also available were metal "hall" or "passage" chairs. The range of metal bedsteads, of different shapes and a myriad decorations, was enormous and included single, double, folding and canopied beds, as well as lounge settees and cradles. Among the garden furniture available were benches, chairs, settees, armchairs, sofas and various types of table. The design of these articles was often very similar to pieces reproduced in periodicals like the London-based Art Journal.

At this period, the generic term "iron furniture" was regularly used to refer to objects in iron proper, wrought iron, cast iron, and even copper or brass. Between 1850 and 1880, however, cast iron predominated, and it was available in a huge selection of motifs and designs. After the piece was cast, it was bronzed or painted brown, grey, black or green; it was then given an enamel or japanned finish. During the last two decades of the century, there was a gradual standardization of metal furniture. During this period, while production of inexpensive iron bedsteads continued, luxury beds were generally made of brass or copper.

In Montreal, two names above all were associated with iron furniture: William Rodden and William Clendinneng. Both men were employed at the Hedge & Bonner foundry (1843-1859) until 1859, at which time Rodden purchased the company and re-named it the Montreal Foundry and City Works. Rodden and Clendinneng then became partners in the running of the foundry and a store. In 1868,

411
Coat and umbrella stand, about 1860-1890
Cast iron, 217 x 102 x 31 cm
Archdiocese of Sherbrooke
Photo Christine Guest/MMFA

Small entrance halls very often contained a simple metal stand for hanging hats and coats. They became common in Victorian homes at the same time as the hall itself. The British magazine *The Art-Union: A Monthly Journal of the Fine Arts* illustrated a stand similar to this one in its August 1846 issue (p. 221).

412
Advertisement for the firm of Rodden & Meilleur of Montreal
Published in the *Business Guide to the City of Montreal* (Montreal: John Lovell, 1860), p. 47
Photo SRP

Clendinneng took over entirely and his son subsequently carried on the business until the early twentieth century. As well as iron furniture, the company manufactured stoves, furnaces, railings and a wide range of ornamental work. At one time, the Stephens, Allans and Molsons all counted among the company's clients. William Rodden was awarded several prizes at the provincial exhibitions of 1853 and 1857, and

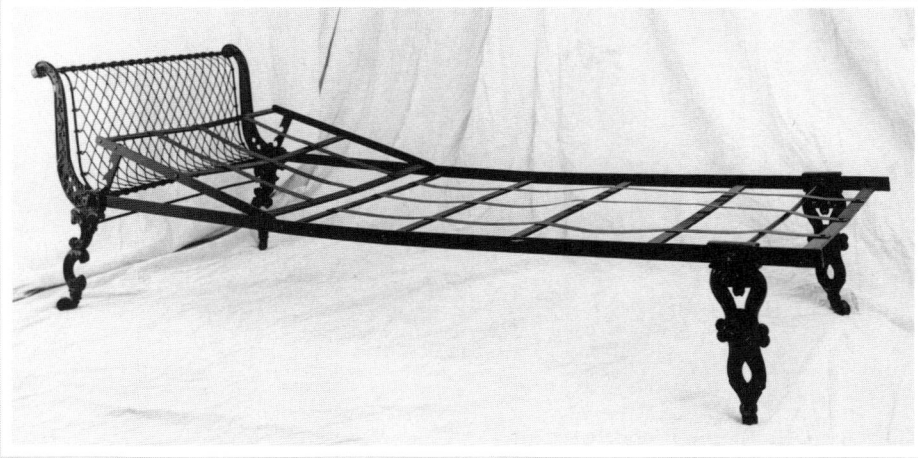

413
Ives & Allen
Rococo-revival bed, between 1860 and 1873
Cast iron, 70 x 76 x 197 cm
Aux Multiples Collections, Quebec City
Photo SRP
The head of this bed is adjustable. It bears the inscription "IVES & ALLEN MONTREAL".

414
Rococo-revival bed head, about 1860
Cast iron, 110.7 x 139.7 cm
The Montreal Museum of Fine Arts,
gift of Mrs. Walter Molson (1950.51.Dm.18)
Photo Christine Guest/MMFA

415
Rococo-revival bed, about 1860
Detail: the head
Cast iron, 100 x 145.6 x 207 cm
Private collection, Rivière-du-Loup
Photo Christine Guest/MMFA

Clendinneng's son was the only exhibitor to present iron garden furniture at the exhibition of 1893. The firm had a high output and marketed its goods increasingly throughout Canada and even abroad. The existence of a number of other large Montreal companies producing metal furniture, such as Meilleur, Rodden [T.M.] & Meilleur (1856-1862), Prowse & McFarlane, Ives & Allen and Surveyer, is proof of the importance of this industry.

In 1862, the Quebec City firm of James Foley, located on de la Fabrique Street, was offering its clients "an assortment of iron bedsteads from the best makers and in the latest fashions, including the Prince of Wales, the Harp, the Gothic, with scrollwork or openwork, folding, etc.". The beds belonging to the Montreal Museum of Fine Arts and a private collection in Rivière-du-Loup, adorned respectively with three ostrich feathers and a harp, seem to correspond accurately to the first two designs mentioned in the issue of *Le Canadien* published on May 20, 1862. Another Quebec City firm, Glover & Fry, sold iron beds from

THE FURNITURE

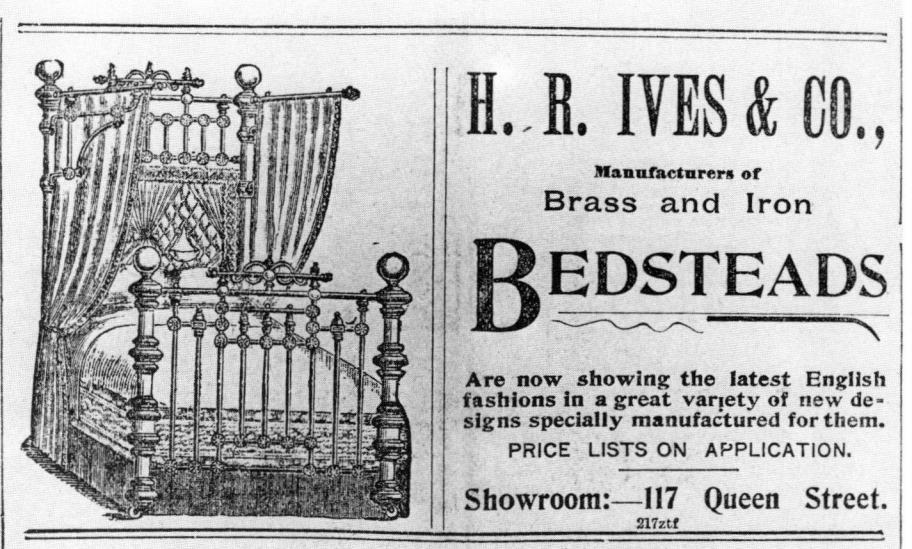

416
Advertisement for the firm of H. R. Ives & Co. of Montreal
Published in the *Montreal Star*, September 15, 1896
Photo SRP

1860 – and possibly earlier – until the turn of the century. Elsewhere in the province, similar products were sold quite widely by George Gale & Son of Waterville, in the Eastern Townships, and by the St. Maurice Iron Foundry of Trois-Rivières.

Several Montreal manufacturers and sellers of wooden and metal furniture did not hesitate to complete their own selections with elegant metal pieces imported from England, France or the United States. In June 1862, the Quebec City firm of Foley advertised that its iron bedsteads came from "factories in Montreal and New York". And in the same month, Glover & Fry also made use of the *Journal de Québec* to promote their recent English and French imports:

The undersigned have just received a shipment of English and French bedsteads, which arrived on the *San Juan* from Le Havre, which, with the assortment of similar articles of English make already in stock, constitute the most complete and extensive range that can be seen in the province of iron and copper bedsteads, for sale at prices bound to stimulate buyers. It is hardly necessary to reiterate the advantages of iron bedsteads over wooden ones as far as health, hygiene and durability are concerned.

The Victorians were, indeed, well aware of the advantages of metal furniture, which combined durability, fire resistance, convenience, comfort and elegance with easy maintenance and coolness in summer. And not forgetting, of course, the hygienic properties that, in Victorian eyes, made iron furniture a major contributor towards the health of its users!

Daniel Drouin and John R. Porter

THE PURSUIT OF ELEGANCE

Dominant Styles and the Evolution of Taste

> Many people who have fairly good taste, are yet from want of training, unable to use it to advantage in house decorations... Good taste is good taste the world over, and it is only the extreme in styles that changes... The love for the beautiful finds a place in every refined mind, and is a germ that desires cultivation, and is ever on the lookout for the means of gratifying that desire.[1]

IT IS HARDLY NECESSARY TO RECALL THAT THE HISTORY OF fine furniture in Victorian Quebec follows a pattern that is far from linear. As in art and architecture, the situation was one of extravagant eclecticism, with formal and stylistic variations inspired by the past rubbing shoulders with others that, in sharp contrast, reflected a forward-looking preoccupation with innovation and reform. It was a situation rife with oppositions, overlappings and paradoxes, influenced by many external factors. Against this constantly changing backdrop even the Victorians themselves sometimes felt lost, especially since unanimity on the exact nature of the "good taste" so eagerly sought by all was hard to attain.

Now, a century later, we clearly need to set our own tastes and sensibilities aside if we wish to fully grasp those of the Victorians. Just as our lifestyles and domestic customs will undoubtedly be a source of some astonishment to our great-grandchildren, it is quite natural that those of our own great-grandparents should occasionally leave us baffled. In the realm of taste, our aim should surely be to understand rather than to share the now-outmoded perceptions and choices of our forefathers. For in their fusing of historical styles, they felt themselves to be in the very forefront of fashion. They were entirely supported in this view, moreover, by the official doctrines and models promoted by the great universal exhibitions.[2] It must also be conceded that what is generally considered desirable in the way of decor and lighting for living spaces can alter utterly from one generation to the next. A statement taken from the "furnishing" section of the *Album de la Minerve* in 1873 serves to illustrate the point:

> The fear of *darkening* a room by hangings, paintings and curtains is the result of a prejudice. Everyone knows today that there is nothing more *furnishing*, *decorative*, comfortable and *warm* to the eye than tones that are dark and, as a consequence, rich.[3]

It should not be inferred from this remark, however, that the interiors of Victorian homes were invariably sombre and overcrowded, for this widespread and enduring view is something of an over-simplification. Nor was all the furniture of the period an exquisitely crafted and veneered expression of

417
Greek-revival easy chair, about 1890-1900
Painted wood and upholstery, 98 x 74 x 80 cm
Musée Laurier, Arthabaska
Photo Christine Guest/MMFA

the cabinetmaker's art. Although present-day experts tend to favour pieces in richly carved wood, the most expensive and highly valued articles at the time were often generously upholstered seats of one kind or another covered in luxurious fabrics.[4] In fact, the reputation of a furniture maker like Noël Pratte depended as much on his skills as an upholsterer-decorator as on his fine cabinetwork.[5]

It should also be remembered that the "Victorian" style meant more than simply rococo-revival furniture made of mahogany and decorated with carved roses. As readers will already have begun to realize, the reality of the situation was far more complex. Throughout our research, we have found in contemporary sources evidence of a world of styles that knew virtually no bounds, either spatial or temporal. Apart from the mysterious forms labelled "antique", "classical" and "modern", there is mention of the "English", "American", "Japanese", "French", "Parisian", "Greek-revival", "Flemish-

Renaissance", "Louis XIV", "Louis XV" (rococo revival), "Louis XVI", "Elizabethan" (or "Queen Elizabeth") and "Queen Anne", not forgetting, of course, the "Gothic", "Renaissance", "Empire" and "Eastlake" styles! And even the labels do not tell us much about the furniture itself, for the names and categories attached to it were often just as fanciful as the liberties taken by the manufacturers in their borrowings and blendings from the original historical sources. Brimful of eclectic pastiches and hybrid creations, the Victorian era was not a period of true renaissance but rather — to borrow the term employed by Maurice Rheims — of "senescence".[6] More often than not a cabinetmaker's creative energy would be restricted to technical virtuosity or the capacity to produce a very wide range of furniture. Owen McGarvey for example, like many of his competitors, fell into the trap of overdoing the technique of marquetry, often uniting in a single piece of furniture countless numbers of wood fragments from dozens of different varieties. In 1882, he exhibited a "richly-carved pedestal table of black walnut with inlaid octagonal top":

> The outer border of this table top is formed of carved shells, and the remaining design is formed of coloured marquetrie containing not less than nine thousand pieces of wood. Its centre is occupied by a sixteen pointed star of diamond shape and six different coloured woods, and grouped round this are eight panels representing as many various subjects, such as an Indian chief, George Washington, birds and floral designs. The whole design is extremely pleasing and the figures are remarkably clear and well brought out — indeed it is a splendid piece of art workmanship.[7]

It is also interesting to note that since the 1860s this same McGarvey had on offer in his store no less than thirty-two models of chair, ranging from the most basic to items of quite incredible luxury and cost.[8]

The concrete examination of furniture from the period between 1840 and 1900 can hold as many surprises as the study of documentary sources. For example, there is the curious curule chair, based on a model employed in Ancient Rome and then successively rediscovered and adapted during the Renaissance, under the Directoire and the Empire, and yet again in Victorian times.[9] This Victorian version is an extremely free interpretation that includes a number of Renaissance-inspired decorative elements; indeed, in this particular example the classical X-shaped under-frame is lacking and only the saddle-shaped upper part recalls the genuine curule chair. In another version, though, it is only the legs that are truly "curule", while the upholstery, the carving, and the beaver depicted on the back bear no relation whatever to the original prototype!

There has already been mention of the criticisms expressed by Napoléon Aubin in 1847 of the sumptuous furnishings of *bourgeois* interiors, which revealed according to him "neither taste nor talent". "Any boor", wrote the journalist, "suddenly enriched by a stroke of luck, can order from his furniture maker the most luxurious objects and fabrics; but only a well-bred, sensitive, educated man is able to suggest to an artist well-chosen themes for paintings".[10] Setting aside his desire to enlarge the potential clientele of Quebec artists, Aubin was raising one of the crucial problems faced by the new rich and those members of the middle classes eager to surround themselves with a decor they felt reflected their social and financial position. In the

418
Renaissance-revival curule chair, 1914
110 x 76 x 52 cm
Private collection, Quebec City
Photo Christine Guest/MMFA

Victorian taste endured long after the death of the Queen in 1901, and during the early twentieth century was still sometimes expressed in the acquisition of eclectic furniture from abroad. This chair, which is part of an eleven-piece drawing-room suite, was purchased from a manufacturer in Venice, Italy, on February 28, 1914, by Aimé Laferrière, a shopkeeper from Pierreville, Quebec. His brother David, a lumber dealer and mayor of Pierreville, bought a ten-piece suite. Some of the pieces puchased by Aimé now belong to the Soeurs de l'Assomption in Nicolet.

419
Drawing-room chair, about 1890
Black walnut, 107.5 x 47.2 x 64.6 cm
Canadian Museum of Civilization, Hull (984.56.1)
Photo Christine Guest/MMFA

face of a lack of tradition or personal knowledge, reinterpretations of historical styles appealed both because they were aesthetically "safe" and because they were often associated with the prestige of old European nobility and monarchs of the past. The decoration of rooms in the various Louis styles or, especially, the very popular rococo-revival was moreover facilitated by the "furniture and furnished room plans" that some *meubliers*-decorators imported from Europe.[11] The mistress of the house and her proud husband, invited to decide among a number of alternatives, appreciated a process that gave them the feeling they were making a personal choice in the realm of elegance, fashion and good taste.

In the final decades of the century, the decorative repertoire became even wider, and the various services offered by *meubliers*-upholsterers increased in importance. However, in the face of the absurdities of rampant eclecticism and the many excesses committed in the name of good taste, there was a reaction, especially in England and the United States, against the power wielded by unqualified "decorators". In spite of considerable resistance, the winds of reform began to blow, causing ripples that affected both theories of interior decoration and the design of furniture itself. *The Scientific Canadian* gave off reverberations of the debate by reprinting in its November 1880 issue an article published earlier by the London-based magazine *Builder*, entitled "Is the Prevalent Taste for 'Art Furniture' and Bric-à-Brac Indicative of a Sound or Healthy Aesthetic Culture".[12] It is interesting to note how the article makes a number of points that echo ideas expressed by Napoléon Aubin in 1847.

LIVING IN STYLE

420

Drawing-room Furniture (in the Louis XV Style),
about 1844

Chromolithograph published in the *Garde-Meuble ancien et moderne : collection de tentures*
(Paris: D. Guilmard, 33rd issue, plate no. 88)
Smithsonian Institution Libraries,
Cooper-Hewitt Branch, New York
Photo Ken Pelka, Art Resource, New-York

The lower part of the chromolithograph is entitled: "Floor Plan of the Drawing Room Showing the Position of Each Piece of Furniture".

Seen globally, then, Victorian furniture does not constitute a homogeneous whole. Despite its marked leaning towards forms from the past, it did undeniably evolve, particularly to the extent that it was affected by the major reform movements that swept through Western societies during the last quarter of the century. We will now attempt to identify the main elements of that evolution by examining the principal styles of Quebec furniture and classifying them under the two broad categories of "historicism" and "reformism". First, however, at the risk of seeming repetitive, a few important points must be made.

In a Victorian room, an article of furniture was hardly autonomous: it was part of an ensemble of furniture that itself was integrated into a decor in

421
Drawing-room Interior, about 1850
Chromolithograph published in the *Garde-Meuble ancien et moderne : collection de tentures*
(Paris : D. Guilmard, 74th issue, plate no. 212)
Smithsonian Institution Libraries,
Cooper-Hewitt Branch, New York
Photo Ken Pelka, Art Resource, New-York

422
Notman Studio, Montreal
Mrs. Williams' drawing room, Trafalgar Avenue, Montreal, 1887
Photograph
McCord Museum of Canadian History, Montreal, Notman Photographic Archives (83,214 Misc-II)

which mouldings, wallpapers, hangings, carpets, cushions, sculptures and decorative art objects of all sorts contributed towards the physical and aesthetic well-being of the users. Adding to this already chaotic environment, where the single object tended to be swallowed up by the whole, was a veritable host of knick-knacks and souvenirs. When we examine the stylistic characteristics of a particular piece, therefore, it should be remembered that in its original context it took much of its significance from being part of an eclectic accumulation of often entirely disparate objects. In addition, a piece of furniture that showed no signs of, say, exoticism in its shape or ornamentation could be "contaminated" by this fashion via the proximity of other

decorative items (a Japanese screen, for example). And, of course, the clients of a *meublier*-decorator were often less concerned with the particular style of a piece of furniture than they were with the comfort, blatant luxury and general effect of the interior decor.

As far as the various revival styles themselves are concerned, it should be noted that they did not follow successively one upon the other. Generally speaking, they flourished simultaneously and even intermingled, and they were not all equally important in terms of popularity, distribution and duration. The Gothic-revival and Elizabethan-revival styles had, for instance, nothing like the impact of the rococo and Renaissance revivals. And while Quebec Victorian furniture certainly shares many important characteristics with its counterparts from France and England, it also shows proof of some quite individual preferences and interpretations. While proximity to the United States certainly had its effect, it would be wrong to assume that Quebec furniture was a slavish imitation of that produced in America. The catalogue of decorative motifs that appears below illustrates the originality of Quebec's furniture makers just as clearly as it demonstrates their receptivity to outside influences.[13]

423
Rococo-revival wall mirror
Walnut, 186.25 x 90 cm
Musée de la civilisation, Quebec City (88-40)
Photo Christine Guest/MMFA

424
Rococo-revival mirror, detail of figure 133
Gilded wood, 295 x 125 cm
Musée de la civilisation, Quebec City (89-51)
Photo Christine Guest/MMFA

* * *

VICTORIAN HISTORICISM

The most popular style in Quebec during the Victorian era was the rococo-revival. Closely associated with France and particularly the extraordinarily luxurious interiors of the great eighteenth-century monarchs, the rococo revival was at its height between 1840 and 1870, although it remained a favourite of the middle classes for a good deal longer. In fact, a number of the styles of the period persisted for many decades, and it is this difficulty of

425
Rococo-revival bergère chair
Black walnut, 128 x 78 x 100 cm
Musée Pierre-Boucher du Séminaire de Trois-Rivières
Photo Christine Guest/MMFA

This bergère chair with armrests in the shape of griffins was used as a ceremonial chair. Although rococo-revival furniture borrowed heavily from the formal vocabulary of the Louis XV style, the Victorian influence can be seen here in the exaggerated shapes and the high relief of the carving.

426
Rococo-revival balloon-back chair
92 x 43 x 53 cm
Augustinian monastery of the l'Hôtel-Dieu de Québec
Photo Christine Guest/MMFA

assigning definite limits to an individual style which accounts to some degree for the differences of opinion among international scholars regarding their chronology.

During the Victorian era, the rococo-revival style was generally referred to as "Louis XIV" or "Louis XV". It consisted in fact of a rather loose interpretation of certain formal and decorative features of the two styles. The elegance, lightness and delicacy of carving demonstrated by the furniture is evidence, however, of the predominance of the Louis XV influence. These qualities were embodied in a systematic use of the curve and the counter-curve – notably in slender cabriole legs – and of rich decoration that featured simultaneously 'S' and 'C' scrolls, rocaille motifs, and garlands of foliage, flowerets and roses. Given the relatively flexible borderline between the Louis XV and Louis XIV forms, a number of elements were borrowed from the latter, including diaper motif grounds, ribbons, interlacing, acanthus leaves, palmettes, shells and griffins. The drawing-room suites, mirrors, centre tables, bergère chairs, sofas, armchairs and other seats of all kinds created in the style show an almost infinite range of decorative combinations drawn from this repertoire. In the dining room, the large sideboard was given a place of honour and was frequently ornamented with naturalistic motifs appropriate to its function. While still showing the occasional crest in the form of a cross-bow and the ubiquitous curves of 'S' and 'C' scrolls, it often bore carvings evoking the pleasures of the table: hunting scenes, birds and fish of all kinds, fruit and

427

428

vegetables. In fact, the repertoire employed for sideboards by Quebec decorators is similar in many ways to that used (for the most part a good deal earlier) by the great furniture designers working in Paris in the 1850s.

The Renaissance-revival style also adapted itself well to the challenges presented by the sideboard. In September 1865, André Molinelli, a furniture maker recently arrived in Montreal, presented in that city "a Renaissance-style buffet, in polished walnut, with carving representing various hunting and fishing scenes, the whole of quite remarkable workmanship".[14] Later, Azarie Lavigne also adopted the "Molinelli style, so appreciated and so fashionable in Montreal".[15] However, despite the brevity of the description and the absence of any tangible evidence, it seems likely that Molinelli's "Renaissance" style was much closer to what we know as rococo-revival! If we examine the Renaissance-revival sideboard belonging to the Montreal Museum of Fine Arts, we can see that it is an extremely well-proportioned piece whose presence owes much to its architecturally-inspired iconography. Harmony and balance have been achieved principally through a skilful use of the straight line, and there is no excessive ornamental carving. The quality of the veneers and the dignity of the classically-inspired head blend beautifully with the broken pediment, the fine elevation and the subtle interplay of projections and recesses.

The Renaissance-revival style, at its height between 1860 and 1880, was the second most popular style in Victorian Quebec. It was manifested in a number of fine bedroom and drawing-room suites and, of course, the famous

427
Attributed to William Drum
(about 1808-1876)
Balloon-back chair, about 1851
Black walnut, 83.5 x 52 x 47.5 cm
Canadian Museum of Civilization, Hull (A-4857)
Photo Christine Guest/MMFA

This chair, whose back is decorated with a beaver, is believed to have been presented both at the Great Exhibition in London, in 1851, and the Paris exhibition of 1855. Colonel William Rhodes (1821-1892), owner of a villa in Quebec City called Benmore, apparently bought the piece directly from Drum at the Paris fair.

428
Rococo-revival drawing-room chair
Walnut, 89.2 x 48.2 x 60.8 cm
Musée de la civilisation, Quebec City (76-235)
Photo Christine Guest/MMFA

THE FURNITURE

429
Francis-Pierre Gauvin (1866-1934)
Naturalistic sideboard, about 1890-1900
Walnut, bird's-eye and figured maple veneer,
275 x 187 x 60 cm
Musée de la civilisation, Quebec City (90-2226)
Photo Brian Merrett/MMFA

430
Dining-room Sideboard-dresser (Mahogany), about 1855
Chromolithograph published in the *Garde-Meuble ancien et moderne : collection de meubles* (Paris : D. Guilmard, 103rd issue, plate no. 603)
Bibliothèque Forney, Paris

fitted bookcase from Ravenscrag. With its iconography closely associated with the prosperity of the Florentine bankers of the Italian Renaissance, it was naturally much appreciated by the wealthy *bourgeoisie*. The Renaissance-revival armchair accompanied by a foot-rest or stool belonging to the Sainte-Anne School in La Pocatière was photographed by Marius Barbeau in 1951; with its chamfered under-frame, the caryatids adorning its arms, its balusters and the cartouche decorated with a medallion, it is a typical example of the style. The lady's chair from the collection of the Montreal Museum of Fine Arts employs fundamentally the same decorative vocabulary but also presents, in the hand-embroidered fabric that covers it, an example of how Victorian women occasionally contributed to the household decor. The floral motifs so popular at the time are embroidered in cross stitch on a canvas ground and accented with beadwork.[16] Another chair, covered with a more recent floral needlepoint, shows a Renaissance-inspired cresting combined with a number of rococo-revival decorative elements (the legs and rose motifs of the under-frame, for example).

Another style that can be accurately described as "hybrid" was the Elizabethan revival, whose popularity in England was bolstered by the publication during the 1830s of works by J. C. Loudon — the *Encyclopedia of Cottage, Farm and Villa Architecture* — and of Joseph Nash — *Mansions of England in the Old Time*. The label "Elizabethan" refers, of course, to the reign of Elizabeth I of England, which is to say the latter half of the sixteenth century. The Elizabethan revival form was also influenced by furniture executed under the

432
Rococo-revival drawing-room chair
Black walnut and tapestry, 121.5 x 60.5 x 54 cm
Serge Joyal Collection, Montreal
Photo Christine Guest/MMFA

431
Renaissance-revival sideboard,
about 1875-1890
Black walnut, figured walnut, basswood and marble, 300 x 243 x 68 cm
The Montreal Museum of Fine Arts, purchase, Association of Volunteer Guides (1991.Df.1 a-b)
Photo Christine Guest/MMFA

Like many o¡f the pieces that now belong to religious or public institutions, this sideboard was originally intended for domestic use. It belonged successively to Ernest Cormier's father, Dr. Isaïe Cormier, who lived on Sherbrooke Street West in Montreal, to his brother Amédée, who lived in L'Assomption, and to the Soeurs des Saints-Noms-de-Jésus-et-de-Marie (via one of Amédée's daughters).

reigns of Charles I and Charles II, during the seventeenth century, and in fact contains elements of the Jacobean, Stuart, Tudor and William and Mary styles! In spite of these complex origins, however, an Elizabethan-revival chair can be recognized by the bead, cable, spiral and ball motifs that decorate the uprights and the high, narrow, padded back with floral decorations.[17] In light of the fluidity of this particular style, though, and the liberties taken by furniture makers with the various decorative repertoires, we have reason to wonder about the exact nature of the furniture given this label in Quebec City and Montreal newspapers between 1850 and 1875. It is possible that some confusion existed between the Elizabethan-revival and the Gothic-revival, even taking account of the interpretation offered by Loudon himself.[18] The fact that certain historical photographs show chairs that combine elements from the two styles reinforces this notion.

Like the Elizabethan-revival, the Gothic-revival style gained much impetus from the new interest in the Middle Ages stimulated by the writings of Sir Walter Scott and the work of the architect Augustus Welby Northmore Pugin (1812-1852). The style was, however, considerably less popular in Quebec than in the United States.[19] The interior decor of the ground floor of the old

THE FURNITURE

433
Marius Barbeau (1883-1969), Ottawa
Renaissance-revival armchair and footstool from the parlour of the Collège Sainte-Anne in La Pocatière, 1951
Photograph
Canadian Museum of Civilization, Hull, Marius Barbeau Collection (J-9872)

434
Renaissance-revival lady's chair, about 1875
Black walnut, 116 x 67 x 60 cm
The Montreal Museum of Fine Arts, purchase, Miss Harriette J. MacDonnell Bequest (1990.Df.2)
Photo Christine Guest/MMFA

Baumgarten house in Montreal was thus something of an exception. It was more common to see the Gothic-revival vocabulary employed in libraries and other masculine rooms with the aim of underlining the intellectual and moral qualities of their users. In spite of a few stylistic divergences, this was the goal of the design for a bookcase kept in the Roy dit Belleau Collection of the Canada Parks Service. The Gothic-revival chair, usually used as an occasional chair, can be recognized by its solid frame, its long, clean lines and, of course, its use of elements from Gothic architecture, including Gothic arches, mullions, trefoil or quatrefoil rosettes, crockets and spiked or finial tops. The Gothic-revival occasional chair from the archbishop's palace in Sherbrooke, executed towards the turn of the century, combines several of these features.

437

438

The collecting of genuinely antique furniture or the acquisition of high-quality reproductions was another manifestation of Victorian historicism. Both were imported into Quebec from abroad, frequently at great cost. As well as the many antique pieces we know to have adorned the homes of rich Montrealers like the Angus family, we have traced several very fine copies of Boulle furniture (from the period of Napoleon III) to the homes of the Tourangeaus of Quebec City, for example, and the Papineaus of Montebello. Other examples once belonging to wealthy members of the *bourgeoisie* have since been bequeathed to private institutions.

439

435

436

THE DESIGN REFORM MOVEMENT

During the 1870s, a period marked by an increasing taste for historical styles, there emerged simultaneously a design reform movement that reacted against the abuse of past forms, eclecticism and poor design, and advocated a return to simplicity. Until the end of the Victorian era, this predominantly English and American movement sparked a wealth of articles and debates in the newspapers and magazines of the time. From the early 1880s, treatises sprinkled with references to "the beautiful", "the aesthetic" and "good taste" began to appear in Quebec, notably in the pages of *The Scientific Canadian*. These writings had a decisive influence on the form and ornamentation of a number of pieces of furniture conceived under the reformist banner.[20]

In the United States, the design reform movement was identified to a great extent with the so-called Eastlake style, named for the Englishman Charles Locke Eastlake (1836-1906). Eastlake, trained as an architect and active as a critic on aesthetic issues, gained renown with the publication in 1868 of his

435
Elizabethan-revival chair, about 1870
Wood, 114 x 50 x 56 cm
Sœurs de la Congrégation Notre-Dame – Villa Maria, Montreal
Photo Christine Guest/MMFA

436
Gothic-revival occasional chair, about 1900
105 x 59 x 64 cm
Archdiocese of Sherbrooke
Photo Christine Guest/MMFA

THE FURNITURE 453

437
George-Étienne Cartier seated on a chair showing the influence of the Elizabethan and Gothic revivals, about 1853
Photograph
National Archives of Canada, Ottawa (C-8360)

438
Pierre Drouin (1815-1860) or Honoré Roy (1821-1892)
Design for a double bookcase
Crayon on paper, 35 x 39.1 cm
Environment Canada, Parks Service, Quebec region (EX 86.3.137)
Photo SRP

439
Boulle cabinet
Black-lacquered wood with inlay and brass fittings, 105 x 115 x 43 cm
Sœurs oblates de Béthanie, Sainte-Marie-de-Beauce
Photo Jean-Pierre Labiau/MOBIVIQ

book *Hints on Household Taste*, which defended a certain type of simple, well-designed furniture. The book was an enormous success and was reprinted four times in England and six times in the United States after 1872. Completely opposed to decorative extravagance and to the heavy varnishes and stains of the various revival styles, Eastlake advocated a return to simplicity, traditional joining techniques, solid structures and high-quality materials. Unlike certain proponents of the design reform movement, he did not restrict himself to ornamentation drawn from the fashionable medieval repertoire. He saw beauty and simplicity as virtually synonymous, and preferred stylized motifs to naturalistic ones. Following the Philadelphia Exposition of 1876, in response to popular demand, a number of American furniture makers enthusiastically adopted Eastlake's ideas. Some of the "Eastlake-style" furniture produced was of high quality, but certain manufacturers made extensive use of machine work to produce and market inexpensive pieces that actually seriously transgressed Eastlake's principles. In spite of his attempt to dissociate himself from such creations in the 1878 re-edition of *Hints on Household Taste*, furniture linked to his name continued to gain in popularity in the United States until about 1890.[21]

Eastlake-style furniture can be recognized by its use of rectilinear forms, strongly-grained hard wood, occasionally of coloured glazed tiles, and of restrained decorative additions often executed by machine, including balustered crowns, applied mouldings, spindles, geometric motifs (incised parallel grooving, triangles, radiating semi-circles, bevelling, chamfering and fluting), and stylized floral and plant motifs. We know that Eastlake-style furniture was available in Quebec in 1880, for during that year McGarvey's clients were able to admire in his Montreal store a sideboard of some sophistication:

> An old fashioned English sideboard, such as our great-grandfathers used and prized, now claims attention. It is by courtesy styled "Eastlake", and ornamented with Minton tiles and mosaics – very quaint, very fashionable, and very useful.[22]

Although Eastlake did more than any other Englishman of his time to focus North American attention on the notion of "beauty", he nevertheless represented only one branch of what was known as the Aesthetic movement. Following in the footsteps of the architect Pugin and the artist and critic John Ruskin, men like Bruce Talbert, William Burges and Edward William Godwin all contributed towards the reform of popular taste by defending historical principles that included a respect for materials, simplicity of design and handcrafting. Deploring the negative effects of the industrialization of manufacturing processes, such as the extravagant ornamentation of furniture and the massive production of all sorts of tasteless decorative objects, they carried on a dedicated crusade in defence of "art furniture".

In November 1880, *The Scientific Canadian* published an article to which we have already referred taken from the London magazine *Builder*. This article challenged the aesthetic theory according to which "art and artistic feeling are as much shown in the designs of furniture and other accessories as in what have been hitherto considered the higher or 'fine' arts of sculpture and

440
Eastlake-style bonheur-du-jour, about 1880-1900
Congrégation de Notre-Dame, Montreal
Photo ministère des Affaires culturelles, Montreal, Inventaire des biens culturels (77-095-35)

441
Eastlake-style armchairs, about 1880-1900
"Economy", 196 x 71 x 75 cm
"Justice", 171 x 62 x 70.5 cm
"Well-being", 162 x 62 x 72 cm
Les Coopérants insurance company
Photo Brian Merrett/MMFA
These three chairs once adorned the board room of the former "Société des artisans canadiens-français de Montréal" (Les Coopérants).

THE FURNITURE

442
Eastlake-style chair, about 1880-1900
Black walnut and imitation leather,
94.5 x 50 x 54 cm
The Montreal Museum of Fine Arts, gift of the
Congrégation des soeurs grises de Montréal (1990.Df.1)
Photo Christine Guest/MMFA

The Eastlake influence is evident in the chair's clean lines and incised geometric motifs, and in the machine-made decorative elements. This type of chair could be found in either the dining room or the drawing room.

443
Lower right-hand door of an Eastlake-style sideboard, about 1880-1900
Detail of figure 202
215 x 137 x 52 cm
Musée Laurier, Arthabaska
Photo Christine Guest/MMFA

painting".[23] The article also criticized the borrowing by the defenders of "art furniture", in the name of "good taste", of decorative elements from foreign traditions. Another article in the same issue, based on one that had appeared in the *American Cabinet Maker*,[24] discussed the "New Queen Anne Style". Closely linked to the Aesthetic movement, the Queen Anne style was ironically described as "severe", "austere" and "uncomfortable".

> The little joints and inlaid spots are very "nice", and the little skewer legs vibrate sympathetically at a touch, so light are they. There is something weakly and feminine about this style which goes to our hearts. Yet the inoffensiveness, unwarmed by some character, some *chic*, is in itself sometimes an offence.

Two years later, however, in the same publication, a New York writer defended the fundamental principles of the Aesthetic movement, underlining the importance of the decor of ordinary life and recommending

> ... a seeking to surround the home and every day life with objects of true beauty, to fill the mind and higher thought, with soft, refining influences that may lift us out of the narrow sphere into which the prosaic duty of every day life induces us.[25]

Whatever the view taken, these articles confirm that Quebec's citizens were aware of the aims and principles of the Aesthetic movement: to design and create functional everyday objects that were beautiful – even if manufactured industrially – and thereby to contribute to the formation of popular taste; and to unite architecture with decoration, furniture with architecture, and the "fine arts" with the applied arts. The design reform movement, which began around 1850, influenced furniture directly by recommending that it be

made by firms employing trained architects and artists as designers. From 1880 to the start of the First World War, the term "art furniture" was applied to a wide range of productions, which, depending on the manufacturer, could be in either simple or complex shapes, with flat and angled planes or generous curves, using styles and ornamentation of historical or exotic inspiration. Stylized motifs – especially floral images – were, however, extremely common, along with inlays and marquetry, ebonizing, japanning, and additions of gold leaf. Despite certain obvious differences, the settee and occasional chair belonging to the archbishop's palace of Chicoutimi and the "lady's writing desk" in the collection of the McCord Museum were each created under this same banner. Of particular note are the small petalled flowers, so typical of the movement, which recall the geometric designs of the contemporary American furniture maker Daniel Pabst.[26]

A number of contemporary documentary sources indicate that the latest fashions in "aesthetic" furniture had their influence in Quebec. In September 1880, Owen McGarvey had in stock "a Queen Anne bedroom set of nine pieces, in ebony and gilt, ornamented very tastefully with floral decorations".[27] Two years later, he presented more furniture in the same style at his stand at the Crystal Palace, including "an ebony Queen Anne table with colored marquetrie top especially noticeable for its original design, magnificent clear finish and perfect color blending".[28] Certain rival *meubliers* were more attracted by the "Japanese" style, another important thread in the fabric of the Aesthetic movement.

Japan re-established trade relations with Europe in 1854 and eight years later participated for the first time in a universal exhibition. From this point on, the British market was inundated with ceramics, lacquer work, prints,

444

Central section of the back of a love seat, Aesthetic movement, 1890
Detail of figure 178
Black walnut, 108.5 x 146 x 70 cm
Bishop's palace of Chicoutimi
Photo Christine Guest/MMFA

445

Occasional chair, Aesthetic movement, about 1880-1900
Painted wood, 84.5 x 56.3 x 54.7 cm
McCord Museum of Canadian History, Montreal, (UADE 18)
Photo Christine Guest/MMFA

THE FURNITURE

446
Bonheur-du-jour, Aesthetic movement, about 1880-1900
Painted wood, 144.8 x 82.6 x 47.7 cm
McCord Museum of Canadian History, Montreal, (M 976.131)
Photo Christine Guest/MMFA

447
Pedestal table, Aesthetic movement, about 1880-1900
Painted wood and marquetry, 75 x 64 (diam.) cm
McCord Museum of Canadian History, Montreal, (M 18975)
Photo Christine Guest/MMFA

tableware and small ornaments of all kinds produced in the "land of the rising sun". The same phenomenon was repeated in the United States, moreover, following the Philadelphia Exposition of 1876. The public on both sides of the Atlantic displayed an enormous appetite for things Japanese, and this taste was stimulated by the publication of a host of books and illustrated articles.[29] Adherents of the design reform movement also appreciated the expressive lines, the colour and the asymmetry of Japanese art. In fact, the label "art furniture" was often applied indiscriminately at this period to the Anglo-Japanese style characterized by ebonized wood, inlay, marquetry, stylized motifs and a frequent use of bamboo and rattan – both as popular as they were inexpensive. The principal proponent of the "Japanese" style within the Aesthetic movement was E. W. Godwin. In 1881, D. S. Rickaby of Quebec City was selling "Drawing-room Furnishings in the latest styles, 'Japanese' and 'American'".[30] And a year earlier, the Montreal furniture maker James Wright had had the Notman studio photograph two curious "cupboards" of Japanese inspiration; these striking pieces combine a skilful use of panels of mirror and of short, diagonally arranged planks, contrasting materials and the decorative effects of asymmetrically-positioned figured scenes.[31]

As well as its taste for Japan, the Aesthetic movement showed a marked but less lasting interest in exotic forms associated with the Orient in general. In some turn-of-the-century interiors this was reflected in the "cosy corner", that small area of a room intended to create a particular atmosphere (examples were Annie Morrice's bedroom in the house on Redpath Street, and the

smoking room of The Homestead, the Harrison Stephen house, both in Montreal). The "Moorish" or "Turkish" style featured ottomans and generously padded armchairs covered in velvet and elaborately trimmed with fringing and tassels. In contrast to the furniture of the cabinetmaker and carver, upholsterer's creations such as these were more susceptible to the vagaries of fashion and considerably more difficult to preserve in good condition. The Musée de la civilisation possesses a few examples, and the Notman Photographic Archives contain a series of photographs of drawing-room furniture of this type created by the manufacturer Tombyll in 1892 and 1893.[32]

This "exotic" dimension of the Aesthetic movement obviously contributed to abuses by encouraging the fashion for ostentatious upholstery, hangings, accumulation and eclecticism that marked the final decades of the nineteenth century. As a result, the principles of interior decoration propounded by John Ruskin were sometimes contested by other tastemakers. An article that appeared in *The Scientific Canadian* in November 1881, apparently taken from a British publication, made the point that extensive "borrowing"

448
Notman Studio, Montreal
Whatnot, Aesthetic movement, made by James Wright, 1880
Photograph
McCord Museum of Canadian History, Montreal, Notman Photographic Archives (56,062-BII)
The ceramic tiles that ornament this piece were apparently made at the famous Minton factory in Stoke-on-Trent, England.

449
Notman Studio, Montreal
Whatnot, Aesthetic movement, made by James Wright, 1880
Photograph
McCord Museum of Canadian History, Montreal, Notman Photographic Archives (56,061-BII)
The short diagonally-arranged planks of this piece, and the small balusters to be seen on its crown, relate it formally to a "Queen Anne style sideboard" reproduced in the December 1878 issue of the *Canadian Mechanics' Magazine and Patent Office Record* (p. 384).

450
Embroideries for Sofas and Ottomans
Engraving published in the *Canadian Illustrated News*, September 13, 1873
National Archives of Canada, Ottawa (C-59350)

THE FURNITURE

451

452

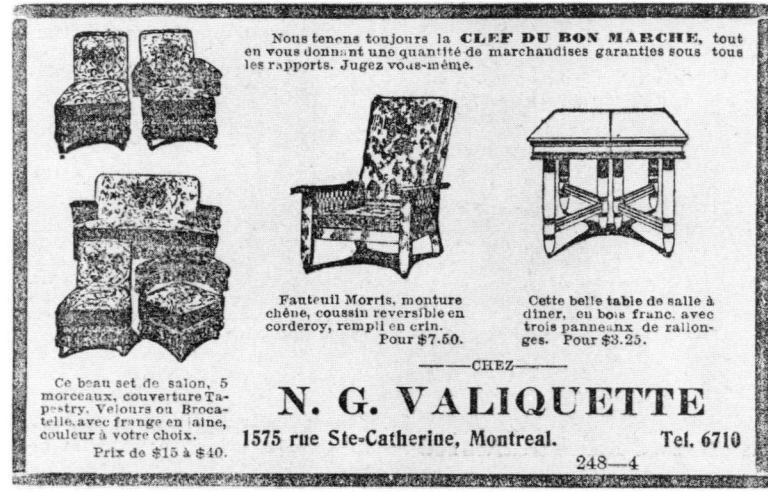

453

454

451
Notman Studio, Montreal
Armchairs made by R. N. Tombyll, 1892
Photograph
McCord Museum of Canadian History, Montreal,
Notman Photographic Archives (99,064 Misc-II)

452
Notman Studio, Montreal
Armchairs made by R. N. Tombyll, 1893
Photograph
McCord Museum of Canadian History, Montreal,
Notman Photographic Archives (101,903 Misc-II)

453
Moorish-style love seat, about 1890-1900
Wood, upholstery fabric and braiding,
94.2 x 117 x 56 cm
Musée de la civilisation, Quebec City (80-766)
Photo Christine Guest/MMFA

454
Advertisement for the firm of N. G.
Valiquette of Montreal
Published in *La Presse*, August 26, 1897
National Library of Canada, Ottawa (NC-17947)

from foreign styles conflicted with a society's traditional way of life and the fundamental characteristics of its vernacular architecture:

> In these matters we are but too apt to forget that the style of decoration suitable to the sunny climes of the South and East, and most in harmony with the habits and customs of its peoples, are in a great measure, if not altogether, unsuited to our insular situation and domestic habits. We may adapt them (or rather what is good in them) to our purpose, and we may derive many valuable lessons in form and colour from them; but to transplant them in their original form is a grave error. . . we have the Moresque or Moorish style of decoration — a combination of some of the best features of the Egyptian, the Greek, the Roman, the Byzantine, and Arab styles, admirably adapted to the land of cloudless skies, where shade and coolness were a necessity, and only to be got by a particular style of architecture with open courts for light and ventilation; but in our "muggy" climate, where we have but too little sun and plenty of wind, such a style of decoration is, to say the least of it, unsuitable. Many of its beautiful geometric diapers and ornaments we may use with advantage, and the lessons in color which it teaches cannot be over-estimated. But to make our rooms exact counterparts of the beautiful halls of the Alhambra (even if we could) would be simply ridiculous.[33]

In 1897, an advertisement run by the Montreal dealer N. G. Valiquette showed images of Moorish-style furniture side by side with a solid-looking

455
William Morris (1834-1896) and Morris & Company
Minstrel Angels, 1882
Coloured glass, painted glass and lead,
64.7 x 78.7 cm
The Montreal Museum of Fine Arts, gift of the David A. P. Watt family (1918.Dg.3)
Photo Christine Guest/MMFA

This stained-glass panel is one of a pair ordered from the firm of Morris & Company in March 1882 by David Watt of Montreal. The figures of *Minstrel Angels* are based on drawings executed by William Morris in 1873 for the windows of the chapel of Jesus College, Cambridge.

456
"Morris" armchair, Arts and Crafts style
Oak, 107 x 69 x 54 cm
Louis Zaor Collection, Quebec City
Photo Christine Guest/MMFA

454 chair of elegant design. This oak chair was identified as a "Morris armchair", a reference to the Englishman William Morris (1834-1896), a major reformist in the field of the applied arts. Morris, whose ideological position was close to that of Charles Locke Eastlake, was one of the leaders of the Arts and Crafts movement, which, in a reaction against industrialized mass production, aimed to reinstate handcrafts in a central position. A great admirer of medieval craft forms, Morris advocated the strictest simplicity in the design of furniture and domestic interiors. He and his collaborators designed and pro-
455 duced a wide range of objects, including wallpaper, tapestries, stained glass and furniture. Their hand-made furniture was not distributed widely, however, for it was costly to produce and thus beyond the reach of the masses; but it did stimulate a widespread interest in simple, well-built furniture that emphasized the natural beauties of wood. In a situation mirroring the paradoxical commercialization of the "Eastlake" style, Morris' defence of ancient hand skills led, in both England and the United States, to the mass-production of cheap oak furniture whose form followed its function. With its rectilinear shapes, its stylized plant motifs and the griffin heads – looking
456 remarkably like medieval gargoyles – adorning its armrests, the "Morris armchair" is typical of this type of furniture. More than any other branch of the design reform movement, Morris's Arts and Crafts style was responsible for finalizing the break with Victorian historicism and opening the way to the Modern movement which, after the fever of Art nouveau, the excesses of the Edwardian period and the tragic interruption of the Great War, was to gradually dominate the twentieth century.

These two great trends, the historicist and the reformist, gave birth to interiors and furniture whose eclecticism and hybridity make them hard to classify. George Stephen, for example, the richest Montrealer of his

THE FURNITURE

457
Notman Studio, Montreal
Drawing room of the George Stephen
house, Montreal, 1884
Photograph
McCord Museum of Canadian History, Montreal,
Notman Photographic Archives (73,825 Misc-II)

generation, stopped at nothing in his attempt to create a drawing room he felt would do him justice. The room included a coffered ceiling of medieval inspiration, a wall panelling of various types, Moorish-style furniture, a Chinese screen, a myriad of objects of all sizes and descriptions, and paintings that illustrate a quintessentially Victorian taste. The same indiscriminate blending — of rococo-revival and Eastlake-style elements, for example — can also be seen in single items of furniture. To make sense of such mixtures, the observer often has no choice but to identify the various elements one by one, using a specialized vocabulary that takes no account of stylistic boundaries.[34]

Quite apart from its structural characteristics, Victorian furniture reflected the fluctuating tastes of its users in its employment of a vast repertoire of decorative motifs, of human, animal, plant and miscellaneous origin. The study of these motifs allows us both to identify various elements peculiar to Quebec furniture and to confirm and reassess the brief stylistic examination here outlined of a body of furniture that will always resist classification.

John R. Porter

458
W. Doherty
Eastlake-style harmonium with rococo-revival ornamentation, about 1880-1900
188 x 152 x 62 cm
Village québécois d'antan, Drummondville
The Doherty firm was located in Elington, Ontario.

1. "Simple Ways and Means for Decorating the Home", *The Scientific Canadian*, November 1882, p. 335. These views can apparently be attributed to a contributor to *Builder and Wood-Worker*, a New York periodical to which the author makes specific reference on p. 338.

2. On the subject of the universal exhibition held in Paris in 1878, see Pierre Kjellberg, "Le bon goût il y a cent ans", *Connaissance des arts*, no. 321, November 1978, pp. 106-113.

3. *Album de la Minerve*, May 25, 1873, p. 339 (trans.).

4. See Edward S. Cooke Jr. (ed.), *Upholstery in America & Europe from the Seventeenth Century to World War I* (New York and London: W. W. Norton & Co., 1987).

5. *Industries of Canada, City of Montreal, Historical and Descriptive Review, Leading Firms and Moneyed Institutions* (Montreal: Gazette, 1886), p. 159.

6. Maurice Rheims, "Histoire du mobilier. Le décor de la vie", (pp. 1074-1165) in Jean Poirier (ed.), *Histoire des moeurs*, vol. I: *Les coordonnées de l'homme et la culture matérielle* (Paris: Gallimard, 1990) (Encyclopédie de la Pléiade, vol. 47), p. 1133.

7. *The Gazette*, September 20, 1882, p. 5.

8. R.W.S. Mackay, *The Montreal Directory for 1865-1866* (Montreal: Lovell, 1866), p. 470.

9. There is an almost identical specimen in the collection of the Soeurs de l'Assomption, in Nicolet.

10. *Le Canadien*, October 15, 1847, p. 2 (trans.).

11. *L'Événement*, May 7, 1870. The rococo-revival "drawing-room interior" reproduced here recalls in a number of ways the rooms in Victorian Quebec furnished in this style. The upstairs drawing-room in the house built in 1860 by the architect Charles Baillairgé for a dentist called Baillargeon, situated on Sainte-Ursule Street in Quebec City, is an example that comes to mind.

12. See pp. 354-355 of this issue of *The Scientific Canadian*.

13. These remarks on the various revival styles take account of many studies as well as of recorded observations of my colleague Micheline Huard. On the specific subject of Quebec furniture, see the article by Georges-Pierre Léonidoff and Jean-Pierre Labiau entitled "Un mobilier sans influence", *Continuité*, no. 38, winter 1988, pp. 26-29. For a broader view see a number of works, including John Gloag, *A Complete Dictionary of Furniture* (New York: The Overlook Press, 1991); Milo M. Naeve, *Identifying American Furniture: A Pictorial Guide to Styles and Terms, Colonial to Contemporary* (Nashville: AASLH, 1981); Kathryn McNerney, *Victorian Furniture: Our American Heritage* (Paducah: Collector Books, 1981).

14. *La Minerve*, September 28, 1865, p. 1 (trans.).

15. *La Minerve*, April 26, 1869, p. 3 (trans.).

16. This chair comes from the house of the parents of the late artist Simone Hudon, wife of Henri Beaulac, located on Laurier Street in Quebec City (near Jeanne-d'Arc Park). According to oral tradition, the embroidery was the work of Simone Hudon's grandmother.

17. See R. W. Symonds and B. B. Whineray, *Victorian Furniture* (London: Studio Editions, 1987), *passim*.

18. *Ibid.*, p. 20.

19. See John Gloag, "Nineteenth Century Gothic Furniture in England", *Antiques*, June 1972, pp. 1046-1051; Katherine Susman Howe, "The Gothic Revival Style in America, 1830-1870", *Antiques*, May 1976, pp. 1014-1023.

20. Many of the views expressed here on the reform movement and the various types of furniture associated with it are confirmed by Léonidoff and Labiau, Gloag and Naeve (see n. 13). I would like also to acknowledge Claire Desmeules' valuable contribution to the initial analysis of the various aspects of the reform movement.

21. In an article entitled "Eastlake-influenced Furniture", Mary Jean Madigan notes that while Eastlake preferred handwork he did recognize the advantages of the machine in increasing the accessibility of good furniture (p. 55). See Mary Jean Madigan (intro.), *Nineteenth Century Furniture: Innovation, Revival and Reform* (Watson: Guptill [An Art and Antiques Book], 1982), pp. 52-59.

22. *The Gazette*, September 20, 1880, p. 2. The "Minton tiles" referred to in the article came from the famous Minton ceramic factory at Stoke-on-Trent, Staffordshire, England. The Mintons regularly took part in international exhibitions after 1851. In addition to porcelain and pottery, they also produced a wide variety of decorative painted tiles which were popular with a broad segment of the public. Many examples of their patent tiles bearing the mark of Minton, Hollins & Co. were displayed at the Philadelphia exhibition of 1876.

23. "Is the Prevalent Taste for 'Art Furniture' and Bric-à-Brac Indicative of a Sound or Healthy Aesthetic Culture", p. 354.

24. P. 370. At the outset, the author takes pleasure in emphasizing the historical ambiguity of this fashionable style thus: "What people now call Queen Anne fashions, with a charming indifference to trammels of dates, are the fashions of the three Georges, the 'Marie Antoinette style' (under that queen the Louis XV furniture and decoration, whilst still sumptuous, became refined and moderate), and especially everything which came in during the Empire (Napoleon I). Now, as Anne died in 1714, and Napoleon resigned his crown in 1815, there are just a hundred years of perhaps the most remarkable changes and developments in art which ever occurred in a century, all named after Anne, whose tastes, strictly speaking, belonged to her father's generation."

25. "Simple Ways and Means for Decorating the Home", *The Scientific Canadian*, November 1882, p. 335.

26. See David Hanks, "Daniel Pabst", in Madigan, *op. cit.*, pp. 42-43.

27. *The Gazette*, September 20, 1880, p. 2.

28. *The Gazette*, September 20, 1882, p. 5.

29. In 1880, it was possible to obtain from the publisher of *The Scientific Canadian*, located at 243 Saint-Denis Street in Montreal, D. H. Maser's *Book of Japanese Ornamentation, comprising designs for the use of painters, decorators, designers, silversmiths and many other purposes*. See the detailed description of this work that appears in *The Scientific Canadian*, July 1880, p. 218.

30. *L'Électeur*, December 23, 1881, p. 2 (trans.).

31. The two photos bear the inscription "Piece of furniture for Mr. Wright" and the second is dated March 4, 1880. At this period James Wright had his establishment at 32 Saint-Antoine Street (*The Gazette*, December 3, 1878, p. 1). Wright won two first prizes and a silver medal at the provincial exhibition of 1884 (*The Montreal Daily Star*, September 10, 1884, p. 2).

32. See nos. 99,064 to 99,067-Misc. II and 101,902 to 101,904-Misc. II.

33. P. 346. The year before, an article taken from the London-based *Builder* had already criticized the excessive use of "Japanese jars" and "borrowed decorations" (*The Scientific Canadian*, November 1880, pp. 354-355).

34. See Claire Desmeules, "Le vocabulaire du meuble", *Continuité*, no. 38, winter 1988, pp. 32-33.

DECORATIVE MOTIFS

INSPIRED BY A BROAD RANGE OF STYLES AND CULTURES, THE furniture commonly known as "Victorian" has, with time, become synonymous with incongruous extravagance. However, even though the often exaggerated decoration of such furniture has contributed largely to this negative view, it has never been the object of an in-depth study. In European and American works on the subject, there exists no systematic catalogue or detailed analysis of the decorative motifs employed in nineteenth-century furniture, and the same lack can be felt in the literature dealing with the ornamentation of Quebec Victorian furniture. Such a study is, then, well overdue, if we are to better understand the context within which the furniture of the period was created and used, and to better appreciate the meaning and significance of its decoration.

THE CORPUS: GATHERING AND CLASSIFICATION
The rich documentary collection built up over the years by researchers working on the MOBIVIQ project has served as our data bank. As well as the hundreds of pieces of Victorian furniture catalogued that belong to museums, institutions and private owners, the study includes a large number of period photographs and historical illustrations taken from various archival sources, both public and private; the corpus is completed by several dozen extracts taken from nineteenth-century newspapers and magazines. Some 1,022 distinct ornamental elements have been identified; this number includes all varying motifs appearing on the same piece of furniture and all unique subjects, but not doubles or repeated motifs. For example, each of the seven different figures on the screen belonging to the bishop's palace of Trois-Rivières, and each of the carved male heads on the drawing-room suite by the furniture maker Gourdeau count as individual references, while figurative elements appearing on supports (espagnolettes) count, as do caryatids, columns and feet, as only a single motif.[1]

This catalogue of motifs present in Victorian furniture, of which compilation ceased in January 1992, consists of over two hundred groupings. As new discoveries are made, fresh examples will almost certainly be added to the list, which has been classified according to a model similar to that employed by

459
Naturalistic screen, 175 x 67 x 49 cm
Bishop's palace of Trois-Rivières
Photo Jean-Pierre Labiau/MOBIVIQ

460
Omer Marchand (1872-1936) and the sculptors Bouthier and Proulx. **Term, telamon and grotesque adorning a Renaissance-revival hotel sideboard**, 1900
Detail of figure 250
Oak, 285 x 360 x 60 cm
Raymond Fabien and Marthe Fabien-Lapalme Collection, Anjou. Photo Christine Guest/MMFA

the *Thesaurus iconographique*.[2] Four main organizational categories proved sufficient in ordering the material. All decorative elements observed in the furniture can thus be classified under one or other of four types of image: human (anthropomorphic), animal (zoomorphic), plant (phytomorphic) or other (miscellaneous). This latter category includes heraldic motifs, and decorative elements inspired by religious objects, musical instruments and architecture. This system of classification is based on the relative symbolic importance of the various images, rather than on their popularity.

Of the four categories identified, plant images account for over half of the motifs employed (56%). Animals of one kind or another appear on close to one quarter of the furniture (24%), while human and other images are featured much less frequently (10% each). Quebec furniture makers generally employed the human figure to decorate furniture in the Renaissance-revival and rococo-revival modes, while decorative elements such as Gothic pinnacles and lancet arches, and Renaissance pediments and cornices, are to be found in pieces inspired more specifically by these styles. Plant motifs are part of the general decorative language of furniture rather than being linked closely to any particular form. Even the sunflower, which served as a key symbol of the Aesthetic movement, fulfilled a general ornamental function, as illustrated by the bedroom sets photographed for Marius Barbeau by Edwards.[3] In a most perfect example of eclecticism, a suite in the Eastlake style is adorned with griffins, garlands, vases, flowers and even colonnettes with floral capitals – all motifs that are quite unrelated to the basic form and style of the furniture.

Although there are a few rare pieces bearing only a single decorative element, most of those recorded are richly ornamented, and very little Victorian furniture remained entirely undecorated. The situation is illustrated quite clearly in the table entitled "Ornamentation according to types of furnitures", which has been developed from the four main divisions previously defined and a typological analysis of the furniture recorded. Owing to the widespread presence of large drawing-room mirrors and frames for works of art, which rarely receive documentary mention but are very clearly visible in contemporary photographs, a division labelled "decorative furniture" has been added to the nine categories of furniture defined according to their function. There is also a category that includes ornamental mouldings and decorative ironware. In some cases the percentage of images of a particular class occurring in the various types of furniture is quite revealing; for example, animal images appear more frequently in the case furniture category than in any other. It is worth noting that this category includes sideboards and dressers, both items well-suited to zoomorphic ornamentation, particularly if the decorative theme is related to food.

pp.480-4

POSITION OF THE MOTIFS AND DECORATIVE TECHNIQUES

According to the type of piece being decorated, a variety of motifs might be used to ornament the yoke rail, apron, arm stumps and legs of seat furniture, the doors, cornice and uprights of cupboards, the apron and under-frame of tables, the head and foot of bedsteads and the frames of mirrors and paintings. Some items combine diverse motifs; examples of this are the narrative pieces which, like the marriage bed belonging to the Musée de la civilisation,

461

462

actually tell a story. There is no other way of characterizing this decorative ensemble, where bird, animal, flower and fruit images combine to adorn the bed's head and foot. Not all ornamentation is so eloquent, however, and there are many motifs whose function is strictly decorative, especially in cases of inlay and marquetry.[4]

Together with painting, these techniques – especially popular during the 1880s – allowed furniture makers to extend the repertoire of decorative motifs, which had hitherto been either applied or carved. In some cases the techniques were employed to help create the decorative elements of a particular style, in others they enabled a maker to display all his skill in a "masterpiece" to be displayed at one of the furniture shows that were part of the large provincial and universal exhibitions. This was the aim of the piece created by Louis Lecomte for the provincial exhibition held in Quebec City in 1877, a table consisting of 2,649 pieces of wood and measuring three feet in diameter. In his depiction of a bouquet of flowers, Lecomte employed thirty-eight different varieties of wood and the piece took him thirteen months to complete![5]

HUMAN IMAGES

Considered the most exalted decorative category, the human figure, real or imaginary, appears most frequently in the seat furniture division. Although this can be explained largely by the widespread use of the Renaissance-revival and rococo-revival styles in furniture intended for the drawing room – the room where the need to "show off" was at its most imperative – account must also be taken of the more specific influence of the great European and American furniture makers. Among the latter, Belter, Pabst, Roux and Jeliff were, according to U.S. scholars, largely responsible for the growing popularity in North America of the use of human images as a decorative element. Settees and armchairs by these craftsmen ornamented with human heads are illustrated frequently in monographs and articles on their work.[6] It is impossible, however, to establish the source and diffusion of the human motif since all North American furniture makers of the period, including those in Quebec, had access to pattern books and widely-used designs.[7]

461
Rococo-revival bed
Detail: the head
120 x 152 x 216 cm
Musée de la civilisation, Quebec City, purchase, gift of Alfred Savard (91-1217)
Photo Christine Guest/MMFA

A decorative motif featuring two birds ornamented the crown of a cabinet exhibited by the Parisian cabinetmaker Tahan at the London exhibition of 1851. It reappears on several pieces of Quebec Victorian furniture, including the naturalistic screen belonging to the bishop's palace of Trois-Rivières (459) and the Renaissance-revival bed in the collection of the Batiscan presbytery (223). Another bed from Sainte-Marie de Beauce, in the collection of the Canadian Museum of Civilization in Hull [A 623] since 1957, is similar in various respects to the piece belonging to the Musée de la civilisation in Quebec City.

462
Rococo-revival bed
Detail: the foot
120 x 152 x 216 cm
Musée de la civilisation, Quebec City, purchase, gift of Alfred Savard (91-1217)
Photo Christine Guest/MMFA

463
Top of a pedestal table, Aesthetic movement, about 1880-1900
Detail of figure 447
Painted wood and marquetry, 75 x 64 (diam.) cm
McCord Museum of Canadian History, Montreal (M 18975)
Photo Christine Guest/MMFA

464
Cupid and floral motifs on a rococo-revival wall mirror
Detail of figure 423
Walnut, 186.3 x 90 cm
Musée de la civilisation, Quebec City (88-40)
Photo Christine Guest/MMFA

Of all the recorded motifs employed in Quebec Victorian furniture, it is busts and heads executed in the Belter style that dominate the category of real and imaginary beings, as far as both quantity and variety are concerned. The "imaginary beings" class consists of angels, devils and miscellaneous "grotesques", such as the plant mask carved on the support of a screen in the collection of the Hôtel-Dieu in Quebec City. The human body is depicted in a more complete form in caryatids, espagnolettes, cherubs and a few figures of children – like the one portrayed asleep inside a flower that adorns a chair back. Taken from the decorative repertoire of Boulle furniture, winged cherubs and the cupids often used by Belter were especially popular, particularly on elaborately decorated pieces like the large mirror belonging to the Musée de la civilisation. Male figures occur mainly in representations of heads and busts; indeed, images in this category are rarely seen except as one of the three sub-divisions we have identified: heroes, general depictions – such as the small head wearing a feathered cap, executed in the sixteenth-century style – and portraits.

464

From Anonymous Portraits to Depictions of Heroes

As surprising as it may seem, portraits did occasionally appear as decorative motifs on furniture during the latter half of the century. In 1865, for example, at the agricultural and industrial exhibition held in Montreal, James Thomson presented a sideboard whose mirror was surmounted by a portrait of some unidentified personage of the time. A few years later, in 1871, the Quebec City furniture maker François Gourdeau exhibited a suite taken from the drawing room of a wealthy client. The various male heads that adorned it all differed in feature and hairstyle, indicating that they were indeed portraits (unlike the female figures, which were all identical and less finely carved than the male ones). The practice was not universally appreciated, however, for James Thomson's sideboard sparked criticism. One journalist suggested that, in the name of good taste, the offending portrait be replaced by a head of Ceres or some other legendary character.[8]

465

In fact, some of the most iconographically interesting pieces of furniture display the head of a hero as a decorative element. Ornaments of this type include a splendid Napoleon dominating the cresting rail of a settee, and others in which the place of honour goes to great names from our own history, such as Champlain and Jacques Cartier.

The presumed portrait of Cartier, executed in 1839 by the French painter François Riss (1804-about 1866), was popularized in Quebec during the 1850s following the appearance on the market of a lithograph by Théophile Hamel copied from the Riss work.[9] Hamel's rendering of Cartier, caught up on a tide of emerging nationalism, inspired in its turn a number of artists. As well as being drawn, engraved, sculpted and even integrated into an architectural design, Cartier's likeness also appeared on various articles of furniture, although often in a rather different form from the portrait sketched by Riss. Examples can be seen on the back of a settee, the entablature of a looking-glass from Sir Hugh Allan's library and the top rail of a mirror frame designed in 1866 by Arthur Mingeaud for the lounge of the steamship Québec.[10] It must be pointed out, however, that in the last two cases Cartier's face is part of a design evoking shipping and commerce — activities of special significance for the objects' owners — rather than a celebration of patriotism. In addition, the remarkable group of furniture created by William Drum in 1860 for the Prince of Wales' suite in the parliament buildings included a sofa whose back was decorated with a high-relief head of Jacques Cartier framed by two eagles that, if we are to believe one contemporary journalist, would have impressed Audubon himself.[11]

Similar in design to the Prince of Wales' sofa, the settee belonging to the Augustines of the Hôtel-Dieu in Quebec City, which bears an effigy of Napoleon, presents a simple but striking iconographical programme. In the centre of the piece's wide back rise the shoulders and careworn face of France's first emperor. Covered in decorations and resting on a trophy of banners, the bust is flanked on either side by two imperial eagles. This high-relief carving is a resounding tribute to military genius, an offshoot of the current of Bonapartist sympathy that endured for many years among those fascinated by the romanticism of this historical figure.[12] But the interest of the settee goes further, for the general appearance and iconography of the rococo-revival piece were copied by the author of a sofa presented to Cardinal Taschereau in 1886, but with Champlain in the spotlight, rather than Napoleon.

In fact, the identification of the Champlain figure, which is also framed by two eagles, rests principally on oral tradition. Apart from the moustache and the short beard, and the plausibility of the idea of a tribute to the founder of Quebec City, there are few elements to support such an assertion. We must therefore examine the figure's appearance: wearing a crenel-edged cap, the Champlain on the piece belonging to the archbishop's palace of Quebec City — like the portrayals of Jacques Cartier — recalls the general types borrowed for their costume from Renaissance images. But, unlike the heroic figures, these young men's faces are depicted with great decorative simplicity, in a manner very similar to that employed for female figures.

Female Figures

Far more versatile than their masculine counterparts, women's heads made of wood or metal were applied to a wide variety of furniture. One of the more

465
François Gourdeau (1840-1920)
Head of a man adorning the yoke rail of a Renaissance-revival chair, about 1870
Black walnut, 120 x 45 x 53 cm
The Montreal Museum of Fine Arts, gift of the Succession J. A. DeSève (1986.Df.6)
Photo Christine Guest/MMFA

466
Head of Jacques Cartier adorning the yoke rail of a Renaissance-revival settee, about 1870
Detail of figure 153
Black walnut, 127 x 182 x 87 cm
Musée du Saguenay–Lac-Saint-Jean, Chicoutimi
Photo Christine Guest/MMFA

467
Bust of Napoleon adorning the yoke rail of a Renaissance-revival sofa, about 1875-1890
Detail of figure 152
130 x 220 x 90 cm
Augustinian monastery of the Hôtel-Dieu de Québec, gift of Miss Blanche Côté
Photo John R. Porter/MOBIVIQ

common among the various models employed is the female head shown wearing a diadem or a conical cap with flaps meeting under the chin, inspired by medieval figures; this motif adorns many different objects, including settees, armchairs, beds, tables, sideboards and bookcases, clocks and locks, and even the columns and voussoirs of walls and windows. An example dating from 1851 can be seen on the under-frame of an Elizabethan-style table.[13] In 1888, Franz Sales Meyer mentioned it in his work *Ornamentale Formenlehre* as an example of modern grotesque[14] – an idea supported by the use of the motif on a sideboard by the Parisian cabinetmakers Schmit and Piollet, reproduced in *The Art-workman*.[15] In this example, though, which shows wavy hair arranged on the forehead, the image loses much of its classical spirit and moves closer to the two most striking specimens from the 1870s: the Statue of Liberty and the personage known as "Columbia".[16] Although popular, Columbia did have her competitors; on various pieces of furniture in the Renaissance-revival and rococo-revival styles, preference was often given to "Madame de Pompadour" – a head characterized by long, English-style tresses – or to female profiles inspired by intaglio prints. Both these motifs were employed by the American furniture makers Alexandre Roux and John Jeliff.[17]

ANIMAL IMAGES

The animal kingdom, source of nearly a quarter of the motifs recorded, is well illustrated, although some of the animals depicted are entirely imaginary. Earth, sky and sea each have their representatives: as well as the eight species of mammal, the thirteen species of bird and the six species of fish present in the decorative bestiary of Quebec Victorian furniture, a number of insects and shellfish can be observed. But whether the creatures be large or small, wild or tame, rare or common, indigenous or exotic, it is their principal role to embellish the pieces they adorn. Aside from this function, the significance of these beasts – alive or dead, whole or partial – is derived from the style of the furniture, the position of the motif and the way it is depicted. This is true, moreover, for all the motifs recorded throughout the corpus of catalogued furniture.

Unlike applications of the human figure, the employment of animal motifs is often subject to fixed rules, established by use and supported by a large body of literature. This is the case, for example, of the eagle and the dolphin, which, since Ancient Rome, have symbolized respectively power and the marine world.[18] The same is true of the swan, the heron and the butterfly, all of which became during the nineteenth century distinctive signs of fashionable styles and trends. Certain animals, however, remain exempt from any standard symbolic interpretation. These, through an interplay of references linking them to one or more specific contexts, become emblems. This passage from the world of the symbol, where all is clearly understood and defined, to that of the emblem, where meaning is entirely arbitrary and constantly changing, is well illustrated in Quebec furniture decoration by the use of the beaver and lion motifs.

From Symbol to Emblem: The Case of the Beaver and the Lion
In iconographical repertoires, the beaver, a symbol of chastity, also evokes the

hermit,[19] a symbolism that makes it a quite fitting decorative element for the bed of an unmarried person.[20] In North America, where wealth and civilization were associated with development and trade based on the cutting of wood, this symbolism was no longer entirely suitable.[21] Already during the seventeenth and eighteenth centuries, observation of beaver behaviour had resulted in the animal's image being associated not only with commerce and industry, but also – owing to its complex social organization – with republican ideals and the notion of freedom. When, during the nineteenth century, the work-order-harmony trilogy[22] was added to these concepts, then clearly here was an emblem fit to represent a new nation. Used to symbolize hard work – as a decorative element on a sewing machine, for example – the beaver also served to identify Canadian products. The tables presented by the Hilton firm and by Pierre Roy at the exhibitions of 1851 and 1865 offer proof of this practice.[23] But it is when it appears accompanied by maple leaves on the carved top rail of a mirror or on the back of a ceremonial chair that the beaver fulfils most completely its emblematic function. Under these circumstances, it becomes comparable to the lion, another figure with multiple associations.

Equally evocative of physical and spiritual strength,[24] the lion motif was particularly dear to English hearts during the nineteenth century. The lion was part of the royal coat of arms and as such it was natural to find it decorating furniture intended for use by representatives of governmental power. Some people, however, included the image in the ornamentation of their household furniture without necessarily adhering to the rules of heraldry: an example is the lion rampant wearing a ball and chain and holding a wild rose in its paw featured on the apron of the Levey family sideboard.[25] More often than not, though, only the head and front legs of the big cat were depicted, rather than the whole body.

All sorts of variations, including quite naturalistic images, highly stylized ones and masks, heads of lions roaring or with their jaws shut, were used not only as decorative elements (as applied ornamentation or on the crown of certain pieces) but also as supports (in the form of capitals or armrests). Feline paws – fine or chunky, with or without claws – made fashionable by the Regency style that reigned during the early part of the century, appeared very frequently on the legs of various items of drawing-room or dining-room furniture. While some of these paw feet, especially those adorning settees, were extremely realistically executed, numerous round tables were equipped with

468
Head of Columbia adorning the head of a Renaissance-revival bed, about 1875-1890
Detail of figure 224
230 x 133 x 201 cm
Musée du Séminaire de Québec, gift of Abbé G. Édouard Côté
Photo John R. Porter/MOBIVIQ

469
Beaver and maple leaves decorating a naturalistic mirror
220 x 115 cm
Soeurs des Saints-Noms-de-Jésus-et-de-Marie, Valleyfield
Photo ministère des Affaires culturelles, Montreal, Inventaire des biens culturels (78-292-35)

This mirror, kept until recently at the Vincent d'Indy music school in Outremont, was given to the nuns on April 8, 1927, by Antoinette Valois, wife of Judge Onésime Loranger.

a simple support in which the rendering of the feet was a good deal more abstract.

Imaginary and Strange Animals

The category of fabulous beings, neither entirely real nor entirely imaginary, includes the griffin, that legendary creature with the body of a lion and the head and wings of an eagle. This mythical beast, which is also a heraldic motif, appears sometimes finely carved in the round, at others roughly and simply incised; as a decorative element, it was employed both in furniture of no particular style and in pieces inspired by the Gothic and Renaissance forms. Other fabulous beasts, like the chimera, the dragon and the phoenix, served to enlarge the decorative vocabulary yet further and incidentally prepared the way for the depiction of another very strange animal: the ornithorhynchus, or duck-billed platypus.

It was indeed a surprise to find in the Barbeau collection kept at the Canadian Museum of Civilization, in Hull, a photograph of a carved relief depicting a scaly-bodied animal with the tail of a bird and the beak of a duck. In spite of the rather inaccurate rendering of the coat, the flat, beaver-like tail and the webbed, clawed feet are clear clues to the animal's identity.[26] The existence of the platypus, which is a native of the Australian continent, was not recorded until the late eighteenth century (1789). The anatomical peculiarities of this bizarre survivor from prehistoric times, which although a mammal is also an egg-layer, raised many doubts and taxonomic conundrums. Interestingly, it was during a British Zoological Society conference held in Montreal on September 2, 1884, that the discovery of platypus eggs was first announced. Perhaps interest in the creature as a decorative motif was sparked by the publicity surrounding this important discovery? Given the lack of any detailed information about the piece the idea is a tempting one, especially in view of the wide variety of less exotic animals and birds that were already part of the decorative repertoire.

Birds as Decorative Elements

Many different species of bird were employed in the embellishment of Victorian furniture, no doubt a reflection of the passion for listing and classifying the natural world that marked the century of Darwin.[27] Perching birds (of the passeriforme order, which includes many land birds) appear very frequently, their small round bodies and short beaks often applied to bedsteads or carved on uprights and horizontals, aprons and cross pieces. They are usually depicted in action, flying, feeding, billing and cooing or sitting on their nests. Other larger varieties, such as pheasants and herons, are generally given a more majestic pose, spreading their wings at some choice spot, like the surround of a mirror. All, large and small alike, show some influence of oriental art, although revised and sanctioned by the styles in vogue between 1850 and 1880.

However, the goose that crowns one of the sideboards belonging to the Musée de la civilisation and the few birds of prey recorded seem to have been less susceptible to the orientalism evident in most of the other bird motifs. Although relatively simply executed, an image of a wise owl appears to great effect on the entomologist's cabinet[28] made for Father Léon Provancher, a local expert in the field. The eagle had a quite illustrious career as a decorative motif. Our American neighbours adopted the bald-headed eagle as their emblem in 1782, and many variations on the theme can be found in their furniture.[29] Some of these are similar to the paired birds perched on the back of the settees belonging to the Hôtel-Dieu and the archbishop's palace of Quebec City. But although on the North American continent the eagle motif was not restricted to any particular style, in Europe the great raptor was closely associated with the Empire and Chippendale styles. Both these forms tended to eschew the whole body, preferring to portray the head or the powerful talons grasping a globe, this latter image forming a classical Chippendale foot. This partial use of animals is seen very rarely in still life.

Pigeons and doves, with their small heads, long necks and plump bodies, can easily be distinguished from the squat partridge and grouse (order galliformes), which are usually depicted with their wide tails spread; similarly, the broad beak of the duck, the long fine ones of various shore birds and the crest worn by different varieties of woodpecker all serve to identify the other species that provide the principal decoration on a good number of sideboards and dressers. Dead birds are also depicted and, although the motifs are less varied than in the live versions, these creatures shown hanging by their feet, feathers ruffled and wings drooping, can be extremely revealing.

Still Lifes

The history of the genre tells us that from the sixteenth century on still lifes related to hunting were the closed province of princes and kings who, by commissioning huge paintings of game, reaffirmed their exclusive right to hunt and manifested their taste for venison.[30] References to wealth and privilege are frequent in discussions by nineteenth-century critics of furniture in the French Renaissance style, such as the famous piece by the Parisian Alexandre-Georges Fourdinois presented at the Great Exhibition of 1851.[31] Taking this work as a model,[32] many makers created sideboards and dressers in which the doors or the tympanum of the cornice were decorated with species associated principally with the sport of hunting as perceived and practiced during the last century.[33]

Like the painter Antoine Plamondon, who in 1850 executed a picture depicting three youths hunting *tourtes*, or passenger pigeons, a few carver-cabinetmakers decorated their works with images of the bird whose tasty flesh eventually led to its extinction and who lent its name to one of Quebec's traditional dishes – the savoury meat pie known as *tourtière*. Rather oddly, doves and ducks, both of which were consumed widely,[34] appear very infrequently on dining-room display pieces. In imitation of the masterpieces presented between 1842 and 1862 at the "furniture salons" of the great exhibitions, which were publicized and described in detail in articles appearing in the *Art Journal* and the *Illustrated London News*, many cabinetmakers opted rather for partridge, grouse and other gallinaceous birds.

Whatever game birds are depicted – partridge, spruce grouse or ruffed grouse – they are always rendered in considerable detail and are at times accompanied by some variety of long-billed bird, generally a shore bird such as a woodcock or a sandpiper. Occasionally a woodpecker (possibly a hairy woodpecker) or a duck is added to the group, as in the very fine little panel that adorns a sideboard in the collection of the Séminaire de Québec. The

470
Marius Barbeau (1883-1969), Ottawa
Duck-billed platypus adorning a sideboard that belonged to Mrs. Acton-Bond of Ottawa, 1963
Photograph
Canadian Museum of Civilization, Hull, Marius Barbeau Collection (J-18228)

471
Griffins adorning the back of a Renaissance-revival curule chair, about 1914
Detail of figure 418
110 x 76 x 52 cm
Private collection, Quebec City
Photo Christine Guest/MMFA

472
Perching bird adorning the apron of a rococo-revival console table surmounted by a mirror
Detail of figure 184
79 x 142 x 61 cm (table); 160 cm (mirror)
Private collection, Coaticook
Photo Christine Guest/MMFA

dead body of a hare is seen only very rarely, despite the fact that this motif was reproduced in illustrated magazines and catalogues accessible to Quebec furniture makers[35] and that the painter Krieghoff employed it in several paintings of game apparently intended for English army officers.[36] Members of the deer family were better represented, however, at least in the furniture catalogued.

Animal Sculpture

A few pieces present celebrations in wood of hunting, still considered a noble activity. Deer, carved in the round and depicted not only as spoils of the chase but also as its quarry, belong rather to the category of animal sculpture than that of still life, a genre executed principally in relief. Thus, rather than simply portraying the dead body of a stag, a common motif on decorated sideboards of the period,[37] the images on the sideboard belonging to the Collège de Lévis and the ones recorded in a photograph in the Fonds Brassard are powerful death scenes, recalling the stag hunt with dogs executed by a Brussels furniture maker in 1847. If we compare our examples to the cornice of the cupboard reproduced in the *Art Union*, however, it becomes evident that our makers "Canadianized" the motif. From the massive body, the powerful neck, the broad muzzle and especially the antlers, which show irregular tines and a solid area in the centre, it seems clear that the animal is a caribou. Populations of the once common woodland caribou were decimated as the result of changes in its habitat and the market for its meat.[38]

Images of caribou pursued by hounds were sometimes replaced by depictions of the dogs themselves, as in the canine supports that adorn the second level of a sideboard mirror (Musée de la civilisation, Quebec City). Other animals were also used to evoke successful hunting expeditions and the rich resources of our forests. The sideboard handles in the form of deer, once attributed to Suzor-Coté,[39] or those shaped like beaver, mink and weasels on a sideboard belonging to the Musée du Saguenay – Lac-Saint-Jean, highlight the importance of these various creatures, valued either as the object of recreational hunting or for their fur.

475

477

478

LIVING IN STYLE

The Underwater World

As well as portrayals of furred and feathered animals, we find, from the 1860s on, occasional motifs featuring creatures that live in water. Fish appear carved in relief on the panels of dining-room cupboards and, like game motifs, generally come in groups of two, three or four, sometimes accompanied by an eel or even a lobster. Regardless of the degree of naturalism or stylization, various anatomical features enable us to identify several local species of fish.[40] Salmon and brook char are easily recognized by their smooth, streamlined bodies. Both these varieties were highly popular with fishermen, as was the pugnacious bass, characterized by its large mouth and the irregular shape of its dorsal fin.[41] The American shad,[42] fished both for the sport it provided and for its gastronomic qualities, is a long, slim fish with a characteristic tail divided into two equal parts by a deep V-shaped indention. That it also served as a cabinetmaker's model is proved by a drawing in the collection taken from the workshop of the craftsman Roy dit Belleau.[43] The repertoire of water-animal ornamentation also includes the sturgeon, a fish easily identifiable by its long snout and bony plates. Unknown here until the 1860s, the sturgeon later became one of the species fished commercially. It shared this distinction with the eel, of which ornamental images have been recorded on sideboards and dressers in Rivière-Ouelle and Sainte-Anne-de-la-Pérade.[44]

From among all the furniture listed, only sixteen ichthyological images have been identified. Can this small percentage be attributed to a general indifference to fish as a foodstuff during the last century, owing to its strong flavour?[45] It seems possible, although both French and English decorators advocated the use of hunting and fishing still lifes for dining-room murals.[46] Was their advice taken? If we rely on the photographic evidence, apparently not. The underwater world was decidedly better represented by the ornamental use of shell motifs.

Unlike representations of game and fish, which are confined almost exclusively to the decoration of dining-room furniture, shell images appear on all types of household furniture and ornaments. A purely decorative element, whose use has a long history,[47] the shell may be carved, painted or inlaid; it usually appears near the centre of the piece – for example, on the crown of a seat back, or the middle of the apron of a table. Although a few quite naturalistic shell motifs have been recorded, by far the most popular is the stylized ridged half-circle of the scallop-shell, portrayed either from the outside (convex) or the inside (concave). The shell motif is not restricted to any particular style but appears indiscriminately throughout many, including the Chippendale, Regency, Eastlake, Elizabethan and rococo-revival. It can even be found in iron accessories; in fact, of all the countless moulded metal furniture handles produced, a large percentage of those not shaped like a conventionalized acanthus leaf were an imitation of the curved form of a shell.

PLANT IMAGES

Motifs inspired by the plant world have served as decorative models since time immemorial, and Victorian cabinetmakers used them extensively. In fact, more than half of the ornamental elements identified belong to this category, which includes forty-two distinct motifs (seven varieties of leaf, seventeen of fruit and vegetables, and eighteen of flowers). Perhaps, as R. W.

473

474

475

473
Sideboard presented by Alexandre-Georges Fourdinois at the Great Exhibition held in London in 1851
Engraving published in *Industry of All Nations : The Art-Journal Illustrated Catalogue* (London : George Virtue, 1851), p. 285.
Library of the Montreal Museum of Fine Arts
Photo Christine Guest/MMFA

474
Still life with partridge adorning the lower right-hand door of a Renaissance-revival sideboard, about 1890
Detail of figure 275
White oak, 323 x 264 x 67 cm
Ministère de l'Enseignement supérieur et des Sciences, Gouvernement du Québec
Photo Christine Guest/MMFA

475
Still life with hare and partridge adorning the crown of a rococo-revival sideboard
Detail of figure 199
Mahogany and mahogany veneer, 266 x 200 x 67 cm
Musée du Saguenay–Lac-Saint-Jean, Chicoutimi (A-76.146)
Photo Christine Guest/MMFA

476
Rococo-revival sideboard
207 x 214 x 67 cm
Priests' residence, Séminaire de Québec
Photo Jean-Pierre Labiau/MOBIVIQ

476

Symonds and B. B. Whineray suggest in their study of Victorian furniture,[48] the enormous popularity of this form of decoration, which transcends even stylistic considerations, can be attributed to the need to embellish furniture in order to make it more attractive to potential buyers. In this quest for enhancement, the advent of machine work and of pattern books were particularly useful in the fabrication of furniture, especially seat furniture. Beds and lounge furniture, iron accessories and decorative furniture also provided surfaces admirably suited to plant motifs, either carved, applied, inlaid, painted or incised.

Classical Motifs: The Mediterranean Influence

Plant motifs, then – simple or complex, individual or combined – offered craftsmen a greater range of possibilities for displaying their skill than either human or animal images. The acanthus leaf, which appears extremely frequently, is a case in point. Disparaged by some (Owen Jones in 1856 and Eastlake in 1868), included in the list of desirable "modern" motifs by others (Meyer in 1887),[49] the acanthus takes many forms, sometimes quite naturalistic but more often highly artificial and stylized, like the motifs that appear in the catalogue belonging to the furniture maker Roy dit Belleau,[50] or those taken from the drawing lessons in the collection "Vere Foster's work on Drawing", republished in 1878 by the *Canadian Mechanics' Magazine and Pattent Office Record*.[51] Curved into a "C" shape, twirled into an "S", broadened until it resembled a fleur-de-lis or a palmette, the acanthus could be replaced by no other leaf. Even palm and laurel leaves, which were also part of the classical decorative vocabulary, were little used by comparison: to date, barely a dozen pieces ornamented with these leaves have been recorded. And although certainly more familiar to local craftsmen, oak, maple and ivy leaves figure on only about twenty occasions and their use seems to have been quite restricted.

The Northern Flora

A revival of interest in the medieval style was accompanied by a penchant for indigenous plant motifs. In articles first published in 1870 in the *Art Journal* and partially reprinted eight years later in the *Canadian Mechanics' Magazine*, Edward Hulme sanctioned this type of decoration and published plates showing the possibilities for adapting local plants for ornamental purposes.[52] Oak, ivy and maple leaves were all employed in this way, although the maple leaf was less subject to the vagaries of fashion and was not restricted to any particular style.

Like the beaver, the maple leaf gradually took on emblematic significance. Its inclusion in the ornamentation of the bed head created in 1860 by the Toronto firm of Jacques & Hay for the Prince of Wales' visit, and its use in the frame surrounding the panels painted by Krieghoff for the Quebec parliament are important examples of this function. The large looking-glass belonging to the Soeurs des Saints-Noms-de-Jésus-et-de-Marie offers a particularly good illustration of the issue raised by Hulme concerning naturalistic as opposed to conventionalized treatment. If we examine the leaves closely, it is clear that instead of the foliage of the sugar maple (*acer saccharum*), the carver has depicted that of two other varieties: the silver maple (*acer saccharinum*) at the top, and the Norway maple (*acer platanoides*) in the divided vases at the base of the mirror. This is not unusual. According to Frère Marie-Victorin, the silhouette of the sugar maple leaf served rarely as the image of our emblem, artists generally preferring the more pronounced lobes of the silver maple leaf, and its more jagged edge.[53] The rose motif, with the acanthus one of the most popular decorative images of all, has a similar history.

The Invasion of the Rose

The seats included in the Victorian furniture constituting the corpus at the present time, particularly those in the rococo-revival style, are decorated with an enormous number of rose motifs. While this floral profusion was clearly linked to the notion of luxury, the rose was also sometimes employed in a considerably more moderate fashion.

477
Caribou hunt adorning the crown of a Renaissance-revival sideboard
213 x 132 x 47 cm
Priests' residence, Collège de Lévis
Photo Jean-Pierre Labiau/MOBIVIQ

478
Ermine or mink adorning the left-hand drawer handle of a rococo-revival sideboard
Detail of figure 199
Mahogany and mahogany veneer,
266 x 200 x 67 cm
Musée du Saguenay–Lac-Saint-Jean, Chicoutimi (A-76.146)
Photo Christine Guest/MMFA

THE FURNITURE

479
Still life with fish and lobster adorning the lower left-hand door of a Renaissance-revival sideboard, about 1890
Detail of figure 275
White oak, 323 x 264 x 67 cm
Ministère de l'Enseignement supérieur et des Sciences, Gouvernement du Québec
Photo Christine Guest/MMFA

In the ornamentation of the backs, aprons, under-frames and heads of armchairs, tables and beds, decorators drew their inspiration not only from the creations of their fellow-craftsmen, past and present, but also from popularized versions of the latest scientific discoveries, including those related to that quintessentially Victorian flower, the rose. During the nineteenth century, as the result of advances in hybridization techniques, the cultivation of roses became widespread. Into this context of rapid horticultural development[54] was born the modern rose, round, luscious and perfumed, the perfect response to the aesthetic requirements of Victorians, including the makers and purchasers of furniture.

Of the two thousand varieties of rose available at the time,[55] two seem to have been favoured as a motif: the five-petalled wild rose (*rosa rugosa*) and the cultivated rose (*rosa centifolia*). Depicted at various stages in their flowering, roses were often combined with other decorative elements, sometimes human figures, sometimes animals, but usually the natural accompaniment of other plant motifs. Among the flowers portrayed alongside roses we have identified daisies, sunflowers, dahlias, poppies, irises, orchids, arum lilies, tulips, harebells, convolvulus, daffodils, lilies of the valley and thistles. These flowers, shown in varying numbers, appear either spread out or assembled in a bouquet depending on the shape and area of the piece to be decorated. Roses themselves, and other many-petalled flowers, are almost always shown in a frontal view; different varieties, however, like poppies, harebells and convolvulus, are often shown from the back or in profile. These latter viewpoints, suggested by Meyer (1888), were often employed for isolated motifs (see in particular the Whitehead suite belonging to the Musée de la civilisation).

480

Other Elements in the Floral Repertoire

Several other reflections of Victorian horticultural taste, aside from the rose, were featured in the floral garden of decorative motifs. Indigenous varieties like convolvulus, harebells, arum lilies and thistles, all highly recommended by Edward Hulme and also part of the local landscape, won themselves a place on Quebec furniture. Represented too were the lily, the sunflower, the crocus and the daffodil, all species closely linked to the Aesthetic movement, including the Eastlake style. The employment of dahlias and rhododendrons as motifs reflected the general popularity of the two flowers, the one being fashionable in the first half of the century, the other in the latter.[56]

Decorative floral images did not only appear on furniture in the form of carving, but were also featured on works ornamented with marquetry, inlay and painting. Many are the pieces in papier mâché or wood that, against an orientally-inspired ground of black lacquer, display the profusion of the Victorian garden. The maker J. M. Papineau began to build his reputation for this type of furniture in 1858, with his black painted bedroom set highlighted with gilt and painted motifs.[57] Nevertheless, the richest and most elaborate examples of floral decoration are carved, and it was the favoured expressive technique of several of Quebec's most interesting furniture makers. Two years later, an enthusiastic reviewer compared the workmanship of a bedroom suite carved by Thomas Pariseau to the creations of Pierre-Joseph Redouté, the great floral painting specialist whose major treatise on roses still dominates the field.[58]

Among the very finest examples are the floral bouquets and garlands featured in profusion on the mirrors and tables, and indeed all over the drawing-room furniture carved by Gourdeau. Such opulence can only be matched by the reliefs that adorn some sideboards and dressers, whose panels are embellished with the classical food-related iconography of fruit, vegetables, game and fish.

Carving the Contents of the Larder

From among the positive cornucopia of food-inspired shapes – three-dimensional or incised, rounded or flat, presented in vertical or horizontal festoons – we can identify several kinds of fruit, including apples, pears, plums, cherries, gooseberries, lemons and pomegranates, but also a number of vegetables, such as pumpkins, turnips or swedes, corn cobs, beans and peas. There is also a number of small fruits, like raspberries, blackberries and other field berries, and sometimes even a few nuts are added to complete the feast of ornamental carving.

Although the presence of these foodstuffs accords with what we know of eating habits and market gardening activities at the time,[59] some scholars have seen the use of images of fruit and vegetables at various stages of their development as related to scientific investigation;[60] this seems doubtful, however, especially in the case of the pomegranate, a fruit with an extremely rich symbolic history. It therefore seems prudent to understand this ornamentation as simply the rendering, in accordance with the pervasive naturalism of the period, of motifs drawn from nature. Among the various motifs of edible plants used to decorate household furniture, one of the most popular was a leafy branch bearing bunches of grapes. This image appears on numerous pieces of seat furniture, table aprons and piano legs, as well as on the frames surrounding mirrors and screens. Some decorators, however, preferred scrolling foliage to the vine branch for use as a link or pendant motif.

Between the Real and the Imaginary: The Foliated Scroll

The foliated scroll, or rinceau, is a multi-purpose ornament used highly effectively to give body to cast-iron furniture and to fill in and set off areas of decorative inlay on Boulle furniture. The cut-out wooden leaf shapes used to create the open-work panels on pianos and the carved or applied relief decoration of certain drawing-room cabinets and tables are illustrations of the double decorative and fill-in function of foliated scrollwork. Unfolded, the rinceau becomes a long, ornamental ribbon, just one more item in the wide range of decorative devices used to embellish furniture of every style.

MISCELLANEOUS IMAGES

Over half the motifs that fall into this final category are derived from objects of one sort or another. Among those most frequently employed – without necessarily meeting the standards of the neo-classical style that inspired them – are the closed urns that crown large central fixtures, the heads of Renaissance-revival beds or the cornices of armoires, the carved or painted vases that contain foliage, flowers or fruit, and finally the lyres that serve as pedal boards, seat backs and head boards. Less common motifs in this class, whose usage parameters it is hard to establish precisely, are fans, globes, hel-

480
François Gourdeau (1840-1920)
Roses adorning the support of a Renaissance-revival games table,
about 1870. Detail of figure 294
Black walnut, 78 (diam.) x 91 x 45 cm
The Montreal Museum of Fine Arts, gift of the Succession J. A. DeSève (1987.Df.3)
Photo Christine Guest/MMFA

481
Still life with turnips or swedes adorning the lower left-hand door of a Renaissance-revival sideboard,
about 1880. Detail of figure 358
Walnut and burl walnut, 310.5 x 204 x 61 cm
Musée du Séminaire de Québec, gift of Abbé G. Édouard Côté
Photo Christine Guest/MMFA

mets, mitres and crosses. The symbolic use of such images is sometimes evident, however, as with the addition of a mitre to a bishop's throne, the terrestrial globe that surmounts the ornamented bookcase belonging to Sir Hugh Allan and the crosses that adorn a number of prie-dieus.

Heraldic References: The Presence of History

The motifs belonging to the second group in the class of miscellaneous images, heraldic motifs, are undoubtedly a reflection of humanity's ongoing preoccupation with history. The decorating of objects with escutcheons, badges and monograms can be a way of indicating ownership, membership in a particular group or even occupation. The coats of arms that appear carved or applied on ceremonial chairs intended for religious or political leaders fall into this latter category, while others featured on certain Renaissance-revival seat furniture are more the result of a taste for the decorative vocabulary of a particular style. The presence of some entirely imaginary armorial images — single shields and unfurled parchments — offer further proof of the fashion for heraldic devices. Such motifs are widespread, appearing on seats, cabinets, hall furniture, sideboards and bookcases. The Ravenscrag bookcase belonging to Sir Hugh Allan, with its four carved panels, illustrates how well a piece of this type lends itself to the use of emblems: four trophies of objects, applied on medallions, adorn the panels of the lower part of the case. The first three of these freely composed images relate respectively to Commerce, the Fine Arts (painting, sculpture and architecture) and Literature and History, while the last, with its many battle-related motifs and its inscription, "the State", likely evokes the trilogy of power, order and justice. This magnificent bookcase is inspired by the Renaissance style; a number of other pieces fulfilling the same function were examples of the Gothic revival. It is in these two styles that the integration into cabinetmaking of motifs taken from architecture is most evident.

Architectural References

While the motifs representing lancet, tri-cusped or many-cusped arches, and pinnacles, pendants and rosettes, all taken from the Gothic vocabulary, usually appear on furniture that is Gothic either in form or spirit, this relation is less clear in the case of columns and pilasters. Whether smooth, wreathed or fluted, ornamented with drapery or with floral capitals, columns are commonly found on all types of case furniture, including wardrobes, bookcases,

482
Coat of arms on a Renaissance-revival Speaker's chair, about 1879
Detail of figure 36
White oak, 224 x 81.5 x 69 cm
Archdiocese of Quebec City, kept at the Musée du Séminaire de Québec
Photo Christine Guest/MMFA

The shield bears the arms of Canada's first five provinces: Ontario, Quebec, New Brunswick, Nova Scotia and Manitoba.

483
Fine arts trophy adorning a Renaissance-revival bookcase, about 1864
Detail of figure 41
Black walnut, 347.6 x 550 x 61.6 cm
Allan Memorial Institute, Montreal
Photo Christine Guest/MMFA

ORNAMENTATION ACCORDING TO TYPES OF FURNITURE					
CATEGORIES	Seat furniture	Storage furniture	Support furniture	Beds and lounging furniture	Work furnit
Anthropomorphic images	44	22	13	5	
Zoomorphic images	69	90	35	13	
Phytomorphic images	289	95	78	33	
Miscellaneous images	22	41	7	15	
Totals for each type of furniture	424	248	133	66	

Glass (glasse) Eng.

A large piece of amalgam-coated glass found in any room. The notaries mention the **bureau glass** in a *chambre*, bedroom or servant's room, the **dressing glass** in the bedroom, the **looking glass**, small, in the bedroom, dining room, kitchen, parlour, bathroom, sitting room or room, and the **toilet glass**[39] above the small mahogany toilet table in the bedroom, dining room or other room.

Miroir[40] Fr.

A polished reflecting surface, of varying size depending on the room it stands in or where it is placed. In the *chambre à coucher* it could be large, small or oval. The piece of glass was mounted in a gilt frame or moulding finely carved in *noyer noir*, mahogany or *acajou*, *bambou doré* (gilt bamboo) or *pin*, with a wood frame covered in gilding. It stood on a *pivot*, stand or foot sometimes containing two small drawers, and was placed on the cornice or hung over the mantelpiece in the *salon*. Large looking glasses with rounded tops and gilt and *noyer noir* frames were found in the *cuisine*, the *passage*, the *salle*, the *salle à dîner* or the *salle à manger*, while smaller oval ones adorned the *salle d'entrée*, the *salle de réception*, the *salle de bain* and the *salon*.

The notaries mention the **miroir à barbe**[41] (shaving mirror) on an *acajou* foot in the *chambre à coucher*, the **grand miroir anglais** in the *salon*, the **miroir à toilette** or **miroir de toilette**,[42] large or small, on a table in the *chambre à coucher*, the large **miroir de centre** in finely carved *noyer noir*, the small mirror with brass screws, the **large miroir de cheminée** in the *salon* or *chambre de compagnie*, the **miroir de trumeau**[43] or **miroir trumeau** (pier glass or overmantel glass) in the *salle*, the *chambre de compagnie* or the *passage*.

The newspapers advertised a handsome **miroir à pied** with a gilt frame and a **miroir de fantaisie** for the *chambre à coucher*.

Mirror (miror) Eng.

A large or small polished reflecting surface. Mirrors were placed in bedrooms and dining rooms, and with gilt frames in drawing rooms, kitchens, sitting rooms and parlours.

IV. ELEVATION FURNITURE (STEPS AND STOOLS)

Furniture used for reaching high places or for climbing up to another piece of furniture. *Escabeaux* (step ladders) and *marchepieds* (bed steps) were often replaced by *tabourets* (stools) or *bancs* (benches).

Escabeau (escabot) Fr.

A small piece of furniture with no arms or back[44], used for reaching another piece of furniture, usually the bed or something relatively high. *Escabeaux* (step ladders) were found in the *chambre*, the *cuisine*, the *passage*, the *dépense* (storeroom) and the *tambour* (vestibule). It was a small object, made of *frêne* and composed of two steps and a seat.

The notaries mention the *escabeau de lit*[45] in the chambre à coucher.

Marchepied Fr.

A low piece of furniture consisting of from two to four steps, later covered, of wood, used for climbing into bed and kept in the *chambre à coucher*. The *marchepied* or bed steps could be replaced by a *tabouret de pied* (foot stool).

V. SEAT FURNITURE

A piece of furniture used for resting part or all of the body, with a seat element consisting of a longer or shorter horizontal piece for one or more persons. It is made up of various specific parts: arms or armrests, wings[46] and moveable cushions. The seat and back[47] were usually covered, upholstered and stuffed to make them more comfortable. Seat furniture is divided into various categories according to the number of persons accommodated and the parts of the body that are supported. It is found all over the house.

Chairs had straw or elm-bark[48] bottoms and were made of basketwork[49] or canework.[50] The covering fabrics most used were horsehair, damask, cretonne and chintz, with horsehair and damask predominating in chair covering. The framework was usually of wood.

Armchair[51] Eng.

A wide one-person seat with a back and arms, cane-bottomed, leather-covered. A rarely used term.

Banc Fr.

Maître Jacques et Helmina étaient assis sur un banc de jonc vis-à-vis d'un feu ardent allumé dans l'âtre [Master Jacques and Helmina were sitting on a cane bench beside a brightly-burning fire in the hearth] (Eugène L'Ecuyer, "*La fille du brigand*", 1844, published in *Le répertoire national* or *Recueil de littérature canadienne*, ed. by J. Huston, Montreal: J. M. Valois et Cie., 1893, vol. III, p. 105).

A seat for several people, undecorated, generally long and narrow, with a wooden framework. It can be made of *bois de pin*, of basketwork, have a cane bottom, be stuffed with horsehair and covered with velveteen. Most often found in the *cuisine*, *chambre à coucher* or *chambre de compagnie*. Also found in the *salle à dîner*, *salon*, *passage*, *aile*, *bureau* and *étude*.

The notaries mention the **banc à musique** in the *chambre à coucher* and the *salon*, the **banc de piano** or **à piano**[52] or **de gout pour piano** in the *salon* and *chambre de compagnie*, made of *bois franc* or *noyer* and *bourré de crin* (stuffed with horsehair), the wooden **banc d'office**, the stuffed **banc de bureau** covered *en imitation de cuir* (with imitation leather) in the *bureau*, the **petit banc de pied** or **à pied** *en peluche* (plush-covered) in the *chambre à coucher*, the **banc pour laver** or **à laver**, the **banc percé**[53] for children, and the **banc pliant** *couvert en toile* (canvas-covered folding bench).

The **petit banc** is probably a synonym for a *tabouret* or *escabeau*.

Berçante[54] (chaise berçante) Fr.

A rocking chair, found in the kitchen, passage, dining room, office, drawing room, bedroom and family room. It can be made of basketwork with a cane or basketwork bottom covered in plush, grey damask or horsehair. The frame can be of *noyer noir*, *frêne* or *pin*.

The notaries mention the **berçante d'enfant** (child's rocker), the **berçante de nourrice** (nurse's rocker) and the **berçante perforée d'enfant** (child's close stool rocker).

Berçeuse (chaise berçeuse) Fr.

A rocking chair found in the *chambre à coucher*, *chambre de compagnie*, *cuisine*, *cuisine d'été* (summer kitchen), *salle d'entrée* or the *salon*. It was made of *pin*, covered with *indienne de meuble* (chintz), and could have a horsehair or cane bottom or be made of basketwork.

Bergère (berjère) Fr.

Wide deep armchair with a generally high rounded back[55], cushions on the bottom and padded sides. The *bergère* was wider and deeper than a regular armchair. It could be *grande*, *brodée* (embroidered), stuffed with *crin* or *paille* (straw), either uncovered or covered with *indienne*, *damas*, *damas de laine*, *moire* or *peluche*, and made of carved *noyer noir* or *merisier* (yellow birch). It was found in the *chambre à coucher*, the *chambre de compagnie*, the *salon*, the *salle* or the *aile*.

The notaries mention the **bergère sculptée à l'antique** and the **bergère à ressort**.[56]

Canapé[57] (kanapé) Fr.

A seat for more than one person, upholstered, with a back, wings and arms,

486
Advertisement for the firm of Charles Edmond Pariseau of Montreal
Published in *Le Négociant canadien*, March 14, 1872
Photo SRP

found in the *chambre à coucher*, the *salle à dîner*, *salle d'entrée*, the *salon*, the *salle*, the *passage* and the *cuisine*, which could be made of *noyer noir*, *acajou* or *pin* with a brass surround. It was quilted, and might be covered in *indienne*, *cretonne*, *cuir*, *coton*, *damas de laine*, *damas vert ou rouge* (green or red damask), *moire noire* (black moiré), *toile cirée*[58] (oilcloth), *tapis* or *étoffe bleue*, stuffed or upholstered in *reps* and with a flannel cover.

The notaries mention the **canapé à ressort double s'ouvrant**, the **canapé à ressort**, the **canapé extension** in *damas rouge*, the **canapé-lit**[59] (bed-settee) in the *salle d'entrée*, the *salon* or the *bureau*, stuffed with *crin*, and the **canapé à oreilles**.[60]

The newspapers advertised a *canapé à la mode française* in *damas* and in *crin*.

Causeuse[61] Fr.

Une causeuse et deux fauteuils, aussi de bois satiné et de velours rouge, semblaient attendre d'élégants visiteurs [A love seat and two armchairs also of satiny wood and red velveteen, seemed to await elegant visitors] (Joseph Marmette, *Récits et souvenirs*. Montreal: Beauchemin, 1925 [1872], p. 16).

They saw Major Sternfield seated on a causeuse beside a pretty, child-like creature of sixteen (Rosanna Leprohon, *Antoinette de Mirecourt or Secret Marrying and Secret Sorrowing*. Montreal: McClelland and Stewart Ltd., 1973 [1864], p. 95).

A two-seater sofa or small settee for only two, found in the *salon*, covered in coloured *brocatelle* or *coton* and made of *broches* (wire) or *merisier*. The word was mostly used by furniture dealers in newspaper advertisements of the period.

Chair[62] Eng.

The chair was inviting enough, with its chintz cover and wicker seat, but he would never admit fatigue (Gilbert Parker, *The Pomp of the Lavillettes*. London: Methuen & Co., 1897, p. 114).

A seat for one person, with a seat and back, found mainly in the bedroom, kitchen and dining room, but also in the sitting room, parlour, hall, drawing room, any other room, the library and the passage. Made of black walnut, mahogany, reed or wicker. The seat was cane or rush, covered with rep, damask, plush, horsehair or hair cloth.

The notaries mention various kinds of chair used for different purposes:

a) classified according to the rooms where they are found: the **bedroom chair** in the bedroom; the **common chair** in the kitchen, bedroom, sitting room, other room or parlour; the **dining chair**, of oak, black walnut or mahogany with a cane bottom, in the dining room, sitting room or parlour; the **drawing room chair** in black walnut; the **hall chair**[63] of mahogany in the hall, parlour, passage, drawing room or sitting room; the **kitchen chair** in the kitchen; the **nursing chair**[64] in the sitting room; the **office chair** in the office and the dining room; and the **parlour chair**.[65]

b) classified as adjustable: the **camp chair**[66] in the parlour, office or bedroom; the **folding chair**, cane-seated, in the parlour or the library;

c) classified as being for children: the high or low **child's chair** in the dining room, sitting room, bathroom or breakfast room and the **high chair** in the dining room;

d) classified according to its specific style or characteristic shape: the **step chair** in the pantry; the **serving chair** in the library or drawing room; the **star chair** in the drawing room; the **worked chair** in the drawing room; the **reclining chair** in the drawing room; the **Windsor chair**[67] in the living room or the kitchen; the **fancy chair** in the parlour or dining room; the **Japanese chair** and the **invalid chair** in the sitting room or bedroom; the **night chair** in the bedroom or chamber; the **commode chair**; the **carving chair** in the sitting room; the **piano chair** in the sitting room; the **screen chair** and the **smoking chair**.[68]

Chaise[69] Fr.

A seat for one, with a seat and back, the bottom of which may be stuffed, covered[70] or caned. In several of the sources *chaises* are found in the *chambre à coucher*, the *cuisine*, the *salle à dîner*, the *salle à manger* and the *salon*. They could also stand in the *salle d'entrée*, the *salle*, the *cabinet*, the *bureau*, the *chambre de bain*, the *passage* and the *boudoir*.

A *chaise*, *petite* or *grande*, could be made entirely of *bois franc* (*noyer noir*, *acajou* or mahogany, *merisier*, *cerisier* (cherrywood), *chêne*, *frêne*, *orme*, *bois plié* (bentwood), *érable piqué* (bird's-eye maple)), of *bois mou* (*pin*), or of imported wood (*roseau* [reed], *bois de rose*, *ébène*). The *fond*, *siège* or *fonçure* (bottom) was usually stuffed with *crin*, *empaillée* or *en jonc*, sometimes of *canne* or *paille*, *lacée*. Less commonly the bottom and back might be *en raquette*, *en "rateau"* or *en peau crue*[71] (rawhide). A chaise could be upholstered or covered with *crin*, *indienne*, *moire*, *cuir*, *peau* or *peau crue*, *toile* (canvas), *cretonne*, *coton*, *damas* or *damas de laine*, *peluche* (plush), and stuffed with *laine* (wool) with a round *foncé* back. It could be *sculpté* (carved) with mounting in exotic wood (*acajou*) different from the wood employed for the main frame, which would be of *noyer noir* with small bars.

The notaries mention *chaises* of varying shapes and functions:

a) classified by the room it stands in or by the other piece of furniture it accompanies: the ***chaise à dîner*** or ***de salle à dîner*** or ***de salle à manger*** (dining-room chair) was naturally found in the *salle à dîner* ; it could be made of *noyer noir* or *bois franc*, be *entouré*, stuffed with *toile cirée*, covered with *peluche* or *cuir*, sometimes imitation leather, with a *fond* of *crin*, *cuir* or *jonc*; the ***chaise de cuisine*** is listed in the *cuisine* or the *salle à dîner* ; the ***chaise de bureau*** in the *cuisine*; the ***chaise de parloir*** in the parlour: the ***chaise de salon*** of *noyer noir* covered in *reps* in the *salon*; the ***chaise de passage*** in *bois franc*, imitation *acajou*, *frêne*, *cuir* or *noyer noir*, stuffed with *crin*, with a *fond en jonc* (cane bottom), could stand in the *passage*, the *salle de famille*; the ***chaise de chambre*** (bedroom chair) is also listed;

b) chairs accompanied by an accessory: the ***chaise d'aisance***[72] found mainly in the *chambre à coucher*, the *passage* or the *salon*, was made of hardwood or *pin* and covered with *crin*, *reps* or *velours de coton* (cotton velveteen); the ***chaise à commodité***[73]; the ***chaise à l'aise***; the ***chaise perforée***[74] found in the *chambre à coucher*; the ***chaise percée***[75];

c) chairs that moved: the ***chaise tournante***, without screws, in the *salle*, the *bureau*, the *salle de famille* or the *chambre à coucher*; the ***chaise à dossier reversible***; the ***chaise à bercer***; the ***chaise berceuse***, which might be stuffed with *jonc* with a bottom of *canne* or *jonc* and the back of *jonc*, covered with *crin* or *tapis* with an outer cover of *crin*, when *petite* usually stood in the *chambre à coucher*, but was also found in the *salon* and sometimes in the *salle d'entrée*, the *salle* or the office; the ***chaise berçante***[76], made of *bois franc* (*noyer noir*) with the *fond* and sometimes the *dossier* (back) of *jonc*, *crin*, *canne*, *peau crue*, or with a bottom of *écorce* (bark), with wings and a stuffed or slatted *dossier*, and was found in the *chambre à coucher* and the *chambre de compagnie*, the *salle à dîner*, the *salon*, the *cuisine*, the *salle d'entrée*, and sometimes in the *passage*, the *salle* or the *bureau*; the *petite berçante*, covered with *maroquin* (Morocco leather) or *crin*, was found in the salle d'entrée, the cuisine or the chambre à coucher; and the ***chaise à spring***, of *noyer noir* with a *fond en crin*, in the *salon*;

d) chairs that folded and could be moved around: the ***chaise pliante*** (folding chair) of wood, perforated, in the *chambre à coucher*; and the ***chaise portative*** *en jonc* (portable cane chair) in the *salle à dîner*;

e) chairs classified by style: the ***chaise ancienne***; the ***chaise à la mode*** *en jonc*, *fond en canne*, *à la façon Windsor* (in the Windsor style); the ***chaise bay window***; the ***chaise***

Windsor; the **chaise de fantaisie** covered with *cretonne* in the *chambre* or the *salon*; the **chaise turque**; the **chaise française berçante** in *acajou*; the **chaise Louis XIV** and the **chaise de style Elisabeth**;

f) chairs of no particular style: the **chaise ordinaire** with wings in *peluche blanche* (white plush) in the *salon* or *parloir*; the **chaise commune** or **en bois** (ordinary wooden chair) in the *cuisine*, also in the *chambre à coucher*, the *salle d'entrée*, the *cabinet*, the *salle à dîner* or the *office*, which could be *empaillée en jonc* with a seat of *écorce d'orme* (elm bark);

g) classified according to a specific function: the **chaise à couture** (sewing chair) of mahogany in the *salon*; the **chaise à lire** (reading chair) and the **chaise prie-Dieu** [see Prie-Dieu] (prayer stool or chair) of *noyer noir*, *dorée* (gilded) and covered with *reps* in the *salon*;

h) chairs that could replace another piece of furniture for sitting or lying down: the **chaise bergère** in the *chambre*; the **chaise-canapé** that was part of a bedroom suite; the **chaise fauteuil** of *noyer noir*, *brodée* (embroidered) with wool and beads in the salon; the **chaise à bras** in the *salle à dîner* or the *salon*, *bourrée en crin*, *en cuir*, *en damas couleur marron* (maroon-coloured damask), made of *noyer noir* or *acajou*, covered with *maroquin* or *crin*; the **chaise-lit** and the **chaise-d'escabeau** of *fresne* (ash) or *noyer noir*, found in the *passage* or the *chambre de bain*;

i) chairs for a specific person: the **chaise d'enfant** *haute* (child's high chair), *perforée* (with a hole for a chamber pot) or *pliante* (folding), with a *tablette* (tray), made of *noyer noir* or *bois plié* (bentwood) and covered with *cretonne*, found in the *salle à dîner*, the *chambre* and the *salle d'entrée* as well as the *cabinet*, the *cuisine*, the *chambre à déjeuner* (breakfast room), the *salle* or the *salon*; the **chaise de dame** (lady's chair) in the *salon*; and the **chaise de malade** (invalid chair) *à roues* or *avec roulettes* (with wheels or casters), *bourrée en toile* in the *chambre à coucher*;

j) and other kinds of chair: the **chaise basse** (low chair); the **chaise de camp** of *reps* in the *chambre* and the *salon*; the **chaise de nuit** in the *chambre à coucher* and the *chambre de bain*; the *chaise hamac* (hammock chair) in the *salle à dîner*; and the **chaise à billot**.

Couch Eng.

A long seat found in the hall room, the dining room, the drawing room, the bedroom, the smoking room or the music room.

Divan[77] Fr.

A seat without arms or back, with moveable *coussins* serving as the back and wings, on which several people can sit. A divan could be *rond* (round), covered with *peluche* or *soie* (silk) and placed in the *salle d'entrée*. It was a little-used term, found only three times in documents from 1880 including two mentions in a furniture dealer's inventory.

Easy chair Eng.

A wide deep seat that usually had a high soft back, which could be made of mahogany or black walnut, covered with green worsted damask, and mainly stood in the bedroom or the dining room but is also found in the parlour, sitting room or drawing room.

Fauteuil (*fauteuille*) Fr. and Eng. in one literary source

> *Près de la fenêtre, dont les persiennes adoucissent la lumière trop crue du soleil, un bon fauteuil est installé* [Beside the window, with its closed shutters filtering the glaring sunlight, stands a comfortable armchair] (Françoise [Robertine Barry], *Chroniques du lundi de Françoise*. Quebec City, p. 155).
>
> She threw herself into the *fauteuil* hoping that tears might come to her relief (Leprohon, *op. cit.*, p. 154).

A seat for one, with a back and arms, *à barreau*, *à spring* or *berçant* (rocking). *Fauteuils* are listed as being in the *chambre à coucher*, the *salon*, the *salle à dîner*, the *salle à manger*, the *salle d'entrée*, the *cabinet*, the *salle*, the *office* and the *cuisine*. To make them more comfortable, they were sometimes *bourré en crin* or *en jonc*, *empaillé* or provided with *coussins* (cushions). A *fauteuil* could be upholstered or covered in *cuir* (dark) or imitation *cuir*, *jonc*, *moire, crin, coton, cretonne, toile, indienne, peluche, damas, cramoisi* or *velours* (velveteen). It might also be *brodé en laine* (embroidered with wool), *ouvragé* (carved) sometimes with roses, and made of *bois franc* (*noyer noir, acajou*), with *broches* (spindles) of *bois plié* (bentwood) or *ébène*.

The notaries mention the ***fauteuil à bras***, the ***fauteuil à dame*** (lady's armchair), the ***fauteuil de salon***, the ***fauteuil reversible***, the ***fauteuil perforé*** with a reversible *coussin* of corduroy filled with *crin*, the ***fauteuil à bascule*** (rocking armchair), the ***fauteuil d'aisance*** (close stool chair), the ***fauteuil Morris***[78] and the ***fauteuil de bureau*** with *coussins*.

Lounge[79] Eng.

Form of seat or chaise-longue found in the library, sitting room, bedroom, dining room, parlour, hall or kitchen.

Ottoman/Ottomane Eng. and Fr.

A long padded upholstered seat with springs and a [horse]hair bottom, found in the drawing room, parlour, sitting room and bedroom.

The French-language inventories make one mention, in 1860, of an ***ottomane bourrée***, placed in the *salon* or the *chambre à coucher*.

Prie-Dieu Fr.

A piece of religious furniture for kneeling on while praying, usually found in the bedroom. It was made of *noyer noir* and covered with wine-coloured *velours*.[80] A little-used term as compared to the *chaise prie-Dieu*.

Rocker Eng.

A rocking chair or armchair found in the servant's room, the chamber, the dining room, sitting room or kitchen.

The notaries mention an **easy rocker**.

Rocking chair Eng.

A rocking chair or armchair resting on curved runners called bends connecting the front and back feet allowing the chair to be rocked with a simple body movement. Made of mahogany or black walnut with a cane or hair bottom, it was most often found in the bedroom, but also in the sitting room, dining room, parlour, kitchen, nursery, drawing room or any other room.

Settee[81] Eng.

A long seat with arms and back, mentioned in a document of 1877 as standing in the bedroom, kitchen, parlour, dining room or another room.

The notaries mention the **rocking settee**.

Sofa[82] (sopha, sophat, sauphat, soffat) Fr. and Eng.

> *J'y placerai une causeuse et un grand sofa que tu garniras de multiples coussins et autour duquel tu suspendras d'épaisses tentures pour faire un coin d'intimité où nous irons souvent nous asseoir pour faire la causette et rappeler les souvenirs de nos premières amours* [I will put there a love seat and a big sofa, on which you will scatter lots of cushions and around which you will hang thick drapes to make a cosy private corner where we will often go and sit to talk and recall the memories of our first loves] (René Detertoc, *L'amour ne meurt pas*. Montreal, unpublished, 1930, p. 255).

A piece of furniture kept closed in the daytime, when it was used as seating, and opened at night to serve as a bed. The back was in three sections on a one-piece frame running the length of the sofa; there was an arm and cushions at each end. It could be *à ressort* or sprung, *à rabat* (folding) with a *paillasse* (mattress), and covered with *crin*, *indienne barrée (rayée)* (striped calico), *reps, rip, moire*, mohair sometimes with a flower pattern, *cretonne, toile, damas, coton, velours, peluche, tapis, corde noire* (black cord)[83], stuffed with *laine, paille* or *crin* and covered with *tapis*. Sofas could be made of *bois franc* with surround of *acajou* or *noyer noir*, or made of *noyer noir solide*, *plaqué* (veneered) or *sculpté* (carved), of *acajou solide* or *plaqué* or of *pin imité* (imitation pine), and might be found in the *chambre*, the *salon*, the *salle*, the *salle à dîner*, the *salle d'entrée*, the *cabinet*, the *passage*, the *salle à manger* or the *chambre à diner*.

The notaries mention the ***sofa-rabat*** in the chambre. An advertisement published in 1852 offered a ***sofa à la mode française*** in damas and crin; another in 1840 mentions a ***sofa à la grecque***.

In the English-language inventories the notaries list damask-covered, small, straw and hair cloth, cushion, wooden and mahogany sofas found in the drawing room, dining room, parlour, hall, sitting room, kitchen, bedroom and other rooms.

Stool Eng. and one Fr. mention in an after-death inventory

One-place seat without a back or arms, found in the parlour, drawing room, dining room, bedroom, sitting room, library or salon.

The notaries mention the **footstool** in the parlour or drawing room, the **music stool** (circular and adjustable) of mahogany, the **night stool**, the **piano stool** (rectangular) in the parlour, drawing room or sitting room, and the **guitar stool**.

Tabouret[84] Fr. and one Eng. mention in an after-death inventory

A small, one-place seat with no back or arms, sometimes upholstered and of varying design. It had a *fond en jonc* (cane bottom), could be covered in *coton, peluche, cretonne* or *tapis*, and made of *bois franc* (*cerisier, noyer noir, acajou*), of *ébène* or *plaqué en rose de bois* (with rosewood veneer).

It is listed in the *chambre*, the *chambre à coucher*, the *chambre de compagnie*, the *salon*, the *salle*, the *salle d'entrée*, the *passage* and the dining room.

Tabourin[85] Fr.

A small seat of *acajou* with carving, covered in *crin* or some other high-quality material such as *damas, serge rouge* (red serge) or *velours*. Found in the *chambre à coucher*, the *grande chambre*, the *salle d'entrée* or the *salon*. A little-used term: the *tabourin* possibly replaced the *tabouret de pied* (footstool).

Tête-à-tête Eng.

A seat for only two people with a concave curved back[86], made of mahogany or black walnut and found in the drawing room. A little-used term found only in English documents.

Vis-à-vis [*confident*] Fr.

Piece of furniture on which two people can sit facing each other.[87] A term found twice in advertisements in 1876 and 1885.

VI. BEDS AND LOUNGE FURNITURE

This sort of furniture was used for lying down on, and hence incorporated a horizontal piece of greater or lesser length. Beds were mainly found in the bedroom, of course, but could also be placed in other rooms to accommodate visitors. They could be made of *bois, fer* (iron) or *cuivre* (brass) with a separate or built-in *paillasse* (straw mattress),[88] *sommier* (springs),[89] *couette* (quilt),[90] or *matelas* (mattress).[91]

Some furniture was dual-purpose, as for example the *lit de repos* (couch) for children or adults, and the *meuble de jour* (day bed), which originated as a chaise-longue. It had an adjustable reclining back and was used for daytime naps. It was not wide, and could be used to seat several people.

Banc-lit[92] (*banc à lit*) Fr.

A piece of furniture that served as a bench in the daytime and opened into a bed at night. Found in the *chambre à coucher* or the *cuisine*.

Bed (bede) Eng. and Fr.

Could be small or little, made of brass, with springs and a feather or straw mattress, and was found in the bedroom, the chamber, the kitchen, the kitchen chamber, the parlour, the sitting room, and other rooms.

487
Chair with cane seat and back in the William and Mary style, about 1880
122 x 61 x 67 cm
Soeurs de la Congrégation Notre-Dame – Villa Maria, Montreal
Photo Christine Guest/MMFA
This armchair was almost certainly part of a drawing-room suite. A settee identical in construction and style has been discovered in a private collection in L'Assomption.

The notaries record the **bed-sofa** and the **bunk bed** in the bedroom, the **camp bed**, **double bed**, **folding bed**, the **lounge bed** in the sitting room, the **settle bed** in the kitchen and the **simple bed**.

In Quebec, the word 'bed' or "bede" meant a small sofa bed found usually in the *chambre* or the kitchen.

Ber (berre, bert, baire, bere) Fr.

C'est aujourd'hui la demeure d'une aimable famille, qui montre avec complaisance le petit coin où ma mère dodelinait mon berceau, mon ber comme on disait alors: une expression de Bretagne et de Normandie [Today it is the home of a charming family, who are pleased to show the corner where my mother rocked my cradle, my *ber* as people said then: it was an expression common in Normandy and Brittany] (Louis Fréchette, *Mémoires intimes*. Montreal: Fides, 1961, p. 32).

A child's cradle or cot that can be rocked, of *frêne* or *pin*, found in the *cuisine*, the *chambre à coucher*, the *cabinet* and the *salle d'entrée*.

Berceau Fr.

A small piece of furniture that can be moved about so that a sleeping infant can be supervised. It was placed in the children's *chambre à coucher*, the *cuisine*, the *salle*, the *salle d'entrée* and the *cabinet*.

The notaries mention the **berceau à barattin**[93] in the *salle*, the **berceau d'enfant** (child's cradle), *petit*, *plié* and *suspendu* (made to hang), made of *bois franc* (*noyer noir*, *frêne*) or of *jonc* with the base of *noyer noir* or *osier* (wicker). An English-language inventory mentions the **berceaunette**[94] in the bedroom; a French-language one lists a **bercelonnette**[95] made of *fil de fer tissé* (wire mesh).

Cot[96] Eng.

A portable child's bed or single bed placed in the bedroom or other room.

Couche Fr. and Eng.

A bed, sometimes double, of *bois franc*, found in the kitchen or the *chambre*. A little-used term in French. The newspapers advertised a mahogany *couche* (couch) covered with French damask.

Couchette[97] Fr. and once in Eng. in an after-death inventory

Sur une couchette de bois d'acajou surmontée d'un moustiquaire de mousseline blanche, placée dans une alcôve, un lit de duvet recouvert de draps blancs de fine toile attendait le capitaine [On a mahogany bedstead shrouded in a white muslin mosquito net and standing in an alcove, a feather bed spread with sheets of fine white linen awaited the captain] (Boucher de Boucherville, *op. cit.*, p. 172.)

A piece of furniture for lying down on to sleep or rest. A *couchette* (bedstead) could be *petit*, *simple* or *double*, *pliante* (folding), made of *bois franc* (*noyer noir*, *merisier*, *orme*, *acajou*, mahogany, *frêne* or *cerisier*) of *bois mou* (*noyer tendre* (butternut), *pin*, *bois blanc* (basswood)) or *à corde* or *en fer* (iron) with springs. Mainly listed in the *chambre à coucher* (or *chambre à coucher des étrangers* (visitor's or child's bedroom)), sometimes in the *cuisine*, the *cabinet*, the *salle*, the *salon* or the *salle d'entrée*.

The notaries mention the **couchette à ciel** (bedstead with canopy), of *bois franc*, *simple*, *petite*, *double*, *à barreaux* (with posters) *à grands poteaux*, *à barattin* (barathin), *basse*, *à roulettes en fonte* (with cast-iron wheels), with springs, *bourrée*, *à dossier haut* (high-backed), *grande*, *les barres en bois* (with wooden posters); the **lit à tombeau**,[98] the **couchette anglaise**, the **couchette américaine**, the **couchette d'enfant** (cot or crib), *à barreau*, made of *bois franc* (*noyer noir*, *orme*) or *en fer*, the **couchette française**[99] of *bois franc* (*noyer noir*, *acajou*, veneered mahogany) and the **couchette Windsor**.

Cradle[100] Eng.

Small child's bed suspended from a horizontal bar, made of cherry, located in a room, bedroom or sitting room.

Crib Eng.

Small child's bed suspended from a horizontal bar, made of iron and located in the bedroom.

502 LIVING IN STYLE

Lit Fr.
>*Le lit était immense, en noyer noir, orné de clochetons et de guirlandes* [... a huge bed, made of black walnut and carved with wreaths and pendants] (Robert de Roquebrune,*Testament of My Childhood* [Toronto: University of Toronto Press, 1964], Felix Walter [trans.], p. 151; trans. of de Roquebrune, 1979, p. 168)

A piece of furniture for sleeping or resting, made of *bois de pin* or *fer*, *garni* (with furnishings), might include *roulettes* (castors), *ressorts* (springs), *plumes* (feathers) and *toile* (canvas), possibly stuffed; large or double.

The notaries refer to a **lit anglais** (English), **lit de camp**,[102] **lit d'enfant** (child's),[103] **lit double** (double)[104] *garni* and a **lit simple** (single)[105] or **petit lit** (small).

VII. SUPPORT FURNITURE

Open furniture, without doors, that includes shelves, horizontal bars or other elements; used for hanging clothes, storing objects, displaying china or placing cleaned objects temporarily before putting them away; also, pieces to be placed in strategic positions near other articles of furniture. Unlike storage furniture, support furniture is mobile and can be moved relatively easily. Support furniture is made of unadorned, veneered, imitation, unfinished, varnished or stained wood.

The following pieces fall into the category of support furniture: the *accrochoir*, the *banc à bouquets* or *à fleurs*, the *cheval* or *chevalet à linge*, the *console*, the *dressoir*, the dresser, the *desserte*, the dumb waiter, the *étagère*, the *étendoir à linge*, the *guéridon*, the *jardinière*, the *lave-mains*, the *porte-carte*, the *porte-chapeau*, the *portemanteau*, the *porte-parapluie*, the *patère*, the rack, the stand, the table, the whatnot and the washstand.

Accrochoir Fr.
An object located in the *passage* or the *grenier* (attic). Little-used term.[106]

Banc à bouquets or *à fleurs* Fr.
A small item of furniture, standing on the floor, used to hold vases and pots containing flowers or bouquets. Found in the passage, the *salle à manger* or the *salle d'entrée*.

Banc à chandelles Fr.
Found in the *chambre*, probably a synonym for candle-stand, a kind of pedestal table. It appears only once, in an inventory dating from 1860.

Cheval à linge or *pour le linge*[107] Fr.
A frame made of *bois*, *fonte* or *fer* (about 1880), known in English as a clothes horse, on which linen and clothes were hung to dry. Sometimes quite small, it is usually found in the *cuisine*, the *chambre* or the passage.

Chevalet à linge Fr.
A rack used for drying clothes and linen. Made of *bois de bambou* (bamboo) or *ébène* (ebony). Little-used term.

Console[108] Fr. and Eng.
>*Enfin, une console portant un grand miroir et divers bibelots* [Finally, a console bearing a large mirror and various ornaments] (Léon Gérin, "L'habitant de Saint-Justin.. Contribution à la géographie sociale du Canada" [1898], in Jean-Charles Falardeau and Philippe Garigue *L'habitant de Saint-Justin*, Montréal: PUM, 1968, p. 97)

A table fixed to a wall and supported by two legs at the front, made of walnut or blacknut, the top made of marble; found in the salon, the parlour, the sitting room, the drawing room, the dining room or the bedroom.

488
Rococo-revival prie-Dieu
Walnut, 90.3 x 40 x 43.5 cm
Congrégation Notre-Dame, Montreal
Photo ministère des Affaires culturelles, Montreal,
Inventaire des biens culturels (77-081-35)

489
John W. Ross, Montreal
The Ross family of Montreal gathered around their alligator visiting-card holder, about 1885
Photograph
National Archives of Canada, Ottawa (PA-113071)
The Rosses lived on University Street.

489

Dressoir Fr.

On voit que l'habitant de Saint-Justin a un dressoir bien fourni, qu'il n'est pas contraint de manger à la gamelle, comme le paysan de certaines provinces de France [We see that those who live in Saint-Justin have a well-supplied dresser and are not obliged to eat in the communal dining room, like the peasants in certain French provinces] (Gérin, *op.cit.* p. 95).

A piece of display furniture with several shelves and no doors, used to hold china and other objects used during meals.[109] The *dressoir* is located in a *salle d'entrée*.[110]

Dresser Eng.

A piece with shelves used to hold china and food; found in a room. This little-used term does not appear before 1867.

Desserte[111] Fr.

A small dining-room table or sideboard used to hold the dishes while food is being served. Little-used term.

Dumb waiter[112] Eng.

Small table with a number of round or square trays arranged in decreasing size order around a central column. Found in a drawing room. This term is mentioned only once, in an inventory dating from 1877.

Étagère Fr. (one mention in an English after-death inventory)

A stand consisting of tiers of open shelves, free-standing or fixed to the wall, without doors; sometimes triangular, to fit into a corner; sometimes fitted with a mirror; used to hold books or ornaments. Made of *noyer noir*, *pin*, *bambou* or ebony and found in the *salon*, *salle à dîner* or *chambre*.

The notaries refer to an *étagère à coin* or *de coin* in *noyer noir* and to an ***étagère à glace*** (with mirror). In 1900, there is a reference to an ***étagère-cabinet*** in a drawing room.

Étendoir à linge Fr.

A frame used for drying linen. Mentioned only once.

Guéridon Fr.

Sur un petit guéridon placé au milieu de la chambre, il y avait un superbe bouquet de fleurs dans un vase de

LIVING IN STYLE

cristal [On a small pedestal table in the middle of the room there was a superb bouquet of flowers in a crystal vase] (Boucher de Boucherville, *op. cit.* p. 173).

A small round table with a central support; an accessory in the *salon* or the *salle de séjour*;[113] the top[114] might be in *marbre*, *bois franc* or *pin*. Found in a *chambre* or in a *salle d'entrée*. This little-used term appears only four times, the expression *petite table* (small table) being generally preferred.

Jardinière[115] Fr.

An ornamental piece designed to hold a receptacle for flowers. Made commonly of *noyer noir* or *ébène*, with a top of *marbre*, and found in the *salon* or some other room. The term was little used, flower stand or *banc à bouquets* or *à fleurs* being generally preferred.

Lave-mains (*lavemains*) (*lavabo*) Fr.

Washstand with furnishings, possibly including one or two doors, three drawers (small or large) designed to hold washing utensils.[116] The *table de toilette* was sometimes confused with the *lave-mains*. Made of *bois franc* (mahogany, *acajou*, *noyer noir* or *teint*, *frêne*, *merisier*) or *bois mou* (*bois blanc*, *pin solide* or *imité*), covered in *marbre* and with a *miroir*. Usually found in the *chambre à coucher* and the *chambre de compagnie*, but also in the *cuisine*, the *cabinet*, the *salle* or the *salle d'entrée*.

Patère Fr.

A piece of furniture used to hang clothes, made of *merisier* or *noyer noir* and found in the passage. The term was little used, *porte-chapeaux* being generally preferred.

Porte-carte Fr.

A small stand designed to hold visitors' cards. There are mentions dating from 1878 and 1889 of *porte-cartes* made of *écaille* (tortoiseshell) found in the salon. Little-used term.

Porte-chapeau(x)[117] Fr.

A piece of furniture with one or more pegs designed for hanging hats. Made of *bois franc* (*noyer noir*, *acajou*, *cerisier*, *merisier*, *frêne*, *érable*) and sometimes including a *miroir*. Found most frequently in the passage, the *entrée* and the *chambre*.

Portemanteau[118] (*porte-manteau*) Fr.

A piece of furniture fixed to or set against a wall in the entrance to a house, possessing pegs for hanging clothes and possibly including a *miroir*. Might be *petit* or *grand*, covered in *cuivre noir* or *peau*. Found in the *chambre à coucher*, the *cuisine* or the *chambre de bain*.

Porte-parapluie Fr.

A small piece designed to hold umbrellas and canes; made of *fonte* (cast iron) and found in the passage.

Rack Eng. and Fr.

Used to hang clothing on the wall or to store other objects (only a single mention in one after-death inventory).

The notaries mention a **book rack** in the bathroom and the library, a **cloth rack** in the kitchen and a **clothes rack** in the bedroom, a **Dali rack** in the passage, a **hall** or **hat rack** in the hall, the passage or the bedroom and a **tornel rack** in the bedroom.

Stand[119] Eng. and Fr.

A small piece of furniture on a single foot used to hold objects or clothes. Often described as small, the **stand** is usually found in the bedroom, the parlour, the sitting room and the dining room.

The notaries mention a **coat stand** in the bedroom, a **flower stand** (**fancy, large, china**) in the parlour, with a marble top in the dining room, the drawing room, the hall and the bedroom, a **hall stand** or **hat stand** of black walnut in the hall, a **high stand** with mirror in the bedroom or sitting room, a curled **light stand** in the bedroom, the parlour, the dining room, the sitting room or the chamber, a **music canterbury**[120] **stand** in the drawing room, private office room, bedroom or sitting room, a **night stand** in the bedroom or chamber, a **side stand** in the dining room and a walnut **umbrella stand** in the hall.

Starting in 1846, French notaries mention the *stand* or *accrochoir* and the ***stand à chapeaux*** (used for hanging hats), found in the passage.

Table[121] Fr.

Cette table était couverte des mets, des vins et du café qui composaient un déjeuner canadien de la première société [The table was covered with the dishes, wines and coffee that constituted an upper-class Canadian luncheon] (Philippe Aubert de Gaspé, *Les anciens canadiens*. Montreal: Beauchemin, 1931 [1864], p. 66).

A piece of furniture consisting of a flat slab or board with legs or feet, used to hold various objects (either temporarily or otherwise) or to support another piece of furniture. It may include storage compartments (drawers) and may be placed near a bed or a piece of lounging or seat furniture. It takes many forms and fulfils many functions in different rooms in the house.

a) Classified according to whether or not the board may be modified – by the addition of two, three or even as many as six extensions or panels – or flanked on either side by a folding leaf that allows the table to be enlarged when necessary. In some cases, the board or alternatively the legs may be folded down so it may be stored in a small space. The notaries mention the ***table à panneaux*** (panel table), sometimes described as *petite* and found in the *cuisine*, the *chambre*, the *salle à dîner*, the *salle*, the *passage*, the *bureau*, the *salon*, or the *chambre d'entrée*. The table used for dining is made of *bois franc* (*noyer noir*, *pin*, mahogany, *merisier*) or of *bois mou* (*noyer tendre*). The legs are *tourné* (turned). It is sometimes covered with a *tapis de table ciré* (waxed table cloth).[122] The ***table à volets***[123] (table with sections, four to six), the ***table à ralonge*** or ***à rallonges*** (extending table) made of *noyer noir*, the ***table à rabat***, the ***table à dîner à trois battants*** and the ***table à côtés*** are found variously in the *salle à dîner*, the *salle*, the *cuisine*, the *chambre à coucher* or the *salon*.

b) Classified as extendable or equipped with a slide device making storage easier: the ***table pliante*** (*tabliante*) (folding table) *grande* or *petite*, composed of two panels, is made of *bois franc* (*acajou* or mahogany), *cerisier* [*cerise*], *noyer noir*) or of *bois dur*; the top may be covered in imitation *marbre*. There is also mention of the ***table extensible***, which appears around 1900, in the *salle à dîner* or the *salle d'entrée*, and the ***table à coulisse*** in the *salle à dîner*, made of *frêne* or *noyer noir*.

c) Classified according to its shape: the ***table carrée*** (*quarré*) (square) in *frêne*, *petite* with *tiroirs* (drawers), might be found in the *salon*, the *chambre à coucher*, the *salle à dîner*, the *salle d'entrée*, the *cuisine*, or the *parloir*; the ***table à demi-lune*** (half-moon), *petite* or *protégée par un tapis vert* (covered with a green cloth), is found in the *salon*, the *chambre* or the *passage*; the ***table demi-ronde*** (half-circle) of *noyer noir* appears in the *salle à manger* or the *chambre de compagnie*; the ***table ovale*** (oval), with a *tapis* (cover), with four legs with *roulettes* (castors) or *tournés* (turned), covered in *marbre* and made of *bois blanc*, *bois franc* (*frêne*, *noyer noir*, *merisier*) or *bois mou* (*pin*), appears in the *salon*, the *chambre à coucher*, the *salle de famille*, and the *salle à dîner*; the ***table ronde***, *petite* and on a *pied* (central pillar) or *tripied* (tripod), covered in *velours rouge* (red velvet), *vernie* (varnished), made of *bois franc* (*acajou* or mahogany, *noyer noir*, *merisier*, *frêne*), *bois mou* (*noyer tendre*, *pin*) or *papier mâché*, is found in the *chambre à coucher*, the *salon*, the *salle à dîner*, the *cuisine*, the *salle* or the *passage*.

d) Classified according to its size: the ***petite table***[124] is found mostly in the *chambre à coucher*, but also in the *salle*, the *cuisine*, the *salle à dîner*, the *passage*, the *cabinet*, the *salle d'entrée* and the *parloir*. It may be *teintée* and made of *bois franc* (*merisier*, *acajou* or mahogany, *cerisier*, *noyer noir*), of *bois mou* (solid or imitation *pin*) or of *papier mâché*; the top may be of *marbre* or *vitre* (glass). It may be accompanied by a *miroir* and it may include three *tiroirs*. The ***grande table***,[125] made of *acajou* or *pin*, is found principally in the *cuisine*, but also in the *chambre à coucher* and the *salle à dîner*.

e) Classified according to a function related to the preparation and service of meals: the ***table de cuisine*** or ***à cuisine*** is found, naturally, in the *cuisine*, the ***table à déjeuner*** (luncheon) made of *acajou* and the ***table à desservir*** (clearing) in the *salle à dîner*. The ***table à dîner extensible*** (extendable) may include two or three *panneaux* (panels), three *battants* (flaps), six *volets* (sections), *morceaux* (pieces) or *feuilles* (leaves). This table, extendable or with a *tiroir*, appears mainly in the *salle à dîner* or *à manger*, the *chambre à coucher*, the *cuisine*, the *salle d'entrée*, the *salon* and the *chambre à dîner*. It can be made of *bois franc* (*acajou* or mahogany, *noyer noir*, *merisier*, *frêne*, *chêne*), and is sometimes covered with a *tapis*. The ***table à manger*** is found in the *salle à manger*.

f) Classified according to a function related to personal toilet or rest: the ***table à toilette***[126] (dressing table, washstand) (*table de toilette*, *coiffeuse*, with *pot* (pitcher), *bassin* (basin) and *accessoires* (accessories) appears only in the *chambre à coucher*. It may be *petite* and made of *noyer noir* or *pin*, and is sometimes accompanied by a mirror. The ***table de nuit***[127] (*table à toilette* is more commonly used) is made of *noyer noir*.

g) Classified according to a function related to needlework: the ***table à couture*** (sewing) is in the *salon*; a ***table à ouvrage***[128] (handwork) is mentioned; the ***table pour dames*** (ladies') on *colonnes à spirale* (on spiral columns), made of *bois franc* (*acajou* or mahogany, *noyer noir*, *ébène*) is found in the *chambre à coucher*, the *salon* or the *salle à dîner*.

h) Classified according to a function related to leisure or office work: the ***table de bureau*** (office) with *tablettes* (shelves); the ***table à dessin*** in the *étude* (study); the ***table à écrire*** (writing); the ***table à cartes*** (card) in the salon, the *chambre à coucher*, the *chambre de compagnie*, the *petite salle* and the *salle d'entrée*. It might be made with *bois précieux* (precious wood) (*acajou* or mahogany, *ébène*, *noyer noir*, *merisier*) or protected by a *tapis ciré* (oilcloth). The ***table à jeu***[129] (games) or ***table à jouer*** appears only in the *chambre à coucher* and *de compagnie*; it is *petite*, made of *bois franc* (*merisier*, *acajou* or mahogany), or on *roulettes*. The ***table commune*** (communal) is found in the *cuisine*, the *salle à dîner*, the *salle* or the *salle d'entrée*. A large table called the ***table de famille*** (family) is found in the *cuisine*; it might include six panels and be of *noyer noir*, *pin* or *acajou*; it also appears in the *chambre* and the *salle à dîner*. The ***table de centre*** (centre), may be extendable with panels, may have four feet and be in *bois franc* (*acajou* or mahogany, *ébène*, *noyer noir*, *merisier*, *orme*) or *bois mou* (*bois blanc*, *noyer tendre*); it may be *teint en brun* (stained brown), *ovale*, *petite* and found in the *salon*, the *chambre*, the *cuisine* or the *salle à dîner*; or *grande* and in the *salon*, with a top of *marbre du Tennessee* (Tennessee marble), of *pluche* (*pruche*) (hemlock) or "*marquetée*" *bois de Chine* (marquetry in Chinese wood).[130] The ***table de milieu*** is in *noyer noir* and appears in the *salon*.

i) Classified according to the fact that it accompanies another piece of furniture: the ***table à sopha*** (sofa) in *acajou* appears in the *salon* or the *chambre à coucher*.

j) Classified according to its quality or style: the ***meilleure table de salon*** (best)[131] in *noyer noir*, *marquetrie* or with *glace incrustée de maille* (inlaid mirror); the ***table à la reine Elizabeth***.

Around 1880, there are references to the ***table de fantaisie*** (fancy), found in the *salon*, the top in *pruche*, *cerisier* or *ébène*; also the ***table de trumeau***[132] (pier table).

Table Eng.

A piece of furniture consisting basically of a flat slab or board with three or four legs or feet, used to hold various objects (either temporarily or otherwise) or to support another piece of furniture. In the English inventories the table is found in the kitchen, the bedroom, the dining room, the sitting room, the drawing room, the hall, the parlour, the library, the living room, the passage and the bathroom. It is made of plain or covered hardwood, of blacknut or walnut, pine leaf, plush covered, mahogany, of silver birch or birch leaf, or papier mâché; the top may be in marble.

a) Classified according to its size: the **large table** in mahogany or pine appears in the sitting or dressing room; the **occasional table**[133] and the **small table** in the bedroom, the dining room, the parlour, the kitchen, the sitting room, the drawing room or the nursery.

b) Classified according to the fact that its length may be modified: the **extension table** (extending table) is found in the dining room or the kitchen; the **folding table**, small and of hardwood, in the dining room; and the **fall leaf table** in the parlour.

c) Classified according to its shape: the **corner table** appears in a room, the **oval stained table** in the bathroom, the hardwood **round table** in the parlour, the sitting room, the dining room and the drawing room, the small **square table** in the bedroom and the **oblong table** in the pantry.

d) Classified according to its function or the room where it appears: the **cook's table** in the sitting room; the **dining table** made of plane (plain, plein) wood, with drawers, small, of cherry, mahogany or black walnut found in the dining room, the drawing room or the parlour; the **dinner table** in the dining room of the breakfast room, the **hall table** in the hall or passage, the **kitchen table** (large) in the kitchen or the bedroom, the **office table** in the bedroom and the **parlour table** in the parlour.

e) Classified according to a function related to leisure, work or some other activity: the mahogany or black walnut **card table** in the drawing room, the dining room, the kitchen, the parlour or the bedroom; the mahogany **Loo table**[134] in the drawing room; the **billiard table**; the **work table**[135] (**Chinese**) in the bedroom, the parlour, the sitting room, the dining room, the library or the drawing room; the **breakfast table** in the kitchen or another room; the **tea table**[136] in the sitting room; the **serving table**[137] in the sitting room; the **fancy table (with cloths)** in the sitting room, the parlour, the drawing room or the dining room; the **toilet table**[138] with toilet glass in the bedroom; the **side table**[139] (bedside table) (small) in the dining room, the breakfast room or the parlour; the **dressing table**[140] with glass in the bedroom or the chamber; the **table somno** in the bathroom and the square hardwood **writing table** in the library or the sitting room.

There is also mention of the **basket table** in the drawing room; the black walnut **centre table**[141] with a marble top, found mostly in the parlour, but also in the sitting room, the drawing room and the library; the **fancy table** in the drawing room, the parlour, the dining room or the sitting room; the hardwood **wing table** in the sitting room; the **deal table** in the parlour; the **Pembroke**[142] **table**; the **Chinese table** and the **quartette (quartet) table**.[143]

Whatnot (what-nots) Eng. and Fr.

Mentioned only once in an after-death inventory. A mobile stand consisting of several tiers of shelves used to hold ornaments and other articles. It might be square and found in the parlour, the drawing room, the dining room, the sitting room, the bathroom the salon or some other room; it might be made of black walnut, mahogany or walnut.

Washstand[144] (wash hand stand) Eng.

A piece of furniture which, like the toilet table, is used to hold the utensils needed for personal toilet; made of solid mahogany and found principally in the bedroom and the chamber, but also in the passage, the nursery, the office and the kitchen.

Gynette Tremblay

ALPHABETICAL INDEX OF TERMS

A)
accrochoir (VII)
arm-chair (V)
armoire (I)

B)
banc (V)
banc à bouquets-fleurs (VII)
banc à chandelles (VII)
banc-lit (VI)
bed (VI)
ber (VI)
berçante (V)
berceau (VI)
berceuse (V)
bergère (V)
bibliothèque (I)
bookcase (I)
buffet (I)
bureau (I)
bureau (I)

C)
cabinet (I)
canapé (V)
causeuse (V)
chair (V)
chaise (V)
chest of drawers (I)
cheval à linge (VII)

chevalet à linge (VII)
chiffonnier (I)
commode (I)
console (VII)
cot (VI)
couch (V)
couche (VI)
couchette (VI)
cradle (VI)
crédence (I)
crib (VI)
cupboard (I)

D)
desk (I)
desserte (I)
divan (V)
dressoir (VII)
dresser *(VII)*
dumb waiter (VII)

E)
écran (II)
easy-chair *(V)*
escabeau (IV)
étagère (VII)
étendoir à linge (VII)

F)
fauteuil (V)

G)
garde-robe (I)
guéridon (VII)
glace (III)
glass *(III)*

J)
jardinière (VII)

L)
lave-main (VII)
lit (VI)
lounge [chair] (V)

M)
marchepied (IV)
miroir (III)
mirror (III)

O)
ottoman (V)
ottomane (V)

P)
patère (VII)
porte-carte (VII)
porte-chapeau (VII)
portemanteau (VII)
porte-musique (VII)
porte-parapluie (VII)
prie-Dieu (V)
pupitre (I)

R)
rack (VII)
rocker (V)
rocking-chair (V)

S)
screen (II)
secrétaire (I)
secretary (I)
settee (V)
sideboard (I)
stand (VII)
stool (V)
sofa (V)
sofa (V)

T)
table (VII)
table *(VII)*
tabouret (V)
tabourin (V)
tête-à-tête *(V)*

V)
vis-à-vis (V)

W)
wardrobe (I)
whatnot (VII)
washstand (VII)

---

1 L. H. Huot, *Annuaire du commerce et de l'industrie de Québec pour 1873* (Quebec City: L. H. Huot, 1873), p. 22 (trans.).

2 *L'Opinion publique*, September 21, 1871, p. 462 (trans.).

3 *Journal de Québec*, September 14, 1871, p. 2 (trans.).

4 *L'Opinion publique*, September 21, 1871, p. 462 (trans.).

5 Michel Lessard and Huguette Marquis, *Encyclopédie des antiquités du Québec* (Montreal: Les Éditions de l'Homme, 1971), p. 136 (trans.).

6 *Oeuvres complètes de l'abbé H. R. Casgrain, légendes canadiennes* (Montreal: Beauchemin, 1896), p. 268 (trans.).

7 According to Esther Poisson, "'set' was one of the earliest English terms to enter Quebec French after the Conquest. The oldest use of the term dates back to 1799 in the sense of an *ensemble*, a collection, hence 'set of furniture'". ("Étude du vocabulaire du mobilier d'habitation dans la région des Bois-Francs d'après les journaux publiés depuis 1866", M.A. thesis, Faculté des lettres, Université Laval, 1982, p. 25.)

8 These woods resemble each other closely.

9 A silk or woollen fabric figured with various patterns, red, grey, green or white in colour.

10 Cotton fabric printed in many colours.

11 Silk fabric made to resemble brocade (a silk fabric figured with patterns woven in gold and silver thread). "A nineteenth century silk fabric resembling damask, with a pattern which appears to be embossed" (Jeanne Minhinnick, *At Home in Upper Canada* (Toronto Vancouver: Clarke, Irwin & Company Ltd., 1983), p. 224.

12 A red or white silk fabric, with a longer and more open pile than that of velvet. Always written *pluche* in the inventories.

13 A transversely corded cloth of silk and wool or silk and cotton; sometimes spelt *reppe*, *rept* or *rep*.

14 An old-fashioned term for a wooden chest with a convex lid for storing clothing.

15 A term that appeared in the late nineteenth century, when the *buffet* (sideboard) and the *dressoir* (dresser) were combined to make a single piece: the vaisselier (Nicole Genêt, Luce Vermette and Louise Décarie-Audet, *Les objets familiers de nos ancêtres* (Montreal: Les Éditions de l'Homme, 1974, p. 101).

16 The *armoire* was a development of the *coffre* (chest), the ancestor of all case furniture used in the home (the *bahut*, the *armoire*, the *vaisselier*.) It was the first piece of furniture to arrive in New France. "In middle-class homes [in France], the *armoire* became an essential piece of furniture, given the growing importance of linen in domestic life [...]. At the court of Louis XV *armoires* tended to be relegated to the servants' quarters [...]. Sometimes a built-in cupboard was preferred; this solution, rejected during the nineteenth century, came back into fashion in the twentieth [...]. The *armoire* came back into fashion in the reign of Louis-Philippe [of France]. It became more popular than ever, and was to be found in every bedroom until the early twentieth century, when a new period of eclipse began, so that it has almost disappeared from contemporary furniture." (*Histoire du mobilier*. Paris: Éditions Atlas, 1984, pp. 313-314).

17 This was also the piece of furniture which inspired Émile Nelligan's poem "*Vieille armoire*" at the end of the nineteenth century: "Sleep on, revered jumble of old porcelains,/All shut up, all

cold as dead men's eyes;/Japanese tea-sets that speak of other days/And the rich meals of lovely chatelaines!" (*The Complete Poems of Émile Nelligan*, ed. and trans. by Fred Cogswell. Harvest House, 1983, p. 62).

18 A piece that appeared in the late eighteenth century. "Built into a corner of the room while the house was being constructed, the corner cupboard has only one face, its sides being the whitewashed walls. It was not common, and became popular only in the next century" (Genêt et al., 1974, p. 28 [trans.]). Also called an *encoignure* in French.

19 See cylinder desk, note 33 of this text.

20 "In England, the bureau developed from the chest of drawers in the eighteenth century. It consisted of a flanked by compartments and drawers. It could be used as a desk, or in the bedroom as a place to store linen." (*Le mobilier du XIXe siècle en France et en Europe*. Paris: 1991, p. 291).

21 This was used as a large dressing table with a mirror, and is a term not found in the inventories. It was a typically feminine piece of furniture, also called a *poudreuse* or a *table à poudre* (*Le mobilier du XIXe siècle en France et en Europe*. Paris: 1991, p. 292). "The words *coiffeuse* and *poudreuse* are not found in the language before the mid-nineteenth century. Until then, it was simply called a *toilette*, after its function. The piece of furniture as such is an eighteenth-century creation [...]. During the second Empire the table surmounted by a mirror came back into fashion" (Guillaume Janneau, "De la *toilette* à la '*coiffeuse*' ", *Vie et langage*, no. 263, February 1974, pp. 94, 97.)

22 These were probably porcelain.

23 "This was one of most expensive pieces of furniture in the house", which is why it was found in the reception rooms (*Le mobilier du XIXe siècle en France et en Europe*. Paris: 1991, p. 291.)

25 In the late nineteenth century decorative influences from Japan became more popular than those from China, and references to foreign styles became more common. The Japanese style was in the ascendent from 1860 to 1870. "The vogue for orientalism began in the 1850s, having been popular in the eighteenth century and very early nineteenth century." (Christopher Payne, *19th Century European Furniture (Excluding British)* England: Antique Collectors' Club, 1981, p. 78).

26 According to Charles Platten Woodhouse, "Perhaps even more than in the seventeenth century, when it first appeared, the chest of drawers was a Victorian '*indispensable*'". (*The Victorian Collector's Handbook*. London: George Bell and Sons, 1970, p. 125).

27 "The chiffonnier first appeared in about 1735 along with all the furniture for ladies; it consisted of a vertical series of narrow drawers all the same height" (Guillaume Janneau, "Le chiffonnier", *Vie et langage*, no. 273, December 1974, p. 686.)

28 First seen in the 18th century, the *commode* developed from the *coffre* (chest) and was invented by Charles-André Boulle in 1697.

29 Probably served as a dressing table.

30 *Fantaisie* (fancy) was the opposite of ordinary in newspaper parlance, and implied decorative elements.

31 "A large cupboard with a recessed superstructure containing smaller cupboards with a narrow shelf in front of them. Sometimes described as a hall cupboard". (John Gloag, *A Complete Dictionary of Furniture*. New York: The Overlook Press, 1991, p. 537).

32 A lighter and more delicate lady's desk (*Histoire du mobilier*, 1984, p. 316).

33 "Furniture makers created various kinds of desks, such as the *bureau à cylindre*, in which the work surface was enclosed by a sort of roll-top". (*Histoire du mobilier*, 1984, p. 316). The *pupitre à cylindre* was a *bureau à cylindre*, also known as a *secrétaire à cylindre* or cylinder desk. This was a piece of furniture "with a semi-cylindrical shutter in one piece or of slats that pulled down over the upper pigeonholes and compartments" (Boidi Sassone, *Le mobilier français du XIXe siècle*. Paris: Larousse, 1985, p. 76).

34 "This appeared in about 1780, and was attributed to Hepplewhite: derived from the side table, a piece of furniture placed in earlier times against the dining-room wall, the sideboard remained in use throughout the nineteenth century, alongside the *crédence à vitrine supérieure* (the glass-fronted credence)" (Boidi Sassone, *op. cit.*, p. 293).

35 A term also used in French. The dressing room was a room adjoining the bedroom in which clothes were kept.

36 According to C. Platten Woodhouse, the screen was "one of the most decorative items in Victorian furnishing" (1970, p. 137).

37 A *glace* is a surface that reflects images, mounted in a frame, border or wooden support; the term is reserved for looking glasses forming part of the décor; other sorts of glass were called *miroirs* (mirrors). In Quebec, the words *miroir* and *glace* were interchangeable, though *miroir* was the commoner term. E.-Z. Massicotte points out that the expression *glace de miroir* occurs in the *Édits et Ordonnances* for 1748 (1942, p. 41). It should be remembered that the earliest mirrors were made of tin.

38 A large moveable mirror mounted on a swivel base so that it can be tilted to obtain a full-length view.

39 According to John Gloag, "During the nineteenth century they were usually known as dressing glasses" (1991, p. 671).

40 According to Philippe Aubert de Gaspé, fils, "Few farmers had mirrors" (*Le chercheur de trésors*. Montreal: Réédition-Québec, 1968 [1837], p. 29, trans.). Furthermore, according to Massicotte, "When Montreal was founded, there were various kinds of looking glass. Those for trading were made of tin. Some had horn frames. Mirrors made of glass had wooden frames, either plain or gilded. Some were called toilet mirrors, others came in a leather case ("L'ameublement à Montréal aux XVIIe et XVIIIe siècles" [trans.] *Bulletin des recherches historiques*, vol. XLVIII, no. 2, February 1942, p. 77).

41 "A small circular mirror mounted on an adjustable stand (sometimes on castors), so a man could shave standing". (Nicole De Reyniès, *Le mobilier domestique*. Paris: Imprimerie nationale, 1987, vol. II, p. 258).

42 "A small mirror with a back leg so it can stand upright" (De Reyniès, 1987, p. 956).

43 "A framed mirror occupying a mantelpiece or the wall between two piers" (A. Audouy and G. Thivet, *Terminologie de l'ameublement*. Rodez, Subervie, 1974, p. 70). The upper part of the mirror might comprise a painting.

44 "The word *dossier* (back), as its name implies, originally served to designate that part of a bench, chair or armchair against which the seated person leans his or her back" (Henry Havard, *Dictionnaire de l'ameublement et de la décoration depuis le XIIIe siècle jusqu'à nos jours*. Paris: Maison Quantin, 1890, vol. II, p. 153).

45 Used to climb into bed.

46 "The *oreilles* (wings or lugs) is fixed parts of the chair set at right angles to the back, against which the head can be rested" (De Reyniès, 1987, p. 11).

47 The *dos* (back) of a seat can also be called a *dossier* (Havard, 1890, p. 152).

48 Interwoven maple and elm bark.

49 Process by which a chair was covered with twisted or braided straw plaited with strips of elm or ash bark. Straw-bottomed chairs do not seem to have been very durable, since an advertisement recommends those whose cane-bottomed chairs are broken to replace them with "Gardner's chair with Perforated Marquetry (Veneer)", guaranteeing that "it will never wear out" (*L'Événement*, July 9, 1879, p. 4), (trans.).

50 "*Canne* (cane) is the name for a kind of rattan imported from the East Indies and for its bark cut into narrow strips and used to weave seat furniture. It was only in the 17th century that chairs, armchairs and stools began to be caned. This new material, cleaner and above all more elegant than straw, soon came into general use" (Havard, 1890, vol. I, p. 553). *Canné* (caned): term applied to a piece of furniture the back and/or seat of which are made of strips of cane, wicker or rattan interwoven (*Histoire du mobilier*, 1984, p. 76).

51 "Literally, a chair with arms, a *fauteuil*" (Alessandra Ponte, *Le mobilier anglais du XIXe siècle*. Paris: Larousse, 1986, p. 76 [trans.]).

52 The notaries mention a *banc pour le piano* in the *salon* and a *banc à piano* in the *chambre de compagnie*.

53 "A seat with a twenty-five centimetre hole in the bottom to serve as a toilet seat. The chamber pot was placed either on the ground beneath the chair or on a shelf between the chair legs" (De Reyniès, 1987, p. 676).

54 According to Paul-Louis Martin, "the *chaise berçante* (rocking chair) appeared in Quebec in the early 19th century" (*La berçante québécoise*. Montreal: Les Éditions du Boréal Express, 1973, p. 16).

55 "The high back was formed of one piece with the arms" (Claire Desmeules, "Le vocabulaire du meuble", *Continuité*, no. 38, winter 1988, p. 32).

56 Metal springs became common about 1850.

57 The *canapé* was called a davenport in the United States, but the latter term does not appear in the sources consulted. Antoine Furetière states that the *canapé* and the sofa were the same thing after 1690 (*Le dictionnaire usuel*. Paris: SNL, 1978). In Quebec the two terms are interchangeable in the inventories, though sofa occurs more often.

58 Thin fabric coated with a substance that makes it waterproof while keeping it soft. Mainly used on tables to protect the wood.

59 "However, it seems that the *canapé*, when it first appeared, was thought of more as a piece of furniture for lying down on, or even for sleeping on, than as seating for several people" (Havard, 1890, p. 542 [trans.]).

60 "A settee with wings projecting from the back" (Havard, 1890, vol. I, p. 610 [trans.]).

61 "With a low back, not to go over the shoulders" (Havard, *op.cit.* vol. 1, p. 610 [trans.]).

62 The word 'chair' is here used in the most general sense to include seating with arms such as a smoking chair.

63 This was a narrow, high-backed chair used only in the hall.

64 "A low-seated single chair, between 13 and 15 inches high. A mid-18th century term, though probably in use earlier" (Gloag, 1991, p. 472).

65 "Contemporary term used in the second half of the 18th century to describe a single chair with a pierced, interlaced back splat and carved decoration on the frame [...] Throughout the Victorian period almost any single chair except a bedroom chair or a ponderous balloon-back dining-room chair, could be and often was described as a parlour chair, and by the end of the 19th century the term ceased to have any particular meaning" (Gloag, 1991, pp. 494-495).

66 "During the Renaissance the term 'camp furniture' was used for some light small items that could be easily packed up and carried from place to place. Camp furniture first appeared in the 15th century" (Havard, 1890, vol. I, p. 538).

67 "A generic name for a spindle-backed chair, single or armed. Originated in the early eighteenth century but not associated with George III, as sometimes asserted. Windsor chairs were used in the kitchen and servants' quarters in late Victorian times" (Platten Woodhouse, 1970, p. 124). Very common in the nineteenth century, Windsor chairs always had spindle backs.

68 Smoker's chair or "smoker's chaise: a type of armchair introduced in the 1890s for use in dining rooms and smoking-rooms. A drawer fitted beneath the seat contained a spittoon" (Platten Woodhouse, 1970, p. 138). *Fumeuse*: "an upholstered smoker's chair typical of the second half of the 19th century. A large armrest attached to the top of the back held a box with smoking paraphernalia, hidden under an upholstered lid" (Boidi Sassone, 1985, p. 79).

69 A *chaise* differs from a *tabouret* (stool) in having a back, and unlike a *fauteuil* (armchair) has no arms.

70 "A piece of seat furniture with a permanent covering of some thickness" (De Reyniès, 1987, p. 43).

71 Raw, untanned leather. According to P.-L. Martin, "strips of rawhide from deer, moose, caribou or eels were to be found in bundles in any Quebec farmer's home from the 17th century on. The settlers had learned from the Amerindians how to use them to weave snowshoes, but we do not know at what point during the 18th century someone thought of making chair seats out of them"("Chaises et chaisiers québécois", *Ethnologie québécoise I*. Montreal: Éditions Hurtubise HMH, 1972, p. 149).

72 All these expressions designate a close stool chair.

73 Used in the 17th century: a seat with a hole for a chamber pot.

74 According to an advertisement published in *L'Événement* on July 9, 1878, a *chaise perforée* was veneered with ornamentally perforated plywood.

75 According to Genêt *et al.*, "the expression *chaise percée* was mainly used in the 17th century, *chaise de commodité* in the 18th century" (1974, p. 79).

76 P.-L. Martin describes two types of rocking chair made at this time, one called a *col de cygne* (swan's neck) and the other of a 'Victorian' type (1973, pp. 104 and 117).

77 A *divan* or ottoman was a kind of large sofa or settee of Turkish origin, without back or armrests. "It is actually a wide, deep cushion (Janneau, 1974, p. 278). "The ottoman usually had cushions scattered on it. It was low, thickly padded, of varying length, usually a metre wide, so that several people could sit on it or if necessary sleep on it" (Havard, 1890, vol. II, p. 123).

78 "Made by the William Morris firm from about 1865. A chair of ebonized beechwood, rush-seated and straight-backed" (Platten Woodhouse, 1970, p. 123). "Large easy chair of the late 19th century with adjustable back, loose cushions forming the seat and back rest within a wooden frame" (Joseph Aronson, *The Encyclopedia of Furniture*. New York: Crown Publishers, 1965, p. 312).

79 "Type of couch in late-19th century work, often with one end high as a pillow" (Aronson, 1965, p. 286).

80 "Wine-coloured, wine-red". (Société du parler français au Canada, *Glossaire du parler français au Canada*. Quebec City: Les Presses de l'Université Laval, 1968, p. 697).

81 According to A. Ponte, "a small *canapé* generally forming part of a suite of chairs, with a separate back for each place. When larger, it is called a sofa" (1985, p. 79).

82 In Quebec the term sofa meant the same as *canapé* and was more used.

83 This was probably horsehair.

84 The *tabouret* replaced the *pouf*, which we have found mentioned only once in a literary work: "I looked everywhere, under all the *poufs*, to find the snake" (Françoise [Robertine Barry], *Chroniques du lundi de Françoise*, p. 283). The *pouf* appeared in about 1845. (Havard, 1890, vol. IV, p. 581).

85 "This word [*tabourin*] is first found in the late 17th century, meaning *tabouret* (stool)" (Havard, 1890, p. 1191) [...] Throughout the 16th and 17th centuries the terms *tabour*, *tabourin*, *tambour* and *tambourin* were used interchangeably (Havard, 1890, p. 1167). A recent usage turned up in the card index of the *Trésor de la langue française au Québec* project (TLFQ), Faculté des lettres, Université Laval: "I had my feet up on the tambourin" (Hull, May 1979, spoken by a native of Abitibi).

86 "It was placed beside the corner of the hearth to make a semicircle with another tête-à-tête or an armchair" (Havard, 1890, vol. IV, p. 1,299).

87 "Arranged so that the people sitting found themselves *visage à visage* (face to face)" (Havard, 1890, vol. IV, p. 1,599).

88 A sleeping surface consisting of a large straw-filled cushion the same size as the bed.

89 A sleeping surface originally made of a large cushion stuffed with horsehair, and later a rigid frame, raised or flat, with springs.

90 A large mattress stuffed with feathers or down.

91 A large pallet of cotton or wool for sleeping on. According to E.-Z. Massicotte, instead of the "feather bed, servants and the working classes probably slept on a straw *paillasse* covered with ticking of the coarse local cloth. Sometimes the *paillasse* replaced the *matelas*" (1942, p. 78).

92 No mention before the 19th century. One French writer defines this piece of furniture as "a rustic sofa-bed" (Massicotte, 1942, p. 34).

93 *Barattin* (*barratin*, *barathin*): wooden bedstead with planks running the length of the frame parallel to the sides to hold the cross bars.

94 A hanging, moveable cradle for babies.

95 "A derivative of *berceau*, admitted in 1835. A light cradle, usually of wicker" (A. Hatzfield and A. Darmesteter, *Dictionnaire général de la langue française du commencement du XVIIe siècle à nos jours*. Paris: Delagrave, 1920). A term used in the second half of the 19th century for hanging cradle" (Havard, 1890, vol. I, pp. 295-296).

96 *Cote*: a hanging cradle or sort of camp bed (Société du parler français au Canada, 1968, p. 232).

97 *Couchette* and *lit* (bed and bedstead) seem interchangeable terms.

98 *Lit en tombeau*: covered-in bed: "A bed with a canopy the same size but with an interrupted surface, so that the part over the bedhead is horizontal while the rest slopes down to the bedfoot, so that the canopy is supported by the bed, not hung above it. A *lit en tombeau* could also be folding" (De Reyniès, 1987, p. 250).

99 Synonymous with *lit à la française*: "it had a single bedhead, and the legs extended upwards to hold the canopy" (De Reyniés, 1987, p. 256).

100 A newspaper advertisement of 1851 offered "a new article: a settee cradle".

101 With a mattress and a *paillasse*.

102 A folding or collapsible bed of wood or metal (iron, brass) designed to be moved about.

103 A piece of furniture consisting of a long wide box mounted on feet for a child to sleep in. The sides of the box prevented the infant from falling or climbing out. Generally not moveable.

104 A two-person bed, or any bed more than one metre 30 cm wide.

105 A one-person bed, or any bed one metre 20 cm or less in width.

106 Probably a synonym for *portemanteau* (Belisle, 1969, p. 6) or *patère* (Société du parler français au Canada, 1968, p. 11). Known in English as a clothes-horse: "Light, wooden frames, mounted upon feet, with two or three cross-bars; or made to fold, with two or three leaves; on which clothes and towels are spread to dry" (Gloag, 1991, p. 235).

107 "Rack or framework for hanging towels, used in conjunction with a washstand in the 18th and 19th centuries" (Aronson, 1965, p. 442).

108 "A table fixed to a wall and supported only by one or two legs at the front" (Gloag, 1991, p. 252).

109 "Although from the 13th century on, the *bourgeoisie* and the lesser nobility continued to eat in the kitchen where the meal was prepared, the wealthier classes began to take dinner and supper in the *salle*, the state apartments, and later in luxuriously furnished antechambers. The dresser, therefore, while remaining in the kitchen where it was essential, began to be found in other rooms where meals were eaten" (Havard, 1890, vol. II, p. 199).

110 It should be remembered that in the 19th century the *buffet* and the *dressoir* were put together to make one single piece, the *vaisselier* (Genêt et al., 1974, p. 101).

111 Accepted in French in the late 19th century.

112 This small occasional table appeared during the first half of the 18th century and became an indispensable item in Regency dining rooms" (Ponte, 1986, p. 78).

113 "Usually placed beside an armchair or a bed" (Genêt et al., 1974, p. 139).

114 A horizontal element, sometimes reversible, which constitutes the upper part of something and is sued to close it or to place objects on. A *dessus* (top) is usually fixed, less often moveable. *Dessus* can project beyond, be the same size as, or smaller than, what they rest on.

115 According to N. De Reyniès, "the term *jardinière* appears only in the 19th century, and apparently after 1850" (1987, p. 934). It was found in Quebec about 1885.

116 "Two washstands each with a water container inside, with spouts for the clean water and evacuation holes for the dirty water". *L'Événement*, September 25, 1877, p. 2.

117 A coat rack was attached to the wall, while a hat rack was a standing structure on a base.

118 The *portemanteau* often replaced the *patère*.

119 The equivalent French words are *étagère*, *guéridon* and *console*. The word stand has been accepted in French since 1893 to described a shelf to hold a typewriter.

120 A canterbury was "a small stand with racks or divisions to hold music books" (Gloag, 1991, p. 179).

121 "The table was an indispensable item of furniture for our ancestors, It had many uses – eating, working, writing and playing games – and many people had more than one table in the house" (Genêt et al., 1974, p. 253).

122 A table cover: good-quality fabric, attached or removable, use to cover the top of a table, or all of it.

123 Leaf: "the extra sections that may be added to increase the length of an extending table; also the hinged flap of a gate-leg or drop-leaf table." (Gloag, 1991, p. 424).

124 The *petite table* may have been a console table, drawing-room table or pedestal table.

125 The *grande table* would have required more than one person to move it.

126 "Toilet or dressing tables as such date from the 1830s; these were small, useful items with a marble top and one or more drawers to hold toilet articles, surmounted by a mirror the tilt of which could be adjusted" (A. Hatzfield, *Grand Dictionnaire universel* (Paris: Delagrave, 1865), p. 259).

127 Bedside table.

128 *Travailleuse* (lady's work table): a small piece of furniture with drawers in which women kept their sewing and knitting.

129 "A very ancient game, possibly the ancestor of billiards [...] Bagatelle tables varied greatly in size. Some were one metre 75 long by 50 cm wide, others up to four metres long and one metre wide; but smaller tables were mostly used. They were often supported on a solid wood framework, and consisted of a slab of marble, slate or wood covered with a tightly stretched green baize fabric, surrounded by a rim or edge and stuffed with an elastic material, nowadays usually rubber" (T. De Moulidard, *Grande encyclopédie des jeux, méthodique, universelle, illustrée*. Paris: Montgredin, 1880, p. 190). Bagatelle tables had been advertised in Quebec, in newspapers such as *La Minerve*, *La Gazette de Québec*, *Le Nouvelliste* and *Le Canadien*, since 1778.

130 *Bois de Chine* (Chinese wood): "This is still the name for an exotic wood veneer used in cabinet-making and marquetry; it comes from China and Guyana. It is a brownish-red colour with black grain, and is a very hard wood" (Havard, 1890, p. 814).

131 *Table de salon* (drawing-room table): a centre table of varying size, intended for the drawing room and able to hold a tray. Eventually very ornately carved in relief, completely covered with fabric, it could be many shapes: round, oblong, with a slanting corner, decorated with fretwork, and so on. The term seems to have appeared in the second half of the 19th century" (De Reyniès, 1987, p. 386). The term appears in newspapers of 1857 but was found only once in 1900 in an after-death inventory.

132 A piece of furniture highly fashionable in the 18th century. It belongs to the category of *bureaux* and generally consisted of two sections, the upper one with compartments enclosed by doors and mirrors, the lower section containing drawers and a glass front, a wooden panel or a mirror.

133 "This was a table with no specific function, unlike the sofa table, tea table or games table. Occasional tables varied greatly in size and shape, and were very common in 19th century homes" (Ponte, 1985, p. 79).

134 Loo table: "A circular card table with a central pillar supporting the top and resting upon a base with three or four feet, introduced in the early 19th century, and designed specifically for the round game of cards known originally as lanterloo" (Gloag, 1991, p. 437).

135 "Considered an essential piece of furniture in a lady's sitting room and indispensable to a young lady expected to take her needlework seriously" (Platten Woodhouse, 1970, p. 141). Also called in French a *travailleuse* or a *table à ouvrage* (Payne, 1981, p. 44).

136 No *table à café* nor coffee table was found in the sources consulted.

137 This was a table placed alongside the dining-room wall.

138 "A large dressing table with a mirror. Little distinction is made between the lady's dressing table (*coiffeuse* or *poudreuse*) and the gentleman's *barbière* [often a dressing chest in English]" (Ponte, 1986, p. 11).

139 "Side tables in dining rooms; generally higher than an ordinary table, and fitted with drawers for silver" (Aronson, 1965, p. 378).

140 "Throughout the 18th century, the term toilet or toylet, signified a lady's dressing table furnished with all the apparatus for make-up" (Gloag, 1991, p. 671).

141 The same as a drawing room table (Payne, 1981, p. 44).

142 "A small rectangular table extendable by means of flaps" (Ponte, 1986, p. 78).

143 A nest of tables consisting of three, four or five small tables of decreasing size which can fit one inside another.

144 "An elaboration of the bason, or basin, stand, introduced during the first half of the 19th century, and an essential item in the Victorian bedroom suite" (Gloag, 1991, p. 708).

145 In the 1840s the term was wash-hand stand; it later became abbreviated to washstand.

Select Bibliography

I ARCHIVES AND MANUSCRIPTS

Archives du bureau des brevets, Hull
Original patents.

Archives judiciaires de Québec, Quebec City
Notarial records from the offices of Joseph Allaire, Charles-Henry Andrews, Ferdinand Audet, Louis-Onésime Audet, Jacques Auger, Joseph-Édouard Boily, J.-Boutin Bourassa, William Noble Campbell, J.-Alphonse E. Chaperon, Jean-Baptiste Delâge, Léopold Falardeau, Joseph-Octave Gagné, Alexandre Gauvreau, Charles Grenier, A. Guillet-Tourangeau, Jean-Baptiste Hamel, Victor Laberge, Cyprien Labrèque, E.-Hypolite Laliberté, Edmond Larue, V.-Wenceslas Larue, Louis Leclerc, David Noël, Isaï Nolet, Thomas-M.-Wilbrod Pampalon, Germain-Arthur Paradis, Louis Parent, J.-Édouard Plamondon, Joseph-Edmond Roy, Léon Saint-Amand and Joseph Savard.

Archives judiciaires de Sherbrooke
Notarial records from the offices of Louis-Avila Audet, Georges-Edmond Borlase, François-Xavier David, Jean-Baptiste Gendreau, Joseph-E. Girouard, L.-Hector Jasmin and Charles-Henri Langlois.

Archives judiciaires de Trois-Rivières
Notarial records from the offices of Pierre Désilets, Louis-Adolphe Lord and Télesphore-Eusèbe Normand.

Archives of the Montreal Museum of Fine Arts

Archives du Musée de la civilisation, Quebec City
Correspondence between Mr. and Mrs. Chapais.

Archives of the McCord Museum of Canadian History, Montreal

Archives du Musée du Québec, Quebec City

Archives du Musée du Séminaire de Québec, Quebec City
Suzor-Coté papers.

National Archives of Canada, Ottawa
Individual and industrial census records for Quebec City, Montreal, Trois-Rivières and Sherbrooke: 1842, 1851, 1861, 1871, 1881, 1891 and 1901.

Archives nationales du Québec à Chicoutimi
Notarial records from the offices of Ovide Bossé, Thomas-Zénime Cloutier, Jean Gagné and Lucien Tremblay.

Archives nationales du Québec à Montréal
Notarial records from the offices of Amable Archambault, Joseph Aussem, Édouard-Alexandre Beaudry, Ramon Beaufield, Adolphe Beauvais, Louis Bédard, Joseph Belle, Adolphe-Hector Bernard, Charles-Adrien Berthelot, Pierre Brais, Hugh Brodie, Louis-Théodore Chagnon, Michel Charest, Joseph Chartrand, Félix Chenier, Hyacinthe Denis Côté, Pierre Crevier, Charles Cushing, Alphonse-Clovis Décary, Georges-Hector Demers, Charles-Danau Demuy, Owen-Joseph Devlin, Nicolas-Benjamin Doucet, Louis-Félix Gauvreau, Aimé Geoffrion, Césaire Germain, Joseph Goguet, Jonathan-Abraham Gray, William Anderson Hall, Louis-Gaspard Hétu, Jean-Baptiste Houlé, Alfred-G. Isaacson, John Hilder Isaacson, André Jobin, Joseph-Augustin Labadie, Patrice Lacombe, Louis Lacoste, Eustache Larose, Félix-Hector Leblanc, Cléophas-E. Leclerc, J.-Adrien Legris, William Francis Lighthall, Louis-Séraphin Martin, Pierre Mathieu, Joseph Meilleur, Louis Normandin, Victor Normandin, William Anderson Philips, Isaie-A. Quintal, Félix Rieutord, Aimé-J.-Achille Roberge, James Smith, Ernest-Henri Stuart and Pierre-Charles Valois.

Architectural plans

Archives nationales du Québec à Québec, Quebec City
Notarial records from the offices of Alexis Beaulieu, Joseph Bernard, Paul Bigué, Henri Bolduc, Charles Bourget, Archibald Campbell, William Darling Campbell, John Childs, Alexis Côté, Jean-Baptiste Couillard,

N.B. The highly select bibliography includes the main sources, reference books and articles used in the MOBIVIQ project. Complementary references appear in note form throughout the catalogue.

Claire Desmeules and John R. Porter

Moïse Couture, Charles-Maxime Defoy, John Doyle, Pierre Fournier, Pierre Garon, Nicolas Gauthier, François-Léon Gauvreau, Olivier Grégoire, F.-Marcel Guay, Germain Guay, John Simpson Hossack, Josiah Hunt, François Laroche, Joseph Laurin, Louis Lavoie, Errol Boyd Lindsay, Laughlan T. McPherson, Louis Panet, Joseph Pelchat, Joseph Petitclerc, Louis Prévost, Alexandre-B. Sirois and Édouard Tessier.
Architectural plans: Staveley papers, Chênevert papers.

Archives nationales du Québec à Sherbrooke
Notarial records from the offices of Joseph T.-Lactance Archambault, Pierre Bériau, Michael Boyce, Charles Brin, François-Xavier Bureau, Richard Dickinson, Edouard Pellew Felton, G.-H. Napier, C. A. Richardson, William Ritchie and Daniel Thomas.

Archives nationales du Québec à Trois-Rivières
Notarial records from the offices of J.-Michel Badeau, Laurent-David Craig, Pierre-Laurent Craig, Valère Guillet, Petrus Hubert, Denis-Genest Labarre, Flavien Lottinville and François-Xavier Pratte.

Archives paroissiales de Grondines

Archives de la Société de Jésus, Quebec City

Archives du Séminaire de Québec, Quebec City
Duplicate 189: Cabinetmaker François Bédard's account book.
Varia.

Archives de la ville de Québec, Quebec City

Canadian Centre for Folk Culture Studies, Hull (Canadian Museum of Civilization)
Marius Barbeau papers.

II PRINTED SOURCES

2.1 Commercial directories from the cities of Montreal, Quebec City, Trois-Rivières and Sherbrooke

2.2 Patents, plans and articles on decoration
Canadian Magazine of Science and the Industrial Arts. Patent Office Record (1883-1891).
Canadian Mechanics' Magazine and Patent Office Record (1876-1878).
The Canadian Patent Office Record and Mechanics' Magazine (1873-1875).
List of Canadian Patents from the Beginning of Patent Office, June 1824 to 31st of August 1872. Ottawa, MacLean, Roger & Co., 1882.
The Scientific Canadian, Mechanics' Magazine and Patent Office Record of Canada (1879-1882).

2.3 Catalogues from T. Eaton, Toronto, nos. 5-46 (1888-1901).

2.4 Parliamentary Records
Session records for the years 1861, 1862, 1865, 1876, 1880, 1881, 1885, 1887, 1888 and 1889.

2.5 Provincial Exhibitions
Souvenir albums, catalogues, guides, price lists and reports produced by various provincial exhibition committees.

2.6 World's Fairs
Catalogues, price lists and various reports produced by committees from Canada and abroad [in chronological order], including:
The Industry of All Nations 1851: The Art Journal Illustrated Catalogue. London: George Virtue, 1851.
Official Catalogue of the New York Exhibition of the Industry of All Nations, 1853. New York: George P. Putman & Co., 1853.
Catalogue de la collection envoyée du Canada à l'Exposition universelle de Paris, 1855 et classée d'après le système adopté par la Commission impériale. Paris: Hector Bossange et Fils, 1855.
Catalogue officiel publié par ordre de la Commission impériale, 2nd ed. Paris: E. Panis, 1855.
TACHÉ, Joseph-Charles. *Catalogue raisonné des produits canadiens exposés à Paris en 1855.* Paris: G.-A. Pinard and Dentan et Cie, 1855.
TACHÉ, Joseph-Charles. *Rapport préliminaire du secrétaire du comité exécutif canadien de l'exposition universelle devant avoir lieu à Paris en 1855.* Quebec City: Canada Gazette, 1855.
ROBIN, Charles. *Extrait relatif au Canada, de l'histoire de l'exposition universelle de 1855.* Quebec City: E.R. Fréchette, 1856.
TACHÉ, Joseph-Charles. *Canada at the Universal Exhibition of 1855.* Toronto: John Lovell, 1856.
Extraits du rapport sur l'Exposition de Paris: produits du Canada. Toronto: Stewart Derbishire & George Desbarats, 1857.
The Art Journal Illustrated Catalogue on the International Exhibition 1862. London: James S. Virtue, 1862.
Catalogue of Canadian Collection for the International Exhibition, London, 1862. Montreal: Longmoore & Co. and Montreal Gazette Steam Press, 1862.
Catalogue of the Canadian Contributions to the Dublin Exhibition, 1865.
Dublin International Exhibition of Arts and Manufactures, 1865. Under the Special Patronage of Her Majesty the Queen, Official catalogue. Dublin: John Falconer, 1865.
The Illustrated Catalogue of the Universal Exhibition, The Art Journal. London: Virtue & Co., 1867.
DUCUING, Fr. *L'Exposition universelle de 1867 illustrée.* Paris: Ch. Lahure, 1868, 2 vols.
Catalogue of Canadian Exhibitors at the International Exhibition, Philadelphia. Montreal: Le National, 1876.
TUPPER, Charles. *Antwerp Universal Exhibition 1885, Official Catalogue of the Canadian Section.* [1885].
"The Colonial and Indian Exhibition 1886". *The Art Journal*, 1886 (supplement).
Colonial and Indian Exhibition of 1886: A Revelation of Canada's Progress and Resources: Extracts from British and Colonial Journals. Ottawa: Department of Agriculture, 1888.
DUPUIS, Auguste. *La province de Québec à l'Exposition de Paris 1900.* Quebec City: Darveau, 1901.

2.7 Newspapers
Montreal: *L'Agriculteur*, *L'Aurore des Canadas*, *Les Beaux-Arts*, *La Bibliothèque canadienne*, *Le Bien public*, *Canada-Revue*, *Canadian Illustrated News*, *Le Canard*, *Le Courrier de Montréal*, *Diogenes*, *L'Encyclopédie canadienne*, *The Gazette*, *The Herald*, *La Minerve*, *Le Monde Illustré*, *The Montreal Star*, *The Montreal Transcript*, *Montreal Weekly Witness*, *Le Négociant canadien*, *L'Opinion publique*, *L'Ordre*, *La Patrie* (1854-1858) and *La Patrie* (1879-1900), *Le Pays*, *The Pilot*, *La Presse*, *Star Weekly* and *La Tribune*.
Quebec City: *L'Artisan*, *Le Canadien*, *Le Courrier du Canada*, *L'Écho du peuple*, *L'Électeur*, *L'Événement*, *Le Fantasque*, *Journal de l'Instruction publique*, *Journal de Québec*, *The Morning Chronicle*, *Le Nouvelliste*, *Quebec Daily Mercury*, *The Quebec Daily News*, *The Quebec Daily Telegraph*, *The Quebec Gazette*, *La Scie*, *La Semaine commerciale*, *Le Soleil*, *La Tribune*, *L'Union libérale*, *La Vallée de la Chaudière* [Sainte-Marie-de-Beauce] and *La Vérité*.
Eastern Townships: *The Canadian Times*, *Le Pionnier de Sherbrooke*, *The Sherbrooke Examiner*, *Sherbrooke Gazette and Eastern Townships Advertiser* and *The Stanstead Journal*.
Trois-Rivières: *L'Ère nouvelle*, *Gazette des Trois-Rivières*, *L'Indépendance canadienne* and *Le Trifluvien*.
Abroad: *The Illustrated London News* (1849-1894).

2.8 Books on etiquette and manners
ALQ, Louise d'. *Le savoir-vivre dans toutes les circonstances de la vie.* Paris: Bureaux des causeries familières, 1886 [1st ed. 1877], 2 vols.
BOITARD, M. *Manuel-physiologie de la bonne compagnie, du bon ton et de la politesse.* Paris: Dard, 1863.
CORDONNIER, Émile. *Encyclopédie pratique de la politesse et du savoir-vivre.* Paris: Aristide Quillet, 1930.
DROHOJOWSKA, Mme la comtesse. *De la politesse et du bon ton ou devoirs d'une femme chrétienne dans le monde*, 2nd ed. Paris: Victor Sarlit, 1860.
DUFAUX DE LA JONCHÈRE, E. *Le savoir-vivre dans la vie ordinaire et dans les cérémonies civiles et religieuses.* Paris: Librairie Garnier Frères, 1883.
F.P.B. *Nouveau traité des devoirs du chrétien envers Dieu....* Quebec City: S. Chaperon, 1892.
GENLIS, Madame la comtesse de. *Dictionnaire critique et raisonné des étiquettes de la cour, des usages du monde ... des Français depuis la mort de Louis XIII jusqu'à nos jours.* Paris: P. Mongie, 1818.
Manners. Toronto: McClelland, Goodchild & Stewart Ltd., 1914.
MORTON, Agnes H. *Etiquette.* Philadelphia: The Penn Publishing Co., 1913 [1st ed., 1892].
ROBINSON, Nugent. *Collier's Encyclopaedia of Commercial and Social Information and Treasury of*

Useful and Entertaining Knowledge, rev. ed. New York: Peter Fenelon Collier Publisher, 1882.
SAUVALLE, M. *Mille questions d'étiquette discutées, résolues et classées.* Montreal: Beauchemin, 1907.
STAFFE, La Baronne. *Usages du monde: règles du savoir-vivre dans la société moderne.* Paris: Victor Havard, 1893.
La vraie politesse et le bon ton. Montreal: Eusèbe Senécal, 1873.
WILDEBLOOD, Joan and Peter BRINSON. *The Polite World: A Guide to English Manners and Deportment from the Thirteenth to the Nineteenth Century.* London: Oxford University Press, 1965.

2.9 Commercial Publications

Annual Report of the Quebec Board of Trade. Quebec City: Morning Chronicle, 1868.
The Board of Trade, Montreal, 1893: A Souvenir of the Opening of the New Building. Montreal, 1893.
BORTHWICK, Douglas. *Montreal, Its History, to Which Is Added Biographical Sketches with Photographs of Many of the Principal Citizens.* Montreal: Drysdale, 1875.
BORTHWICK, Douglas. *History of Montreal Including the Streets of Montreal, Their Origin and History.* Montreal, 1897.
Le Canada: courte esquisse de sa position géographique, ses productions, son climat, ses ressources, ses institutions scolaires et municipales, ses pêcheries, chemins de fer, etc. Quebec City: John Lovell, 1860.
Le commerce de Montréal et de Québec et leurs industries en 1889. Montreal: J.J. Kane et Cie, 1889.
The Dominion Annual Register and Review (1882-1886). Toronto: Hunter Rose and Co., 1883-1887.
HUOT, L.H. *Annuaire du commerce et de l'industrie de Québec pour 1873.* Quebec City: L.H. Huot, 1873.
HUTTEMEYER, J.G.C. *Les intérêts commerciaux de Montréal et Québec et leurs manufactures.* Montreal: J.G.C. Huttemeyer, 1889.
Industries of Canada: City of Montreal, Historical and Descriptive Review, Leading Firms and Moneyed Institutions. Montreal: Gazette, 1886.
LANGEVIN, Hector. *Le Canada: ses institutions, ressources, produits, manufactures etc.* Quebec City: Lovell et Lamoureux, 1855.
Montreal Business Sketches with a Description of the City of Montreal, Its Public Buildings and Places of Interest, and the Grand Trunk Works at Point St. Charles, Victoria Bridge, etc. Montreal: Canada Railways Advertising Company and M. Longmoore & Co., 1864.
Montréal fin de siècle: histoire de la métropole du Canada au dix-neuvième siècle. Montreal, 1899.
Montreal Illustrated 1894...: A Brief History of the City from Foundation to the Present Time. Montreal: The Consolidated Illustrating Co., 1894.
Semi-Centennial Report of the Montreal Board of Trade and Report of the Council. Montreal: Gazette, 1893.
TÊTU, Horace. *Résumé historique de l'industrie et des commerces de Québec de 1775 à 1900.* Quebec City, 1899.

2.10 Censuses

Canadian census reports for the years 1851, 1861, 1871, 1881, 1891 and 1901.
SMALL, H.B. *Puissance du Canada: industries et manufactures compilées d'après les dernières statistiques.* Ottawa: Le Pionnier, 1885.

2.11 Literary texts, diaries and travel logs

BÉÏQUE, F.L. *Quatre-vingts ans de souvenirs.* Montreal: Bernard Valiquette and Éditions A.C.F., 1939.
BIART, Lucien. *À travers l'Amérique: nouvelles et récits.* Paris: A. Hennuyer.
BIBAUD, Adèle. *Les fiancés de St-Eustache.* Montreal: Imprimerie du Messager, 1910.
COTTEAU, Edmond. *Promenades dans les deux Amériques 1876-1877.* Paris: Charpentier et Cie, 1887.
DUFFERIN, The Marchioness of. *My Canadian Journal 1872-78: Extracts from My Letters Home Written While Lord Dufferin Was Governor-General.* New York: Appleton & Co., 1891.
FADETTE. *Journal d'Henriette Dessaulles 1874-1880.* Montreal: Hurtubise, 1971.
FRANÇOISE [Robertine Barry]. *Chroniques du lundi de Françoise.* Quebec City.
FRÉCHETTE, Louis. *Mémoires intimes.* Montreal and Paris: Fides, 1961.
GÉRIN, Léon. "L'habitant de Saint-Justin. Contribution à la géographie sociale du Canada", MSRC[1898]. In Jean-Charles Falardeau and Phlippe Garigue. *Léon Gérin et l'habitant de Saint-Justin.* Montreal: PUM, 1968, pp. 49-130.
GÉRIN-LAJOIE, Antoine. *Jean Rivard le défricheur: récit de la vie réelle, suivi de Jean Rivard, économiste.* Montreal: Hurtubise, 1977.
GRANT, George Monro. *Artistic Quebec Described by Pen and Pencil.* Toronto: Belden Brothers, 1888.
HULOT, Baron Étienne. *De l'Atlantique au Pacifique à travers le Canada et les États-Unis.* Paris: Plon, 1888.
LÉVIS, Marquis de. *Visite au Canada.* Châteaudun: Imprimerie typographique, 1896.
LIONNET, Jean. *Chez les Français du Canada.* Paris: Plon, 1908.
LOIR, Adrien. *Canada et Canadiens.* Paris: E. Guilmoto, 1908.
MARCHAND, Joséphine. "Journal-mémoires de madame Raoul Dandurand". Unpublished manuscript, private collection.
MARMETTE, Joseph. *Récits et souvenirs.* Montreal: Beauchemin, 1925.
MARMIER, Xavier. *Les États-Unis et le Canada.* Tours: Alfred Mame, 1898.
Oeuvres complètes de l'abbé H.R. Casgrain. Vol. 1: *légendes canadiennes et variétés.* Montreal: Beauchemin, 1896.
Le Répertoire national. Montréal: J.M. Valois et Cie, 1893, vols. 2 and 3.
ROQUEBRUNE, Robert de. *Testament de mon enfance.* Montreal: Fides, 1979.

2.12 Varia (including pattern books)

Album de la Minerve: journal de la famille, de la mode, de l'économie domestique, de la littérature et des arts. Montreal, 1872-1874 (vols. 1-3).
The Art Journal. London and New York, 1849-1904.
BAIRD, Henry C., ed. *The Painter, Gilder and Varnisher's Companion.* Philadelphia, 1854.
BAIRD, Henry C., ed. *Cabinet Makers' Album of Furniture Comprising a Collection of Designs for the Newest and Most Elegant Styles of Furniture Illustrated by Forty-Eight Large and Beautifully Engraved Plates.* Philadelphia, 1868.
BAIRD, Henry C., ed. *Victorian Gothic and Renaissance Revival Furniture: Two Victorian Pattern Books.* Philadelphia: Athenaeum Library of Nineteenth-Century America, 1977 [reprint of the 1868 ed.].
BLACKIE AND SON. *The Victorian Cabinet-maker's Assistant.* New York: Dover Publications, 1970 [reprint of the 1853 ed.].
Catalogue and Rules of the Library and Reading Room of the Quebec Mechanics' Institute. Quebec City: W. Cown & Son, 1841.
Catalogue of Books in the Library of the Mechanics' Institute of Montreal with the Rules of the Library and Reading Room. Montreal: Owler & Stevenson, 1855.
Catalogue of the Household Furniture... to Be Sold at Spencer Wood. Quebec City: T. Cary, 1851.
Catalogue Sale of Valuable Maple, Mahogany & B. Walnut Household Furniture, Rich China & Glassware, Tapestry, Carpets. Used by H.R.H. The Prince of Wales, To Be Sold at the Residence of Sir W.F. Williams Commander of the Forces, Sherbrooke Street, on Thursday, 27th September [1860]. Montreal, Henry Rose.
DOWNING, A.J. *Cottages Residences: A Series of Designs for Rural Cottages and Cottage Villas and Their Gardens and Grounds Adapted to North America.* New York and London: Wiley & Pietram, 1844.
DOWNING, A.J. *The Architecture of Country Houses.* New York: Dover Publications, 1969 [New York: Appleton, 1850].
DOWNING, A.J. and J.C. LOUDON. *Furniture for the Victorian Home.* New York: Watkins Glenn, The American Life Foundation, 1978.
EASTLAKE, Charles Locke. *Hints on Household Taste.* New York: Dover Publications, 1969 [London: Longmans, Green & Co., 1868].
EISENLOHR, L. and C. WEIGLE, eds. *The Art Workman: A Monthly Journal of Design for the Artist, Artificer and Manufacturer.* London: James Hagger, 1883 (5th series) and London: A. Fischer, 1884 (6th series).
Le Garde-meuble ancien et moderne (furniture journal published in Paris by Désiré Guilmard starting in 1839).
KING, Thomas. *The Modern Style of Cabinet Work Exemplified.* London: H.G. Bohn, 1862.
LOUDON, J.C. *An Encyclopaedia of Cottage, Farm and Villa Architecture and Furniture.* London: Longman, Brown, Green & Longmans, 1842.
MONTGOMERY WARD AND CO. *Catalogue and Buyers' Guide No. 57, Spring and Summer 1895.* New

York: Dover Publications Inc., 1969 [reprint of the original 1895 ed.].
MUTHESIUS, Hermann. *The English House*. New York: Rizzoli, 1987 [Berlin, Wasmuth, 1904].
NICHOLSON, Peter and Michael ANGELO. *The Practical Cabinet Maker, Upholsterer and Complete Decorator*. East Ardsley, Wakefield, England: EP. Publishing Ltd., 1973 [London, 1826].
NOSBAN ET MAIGNE. *Nouveau manuel complet de l'ébéniste et du tabletier*. Paris: Inter-Livres, [reissue of *L'ébéniste* by the Encyclopédie Roret, 1869].
ROUBO, J.A. *Le menuisier en meubles*. Paris: Inter-Livres.
RUSSELL, Willis. *Quebec: As It Was and As It Is, or a Brief History of the Oldest City in Canada, from Foundation to the Present Time, with a Guide for Strangers to the Different Places of Interest Within the City and Adjacent Thereto*. Quebec City: P. Lamoureux, 1857.
VAUX, Calvert. *Villas and Cottages: The Great Architectural Style-Book of the Hudson River School*. New York: Dover Publications Inc., 1970 [Harper & Brother, 1864].
WELLS, Percy A. and John HOOPER. *Modern Cabinet Work Furniture and Fitments*. London: B.T. Batsford, 1909.

III DICTIONARIES AND REFERENCE BOOKS

3.1 General Dictionaries and Reference Books

Dictionnaire biographique du Canada, vols. 7-12 (1836-1900). Quebec City: PUL, 1972-1990.
LEMIRE, Maurice, ed. *Dictionnaire des oeuvres littéraires du Québec*. Vol. 1: Des origines à 1900, 2nd rev. and enlarged ed. Montreal: Fides, 1980.

3.2 Dictionaries and Reference Books on Furniture

Ameublement. Terminologie du mobilier. Cahier du Centre technique du bois no. 13. Paris: Centre technique du bois.
ANTIQUES COLLECTOR'S CLUB. *Pictorial Dictionary of British Nineteenth-Century Furniture Design*. Intro. by Edward Joy, Antiques Collector's Club. Hacker, 1980.
ARONSON, Joseph. *The Encyclopaedia of Furniture*, 3rd ed. New York: Crown Publishers, 1965.
AUDOUY, A. and G. THIVET. *Terminologie de l'ameublement*. Rodez: Imprimerie Subervie, 1974.
AUSSEL, André. *Histoire de l'art: étude des styles du mobilier*. Paris: Dunod, 1975.
BOGER, Louise Ade. *The Complete Guide to Furniture Styles*. New York: Scribner, 1982.
BOUILLET, M.N. *Dictionnaire universel des sciences, des lettres et des arts*. Paris: Hachette, 1884.
BUTLER, Joseph T. and Katleen Eagen JOHNSON. *Field Guide to American Antique Furniture*. A Roundtable Press Book. New York: Facts on File Publications, 1985.
Dictionnaire raisonné universel des arts et métiers. Lyons: Amable Le Roy, 1801.
Encyclopédie du dix-neuvième siècle: répertoire universel des sciences, des lettres et des arts. Paris: Librairie de l'Encyclopédie du 19e siècle, 1877.
FRANKLIN, Alfred. *Dictionnaire historique des arts, métiers et professions*. Paris: A. Welter éd., 1906.
GLOAG, John. *A Complete Dictionary of Furniture*. Ed. by Clive Edwards. New York: The Overlook Press, 1991.
HAVARD, Henri. *Dictionnaire de l'ameublement et de la décoration depuis le XIIIe siècle jusqu'à nos jours*. Paris: Maison Quantin, 1890, 4 vols.
JERVIS, Simon. *Dictionary of Design and Designers*. London: Penguin, 1984.
JONES, Owen. *The Grammar of Ornament*. New York: Dover Publications, 1987 [London: Day & Son, 1856].
KETCHUM, William C. *Chests, Cupboards, Desks and Other Pieces*. New York: Alfred A. Knopf, 1982.
LAMI, O.E. *Dictionnaire encyclopédique et biographique de l'industrie et des arts industriels*. Paris: Librairie des dictionnaires, 1881-1886.
LEDOUX-LEBARD, Denise. *Les ébénistes parisiens du XIXe siècle (1795-1889), leurs oeuvres et leurs marques*. Paris: Les Éditions de l'Amateur, 1984.
LEWIS, Philippa and Gillian DARLEY. *Dictionary of Ornament*. New York: Pantheon Books, 1985.
LOCKWOOD, Luke Vincent. *The Furniture Collector's Glossary*. New York: Da Capo Press, 1967 [New York: The Walpole Society, 1913].
MANAZZA, Paul and Jean-François CIVARDI. *Histoire illustrée des meubles de style*. Paris: De Vecchi, 1989.
NAEVE, Milo M. *Identifying American Furniture. A Pictorial Guide to Styles and Terms, Colonial to Contemporary*. Nashville: The American Association for State and Local History, 1981.
REYNIÈS, Nicole de. *Principes d'analyse scientifique. Le mobilier domestique: vocabulaire typologique*. Inventaire général des monuments et des richesses artistiques de la France. Paris: Imprimerie nationale, 1987, 2 vols.
SCHWARTZ, Marvin D. *Chairs, Tables, Sofas and Beds*. New York: Alfred A. Knopf, 1982.
SWEDBERG, Robert and Harriet SWEDBERG. *Victorian Furniture*. Radnor, Pennsylvania: Wallace-Homestead, 1984, 3 vols.
VERMETTE, Luce. *Répertoire des ébénistes des villes de Montréal et de Québec, 1850-1870*. Ottawa: Parks Canada, 1984. Microfiches.
WOODHOUSE, Charles Platten. *The Victorian Collector's Handbook*. London: George Bell & Sons, 1970.

IV GENERAL STUDIES AND ARTICLES

ACKERMAN, James S. *The Villa Form and Ideology of Country Houses*. Washington: Princeton University Press, 1990.
ARIÈS, Philippe and George DUBY, eds. *Histoire de la vie privée*. Vol. 4: De la Révolution à la Grande Guerre. Paris: Seuil, 1987.
L'art de vivre: Decorative Arts and Design in France 1789-1989. New York: Cooper-Hewitt Museum and Vendome Press, 1989.
BERVIN, George. "Environnement matériel et activités économiques des conseillers exécutifs et législatifs à Québec, 1810-1830". *Bulletin d'histoire de la culture matérielle*, no. 17, (1983), pp. 9-24.
BERVIN, George. *Québec au XIXe siècle: activité économique des grands marchands*. Sillery: Éditions du Septentrion, 1991.
BOUDON, Pierre. "Sur un statut de l'objet: différer l'objet de l'objet". *Communications*, no. 13. Paris: Seuil, 1969, pp. 65-87.
BOURDIEU, Pierre. "Méthode scientifique et hiérarchie sociale des objets". *Actes de la recherche en sciences sociales*, no. 1 (January 1975), pp. 4-6.
BOURDIEU, Pierre. *La distinction: critique sociale du jugement*. "Le sens commun" series. Paris: Éditions de Minuit, 1979.
BOURDIEU, Pierre. *Le sens pratique*. Paris: Éditions de Minuit, 1980.
BURKE, Bolger et al. *In Pursuit of Beauty*. New York: Metropolitan Museum of Art and Rizzoli, 1986.
CAMERON, Christina. "Housing in Quebec before Confederation". *The Journal of Canadian Art History/Annales d'histoire de l'art canadien*, vol. 6, no. 1 (1982), pp. 1-34.
COOPER, J.I. "The Social Structure of Montreal in the 1850's". *The Canadian Historical Association Report 1955-56*, pp. 63-73.
CROSSICK, Geoffrey. *An Artisan Elite in Victorian Society: Kentish London, 1840-1880*. London: Croom Helm, 1978.
DARROCH, A. Gordon and Michael D. ORNSTEIN. "Ethnicity and Occupational Structure in Canada in 1871: The Vertical Mosaic in Historical Perspective". *Canadian Historical Review*, vol. 61, no. 3 (1980).
DAUMARD, Adeline. "Une référence pour l'étude des sociétés urbaines en France aux XVIIIe et XIXe siècles. Projet de code socio-professionnel". *Revue d'histoire moderne et contemporaine*, July 1963, pp. 185-210.
DENVIR, Bernard. *The Early Nineteenth Century: Art, Design and Society, 1789-1852*. London and New York: Longman, 1984.
DENVIR, Bernard. *The Late Victorians: Art, Design and Society, 1852-1910*. London and New York: Longman, 1986.
ÉLEB-VIDAL, Monique and Anne DEBARRE-BLANCHARD. *Architectures de la vie privée: maisons et mentalités, XVIIe - XIXe siècles*. Brussels: Archives d'architecture moderne, 1989.
FAUCHER, Albert. "La notion de luxe chez les Canadiens français au dix-neuvième siècle". *Proceedings and Transactions of the Royal Society of Canada/Délibérations et mémoires de la Société royale du Canada*, 4th series, vol. 11 (1973), pp. 175-180.
FOURASTIÉ, Jean and Françoise. *Histoire du confort*. "Que sais-je?" series. Paris: PUF, 1962.
GAGNON, François-Marc, John BLAND and Élisabeth COLLARD. *La fin d'une époque: Montréal*

1880-1914. Montreal: McCord Museum of Canadian History and McGill, 1977.

GAGNON PRATTE, France. L'architecture et la nature à Québec au XIXe siècle: les villas. Quebec City: Ministère des Affaires Culturelles, 1980.

GAGNON PRATTE, France. Maisons de campagne des Montréalais 1892-1924: l'architecture des frères Maxwell. Montreal: Éditions du Méridien, 1987.

GARRET, Elisabeth Donaghy. At Home: The American Family 1750-1870. New York: Harry N. Abrams Inc., 1990.

GIEDION, Siegfried. La mécanisation au pouvoir: contribution à l'histoire anonyme. Paris: Centre Georges-Pompidou, 1980.

GIROUARD, Mark. The Victorian Country House. New Haven, Connecticut, and London: Yale University Press, 1985.

HARDY, Jean-Pierre. "Niveaux de richesse et intérieurs domestiques dans le quartier Saint-Roch à Québec, 1820-1850". Bulletin d'histoire de la culture matérielle, no. 17, (1983), pp. 63-94.

HARE, John, Marc LAFRANCE and David-Thiery RUDDEL. Histoire de la ville de Québec, 1608-1871. Montreal: Éditions du Boréal and Canadian Museum of Civilization, 1987.

HAUS, Andréa. "Historisme et style dans l'industrie artistique au XIXe siècle". Histoire et critique des arts. November 1977, pp. 22-29.

HUBBARD, R.H. Rideau-Hall: histoire illustrée de la résidence du gouverneur général à Ottawa depuis l'époque victorienne jusqu'à nos jours. Montreal: McGill-Queens University Press, 1979.

IBERVILLE-MOREAU, Luc d'. Montréal perdu. Montreal: Quinze, 1975.

JERVIS, Simon. Le style de la grande époque victorienne. Ottawa: National Gallery of Canada, 1975.

KATZ, Michael B. The People of Hamilton, Canada West: Family and Class in a Mid-Nineteenth-Century City. Cambridge, Massachusetts: Harvard University Press, 1975.

KIMBALL, Fiske. The Creation of the Rococo Decorative Style. New York: Dover Publications, 1980 [Philadelphia Museum of Art, 1943].

KNIGHTS, Peter R. The Plain People of Boston, 1830-1860: A Study in City Growth. New York: Oxford University Press, 1971.

LACELLE, Claudette. Les domestiques en milieu urbain en début du XIXe siècle. Ottawa: Environment Canada-Parks, 1987.

LANGEVIN, Hector. Le Canada, ses institutions, ressources, produits, manufactures. Quebec City: Lovell et Lamoureux, 1855.

LESSER, Gloria. "Trafalgar Lodge: A Rare Exemple of Gothic Revival in Montréal". Canadian Collector, vol. 19, no. 3 (May-June 1984), pp. 49-52.

LINTEAU, Paul-André. "Quelques réflexions autour de la bourgeoisie québécoise, 1850-1914". Revue d'histoire de l'Amérique française, vol. 30, no. 1 (June 1976), pp. 55-66.

LINTEAU, Paul-André, René DUROCHER and Jean-Claude ROBERT. Histoire du Québec contemporain: de la Confédération à la crise (1867-1929). Montreal: Éditions du Boréal, 1989.

MACKAY, Donald. The Square Mile: Merchant Princes of Montreal. Vancouver and Toronto: Douglas & McIntyre, 1987.

MARSAN, Jean-Claude. Montréal en évolution. Montreal: Fides, 1974.

MATHIEU, Jacques, Georges-P. LÉONIDOFF and John R. PORTER. "L'objet et ses contextes". Material History Bulletin/Bulletin d'histoire de la culture matérielle, no. 26 (Fall 1987), pp. 7-18.

MOUSSETTE, Marcel. "Sens et contresens: l'étude de la culture matérielle au Québec". Canadian Folklore canadien, vol. 4, nos. 1-2 (1984), pp. 7-26.

OUELLET, Fernand. "Structure des occupations et ethnicités dans les villes de Québec et de Montréal (1819-1844)". In Éléments d'histoire sociale du Bas-Canada. Montreal: HMH, 1972, pp. 177-205.

PAQUET, Gilles and Jean-Pierre WALLOT. "Structures sociales et niveaux de richesse dans les campagnes du Québec: 1792-1812". Bulletin d'histoire de la culture matérielle, no. 17, pp. 25-44.

PAQUET, Gilles and Jean-Pierre WALLOT. "Groupes sociaux et pouvoir: le cas canadien au tournant du XIXe siècle". Revue d'histoire de l'Amérique française, vol. 27, no. 4 (March 1974), pp. 509-564.

PARISEAU, Gérard. "Le capitalisme triomphant dans le Québec de 1870 à 1900". Proceedings and Transactions of the Royal Society of Canada/Délibérations et mémoires de la Société royale du Canada, 4th series, vol. 11 (1973), pp. 159-174.

PINARD, Guy. Montréal, son histoire, son architecture. Montreal: La Presse, 1988, 3 vols.

PRAZ, Mario. L'ameublement: psychologie et évolution de la décoration intérieure. Paris: Tisné, 1964.

RÉMILLARD, François and Brian MERRETT. Demeures bourgeoises de Montréal: le mille carré doré 1850-1930. Montreal: Éditions du Méridien, 1986.

ROBERT, Jean-Claude. "Les notables de Montréal au XIXe siècle". Histoire sociale, vol. 8, no. 15 (May 1975), pp. 54-76.

ROBERT, Jean-Claude. "Aperçu sur les structures socio-professionnelles des villages de la région nord de Montréal, durant la première moitié du XIXe siècle". Cahiers de géographie du Québec, vol. 28, nos. 73-74 (April-September 1984), pp. 63-72.

SACHKO MACLEOD, Diane. "Art History and Victorian Middle-Class Taste". Art History, vol. 10, no. 3 (September 1987), pp. 328-350.

SCHAPIRO, Meyer. "La notion de style". Style, artiste et société. Paris: Gallimard, 1982, pp. 35-85.

SCHROEDER-GODEHUS, Brigitte and Anne RASMUSSEN. Les fastes du progrès: le guide des expositions universelles 1851-1992. Paris: Flammarion, 1992.

La sculpture française au XIXe siècle. Paris: Ministère de la Culture and Éditions de la Réunion des musées nationaux, 1986.

SNELL, J.G. "The Cost of Living in Canada in 1870". Histoire sociale, vol. 12, no. 23 (May 1979), pp. 186-191.

TRIGGS, Stanley, Brian YOUNG, Conrad GRAHAM and Gilles LAUZON. Le pont Victoria: un lien vital/Victoria Bridge: The Vital Link. Montreal: McCord Museum of Canadian History, 1992.

The Victorians. Intro. by Joan Evans. London: Cambridge University Press, 1966.

WALKLING, Gillian. Upholstery Styles. New York: Van Nostrand Reinhold, 1989.

WHARTON, Edith and Ogden CODMAN, Jr. The Decoration of Houses. New York: W.W. Norton and Co. inc., 1978 [reprint of 1902 ed., Scribner].

V STUDIES AND ARTICLES ON WESTERN FURNITURE

AMES, K. L. "The Rocking Chair in Nineteenth-Century America". Antiques, vol. 103, no. 2 (February 1973), pp. 322-327.

AMES, K. L. "Grand Rapids Furniture at the Time of the Centennial". Winterthur Portfolio, vol. 10 (1975), pp. 23-50.

AMES, K. L. "Designed in France: Notes on the Transmission of French Style to America". Winterthur Portfolio, vol. 12 (1977), pp. 103-114.

AMES, K. L. "Meaning in Artefacts: Hall Furnishings in Victorian America". Journal of Interdisciplinary History, no. 9 (Summer 1978), pp. 19-46.

AMES, Kenneth Leroy. Victorian Furniture: Essays from a Victorian Society. Autumn Symposium: The Victorian Society in America Published as Nineteenth-Century, vol. 8, nos. 3-4, 1982.

"Ameublement". Métiers d'Art, no. 28 (March 1985), 93 pp.

"Art du meuble". Métiers d'Art, nos. 26-27 (October 1984), 123 pp.

BANKS, John. "In the Style of Eastlake Never Construct Ornament... Only Ornament Construction". Antique Showcase, vol. 24, no. 10 (April 1989), pp. 11-14.

BISHOP, Robert. Centuries and Styles of the American Chair, 1640-1970. New York: E.P. Dutton; Toronto and Vancouver: Clarke, Irwin & Co., 1972.

BOIDI SASSONE, Adriana. Le mobilier français du XIXe siècle. Paris: Larousse, 1985.

BOWERING, Ian. "Nineteenth-Century Sofas: Tastes and Styles". Antique Showcase, June 1988, pp. 7-9.

CANTOR, Jay. "When Wine Turns to Vinegar: The Critics' View of `19th-Century America'". Winterthur Portfolio, vol. 7, 1972, pp. 1-27.

CLOUZOT, Henri. "Le décor de la vie sous le Second Empire". La Revue de l'art ancien et moderne, vol. 62, no. 238 (July-August 1922), pp. 120-135.

COOK, Edward S. Jr., ed. *Upholstery in America and Europe from the Seventeenth Century to World War I*. New York and London: W.W. Norton & Co., 1987.

COOPER, Jeremy. *Victorian and Edwardian Furniture and Interiors: From Gothic Revival to Art Nouveau*. London: Thames & Hudson, 1987.

DAVIDSON, Marshall B. and Elisabeth STILLINGER. *The American Wing at the Metropolitan Museum of Art*. New York: The Metropolitan Museum of Art and Alfred A. Knopf, 1985.

DAVIS, Felice. "The Victorian and Their Furniture". *Antiques*, vol. 43, no. 6 (June 1943), pp. 256-259.

DAVIS, Felice. "Victorian Cabinetmakers in America". *Antiques*, vol. 44, no. 3 (September 1943), pp. 111-115.

Design and Industry: The Effects of Industrialisation and Technical Change on Design. London: The Design Council, 1980.

DEVOE, Shirley Spaulding. *English Papier Mâché of the Georgian and Victorian Periods*. Middletown, Connecticut: Wesleyan University Press, 1971.

DOUGLAS, Ed. Polk. "The Furniture of John Henry Belter: Separating Fact from Fiction". *Antiques*, vol. 7, no. 1 (November-December 1990), pp. 112-119.

DUBROW, Eileen and Richard DUBROW. *American Furniture of the Nineteenth-Century: 1840-1880*. Exton, Pennsylvania: Schiffer, 1983.

EARL, Polly Anne. "Craftsmen and Machines: The Nineteenth-Century Furniture Industry". *Technological Innovation and the Decorative Arts, Winterthur Conference Report 1973*. Ed. by M.G. Quimby and Polly Anne Earl. Charlottesville: University Press of Virginia, 1974, pp. 307-329.

ETTEMA, Michael J. "Technological Innovation and Design Economics in Furniture Manufacture". *Winterthur Portfolio*, vol. 16, nos. 2/3 (Summer/Fall 1981), pp. 197-223.

FAIRBANKS, Jonathan. *American Furniture 1620 to the Present*. New York: Richard Marek Publishers, 1981.

FERAY, Jean. *Architecture intérieure en France des origines à 1875*. Paris: Berger-Levrault, 1988.

GERE, Charlotte. *L'époque et son style: la décoration intérieure au XIXe siècle*. Paris: Flammarion, 1989.

GLOAG, John. *Victorian Comfort: A Social History of Design from 1830-1900*. London: Adam and Charles Black, 1961.

GLOAG, John. *A Short Dictionary of Furniture Containing 1,767 Terms Used in Britain and America*. New York: Holt, Rinehart & Winston, 1965.

GLOAG, John. *A Social History of Furniture Design from B.C. 1300 to A.D. 1960*. New York: Crown Publishers, 1966.

HAWLEY, Henry. "American Furniture of the Mid-Nineteenth-Century". *The Bulletin of the Cleveland Museum of Art*, vol. 74, no. 5 (1987), pp. 187-215.

HAWLEY, Henry. "Meubles américains d'influence française". *L'Estampille*, no. 224 (April 1989), pp. 60-71.

Histoire du mobilier. Intro. by Sir John Pope-Hennesy. Paris: Éditions Atlas, 1984.

HORNUNG, Clarence P. *Treasury of American Design and Antiques*. New York: Harry N. Abrams, 1950.

HOWE, Katherine S. and David B. WARREN. *The Gothic Revival Style in America: 1830-1870*. Houston: Museum of Fine Arts, 1976.

IVERSON, Marion Day. *The American Chair, 1630-1890*. New York: Hastings House; Toronto: S.J. Reginald Saunders Publishers, 1957.

JOY, Edward Thomas. *Chairs*, rev. ed. London: Country Life Books, 1980 [The Country Life Library of Antiques, 1968].

KANE, Patricia E. *Three Hundred Years of American Seating Furniture: Chairs and Beds from the Mabel Brady Gorvan and Other Collections at Yale University*. Boston: New York Graphic Society, 1976.

KIMBALL, Fiske. "Victorian Art and Victorian Taste". *Antiques*, vol. 23, no. 3 (March 1933), pp. 103-105.

LASDUN, Susan. *Victorians at Home*. London: Weidenfeld & Nicholson, 1981.

LEHMANN, Colette. *Mobilier Louis-Philippe, Napoléon III*. Paris: Charles Massin.

LEOPOLD, Allison Kyle. *Cherished Objects: Living with and Collecting Victoriana*, New York: Clarkson N. Potter, 1991.

LITTLE, Robert. *The Work of William Morris (1834-1896)*. Montreal: The Montreal Museum of Fine Arts, 1991.

MAAS, John. *The Victorian Home in America*. New York: Hawthorn, 1972.

MADIGAN, Mary Jean (intro.). *Nineteenth Century Furniture: Innovation Revival and Reform*, New York: Art and Antiques Book, 1982.

MARSHALL, John and Ian WILLOX. *The Victorian House*. London: Sidgwick & Jackson, 1986.

MAYHEW, Edgard de N. and Minor MYERS. *A Documentary History of American Interiors from the Colonial Era to 1915*. New York: Charles Scribner's Sons, 1980.

McMURRY, Sally. "City Parlor, Country Sitting Room: Rural Vernacular Design and the American Parlor, 1840-1900". *Winterthur Portfolio*, vol. 20, no. 4 (Winter 1985), pp. 261-280.

McNERNEY, Kathryn. *Victorian Furniture: Our American Heritage*. Paducah, Kentucky: Collector Books [1981].

MEYER, Daniel. "Meubles: oeuvres d'art ou objets utilitaires?" *Connaissance des arts*, no. 433 (March 1988), pp. 86-97.

Le mobilier du XIXe siècle en France et en Europe. Paris: Mengès; London: Sotheby's, 1991.

OSTERGARD, Derek E., ed. *Bent Wood and Metal Furniture 1850-1946*. Washington: The University of Washington Press and The American Federation of Arts, 1987.

OTTO, Celia Jackson. "The Rococo Style in Nineteenth-Century American Furniture". *Antiques*, vol. 88, no. 3 (September 1965), pp. 325-329.

OTTO, Celia Jackson. *American Furniture of the Nineteenth-Century*. New York: The Viking Press, 1965.

PALLOT, Bill G.B. *L'art du siège au XVIIIe siècle en France*. Paris: A.C.R. and Gismondi Éditeurs, 1987.

PAYNE, Christopher. *19th Century European Furniture*. Antique Collector's Club, 1981.

PONTE, Alessandra. *Le mobilier anglais du XIXe siècle*. Paris: Larousse, 1986.

RALSTON, Ruth. "Nineteenth-Century New York Interiors". *Antiques*, vol. 43, no. 6 (June 1943), pp. 266-270.

RHEIMS, Maurice. "Histoire du mobilier". In *Histoire des moeurs*, vol. 1. Paris: Encyclopédie de La Pléiade, 1990, pp. 1074-1165.

RYBCZYNSKI, Witold. *Le confort*. Montreal: Éditions du Roseau, 1989 [Viking Penguin, 1986].

SAVAGE, George. *Histoire de la décoration intérieure*. Paris: Éditions Aimery Somogy, 1967.

SCHWARTZ, Marvin, Edward J. STANEK and Douglas K. TRUE. *The Furniture of John Henry Belter and the Rococo Revival: An Inquiry into the Nineteenth-Century Furniture Design through a Study of the Gloria and Richard Mauney Collection*. New York: E.P. Dutton, 1980.

SMITH, Robert Chester. "Late Classical Furniture in the United States 1820-1850". *Antiques*, vol. 74, no. 6 (December 1958), pp. 519-523.

SMITH, Robert Chester. "Gothic and Elizabethan Revival Furniture 1800-1850". *Antiques*, vol. 75, no. 3 (March 1959), pp. 272-275.

SMITH, Robert Chester. "Rococo Revival Furniture 1850-1870". *Antiques*, vol. 75, no. 5 (May 1959), pp. 471-475.

SMITH, Robert Chester. "Furniture of the Eclectic Decades 1870-1900". *Antiques*, vol. 76, no. 1 (July 1959), pp. 50-53.

SMITH, Robert Chester. "Good Taste in Nineteenth-Century Furniture". *Antiques*, vol. 76, no. 4 (October 1959), pp. 342-345.

STRICKLAND, Peter L. L. "Furniture by the Lejambre Family of Philadelphia". *Antiques*, vol. 113, no. 3 (March 1978), pp. 600-613.

SYMONDS, Robert Wemyss. "From Craft to Industry: The Furniture of the Victorians". *Antiques*, vol. 54, no. 4 (October 1948), pp. 256-258 (part 1); *Antiques*, vol. 54, no. 5 (November 1948), pp. 336-339 (part 2).

SYMONDS, R. W. and B. B. WHINERAY. *Victorian Furniture*. London: Studio Editions, 1987 [London: Country Life, 1962].

THORNTON, Peter. *L'époque et son style: la décoration intérieure 1620-1920*. Paris: Flammarion, 1986.

WAISSENBERGER, Robert. *Vienne 1815-1848: l'époque du Biedermeier*. Paris: Seuil, 1985.

WILSON, Michael I. "Victorian Furniture". *Canadian Collector*, vol. 5, no. 5 (May 1970), pp. 18-21.

VI STUDIES AND ARTICLES ON FURNITURE IN CANADA

BATES, Christina. "Le mobilier de la villa Bellevue en 1848". *Bulletin de recherche* (Parks Canada), no. 175 (August 1982).

CATHCART, Ruth. *Jacques & Hay: 19th Century Toronto Furniture Makers*. Erin, Ontario: The Boston Mills Press, 1986.

DUNNING, Phil. T. "Canadian Cabinetmakers and Victorian Style: The Jacques & Hay Style?". *Canadian Antiques Collector*, November-December 1974, pp. 14-17.

HUBBARD, R.H. *Rideau Hall*. Ottawa: Imprimeur de la Reine, 1967.

KOLTUN, L.A. *The Cabinet Maker's Art in Ontario, 1850-1900*. "Mercure" series, no. 26. Ottawa: National Museum of Man, 1979.

MACKINNON, Joan. *A Checklist of Toronto Cabinet and Chair Makers, 1800-1865*. "Mercure" series, no. 11. Ottawa: National Museum of Man, 1974.

MACKINNON, Joan. *Kingston Cabinet Makers, 1800-1867*. "Mercure" series, no. 14. Ottawa: National Museum of Man, 1976.

MURRAY, Joan. "Victorian Canada". *Canadian Collector*, vol. 5, no. 2 (February 1970), pp. 10-14.

PAIN, Howard. *The Heritage of Upper Canadian Furniture: A Study in the Survival of Formal and Vernacular Styles from Britain, America and Europe, 1780-1900*. Toronto: Van Nostrand Reinhold, 1978.

RYDER, Huia Gwendoline. *Antique Furniture by New Brunswick Craftsmen*. Toronto: Ryerson Press, 1965.

WEBSTER, Donald Blake. "Victorian Furniture in Canada". *Canadian Antiques Collector*, November 1970, pp. 9-12.

WILSON, Anne Elizabeth. "A History of Canadian Furniture: Some Distinguished Canadian Craftmen Contemporary with Duncan Phyfe". *Canadian Homes and Gardens*, vol. 5, no. 5 (May 1928), pp. 40, 52.

WILSON, Anne Elizabeth. "A History of Canadian Furniture". *Canadian Homes and Gardens*, vol. 5, no. 7 (July 1928), pp. 25-27, 51.

VII STUDIES AND ARTICLES ON QUEBEC FURNITURE

BARBEAU, Marius. "Laurentian Wood Carvers". *The Canadian Geographical Journal*, vol. 9, no. 4 (October 1935), pp. 181-190.

BARBEAU, Marius. "$75 for a Fallen Angel: Wood Carvers of Early Canada, Culture from France". *The Sunday Sun* [Vancouver], November 23, 1935, p. 31.

BARBEAU, Marius. "Les derniers de nos artisans". *La Presse* [Montreal], Saturday, February 20, 1937, p. 55.

BARBEAU, Marius. *Québec où survit l'ancienne France*. Quebec City: Librairie Garneau, 1937.

BARBEAU, Marius. *J'ai vu Québec*. Quebec City: Librairie Garneau, 1957.

BOULIZON, Guy. "Le style victorien". *Chez soi*, vol. 4, no. 4 (June 1981), pp. 123-130.

CARUFEL, Hélène de. "Regard sur le mobilier victorien". Pamphlet from an exhibition at the Musée du Québec, 1980.

COLLARD, Elisabeth. "Montreal Cabinet Makers and Chair Makers, 1800-1850: A Checklist". *Antiques*, vol. 105, no. 5 (May 1974), pp. 1132-1146.

DARBÉ, A. "Un pupitre-mosaïque". *La vie forestière*, August-September 1931, pp. 26-28.

DESMEULES, Claire. "Le vocabulaire du meuble". *Continuité*, no. 38 (Winter 1988), pp. 32-33.

DROUIN, Daniel. "Les meubliers du Québec aux expositions provinciales, internationales et universelles, 1850-1900". Master's thesis, Université Laval, October 1992.

LABIAU, Jean-Pierre. "Quelques problèmes soulevés par l'étude du mobilier victorien au Québec". *Perspectives*, no. 4 (Winter 1988), pp. 10-11.

LABIAU, Jean-Pierre. "Le mobilier des XIXe et XXe siècles". *Objets de civilisation*. Quebec City: Musée de la civilisation and Éditions Broquet, 1990, pp. 51-60.

LECLERC, Denise. "Musée du Québec: regard sur le mobilier victorien". *Bulletin d'histoire de la culture matérielle*, no. 12 (Spring 1981). Ottawa: National Museum of Man, pp. 80-87.

LÉONIDOFF, Georges-P. and John R. PORTER. "La recherche universitaire et la mise en valeur des collections de mobilier victorien au Québec". *Muse*, Spring 1986, pp. 22-27.

LÉONIDOFF, Georges-P. and Jean-Pierre LABIAU. "Un mobilier sous influence". *Continuité*, no. 38 (Winter 1988), pp. 26-29.

LESSARD, Michel and Huguette MARQUIS. *Encyclopédie des antiquités du Québec*. Montreal: Éditions de l'homme, 1971.

MARTIN, Paul-Louis. *La berçante québécoise*. Montreal: Boréal-Express, 1973.

McILWRAITH, Jean N. "The Pursuit of the Swan-Necked Rocker: A Quest for the Pitt and Drum Varieties of Rocking Chairs…" *Canadian Homes and Gardens*, vol. 2, no. 11 (November 1925), pp. 60-63.

MORISSET, Gérard. *Coup d'oeil sur les arts en Nouvelle-France*. Quebec City, 1941.

OLIVER, Lucille. *Mobilier québécois*. Paris: Charles Massin, 1979.

PALARDY, Jean. *Les meubles anciens du Canada français*. Paris: Arts et métiers graphiques, 1963.

POISSON, Esther. "Étude du vocabulaire du mobilier d'habitation de la région des Bois-Francs d'après les journaux publiés depuis 1866". Master's thesis, Université Laval, October 1982.

PORTER, John R. *L'avènement de l'industrie et la persistance des pratiques artisanales à l'époque victorienne au Québec: quelques notes exploratoires touchant le cas des meubliers*. Quebec City: Université Laval, 1988 (Actes du CÉLAT, no. 1), pp. 91-96.

PORTER, John R. "L'objet matériel et ses contextes: le cas du meuble de l'époque victorienne au Québec". Transcript from the conference "Les dynamismes culturels en France et au Québec" held in Rennes June 2 and 3, 1988. *Annales de Bretagne et des Pays de l'ouest*, vol. 95, no. 4 (1988), pp. 379-388.

PORTER, John R., ed. *Les meubliers Pierre Drouin et Honoré Roy et l'industrie du meuble à Québec à l'époque victorienne*. Quebec City: Université Laval, 1989 (Cahier du CÉLAT, no. 10).

PORTER, John R. and Jean BÉLISLE. *La sculpture ancienne au Québec: trois siècles d'art religieux et profane*. Montreal: Éditions de l'homme, 1986.

PORTER, John R. and Micheline HUARD. "La création québécoise". *Continuité*, no. 38 (Winter 1988), pp. 18-21.

PRIOUL, Didier and Georges-P. LÉONIDOFF. "Décors victoriens". *Continuité*, no. 38 (Winter 1988), pp. 22-25.

SMITH, J. H. "A French Canadian Restoration at Quebec". *Canadian Homes and Gardens*, vol. 3, no. 9 (1926), pp. 44-45, 56.

"Suzor-Coté aurait-il sculpté ce buffet gardé à Notre-Dame?". *Le Petit Journal*, September 25, 1949.

TARDIF, Richard. "Le confort des vernis". *Summum*, vol. 2, no. 2 (1989), pp. 40-43.

TRÉPANIER, Paul. "Montréal: la maison George Étienne Cartier". *Continuité*, no. 38 (Winter 1988), pp. 30-31.

VALLIÈRE, Suzanne. "Philippe Vallière, ébéniste et manufacturier de meubles". *Cap-aux-Diamants*, vol. 2, no. 1 (Spring 1986), pp. 25-28.

VALLIÈRE, Suzanne. "Philippe Vallière, fournisseur d'ameublement pour les édifices parlementaires". Bulletin de la bibliothèque de l'Assemblée nationale, vol. 21, nos. 2-3, pp. 10-13.

VERMETTE, Luce. "Ébéniste à meublier: l'ébénisterie au Québec au milieu du XIXe siècle". *Canadian Collector*, May 1985, pp. 45-50.

VILDER, André. "Le meuble québécois d'hier à aujourd'hui". *Les idées de ma maison*, no. 54 (September 1988), pp. 81-95.

WEBSTER, Donald Blake. "Quebec Furniture with an English Accent". *Canadian Homes*, July 1969, p. 7.

WEBSTER, Donald Blake, ed. "Furniture of English Québec". *The Book of Canadian Antiques*. Toronto: McGraw-Hill Ryerson, 1974, pp. 54-70.

490

Landscape, about 1900

Stained glass, 133.2 x 130 cm

Musée de la civilisation, Quebec City, gift of the Jesuit Missions (90-703)

Photo Pierre Soulard/Musée de la civilisation

The Victorian fascination with the Middle Ages led to a new interest in stained glass, a long-neglected art. This panel came from Lord Atholstan's house, built on Montreal's Sherbrooke Street in 1893. It was situated above the stone fireplace of the great hall.

List of Art Works Presented in the Exhibition*

John Henry Robinson (1796-1871)
Her Most Gracious Majesty, the Queen Victoria, 1845
Coloured engraving after a work by John Partridge (1790-1872), 67.1 x 54.3 cm
Musée du Québec, Quebec City, (A.42.75.E)

Georges T. Doo (1800-1886)
His Royal Highness the Prince Albert, K. G. & c., 1844
Coloured engraving after a work by John Partridge (1790-1872), 66.9 x 54.9 cm
Musée du Québec, Quebec City, (A.42.76.E)

Louis-Philippe Hébert (1850-1917)
Father Joseph Michaud and Monsignor Ignace Bourget Studying the Plans for Montreal's New Cathedral in the Company of Several Notables, 1902
Bronze bas-relief, 87.4 x 183.3 x 15.5 cm
Musée du Québec, Quebec City (A 77.207 S)

Louis-Philippe Hébert (1850-1917)
St. Philomena, 1898
Polychrome wood, 158.5 cm
The Montreal Museum of Fine Arts, gift of the Soeurs des Saints-Noms-de-Jésus-et-de-Marie (1973.2)

Jean-Baptiste Côté (1832-1908)
Napoleon III, 1870
Wood, 73 x 46.7 x 29.2 cm
Musée du Québec, Quebec City (86.101)

Louis-Philippe Hébert (1850-1917)
Sir Louis-Hippolyte Lafontaine, 1885
Painted plaster, 74.5 x 29.5 x 22 cm
The Montreal Museum of Fine Arts, gift of René Lemire (1988.13)

Louis-Philippe Hébert (1850-1917)
Sir John Alexander Macdonald, 1886
Painted plaster, 74.5 x 28.5 x 25 cm
The Montreal Museum of Fine Arts, gift of René Lemire (1988.14)

Frederick Lessore (1879-1951)
Sir Cornelius Van Horne, 1900-1915
Bronze, 49.8 x 38.1 x 24.1 cm
The Montreal Museum of Fine Arts, gift of William C. Van Horne (1945.947)

Louis-Philippe Hébert (1850-1917)
Sir George Alexander Drummond, about 1886
White marble, 75 cm
The Montreal Museum of Fine Arts, gift of the family of Sir George Alexander Drummond (1923.460)

Théophile Hamel (1817-1870)
Lord Elgin, 1852
Oil on canvas, 77 x 48.9 cm
Musée du Séminaire de Québec (Pc 983.19)

Prince Viktor Hohenlohe-Langenburg (1833-1891)
Madame Albani, about 1890
Marble, 73.5 x 43.5 x 32.5 cm
Musée du Québec, Quebec City (34.714)

Antoine Plamondon (1804-1895)
Self-portrait, 1882
Oil on canvas, 80 x 64 cm
Musée du Séminaire de Québec (PC 983.11 R, 352)

R. Lothée(?)
Louis-Philippe Hébert in His Studio, 1893
Oil on canvas, 46.5 x 32.5 cm
Musée des Arts décoratifs de Montréal

Hiram Powers (1805-1873)
Proserpine, 1852
White marble, 55.9 x 24.1 x 24.1 cm
The Montreal Museum of Fine Arts, gift of Dr. J. Douglas Morgan (1952.1070)

William Raphael (1833-1914)
Downstream, 1892
Oil on canvas, 40.6 x 63.8 cm
The Montreal Museum of Fine Arts, purchase, Horsley and Annie Townsend Bequest (1963.1433)

François B. Deblois (1829?-1913)
The Farm in Vaudreuil, 1875
Oil on canvas, 34.5 x 66.3 cm
The Montreal Museum of Fine Arts, purchase, Horsley and Annie Townsend Bequest (1963.1388)

Otto Reinhold Jacobi (1812-1901)
Splugen Pass, 1855
Oil on canvas, 67.2 x 80 cm
The Montreal Museum of Fine Arts, gift of the Honourable John S. McLennan (1879.83)

Antoine Plamondon (1804-1895)
Still Life with Apples and Grapes, 1870
Oil on canvas, 98.2 x 77.6 cm
The Montreal Museum of Fine Arts, gift of Maurice Corbeil (1983.22)

Narcisse-Virgile Díaz de la Peña (1808-1876)
Two Children with a Kid, 1860
Oil on canvas, 58.4 x 46.4 cm
The Montreal Museum of Fine Arts, gift of Lord Strathcona and family (1927.254)

Otto Reinhold Jacobi (1812-1901)
Portrait of Jane Wiseman Wilson, 1877
Oil on canvas, 63.5 x 51.1 cm
The Montreal Museum of Fine Arts, gift of Miss Esther Wilson Kerry (1976.12)

Paul Peel (1860-1892)
Repose, about 1890
Oil on canvas, 58.1 x 78.1 cm
The Montreal Museum of Fine Arts, Harold W. Lawson Bequest (1979.16)

Jean-Jacques called James Tissot (1836-1902)
October, 1877
Oil on canvas, 216 x 108.7 cm
The Montreal Museum of Fine Arts, gift of Lord Strathcona and family (1927.410)

John Adams-Acton (1830-1910)
The Lady of the Lake, 1864
Carrara marble, 229 cm
Musée du Québec, Quebec City, gift of William Dobell, (G-36.30-S)

---

* Complete information on the artefacts presented in the exhibition appears in the document "Scénario et design de l'exposition *Un art de vivre*" (1992) of which a copy is held in the archives of the Musée de la civilisation in Quebec City.

Index of Names*

Abbott, S.W. 274
Aberdeen, Ishbel Maria Marjoribanks, Lady 228
Aberdeen, J.C. Hamilton-Gordon, Lord 228, 289
Acton-Bond, Mrs. 473
Adams-Acton, John 66, 68, 521
Aitken, James Alfred 140
Albani, Emma Lajeunesse, called Madame 521
Allan, Andrew 204
Allan, family 39, 289, 305,
Allan, Sir Hugh 49, 50, 52, 86, 92, 270, 291, 438, 469, 480
Allan, Sir Hugh Montagu 49, 52, 141, 289, 291
Allard, Célestin 407
Allen, William 381
Andrews, George Henry 55
Angus, Alexander 177
Angus, Bertha 180
Angus, David James 180
Angus, Donald Forbes 180, 183, 185
Angus, Edith 179
Angus, Elspeth Hudson 180
Angus, Frederick F. 185, 189
Angus, Kate Jane 180, 181
Angus, Margaret Forrest 177, 180
Angus, Mary Anne, née Daniels 177, 183, 187
Angus, Mary Henshaw 183, 184
Angus, Maud Mary 180
Angus, Richard Bladworth 66, 140, 176-190, 452
Angus, William Forrest 180
Anne, Queen 464
Anstett, Z.T. 434
Arel, Ferdinand 303, 320, 321, 413, 414
Armstrong, George 271, 275, 277, 285, 293, 320, 321, 421, 422
Armstrong, William 293
Arnton, Ethel 255
Arthur, Duke of Connaugh, prince 73
Ash, John 315
Ahasuerus, King of Persia 216
Atholstan, Hugh Graham, Baron 520
Atkinson, Anthony 132
Atkinson, Henry 64, 132, 133
Atkinson, William 132
Aubert de Gaspé, Philippe, fils 509
Aubert de Gaspé, Philippe-Joseph 45
Aubin, Napoléon 63, 199, 443, 444
Auclair, André 84, 484
Audubon, Jean-Jacques 469
Baillairgé, Charles 60, 75, 101, 326, 464
Baillargeon 464
Baird, Edmond 270, 292

Baird, Henry Carey 406, 412
Baird, James 270, 293
Baker, Charles L. 181, 184, 186
Baker et Julien 371, 423
Baker, John Carpenter 71, 134-136
Baker, Mary Jane 134, 136
Baldwin 437
Baldwin, Robert 34
Balny jeune 408
Barbeau, Charles 23, 24, 159
Barbeau, Elzéar 357
Barbeau, Marius 23, 25, 29, 52, 240, 303, 305, 306, 450, 452, 466, 473
Barnard, Élodie 298
Barnard, Julienne 298
Barocci, Federigo 74
Barrington & Perry 382
Barry, Robertine 198, 209
Bartholdi, Frédéric-Auguste 75
Bartholdy, Félix Mendelssohn 193
Baumgarten, Alfred M.F. 112, 245, 452
Bazin, Neuville 295
Beau, Henri 74
Beaulac, Henri 464
Beaumier, Prosper 235
Bédard, Charles-Olivier 146, 210, 214, 215, 281, 285, 409
Bédard, François 340
Beemer, H.-J. 329
Bégin, Mgr Louis-Nazaire 210, 211
Béique, Mrs. Frédéric-Ligori 94, 106
Beigne, Joseph F. 320, 321
Bélanger, Adolphe 271, 282, 293, 366, 378, 379, 390
Bélanger & Gariépy 295
Bélanger, Émile 45
Bélanger, Octave 45
Bell-Smith, Frederic Marlett 234
Bellows, Albert Fitch 140
Belter, John Henry 287, 289, 293, 467, 468
Bender 395
Berchoux, Joseph 248
Bergeron, Stanislas 309
Berlinguet, François-Xavier 278
Berlinguet, Louis-Flavien 60, 61, 340, 348, 404
Berlinguet, Louis-Thomas 60, 61, 64, 84, 133, 340, 348, 404
Bernard, Henry 234
Bertrand, Édouard 52, 291, 305, 306
Bertrand, Narcisse 23
Beyd & Co. 367
Bigaouette, Félix 310, 320, 321
Bicknell & Comstock 112
Bilodeau, Marie-Aglaé 199, 221
Bisset, George 334
Bistodeau, Eugène 274, 299, 322
Blais et Lemay 293
Blanchet, Joseph-Goderic 47

Bohle & Hendery 76, 78
Bohle, Peter 76
Boitard 241
Borden, Sir Robert Laird 186
Borthwick, John Douglas 288
Boswell 284
Boucher, Bruno 314
Bouguereau, William-Adolphe 66, 67
Boulle, André-Charles 401, 509
Bourassa, Napoléon 45, 71, 73, 211,
Bourdon aîné 407, 409
Bourget, Mgr Ignace 41, 44, 72, 83, 521
Bourinot, John George 64
Bouthier 160, 278, 280, 291, 466
Bouthillier, Anne-Elmire 229
Bowles 324
Boxer, Edward 484
Boxer, F.N. 433
Boxer, Jemima 484
Boyd Lindsay, Errol 230
Brassard, Sylvio 24, 25
Brehaut, William Henry 210
Bresse, Guillaume 396
Brien dit Desrochers, Benjamin 220
Brochu, Blanche 303
Brochu, Luce 351
Brochu, Lucille 303
Brouillette, Charles 24
Brown 83
Brown, David S. 218, 407
Browne, Goodlatte Richardson 331
Browne, John James 110
Bullet, Charles 64, 83
Burges, William 131, 455
Burstall, Edward 408, 412
Bush 135
Butters 96
Butters, Mrs. I. 94
Byron, George, called Lord 51
Cameron, J.R. 380
Canadian Pacific Railway Workshops, Hochelaga 185
Canova, Antonio 80
Capistran, Christophe 315
Cappelli, Louis see Capello, Luigi
Cappello, Luigi 73, 395
Carbonneau, Joseph 303
Cardinal, Thomas 359
Carlisle, Frederick 366
Carlisle, John 278
Carlisle, William Ogle 378
Caron, Augustin 353, 355
Caron, Charles 397
Caron, Marie-Joséphine 249
Caron, René-Édouard 249
Caron, Mrs. René-Édouard, née Joséphine Deblois 77, 79

---

* This index was drawn up by Daniel Drouin with the assistance of Andréanne Bolduc. The names of furniture makers and companies that manufactured or commercialized furniture are in *italics*.

LIVING IN STYLE

Cartier, Sir George Étienne 34, 39, 454
Cartier, Jacques 26, 51, 52, 54, 75, 469, 470, 481
Casault, Abbé Louis-Jacques 61
Casgrain, Abbé Henri-Raymond 28, 488
Castonguay, Théodore 293
Caverhill, Marjorie 59
Cérès 75
Chabert, Abbé Joseph 80
Chamberland, Philomène 299
Champlain, Samuel de 469, 481
Chapais, Amélie 295
Chapais, family 200
Chapais, Georgina Dionne 295, 298, 345
Chapais, Jean-Charles 295, 296, 298, 345
Chapais, Sir Thomas 298
Chapleau, Marie-Louise, née King 228
Chapleau, Zéphirin 222
Charette, François-Athanase de 234
Charland et Lahaise 277
Charles I, King 451
Charles II, King 451
Chartré, Zéphirin 101
Chauvin, Jean 20
Chrétien, Charles 342
Clark 437
Claudet 379, 387
Clavette, Catherine 353
Clavette, Charles 353, 358, 361
Clavette, Jean-Baptiste 353
Clavette, Marguerite 353
Cleghorn, James Power 140
Clément, Joseph-Ludger 280
Clément, Mrs. 99
Clendinneng, William 438, 439
Cleopatra 185
Clerc, Émile 415
Clifford, Mrs. James 77, 81
Clutterbuck, Charles 77
Cochrane, Miss 389
Cockburn, James Pattison 139
Coleridge, Francis George 415
Collard, Elizabeth 270
Compagnie de meubles d'Ontario 293
Constable, John 66
Constant, Jean-Joseph-Benjamin 66
Constantine, R. 375, 390
Cormier, Amédée 451
Cormier, Ernest 451
Cormier, Isaïe 451
Corot, Jean-Baptiste-Camille 66
Côté, Jean-Baptiste 23, 275, 299, 303, 521
Côté, O.C. 23, 29, 484
Cotter 370
Cottier and Company 184
Cotton, E.T. 370, 371
Cousin, Paul 75, 76, 303
Coyle, James 324
Coysh, W.R. 274, 277, 278
Craig, Joseph A.I. 271, 277, 282, 320, 321, 366, 367, 375, 382, 390
Craig, Thomas 276, 329
Creelman, Adam Rutherford 209
Crémazie, Octave 19

Dagg, Georgiana 141
Dagneau, Jean-Ferdinand 221
Dalou, Aimé-Jules 75
D'Alq, Louise 193, 194, 220
D'Alquié de Rieupeyroux, Louise see D'Alq, Louise
Daly, César 109
Dandurand, Raoul 119, 289
Dandurand, Mrs. Raoul, née Joséphine Marchand 101, 119, 289
Daniels, Kendall & Company 286, 290
D'Arcy McGee, Thomas 39, 40
Darwin, Charles 472
Dauphin, Charles-Olivier 84
David, Jacques-Louis 80
Davidson, Thomas 236
Davis, Alexander Jackson 95
Dawson, John William 280
Deblois, Alfred 353, 355
Deblois, François-B. 521
De Bonald, Guillaume S. 423
Dechêne, Louise Saint-Jacques 92
Decker & Son 284
Degas, Hilaire-Germain-Edgar 66
Delmas, G. 490
Desbarats, George-Édouard 94
Désilets, Johny 192
Desrochers, Édouard 23
Dessaulles, family 91
Dessaulles, Georges-Casimir 91
Dessaulles, Henriette 91, 117, 258
Désy, Léopold 418
Díaz de la Peña, Narcisse-Virgile 521
D'Iberville-Moreau, Luc 52
Dion 23
Dion, Eusèbe 320, 321
Dionne, Amable 249, 295
Dionne, Georgina see Chapais, Georgina Dionne
Dionne, Joseph 232, 484
Dionne, Louise-Adèle 249
Dobell, Richard Reid 66, 89, 123, 125
Doddridge, A.P. 100
Dogherty Brothers 390
Dogherty, W.F. 366, 378, 390, 423
Doherty, W. 463
Domenichino, Domenico Zampieri, called 73
Donohue, Thomas 359
Doo, Georges T. 20, 521
Doré, Gustave 66
Dorion, Sir Antoine-Aimé 34, 94
Doutre, Joseph 201, 221
Downing, Andrew Jackson 93, 95, 185, 206, 222, 259, 430
Drouin, François 351
Drouin, Pierre 274, 280, 290, 316, 349-360, 404-406, 454
Drouin, Pierre, père 349
Drouin & Roy 315, 355-359
Drum Cabinet Manufacturing Company 277, 328, 329, 330, 332, 333, 347
Drum, Hugh 324
Drum, Isaac 329, 341
Drum, Samuel-Wilson 326, 329, 341

Drum, William 23, 52, 57-61, 164, 165, 168, 173, 270, 271, 274-278, 281, 290, 293, 295, 297, 299, 300, 303, 305, 311, 315, 320, 321, 323-349, 353, 367, 371, 375, 379, 381, 382, 384-386, 390, 395, 404, 421, 437, 449, 469, 487
Drummond, Sir George Alexander 66, 293, 493, 521
Dubord, Hippolyte 352
Dubuc, J. E. A. 106
Dufferin, F.T.H.-T. Blackwood, Lord 44, 234
Dufferin, H.G.H. Blackwood, Lady 234
Duhamel, Jean-Baptiste 315
Dumaige, Étienne-Henri 185
Duncan, James 40, 67, 68, 76
Duncanson, Robert 134
Dupré, Jules 185
Durham, John George Lambton, Lord 34
Eastlake, Charles Locke 122, 131, 239, 453-455, 461, 464, 477
Eaton 36, 285, 288
Eaton, J.O. 135
Eaton, Timothy 285, 288, 421
Eaton, Wyatt 134, 135
Ebbinghousen 293, 409
Edison, Thomas 103
Edson, Allan Aaron 71, 134, 135
Edson & Co., M.G. 417, 431
Edward VII see Wales, Edward Prince of
Edwards, William Bertrand 25, 29, 466
Edwin 135
Eleb-Vidal, Monique 107, 117, 226
Elgin, James Bruce, Lord 60, 61, 404, 521
Elizabeth I, Queen 450
Ellis, Sarah Stickney 194, 220
Ellis, William 220
Elot dit Julien, Olivier 351
Erard 395
Escosura, Ignacio Leon y 234
Escoubès 280, 291
Esther 216
Ethier 280, 281
Ettema, Michael-J. 335
Evans, Catherine 139
Ewing, John 320, 321
Fabre et Gravel 222
Falardeau, Antoine-Sébastien 73, 74
Falardeau, Hilaire 278, 281
Farley, Mrs. 389
Ferland, Abbé Jean-Baptiste-Antoine 209
Fichot, Charles 291, 306
Fiset, Jourdain 259, 484
Fitzgerald, C. 234
Floyd, J.W. 436
Foisy, Thomas F.G. 78
Foley, James 439, 440
Forget called Despatis, Joseph 366
Forgues, Simon 351
Fortier, family 287, 289
Foster 233
Foster, Mrs. 236
Fourdinois, Alexandre-Georges 473, 476
Fowler, Alexander G. 52
Fox, Thomas 175, 408, 410
Fraser, John Arthur 71

Fréchette, Louis 88
Frederick the Great, King 133
Freys, Marie-Louise 349
Friend, Washington F. 70
Frontenac, Louis de Buade, Count 484
Furetière, Antoine 509
Gadd, Joseph 203
Gage, G.T. 320, 321
Gagliardi, Pietro 74
Gagné, Marguerite 354
Gagnon, Thomas 293
Gale & Son, George 440
Gardner, 128, 509
Gariepy, Edgar 22, 28, 79, 208, 211
Garneau, François-Xavier 22, 45
Garneau, Pierre 409
Gauthier et Frères 303
Gauvin, Francis-Pierre 150, 172, 432, 450
Gauvin, Pierre 75, 76
Gauvreau, Jean-Marie 291
Géraux, Louise 353
Gere, Charlotte 122
Gérin-Lajoie, Antoine 45, 221
Gérin-Lajoie, Elzéar 233
Ghent, Peter 234, 235
Gibb, Benaiah 64
Giedion, Siegfried 26, 415, 421
Gignac, Joseph-Honoré 365, 389
Giguère, J.-B. 355
Gillow 408
Gilman, Francis Edward 217, 218
Gilmour, Arthur de Cresse 134-136
Gilmour, Arthur Henry 71, 134-136
Gilmour, Mary Jane see Baker, Mary Jane
Girouard, Mark 90
Giroux, Yves 355
Glover & Fry 275, 439, 440
Godwin, Edward William 455, 458
Goodwin, Henry 295, 296
Goss and Magoon 286
Gouin, Paul 23
Goulden, James 280, 282
Gourdeau, Athala 222
Gourdeau, Édouard, fils 303
Gourdeau, Édouard, père 299, 303, 340
Gourdeau, François-Xavier 144, 171, 210, 274, 277, 299-303, 367, 375, 385, 390, 395, 404, 435, 465, 468, 469, 479, 485
Grant, I. 416
Grant, Thomas Hunter 329
Gray 234
Greaves et Fils, W. 437
Greeley, Horace 135
Grenier, Marie-Esther 359
Grzimek, Bernhard 484
Guay, Bénoni 88
Guerrand, Roger-Henri 252
Guilbault, Marie-Dina 235
Guilmard, Désiré 361, 404-407
Gurd 88
Haberer, Eugene 362
Hague, family 219, 420
Hague, George 109, 114, 124, 420, 431
Hague, J. Anderson 234

Hale, J.P. 284
Hamel, Charles 357
Hamel, Eugène 61, 73, 74, 395
Hamel, Ferdinand 295-298
Hamel, Théophile 60, 61, 77, 79, 83, 404, 469, 484, 521
Hamel, Reverend Thomas 395
Hamilton, John 130, 179
Hammond, R. 381
Hanhart, M. & N. 274
Haney & Co., Jess 433
Hanks, David 412
Hanna, David B. 180
Hardy, Haywood 234
Harrison, John 232
Hart, Ezekiel 230
Hartland, Henry Albert 234, 235
Hasley, George 340
Havard, Henri 191
Hawkins 234
Hay & Co., R. 278, 327, 382
Hébert, Louis-Philippe 42, 66, 75, 521
Hedge & Bonner 438
Heintzman, Theodor August 199
Hendery, Robert 76
Héribel 367
Herring, John Frederick 234
Hicks, M.X. 281
Hill, J. 114, 115, 227
Hill, James Jerome 178
Hilton, John 53, 270-273, 276, 277, 281, 293, 365, 375, 376, 426, 471, 484
Hilton, John & William 26, 50, 52-54, 58, 162, 163, 270, 273, 274, 275, 278, 292-294, 311, 320, 321, 365, 366, 375-378, 380, 381, 390, 418, 427
Hilton, William 270, 365, 375-377, 384, 426
Hincks, Sir Francis 60
Hitchcock, Lambert 277
Hobbs, Thomas 350
Hodgson, William 206
Hohenlohe-Langenburg, Prince Viktor, Count Gleichen 521
Holt, John Henderson 130
Home, Mrs. William 23
Hope, William 140
Hopkins, E.C. 185, 190
Hopkins, John William 52, 180, 181, 185, 187, 190, 377
Hosmer, Charles Rodolph 66, 140
Houghton, T. 100
Hover 423
Hudon, Simone 464
Hulmes, Edward 477, 478
Hunt, James 325
Hunter, Thomas 341
Hunzinger, George 420, 421, 430
Huot, Charles 73
Huot, L.H. 396
Hutchison, Alexander Cooper 179
Ingres, Jean-Auguste-Dominique 73
Ives & Allen 439
Ives & Co., H.R. 440
Jackson, Ruth 189
Jacobi, Otto Reinhold 70, 71, 135, 521

Jacques & Hay 55, 56, 58, 269, 276, 278, 280, 285, 327, 382, 477
James, Henry 179
Jancowski 404, 405
Jeliff, John 467, 470, 484
Jobin, Louis 23, 75, 76, 347, 397
Johnston, Helen 234
Jolin, François 355
Jones, J. Clinton 235
Jones, Owen 477
Jones, Russell 261, 293
Jongers, Alphonse 184, 185
Joyal, Serge 407
Julien, Octave-Henri 382
Jump, Edward 44, 192
Kandahar, Roberts, Field-Marshal of 138
Kay, William Frederick 141
Kennedy, Henry 234
King, E. 234
King, Oliver 203
King, William 212, 428, 430
Kohn, Jacob & Josef 276, 288, 428
Kotchenreiter 234
Krieghoff, Cornelius 23, 67-68, 135, 140, 274, 474, 477
Labelle, Father Antoine 40
Labelle, H.P. 233, 235, 271, 282, 286, 289, 366, 367
Lacasse, Marie-Rose Délima 213
Lacelle, Claudette 118
Lachance, Caroline 216, 222
Lachance, Xavier 216
Lacroix, Édouard 358
Lafleur, François 375, 404, 410, 434
Lafontaine, Sir Louis-Hippolyte 34, 521
Laforest, Philomène 222
Lamarre, Joseph 23
Lambkins Furniture Co. 134
Lamontagne, Joseph-Guillaume 222
Lamothe, Onésime 315
Lamprecht, William 73, 80
Langelier, Charles 122
Laperrière, Aimé 444
Laperrière, David 444
Lapointe, Frederic 121, 277, 282-285, 287, 290
Laroche, Alphonse 359
Larose, Ludger 202
Laurier, Sir Wilfrid 44
Laurier, Lady Zoé, née Lafontaine 233
Laval, Mgr François de 61
Lavigne, Azarie 23, 271, 277, 320, 321, 366, 375, 377, 378, 389, 390, 404, 449
Lawford & Nelson 55
Lazarus, Frances 230
Leache 236
Leberenz 234
Lebuffe, Jean 315
Leclerc dit Francoeur, Thomas 355
Lecomte, Louis 373, 467
Leduc, Ozias 73
Leeming, John 76, 80
Le Gardeur, family 223
Légaré, Joseph 61, 64, 68, 132
Leggo, William Augustus 38
Lejambre, family 406

Lemay, Pamphile 81
Lemieux, Charles-Eusèbe 61
Lemire, Joseph 309
Leprohon, Louis-Xavier 64, 133
Lessore, Frederick 521
Levasseur, Émérance 299, 303
Levasseur, Nazaire 300, 302, 303
Levasseur, Théophile 302, 303
Levey, Charles Eleazar 242, 484
Levey, family 471
Lévis, Marquis de 227
Leyde, Otto Theodor 234
L'Heureux, Louis 315
L'Hoist, Jean 280
Lisgar, John Young, Baron 113
Livernois, Jules-Ernest 60, 65, 71, 72, 276, 420
Livernois, Jules-Isaï Benoit de 68
Lloyd, A. Thomas 76
Lonclas, Alphonse 59
Long, William 320, 321
Loranger, Onésime 471
Lorne, J.D.S. Campbell, Marquis of 67, 77, 81, 214
Loss 35
Lothée, R. 521
Loudon, John Claudius 99, 222, 450, 451
Louis XV, King 225, 508
Louis-Philippe I, King 248, 508
Louise, Marchioness of Lorne, Princess 67, 78, 81, 203, 214
Lowe, Peter 132
Lyman, family 124
Lynch, Édouard 313
Lynch, William 275, 304, 312, 313, 320, 321
Macdonald, Sir John Alexander 34, 178, 281, 287, 521
MacDuff 86
Mackenzie, Hector 67, 131, 140, 141
MacKenzie, John Gordon 140
Mackmurdo, Arthur Heygate 131
MacPherson, Colonel 114, 210, 211, 218
Madigan, Mary Jean 464
Maisonneuve, Paul de Chomedey de 75
Maitland, Edward 80
Mallet, Mother Marie-Anne-Marcelle 43
Manceau, Évariste 359
Maranda, Pierre 340
Maratta, Carlo 74
Marchand, Félix-Gabriel 219
Marchand, Gabriel 219, 220
Marchand, Jean-Omer 160, 278, 280, 466
Marchand, Joséphine see Dandurand, Madame Raoul
Marchand, Marguerite 219
Marchand, Rose-Anna, née Chaput 219
Marcoux, Joseph 351
Marcoux, Moïse 418
Marie-Victorin, Conrad Kirouac, dit frère 477
Marmette, Joseph 45
Marsh, W.E. 130
Martel, Curé Joseph-Stanislas 281
Martin, Charles F. 189
Martin, Margaret Angus 189
Martin, Paul-Louis 485, 509
Martin, Thomas Mower 134, 135

Martineau 428
Martinelli, Giovanni 74
Maser, D.H. 464
Mason & Hamlin 306
Mason, James 233
Massicotte, Édouard-Zotique 509, 510
Masson 254
Masson, Wilfrid-Antoine 292
Matte, Eustache 355
Matthews, Willie 17
Max, Gabriel Cornelius von 66
Maxham, Andrew J. 286
Maxwell, Edward 184, 186, 190
Maxwell, William Sutherland 188
Mayer, G.D. 344, 421
McArthur & Spence 55
McCarthy, Edward 235
McDonald, Charles 297
McDonald, Sarah 231
McDonald, W.M. 397
McDougall, Mrs. A.G. 283
McDougall, John 335
McGarr, Mary-Ann 235
McGarvey, John 273
McGarvey, Owen 158, 159, 272-278, 281, 282, 289, 290, 292, 304, 322, 365, 366, 369, 371, 374, 375, 378, 379, 381-384, 388, 390, 393, 394, 401, 404, 405, 415, 418, 420-423, 430, 431, 437, 443, 455, 457
McGarvey & Son, Owen 273, 287, 365, 366, 374, 378, 390, 393, 394, 418, 422
McGill, family 39
McGill, Peter 270
McIntyre, Duncan Eberts 178
McKay, Lauchlan 395
McLaughlin, Samuel 37
McLennan, Misses 59
McMaster, William 277
McRae 35
Meakins, C.W. 389
Meeks, J. & J.W. 286, 287, 289, 409
Meeks, John 287
Meeks, Joseph 287, 289, 409
Meeks, Joseph W. 287, 289, 409
Meighen, Mrs. Robert 138
Meighen, Robert 138
Meilleur & Cie 390
Meissonier, Jean-Louis-Ernest 66
Meloche, Edmond 73
Melot, Michel 29
Mercier 248
Méthot, Philéas 232
Meyer, Daniel 29
Meyer, Franz Sales 470, 477, 478
Michelot, Alexis 280, 291
Michaud, Father Joseph 42, 521
Mignard, Pierre 72
Milot, Jocelyne 361
Mingeaud, Arthur 26, 52-54, 291-293, 341, 469
Minton 459, 464
Minton, Hollins & Co. 464
Moisan, Laurent 23
Moles, Abraham 80
Molinelli, André 367, 375, 377, 390, 449
Molson, family 39

Molson, John 270, 326, 438
Molson, John Thomas 430
Molson, John William, Sr. 39
Molson, William 39
Monet, Claude 66
Monier, Joseph 340
Montpetit, André-Napoléon 386
Montreal Foundry and City Works 438
Moore, William W. 320, 321, 417
Moreau, Eusèbe 213
Moreau, Mrs. Eusèbe see Lacasse, Marie-Rose Délima
Moreau, Rose-de-Lima (Mary) see Roy, Mrs. Arsène
Morel, François-Xavier 353
Morel, Octave 23, 275
Morgan, Henry 233, 284, 288, 366
Morgan, Henry James 64
Morgan, R. 395
Morisset, Gérard 20
Morland, George 234
Morrice, Annie 108, 109, 205, 235, 265, 458
Morrice, James 366, 381
Morrin, Joseph 139
Morris, Andrew 67
Morris & Company 461
Morris, William 64, 131, 184, 187, 189, 461, 510
Mountain, George Jehoshaphat 77
Mozart, Wolfgang Amadeus 193
Muerrle, C.A. 114, 211
Müller, Daniel 73
Munier 234
Musson, John 139
Muthesius, Hermann 111, 238
Muthesius, Stephan 95, 98
Napoléon I, Emperor 132, 133, 464, 469, 470, 484
Napoléon III, Emperor 109, 452
Nash, Joseph 450
Neil, Robert 335
Nelligan, Émile 193, 221, 508
Nelson 234
Nelson, Horatio, Viscount 133
Nestfield, William Eden 111
New York Piano Co. 203, 284
Nicol, J. 287
Nightingale, D. 293
Nolet, Joseph 358
Noreau, Jean 355
Norman, W.C. 281
Notman, William 17, 39, 41, 71, 73, 135, 204, 280, 418, 425, 458
Notman, William McFarlane 137
O'Brien, Lucius Richard 70, 71
Ogilvie, family 39
Ogilvie, William Watson 234
Oisel, F. 395
Olmstead, Frederick Law, Jr. 188
Oshawa Cabinet Factory 367, 369
Ouellet, Fabien 303
Overbeck, Johann Friedrich 73
Pabst, Daniel 406, 412, 457, 467
Pageau, Hector 423
Palardy, Jean 20
Panet, Marie 249

INDEX 525

Papineau, family 91, 420, 452
Papineau, Jean-Marie 287, 320, 321, 370, 404, 478
Papineau, Louis-Joseph 22, 34, 39, 76, 79, 206, 210, 211, 229
Paquet, Amable 351
Paquet, Marie 351, 357
Paquet, Zéphirin 210
Parent, Étienne 45
Parent, Joseph 340
Pariseau, Charles-Edmond 271, 281, 293, 367, 404, 497
Pariseau, Thomas 27, 478
Parks, J.G. 206, 229
Parme, Charles III, Duke of 73
Parsons, S.R. 274, 277, 281, 282, 320, 321
Partridge, John 20, 521
Pasqualoni, Vincenzo 61, 73
Paton, Noel Joseph 184
Paton, Walter Hugh 234
Paxton, Sir Joseph 377
Peachy, Joseph-Ferdinand 97
Peel, Paul 521
Perrault & Cie 290
Perrault, Marie-Louise 230
Perrot, Michèle 104
Perry 134
Perry, J.D. 135
Perry, James M. 390
Pfeiffer, Dorothy, called Mrs. Gordon 23
Pichet, Jean 315
Pie IX, Pope 61
Pigeon, Lumina 293
Pinard, Guy 52
Piollet 470
Plamondon, Antoine 72, 473, 521
Plante & Vézina 293
Pleyel 395
Plimpton 422
Poisson, Esther 508
Pollard, Sidney 337
Pompadour, Jeanne-Antoinette Poisson, Madame de 470
Porter, John William 429
Porter, Robert Shipp 429
Portugais, Lemay & Cie 293
Powers, Hiram 521
Pratt, Noël see *Pratte, Noël*
Pratte, John 305
Pratte, Noël 271, 291, 305, 320, 321, 366, 384, 442
Préfontaine, A. 104
Préfontaine, Thomas 104
Price, William 36
Pringle, Thomas 220
Proulx 160, 278, 280, 466
Proulx, Joseph 315
Provancher, Abbé Léon 284, 472
Provencher, Jean 485
Prowse & McFarlane 439
Pugin, Augustus Welby Northmore 451, 455
Racine, Mgr Dominique 47
Raffaëlli, Jean-François 66
Rainville 29
Ramsay & McArthur 381
Raphael, Raffaello Sanzio, called 72, 76, 133
Raphael, William 69-71, 521

Rasco, Francis 293
Rastel de Rocheblave, Pierre de 229
Raymond, Charles 423
Readhead, Thomas M. 381
Redouté, Pierre-Joseph 478, 485
Redpath, family 289, 305
Redpath, Peter 52
Reed & Meakins 375, 381, 387, 389, 390
Renaud, Jacques 340
Renaud, King et Patterson 288, 289, 366
Reni, Guido 72, 74
Reyniès, Nicole de 26, 489, 511
Rheims, Maurice 443
Rhodes, Captain 381
Rhodes, Catherine 410
Rhodes, Godfrey 408, 410
Rhodes, William 449
Richard, Joseph 359
Richards, John 335
Richardson, Henry Hobson 111, 182
Rickaby, David S. 276, 288, 428, 458
Rickaby, John 293
Rickaby, T. 278
Riley, B. 134
Rimbaud, Arthur 241
Riss, François 469
Robb, M.E. 219
Robbe, Louis-Marie 141
Roberge, Father Thomas 210
Robertson, Charles 293, 346
Robin, Charles 320, 321
Robinson, John Henry 20, 521
Robitaille, François-Xavier 357
Robitaille, Sophie 354, 357-360
Rodden & Meilleur 438, 439
Rodden, Thomas M. 439
Rodden, William 390, 438, 439
Rodin, Auguste 66
Roquebrune, Robert Laroque de 223, 233, 238, 246
Roger, Adolphe 135
Roret 407
Rose, John 55, 56
Ross, Daniel Alexander 395
Ross, family 504
Ross, James 66, 115, 289
Ross, John W. 504
Ross, Mrs. 283
Rousseau, Edmond 209
Routier, Joseph 354, 355, 357-360
Routier, Joseph, père 354
Routhier & Compagnie, Joseph 359
Roux, Alexandre 467, 470, 484
Roy 76
Roy, Anne-Marie, called Sister Saint-Nazaire 301
Roy, A.R. 45
Roy, Mrs. Arsène, née Mary Moreau 300, 301
Roy, Étienne 353
Roy, Honoré 274, 280, 290, 316, 340, 349, 350, 353-361, 404-406, 433, 437, 454, 475, 477
Roy, Honoré 293
Roy & Cie, Honoré 357, 358
Roy, Joséphine 353
Roy, Mgr Lionel 301

Roy, Louis 353, 355
Roy, Marie-Joséphine, called Marcelline 353, 354
Roy, Marie-Marguerite-Adéline 353, 354
Roy, Michel 277
Roy, Pierre, alias "Puff Roy" 23, 274, 281, 293, 299, 367, 382, 390, 392, 401, 404, 471
Roy, Victor 49, 52
Roy dit Belleau, Honoré see Roy, Honoré
Roy & Clavette 357, 358
Rubens, Peter Paul 73, 248
Ruel, family 242
Ruelland, Ludger 213
Ruolz, Henri, Count 244
Ruskin, John 455, 459
Russell, John 429
Russell, Tom 429
Russell, Willis 281, 334, 335
Rybczynski, Witold 89, 225
Saint-Amand, Onésime 431-434
Saint-Laurent, Jean-Baptiste 404, 434
Saint-Nazaire, Sister see Roy, Anne-Marie
Saint-Ours, Charles de 223
Saint-Ours, family 223
Sandham, Henry 71, 73, 135
Santore 234
Savage & Lyman 76, 78
Sawyer, William 67
Sax, abbé Pierre-Télesphore 80
Saxe-Coburg-Gotha, Albert, Prince of 20, 129, 363, 386, 521
Schreyer, Adolf 234
Schmit, Frédéric 470
Scott, Sir Walter 66, 451
Scott, Walter A. see *Scott & Sons, William*
Scott, William 277, 366, 369, 378
Scott, William W. see *Scott & Sons, William*
Scott & Sons, William 277, 278, 289
Scully, Vincent 185
Seargeant, Lewis James 116
Sellens, Alvin 437
Sharpe, Edward 73
Sharpe, W. 98
Shaw & Frère 293
Shaw, Henry J. 288-290, 366, 390, 409
Shaw, John 325
Shaw, Richard Norman 111, 131, 181
Shaw, S.J. 437
Simard, Crispin 342
Simard, Z. 293
Simon, Jules 193
Skaife, Lewis 231
Smith, A.N. 417, 431
Smith, Andrew McKay 141
Smith, Charles Alexander 74
Smith, Donald Alexander see Strathcona
Smith, Gustave 80
Smith, Harcourt 130
Smith Hall 234
Snyders, Frans 248
Somerville, Martin 67, 376
Souci, Adolphe 359
Southgate 81
Spence, John C. 382, 389
St. Maurice Iron Foundry 440

Stanton, Ann Letta Augusta 134, 136
Statt 367
Staunton, A.A. 68
Staveley, Edward Black 98
Staveley, Harry 97, 98, 100
Steel, James 274, 277, 285, 293
Steele, Alexander Denton 179
Stephen, family 289, 305
Stephen, George, Baron Mount Stephen 52, 111, 122, 130, 138, 178, 244, 257, 258, 429, 461, 462
Stephens, Harrison 114, 115, 227, 438, 458
Stewart, Mrs. David M. 57
Stewart, May B. 57, 59
Stoneham, S.F. 207, 222
Strange, Thomas Bland 395
Strathcona, Donald Alexander Smith, Baron 66, 140, 178, 403
Stuart, Ernest-Henri 141
Stuart-Henry 96, 124
Surveyer, L.J.A. 439
Suzor-Coté, Marc-Aurèle de Foy 74, 409, 474
Symonds, Robert Wemyss 476
Taché, Eugène-Étienne 76, 77
Taché, Joseph-Charles 387
Tahan, Jean-Pierre-Alexandre 284, 467
Tail, Thomas 231
Talbert, Bruce J. 455
Taschereau, Charles 249
Taschereau, Elzéar-Alexandre 469
Taschereau, Gabriel-Elzéar 249
Taschereau, Gabrielle 249
Taschereau, Jean-Thomas 249
Taschereau, Jean-Thomas, père 249
Taschereau, Louis-Alexandre 22, 249
Taschereau, Michel 249
Taylor, Miss 389
Tees, D. & J. 311, 312, 320, 321
Tees, David 278, 311, 312, 320, 321
Tees & Cie 421
Tees, family 390
Tees, Joseph 311, 312, 320, 321
Tennyson, Alfred Lord 184
Têtu, Cirice 101
Thivierge, Émérance 355
Thompson, Esther 324
Thompson, James see Thomson, James
Thompson, Richard 485
Thomson, James 52, 280, 289, 291, 305, 366, 375, 377, 382, 390, 418, 419, 431, 468
Thonet, Michael 427, 428
Thoren, Karl Kasimir Otto von 234
Thornton, John 274, 285
Tigh, J.B. 235
Tissot, Jean-Jacques, called James 521
Titien, Tiziano Vecellio, called 73
Tombyll, R.N. 424, 425, 431, 459, 460
Tourangeau, family 452
Traquair, Ramsay 22, 79
Tremblay, Jean-Baptiste 325
Tudor-Hart, Percival 410
Tupper, Sir Charles 388
Turgeon, P. 353
Turner, Joseph Mallord William 66
Twose, Samuel 320, 321, 367

Underwood, J. 280
The Universal Commode Cabinet 422, 423
Usborne, George William 132
Valiquette, N.G. 422, 423, 460
Vallée, Louis-Prudent 53
Vallière, Jean-Olivier 271, 276, 278, 293, 324, 346, 404, 407, 413
Vallière, Philippe 23, 61, 169, 270, 271, 274, 276, 278, 280, 284, 285, 287, 291, 292, 295-300, 303, 305, 311, 320, 321, 341, 345, 367, 369, 375, 379, 385, 386, 390, 395-397, 401, 428, 487
Valois, Antoinette 471
Van Horne, Sir William Cornelius 65, 140, 178, 289, 521
Vanderbilt II, Cornelius 181
Vandry, Edmond 429
VanKoughnet, Philip Michael Matthew Scott 58
Vardon et Hogan 278
Varigny, Henry de 389
Vass, A.H. 293
Vaughan, Mrs. 195
Vaux, Calvert 94
Veblen, Thorstein Bunde 179
Veniere-Nicol, N. 404
Venner, William 358
Victoria, Queen 20, 27, 34, 47, 55, 60, 61, 77, 81, 119, 129, 214, 290, 348, 375, 386-388, 390, 401, 403, 431, 444, 485, 520, 521
Vogt, Adolphe 67, 70, 71, 134-136, 140
Vose & Sons 284
Wales, Edward Prince of 55-59, 186, 278, 279, 281, 345, 346, 369-371, 387, 469, 477
Walker, Horatio 21, 71
Ward, Alfred 293
Warner, Henry 395
Warren, Mrs. 389
Washington, George 390, 443
Watson, William 293
Watt, David 461
Way, Charles Jones 234, 235
Webb, Philip 111
Weber, Albert 284
Weil & Braunsdorf 286
Welling, Louise 232, 484
Welsbach 102
Wharton, Edith 179
Whineray, B.B. 476
Whistler, James Abbott MacNeil 66
Whitehead, family 23, 210, 433
Whiteside & Co. 320, 321
Whitney, Edwin R. 434
Wilder, H.A. 366, 378
Wiles, L.M. 135
Wilkie, Daniel 139
William, Robert 277, 293
Williams, family 137
Williams, J. 436
Williams, Mrs. 446
Williams, Paul 485
Wilson, Elizabeth 324
Wilson, George 417
Wilson, Jane Wiseman 521
Wilson, Richard 185
Wily, Daniel Berkly 52, 180, 181, 185, 190

Wolfe, James 133
Wood 114
Woodley, Joseph 431
Woodward, John 274
The Wooton Desk Company 293, 493
Wordsworth, William 185
Wright, James 458, 459, 464
Wright, Janet 95
Wright, M. 135
Würtele, Fred C. 97
Wyant, Alexander Helwig 134, 135
Young, John 23, 348
Zaor, Louis 303
Zapponi, Hipolito 291, 292
Zugel, Henrich Johann 140